Data Abstraction
& Problem Solving
with JAVA™

W A L L S
A N D
M I R R O R S

Data Abstraction & Problem Solving with JAVA™

WALLS AND MIRRORS

3rd Edition

Janet J. Prichard
Bryant University

Frank Carrano
University of Rhode Island

International Edition contributions by
Indrajit Banerjee
Bengal Engineering and Science University

PEARSON

Boston   Columbus   Indianapolis   New York   San Francisco   Upper Saddle River
Amsterdam   Cape Town   Dubai   London   Madrid   Milan   Munich   Paris   Montreal   Toronto
Delhi   Mexico City   Sao Paulo   Sydney   Hong Kong   Seoul   Singapore   Taipei   Tokyo

Editorial Director: Marcia Horton
Editor-in-Chief: Michael Hirsch
Editorial Assistant: Stephanie Sellinger
Marketing Manager: Yezan Alayan
Marketing Coordinator: Kathryn Ferranti
Vice President, Production: Vince O'Brien
Managing Editor: Jeff Holcomb
Senior Production Project Manager: Marilyn Lloyd
Publisher, International Edition: Angshuman Chakraborty

Acquisitions Editor, International Edition: Arunabha Deb
Publishing Assistant, International Edition: Shokhi Shah
Senior Operations Supervisor: Alan Fischer
Operations Specialist: Lisa McDowell
Text Designer: Sandra Rigney
Cover Designer: Jodi Notowitz
Cover Image: Getty Images/Steve Wall
Full-Service Vendor: GEX Publishing Services
Printer/Binder: Courier Stoughton

Credits and acknowledgments borrowed from other sources and reproduced, with permission, in this text-book appear on appropriate page within text.

Authorized adaptation from the United States edition, entitled Data Abstraction and Problem Solving with Java: Walls and Mirrors, 3rd edition, ISBN 978-0-13-212230-6 by Frank M. Carrano and Janet J. Prichard published by Pearson Education © 2011.

If you purchased this book within the United States or Canada you should be aware that it has been imported without the approval of the Publisher or the Author.

British Library Cataloguing-in-Publication Data
A catalogue record for this book is available from the British Library

Many of the designations by manufacturers and seller to distinguish their products are claimed as trademarks. Where those designations appear in this book, and the publisher was aware of a trademark claim, the designa-tions have been printed in initial caps or all caps.

10 9 8 7 6 5 4 3 2 1—CRS—14 13 12 11 10

ISBN 10: 0-273-75120-4
ISBN 13: 978-0-273-75120-5

Brief Contents

Contents

Preface

Welcome to the third edition of *Data Abstraction and Problem Solving with Java: Walls and Mirrors*. Java is a popular language for beginning computer science courses. It is particularly suitable to teaching data abstraction in an object-oriented way.

This book is based on the original *Intermediate Problem Solving and Data Structures: Walls and Mirrors* by Paul Helman and Robert Veroff (© 1986 by Benjamin Cummings Publishing Company, Inc.). This work builds on their organizational framework and overall perspective and includes technical and textual content, examples, figures, and exercises derived from the original work. Professors Helman and Veroff introduced two powerful analogies, walls and mirrors, that have made it easier for us to teach—and to learn—computer science.

With its focus on data abstraction and other problem-solving tools, this book is designed for a second course in computer science. In recognition of the dynamic nature of the discipline and the great diversity in undergraduate computer science curricula, this book includes comprehensive coverage of enough topics to make it appropriate for other courses as well. For example, you can use this book in courses such as introductory data structures or advanced programming and problem solving. The goal remains to give students a superior foundation in data abstraction, object-oriented programming, and other modern problem-solving techniques.

New in this edition

Uses Java 6:   This edition has been thoroughly revised to be compatible with the latest release of Java, known as Java 6. All code has been completely revised to be Java 6 compliant. Generics are also an important part of Java 6, and this material is discussed in depth in Chapter 9, and then used throughout the remainder of the collections in the text.

Enhanced Early Review of Java: We have increased the amount of coverage of the Java language in the first chapter of the book to help students make the transition from their introduction to Java course to this course. Chapter 1 provides a concise review of important Java material, including brief discussions on constructors, object equality, inheritance, and the *Array* class. A discussion of the *Console* class from Java 6 was also added to Chapter 1. Chapter 9 focuses on advanced Java techniques, and includes an enhanced discussion of how to create an iterator class.

Linked List: The node class for linked lists has been simplified. The implementation now assumes the node class is package access only, and the other classes in the same package have direct access to the data within a node. Students are asked to explore the implications of making the data private in a node as an exercise.

Updates the Use of the Java Collections Framework: The Java Collections Framework is discussed throughout the text, with a section added to show the JFC classes that parallel those presented in the text. The Deque class, added in Java 6, is presented in Chapter 8.

Other enhancements: Additional changes aimed at improving the overall usability of the text include new exercises and a new cleaner design that enhances the book's readability.

TO THE STUDENT

Thousands of students before you have read and learned from *Walls and Mirrors*. The walls and mirrors in the title represent two fundamental problem-solving techniques that appear throughout the book. Data abstraction isolates and hides the implementation details of a module from the rest of the program, much as a wall can isolate and hide you from your neighbor. Recursion is a repetitive technique that solves a problem by solving smaller problems of exactly the same type, much as mirror images that grow smaller with each reflection.

This book was written with you in mind. As former college students, and as educators who are constantly learning, we appreciate the importance of a clear presentation. Our goal is to make this book as understandable as possible. To help you learn and to review for exams, we have included such learning aids as margin notes, chapter summaries, self-test exercises with answers, and a glossary. As a help during programming, you will find Java reference materials in Chapter 1, and inside the covers. You should review the list of this book's features given later in this preface under the section "Pedagogical Features."

The presentation makes some basic assumptions about your knowledge of Java as reviewed in Chapter 1. Some of you may need to review this language or learn it for the first time by consulting this chapter. Others will find that they already know most of the constructs presented in Chapter 1. You will need to know about the selection statements *if* and *switch*; the iteration statements *for*, *while*, and *do*; classes, methods, and arguments; arrays; strings; and files. In addition to the material in Chapter 1, this book discusses advanced Java topics such as generics and iterators in Chapter 9. We assume no experience with recursive methods, which are included in Chapters 3 and 6.

All of the Java source code that appears in this book is available for your use. Later in this preface, the description of supplementary materials explains how to obtain these files. See page 21—Supplemental Materials—for instructions on how to access these files.

TO THE INSTRUCTOR

This edition of *Walls and Mirrors* uses Java 6 to enhance its emphasis on data abstraction and data structures. The book carefully accounts for the strengths and weaknesses of the Java language and remains committed to a pedagogical approach that makes the material accessible to students at the introductory level.

Prerequisites

We assume that readers either know the fundamentals of Java or know another language and have an instructor who will help them make the transition to Java. By using Chapter 1, students without a strong Java background can quickly pick up what they need to know to be successful in the course. In addition, the book formally discusses Java classes. Included are the basic concepts of a class, inheritance, polymorphism, interfaces, and packages. Although the book provides an introduction to these topics in connection with the implementations of abstract data types (ADTs) as classes, the emphasis of the book remains on the ADTs, not on Java. The material is presented in the context of object-based programming, but it assumes that future courses will cover object-oriented design and software engineering in detail, so that the focus can remain on data abstraction. We do, however, introduce the Unified Modeling Language (UML) as a design tool.

Organization

The chapters in this book are organized into two parts. In most cases, Chapters 1 through 11 will form the core of a one-semester course. Chapters 1 or 2 might be review material for your students. The coverage given to Chapters 11 through 15 will depend on the role the course plays in your curriculum.

Flexibility

The extensive coverage of this book should provide you with the material that you want for your course. You can select the topics you desire and present them in an order that fits your schedule. A chapter dependency chart follows, and shows which chapters should be covered before a given chapter can be taught.

Part 1: Problem-Solving Techniques. The first two chapters in Part 1 resemble an extension of an introductory course in that their emphasis is on major issues in programming and software engineering. Chapter 3 introduces recursion for those students who have had little exposure to this important topic. The ability to think recursively is one of the most useful skills that a

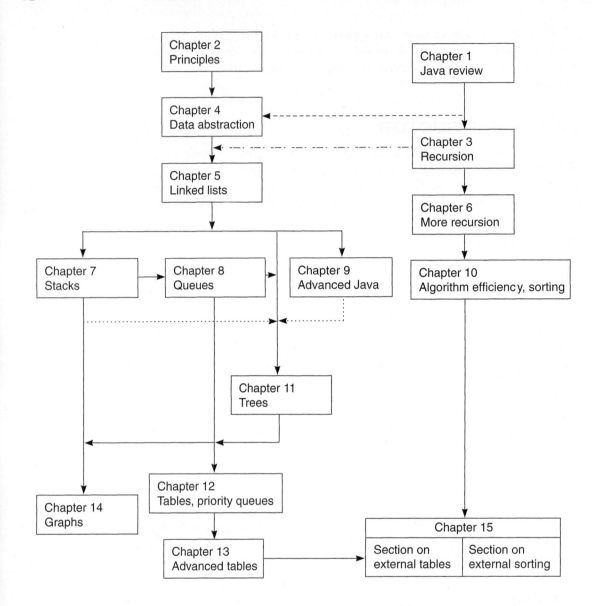

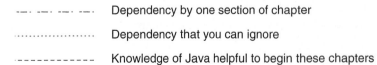

Dependency by one section of chapter

Dependency that you can ignore

Knowledge of Java helpful to begin these chapters

computer scientist can possess and is often of great value in helping one to understand better the nature of a problem. Recursion is discussed extensively in this chapter and again in Chapter 6 and is used throughout the book. Included examples range from simple recursive definitions to recursive algorithms for language recognition, searching, and sorting.

Chapter 4 discusses data abstraction and abstract data types (ADTs) in detail. After a discussion of the specification and use of an ADT, the chapter discusses Java classes, interfaces, and packages, and uses them to implement ADTs. Chapter 5 presents additional implementation tools in its discussion of Java reference variables and linked lists.

You can choose among the topics in Part 1 according to the background of your students and cover these topics in several orders.

Part 2: Problem Solving with Abstract Data Types.   Part 2 continues the use of data abstraction as a problem-solving technique. Basic abstract data types such as the stack, queue, binary tree, binary search tree, table, heap, and priority queue are first specified and then implemented as classes. The ADTs are used in examples and their implementations are compared.

Chapter 9 extends the treatment of Java classes by covering inheritance, the relationships among classes, generics, and iterators. Chapter 10 formalizes the earlier discussions of an algorithm's efficiency by introducing order-of-magnitude analysis and Big O notation. The chapter examines the efficiency of several searching and sorting algorithms, including the recursive mergesort and quicksort.

Part 2 also includes advanced topics—such as balanced search trees (2-3, 2-3-4, red-black, and AVL trees) and hashing—that are examined as table implementations. These implementations are analyzed to determine the table operations that each supports best.

Finally, data storage in external direct access files is considered. Mergesort is modified to sort such data, and external hashing and B-tree indexes are used to search it. These searching algorithms are generalizations of the internal hashing schemes and 2-3 trees already developed.

In Part 1, you can choose among topics according to your students' background. Three of the chapters in this part provide an extensive introduction to data abstraction and recursion. Both topics are important, and there are various opinions about which should be taught first. Although in this book a chapter on recursion both precedes and follows the chapter on data abstraction, you can simply rearrange this order.

Part 2 treats topics that you can also cover in a flexible order. For example, you can cover all or parts of Chapter 9 on advanced Java topics either before or after you cover stacks (Chapter 7). You can cover algorithm efficiency and sorting (Chapter 10) any time after Chapter 6. You can introduce trees before queues or graphs before tables, or cover hashing, balanced search trees, or priority queues any time after tables and in any order. You also can cover external methods (Chapter 15) earlier in the course. For example, you can cover external sorting after you cover mergesort in Chapter 10.

Data Abstraction

The design and use of abstract data types (ADTs) permeate this book's problem-solving approach. Several examples demonstrate how to design an ADT as part of the overall design of a solution. All ADTs are first specified—in both English and pseudocode—and then used in simple applications before implementation issues are considered. The distinction between an ADT and the data structure that implements it remains in the forefront throughout the discussion. The book explains both encapsulation and Java classes early. Students see how Java classes hide an implementation's data structure from the client of the ADT. Abstract data types such as lists, stacks, queues, trees, tables, heaps, and priority queues form the basis of our discussions.

Problem Solving

This book helps students learn to integrate problem-solving and programming abilities by emphasizing both the thought processes and the techniques that computer scientists use. Learning how a computer scientist develops, analyzes, and implements a solution is just as important as learning the mechanics of the algorithm; a cookbook approach to the material is insufficient.

The presentation includes analytical techniques for the development of solutions within the context of example problems. Abstraction, the successive refinement of both algorithms and data structures, and recursion are used to design solutions to problems throughout the book.

Java references and linked list processing are introduced early and used in building data structures. The book also introduces at an elementary level the order-of-magnitude analysis of algorithms. This approach allows the consideration—first at an informal level, and then more quantitatively—of the advantages and disadvantages of array-based and reference-based data structures. An emphasis on the trade-offs among potential solutions and implementations is a central problem-solving theme.

Finally, programming style, documentation including preconditions and postconditions, debugging aids, and loop invariants are important parts of the problem-solving methodology used to implement and verify solutions. These topics are covered throughout the book.

Applications

Classic application areas arise in the context of the major topics of this book. For example, the binary search, quicksort, and mergesort algorithms provide important applications of recursion and introduce order-of-magnitude analysis. Such topics as balanced search trees, hashing, and file indexing continue the discussion of searching. Searching and sorting are considered again in the context of external files.

Algorithms for recognizing and evaluating algebraic expressions are first introduced in the context of recursion and are considered again later as an application of stacks. Other applications include, for example, the Eight Queens problem as an example of backtracking, event-driven simulation as an application of queues, and graph searching and traversals as other important applications of stacks and queues.

Pedagogical Features

The pedagogical features and organization of this book were carefully designed to facilitate learning and to allow instructors to tailor the material easily to a particular course. This book contains the following features that help students not only during their first reading of the material, but also during subsequent review:

- Chapter outlines and previews

- Key Concepts boxes

- Margin notes

- Chapter summaries

- Cautionary warnings about common errors and misconceptions

- Self-test exercises with answers

- Chapter exercises and programming problems. The most challenging exercises are labeled with asterisks. Answers to the exercises appear in the *Instructor's Resource Manual.*

- Specifications for all major ADTs in both English and pseudocode

- Java class definitions for all major ADTs

- Examples that illustrate the role of ADTs in the problem-solving process

- Appendixes, including a review of Java

- Glossary of terms

SUPPLEMENTAL MATERIALS

The following supplementary materials are available online to all readers of this book at www.pearsonhighered.com/cssupport.

- *Source code* of all the Java classes, methods, and programs that appear in the book

- *Errata*: We have tried not to make mistakes, but mistakes are inevitable. A list of detected errors is available and updated as necessary. You are invited to contribute your finds.

The following instructor supplements are only available to qualified instructors. Please visit Addison-Wesley's Instructor Resource Center (www.pearsonhighered.com/irc) or contact your local Addison-Wesley Sales Representative to access them.

- *Instructor's Guide with Solutions*: This manual contains teaching hints, sample syllabi, and solutions to all the end-of-chapter exercises in the book.

- *Test Bank*: A collection of multiple choice, true/false, and short-answer questions

- *PowerPoint Lectures*: Lecture notes with figures from the book

TALK TO US

This book continues to evolve. Your comments, suggestions, and corrections will be greatly appreciated. You can contact us through the publisher at computing@aw.com, or:

Computer Science Editorial Office
Addison-Wesley
501 Boylston Street, Suite 900
Boston, MA 02116

ACKNOWLEDGMENTS

The suggestions from outstanding reviewers have, through the past few editions, contributed greatly to this book's present form. In alphabetical order, they are:

Ronald Alferez—*University of California at Santa Barbara*
Claude W. Anderson—*Rose-Hulman Institute of Technology*
Don Bailey—*Carleton University*
N. Dwight Barnette—*Virginia Tech*
Jack Beidler—*University of Scranton*
Elizabeth Sugar Boese—*Colorado State University*
Debra Burhans—*Canisius College*
Tom Capaul—*Eastern Washington University*
Eleanor Boyle Chlan—*Johns Hopkins University*
Chakib Chraibi—*Barry University*
Jack N. Donato—*Jefferson Community College*
Susan Gauch—*University of Kansas*
Mark Holliday—*Western Carolina University*
Lily Hou—*SUN Microsystems, Inc.*
Helen H. Hu—*Westminster College*
Lester I. McCann—*The University of Arizona*
Rameen Mohammadi—*SUNY, Oswego*
Narayan Murthy—*Pace University*
Thaddeus F. Pawlicki—*University of Rochester*

Timothy Rolfe—*Eastern Washington University*
Hongjun Song—*University of Memphis*

For their peer reviews of the international edition, we would like to thank:

Arup Kumar Bhattacharjee—*RCC Institute of Information Technology*
Soumen Mukherjee—*RCC Institute of Information Technology*

We especially thank the people who produced this book. Our editors at Addison-Wesley, Michael Hirsch and Stephanie Sellinger, provided invaluable guidance and assistance. Also, Marilyn Lloyd, Linda Knowles, Yez Alayan and Kathryn Ferranti contributed their expertise and care during the final production and in the marketing of the book.

Many other wonderful people have contributed in various ways. They are Doug McCreadie, Michael Hayden, Sarah Hayden, Andrew Hayden, Albert Prichard, Frances Prichard, Sarah Mason, Karen Mellor, Maybeth Conway, Ted Emmott, Lorraine Berube, Marge White, James Kowalski, Ed Lamagna, Gerard Baudet, Joan Peckham, Victor Fay-Wolfe, Bala Ravikumar, Karl Abrahamson, Ronnie Smith, James Wirth, Randy Hale, John Cardin, Gail Armstrong, Tom Manning, Jim Abreu, Bill Harding, Hal Records, Laurie MacDonald, Ken Fougere, Ken Sousa, Chen Zhang, Suhong Li, Richard Glass, and Aby Chaudhury. In special memory of Wallace Wood.

Numerous other people provided input for the previous editions of *Walls and Mirrors* at various stages of its development. All of their comments were useful and greatly appreciated. In alphabetical order, they are: Stephen Alberg, Vicki Allan, Jihad Almahayni, James Ames, Andrew Azzinaro, Tony Baiching, Don Bailey, Wolfgang W. Bein, Sto Bell, David Berard, John Black, Richard Botting, Wolfin Brumley, Philip Carrigan, Stephen Clamage, Michael Clancy, David Clayton, Michael Cleron, Chris Constantino, Shaun Cooper, Charles Denault, Vincent J. DiPippo, Suzanne Dorney, Colleen Dunn, Carl Eckberg, Karla Steinbrugge Fant, Jean Foltz, Marguerite Hafen, George Hamer, Judy Hankins, Lisa Hellerstein, Mary Lou Hines, Jack Hodges, Stephanie Horoschak, John Hubbard, Kris Jensen, Thomas Judson, Laura Kenney, Roger King, Ladislav Kohout, Jim LaBonte, Jean Lake, Janusz Laski, Cathie LeBlanc, Urban LeJeune, John M. Linebarger, Ken Lord, Paul Luker, Manisha Mande, Pierre-Arnoul de Marneffe, John Marsaglia, Jane Wallace Mayo, Mark McCormick, Dan McCracken, Vivian McDougal, Shirley McGuire, Sue Medeiros, Jim Miller, Guy Mills, Cleve Moler, Paul Nagin, Rayno Niemi, Paul Nagin, John O'Donnell, Andrew Oldroyd, Larry Olsen, Raymond L. Paden, Roy Pargas, Brenda C. Parker, Keith Pierce, Lucasz Pruski, George B. Purdy, David Radford, Steve Ratering, Stuart Regis, J. D. Robertson, John Rowe, Michael E. Rupp, Sharon Salveter, Charles Saxon, Chandra Sekharan, Linda Shapiro, Yujian Sheng, Mary Shields, Carl Spicola, Richard Snodgrass, Neil Snyder, Chris Spannabel, Paul Spirakis, Clinton Staley, Matt Stallman, Mark Stehlick, Harriet Taylor, David Teague, David Tetreault, John Turner, Susan Wallace, James E. Warren, Jerry Weltman, Nancy Wiegand, Howard Williams, Brad Wilson, Salih Yurttas, and Alan Zaring.

Thank you all.

F. M. C.
J. J. P.

PART ONE

Problem-Solving Techniques

The primary concern of the six chapters in Part One of this book is to develop a repertoire of problem-solving techniques that form the basis of the rest of the book. Chapter 1 begins by providing a brief overview of Java fundamentals. Chapter 2 describes the characteristics of a good solution and the ways to achieve one. These techniques emphasize abstraction, modularity, and information hiding. The remainder of Part One discusses data abstraction for solution design, more Java for use in implementations, and recursion as a problem-solving strategy.

CHAPTER 1

Review of Java Fundamentals

This book assumes that you already know how to write programs in a modern programming language. If that language is Java, you can probably skip this chapter, returning to it for reference as necessary. If instead you know a language such as C++, this chapter will introduce you to Java.

It isn't possible to cover all of Java in these pages. Instead this chapter focuses on the parts of the language used in this book. First we discuss basic language constructs such as variables, data types, expressions, operators, arrays, decision constructs, and looping constructs. Then we look at the basics of program structure, including packages, classes, and methods, with a brief introduction to inheritance. We continue with useful Java classes, exceptions, text input and output, and files.

27

1.1 Language Basics

Let's begin with the elements of the language that allow you to perform simple actions within a program. The following sections provide a brief overview of the basic language constructs of Java.

Comments

A variety of commenting styles are available in Java

Each comment line in Java begins with two slashes (//) and continues until the end of the line. You can also begin a multiple-line comment with the characters /* and end it with */. Although the programs in this book do not use /* and */, it is a good idea to use this notation during debugging. That is, to isolate an error, you can temporarily ignore a portion of a program by enclosing it within /* and */. However, a comment that begins with /* and ends with */ cannot contain another comment that begins with /* and ends with */. Java also has a third kind of comment that is used to generate documentation automatically using *javadoc*, a documentation utility available in the Software Development Kit (SDK). This comment uses a /** to start and a */ to end.

Identifiers and Keywords

A Java **identifier** is a sequence of letters, digits, underscores, and dollar signs that must begin with either a letter or an underscore. Java distinguishes between uppercase and lowercase letters, so be careful when typing identifiers.

Java is case sensitive

You use identifiers to name various parts of the program. Certain identifiers, however, are reserved by Java as **keywords,** and you should not use them for other purposes. A list of all Java keywords appears inside the front cover of this book. The keywords that occur within Java statements in this book are in boldface.

Variables

A variable contains either the value of a primitive data type or a reference to an object

A variable, whose name is a Java identifier, represents a memory location that contains a value of a primitive data type or a reference. You **declare** a variable's data type by preceding the variable name with the data type, as in

```
double radius;  // radius of a sphere
String name;    // reference to a String object
```

Note that the second declaration does not create a *String* object, only a variable that stores the location of a *String* object. You must use the *new* operator to create a new object.

Primitive Data Types

The primitive data types in Java are organized into four categories: boolean, character, integer, and floating point. For example, the following two lines declare variables of the primitive type *double*.

```
double radius;
double radiusCubed;
```

Some of the data types are available in two forms and sizes. Figure 1-1 lists the available primitive data types.

A boolean value can be either *true* or *false*. You represent characters by enclosing them in single quotes or by providing their Unicode integer value (see Appendix B). Integer values are signed and allow numbers such as −5 and +98. The floating-point types provide for real numbers that have both an integer portion and a fractional portion. Character and integer types are called **integral types.** Integral and floating-point types are called **arithmetic types.**

A value of a primitive type is not considered to be an object and thus cannot be used in situations where an object type is expected. For this reason, the package *java.lang* provides corresponding **wrapper classes** for each of the primitive types. Figure 1-1 also lists the wrapper class corresponding to each of the primitive types.

> A wrapper class is available for each primitive data type

Each of these classes provides a constructor to convert a value of a primitive type to an object when necessary. Once such an object has been created, the value contained within the object cannot be modified. Here is a simple example involving integers:

```
int x = 9;
Integer intObject = new Integer(x);
System.out.println("The value stored in intObject = "
                    + intObject.intValue());
```

> You can represent the value of a primitive data type by using a wrapper class

Category	Data Type	Wrapper Class
Boolean	boolean	Boolean
Character	char	Character
Integer	byte	Byte
	short	Short
	int	Integer
	long	Long
Floating point	float	Float
	double	Double

FIGURE 1-1

Primitive data types and corresponding wrapper classes

The class *Integer* has a method *intValue* that retrieves the value stored in an *Integer* object. Classes corresponding to the other primitive types provide methods with similar functionality.

Java has a feature called **autoboxing** that makes it easier to convert from a primitive type to their equivalent wrapper class counterparts. In the previous example, we explicitly created a new *Integer* object to store the value 9. With autoboxing, we can simply write

```
Integer intObject = 9;
```

The compiler automatically adds the code to convert the integer value into the proper class (*Integer* in this example).

The reverse process of converting an object of one of the wrapper classes into a value of the corresponding primitive type is called **auto-unboxing.** In the example

```
int x = intObject + 1;
```

the compiler again automatically generates the code to convert the *Integer* object *intObject* to a primitive type (*int* in this example) so that the expression can be evaluated.

References

A reference variable contains an object's location in memory

Java has one other type, called a reference, that is used to locate an object. Unlike other languages, such as C++, Java does not allow the programmer to perform any operations on the reference value. When an object is created using the *new* operator, the location of the object in memory is returned and can be assigned to a reference variable. For example, the following line shows the reference variable *name* being assigned the location of a new *string* object:

```
String name = new String("Sarah");
```

A special reference value of *null* is provided to indicate that a reference variable has no object to reference.

Literal Constants

Literal constants indicate particular values within a program

You use literal constants to indicate particular values within a program. In the following expression, the 4 and 3 are examples of literal constants that are used within a computation.

```
4 * Math.PI * radiusCubed / 3
```

You can also use a literal constant to initialize the value of a variable. For example, you use *true* and *false* as the values of a boolean variable, as we mentioned previously.

You write decimal integer constants without commas, decimal points, or leading zeros.[1] The default data type of such a constant is either *int*, if small enough, or *long*.

You write floating constants, which have a default type of *double*, with a decimal point. You can specify an optional power-of-10 multiplier by writing *e* or *E* followed by the power of 10. For example, *1.2e-3* means 1.2×10^{-3}.

Character constants are enclosed in single quotes—for example, `'A'` and `'2'`—and have a default type of *char*. You write a **literal character string** as a sequence of characters enclosed in double quotes.

Several characters have names that use a backslash notation, as given in Figure 1-2. This notation is useful when you want to embed one of these characters within a literal character string. For example, the statement

```
System.out.println("Hello\n Let\'s get started!");
```

uses the **new-line character** \n to place a new-line character after the string *Hello*. You will learn about this use of \n in the discussion of output later in this chapter. You also use the backslash notation to specify either a single quote as a character constant (\') or a double quote (\") within a character string.

Named Constants

Unlike variables, whose values can change during program execution, named constants have values that do not change. The declaration of a named constant is like that of a variable, but the keyword *final* precedes the data type. For example,

```
final float DEFAULT_RADIUS = 1.0;
```

Do not begin a decimal integer constant with zero

The value of a named constant does not change

Constant	Name
\n	New line
\t	Tab
\'	Single quote
\"	Double quote
\0	Zero

FIGURE 1-2

Some special character constants

1. Octal and hexadecimal constants are also available, but they are not used in this book. An octal constant begins with *0*, a hex constant with *0x* or *0X*.

Named constants
make a program
easier to read and
modify

declares *DEFAULT_RADIUS* as a named floating-point constant. Once a named constant such as *DEFAULT_RADIUS* is declared, you can use it, but you cannot assign it another value. By using named constants, you make your program both easier to read and easier to modify.

Assignments and Expressions

You form an expression by combining variables, constants, operators, and parentheses. The **assignment statement**

```
radius = initialRadius;
```

An assignment
statement assigns
the value of an
expression to a
variable

assigns to a previously declared variable *radius* the value of the **expression** on the right-hand side of the **assignment operator** =, assuming that *initialRadius* has a value. The assignment statement

```
double radiusCubed = radius * radius * radius;
```

also declares *radiusCubed*'s data type, and assigns it a value.

Arithmetic expressions. You can combine variables and constants with **arithmetic operators** and parentheses to form **arithmetic expressions**. The arithmetic operators are

*	Multiply	+	Binary add or unary plus
/	Divide	-	Binary subtract or unary minus
%	Remainder after division		

Operators have a
set precedence

The operators *, /, and % have the same precedence,[2] which is higher than that of + and -; unary operators[3] have a higher precedence than binary operators. The following examples demonstrate operator precedence:

a - b / c means	*a - (b / c)*	(precedence of / over -)
-5 / a means	*(-5) / a*	(precedence of unary operator -)
a / -5 means	*a / (-5)*	(precedence of unary operator -)

Arithmetic operators and most other operators are **left-associative.** That is, operators of the same precedence execute from left to right within an expression. Thus,

---

2. A list of all Java operators and their precedences appears inside the back cover of this book.
3. A unary operator requires only one operand, for example, the - in -5. A binary operator requires two operands, for example, the + in 2 + 3.

```
a / b * c
```

means

```
(a / b) * c
```

Operators are either left- or right-associative

The assignment operator and all unary operators are **right-associative,** as you will see later. You can use parentheses to override operator precedence and associativity.

Relational and logical expressions.   You can combine variables and constants with parentheses; with the **relational,** or **comparison, operators** <, <=, >=, and >; and with the **equality operators** == (equal to) and != (not equal to) to form a **relational expression.** Such an expression evaluates to *false* if the specified relation is false and to *true* if it is true. For example, the expression 5 != 4 has a value of *true* because 5 is not equal to 4. Note that equality operators have a lower precedence than relational operators. Also note that the equality operators work correctly only with the primitive types and references. The == operator determines only whether two reference variables are referencing the same object, but not whether two objects are equal.

Equality operators work correctly only with primitive types and references

You can combine variables and constants of the arithmetic types, relational expressions, and the **logical operators** && (and) and || (or) to form **logical expressions,** which evaluate to *false* if false and to *true* if true. Java evaluates logical expressions from left to right and stops as soon as the value of the entire expression is apparent; that is, Java uses **short-circuit evaluation.** For example, Java determines the value of each of the following expressions without evaluating *(a < b)*:

Logical expressions are evaluated from left to right

Sometimes the value of a logical expression is apparent before it is completely examined

```
(5 == 4) && (a < b)   // false since (5 == 4) is false
(5 == 5) || (a < b)   // true since (5 == 5) is true
```

Implicit type conversions for the primitive numeric types.   Automatic conversions from one numeric data type to another can occur during assignment and during expression evaluation. For assignments, the data type of the expression on the right-hand side of the assignment operator is converted to the data type of the item on the left-hand side just before the assignment occurs. Floating-point values are truncated—not rounded—when they are converted to integral values.

Conversions from one data type to another occur during both assignment and expression evaluation

During the evaluation of an expression, any values of type *byte*, *char*, or *short* are converted to *int*. These conversions are called **integral promotions.** After these conversions, if the operands of an operator differ in data type, the data type that is lower in the following hierarchy is converted to one that is higher (*int* is lowest):

```
int  →  long  →  float  →  double
```

For example, if A is *long* and B is *float*, A + B is *float*. A copy of A's *long* value is converted to *float* prior to the addition; the value stored at A is unchanged.

Explicit type conversions for primitive numeric types.   Numeric conversions from one type to another are possible by means of a **cast**. The cast operator is a unary operator formed by enclosing the desired data type within parentheses. Thus, the sequence

```
double volume = 14.9;
System.out.print((int)volume);
```

You convert from one numeric type to another by using a cast

displays 14.

Multiple assignment.   If you omit the semicolon from an assignment statement, you get an **assignment expression.** You can embed assignment expressions within assignment expressions, as in *a = 5 + (b = 4)*.

This expression first assigns 4 to *b* and then 9 to *a*. This notation contributes to the terseness of Java and is sometimes convenient, but it can be confusing. The assignment operator is right-associative. Thus, *a = b = c* means *a = (b = c)*.

Other assignment operators.   In addition to the assignment operator =, Java provides several two-character assignment operators that perform another operation before assignment. For example,

a += b means *a = a + b*

Other operators, such as -=, *=, /=, and %=, have analogous meanings.

The operators ++ and -- are useful for incrementing and decrementing a variable

Two more operators, ++ and --, provide convenient incrementing and decrementing operations:

++a means *a += 1*, which means *a = a + 1*

Similarly,

--a means *a -= 1*, which means *a = a - 1*

The operators ++ and -- can either precede their operands, as you just saw, or follow them. Although a++, for instance, has the same effect as ++a, the results differ when the operations are combined with assignment. For example,

b = ++a means *a = a + 1; b = a*

Here, the ++ operator acts on *a before* the assignment to *b* of *a*'s new value. In contrast,

b = a++ means *b = a; a = a + 1*

The assignment operator assigns *a*'s old value to *b* before the ++ operator acts on *a*. That is, the ++ operator acts on *a after* the assignment. The operators ++

and `--` are often used within loops and with array indexes, as you will see later in this chapter.

In addition to the operators described here, Java provides several other operators. A summary of all Java operators and their precedences appears inside the back cover of this book.

Arrays

An array is a collection of **elements**, **items**, or **values** that have the same data type. Array elements have an order: An array has a first element, a second element, and so on, as well as a last element. That is, an array contains a finite, limited number of elements. Like objects, an array does not come into existence until it is allocated using the *new* statement. At that time, you specify the desired size of the array. Because you can access the array elements directly and in any order, an array is a **direct access**, or **random access**, data structure.

An array is a collection of data that has the same type

You can access array elements directly and in any order

One-dimensional arrays. When you decide to use an array in your program, you must declare it and, in doing so, indicate the data type of its elements. The following statements declare a **one-dimensional array**, *maxTemps*, which contains the daily maximum temperatures for a given week:

```
final int DAYS_PER_WEEK = 7;
double [] maxTemps = new double[DAYS_PER_WEEK];
```

The bracket notation *[]* declares *maxTemps* as an array. The array is then allocated memory for seven floating-point elements.

The declared length of an array is accessible using the data field *length* associated with the array. For example, *maxTemps.length* is 7. You can refer to any of the floating-point elements in *maxTemps* directly by using an expression, which is called the **index**, or **subscript**, enclosed in square brackets. In Java, array indexes must have integer values in the range 0 to *length* − 1, where *length* is the data field just described. The indexes for *maxTemps* range from 0 to *DAYS_PER_WEEK* − 1. For example, *maxTemps[4]* is the fifth element in the array. If *k* is an integer variable whose value is 4, *maxTemps[k]* is the fifth element in the array, and *maxTemps[k+1]* is the sixth element. Also, *maxTemps[++k]* adds 1 to *k* and then uses the new value of *k* to index *maxTemps*, whereas *maxTemps[k++]* accesses *maxTemps[k]* before adding 1 to *k*. Note that you use one index to refer to an element in a one-dimensional array.

Use an index to specify a particular element in an array

An array index has an integer value greater than or equal to 0

Figure 1-3 illustrates the array *maxTemps*, which at present contains only five temperatures. The last value in the array is *maxTemps[4]*; the values of *maxTemps[5]* and *maxTemps[6]* are 0.0, the default initial value for floating-point numbers.

You can initialize the elements of an array when you declare it by specifying an **initializer list**. The initializer list is a list of values separated by commas and enclosed in braces. For example,

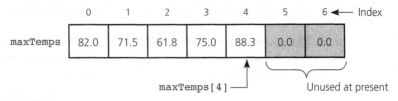

FIGURE 1-3

A one-dimensional array of at most seven elements

You can initialize an array when you declare it

```
double [] weekDayTemps = {82.0, 71.5, 61.8, 75.0, 88.3};
```

initializes the array *weekDayTemps* to have five elements with the values listed. Thus, *weekDayTemps[0]* is 82.0, *weekDayTemps[1]* is 71.5, and so on.

You can also declare an array of object references. The declaration is similar to that of an array of primitive types. Here is a declaration of an array for ten *String* references:

```
String[] stuNames = new String[10];
```

Note that all of the references will have the initial value *null* until actual *String* objects are created for them to reference. The following statement creates a *String* object for the first element of the array:

```
stuName[0] = new String("Andrew");
```

Multidimensional arrays. You can use a one-dimensional array, which has one index, for a simple collection of data. For example, you can organize 52 temperatures linearly, one after another. A one-dimensional array of these temperatures can represent this organization.

An array can have more than one dimension

You can also declare **multidimensional arrays.** You use more than one index to designate an element in a multidimensional array. Suppose that you wanted to represent the minimum temperature for each day during 52 weeks. The following statements declare a **two-dimensional array,** *minTemps*:

```
final int DAYS_PER_WEEK = 7;
final int WEEKS_PER_YEAR = 52;

double[][] minTemps = new
                 double[DAYS_PER_WEEK][WEEKS_PER_YEAR];
```

These statements specify the ranges for two indexes: The first index can range from 0 to 6, while the second index can range from 0 to 51. Most people picture a two-dimensional array as a rectangular arrangement, or **matrix,** of elements

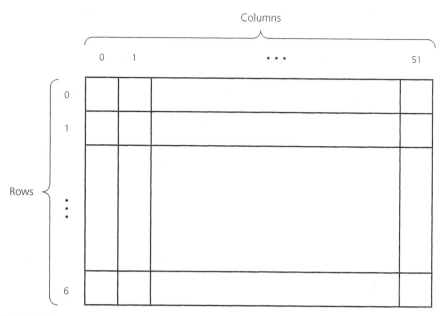

FIGURE 1-4

A two-dimensional array

that form rows and columns, as Figure 1-4 indicates. The first dimension given in the definition of *minTemps* is the number of rows. Thus, *minTemps* has 7 rows and 52 columns. Each column in this matrix represents the seven daily minimum temperatures for a particular week.

To reference an element in a two-dimensional array, you must indicate both the row and the column that contain the element. You make these indications of row and column by writing two indexes, each enclosed in brackets. For example, *minTemps[1][51]* is the element in the 2nd row and the 52nd column. In the context of the temperature example, this element is the minimum temperature recorded for the 2nd day (Monday) of the 52nd week. The rules for the indexes of a one-dimensional array also apply to the indexes of multidimensional arrays.

In a two-dimensional array, the first index represents the row, the second index represents the column

As an example of how to use a two-dimensional array in a program, consider the following program segment, which determines the smallest value in the previously described array *minTemps*:

```
// minTemps is a two-dimensional array of daily minimum
// temperatures for 52 weeks, where each column of the
// array contains temperatures for one week.

// initially, assume the lowest temperature is
// first in the array
double lowestTemp = minTemps[0][0];
int dayOfWeek = 0;
int weekOfYear = 0;
```

An example of using a two-dimensional array

```
// search array for lowest temperature
for (int weekIndex = 0; weekIndex < WEEKS_PER_YEAR;
                                    ++weekIndex) {
   for (int dayIndex = 0; dayIndex < DAYS_PER_WEEK;
                                    ++dayIndex) {
     if (lowestTemp > minTemps[dayIndex][weekIndex]) {
       lowestTemp = minTemps[dayIndex][weekIndex];
       dayOfWeek = dayIndex;
       weekOfYear = weekIndex;
     }  // end if
   } // end for
} // end for
// Assertion: lowestTemp is the smallest value in
// minTemps and occurs on the day and week given by
// dayOfWeek and weekOfYear; that is, lowestTemp ==
// minTemps[dayOfWeek][weekOfYear].
```

It is entirely possible to declare *minTemps* as a one-dimensional array of 364 (7 * 52) elements, in which case you might use *minTemps[81]* instead of *minTemps[4][11]* to access the minimum temperature on the 4th day of the 11th week. However, doing so will make your program harder to understand!

Although you can declare arrays with more than two dimensions, it is unusual to have an array with more than three dimensions. The techniques for working with such arrays, however, are analogous to those for two-dimensional arrays.

You can initialize the elements of a two-dimensional array just as you initialize a one-dimensional array. You list the initial values row by row. For example, the statement

```
int[][] x = {{1,2,3},{4,5,6}};
```

initializes a 2-by-3 array *x* so that it appears as

1	2	3
4	5	6

That is, the statement initializes the elements *x[0][0]*, *x[0][1]*, *x[0][2]*, *x[1][0]*, *x[1][1]*, and *x[1][2]* in that order. In general, when you assign initial values to a multidimensional array, it is the last, or rightmost, index that increases the fastest.

1.2 Selection Statements

Selection statements allow you to choose among several courses of action according to the value of an expression. In this category of statements, Java provides the *if* statement and the *switch* statement.

The *if* Statement

You can write an *if* statement in one of two ways:

if (*expression*)
    statement₁

An *if* statement has two basic forms

or

if (*expression*)
    statement₁
else
    statement₂

where *statement₁* and *statement₂* represent any Java statement. Such statements can be **compound;** a compound statement, or **block,** is a sequence of statements enclosed in braces. Though not a requirement of Java, this text will always use a compound statement in language constructs, even if only a single statement is required.

If the value of *expression* is `true`, *statement₁* is executed. Otherwise, the first form of the *if* statement does nothing, whereas the second form executes *statement₂*. Note that the parentheses around *expression* are required.

Parentheses around the expression in an *if* statement are required

For example, the following *if* statements each compare the values of two integer variables a and b:

```java
if (a > b) {
   System.out.println(a + " is larger than " + b + ".");
} // end if
System.out.println("This statement is always executed.");

if (a > b) {
   larger = a;
   System.out.println(a + " is larger than " + b + ".");
}
else {
   larger = b;
   System.out.println(b + " is larger than " + a + ".");
} // end if

System.out.println(larger + " is the larger value.");
```

You can nest *if* statements in several ways, since either *statement*₁ or *statement*₂ can itself be an *if* statement. The following example, which determines the largest of three integer variables *a*, *b*, and *c*, shows a common way to nest *if* statements:

You can nest *if* statements

```
if ((a >= b) && (a >= c)) {
   largest = a;
}
else if (b >= c) {      // a is not largest at this point
   largest = b;
}
else {
   largest = c;
} // end if
```

The *switch* Statement

When you must choose among more than two courses of action, the *if* statement can become unwieldy. If your choice is to be made according to the value of an integral expression, you can use a *switch* statement.

A *switch* statement provides a choice of several actions according to the value of an integral expression

For example, the following statement determines the number of days in a month. The *int* variable *month* designates the month as an integer from 1 to 12.

```
switch (month) {
   // 30 days hath Sept., Apr., June, and Nov.
   case 9: case 4: case 6: case 11:
      daysInMonth = 30;
      break;
   // all the rest have 31
   case 1: case 3: case 5: case 7: case 8: case 10: case 12:
      daysInMonth = 31;
      break;

   // except February
   case 2:   // assume leapYear is true if leap
             // year, else is false
      if (leapYear) {
         daysInMonth = 29;
      }
      else {
         daysInMonth = 28;
      } // end if
      break;

   default:
      System.out.println("Incorrect value for Month.");
} // end switch
```

Without a *break* statement, execution of a *case* will continue into the next *case*

Parentheses must enclose the integral `switch` expression—*month*, in this example. The `case` labels have the form

case *expression:*

where *expression* is a constant integral expression. After the `switch` expression is evaluated, execution continues at the `case` label whose expression has the same value as the `switch` expression. Subsequent statements execute until either a `break` or a `return` is encountered or the `switch` statement ends.

It bears repeating that unless you terminate a `case` with either a `break` or a `return`, execution of the `switch` statement continues. Although this action can be useful, omitting the `break` statements in the previous example would be incorrect.

If no `case` label matches the current value of the `switch` expression, the statements that follow the `default` label, if one exists, are executed. If no `default` exists, the `switch` statement exits.

1.3 Iteration Statements

Java has three statements—the `while`, `for`, and `do` statements—that provide for repetition by iteration—that is, loops. Each statement controls the number of times that another Java statement—the **body**—is executed. The body can be a single statement, though this text will always use a compound statement.

The `while` Statement

The general form of the `while` statement is

while (*expression*)
   statement

As long as the value of *expression* is `true`, *statement* is executed. Because *expression* is evaluated before *statement* is executed, it is possible that *statement* will not execute at all. Note that the parentheses around *expression* are required.

A ***while*** statement executes as long as the expression is true

Suppose that you wanted to compute the sum of a list of integers stored in an array called *myArray*. The following `while` loop accomplishes this task:

```
int sum = 0;
int index = 0;
while (index <= myArray.length) {
  sum += myArray[index];
} // end while
```

The *break* and *continue* statements. You can use the `break` statement—which you saw earlier within a `switch` statement—within any of the iteration statements. A `break` statement within the body of a loop causes the loop to exit immediately. Execution continues with the statement that follows the loop. This use of `break` within a `while`, `for`, or `do` statement is generally considered poor style.

Use of a ***break*** statement within a loop is generally poor style

The `continue` statement stops only the current iteration of the loop and begins the next iteration at the top of the loop. The `continue` statement is valid only within *while*, *for*, or *do* statements.

The *for* Statement

The *for* statement provides for counted loops and has the general form

A **for** statement lists the initialization, testing, and updating steps in one location

```
for (initialize; test; update)
   statement
```

where *initialize*, *test*, and *update* are expressions. Typically, *initialize* is an assignment expression that initializes a counter to control the loop. This initialization occurs only once. Then, if *test*, which is usually a logical expression, is `true`, *statement* executes. The expression *update* executes next, usually incrementing or decrementing the counter. This sequence of events repeats, beginning with the evaluation of *test*, until the value of *test* is `false`. As with the previous constructs, *statement* is usually a compound statement.

For example, the following *for* statement sums the integers from 1 to *n*:

```
int sum = 0;
for (int counter = 1; counter <= n; ++counter) {
   sum += counter;
} // end for

// this statement is always executed
int x = 0;
```

If *n* is less than 1, the *for* statement does not execute at all. Thus, the previous statements are equivalent to the following *while* loop:

```
int sum = 0;
int counter = 1;
while (counter <= n) {
   sum += counter;
   ++counter;
}  // end while
// this statement is always executed
int x = 0;
```

In general, the logic of a *for* statement is equivalent to

A **for** statement is equivalent to a **while** statement

```
initialize;
while (test) {
    statement;
    update;
} // end while
```

with the understanding that if *statement* contains a `continue`, *update* will execute before *test* is evaluated again.

The following two examples demonstrate the flexibility of the `for` statement:

```
for (byte ch = 'z'; ch >= 'a'; --ch) {
// ch ranges from 'z' to 'a'
    statements to process ch
}  // end for
```

```
for (double x = 1.5; x < 10; x += 0.25) {
// x ranges from 1.5 to 9.75 at steps of 0.25
    statements to process x
}  // end for
```

The *initialize* and *update* portions of a `for` statement each can contain several expressions separated by commas, thus performing more than one action. For example, the following loop raises a floating-point value to an integer power by using multiplication:

```
// floating-point power equals floating-point x
// raised to int n; assumes integer expon
for (power = 1.0, expon = 1; expon <= n; ++expon){
    power *= x;
}   // end for
```

Both *power* and *expon* are assigned values before the body of the loop executes for the first time.

Because the `for` statement consolidates the initialization, testing, and updating steps of a loop into one statement, Java programmers tend to favor it over the `while` statement. For example, notice how the following `while` loop sums the values in an array *x*:

A **for** statement is usually favored over the **while** statement

```
sum = 0;
int i = 0;
while (i < x.length) {
    sum += x[i];
    i++;
} // end while
```

This loop is equivalent to the following `for` statement:

```
for (int i = 0, sum = 0; i < x.length; sum += x[i++]) {
}
```

In fact, this `for` statement has an empty body!

You can omit any of the initialization, testing, and updating steps in a **for** statement, but you cannot omit the semicolons

You can omit any of the expressions *initialize*, *test*, or *update* from a *for* statement, but you cannot omit the semicolons. For example, you can move the *update* step from the previous *for* statement to the body of the loop:

```
for (int i = 0, sum = 0; i < x.length; ) {
    sum += x[i++];
} // end for
```

You also could omit both the initialization and the update steps, as in the following loop:

```
for ( ; x > 0; ) {
    statements to process nextValue in inputLine
} // end for
```

This *for* statement offers no advantage over the equivalent *while* statement:

```
while (x > 0)
```

Although you can omit the *test* expression from *for*, you probably will not want to do so, because then the loop would be infinite.

The *for* loop and arrays.   Java provides a loop construct that simplifies iteration through the elements of an array. A logical name for this loop construct would be the "foreach" loop, but the language developers wanted to avoid adding a new keyword to the language. So the new form of the *for* loop is often referred to as the "enhanced for loop."
The syntax for the enhanced for loop when used with arrays is as follows:

```
for (ArrayElementType variableName :  arrayName)
    statement
```

where *ArrayElementType* is the type of each element in the array, and *arrayName* is the name of the array you wish to process element by element. The loop begins with the *variableName* assigned the first element in the array. With each iteration of the loop, *variableName* is associated with the next element in the array. This continues until all of the elements in the array have been processed. For example:

```
String[] nameList = { "Janet", "Frank", "Mike", "Doug"};
for (string name: nameList) { // for each name in nameList
    System.out.println(name);
} // end for
```

is equivalent to the following:

```
String[] nameList = { "Janet", "Frank", "Mike", "Doug"};
for (int index=0; index < nameList.length; index++) {
   System.out.println(nameList[index]);
} // end for
```

The *do* Statement

Use the *do* statement when you want to execute a loop at least once. Its general form is

```
do {
    statement
} while (expression);
```

A *do* statement loops at least once

Here, *statement* executes until the value of *expression* is `false`.

For example, suppose that you execute a sequence of statements and then ask the user whether to execute them again. The *do* statement is appropriate, because you execute the statements before you decide whether to repeat them:

```
char response;
do {
    . . . (a sequence of statements)
    ask the user if they want to do it again
    store user's response in response
}   while ( (response == 'Y') || (response == 'y') );
```

1.4 Program Structure

Let's begin our discussion of program structure with the simple Java application in Figure 1-5 that computes the volume of a sphere. It consists of two classes, `SimpleSphere` and `TestClass`. Each of these classes is contained in a separate file that has the same name as the class, with `.java` appended to the end. A typical Java program consists of several classes, some of which you write and some of which you use from the Java Application Programming Interface (API). A Java application has one class that contains a method `main`, the starting point for program execution. Running the program in Figure 1-5 produces the following output:

Each Java application must contain at least one class that has a method *main*

```
The volume of a sphere of radius 19.1 inches is 29186.95
```

This application includes all of the basic elements of Java program structure (packages, classes, data fields, and methods). The sections that follow discuss each of these elements.

File `SimpleSphere.java`

1. Indicates `SimpleSphere` is part of a package ---->	`package MyPackage;`
2. Indicates class `Math` is used by `SimpleSphere` -->	`import java.lang.Math;`
3. Begins class `SimpleSphere` ------------------------->	`public class SimpleSphere {`
4. Declares a private data field `radius` ----------------->	`  private double radius;`
5. Declares a constant ------------------------------------>	`  public static final double DEFAULT_RADIUS = 1.0;`
6. A default constructor ---------------------------------->	`  public SimpleSphere() {`
7. Assignment statement --------------------------------->	`    radius = DEFAULT_RADIUS;`
	`  } // end default constructor`
8. A second constructor ----------------------------------->	`  public SimpleSphere(double initialRadius) {`
9. Assignment statement --------------------------------->	`    radius = initialRadius;`
	`  } // end constructor`
10. Begins method `getRadius` -------------------------->	`  public double getRadius() {`
11. Returns data field `radius` --------------------------->	`    return radius;`
	`  } // end getRadius`
12. Begins method `getVolume` -------------------------->	`  public double getVolume() {`
13. A comment -->	`  // Computes the volume of the sphere.`
14. Declares and assigns a local variable ---------------->	`    double radiusCubed = radius * radius * radius;`
15. Returns result of computation ----------------------->	`    return  4 * Math.PI * radiusCubed / 3;`
	`  } // end getVolume`
16. Ends class `SimpleSphere` -------------------------->	`} // end SimpleSphere`

File `TestClass.java`

17. Indicates `TestClass` is part of a package --------->	`package MyPackage;`
18. Begins class `TestClass` ----------------------------->	`public class TestClass {`
19. Begins method `main` --------------------------------->	`  static public void main(String[] args) {`
20. Declares reference `ball` ---------------------------->	`    SimpleSphere ball;`
21. Creates a `SimpleSphere` object -------------------->	`    ball = new SimpleSphere(19.1);`
22. Outputs results --------------------------------------->	`    System.out.println("The volume of a sphere of radius "`
23. Continuation of output string ---------------------->	`            + ball.getRadius() + " inches is "`
24. Continuation of output string ---------------------->	`            + (float)ball.getVolume()`
	`            + "cubic inches\n");`
	`  } //end main`
25. Ends class `TestClass` ------------------------------->	`} // end TestClass`

FIGURE 1-5

A simple Java application

Packages

Java packages provide a mechanism for grouping related classes. To indicate that a class is part of a package, you include a *package* statement as the first program line of your code. For example, lines 1 and 17 in Figure 1-5 indicate that both of these classes, *SimpleSphere* and *TestClass*, are in the package *MyPackage*. The format of the *package* statement is

package *package-name;*

To include a class in a package, begin the class's source file with a **package** statement

Java assumes that all of the classes in a particular package are contained in the same directory. Furthermore, this directory must have the same name as the package.

The Java API actually consists of many predefined packages. Some of the more common of these packages are *java.lang*, *java.util*, and *java.io*. The dot notation in these package names directly relates to the directory structure containing these packages. In this case, all of the directories corresponding to these packages are contained in a parent directory called *java*.

Place the files that contain a package's classes in the same directory

import **statement.**   The *import* statement allows you to use classes contained in other packages. The format of the *import* statement is as follows:

import *package-name.class-name;*

The **import** statement provides access to classes within a package

For example, line 2 in Figure 1-5 imports the class *Math* from the package *java.lang*. The following line also could have been used:

import java.lang.*;

In this case, the * indicates that all of the items from the package *java.lang* should be imported. Actually, this particular line can be omitted from the program, since *java.lang* is implicitly imported to all Java code. Explicitly importing *java.lang.Math* makes it clear to others who read your code that you are using the class *Math* in this code.

Classes

An object in Java is an instance of a class. You can think of a class as a data type that specifies the data and methods that are available for instances of the class. A class definition includes an optional subclassing modifier, an optional access modifier, the keyword *class*, an optional *extends* clause, an optional *implements* clause, and a class body. Figure 1-6 describes each of the components of a class.

An object is an instance of a class

A Java class defines a new data type

When a new class is created in Java, it is either specifically made a subclass of another class through the use of the *extends* clause or it is implicitly a subclass of the Java class *Object*. Creating a subclass is known as inheritance and is discussed briefly in Chapter 4 and in depth in Chapter 9 of this text.

To create an **object** or **instance** of a class, you use the *new* operator. For example, the expression

new SimpleSphere()

creates an instance of the type *SimpleSphere*.

Component	Syntax	Description
Subclassing modifier (use only one)	`abstract`	Class must be extended to be useful.
	`final`	Class cannot be extended.
Access modifiers	`public`	Class is available outside of package.
	no access modifier	Class is available only within package.
Keyword `class`	`class class-name`	Class should be contained in a file called `class-name.java`.
`extends` clause	`extends superclass-name`	Indicates that this class is a subclass of the class `superclass-name` in the `extends` clause.
`implements` clause	`implements interface-list`	Indicates the interfaces that this class implements. The `interface-list` is a comma-separated list of interface names.
Class body	Enclosed in braces	Contains data fields and methods for the class.

FIGURE 1-6

Components of a class

Now let's briefly examine the contents of the class body: data fields and methods.

Data Fields

Data fields are class members that are either variables or constants. Data field declarations can contain modifiers that control the availability of the data field (access modifiers) or that modify the way the data field can be used (use modifiers). The access modifiers are effective only if the class is declared `public`. Although this text uses only a subset of the modifiers, Figure 1-7 shows them all for completeness.

Type of modifier	Keyword	Description
Access modifier (use only one)	**public**	Data field is available everywhere (when the class is also declared *public*).
	private	Data field is available only within the class.
	protected	Data field is available within the class, available in subclasses, and available to classes within the same package.
	No access modifier	Data field is available within the class and within the package.
Use modifiers (all can be used at once)	**static**	Indicates that only one such data field is available for all instances of this class. Without this modifier, each instance has its own copy of a data field.
	final	The value provided for the data field cannot be modified (a constant).
	transient	The data field is not part of the persistent state of the object.
	volatile	The value provided for the data field can be accessed by multiple threads of control. Java ensures that the freshest copy of the data field is always used.

FIGURE 1-7

Modifiers used in data field declarations

Data fields are typically declared *private* or *protected* within a class, with access provided by methods in the class. Hence, a method within a class has access to all of the data fields declared in the class. This allows the developer of the class to maintain control over how the data stored within the class is used.

A class's data fields should be **private** or **protected**

Methods

Methods are used to implement operations. The syntax of a method declaration is as follows:

```
access-modifier use-modifiers return-type
                method-name (formal-parameter-list) {
   method-body
}
```

Usually, each method should perform one well-defined task. For example, the following method returns the larger of two integers:

A method definition implements a method's task

```java
public static int max(int x, int y) {
  if (x > y) {
    return x;
  }
  else {
    return y;
  } // end if
}  // end max
```

Method modifiers can be categorized as access modifiers and use modifiers, with the access modifier typically appearing first. In the example just given, the access modifier *public* appears first, followed by the use modifier *static*. Again, although this text uses only a subset of modifiers, Figure 1-8 shows them all for completeness.

The return type of a **valued method**—one that returns a value—is the data type of the value that the method will return. The body of a valued method must contain a statement of the form

A valued method must use **return** to return a value

```
return expression;
```

where *expression* has the value to be returned. A method can also return a reference to an object. For the method *max*, the return type is *int*. The type of the value must be specified immediately before the method name. If the method does not have a value to return, the return type is specified as *void*.

After the method name, the formal parameter list appears in parentheses. You declare a formal parameter by writing a data type and a parameter name, separating it from other formal parameter declarations with a comma, as in

```
int x, int y
```

Type of modifier	Keyword	Description
Access modifier (use only one)	**public**	Method is available everywhere (when the class is also declared as *public*).
	private	Method is available only within the class (cannot be declared *abstract*).
	protected	Method is available within the class, available in subclasses, and available to classes within the same package.
	No access modifier	Method is available within the class and to classes within the package.
Use modifiers (all can be used at once)	**static**	Indicates that only one such method is available for all instances of this class. Since a *static* method is shared by all instances, the method can refer only to data fields that are also declared *static* and shared by all instances.
	final	The method cannot be overridden in a subclass.
	abstract	The method must be overridden in a subclass.
	native	The body of the method is not written in Java but in some other programming language.
	synchronized	The method can be run by only one thread of control at a time.

FIGURE 1-8

Modifiers used in a method declaration

When you **call,** or **invoke,** the method *max*, you pass it **actual arguments** that correspond to the formal parameters with respect to number, order, and data type. For example, the following method contains two calls to *max*:

When you call a method, you pass it actual arguments that correspond to the formal parameters in number, order, and data type

```
public void printLargest(int a, int b, int c) {
   int largerAB = max(a, b);
   System.out.println("The largest of "+ a + ", " + b + ", "
              | " and " + c + " is " + max(largerAB, c));
} // end printLargest
```

An actual argument
passed by value is
copied within the
method

Arguments passed to Java methods are **passed by value.** That is, the method makes local copies of the values of the actual arguments—a and b, for example—and uses these copies wherever x and y appear in the method definition. Thus, the method cannot alter the actual arguments that you pass to it.

Passing an array to a method. If you want a method to compute the average of the first *n* elements of a one-dimensional array, you could declare the method as follows:

```
public static double averageTemp(double[] temps, int n)
```

You can invoke the method by writing

```
double avg = averageTemp(maxTemps, 6);
```

Arrays are always
passed by refer-
ence to a method

where *maxTemps* is declared an integer array of any length, and *maxTemps* is the previously defined array.

The location of the array is passed to the method. You cannot return a new array through this value, but the method can modify the contents of the array. This restriction avoids the copying of perhaps many array elements. Thus, the method *averageTemp* could modify the elements of *maxTemps*.

An argument that is
a reference can be
used to directly
access the object or
array

So note that when the formal parameter is an object or an array, the actual argument is a reference value that is copied. This means that you can change the contents of the array or object, but not the value of the reference itself. For example, you cannot have a method that creates a new object for a reference in the parameter list. If it does, the new reference value will simply be discarded when the method terminates, and the original reference to the object will be left intact.

Java has a feature that allows a method to have a variable number of arguments of the same type. When defining the method, the rightmost parameter of the method uses the ellipses (three consecutive dots) to indicate that any number of arguments of that type can be specified. For example:

```
public static int max(int... numbers) {

   int maximum = Integer.MIN_VALUE;
   for (int num : numbers) {
     if (maximum < num){
       maximum = num;
     } // end if
   } // end for
   return maximum;
} // end max
```

Note that the variable arguments can be accessed as an array, where the formal parameter name is used as the name of the array within the method. This also means that you can use the same techniques you use to process arrays, such as using the enhanced for loop as demonstrated here.

Constructors.   There is one special kind of method called a **constructor.** Constructor methods have the same name as the class and no return type. The constructor is executed only when a new instance of the class is created. A class can contain multiple constructors, differentiated by the number and types of the parameters. The actual arguments you provide when creating a new instance determine which constructor is executed.

A constructor allocates memory for an object and can initialize the object's data to particular values. A class can have more than one constructor, as is the case for the class *SimpleSphere*.

The first constructor in *SimpleSphere* is the **default constructor.** A default constructor by definition has no parameters. Typically, a default constructor initializes data fields to values that the class implementation chooses. For example, the implementation

```
public SimpleSphere() {
   radius = DEFAULT_VALUE; // DEFAULT_VALUE = 1.0
} // end default constructor
```

sets *radius* to 1.0. The following statement invokes the default constructor, which creates the object *unitSphere* and sets its radius to 1.0:

```
SimpleSphere unitSphere = new SimpleSphere();
```

The next constructor in *SimpleSphere* is

```
public SimpleSphere(double initialRadius) {
   setRadius(initialRadius);
} // end constructor
```

It creates a sphere object of radius *initialRadius*. You invoke this constructor by writing a declaration such as

```
SimpleSphere mySphere = new SimpleSphere(5.1);
```

In this case, the object *mySphere* has a radius of 5.1.

If you omit all constructors from your class, the compiler will generate a default constructor—that is, one with no parameters—for you. A **compiler generated default constructor**, however, might not initialize data fields to values that you will find suitable.

If you define a constructor that has parameters, *but you omit the default constructor*, the compiler will not generate one for you. Thus, you will not be able to write statements such as

```
SimpleSphere defaultSphere = new SimpleSphere();
```

How to Access Members of an Object

You can access data fields and methods that are declared *public* by naming the object, followed by a period, followed by the member name:

A reference to the private data field **radius** would be illegal within this program

```
static public void main(String[] args) {
  SimpleSphere ball = new SimpleSphere(19.1);
  System.out.println("The volume of a sphere of radius "
                     + ball.getRadius() + " inches is "
                     + (float)ball.getVolume()
                     + "cubic inches\n");
} //end main
```

An object such as *ball* can, upon request, return its radius and compute its volume. These requests to an object are called **messages** and are simply calls to methods. Thus, an object responds to a message by acting on its data. To invoke an object's method, you qualify the method's name—such as *getRadius*—with the object variable—such as *ball*.

The previous program is an example of a **client** of a class. A client of a particular class is simply a program or module that uses the class. We will reserve the term **user** for the person who uses a program. You can also access members of a class that are declared *static* (data fields or methods that are shared by all instances of the class) by using the class name followed by the name of the static member. For example, the *static* field *DEFAULT_RADIUS* declared in line 5 of Figure 1-5 can be accessed outside of the class as follows:

```
SimpleSphere.DEFAULT_RADIUS;
```

Class Inheritance

A brief discussion of inheritance is provided here, since it is a common way to create new classes in Java. A more complete discussion of inheritance appears in Chapter 9.

Suppose that we want to create a class for colored spheres, knowing that we have already developed the class *SimpleSphere*. We could write -an entirely new class for the colored spheres, but if the colored spheres are actually like the spheres in the class *SimpleSphere*, we can reuse the *SimpleSphere* implementation and add color operations and characteristics by using inheritance. Here is an implementation of the class `ColoredSphere` that uses inheritance:

```java
import java.awt.Color;
public class ColoredSphere extends SimpleSphere {
  private Color color;

  public ColoredSphere(Color c) {
    super();
    color = c;
  } // end constructor

  public ColoredSphere(Color c, double initialRadius) {
    super(initialRadius);
    color = c;
  } // end constructor

  public void setColor(Color c) {
    color = c;
  } // end setColor

  public Color getColor() {
    return color;
  } // end getColor
} // end ColoredSphere
```

A class derived from the class **_SimpleSphere_**

SimpleSphere is called the **base class** or **superclass,** and *ColoredSphere* is called the **derived class** or **subclass** of the class *SimpleSphere*. The definition of the subclass includes an *extends* clause that indicates the superclass to be used. When you declare a class without an *extends* clause, you are implicitly extending the class *Object*, so *Object* is its superclass.

The subclass inherits the contents of the superclass, details of which are discussed in Chapter 9. For the moment, suffice it to say that the subclass will have all of the public members of the superclass available. Any instance of the subclass is also considered to be an instance of the superclass and can be used in a program anywhere that an instance of the superclass can be used. Also, any of the publicly defined methods or variables that can be used with instances of the superclass can be used with instances of the subclass. The subclass instances also have the methods and variables that are publicly defined in the subclass definition.

Public members of the superclass are available in the subclass

In the constructor for the *ColoredSphere* class, notice the use of the keyword **super**. You use this keyword to call the constructor of the superclass, so *super()* calls the constructor *SimpleSphere()*, and *super(initialRadius)* calls the constructor *SimpleSphere(double initialRadius)*. If the subclass constructor explicitly calls the superclass constructor, the call to *super* must precede all other statements in the subclass constructor. Note that if a subclass

A constructor in a subclass should invoke **_super_** to call the constructor of the superclass

constructor contains no call to the superclass constructor, the default superclass constructor is implicitly called.

If a subclass needs to call a method defined in the superclass, the call is preceded by the keyword *super*. For example, to make a call to the method *getVolume* from within the class *ColoredSphere*, you would write the following:

```
super.getVolume()
```

Here is an example of a method that uses the *ColoredSphere* class:

```
public void useColoredSphere() {
  ColoredSphere redBall =
      new ColoredSphere(java.awt.Color.red);
  System.out.println("The ball volume is " +
                      redBall.getVolume());
  System.out.println("The ball color is " +
                      redBall.getColor());
  // other code here...
} // end useColorSphere
```

This method uses the constructor and the method *getColor* from the subclass *ColoredSphere*. It also uses the method *getVolume* that is defined in the superclass *SimpleSphere*.

1.5 Useful Java Classes

The Java Application Programming Interface (API) provides a number of useful classes. The classes mentioned here are ones that are used within this text.

The *Object* Class

Every Java class inherits the methods of the class **Object**

Java supports a single class inheritance hierarchy, with the class *Object* as the root. Thus, the class *Object* provides a number of useful methods that are inherited by every Java class. In some cases, it is common for a class to redefine, or override, the version of the method inherited from *Object*. The paragraphs that follow summarize some of the more useful methods from the class *Object*.

```
public boolean equals(Object obj)
```

Default *equals* as defined in the class *Object* compares two references

Indicates whether some other object is "equal to" this one. As defined in the class *Object*, equality is based upon references—that is, upon whether both of the references are referencing the same object. This is referred to as shallow equality.

Let's examine the equals method for objects a bit further. Suppose we have the following code:

```
SimpleSphere s1 = new SimpleSphere();
SimpleSphere s2 = s1;
if (s1.equals(s2)) {
  System.out.println("s1 and s2 are the same object" );
} // end if
```

This will produce the following output:

```
s1 and s2 are the same object
```

It is common for a class to redefine this method for deep equality—in other words, to check the equality of the contents of the objects.

Suppose that you want to determine whether two spheres have the same radius. For example,

```
SimpleSphere s1 = new SimpleSphere(2.0);
SimpleSphere s3 = new SimpleSphere(2.0);
if (s1.equals(s3)) {
  System.out.println("s1 and s3 have the same radius");
}
else {
  System.out.println("s1 and s3 have different radii");
} // end if
```

will produce the output

```
s1 and s3 have different radii
```

which is not true! Both *s1* and *s3* have a radius of 2.0. Remember that the default *equals* compares two references; they differ here because they reference two distinct objects. If you want to have *equals* check the values contained in the object for equality, you must redefine *equals* in the class. Here is an example of such an *equals* for the class *SimpleSphere*:

Customizing ***equals*** *for a class*

```
public boolean equals(Object rhs) {
  return ((rhs instanceof SimpleSphere) &&
          (radius == ((SimpleSphere)rhs).radius));
} // end equals
```

An ***equals*** method that determines whether two spheres have the same radius

Notice that the parameter of *equals* is of type *Object*. Remember, we are overriding this method as inherited from the class *Object*, and the parameter list and return value must match. Also notice that we are explicitly checking to make sure that the object parameter *rhs* is an instance of the class *SimpleSphere* by using the *instanceof* operator. If the incoming object *rhs* is an instance of the class *Simplephere* (or one of its subclasses), *instanceof* will return *true*; otherwise, the operator returns *false*. Thus, the *equals* method will return *false* when *rhs* is of a class other than *Sphere*. If the *instanceof* operator returns *true*, the boolean expression proceeds to check whether the data fields are equal. In this example, the data field of the class *SimpleSphere* is a primitive type. If an object is used as a data field, *equals* may have to be defined for that object's class as well. It is up to the designer to decide how "deep" the equality checks must be for a particular class.

Other useful *Object* methods include the following:

protected void finalize()

> Java has a garbage collection mechanism to destroy objects that a program no longer needs. When a program no longer references an object, the Java runtime environment marks it for garbage collection. Periodically, the Java runtime environment executes a method that returns the memory used by these marked objects to the system for future use. The garbage collector calls the *finalize* method on an object when it determines that there are no more references to the object.

public int hashCode()

> Associated with each object is a unique identifying value called a hash code. This method returns the hash code for the object as an integer.

public String toString()

> Returns a string that "textually represents" this object. As defined in the class *Object*, this method returns a string that contains the name of the class of which the object is an instance, followed by the at sign character (*@*), and ending with the unsigned hexadecimal representation of the hash code of the object. For example, given the statement

> Sphere mySphere = **new** Sphere();

> the method call *mySphere.toString()* will return a string similar to *Sphere@733f42ab*.

The *Array* Class

This class contains various static methods for manipulating arrays. Many of the methods have unique specifications for each of the primitive types (*boolean*, *byte*, *char*, *short*, *int*, *long*, *float*, *double*). To simplify the presentation of these methods, *ptype* will be used as a placeholder for a primitive type. Though only the methods for the primitive types are specifically discussed, many of the methods also support an array of elements of type *Object* and generic types.

```
public static ptype[] copyOf(ptype[] original, int newLength)
```

Copies the specified array of primitive types, truncating or padding (if needed) so the copy has the specified length. If padding is necessary, the numeric types will pad with zero, *char* will pad with *null*, and *boolean* will pad with *false*.

```
public static ptype[] copyOfRange(ptype[] original,
                         int beginIndex, int endIndex)
```

Copies the range *beginIndex* to *endIndex-1* of the specified array into a new array. The index *beginIndex* must lie between zero and *original.length*, inclusive. As long as there are values to copy, the value at *original[beginIndex]* is placed into the first element of the new array, with subsequent elements in the original array placed into subsequent elements in the new array. Note that *beginIndex* must be less than or equal to *endIndex*. The length of the returned array will be *endIndex- beginIndex*.

```
public static String toString(ptype[] a)
```

Returns a string representation of the contents of the specified array. The resulting string consists of a list of the array's elements, separated by a comma and a space, enclosed in square brackets ("[]"). It returns *null* if the array is null.

```
public static int binarySearch(ptype[] a, ptype key)
```

Searches the array for the *key* value using the binary search algorithm. The array must be sorted before making this call. If it is not sorted, the results are undefined. If the array contains duplicate elements with the *key* value, there is no guarantee which one will be found. For floating point types, this method considers all *NaN* values to be equivalent and equal. The method is not defined for *boolean* or *short*.

```
public static void sort(ptype[] a)
```

Sorts the array into ascending order. For floating point values, the method uses the total order imposed by the appropriate *compareTo* method and all *NaN* values are considered equivalent and equal. This method is not defined for *boolean* or *short*.

String Classes

Java provides three classes that are useful when working with strings: *String*, *StringBuffer*, and *StringTokenizer*. The class *String* is a nonmutable string type; once the value of the string has been set, it cannot be modified. The class *StringBuffer* implements a mutable sequence of characters; it provides many of the same operations as the *String* class plus others for changing the characters stored in the string. Although at first glance it would seem reasonable for us to simply study *StringBuffer*, using *String* is more efficient. In fact, many methods within the Java API use the class *String*. The last class, *StringTokenizer*, provides methods for breaking strings into pieces.

The class *String*.   Earlier, you saw that Java provides literal character strings, such as

```
"This is a string."
```

This section describes how you can create and use variables that contain such strings. Java provides a class *String* in the package *java.lang* to support nonmutable strings. A nonmutable string is one that cannot be changed once it has been created. Instances of the *String* class can be combined to form new strings, and numerous methods are provided for examining *String* objects. Our presentation includes only some of the possible operations on strings.

You can declare a string reference *title* by writing

```
String title;
```

When you initialize a string variable with a string literal, Java actually creates a *String* object to store the string literal and assigns the reference to the variable. Thus, you can assign a *String* reference by writing

```
String title = "Walls and Mirrors";
```

You can subsequently assign another string to *title* by using an assignment statement such as

```
title = "J Perfect's Diary";
```

Note that this actually creates a new *String* instance for *title* to reference.

Use the method *length* to determine a string's length

In each of the previous examples, *title* has a length of 17. You use the method *length* to determine the current length of a string. Thus, *title.length()* is equal to 17.

Use *charAt* to reference any character within a string

You can reference the individual characters in a string by using the method *charAt* with the same index that you would use for an array. Thus, in the previous example, *title.charAt(0)* contains the character *J*, and *title.charAt(16)* contains the character *y*.

You should not use the == operator to test whether two strings are equal. Using the == operator determines only whether the references to the strings are the same; it does not compare the contents of the *String* instances.

You can compare strings by using the *compareTo* method. Not only can you determine whether two strings are equal, but you can also determine which of two strings comes before the other according to the Unicode table. The *compareTo* method is used as follows:

```
string1.compareto(string2)
```

Use **compareTo** to compare two strings

The character sequence represented by the *String* object *string1* is compared to the character sequence represented by the argument *string2*. The result is a negative integer if *string1* precedes *string2*. The result is a positive integer if *string1* follows *string2*. The result is zero if the strings are equal. The ordering of two strings is analogous to alphabetic ordering, but you use the Unicode table instead of the alphabet. The following expressions demonstrate the behavior of *compareTo*:

```
"dig".compareTo("dog")      //returns negative
"Star".compareTo("star")    //returns negative
"abc".compareTo("abc")      //returns zero
"start".compareTo("star")   //returns positive
"d".compareTo("abc")        //returns positive
```

You can concatenate two strings to form another string by using the + operator. That is, you place one string after another to form another string. For example, if

```
String s = "Com";
```

the statements

```
String t = s + "puter";
s += "puter";
```

Use the **+** operator to concatenate two strings

assign the string *"Computer"* to each of *t* and *s*. Similarly, you can append a single character to a string, as in

```
s += 's';
```

Besides adding two strings together, you can also concatenate a string and a value of a primitive type together by using the + operator. For example,

```
String monthName = "December";
int day = 31;
int year = 02;
String date - monthName + " " + day + ", 20" + year;
```

assigns the string *"December 31, 2002"* to *date*.

As we mentioned earlier, the class *Object* has a method called *toString* that returns a string that "textually represents" an object. The result of the *toString* method is often combined with other strings by means of the + operator.

You can examine a portion of a string by using the method

Use *substring* to access part of a string

```
public String substring(int beginIndex, int endIndex)
```

The first parameter, *beginIndex*, specifies the position of the beginning of the substring. (Remember that 0 is the position of the first character in the string.) The end of the substring is at position *endIndex* - 1. For example, in

```
title = "J Perfect's Diary";
```

title.substring(2, 9) is the string *"Perfect"*.

Other useful *String* methods include the following:

Other useful *String* methods

```
public int indexOf(String str, int fromIndex)
```

Returns the index of the first substring equal to *str*, starting from the index *fromIndex*.

```
public String replace(char oldChar, char newChar)
```

Returns a string that is obtained by replacing all characters *oldChar* in the string with *newChar*.

```
public String trim()
```

Returns a string that has all leading and trailing spaces in the original string removed.

Instances of the class *String-Buffer* are strings that you can alter

The class *StringBuffer*.   In some situations, it is useful to be able to alter the sequence of characters stored in a string. But class *String* supports only nonmutable strings. To create mutable strings (strings that can be modified) use the class *StringBuffer* from the package *java.lang*. This class provides the same functionality as the class *String*, plus the following methods that actually modify the value stored in the *StringBuffer* object:

```
public StringBuffer append(String str)
```

Appends the string *str* to this string buffer.

```
public StringBuffer insert(int offset, String str)
```

The string *str* is inserted into this string buffer at the index indicated by *offset*. Any characters originally above that position are moved up and the length of this string buffer increased by the length of *str*. If *str* is *null*, the string *"null"* is inserted into this string buffer.

```
public StringBuffer delete(int start, int end)
```

Removes the characters in a substring of this string buffer starting at index *start* and extending to the character at index *end - 1* or to the end of the string buffer if no such character exists. If *start* is equal to *end*, no changes are made. This method may throw *StringIndexOutOfBoundsException* if the value of *start* is negative, greater than the length of the string buffer, or greater than *end*.

```
public void setCharAt(int index, char ch)
```

The character at index *index* of this string buffer is set to *ch*. This method may throw *IndexOutOfBoundsException* if the value of *index* is negative or is greater than or equal to the length of the string buffer.

```
public StringBuffer replace(int start, int end,
                            String str)
```

Replaces the characters in a substring of this string buffer with characters in the specified string *str*. The substring to be replaced begins at index *start* and extends to the character at index *end - 1* or to the end of the string buffer if no such character exists. The substring is removed from the string buffer, and then the string *str* is inserted at index *start*. If necessary, the string buffer is lengthened to accommodate the string *str*. This method may throw *StringIndexOutOfBoundsException* if the value of *start* is negative, greater than the length of the string buffer, or greater than *end*.

The class *StringTokenizer*. Another useful class when working with strings is *StringTokenizer* in the package *java.util*. This class allows a program to break a string into pieces or **tokens.** The tokens are separated by characters known as delimiters. When you create a *StringTokenizer* instance, you must specify the string to be tokenized. Other constructors within *StringTokenizer* allow you to specify the delimiting characters and whether the delimiting characters themselves should be returned as tokens. Here is brief description of the three constructors for *StringTokenizer*:

> Instances of the class *String-Tokenizer* are strings that you can break into pieces called tokens

```
public StringTokenizer(String str)
```

This constructor creates a string tokenizer for the specified string *str*. The tokenizer uses the default delimiter set, which is the space character, the tab character, the newline character, the carriage-return character, and the form-feed character. Delimiter characters themselves are not treated as tokens.

```
public StringTokenizer(String str, String delim)
```

This constructor creates a string tokenizer for the specified string *str*. All characters in the *delim* string are the delimiters for separating tokens. Delimiter characters themselves are not treated as tokens.

```
public StringTokenizer(String str, String delim,
                       boolean returnTokens)
```

This constructor creates a string tokenizer for the specified string *str*. All characters in the *delim* string are the delimiters for separating tokens. If the *returnTokens* flag is true, the delimiter characters are also returned as tokens. Each delimiter is returned as a string of length 1. If the flag is false, the delimiter characters are skipped and serve only as separators between tokens.

StringTokenizer also provides the following methods for retrieving tokens from the string:

```
public String nextToken()
```

Returns the next token in the string. If there are no more tokens in the string, it throws the exception *NoSuchElementException*. Exceptions are discussed in the next section.

```
public boolean hasMoreTokens()
```

Returns *true* if the string contains more tokens.

1.6 Java Exceptions

Many programming languages, including Java, support a mechanism known as an **exception,** which handles an error during execution. A method indicates that an error has occurred by **throwing** an exception. The exception returns to the point at which you invoked the method, where you **catch** the exception and deal with the error condition.

An exception is a mechanism for handling an error during execution

Catching Exceptions

To handle an exception, Java provides *try-catch* blocks. You place the statement that might throw an exception within a *try* block. The *try* block must be followed by one or more *catch* blocks. Each *catch* block indicates the type of exception you want to handle. A *try* block can have many *catch* blocks associated with it, since even a single statement may be capable of throwing more than one type of exception. Also, the *try* block can contain many statements, any of which might throw an exception. Here is the general syntax for a *try* block:

*Use a **try** block for statements that can throw an exception*

```
try {
  statement(s);
}
```

The syntax for a *catch* block is as follows:

```
catch (exceptionClass identifier) {
  statement(s);
}
```

Use a **catch** block for each type of exception that you handle

When a statement in the *try* block actually throws an exception, the remainder of the *try* block is abandoned, and control is passed to the *catch* block that corresponds to the type of exception thrown. The statements in the *catch* block then execute, and upon completion of the *catch* block, execution resumes at the point following the last *catch* block.

The system decides which *catch* block to execute by considering the *catch* blocks in the order in which they appear, using the first one that produces a legal assignment of the thrown exception and the argument specified in the *catch* block. Thus, you must order the *catch* blocks so that the most specific exception classes appear before the more general exception classes; otherwise, the code will not compile. For example,

```
try {
  int result = 99 / 0;
  // other statements appear here
} // end try
catch (Exception e) {
  System.out.println("Something else was caught");
} // end catch
catch (ArithmeticException e) {
  System.out.println("ArithmeticException caught");
} // end catch
```

The order of these two **catch** blocks is incorrect

compiles with an error message similar to the following:

```
TestExceptionExample.java:43: exception
  java.lang.ArithmeticException has already been caught
    catch (ArithmeticException e) {
    ^
1 error
```

To get the code to compile successfully, you must switch the order of the *catch* blocks.

The following program demonstrates what happens when an exception is thrown and not caught. Figure 1-9 illustrates these events.

```
class ExceptionExample {
  private int [] myArray;

  public ExceptionExample() {
    myArray = new int[10];
  } // end default constructor
```

This program does not handle the exception that is thrown and, therefore, execution terminates

```java
public void addValue(int n, int value) {
  // add value to element n by calling addOne n times
  for (int i = 1; i <= value; i++) {
    addOne(n);
  } // end for
} // end addValue

public void addOne(int n) {
  // add 1 to the element n
    myArray[n] += 1;
} // end addOne
} end ExceptionExample

public class TestExceptionExample {
  public static void main(String[] args) {
    ExceptionExample e1 = new ExceptionExample();
    e1.addValue(99, 3); // add 3 to element 99
  } // end main
} // end TestExceptionExample
```

The method *addOne* causes *ArrayIndexOutOfBoundsException* from *java.lang* to be thrown when an attempt is made to access *myArray[99]*. Since *addOne* does not provide a handler for the exception (Point 1 in Figure 1-9), the method terminates and the exception is propagated back to *addValue* to the point where *addOne* was called. The method *addValue* also does not provide an exception handler, so it also terminates (Point 2 in Figure 1-9) and the exception is propagated back to *main*. Since *main* is the main method of the program, and the exception is not handled in *main* (Point 3 in Figure 1-9), the program terminates, and an error message similar to the following is displayed on the screen:

```
java.lang.ArrayIndexOutOfBoundsException: 99
  at ExceptionExample.addOne(ExceptionExample.java)
  at ExceptionExample.addValue(Compiled Code)
  at TestExceptionExample.main(TestExceptionExample.java)
```

Notice that the error message for the exception includes a **stack trace,** the sequence of method calls that led to the exception being thrown. This is the default behavior when no exception handler is provided. The message may also contain information specific to the exception at hand; in this case, it contains the index value 99 that caused the exception to be thrown.

This code does not indicate that the method *addOne* might throw the exception *ArrayIndexOutOfBoundsException*. The method's documentation should indicate the exceptions it might throw.

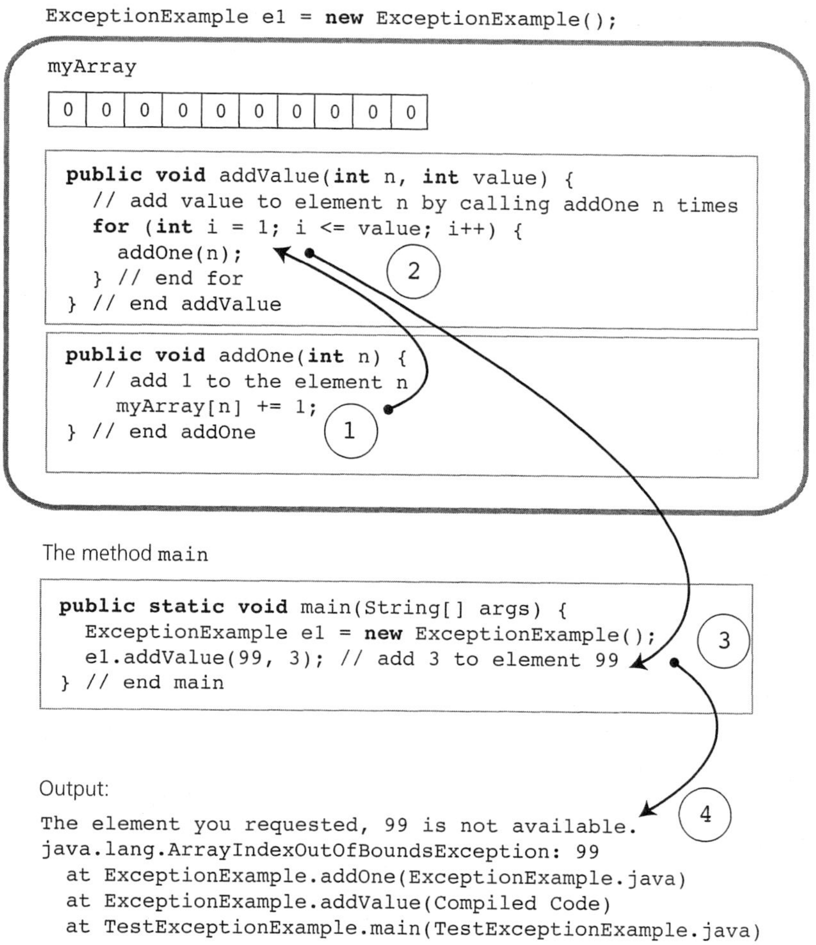

```
ExceptionExample e1 = new ExceptionExample();
```

FIGURE 1-9

Flow of control in a simple Java application

The exception *ArrayIndexOutOfBoundsException* could be caught at any point in the sequence of method calls. For example, *addOne* in the class *ExceptionExample* could be rewritten as follows to catch the exception:

```
public void addOne(int n) {
  try {
    myArray[n] += 1;
  } // end try
  catch (ArrayIndexOutOfBoundsException e) {
    System.out.println("The element you requested, " +
                       n + ", is not available.");
  } // end catch
} // end addOne
```

An example of han-dling an exception

This version of *addOne* produces the following output:

```
The element you requested, 99, is not available.
The element you requested, 99, is not available.
The element you requested, 99, is not available.
```

The method *addOne* is called three times by *addValue* when *e1.addValue(99,3)* executes, and hence the exception is thrown three times. When the exception was not handled, the program terminated the first time the exception occurred. By adding a *catch* block to handle the exception, we allow the code to continue execution.

Although the *addOne* method is where *ArrayIndexOutOfBounds-Exception* is thrown, it is not necessarily the best place to handle the exception. For example, if the call *e1.addValue(99, 10000)* executed, the message printed by *addOne* would have appeared 10,000 times! In this case it makes more sense for the handler to appear in the *addValue* method, and not in the *addOne* method. This assumes that *addOne* no longer handles the exception but propagates it back to *addValue*. Here is the code for *addValue* with the exception handler:

An improved way to handle an exception

```java
public void addValue(int n, int value) {
    try {
        for (int i = 1; i <= value; i++) {
            addOne(n);
        } // end for
    } // end try
    catch (ArrayIndexOutOfBoundsException e) {
        System.out.println("The element you requested, " +
                           n + " is not available.");
        e.printStackTrace();
    } // end catch
} // end addValue
```

This method produces the following output:

```
The element you requested, 99 is not available.
java.lang.ArrayIndexOutOfBoundsException: 99
    at ExceptionExample.addOne(ExceptionExample.java)
    at ExceptionExample.addValue(Compiled Code)
    at TestExceptionExample.main(TestExceptionExample.java)
```

When *addOne* throws the exception *ArrayIndexOutOfBoundsException*, it is propagated back to *addValue*. The method *addValue* abandons execution of the statements in the *try* block, executes the statement in the *catch* block, and resumes execution after the last *catch* block. The message is printed only once, since the *for* loop is inside the *try* block, which is abandoned when the exception occurs. If the *try* block was placed inside the *for* loop (around the call to *addOne*), the exception would be thrown and handled at each iteration of the loop, causing the message to be printed multiple times.

The *catch* block also contains the method call *e.printStackTrace()*. Recall that the *catch* block specifies the type of exception handled and an identifier. This identifier provides a name for the caught exception that can be used within the *catch* block. In this case, the method *printStackTrace* is called for the exception object *e*. The *printStackTrace* method is one of many methods available to exception objects. Other uses of the exception name in the *catch* block are discussed in the next section on throwing exceptions.

You may have noticed that some exceptions from the Java API cannot be totally ignored. You must provide a handler for these exceptions. For example, in the class *java.io.FileInputStream*, the constructor will throw *java.io.FileNotFoundException* if the file specified cannot be found. In this case, the compiler will complain if no exception handler is provided. For example, compiling the following code:

Some exceptions must be handled

```
import java.io.*;
public class TestExceptionExample {
  public static void getInput(String fileName) {
    FileInputStream fis;
    fis = new FileInputStream(fileName);
    // file processing code appears here
  } // end getInput

  static public void main(String[] args) {
    getInput("test.dat");
  } // end main
} // end TestExceptionExample
```

produces a compilation error message similar to the following:

```
TestExceptionExample.java:5: unreported exception
java.io.FileNotFoundException must be caught, or declared
to be thrown
    fis = new FileInputStream(fileName);
          ^

1 error
```

One way to resolve this error message is to provide an exception handler within the *getInput* method as follows:

```
public static void getInput(String fileName) {
  FileInputStream fis;
  try {
    fis = new FileInputStream(fileName);
    // file processing code appears here
  } // end try
```

```
    catch (FileNotFoundException e) {
      System.out.println("The file " + fileName +
                         " is not available");
      System.out.println(e);
    } // end catch
    System.out.println("After try-catch blocks");
  } // end getInput
```

Output similar to the following results when the file named *test.dat* does not exist:

```
The file test.dat is not available
java.io.FileNotFoundException: test.dat
  at java.io.FileInputStream.<init>(FileInputStream.java:56)
  at TestExceptionExample.getInput(TestExceptionExample.java)
  at TestExceptionExample.main(TestExceptionExample.java)
After try-catch blocks
```

Two types of exceptions: checked and runtime

Java has two types of exceptions: checked exceptions and runtime exceptions. The exception *java.io.FileNotFoundException* is an example of a checked exception. **Checked exceptions** are instances of classes that are subclasses of the *java.lang.Exception* class. They must be handled locally or explicitly thrown from the method (as discussed in the next section). They are typically used when the method encounters a serious problem. In some cases, the error may be considered serious enough that the program should be terminated.

Runtime exceptions occur when the error is not considered as serious. These types of exceptions can often be prevented by fail-safe programming. For example, it is fairly easy to avoid allowing an array index to go out of range, a situation that causes the runtime exception *ArrayIndexOutOfBoundsException* to be thrown. Runtime exceptions are instances of classes that are subclasses of the *java.lang.RuntimeException* class. *RuntimeException* is a subclass of *java.lang.Exception* that relaxes the requirement forcing the exception to be either handled locally or explicitly thrown by the method.

The *finally* block.   As an option, you can follow the last *catch* block with a *finally* block that has the following form:

```
finally {
  statement(s);
}
```

This block is executed whether or not an exception is thrown within the *try* block. If an exception is thrown, the appropriate *catch* block executes and then the *finally* block executes. If no exception is thrown, the *finally* block executes upon completion of the *try* block. Note that you can have a *finally* block even if no *catch* block is present. Later in this chapter—in the section *File Input and Output*—you will see an example of a *finally* block that deals with a file when the program no longer needs it.

Throwing Exceptions

As we've mentioned, all exceptions in Java are instances of the class `java.lang.Exception` or one of its subclasses. When a method specification contains a `throws` clause, it also specifies the type of exception that the method can throw. If the method can throw more than one type of exception, each is listed after the `throws` clause, separated by commas. For example, here is the method header for one of the constructors for `FileInputStream`:

```
public FileInputStream(String name)
                throws FileNotFoundException
```

*A **throws** clause indicates that a method might throw an exception*

The `throws` clause indicates that a method may throw an exception if an error occurs during its execution. In this case, the constructor will throw the exception `FileNotFoundException` if the file specified by `name` can't be opened.

An exception is thrown when the `throw` statement is executed. The syntax of this statement is

```
throw reference
```

where *reference* refers to an instance of a subclass of the class `java.lang.Exception`. When the `throw` statement executes, the remaining code in the `try` block or method is ignored. Typically, a `throw` statement will appear as follows:

```
throw new exceptionClass(stringArgument);
```

*Use a **throw** statement to throw an exception*

where *exceptionClass* is the type of exception you want to throw, and *stringArgument* is an argument to the *exceptionClass* constructor that specifies the detail message, a more detailed description of what may have caused the exception.

In certain situations, the Java API will have a predefined exception class that will suit the exception needs of your program. For example, the Java API has an exception `java.lang.IndexOutOfBoundsException` that could be used when an array's index is out of range.

You may also want to define your own exception class. Usually, you use `Exception` or `RuntimeException` as the base class for the exception. Base your decision as to which one to use upon how you want other parts of the program to treat the exception. If you don't want the exception to be ignored, extend `Exception`. If you don't care whether the exception is ignored, or if you have indicated in your precondition how the exception could be avoided, you might choose to extend `RuntimeException`. In either case, your class will

You can define your own exception class

inherit the same set of methods. Often, a constructor that includes a string parameter is provided. For example,

```
class MyRuntimeException extends RuntimeException {
  public MyRuntimeException(String s) {
    super(s);
  } // end constructor
  // All other methods are inherited.
}  // end MyRuntimeException

class MyException extends Exception {
  public MyException(String s) {
    super(s);
  } // end constructor
  // All other methods are inherited.
  // This exception must be handled in or
  // propagated from the method in which it occurs.
}  // end MyException
```

Once you've defined the new exception class, you can use it in the *throw* statement and *catch* blocks of your program. The constructor provides a way to identify the condition that caused the exception to occur. When constructing the new exception, you can include a string that describes the error condition. For example,

```
throw new MyException("MyException: Provide reason");
```

A variety of methods available for exception objects provide access to this detailed message. For example, the methods *printStackTrace*, *getMessage*, and *toString* are just a few of the methods that include this detailed message in their output.

If you throw an exception that is not an instance of *RuntimeException* or one of its subclasses, you must either handle the exception within the method, using *try-catch* blocks, or throw the exception explicitly from the method. To indicate that the exception will be thrown by the method, you include a *throws* clause in the method's specification as follows:

```
public void myMethod() throws MyException {
  // some code here...
  throw new MyException("MyException was thrown: reason");
} // end myMethod
```

Any method that calls *myMethod* must either provide a *catch* block for instances of *MyException* or contain a *throws* clause of its own for *MyException*.

1.7 Text Input and Output

Some Java applications read input from a keyboard and write output to a monitor, often referred to as console I/O. Such input and output consist of **streams,** which are simply sequences of characters that either come from an input source or go to an output destination.

The class of an input stream is *InputStream*, and the class of an output stream is *PrintStream*. The package *java.io* provides these classes and others related to input and output. The class *java.lang.System* provides three Standard streams: *System.in* for the **standard input stream,** *System.out* for the **standard output stream,** and *System.err* for the **standard error stream,** which also is an output stream. Java 6 introduced the *Console* class as an alternative to the Standard Streams. This section provides a brief introduction to simple input and output followed by a discussion of the *Console* class.

A stream is a sequence of characters that either come from or go to an I/O device

Input

As we just mentioned, the input stream *System.in* typically corresponds to keyboard input. But this source in its raw form—a sequence of bytes—cannot readily be used. Java provides a number of classes that facilitate getting the raw data into a form that is easily used within a program. The discussion here will present two approaches to getting input from the console; the first is based on character streams, and the second on the *Scanner* class.

InputStream-Reader converts a stream of bytes to a sequence of characters

Character Streams.   The class *InputStreamReader* transforms a given raw byte stream into a sequence of characters. But dealing with an input stream on a character-by-character basis is tedious. The class *BufferedReader* provides additional facilities that allow the character data to be read as a block or line of characters at a time. *BufferedReader* works with a given instance of *Input-StreamReader*. The following code shows how to use these classes to read a line of input into the string *nextLine*:

```
BufferedReader stdin = new BufferedReader(
        new InputStreamReader(System.in));

String nextLine = stdin.readLine();
```

The *BufferedReader* method *readLine()* retrieves the next line of input as an instance of *String*.

*Using **Buffered-Reader** with **InputStream** allows the **read-Line** method to be used*

But what if the program needs to view the characters in the string *next-Line* as a sequence of integers instead of as a sequence of characters? When the desired input value is not a string, it is usually a value of a primitive type. All of the primitive types provide a method for converting a string to the primitive type. For example, the class *Integer* provides the method *parseInt*. First, you extract the string containing the primitive type from *nextLine*, using the

Use **String-Tokenizer** to break the string into tokens, then convert each token to a value of the primitive type

StringTokenizer class seen earlier. Then, you apply the method that converts the string to a primitive type value. The following code demonstrates this technique by extracting two integers x and y from *nextLine*:

```
BufferedReader stdin = new BufferedReader(
          new InputStreamReader(System.in));

String nextLine = stdin.readLine();

StringTokenizer input = new StringTokenizer(nextLine);
x = Integer.parseInt(input.nextToken());
y = Integer.parseInt(input.nextToken());
```

The *Scanner* Class.   The *Scanner* class makes it easier to get strings and primitive types from keyboard input, *String* objects, and files. The *Scanner* class is located in the *java.util* package, so any code that uses the *Scanner* class should include the statement

```
import java.util.Scanner;
```

A *Scanner* object can be used to break its input into tokens using a delimiter pattern. The default pattern matches any white space, including blanks, tabs, and carriage returns. This pattern can be set and changed using various methods in the *Scanner* class in conjunction with the *Pattern* class. The *Scanner* class also provides various *next* methods to retrieve tokens from the input and convert them to primitive type values and strings. Here is a brief summary of the more useful *next* methods as described in the Java API:

Method	Description
`String next()`	Finds and returns the next complete token from this scanner.
boolean `nextBoolean()`	Scans the next token of the input into a boolean value and returns that value.
double `nextDouble()`	Scans the next token of the input as a double.
float `nextFloat()`	Scans the next token of the input as a float.
int `nextInt()`	Scans the next token of the input as an int.

String nextLine()	Advances this scanner past the current line and returns the input that was skipped.
long nextLong()	Scans the next token of the input as a long.
short nextShort()	Scans the next token of the input as a short.

Note that these methods scan the next token of the input and convert the value to the specified type. If the next token cannot be properly interpreted as the specified type (for example *float* in the case of *nextFloat()*), then an *InputMismatchException* is thrown. These methods will also throw *NoSuchElementException* if the input has been exhausted, and *Illegal-StateException* if the scanner is closed.

Suppose that you wanted to compute the sum of integers that you enter at the keyboard. Note that the *Scanner* class does not provide any easy way to detect the end of an input line, so we will use a negative value or zero to indicate the end of the list of integers. The following code accomplishes this task:

```
int nextValue;
int sum=0;
Scanner kbInput = new Scanner(System.in);

nextValue = kbInput.nextInt();
while (nextValue > 0) {
  sum += nextValue;
  nextValue = kbInput.nextInt();
} // end while
kbInput.close();
```

Note the use of the *Scanner* class constructor with *System.in* (of type *InputStream*) to specify that the input will be from the keyboard. The *Scanner* class also provides constructors for the *String* and *File* data types. The method *close* simply closes the *Scanner* object.

If you are concerned that the user might enter a non-integer value in the list, you can use exception handling to react to that error. You can also use the method *hasNextInt*. This method returns *true* if the next token is an integer value, *false* otherwise. Similar methods exist for the other primitive types and strings.

Output

Java provides the methods *print* and *println* to write character strings, primitive types, and objects to the standard output stream *System.out*. The method *println* differs from *print* in that it terminates a line of output so that subsequent output will start on the next line. When the argument is a

The methods **print** and **println** write to an output stream

string, it is simply placed in the output stream. For example, the following program segment uses *println* with a *String* argument:

```
int count = 5;
double average = 20.3;
System.out.println("The average of the " + count
     + " distances read is " + average
     + " miles.");
```

produces the following output:

```
The average of the 5 distances read is 20.3 miles.
```

As we mentioned in the section on strings, the operator + can be used to concatenate strings with other strings, primitive types, and objects. Thus, the previous statements concatenate the string *"The average of the "* to the string that represents the value of *count*, and so on.

When *println*'s argument is a primitive type or an object, the *static* method *valueOf* from the *String* class is used to determine the corresponding string value that is placed on the output stream. For primitive types, this is a simple string representation of the value. For objects, this is ultimately the value returned by the object's *toString* method. Thus, for example, using the method *toString* as defined in the class *Object*, the statements

The method **toString** is implicitly invoked when an object is an argument of **println**

```
SimpleSphere mySphere = new SimpleSphere();
System.out.println(mySphere);
```

will produce output similar to

```
SimpleSphere@733f42ab
```

You usually override *toString* with your own version. Here is an example that could be used in the class *SimpleSphere*:

```
public String toString() {
   return ("SimpleSphere: radius = " + radius);
} // end toString
```

Now if you execute the statements

```
SimpleSphere mySphere = new SimpleSphere();
System.out.println(mySphere);
```

the output appears as follows:

```
SimpleSphere: radius = 1.0
```

One of the problems with the *print* and *println* methods is the lack of formatting abilities. Java provides a C-style formatted output method called *printf*. This method uses the new variable arguments feature, and has the following format:

```
printf(String format, Object... args)
```

With the new autoboxing feature, the arguments can also be of a primitive type. The format string may contain fixed text and one or more embedded **format specifiers.** For example:

```
String name = "Jamie";
int x = 5, y = 6;
int sum = x + y;
System.out.printf("%s, %d + %d = %d", name, x, y, sum);
```

produces the output:

```
Jamie, 5 + 6 = 11
```

In this example, each of the format specifiers has a corresponding argument value that is placed into the format string upon output. The format specifiers in this example are of the simplest form—they start with the % character and contain only a **conversion** character. The conversion characters for common data types are:

Conversion Character	Data Type
b	boolean
s	String — this is also used with objects and the *toString* method
c	character
d	decimal integer
e	decimal number (formatted in computerized scientific notation)
f	decimal number

A more complete form of the format specifier is as follows:

```
%[width][.precision]conversion
```

The *width* specifies the minimum field width that the value should be printed within. When printing decimals numbers, the *precision* specifies the number of digits of *precision* to be printed after the decimal point. When using precision with strings, it represents a maximum number of characters. Figure 1-10 shows some examples with the corresponding output.

The `Console` Class

Java 6 introduced the Console class to access the character-based console device associated with the current Java virtual machine. Java provides a pre-defined object of type *Console*, as defined in the package *java.io*, that has many of the same capabilities provided by the Standard streams. This *Console* object can be accessed as follows:

```
Console myConsole = System.console();
```

If the JVM running this code has a console available, it returns a reference to it. But if the JVM does not have a console device available, this call will return *null*. So code such as the following often accompanies an attempt to access the console:

```
if (myConsole == null) {
    System.err.println("No console available.");
    System.exit(1);
} // end if
```

Similar to the *BufferedReader* class, the *Console* class also provides a *read-Line()* method to retrieve a line of text from the console. It also defines a second *readLine* method of the form

```
String readLine(String fmt, Object... args)
```

This version provides the ability to create a formatted prompt, and then reads a single line of text from the console. The formatting of the prompt string works much like the *printf* method described earlier in this section.

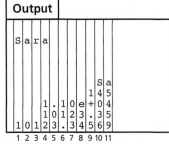

```
String name = "Sarah";
double y = 10123.34568;
int n = 145;
System.out.printf("%.4s\n", name);
System.out.printf("%10.2s\n", name);
System.out.printf("%10d\n", n);
System.out.printf("%10.2e\n", y);
System.out.printf("%10.2f\n", y);
System.out.printf("%5.5f\n", y);
```

FIGURE 1-10

Formatting examples with *printf*

The Console class also provides two methods for the input of a user password:

```
char[] readPassword()
char[] readPassword(String fmt, Object... args)
```

These methods behave similarly to the *readLine* method, but have two important differences. First, when the user enters data at a point in the program where *readPassword* is being executed, it is not echoed back to the console, so it can't be seen by the user (this is what we expect when we type in a password). This is an important feature for helping users maintain password security. Second, the characters typed for the password are entered into a character array, not a *String*. Once the password has been verified, it is strongly suggested that the array holding the password be overwritten with blanks or some other character to minimize the lifetime of the password in memory.

Output to the console is accomplished using the following method:

```
Console printf(String format, Object... args)
```

Alternatively, you can use this method

```
PrintWriter writer()
```

to retrieve a *Printwriter* object that has methods print and println similar to those used with *System.out*.

The following example shows how the *Console* class could be used to prompt for a username and password.

```
import java.io.Console;
import java.util.Arrays;
import java.io.Printwriter;

public class ConsoleExample {

  static boolean validateLogin(String username,
                               char[] password) {
    // Would put code in here to validate the user login
    return true;
  }  // end validateLogin

  public static void main (String args[]){
    Console cons = System.console();
    if (cons == null) {
      System.err.println("No console available.");
      System.exit(1);
    } // end if
    PrintWriter consOutput = cons.writer();
```

```
    String username = cons.readLine("Username: ");
    char [] password = cons.readPassword("Password: ");

    if (validateLogin(username, password)) {
      // At this point you have validated the password
      consOutput.println("User " + username +
                         "successfully logged in");
      // Now wipe out the password from memory
      Arrays.fill(password, ' ');
      // And let the user start his or her session...
    } // end if

  } // end main
} // end ConsoleExample
```

One interesting thing to note here is that if you try to use the *Console* class from some of the Integrated Development Environments (IDEs) such as Eclipse or NetBeans, the IDE may run the JVM in the background, and hence when you execute the above code you will most likely get the message "No console available." But if you execute the program from the command prompt using the java command, it will work as expected.

1.8 File Input and Output

You have used **files** ever since you wrote your first program. In fact, your Java source program is in a file that you probably created by using a text editor. You can create and access such files outside of and independently of any particular program. Files can also contain data that is either read or written by your program. It is this type of file that concerns us here.

A file is a sequence of components of the same data type

A file is a sequence of components of the same data type that resides in auxiliary storage, often a disk. Files are useful because they can be large and can exist after program execution terminates. In contrast, variables of primitive data types and objects, for example, represent memory that is accessible only within the program that creates them. When program execution terminates, the operating system reuses this memory and changes its contents.

Since files can exist after program execution, they not only provide a permanent record for human users, they also allow communication between programs. Program *A* can write its output into a file that program *B* can use later for input. However, files that you discard after program execution are also not unusual. You use such a file as a scratch pad during program execution when you have too much data to retain conveniently in memory all at once.

It is useful to contrast files with their closest Java relatives, arrays. Files and arrays are similar in that they are both collections of components of the same type. For example, just as you can have an array of elements whose type is *char*, so also can you have a file of elements whose type is *char*. In both cases, the components are characters. However, in addition to the previous distinction between files and all other data types—files can exist after program execution and arrays cannot—files and arrays have two other differences:

- **Files grow in size as needed; arrays have a fixed size.** When you declare an array, you specify its maximum size. Thus, a fixed amount of memory represents the array. A well-written program always checks that an array can accommodate a new piece of data before attempting to insert it. If the array cannot accommodate the data, the program might have to terminate with a message of explanation. You can increase the array size—hopefully by changing the value of a named constant—and compile and run the program again.[4] On the other hand, if you declare the array's maximum size to be larger than you need, you waste memory. In contrast, the size of a file is not fixed. When the system first creates a file, the file requires almost no storage space. As a program adds data to the file, the file's size increases as necessary, up to the limit of the storage device. Thus, at any given time, the file occupies only as much space as it actually requires. This dynamic nature is a great advantage.

- **Files provide both sequential and random access; arrays provide random access.** If you want the 100th element in the one-dimensional array x, you can access it directly by writing x[99]; you do not need to look at the elements x[0] through x[98] first. You could choose, of course, to process an array's elements sequentially, but you would do so by accessing each successive element directly and independently of any other element.

   However, you can access elements in a file either directly or sequentially. If you want the 100th element in a file, you can access it directly by position without first reading past the 99 elements that precede it. On the other hand, you could also read all of the first 100 elements one at a time, in sequential order, without specifying any element's position.

Files are classified as follows. A **text file** is a file of characters that are organized into lines. The files that you create—by using an editor—to contain your Java programs are text files. Because text files consist of characters, and accessing characters by position number is usually not convenient, you typically process a text file sequentially. A file that is not a text file is called a **binary file** or sometimes a **general file** or a **nontext file.**

---

4. Chapter 4 describes resizable arrays. If you reach the end of such an array, you can increase its size during execution. However, this process requires copying the old array into the new array.

Text Files

Text files are designed for easy communication with people. As such, they are flexible and easy to use, but they are not as efficient with respect to computer time and storage as binary files.

One special aspect of text files is that they *appear* to be divided into lines. This illusion is often the source of much confusion. In reality, a text file—like any other file—is a sequence of components of the same type. That is, a text file is a sequence of characters. A special **end-of-line symbol** creates the illusion that a text file contains lines by making the file *behave* as if it were divided into lines. On some systems this end-of-line symbol is simply a carriage return, while on others it consists of a carriage return and line feed character. You need not worry about how your system actually views the end-of-line symbol; this is taken care of by the Java runtime system.

A text file
contains lines
of characters

When you create a text file by typing data at your keyboard, each time you press the Enter or Return key, you insert one end-of-line symbol into the file. When an output device, such as a printer or monitor, encounters an end-of-line symbol in a text file, the device moves to the beginning of the next line. In Java, you can specify this end-of-line symbol by using the character \n.

Files end with a
special end-of-file
symbol

In addition, you can think of a special **end-of-file symbol** that follows the last component in a file. Such a symbol may or may not actually exist in the file, but Java behaves as if one did. Figure 1-11 depicts a text file with these special symbols.

Note that the *Scanner* class presented in the previous section can be used to process text files in a manner very similar to the way we handled input from the keyboard. The *Scanner* class has two constructors that can be used to create *Scanner* objects for input files:

```
Scanner(InputStream source)
```

Constructs a new *Scanner* that produces values scanned from the specified input stream.

```
Scanner(File source)
```

Constructs a new *Scanner* that produces values scanned from the specified file.

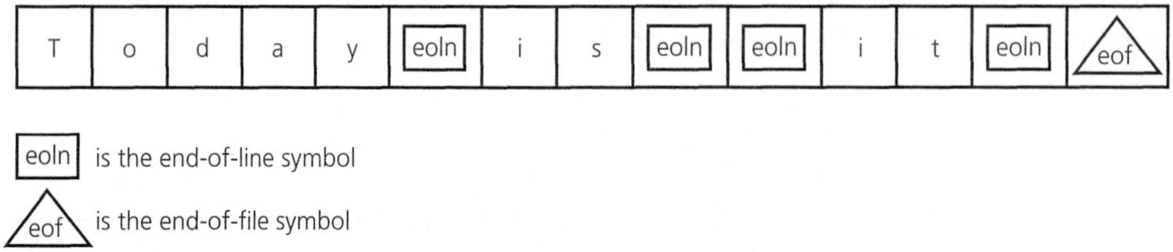

T	o	d	a	y	eoln	i	s	eoln	eoln	i	t	eoln	/eof\

eoln   is the end-of-line symbol

/eof\   is the end-of-file symbol

FIGURE 1-11

A text file with end-of-line and end-of-file symbols

The first constructor allows for any type of *InputStream*, including *System.in* and objects of the subclass *FileInputStream*. The second constructor is based upon the class *File*. This class is part of the *java.io* package. It provides an abstraction for the file within a program. Instances of the class *File* are not used directly for input and output, but for getting characteristics of a file, such as its access mode. The first constructor creates a scanner for the specified file using the *File* class. Here is a simple example that uses the *Scanner* class to read a first name, last name, and age from each line of a file called *Ages.dat* and prints it to standard output:

```
String fname, lname;
int age;
Scanner fileInput;
File inFile = new File("Ages.dat");

try {
  fileInput = new Scanner(inFile);

  while (fileInput.hasNext()) {
    fname = fileInput.next();
    lname = fileInput.next();
    age = fileInput.nextInt();
    age = fileInput.nextInt();
    System.out.printf("%s %s is %d years old.\n",
                      fname, lname, age);
  } // end while

  fileInput.close();

} // end try
catch (FileNotFoundException e) {
  System.out.println(e);
} // end catch
```

Note that here the *hasNext* method is used to determine if the end-of-file symbol has been reached—when the end-of-file is reached, there are no more tokens in the file to be processed. Also, the code above would need to import the classes *File* and *FileNotFoundException* from the package *java.io*, and the *Scanner* class from the package *java.util*.

Alternatively, text input files can be processed using the classes *FileInputStream* and *FileReader*. Output files are also supported by two main classes: *FileOutputStream* and *PrintWriter*. When using these classes, actual read or write access to the file is done through streams. A variety of tasks related to processing files using streams are now presented.

Use streams to access a file

Opening a stream to a file. Before you can read from or write to a file, you need to **open** a stream to the file. That is, you need to create a stream instance.

You must initialize, or open, a stream before you can use it

One way to open a stream to a file for reading is to use the class *FileReader* and provide the file's name when you declare the file stream. For example,

```
FileReader inStream = new FileReader("Ages.dat");
```

declares an input stream variable *inStream* and associates it with the file named *Ages.dat*. The file name can be either a literal c-onstant, as it is here, or a string variable.

Alternatively, you can use an instance of *File* by writing

```
File inFile = new File("Ages.dat");
FileReader inStream = new FileReader(inFile);
```

Unfortunately, the methods available from the class *FileReader* do not lend themselves very well to text processing. Because of this, the stream instance is usually embedded within an instance of the class *BufferedReader*. (This is the same class that we used to read input from the keyboard.) *BufferedReader* provides the method *readLine* for obtaining a line of text as a *String* object. A line is considered to be terminated by an end-of-line character, as we mentioned earlier. Here is an example of opening a stream to a file and adding the functionality of the class *BufferedReader*:

The method **read-Line** reads a line of text as a string

```
FileReader fr = new FileReader("Ages.dat");
BufferedReader input = new BufferedReader(fr);
```

Often, this is combined into a single statement:

```
BufferedReader input = new BufferedReader(
                       new FileReader("Ages.dat"));
```

If the file is not found, an exception is thrown

Note that the *FileReader* constructor will throw the exception *File-NotFoundException* if the file is not found. Since this is a checked exception, the statement must be enclosed in a *try* block. Therefore, the actual code used to open a stream to a text file would be similar to the following:

```
BufferedReader input;
try {
  input = new BufferedReader(new FileReader("Ages.dat"));
  // read data from file
} // end try
catch (FileNotFoundException e) {
  e.printStackTrace();
  System.exit(1); // File not found so exit
} // end catch
```

Now, using the instance of *BufferedReader*, data can be read from the file. As with keyboard input, you can use a *StringTokenizer* to break up the string returned by *readLine* into tokens for easier processing. But how do you know when you have read all of the data in the file? *BufferedReader* provides a method *ready* that determines whether the underlying character stream is ready. This method returns a boolean value that can be used in a *while* loop to determine whether more data is available in the file, as follows:

The method **ready** can be used to determine whether the file contains more data

```
StringTokenizer line;
while (input.ready()) {
    line = new StringTokenizer(input.readLine());
    // process line of data
    ...

} // end while
```

You can also detect when the end of the file is reached by checking whether the method *readLine* returns *null*. For example, the following loop will process all of the lines in the file:

```
StringTokenizer line;
String inputLine;
while ((inputLine = input.readLine()) != null) {
  line = new StringTokenizer(inputLine);
  // process line of data
  ...

} // end while
```

The method *readLine* can throw the exception *IOException*, another checked exception. Also, *readLine* must appear within the same *try* block that creates the *BufferedReader* instance; otherwise, the compiler won't be able to verify that the instance has been initialized properly. One way you can handle this is simply to add another *catch* block for the *IOException* to the *try* statement. Or, since *FileNotFoundException* is a subclass of *IOException*, you can use a single *catch* block as follows:

```
BufferedReader input;
StringTokenizer line;
String inputLine;
try {
  input = new BufferedReader(new FileReader("Ages.dat"));
  while ((inputLine = input.readLine()) != null) {
    line = new StringTokenizer(inputLine);
    // process line of data
    ...

  }
} // end try
```

```
catch (IOException e) {
  System.out.println(e);
  System.exit(1); // I/O error, exit the program
} // end catch
```

File output.   To write text to a file, you need to open an output stream to the file. One way to open a file for writing is to use the class *FileWriter* and provide the file's name when you declare the file stream. For example,

Open an output
stream to a file
before writing to it

```
FileWriter outStream = new FileWriter("Results.dat");
```

declares an output stream variable *outStream* and associates it with the file named *Results.dat*. The file name can be a literal constant, as it is here, or a string variable. If the file *Results.dat* does not exist, a new empty file with this name is created. If the file *Results.dat* already exists, opening it erases[5] the data in the file.

Like *FileReader*, the *FileWriter* class itself does not provide useful methods for writing data to the file. Another class, *PrintWriter*, provides two methods: *print* and *println*. These methods are already familiar to you; they are the same methods used by *System.out*. Here is a simple example of writing data to a file:

```
try {
  PrintWriter output = new PrintWriter(
        new FileWriter("Results.dat"));
  output.println("Results of the survey");
  output.println("Number of males: " + numMales);
  output.println("Number of females: " + numFemales);

  // other code and output appears here...
} // end try

catch (IOException e) {
  System.out.println(e);
  System.exit(1); // I/O error, exit the program
} // end catch
```

Closing a file.   When you have finished using a file, you should close the stream associated with that file. To close a stream (input or output), you use the method *close* as follows:

When you are
finished using a file,
call **close** to close
the stream

```
myStream.close();
```

The file associated with this stream is no longer available for input or output until you open it again.

_____

5. The data might not actually be erased, but the file will behave as if it were empty.

Adding to a text file.   When you open a stream to a file for writing, you can specify a second argument in addition to the file's name to indicate whether the file should be replaced or appended. If this second argument to the *FileOutputStream* constructor is *true*, the file is appended rather than replaced. For example,

```
PrintWriter ofStream = new PrintWriter(
        new FileOutputStream("Results.dat", true));
```

You can append
data to a file

This retains the old contents of the file *Results.dat*, and you can write additional components.

Copying a text file.   Suppose that you wanted to make a copy of the text file associated with the stream variable *original*. Copying a text file requires some work and provides a good example of the statements you have just studied. The approach taken by the following method copies the file one line at a time:

```
public static void copyTextFile(String originalFileName,
                                String copyFileName) {
// ------------------------------------------------------
// Makes a duplicate copy of a text file.
// Precondition: originalFileName is the name of an existing
// external text file, and copyFileName is the name of the
// text file to be created.
// Postcondition: The text file named copyFileName is a
// duplicate of the file named originalFileName.
// ------------------------------------------------------
  BufferedReader ifStream = null;
  PrintWriter ofStream = null;

  try {
    ifStream = new BufferedReader(
              new FileReader(originalFileName));
    ofStream = new PrintWriter(new FileWriter(copyFileName));
    String line;

    // copy lines one at a time from given file
    // to new file
    while ((line = ifStream.readLine()) != null) {
      ofStream.println(line);
    }  // end while
  }  // end try
  catch (IOException e) {
    System.out.println("Error copying file");
  }  // end catch
```

```
      finally {
        try {
          ifStream.close(); // close the files
          ofStream.close();
        } // end try
        catch (IOException e) {
         e.printStackTrace();
        }  // end catch
      } // end finally
  }   // end copyTextFile
```

The *finally* block allows the files to be closed regardless of whether an exception is thrown. It is executed after correct execution of the *try* block or after an exception is handled in a *catch* block.

Searching a text file sequentially.   Suppose that you have a text file of data about a company's employees. For simplicity, assume that this file contains two consecutive lines for each employee. The first line contains the employee's name, and the next line contains data such as salary.

Given the name of an employee, you can search the file for that name and then determine other information about this person. A **sequential search** examines the names in the order in which they appear in the file until the desired name is located. The following method performs such a sequential search, given a class to represent a person:

```
public class Person {
  private String name;
  private double salary;

  public Person(String n, double s) {
    name = n;
    salary = s;
  }  // end constructor
  // other methods appear here
}  // end Person

public static Person searchFileSequentially(
                    String fileName, String desiredName) {
  // ----------------------------------------------------
  // Searches a text file sequentially for a desired person.
  // Precondition: fileName is the name of a text file of
  // names and data about people. Each person is represented
  // by two lines in the file: The first line contains the
  // person's name, and the second line contains the person's
  // salary. desiredName is the name of the person sought.
  // Postcondition: If desiredName was found in the file,
  // a Person object that contains the person's
```

```java
// name and data is returned. Otherwise, the value null
// is returned to indicate that the desiredName was not
// found. The file is unchanged and closed.
// -------------------------------------------------------
BufferedReader ifStream = null;
String nextName = null;
String nextSalary = null;
boolean found = false;

try {
   ifStream = new BufferedReader(new FileReader(fileName));
   while (!found &&
           (nextName = ifStream.readLine()) != null) {
     nextSalary = ifStream.readLine();
     if (nextName.compareTo(desiredName) == 0) {
       found = true;
     } // end if
   } // end while
} // end try
catch (IOException e) {
   System.out.println("Error processing file");
   return null;
} // end catch
finally {
   if(ifStream != null) {
     try {
       ifStream.close(); // close the file
     } // end try
     catch (IOException e) {
       System.out.println("Error closing file");
     } // end catch
   } // end if
} // end finally
if (found) {
   return new Person(nextName,
                   Double.parseDouble(nextSalary));
}
else {
   return null;
} // end if
} // end searchFileSequentially
```

This method needs to look at all the names in the file before determining that a particular name does not occur. If the names were in alphabetical order, you could determine when the search had passed the place in the file that should have contained the desired name, if it existed. In this way, you could terminate the search before you needlessly searched the rest of the file.

Object Serialization

In the method *searchFileSequentially*, we assumed that all of the information about a person had been placed in a text file in a very specific format. In that example, the data fields were strings and primitive values, so it was simply a matter of writing the name data field on one line and the salary on the next line. But what about situations in which the data is more complex? For example, suppose that the *Person* class also kept track of the person's dependents by using an ADT list.[6] To save this information to a text file involves a more complicated scheme, since we may not know beforehand how many dependents an employee has.

Object serialization transforms an object into a sequence of bytes

When data is stored to a file for later use by the same program or another program, it is called **data persistence.** Normally, any information stored in the various variables and data structures in a program is lost when the program terminates execution. In many cases, however, it is desirable to save the data to a file for later retrieval before terminating the program. Java provides a mechanism for creating persistent objects, called **object serialization.** Serialization is the process of transforming an object into a sequence of bytes that represents the object. Deserialization is the process of transforming a sequence of bytes back into an object. Once an object is serialized, it can be stored in a file and read back at a later time using deserialization.

Any object that is to be saved using object serialization must implement the interface *java.io.Serializable*. This interface is somewhat unique in that it contains no methods. It is used to signal the compiler that the instances of this class may need to have their state serialized or deserialized.

One interesting aspect of object serialization is that when an object is serialized, all objects that it references are also serialized, as long as the referenced objects are instances of a class that implements the *Serializable* interface. For example, suppose that the following is the *Person* class described earlier:

```java
import java.io.Serializable;

public class Person implements Serializable {
  private String name;
  private double salary;
  private Person[] dependents;
  private int numDepend = 0;

  public Person(String n, double s) {
    name = n;
    salary = s;
    // assume that ListArrayBased also implements the
    // Serializable interface
    dependents = new Person[25];
  } // end constructor
```

---

6. Chapter 4 introduces the ADT list.

```
   public void addDependent(Person p) {
     numDepend++;
     dependents[numDepend] = p;
   } // end addDependent

   public String getName() {
     return name;
   } // end getName

   // other methods for class appear here
} // end Person
```

When an instance of the *Person* class is serialized, all of the referenced objects are also serialized—the *String* object *name* and the list *dependents*. You accomplish the actual serialization of an object by using the *writeObject* method of the stream class *ObjectOutputStream*. Much like *PrintWriter*, *ObjectOutputStream* adds functionality to *FileOutputStream*. The following statements save a *Person* object *p* to a file *EmployeeDB.dat*:

```
ObjectOutputStream ooStream = new ObjectOutputStream(
             new FileOutputStream("EmployeeDB.dat"));
ooStream.writeObject(p);
```

When the object is deserialized, both it and the objects it originally referenced will be restored to their original state. To do this, use the *readObject* method of the stream class *ObjectInputStream*. Like the *BufferedReader*, *ObjectInputStream* adds functionality to *FileInputStream*. The following statements retrieve a *Person* object *p* from a file *EmployeeDB.dat*:

```
ioStream = new ObjectInputStream(
                new FileInputStream("EmployeeDB.dat"));
nextPerson = (Person)ioStream.readObject());
```

The following method demonstrates how the file could be searched sequentially for a particular person (this method parallels the method given for text files):

```
public static Person searchFileSequentially(
                  String fileName, String desiredName) {
   // --------------------------------------------------------
   // Searches a text file sequentially for a desired person.
   // Precondition: fileName is the name of a binary file
   // of Person objects. desiredName is the name of the person
   // sought.
   // Postcondition: If desiredName was found in the file,
   // a Person object that contains the person's
```

```
      // name and data is returned. Otherwise, the value null
      // is returned to indicate that desiredName was not
      // found. The file is unchanged and closed.
      // ---------------------------------------------------------
      ObjectInputStream ioStream = null;
      Person nextPerson = null;
      boolean found = false;

      try {
        ioStream = new ObjectInputStream(
                                      new FileInputStream(fileName));
        while (!found && (nextPerson =
                  (Person)ioStream.readObject()) != null) {
          if (nextPerson.getName().compareTo(desiredName) == 0) {
            found = true;
          } // end if
        } // end while
      } // end try
      catch (IOException e) {
        System.out.println("Error processing file");
        return null;
      } // end catch
      catch (ClassNotFoundException e) {
        System.out.println("Unexpected object type in file");
        return null;
      } // end catch
      finally {
        //Close the ObjectInputStream
        try {
          if (ioStream != null) {
            ioStream.close();
          }
        } catch (IOException ex) {
          ex.printStackTrace();
        } // end catch
      } // end finally
      if (found) {
        return nextPerson;
      }
      else {
        return null;
      } // end if

    } // end searchFileSequentially
```

Summary

1. Each comment line in Java begins with two slashes (//) and continues until the end of the line.

2. A Java identifier is a sequence of letters, digits, underscores, and dollar signs that must begin with either a letter or an underscore.

3. The primitive data types in Java are organized into four types: integer, character, floating point, and boolean.

4. A Java reference is used to locate an object. When an object is created using the *new* operator, the location of the object in memory is returned and can be assigned to a reference variable.

5. You define named constants by using a statement of the form

   ```
   final   type-identifier = value;
   ```

6. Java uses short-circuit evaluation for expressions that contain the logical operators && (and) and || (or). That is, evaluation proceeds from left to right and stops as soon as the value of the entire expression is apparent.

7. An array is a collection of references that have the same data type. You can refer to the elements of an array by using an index that begins with zero. First the array must be instantiated with the number of elements desired. Then you can assign the references of the array an object.

8. The general form of the **if** statement is

   ```
   if (expression)
       statement₁
   else
       statement₂
   ```

   If *expression* is true, *statement₁* executes; otherwise, *statement₂* executes.

9. The general form of the **switch** statement is

   ```
   switch (expression) {
     case constant₁:
       statement₁
       break;
       . . .
     case constantₙ: case constantₙ₊₁:
       statementₙ
       break;
     default:
       statement
   }
   ```

   The appropriate *statement* executes according to the value of *expression*. Typically, *break* (or sometimes *return*) follows the statement or statements after each *case*. Omitting *break* causes execution to continue to the statement(s) of the *case* that follows.

10. The general form of the `while` statement is

    while (*expression*)
        statement

    As long as *expression* is true, *statement* executes. Thus, it is possible that *statement* will never execute.

11. The general form of the `for` statement is

    for (*initialize; test; update*)
        statement

    where *initialize*, *test*, and *update* are expressions. Typically, *initialize* is an assignment expression that occurs only once. Then if *test*, which is usually a logical expression, is true, `statement` executes. The expression `update` executes next, usually incrementing or decrementing a counter. This sequence of events repeats, beginning with the evaluation of *test*, until *test* is false.

12. The enhanced `for` loop makes it easier to process arrays. The general form of this loop is:

    for (*ArrayElementType variableName: arrayName*)
        statement

13. The general form of the `do` statement is

    do
        statement
    while (*expression*);

    Here, *statement* executes until the value of *expression* is false. Note that *statement* always executes at least once.

14. The filename for a Java source code file has the same name as the class it contains, with `.java` appended to the end.

15. Java packages provide a mechanism for grouping related classes. To indicate that a class is part of a package, you include a `package` statement as the first program line of your code.

16. To use classes contained in other packages, you must include an `import` statement before the class definition. The format of the `import` statement is

    import `package-name.class-name;`

17. An object in Java is an instance of a class. A class can be thought of as a data type that specifies the data and methods that are available for instances of the class. A class definition includes an optional subclassing modifier, an optional access modifier, the keyword `class`, an optional `extends` clause, an optional `implements` clause, and a class body.

18. Data fields are class members that are either variables or constants. Data field declarations can contain modifiers that control the availability of the data field (access modifiers) or that modify the way the data field can be used (use modifiers).

19. Methods are used to implement object behaviors. The general form of a method definition is

```
access-modifier  use-modifier  type  name(formal-parameter-list) {
    body
}
```

   A valued method returns a value by using the `return` statement. A *void* method can use `return` to exit.

20. When you invoke a method, the actual arguments must correspond to the formal parameters in number, order, and type.

21. A method makes local copies of the values of any arguments that are passed. Thus, the arguments remain unchanged by the method. When the argument is a reference, a method can modify the object it references, but not the value of the reference variable itself.

22. Members of a class should be declared as `public` or `private`. The client of the class—that is, the program that uses the class—cannot use members that are `private`. However, the implementations of methods within the class implementation can use them. Typically, you should make the data fields of a class `private` and provide `public` methods to access some or all of the data fields.

23. You can access data fields and methods that are declared `public` by naming the object, followed by a period, followed by the member name.

24. A Java class contains at least one constructor, which is an initialization method.

25. If you do not define any constructors for a class, the compiler will generate a default constructor—that is, one without parameters—for you.

26. Inheritance allows a new class to be defined based on the data fields and methods of an existing class while adding its own functionality. This enhances our ability to reuse code.

27. A class that is derived from another class is called the derived class or subclass. The class from which the subclass is derived is called the base class or superclass.

28. When defining a subclass, the class name is followed by an `extends` clause that names the superclass. If there is no extends clause, the class is implicitly a subclass of `Object`.

29. The `equals` method defined in the class `Object` is based on reference equality; it simply checks to see if two references refer to the same object. This is known as shallow equality.

30. It is common for a class to redefine the equals method for deep equality—in other words, to check the equality of the contents of the objects.

31. The `Array` class contains various static methods for manipulating arrays.

32. A string is a sequence of characters. The `String` class supports nonmutable strings, while the `StringBuffer` class supports mutable strings. In the `String` class, you can access the entire string, a substring, or the individual characters. In the `StringBuffer` class, you can access and actually manipulate the entire string, a substring, or the individual characters.

33. Exceptions are used to handle errors during execution. A method indicates that an error has occurred by throwing an exception. When an exception occurs, the statements within the `catch` block that correspond to the exception are executed.

34. The method `System.out.println` places a value into an output stream. Reading a value from an input stream is easier when the `Scanner` class is used.

35. In Java, files are accessed using the `Scanner` class or streams.

36. The `Console` class provides an alternative way to get input and output from the console of the current program execution environment.

37. Data persistence is supported in Java through object serialization. You serialize an object by using the method `writeObject` from the stream class `ObjectOutputStream`, and you deserialize an object by using the method `readObject` from the stream class `ObjectInputStream`.

Cautions

1. Remember that = is the assignment operator; == is the equality operator.

2. Do not begin a decimal integer constant with zero. A constant that begins with zero is either an octal constant or a hexadecimal constant.

3. Without a `break` statement, execution of a `case` within a switch statement will continue into the next `case`.

4. You must be careful that an array index does not exceed the size of the array. Java will throw the exception `ArrayIndexOutOfBounds` if an index value is less than zero or greater than or equal to the length of the array.

5. If you define a constructor for a class but do not also define a default constructor, the compiler will not generate one for you. In this case, a statement such as

```
MyNewClass test = new MyNewClass();
```

is illegal.

6. When using an IDE, the `Console` object is often not accessible since the JVM executes as a background process.

7. Opening an existing file for output erases the data in the file, unless you specify append mode.

Self-Test Exercises

1. To use each of the following Java classes in your program, indicate an `import` statement that would allow the program to use each of the following methods. If one is not needed, then state so. You may need to do a little research to determine the appropriate package.

   a. **static int** round(**float** a) in the class Math

   b. **void** println(String x) in the class PrintWriter

   c. **boolean** isEmpty() in the class Vector

   d. **int** getErrorCode() in the class SQLException

2. What are the differences between the three types of comments in Java?

3. The syntax of a method declaration is as follows:

```
access-modifier use-modifiers return-type
                method-name (formal-parameter-list) {
   // method-body
}
```

   What are the possible values for `access-modifier` and `use-modifier`?

4. Using the `SimpleSphere` class shown in Figure 1-5, and the following declarations, are the statements below correct or will they generate a compiler error? If they will generate a compiler error, explain why.

```
SimpleSphere myBall = new SimpleSphere(4.695);
```

   a. `myBall.radius = 5.0;`

   b. `int rad = myBall.getRadius();`

   c. `float d = myBall.getDiameter();`

   d. `myBall.DEFAULT_RADIUS = 5.0;`

5. What is meant by "short circuit operator" in a boolean expression? Give an example.

6. What is the difference between checked exceptions and unchecked exceptions?

Exercises

1. What is the output of the following program?

```
class SwitchDemo {
   public static void main(String[] args) {

      int month = 3;
      switch (month) {
         case 1:   System.out.print("January"); break;
         case 2:   System.out.print("February"); break;
         case 3:   System.out.print("March");
         case 4:   System.out.print("April");
         case 5:   System.out.print("May"); break;
         case 6:   System.out.print("June"); break;
      }
   }
}
```

2. Evaluate the following expressions:

   a. `4 + 3 * 11 / 2.0 - (-2)`

   b. `4.6 - 2.0 + 3.2 - 1.1 * 2`

   c. `23 % 4 - 23 / 4`

   d. `12 / 3 * 2 + (int)(2.5 * 10)`

3. The following code results in compile time error storing the values of an *int* variable to a *byte* variable. Identify the problem with the code and provide the solution.

```
public static void coversion ()
{
   int a = 1100;
   byte b = a;
   System.out.println("Value of Byte Variable b = "+b );
}
```

4. What is the output of the following program? If it is an infinite loop, state so.

```
class Sample {
   public static void main(String[] args) {
      byte c = 0;
      for (; c <= 127; c++);
      System.out.println("c = "+c);
   }
}
```

5. What is the problem with the following code?

```
if (amount = 0) {
   System.out.println("Sorry, there are none left");
}
```

6. Given the following if statement:

```
if (x <= 0) {
   if (x <= 100)
      System.out.println("Statement A");
   else
      System.out.println("Statement B");
}
else {
   if (x > 10)
      System.out.println("Statement C");
   else
      System.out.println("Statement D");
}
```

Using relational operators, give the range of values for *x* that produce the following output:

a. Statement A

b. Statement B

c. Statement C

d. Statement D

7. Write a program that reads the value of x and evaluates the following function

$$y = \begin{cases} 1 & \text{for } x > 0 \\ 0 & \text{for } x = 0 \\ -1 & \text{for } x < 0 \end{cases}$$

using

a. nested if statements

b. else if statements

8. What is the output of the following statement?

```
System.out.println("John said \"It should be located in" +
                   "C:\\myfiles\" \n in a worried tone.\"");
```

9. For each set of following statements, indicate the number of times the statement `System.out.print("x");` is executed. If it is an infinite loop, indicate so.

a. `x = 12;`
`while (x > 0) {`
`    System.out.print("x");`
`    x = x - 2;`
`}  // end while`
	b. `x = 3;`
	`do {`
	`    System.out.print("x");`
	`    x--;`
	`} while (x < 0);`

c. `x = 5;`
`while (x > 0) {`
`    System.out.print("x");`
`}  // end while`
	d. `x = 3;`
	`do {`
	`    System.out.print("x");`
	`    x = x + 2;`
	`} while (x <= 9);`

e. `for (i = 0; i <= 99; i++)`
`    System.out.print("x");`
	f. `for (i = 84; i <= 96; i++)`
	`    for (j = 7; j < 10; j++ )`
	`        System.out.println("x");`

10. Correct the code to rectify the compile time error.

```
public class Forloop
{
  public static void main(String[] args)
    {
      int factorial = 1;
        for (int count=1; count < 11)
        {
          System.out.println(factorial *= count);
          count ++;
        }
    }
}
```

11. Given a class `Pet` as started in the following example, add two constructors—one to create pets with a name, the other to create pets with a name and an age.

```
class Pet {
  private String name;
  private int age;
  // add constructors here
```

12. Suppose you have the following class:

```
class Second {
  private int x;
  public int z;

  public int sum() {
    return x + y + z;
  } // end sum

  private void reset(int a, int b, int c) {
    x = a;   y = b;   c = z;
  } // end reset

  public boolean check(float x) {
    return x < 0;
  } // end check
}   // end Second
```

Given the following declaration,

```
Second myClass = new Second();
```

indicate for each statement (which might appear in testing code) if it is *legal* or *illegal* (will cause an error).

a. `myClass.x = 5;`

b. `myClass.z = 5;`

c. `myClass.sum(x);`

d. `int ans = myClass.sum();`

e. `myClass.reset(1, 2, 3);`

f. `boolean x = myClass.check(11.2);`

13. Given the following class `Complex`, complete the following questions:

```
class Complex {
  private int real;
  private int imaginary;
  public Complex(int r, int i) {
    real = r;
    imaginary = i;
  }   // end constructor
```

```
    public String toString() {
      return real + " + " + imaginary + "i";
    } // end toString
} //end class Complex
```

a. Write a statement that creates a complex number 3 + 2i called *c1*.

b. Write a statement that creates a complex number 4 − 5i called *c2*.

c. Write a statement that prints a complex number called *c1*.

d. For the class *Complex*, modify the *toString* method so that if the real or imaginary part is zero, it is not placed in the string. If both are zero, then just print zero. Finally, if the imaginary part is 1 or -1, simply print + i instead of + 1i and − i instead of − 1i.

e. For the class *Complex*, add the following methods:

```
public Complex add(Complex val)
// returns a Complex number whose value is (this + val)
public Complex subtract(Complex val)
// returns a Complex number whose value is (this - val)
public Complex multiply(Complex val)
// returns a Complex number whose value is (this * val)
```

f. Add a *main* program with test code that demonstrates that the above methods are working properly.

14. Write a class *Address* that contains the street, city, and zip code. Provide one or more methods to initialize these values, and a method called *toString* that returns a *String* representation that contains all of these values.

15. Identify the error in the following code.

```
class Sample {
  public static void main(String[] args) {
    int i = 200;
    {
        int i = 100;
    }
  }
}
```

16. Given this code segment,

```
try {
  // statements appear here...
}
catch (IOException ex) {
  System.out.println("I/O error!");
}
catch (NumberFormatException ex) {
  System.out.println("Bad input!");
}
```

```
finally {
  System.out.println("Finally!");
}
System.out.println("Done!");
```

a. what will be printed if an *FileNotFoundException* occurs in the *try* block?

b. what will be printed if an *ArrayIndexOutOfBounds* occurs in the *try* block?

c. what will be printed if no exception occurs in the *try* block?

d. what would happen if the following *catch* clause was added as the first *catch* clause in the code?

```
catch (Exception ex) {
  System.out.println("Error!");
}
```

17. What is the output of the following code?

```
class Sample {
  public static void main(String[] args) {
    int a = 200;
    if ( a = 100 )
    {
      System.out.println(" hello ");
    }
    else
    {
      System.out.println(" world ");
    }
  }
}
```

Programming Problems

1. Create an application called *Registrar* that has the following classes:

   A *Student* class that minimally stores the following data fields for a student:

   - name
   - student id number
   - number of credits
   - total grade points earned

   The following methods should also be provided:

   - A constructor that initializes the name and id fields
   - A method that returns the student name field
   - A method that returns the student ID field
   - A method that determines if two student objects are equal if their student id numbers are the same (override *equals* from the class *Object*)
   - Methods to set and retrieve the total number of credits

- Methods to set and retrieve the total number of grade points earned
- A method that returns the GPA (grade points divided by credits)

An *Instructor* class that minimally stores the following data fields for an instructor:

- name
- faculty id number
- department

The following methods should also be provided:

- A constructor that initializes the name and id fields
- Methods to set and retrieve the instructor's department

A *Course* class that minimally stores the following data for a course:

- name of the course
- course registration code
- maximum number of 35 students
- instructor
- number of students
- students registered in the course (an array)

The following methods should also be provided:

- A constructor that initializes the name, registration code, and maximum number of students
- Methods to set and retrieve the instructor
- A method to search for a student in the course; the search should be based on an ID number.
- A method to add a student to the course. If the course is full, then an exception with an appropriate message should be raised (try creating your own exception class for this). Also, be sure that the student is not already registered in the course. The list of students should be in the order that they registered.
- A method to remove a student from the course. If the student is not found, then an exception with an appropriate message should be raised (use the same exception class mentioned above).
- A method that will allow Course objects to be output to a file using object serialization
- A method that will allow Course objects to be read in from a file created with Object serializtion

You will note that the *Student* and *Instructor* classes described above have some commonality. Create a *Person* class that captures this commonality and uses it as a base class for *Student* and *Instructor*. This class should be responsible for the *name* and *id* fields and also provide a *toString* method that returns a string of the form *name, id*. This will be the inherited *toString* method for the *Student* and *Instructor* classes.

a. Draw a UML diagram for this application.

b. Implement the previous classes in Java. Write a main program that can serve as a test class that tests all of the methods created and demonstrates that they are working.

c. Write a second main program that provides a menu to allow the user to

   i. create a course, prompting the user for all of the course information,

   ii. add students to the course,

   iii. check to see if a student is registered in the course, and

   iv. remove a student from the course.

d. Add to the previous menu the ability to save a course using object serialization. Also add a menu choice to read in a course from a file given the course code. Come up with a system of naming the file so that the user need only be asked the course code to load the course information from a file.

CHAPTER 2

Principles of Programming and Software Engineering

This chapter summarizes several fundamental principles that serve as the basis for dealing with the complexities of large programs. The discussion both reinforces the basic principles of programming and demonstrates that writing well-designed and well-documented programs is cost-effective. The chapter also presents a brief discussion of algorithms and data abstraction and indicates how these topics relate to the book's main theme of developing problem-solving and programming skills. In subsequent chapters, the focus will shift from programming principles to ways of organizing and using data. Even when the focus of discussion is on these new techniques, you should note how all solutions adhere to the basic principles discussed in this chapter.

2.1 Problem Solving and Software Engineering

Where did you begin when you wrote your last program? After reading the problem specifications and procrastinating for a certain amount of time, most novice programmers simply begin to write code. Obviously, their goal is to get their programs to execute, preferably with correct results. Therefore, they run their programs, examine error messages, insert semicolons, change the logic, delete semicolons, pray, and otherwise torture their programs until they work. Most of their time is probably spent checking both syntax and program logic. Certainly, your programming skills are better now than when you wrote your first program, but will you be able to write a really large program by using the approach just described? Maybe, but there are better ways.

Coding without a solution design increases debugging time

Realize that an extremely large software development project generally requires a team of programmers rather than a single individual. Teamwork requires an overall plan, organization, and communication. A haphazard approach to programming will not serve a team programmer well and will not be cost-effective. Fortunately, an emerging engineering field related to a branch of computer science—**software engineering**—provides techniques to facilitate the development of computer programs.

Software engineering facilitates development of programs

Whereas a first course in computer science typically emphasizes programming issues, the focus in this book will be on the broader issues of problem solving. This chapter begins with an overview of the problem-solving process and the various ways of approaching a problem.

What Is Problem Solving?

Here the term **problem solving** refers to the entire process of taking the statement of a problem and developing a computer program that solves that problem. This process requires you to pass through many phases, from gaining an understanding of the problem to be solved, through designing a conceptual solution, to implementing the solution with a computer program.

A solution specifies algorithms and ways to store data

Exactly what is a solution? Typically, a **solution** consists of two components: algorithms and ways to store data. An **algorithm** is a step-by-step specification of a method to solve a problem within a finite amount of time. One action that an algorithm often performs is to operate on a collection of data. For example, an algorithm may have to put new data into a collection, remove data from a collection, or ask questions about a collection of data.

Perhaps this description of a solution leaves the false impression that all the cleverness in problem solving goes into developing the algorithm and that how you store your data plays only a supporting role. This impression is far from the truth. You need to do much more than simply store your data. When constructing a solution, you must organize your data collection so that you can operate on the data easily in the manner that the algorithm requires. In fact, most of this book describes ways of organizing data.

When you design a solution to a given problem, you can use several techniques that will make your task easier. This chapter introduces those techniques, and subsequent chapters will provide more detail.

The Life Cycle of Software

The development of good software involves a lengthy and continuing process known as the software's **life cycle.** This process begins with an initial idea, includes the writing and debugging of programs, and continues for years to involve corrections and enhancements to the original software. Figure 2-1 pictures the nine phases of the software life cycle as segments on a water wheel.[1] This arrangement suggests that the phases are part of a cycle and are not simply a linear list. Although you start by specifying a problem, typically you move from any phase to any other phase. For example, testing a program can suggest changes to either the problem specifications or the solution design. Also notice that the nine phases surround a documentation core in the figure. Documentation is not a separate phase, as you might expect. Rather, it is integrated into all phases of the software life cycle.

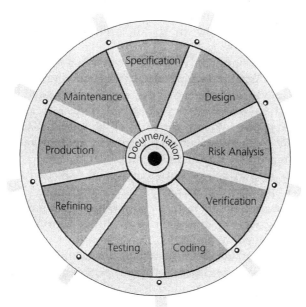

FIGURE 2-1

The life cycle of software as a water wheel that can rotate from one phase to any other phase

---

1. Thanks to Raymond L. Paden for suggesting that the "wheel" be a "water wheel."

Within the last few years, incremental and iterative development methods have emerged. These methods apply the first seven phases (specification, design, risk analysis, verification, coding, testing, and refinement) incrementally in a circular pattern. The refinement phase is where the next changes (or refinements) to the system are considered, leading the development back to the specification phase. Using this approach, a portion of the overall system is developed initially, and then refinements to the solution are incorporated. Once the system is complete, it then moves to the production and maintenance phases. When using an object-oriented language such as Java, this means that the initial development may involve building a subset of objects, then incrementally enhancing these objects and adding new objects until the system is complete and ready for production.

Here, then, are the phases in the life cycle of typical software. Although all phases are important, only those that are most relevant to this book are discussed in detail.

Phase 1: Specification.   Given an initial statement of the software's purpose, you must specify clearly all aspects of the problem. Often the people who describe the problem are not programmers, so the initial problem statement might be imprecise. The specification phase, then, requires that you bring precision and detail to the original problem statement and that you communicate with both programmers and nonprogrammers.

Make the problem
statement precise
and detailed

Here are some questions that you must answer as you write the specifications for the software: What is the input data? What data is valid and what data is invalid? Who will use the software and what user interface should be used? What error detection and error messages are desirable? What assumptions are possible? Are there special cases? What is the form of the output? What documentation is necessary? What enhancements to the program are likely in the future?

Prototype programs
can clarify the
problem

One way to improve communication among people and to clarify the software specifications is to write a **prototype program** that simulates the behavior of portions of the desired software product. For example, a simple—even inefficient—program could demonstrate the proposed user interface for analysis. It is better to discover any difficulties or to change your mind now than to do so after programming is underway or even complete.

Your previous programming assignments probably stated the program specifications for you. Perhaps aspects of these specifications were unclear and you had to seek clarification, but most likely you have had little practice in writing your own program specifications.

Phase 2: Design.   Once you have completed the specification phase, you must design a solution to the problem. Most people who design solutions of moderate size and complexity find it difficult to cope with the entire program at once. The best way to simplify the problem-solving process is to divide a large problem into small, manageable parts. The resulting program will contain **modules,** which are self-contained units of code.

When using an object-oriented language such as Java, these modules take the form of objects. As discussed in Chapter 1, objects are implemented using classes. Classes should be designed so that the objects are independent, or **loosely coupled.** Coupling is the degree to which objects in a program are interdependent. If every object in a program is connected to every other object in the program, that is called highly coupled, and it means that the flow of information between objects is potentially high. If the objects are loosely coupled, changes in one object will have minimal effects on other objects in the program.

Loosely coupled objects are independent

Classes should also be designed so that objects are highly cohesive. Cohesion is the degree to which the data and methods of an object are related. Ideally, each object should represent one component in the solution. Methods within an object should also be highly cohesive, each should perform one well-defined task.

Highly cohesive methods each perform one well-defined task

During the design phase, it is also important that you clearly specify the object interactions. Objects interact by sending messages to each other through method calls, which in turn represents the **data flow** among objects. When designing the methods, you should provide answers to these questions: What data within the object is utilized by the method? What does the method assume? What actions does the method perform, and is the data stored in the object changed after the method executes? Thus you should specify in detail the assumptions, input, and output for each method.

Specify each method's purpose, assumptions, input, and output

For example, if you as program designer needed to provide a method for a shape object that moves it to a new location on the screen, you might write the following specification:

The method will receive an (*x*, *y*) coordinate.
The method will move the shape to the new location on the screen.

You can view these specifications as the terms of a **contract** between your method and the code that calls it.

Specifications as a contract

If you alone write the entire program, this contract helps you systematically decompose the problem into smaller tasks. If the program is a team project, the contract helps delineate responsibilities. Whoever writes the move method must live up to this contract. After the move method has been written and tested, the contract tells the rest of the program how to call the move method properly and lets it know the result of doing so.

It is important to notice, however, that a method's contract does not commit the method to a particular way of performing its task. If another part of the program assumes anything about the method, it does so at its own risk. Thus, for example, if at some later date you rewrite your method to use a different algorithm for moving the shape on the screen, you should not need to change the rest of the program at all. As long as the new method honors the terms of the original contract, the rest of the program should be oblivious to the change.

A method's specification should not describe a method of solution

This discussion should not be news to you. Although you might not have explicitly used the term "contract" before, the concept should be familiar. You write a contract when you write a method's **precondition,** which is a statement of the conditions that must exist at the beginning of a method, as well as when you write its **postcondition,** which is a statement of the conditions at

Method specifications include precise preconditions and postconditions

the end of a method. For example, the move method that adheres to the previous contract could appear in pseudocode[2] as

First-draft
specifications

```
move(x, y)
// Moves a shape to a new location on the screen.
// Precondition: The calling code provides an
// (x, y) pair, both integers.
// Postcondition: The shape is moved to the new
// location.
```

These particular pre- and postconditions are actually deficient, as may be the case in a first-draft contract. For example, does "moved" mean that the shape is moved relative to its previous location by *(x, y)* or that the shape is moved to the new coordinate location *(x, y)*? What is the range of values for *x* and *y*? While implementing this method, you might assume that "moved" means the shape is moved to a new coordinate location *(x, y)* and that the range for *x* and *y* is 0 through 100. Imagine the difficulties that can arise when another person tries to use *move* to move a shape relative to its previous location using *(-5, -5)*. This user does not know your assumptions unless you document them by revising the pre- and postconditions, as follows:

Revised
specifications

```
move(x, y)
// Moves a shape to coordinate (x, y) on the screen.
// Precondition: The calling code provides an
// (x, y) pair, both integers, where
// 0 <= x <= MAX_XCOOR, 0 <= y <= MAX_YCOOR, where
// MAX_XCOOR and MAX_YCOOR are class constants that
// specify the maximum coordinate values.
// Postcondition: The shape is moved to coordinate
// (x, y).
```

When you write a precondition, begin by describing the method's formal parameters, mention any class named constants that the method uses, and finally list any assumptions that the method makes. Similarly, when you write a postcondition, begin by describing the method's effect on its parameters—or in the case of a valued method, the value it returns—and then describe any other action that has occurred. (Although people tend to use the words parameter and argument interchangeably, we will use parameter to mean formal parameter and argument to mean actual argument.)

In an object-oriented system, a method may also change the state of an object. Object state refers to the data that an object holds. In this example, a shape object has two data values that represent its location on the screen. The *move* method actually modifies these values within the object so that the effect

---

2. Pseudocode in this book appears in italics.

is to move the shape to a different location on the screen. Note that the post-condition in the *move* method reflects this change of object state.

Novice programmers tend to dismiss the importance of precise documentation, particularly when they are simultaneously designer, programmer, and user of a small program. If you design *move* but do not write down the terms of the contract, will you remember them when you later implement the method? Will you remember how to use *move* weeks after you have written it? To refresh your memory, would you rather examine your Java code or read a simple set of pre- and postconditions? As the size of a program increases, good documentation becomes even more important, regardless of whether you are the sole author or part of a team.

Precise documentation is essential

You should not ignore the possibility that you or someone else has already implemented some of the required objects and methods. Java facilitates the reuse of software components, which are typically organized into class libraries that group classes into packages containing compiled code. That is, you will not always have access to a method's Java code. The Java **Application Programming Interface** (API) is an example of one such collection of preexisting software. For example, you know how to use the static method *sqrt* contained in the Java API package *java.lang.Math*, yet you do not have access to its source statements, because it is precompiled. You know, however, that if you pass *sqrt* an expression of type *double*, it will return the square root of the value of that expression as a *double*. You can use *java.lang.Math.sqrt* even though you do not know its implementation. Furthermore, it may be that *java.lang.Math.sqrt* was written in a language other than Java! There is so much about *java.lang.Math.sqrt* that you do not know, yet you can use it in your program without concern, *as long as you know its specifications*.

Incorporate existing software components into your design

If, in the past, you have spent little or no time in the design phase for your programs, you must change this habit! The end result of the design phase should be a solution that is easy to translate into the constructs of a particular programming language. By spending adequate time in the design phase, you will spend less time when you write and debug your program.

We will resume our discussion of design later.

Phase 3: Risk analysis.   Building software entails risks. Some risks are the same for all software projects and some are peculiar to a particular project. You can predict some risks, while others are unknown. Risks can affect a project's timetable or cost, the success of a business, or the health and lives of people. You can eliminate or reduce some risks but not others. Techniques exist to identify, assess, and manage the risks of creating a software product. You will learn these techniques if you study software engineering in a subsequent course. The outcome of risk analysis will affect the other phases of the life cycle.

You can predict and manage some, but not all, risks

Phase 4: Verification.   Formal, theoretical methods are available for proving that an algorithm is correct. Although research in this area is incomplete, it is useful to mention some aspects of the verification process.

An **assertion** is a statement about a particular condition at a certain point in an algorithm. Preconditions and postconditions are simply assertions about conditions at the beginning and end of methods.

Java supports an assertion statement that allows you to test a condition at a certain point in a program. The Java assertion statement has two forms:

assert *booleanExpression*;
assert *booleanExpression* : *valueExpression*;

In the first form, if *booleanExpression* is false, an `AssertionError` is thrown with no further detail information. In the second form, if *booleanExpression* is false, the *valueExpression* is evaluated and sent to the `AssertionError` constructor so as to provide more detailed information about the failed assertion. In many instances, the *valueExpression* is simply a string that describes the problem. Here is a simple example of an *assert* statement in a program:

```
public static void main(String[] args) {
   Scanner reader = new Scanner(System.in);
   System.out.print("Enter your score: ");
   int score = reader.nextInt();
   assert score>=0 && score <= 100 :
         "Score "+score+" is not in range 0-100";
   // Continue processing score
   System.out.println("Processing score...");
}
```

So if a value out of range is entered by the user, a message similar to the following will appear:

```
Exception in thread "main" java.lang.AssertionError:
      Score -23 is not in range 0-100
      at AssertionClass.main(AssertionClass.java:9)
```

Note that for the *assert* statement to be executed in a program, you must make sure that the compiler settings enable assertions. In most Integrated Development Environments (IDEs), this feature is usually turned off by default, and so the assertion statements will be ignored.

An **invariant** is a condition that is always true at a particular point in an algorithm. A **loop invariant** is a condition that is true before and after each execution of an algorithm's loop. As you will see, loop invariants can help you to write correct loops. By using invariants, you can detect errors before you begin coding and thereby reduce your debugging and testing time. Overall, invariants can save you time.

You can prove the correctness of some algorithms

Proving that an algorithm is correct is like proving a theorem in geometry. For example, to prove that a method is correct, you would start with its preconditions—which are analogous to the axioms and assumptions in geometry—and demonstrate that the steps of the algorithm lead to the post-conditions. To do so, you would consider each step in the algorithm and show that an assertion before the step leads to a particular assertion after the step.

By proving the validity of individual statements, you can prove that sequences of statements, and then methods, and finally the program itself are correct. For example, suppose you show that if assertion A_1 is true and statement S_1 executes, assertion A_2 is true. Also, suppose you have shown that assertion A_2 and statement S_2 lead to assertion A_3. You can then conclude that if assertion A_1 is true, executing the sequence of statements S_1 and S_2 will lead to assertion A_3. By continuing in this manner, you eventually will be able to show that the program is correct.

Clearly, if you discovered an error during the verification process, you would correct your algorithm and possibly modify the problem specifications. Thus, by using invariants, it is likely that your algorithm will contain fewer errors *before* you begin coding. As a result, you will spend less time debugging your program.

You can formally prove that particular constructs such as `if` statements, loops, and assignments are correct. An important technique uses loop invariants to demonstrate the correctness of iterative algorithms. For example, we will prove that the following simple loop computes the sum of the first *n* elements in the array `item`:

```
// computes the sum of item[0], item[1], . . .,
// item[n-1] for any n >= 1
int sum = 0;
int j = 0;
while (j < n) {
  sum += item[j];
  ++j;
} // end while
```

Before this loop begins execution, `sum` is 0 and `j` is 0. After the loop executes once, `sum` is `item[0]` and `j` is 1. In general,

`sum` is the sum of the elements `item[0]` through `item[j-1]`   Loop invariant

This statement is the invariant for this loop. The invariant for a correct loop is true at the following points:

- Initially, after any initialization steps, but before the loop begins execution

- Before every iteration of the loop

- After every iteration of the loop

- After the loop terminates

For the previous loop example, these points are as follows:

```
int sum = 0;
int j = 0;
                    ←the invariant is true here
while (j < n) {
                    ←the invariant is true here
  sum += item[j];
  ++j;
                    ←the invariant is true here
}  // end while
                    ←the invariant is true here
```

You can use these observations to prove the correctness of an iterative algorithm. For the previous example, you must show that each of the following four points is true:

Steps to establish the correctness of an algorithm

1. **The invariant must be true initially,** before the loop begins execution for the first time. In the previous example, *sum* is 0 and *j* is 0 initially. In this case, the invariant states that *sum* contains the sum of the elements *item[0]* through *item[-1]*; the invariant is true because there are no elements in this range.

2. **An execution of the loop must preserve the invariant.** That is, if the invariant is true before any given iteration of the loop, you must show that it is true after the iteration. In the example, the loop adds *item[j]* to *sum* and then increments *j* by 1. Thus, after an execution of the loop, the most recent element added to *sum* is *item[j-1]*; that is, the invariant is true after the iteration.

3. **The invariant must capture the correctness of the algorithm.** That is, you must show that if the invariant is true when the loop terminates, the algorithm is correct. When the loop in the previous example terminates, *j* contains *n*, and the invariant is true: *sum* contains the sum of the elements *item[0]* through *item[n-1]*, which is the sum that you intended to compute.

4. **The loop must terminate.** That is, you must show that the loop will terminate after a finite number of iterations. In the example, *j* begins at 0 and then increases by 1 at each execution of the loop. Thus, *j* eventually will equal *n* for any $n \geq 1$. This fact and the nature of the *while* statement guarantee that the loop will terminate.

Not only can you use invariants to show that your loop is correct, but you can also use them to show that your loop is wrong. For example, suppose that the expression in the previous *while* statement was *j <= n* instead of *j < n*. Steps 1 and 2 of the previous demonstration would be the same, but Step 3 would differ: When the loop terminated, *j* would contain $n + 1$ and, because the invariant would be true, *sum* would contain the sum of the elements `item[0]` through `item[n]`. Since this is not the desired sum, you know that something is wrong with your loop.

Notice the clear connection between Steps 1 through 4 and **mathematical induction.**[3] Showing the invariant to be true initially, which establishes the **base case,** is analogous to establishing that a property of the natural numbers is true for zero. Showing that each iteration of the loop preserves the invariant is the **inductive step.** This step is analogous to showing that if a property is true for an arbitrary natural number k, then the property is true for the natural number $k + 1$. After proving the four points just described, you can conclude that the invariant is true after every iteration of the loop—just as mathematical induction allows you to conclude that a property is true for every natural number.

Identifying loop invariants will help you to write correct loops. You should state the invariant as a comment that either precedes or begins each loop, as appropriate. For example, in the previous example, you might write the following:

```
// Invariant: 0 <= j <= n and
// sum = item[0] +...+ item[j-1]
while (j < n)
   . . .
```

State loop invariants in your programs

You should confirm that the invariants for the following unrelated loops are correct. Remember that each invariant must be true both before the loop begins and after each iteration of the loop, including the final one. Also, you might find it easier to understand the invariant for a *for* loop if you temporarily convert it to an equivalent *while* loop.

For example, a *for* loop of the form

```
for (initialize; test; update) {
   statement(s)
} // end for
```

can be rewritten as

```
initialize;
while (test) {
   statement(s)
   update;
} // end while
```

---

3. A review of mathematical induction appears in Appendix D.

Here are a few more examples of loop invariants:

```
// Computes an approximation to e^x for a real x
double t = 1.0, s = 1.0;
int k = 1;
// Invariant: t == x^(k-1)/(k-1)! and
//  s == 1+x+x^2/2!+...+x^(k-1)/(k-1)!
while (k <= n) {
   t *= x/k;
   s += t;
   ++k;
}  // end while

// Computes n! for an integer n >= 0
int f = 1;
// Invariant: f == (j-1)!
for (int j = 1; j <= n; ++j) {
   f *= j;
}  // end for
```

Phase 5: Coding. The coding phase involves translating the design into a particular programming language and removing the syntax errors. Although this phase is probably your concept of what programming is all about, it is important to realize that the coding phase is not the major part of the life cycle for most software—actually, it is a relatively minor part.

Phase 6: Testing. During the testing phase, you need to remove as many logical errors as you can. One approach is to test the individual methods of the objects first, using valid input data that leads to a known result. If certain data must lie within a range, include values at the endpoints of the range. For example, if the input value for n can range from 1 to 10, be sure to include test cases in which n is 1 and 10. Also, include invalid data to test the error-detection capability of the program. Try some random data, and finally try some actual data. Testing is both a science and an art. You will learn more about testing in subsequent courses.

Phase 7: Refining the solution. The result of Phases 1 through 6 of the solution process is a working program, which you have tested extensively and debugged as necessary. If you have a program that solves your original problem, you might wonder about the significance of this phase of the solution process.

Often the best approach to solving a problem is first to make some simplifying assumptions during the design of the solution—for example, you could assume that the input will be in a certain format and will be correct—and next to develop a complete working program under these assumptions. You can then add more sophisticated input and output routines, additional features, and more error checks to the working program.

Thus, the approach of simplifying the problem initially makes a refinement step necessary in the solution process. Of course, you must take care to ensure that the final refinements do not require a complete redesign of the solution. You can usually make these additions cleanly, however, particularly when you have used a modular design. In fact, the ability to proceed in this manner is one of the key advantages of having a modular design! Also, realize that any time you modify a program—no matter how trivial the changes might seem—you must thoroughly test it again.

Changes to a program require that you test it again

This discussion illustrates that the phases within the life cycle of software are not completely isolated from one another and are not linear. To make realistic simplifying assumptions early in the design process, you should have some idea of how you will account for those assumptions later on. Testing a program can suggest changes to its design, but changes to a program require that you test the program again.

Phase 8: Production. When the software product is complete, it is distributed to its intended users, installed on their computers, and used.

Phase 9: Maintenance. Maintaining a program is not like maintaining a car. Software does not wear out if you neglect it. However, users of your software invariably will detect errors that you did not discover during the testing phase. Correcting these errors is part of maintaining the software. Another aspect of the maintenance phase involves enhancing the software by adding more features or by modifying existing portions to suit the users better. Rarely will the people who design and implement the original program perform this maintenance step. Good documentation then becomes even more important.

Correcting user-detected errors and adding features are aspects of software maintenance

Is a program's life cycle relevant to your life? It definitely should be! You should view Phases 1 through 7 as the steps in a problem-solving process. Using this strategy, you first design and implement a solution (Phases 1 through 6) based on some initial simplifying assumptions. The outcome is a well-structured program that solves a somewhat simplified problem. The last step of the solution process (Phase 7) refines your work into a sophisticated program that meets the original problem specifications.

What Is a Good Solution?

Before you devote your time and energy to the study of problem-solving techniques, it seems only fair that you see at the outset why mastery of these techniques will help to make you a good problem solver. An obvious statement is that the use of these techniques will produce good solutions. This statement, however, leads to the more fundamental question, what *is* a good solution? A brief attempt at answering this question concludes this section.

Because a computer program is the final form your solutions will take, consider what constitutes a good computer program. Presumably, you write a program to perform some task. In the course of performing that task, there is a real and tangible **cost**. This cost includes such factors as the computer resources (computing time and memory) that the program consumes, any difficulties encountered by those who use the program, and the consequences of a program that does not behave correctly.

However, the costs just mentioned do not give the whole picture. They pertain to only one phase of the life cycle of a solution—the phase in which it is an operational program. In assessing whether or not a solution is good, you also must consider the phases during which you developed the solution and the phases after you wrote the initial program that implemented the solution. Each of these phases incurs costs, too. The total cost of a solution must take into account the value of the time of the people who developed, refined, coded, debugged, and tested it. A solution's cost must also include the cost of maintaining, modifying, and expanding it.

Thus, when calculating the overall cost of a solution, you must include a diverse set of factors. If you adopt such a multidimensional view of cost, it is reasonable to evaluate a solution against the following criterion:

A multidimensional view of a solution's cost

A solution is good if the total cost it incurs over all phases of its life cycle is minimal.

It is interesting to consider how the relative importance of the various components of this cost has changed since the early days of computing. In the beginning, the cost of computer time relative to human time was extremely high. In addition, people tended to write programs to perform very specific, narrowly defined tasks. If the task changed somewhat, a new program was written. Program maintenance was probably not much of an issue, so there was little concern if a program was hard to read. A program typically had only one user, its author. As a consequence, programmers tended not to worry about misuse or ease of use of their programs; a program's interface generally was not considered important.

In this type of environment, one cost clearly overshadowed all others: computer resources. If two programs performed the same task, the one that required less time and memory was better. How things have changed! Since the early days of computers, computing costs have dropped dramatically, thus making the value of the problem solver's and programmer's time a much more significant factor in the cost of a solution. Another consequence of the drop in computing costs is that computers now are used to perform tasks in a wide variety of areas, many of them nonscientific. People who interact with computers often have no technical expertise and no knowledge of the workings of programs. People want their software to be easy to use.

Today, programs are larger and more complex than ever before. They are often so large that many people are involved in their design, use, and mainte- nance. Good structure and documentation are thus of the utmost importance. As programs perform more highly critical tasks, the prices for malfunctions will soar. Thus, society needs both well-structured programs and techniques for formally verifying their correctness. People will not and should not entrust their livelihoods—or their lives—to a program that only its authors can under- stand and maintain.

Programs must be well structured and documented

These developments have made obsolete the notion that the most efficient solution is always the best. If two programs perform the same task, it is no longer true that the faster one is necessarily better. Programmers who use every trick in the book to save a few microseconds of computing time at the expense of clarity are not in tune with the cost structure of today's world. You must write programs with people as well as computers in mind.

At the same time, do not get the false impression that the efficiency of a solution is no longer important. To the contrary, in many situations efficiency is the prime determinant of whether a solution is even usable. The point is that a solution's efficiency is only one of many factors that you must consider. If two solutions have approximately the same efficiency, other factors should dominate the comparison. However, when the efficiencies of solutions differ *significantly*, this difference can be the overriding concern. The stages of the problem-solving process at which you should be most concerned about efficiency are those during which you develop the underlying methods of solution. The choice of a solution's components—the algorithms and ways to store data—rather than the code you write, leads to significant differences in efficiency.

Efficiency is only one aspect of a solution's cost

Another factor in software development costs is code reusability. Making use of existing code can reduce the cost and time needed to develop a solution. It also reduces maintenance costs since reused components are generally well designed and more comprehensively tested. Within the software development process, code reuse typically emerges in two ways. First, components available from code libraries and open source repositories can often be adapted and used in a system. Note that the original design of these off-the-shelf components is completely independent of the current software development activity, yet these components are adapted and refined to be part of the current solution. The second way that code reuse emerges is when components within a project are designed in such a way that allows them to be the basis for more specific components later in the development process.

Code reuse can reduce a solution's cost

This book advocates a problem-solving philosophy that views the cost of a solution as multidimensional. This philosophy is reasonable in today's world, and it likely will be reasonable in the years to come.

2.2 Achieving an Object-Oriented Design

You have seen the importance of specifying the objects during the design of a solution, but how do you determine the objects in the first place? The techniques that help you determine the objects for a particular solution are the subject of entire texts and future courses; these techniques quickly go beyond this book's scope. This section will provide an overview of two general design techniques—abstraction and information hiding—which is followed by a discussion of object-oriented design and functional decomposition.

Abstraction and Information Hiding

Procedural abstraction.   When you design a method as part of a solution to a problem, each method begins as a box that states what it does but not how it does it. No one box may "know" how any other box performs its task—it may know only what that task is. For example, if one part of a solution is to sort some data, one of the boxes will be a sorting algorithm, as Figure 2-2 illustrates. The other boxes will know that the sorting box sorts, but they will not know how it sorts. In this way, the various components of a solution are kept isolated from one another.

Specify what to do, not how to do it

Procedural abstraction separates the purpose of a method from its implementation. Abstraction specifies each method clearly *before* you implement it in a programming language. For example, what does the method assume and what action does it take? Such specifications will clarify the design of your solution because you will be able to focus on its high-level functionality without the distraction of implementation details. In addition, these principles allow you to modify one part of a solution without significantly affecting the other parts. For example, you should be able to change the sorting algorithm in the previous example without affecting the rest of the solution.

Specify what a method does, not how to do it

Specifications do not indicate how to implement a method

As the problem-solving process proceeds, you gradually refine the boxes until eventually you implement their actions by writing actual Java code. Once a method is written, you can use it without knowing the particulars of its algorithm as long as you have a statement of its purpose and a description of its parameters. Assuming that the method is documented properly, you will be able to use it knowing only its declaration and its initial descriptive comments; you will not need to look at its implementation.

Procedural abstraction is essential to team projects. After all, in a team situation, you will have to use methods written by others, frequently without knowledge of

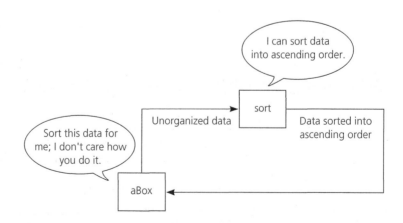

FIGURE 2-2

The details of the sorting algorithm are hidden from other parts of the solution their algorithms. Will you actually be able to use such a method without studying its code? In fact, you do so each time you use a method from the Java API, such as `Math.sqrt`, as was noted earlier.

Data abstraction.   Consider now a collection of data and a set of operations on the data. The operations might include ones that add new data to the collection, remove data from the collection, or search for some data. **Data abstraction** focuses on what the operations do instead of on how you will implement them. The other modules of the solution will "know" *what* operations they can perform, but they will not know *how* the data is stored or *how* the operations are performed.

Specify what you will do to data, not how to do it

For example, you have used an array, but have you ever stopped to think about what an array actually is? You will see many pictures of arrays throughout this book. This artist's conception of an array might resemble the way a Java array is implemented on a computer, and then again it might not. The point is that you are able to use an array without knowing what it "looks like"—that is, how it is implemented. Although different systems may implement arrays in different ways, the differences are transparent to the programmer. For instance, regardless of how the array *years* is implemented, you can always store the value 1492 in location *index* of the array by using the statement

```
years[index] = 1492;
```

and later write out that value by using the statement

```
System.out.println(years[index]);
```

Thus, you can use an array without knowing the details of its implementation, just as you can use the method `Math.sqrt` without knowing the details of its implementation.

Most of this book is about data abstraction. To enable you to think abstractly about data—that is, to focus on what operations you will perform on the data instead of how you will perform them—you should define an **abstract data type,** or **ADT.** An ADT is a collection of data *and* a set of operations on the data. You can use an ADT's operations, if you know their specifications, without knowing how the operations are implemented or how the data is stored.

Ultimately, someone—perhaps you—will implement the ADT by using a **data structure,** which is a construct that you can define within a programming language to store a collection of data. For example, you might store some data in a Java array of integers or in an array of objects or in an array of arrays.

An ADT is not a fancy name for a data structure

Within problem solving, abstract data types support algorithms, and algorithms are part of what constitutes an abstract data type. As you design a solution, you should develop algorithms and ADTs in tandem. The global algorithm that solves a problem suggests operations that you need to perform on the data,

Develop algorithms and ADTs in tandem

which in turn suggest ADTs and algorithms for performing the operations on the data. However, the development of the solution may proceed in the opposite direction as well. The kinds of ADTs that you are able to design can influence the strategy of your global algorithm for solving a problem. That is, your knowledge of which data operations are easy to perform and which are difficult can have a large effect on how you approach a problem.

As you probably have surmised from this discussion, you often cannot sharply distinguish between an "algorithms problem" and a "data structures problem." Frequently, you can look at a program from one perspective and feel that the data structures support a clever algorithm and then look at the same program from another perspective and feel that the algorithms support a clever data structure.

Information hiding.   As you have seen, abstraction tells you to write specifications for each module that describe its outside, or **public,** view. However, abstraction also helps you to identify details that you should hide from public view—details that should not be in the specifications but should be **private.** The principle of **information hiding** tells you not only to hide such details within a module, but also ensures that no other module can tamper with these hidden details.

> All modules and ADTs should hide something

Information hiding limits the ways in which you need to deal with methods and data. As a user of a module, you do not worry about the details of its implementation. As an implementer of a module, you do not worry about its uses.

Object-Oriented Design

> Objects encapsulate data and operations

One way to achieve an object-oriented design is to develop **objects** that combine data and operations to produce a representation of a real-life entity or abstraction. Such an **object-oriented** approach to modularity produces a collection of objects that have behaviors.

Although you may have never thought about it before, you can view many of the things around you as objects. The alarm clock that awoke you this morning **encapsulates** both time and operations such as "set the alarm." To *encapsulate* means to encase or enclose; thus, encapsulation is a technique that hides inner details. Whereas methods encapsulate actions, objects encapsulate data as well as actions. Even though you request the clock to perform certain operations, you cannot see how it works. You see only the results of those operations.

> Encapsulation hides inner details

Suppose that you want to write a program to display a clock on your computer screen. To simplify the example, consider a digital clock without an alarm, as Figure 2-3 illustrates. You would begin the task of designing a modular solution by identifying the objects in the problem.

Several techniques are available for identifying objects, but no single one is always the best approach. One simple technique[4] considers the nouns and

---

4. This technique is not foolproof. The problem specification must use nouns and verbs consistently. If, for example, "display" is sometimes a verb and sometimes a noun, identifying objects and their operations can be unclear.

FIGURE 2-3

A digital clock

verbs in the problem specifications. The nouns will suggest objects whose actions are indicated by the verbs. For example, you could specify the clock problem as follows:

> The program will maintain a digital clock that displays the time in hours and minutes. The hour indicator and minute indicator are both digital devices that display values from 1 to 12 and 0 to 59, respectively. You should be able to set the time by setting the hour and minute indicators, and the clock should maintain the time by updating these indicators.

Specifications for a program that displays a digital clock

Even without a detailed problem specification, you know that one of the objects is the clock itself. The clock performs operations such as

```
Set the time
Advance the time
Display the time
```

The hour indicator and minute indicator are also objects and are quite similar to each other. Each indicator performs operations such as

```
Set its value
Advance its value
Display its value
```

In fact, both indicators can be the same type of object. A set of objects that have the same type is called a **class**. Thus, what you need to specify is not a particular object, but a class of objects. In fact, you need a class of clocks and a class of indicators. A clock object, which is an **instance** of the clock class, will then contain two indicator objects, which are instances of the indicator class.

An object is an instance of a class

Chapter 4 discusses encapsulation further and, in particular, its relationship to Java classes. In subsequent chapters, you will study various ADTs and their implementations as Java classes. The focus will be on data abstraction and encapsulation. This approach to programming is **object based.**

Object-oriented programming, or **OOP,** adds two more principles to encapsulation:

KEY CONCEPTS

Three Principles of Object-Oriented Programming

1. Encapsulation: Objects combine data and operations.

2. Inheritance: Classes can inherit properties from other classes.

3. Polymorphism: Objects can determine appropriate operations at execution time.

Classes can **inherit** properties from other classes. For example, once you have defined a class of clocks, you can design a class of alarm clocks that inherits the properties of a clock but adds operations to provide an alarm. You will be able to produce an alarm clock quickly because the clock portion is done. Thus, **inheritance** allows you to reuse classes that you defined earlier—perhaps for different but related purposes—with appropriate modification.

Inheritance may make it impossible for the compiler to determine which operation you require in a particular situation. However, **polymorphism**—which literally means *many forms*—enables this determination to be made at execution time. That is, the outcome of a particular operation depends upon the objects on which the operation acts. For example, if you use the + operator with numeric operands in Java, addition occurs, but if you use it with string operands, concatenation occurs. Although in this simple example, the compiler can determine the correct meaning of +, polymorphism allows situations in which the meaning of an operation is unknown until execution time.

Chapter 8 discusses inheritance and polymorphism further.

> The + operator has multiple meanings

Functional Decomposition

Generally, an object-oriented approach initially focuses on the data aspects of the design. But equally important is the design of the methods that implement the behavior of the objects. Recall that we want the methods within a class to be highly cohesive—they should represent a single task to be performed in an object. Functional decomposition (also referred to as top down design) can help us break down complex tasks within an object into more manageable single-purpose tasks and subtasks.

The philosophy of functional decomposition is that you should address a task at successively lower levels of detail. Consider a simple example. Suppose that you wanted to find the median among a collection of test scores. Figure 2-4 uses a **structure chart** to illustrate the hierarchy of, and interaction among, the methods that solve this problem. At first, each method is little more than a statement of *what* it needs to solve and is devoid of detail. You refine each method by partitioning it into additional smaller methods. The result is a hierarchy of methods; each method is refined by its successors, which solve smaller problems and contain more detail about *how* to solve the problem than their predecessors. The refinement process continues

> A structure chart shows the relationship among methods

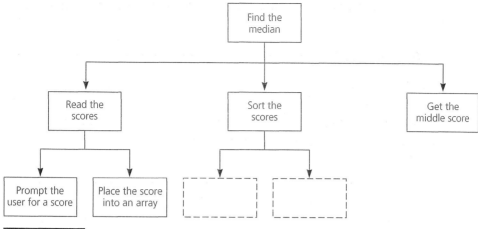

FIGURE 2-4

A structure chart showing the hierarchy of methods

until the methods at the bottom of the hierarchy are simple enough for you to translate directly into Java code that solves very small, independent problems.

Notice in Figure 2-4 that you can break the solution down into three independent tasks:

```
Read the test scores
Sort the scores
Get the "middle" score
```

A solution consisting of independent tasks

If the three methods in this example perform their tasks, then by calling them in order you will correctly find the median, regardless of *how* each method performs its task.

You begin to develop each method by dividing it into subtasks. For example, you can refine the task of reading the test scores by dividing it into the following two subtasks:

```
Prompt the user for a score
Place the score into an array
```

Subtasks

You continue the solution process by developing, in a similar manner, methods for each of these two tasks. Finally, you can use pseudocode to specify the details of the algorithms.

General Design Guidelines

Typically, you use object-oriented design (OOD), functional decomposition (FD), abstraction, and information hiding when you design a solution to a problem. The following design guidelines summarize an approach that leads to modular solutions.

KEY CONCEPTS

Design Guidelines

1. Use OOD and FD together to produce modular solutions. That is, develop abstract data types and algorithms in tandem.
2. Use OOD for problems that primarily involve data.
3. Use FD to design algorithms for an object's operations.
4. Consider FD to design solutions to problems that emphasize algorithms over data.
5. Focus on *what*, not *how*, when designing both ADTs and algorithms.
6. Consider incorporating previously written software components into your design.

Modeling Object-Oriented Designs Using UML

The **Unified Modeling Language (UML)** is a modeling language used to express object-oriented designs. UML provides specifications for both diagrams and text-based descriptions. The diagrams are particularly useful in showing the overall design of a solution, including class specifications and the various ways that the classes interact with each other. It is fairly common to have a number of classes involved in a solution, and thus the ability to show the interaction among classes is one of the strengths of UML.

This text focuses on the design of the classes themselves, and therefore only the class diagrams and associated syntax are presented here. Class diagrams specify the name of the class, the data members of the class, and the operations. Figure 2-5 shows a class diagram for the class `Clock` discussed earlier. The top section contains the class name. The middle section contains the data members that represent the data in the class, and the bottom section contains the operations. Note that the diagram is quite general; it does not really dictate how the class is actually implemented. It typically represents a conceptual model of the class that is language independent.

In conjuction with the class diagrams, UML also provides a text-based notation to represent the data members and operations for classes. This notation can be incorporated into the class diagrams, but usually not to the fullest extent because it tends to clutter the diagrams. This text-based representation is used to describe the classes in this text, because it provides a more complete specification than the diagrams.

The UML syntax for data members is

$$visibility\ name:\ type = defaultValue$$

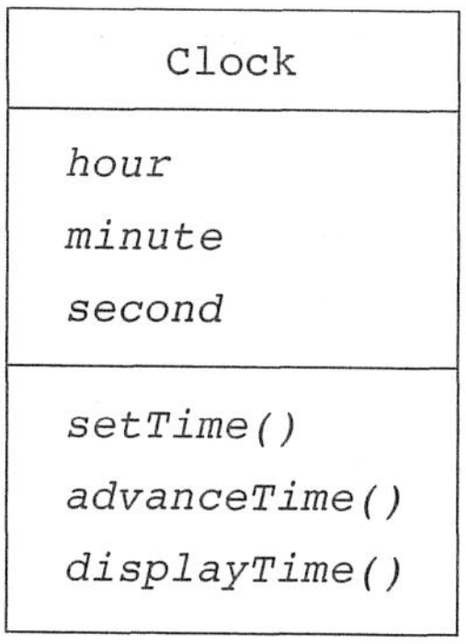

```
┌─────────────────────────┐
│          Clock          │
├─────────────────────────┤
│  hour                   │
│  minute                 │
│  second                 │
├─────────────────────────┤
│  setTime()              │
│  advanceTime()          │
│  displayTime()          │
└─────────────────────────┘
```

FIGURE 2-5

UML diagram for the class *clock*

where

- *visibility* is + (*public*) or – (*private*). A third possibility is # (*protected*), which is discussed in Chapter 9.

- *name* is the name of the data member.

- *type* is the data type of the data member.

- *defaultValue* is an initial value for the data member.

As seen in the class diagrams, at a minimum the name should be provided. The *defaultValue* is used only in situations where a default value is appropriate. In some cases you may also want to omit the *type* of the data member and leave it to the implementation to provide that detail. This text will use the following names for common argument types: *integer* for integer values, *float* for floating-point values, *boolean* for boolean values, and *string* for string values. Note that these names do not necessarily match the corresponding Java data types because this notation is meant to be language independent.

Here is the text-based notation for the data members in the class *Clock* shown in Figure 2-5:

-hour: integer

-minute: integer

-second: integer

The data members *hour*, *minute*, and *second* are declared private, as suggested by the concept of information hiding.

The UML syntax for operations is more involved:

visibility name(parameter-list): return-type {property-string} where

■ *visibility* is the same as specified for data members.

■ *name* is the name of the operation.

■ *parameter-list* contains comma-separated parameters whose syntax is as follows:

direction name: type = defaultValue

where

■ *direction* is used to show whether the parameter is used for input (*in*), output (*out*), or both (*inout*).

■ *name* is the parameter.

■ *type* is the data type of the parameter.

■ *defaultValue* is a value that should be used for the parameter if no argument is provided.

■ *return-type* is the data type of the result of the operation. If the operation does not return a value, this is left blank.

■ *property-string* indicates property values that apply to the operation.

Like the class diagrams for data members, the class diagrams for operations at a minimum provide the *name* of the operation. Sometimes the *parameter-list* is included if it clarifies the understanding of the class functionality.

The *property-string* has a variety of possible values, but of interest in this text is the property *query*. It is a way to indicate that the operation does not modify any data in the class.

Here is the text-based notation for the operations in the class *Clock*:

```
+setTime(in hr: integer, in min: integer, in sec: integer)
-advanceTime()
+displayTime() {query}
```

Here we specified the operations *setTime* and *displayTime* as public, and *advanceTime* as private. The function *displayTime* also has the property *query* specified, as an indication that it does not change any of the data; the function is used only to display the data.

UML class diagrams provide additional notation to illustrate relationships between classes. Suppose that you are asked to model a banking system application. The specification is as follows:

Design a banking system that assigns checking and savings accounts to customers. The bank information includes a name and routing number. Both types of accounts allow balance retrieval, deposits, and withdrawals. A customer may have multiple accounts. Each customer's name and address are stored in the system, and each account has a number assigned to it. Savings accounts earn interest and checking accounts charge for each check when the balance falls below a minimum amount. These adjustments are reflected when the customer requests the current account balance.

Several classes might be designed to represent the various aspects of a bank, as illustrated in Figure 2-6. These classes include a `Bank` class, an `Account` class, and a `Customer` class. Associations between classes are shown with a line, with the option to specify the **cardinality** between the associations. For example, a customer can have one or more accounts, which is illustrated with the notation "1...*" (one to many). Classes may also have different types of relationships with each other. For example, the `Savings` and `Checking` account classes are both derived from the `Account` class, and they inherit the `Account` class's data members and operations. Inheritance is represented with an open triangle pointing to the parent class. Note that the `Checking` and `Savings` classes have their

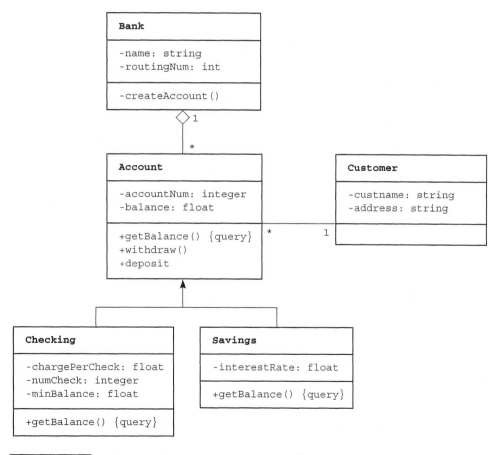

FIGURE 2-6

UML diagram for a banking system

own *getBalance* functions, which **override,** or replace, the *getBalance* function of the parent class, in order to make the necessary calculations for charges and interest. A class may also have a relationship with another class by containing an instance of that class as part of its definition. In the banking example, a bank contains one or more accounts. This type of relationship is called **containment** and is represented by positioning a diamond next to the containing class. Inheritance and containment are discussed in more detail in Chapter 9.

Advantages of an Object-Oriented Approach

The time that you expend on program design can increase when you use object-oriented programming (OOP). In addition, the solution that OOP techniques produce will typically be more general than is absolutely necessary to solve the problem at hand. The extra effort that OOP requires, however, is usually worth it.

When using object-oriented design in the solution to a problem, you need to identify the classes that are involved. You identify the purpose of each class and how it interacts with other classes. This leads to a specification for each class that identifies the operations and data. You then focus on the implementation details for each of the classes, including the use of top-down design to facilitate the development of the operations. It is easier to do the implementation when you focus on one class at a time.

Once you have implemented a class, you must test it at two different levels. First, you must test the class operations. This is usually done by writing a small program that calls the various operations and tests the results against the specifications provided for the operation. Once you have tested each individual class in this way, you should test scenarios in which the classes are expected to work together to solve the larger problem.

When you identify the classes involved in your solution, you will often find that you want a family of related classes. This stage of the design process is time-consuming, particularly if you have no existing classes upon which to build. Once you have implemented a class (called the **ancestor class**), the implementation of each new class (the **descendant class**) proceeds more rapidly, because you can reuse the properties and operations of the ancestor class. For example, as was mentioned earlier, once you have defined a class of clocks, you can design a class of alarm clocks that inherits the properties of a clock but adds operations to provide an alarm. The implementation of the class of alarm clocks would have been much more time-consuming if you did not have a class of clocks on which to base it. Looking ahead, you can reuse previously implemented classes in future programs, either as is or with modifications that can include new classes derived from your existing ones. This reuse of classes can actually reduce the time requirements of an object-oriented design.

OOP also has a positive effect on other phases of the software life cycle, such as program maintenance and verification. You can make one modification to an ancestor class and affect all of its descendants. Without inheritance, you would need to make the same change to many modules. In addition, you can add new features to a program by adding descendant classes that do not affect

A family of related classes

Reuse existing classes

Program maintenance and verification are easier when you use inheritance

their ancestors and, therefore, do not introduce errors into the rest of the program. You can also add a descendant class that modifies its ancestor's original behavior, even though that ancestor was written and compiled long ago.

2.3 A Summary of Key Issues in Programming

Given that a good solution is one that, in the course of its life cycle, incurs a small cost, the next questions to ask are, what are the specific characteristics of good solutions, and how can you construct good solutions? This section summarizes the answers to these very difficult questions.

The programming issues that this section discusses should be familiar to you. However, it is usually the case that the novice programmer does not truly appreciate their importance. After the first course in programming, many students still simply want to "get the thing to run." The discussion that follows should help you realize just how important these issues really are.

One of the most widespread misconceptions held by novice programmers is that a computer program is "read" only by a computer. As a consequence, they tend to consider only whether the computer will be able to "understand" the program—that is, will the program compile, execute, and produce the correct output? The truth is, of course, that other people often must read and modify programs. In a typical programming environment, many individuals share a program. One person may write a program, which other people use in conjunction with other programs written by other people, and a year later, a different person may modify the program. It is therefore essential that you take great care to design a program that is easy to read and understand.

People read programs, too

You should always keep in mind the following six issues of program structure and design:

KEY CONCEPTS

Six Key Programming Issues
1. Modularity
2. Modifiability
3. Ease of use
4. Fail-safe programming
5. Style
6. Debugging

Modularity

Using object-oriented design for software development inherently leads to a modular design. As this book will continually emphasize, you should strive for modularity in all phases of the problem-solving process, beginning with the initial design of a solution. You know from the earlier discussion of object-oriented design that many programming tasks become more difficult as the size and complexity of a program grows. Modularity slows the rate at which the level of difficulty grows. More specifically, modularity has a favorable impact on the following aspects of programming:

Modularity facilitates programming

- **Constructing the program.** The primary difference between a small modular program and a large modular program is simply the number of modules each contains. Because the modules are independent, writing one large modular program is not very different from writing many small, independent programs. On the other hand, working on a large nonmodular program is more like working on many interrelated programs simultaneously. Modularity also permits team programming, where several programmers work independently on their own modules before combining them into one program.

Modularity isolates errors

- **Debugging the program.** Debugging a large program can be a monstrous task. Imagine that you type a 10,000-line program and eventually get it to compile. Neither of these tasks would be much fun. Now imagine that you execute your program and, after a few hundred lines of output, you notice an incorrect number. You should anticipate spending the next day or so tracing through the intricacies of your program before discovering a problem such as an erroneous arithmetic expression.

  A great advantage of modularity is that the task of debugging a large program is reduced to one of debugging many small programs. When you begin to code a module, you should be almost certain that all other modules coded so far are correct. That is, before you consider a module finished, you should test it extensively, both separately and in context with the other modules, by calling it with actual arguments carefully chosen to induce all possible behaviors of the modules. If this testing is done thoroughly, you can feel fairly sure that any problem is a result of an error in the last module added. *Modularity isolates errors.*

  More theoretically, as was mentioned before, you can use formal methods to establish the correctness of a program. Modular programs are amenable to this verification process.

Modular programs are easy to read

- **Reading the program.** A person reading a large program may have trouble seeing the forest for the trees. Just as a modular design helps the programmer cope with the complexities of solving a problem, so too will a modular program help its reader understand how the program works. A modular program is easy to follow because the reader can get a good idea of what is going on without reading any of the code. A well-written method can be understood fairly well from only its name, initial comments, and the names of the other methods that it calls. Readers of a program need to study actual code only if they require a detailed understanding of how the program operates. Program readability is discussed further in the section on style later in this chapter.

- **Modifying the program.** Modifiability is the topic of the next section, but as the modularity of a program has a direct bearing on its modifiability, a brief mention is appropriate here. A small change in the requirements of a program should require only a small change in the code. If this is not the case, it is likely that the program is poorly written and, in particular, that it is not modular. To accommodate a small change in the requirements, a modular program usually requires a change in only a few of its modules, particularly when the modules are independent (that is, loosely coupled) and each module performs a single well-defined task (that is, is highly cohesive).

  Modularity isolates modifications

  When making changes to a program, it is best to make a few at a time. By maintaining a modular design, you can reduce a fairly large modification to a set of small and relatively simple modifications to isolated parts of the program. *Modularity isolates modifications.*

- **Eliminating redundant code.** Another advantage of modular design is that you can identify a computation that occurs in many different parts of the program and implement it as a method. Thus, the code for the computation will appear only once, resulting in an increase in both readability and modifiability. The example in the next section demonstrates this point.

  Modularity eliminates redundancies

Modifiability

Imagine that the specification for a program changes after some period of time. Frequently, people require that a program do something differently than they specified originally, or they ask that it do more than they requested originally. This section offers two examples of how you can make a program easy to modify: through the use of methods and named constants.

Methods.   Suppose that a library has a large program to catalog its books. At several points, the program displays the information about a requested book. At each of these points, the program could include a *System.out.println* statement to display the book's call number, author, and title. You could also replace each occurrence of this statement with a call to a method *displayBook* that displays the same information about the book. Alternatively, you could provide an implementation of the method *toString* in the book class that contains the information you want to display about a book. The method *toString* is invoked when a book object appears in a *System.out.println* statement.

Not only does the use of a method such as *displayBook* have the obvious advantage of eliminating redundant code, it also makes the resulting program easier to modify. For example, to change the format of the output, you need to change only the implementation of *displayBook* instead of numerous occurrences of the *System.out.println* statement. If you had not used a method, the modification would have required you to make changes at each point where the program displays the information. Merely finding each of these points could be difficult, and you probably would overlook a few. In this simple example, the advantages of using methods should be clear.

Methods make a program easier to modify

For another illustration, recall the earlier example of a solution that, as one of its tasks, sorted some data. Developing the sorting algorithm as an independent module and eventually implementing it as a method would make the program easier to modify. For instance, if you found that the sorting algorithm was too slow, you could replace the sort method without even looking at the rest of the program. You could simply "cut out" the old method and "paste in" the new one. If instead the sort was integrated into the program, the required surgery might be quite intricate.

In general, be concerned if you need to rewrite a program to accommodate small modifications. Usually, it is easy to modify a well-structured program slightly: Because each module solves only a small part of the overall problem, a small change in problem specifications usually affects only a few of the modules.

Named constants
make a program
easier to modify

Named constants.   The use of named constants is another way to enhance the modifiability of a program. For example, the restriction that an array must be of a predefined, fixed size causes a bit of difficulty. Suppose that a program uses an array to process the SAT scores of the computer science majors at your university. When the program was written, there were 202 computer science majors, so the array was declared by

```
int [] scores = new int[202];
```

The program processes the array in several ways. For example, it reads the scores, writes the scores, and averages the scores. The pseudocode for each of these tasks contains a construct such as

```
for (index = 0 through 201)
   Process the score
```

If the number of majors changes, not only must you revise the declaration of *scores*, but you must also change each loop that processes the array to reflect the new array size. In addition, other statements in the program might depend on the size of the array. A 202 here, a 201 there—which to change?

On the other hand, if you use a named constant such as

```
final int NUMBER_OF_MAJORS = 202;
```

you can declare the array by using

```
int [] scores = new int[NUMBER_OF_MAJORS];
```

and write the pseudocode for the processing loops in this form:

```
for (index = 0 through NUMBER_OF_MAJORS - 1)
   Process the score
```

If you write expressions that depend on the size of the array in terms of the constant *NUMBER_OF_MAJORS* (such as *NUMBER_OF_MAJORS - 1*), you can change the array size simply by changing the definition of the constant and compiling the program again.

Ease of Use

Another area in which you need to keep people in mind is the design of the user interface. Humans often process a program's input and output. Here are a few obvious points:

- In an interactive environment, the program should always prompt the user for input in a manner that makes it quite clear what it expects. For example, the prompt "?" is not nearly as enlightening as the prompt "Please enter account number for deposit." You should never assume that the users of your program will know what response the program requires.

  Prompt the user for input

- A program should always echo its input. Whenever a program reads data, either from a user or from a file, the program should include the values it reads in its output. This inclusion serves two purposes: First, it gives the user a check on the data entered—a guard against typos and errors in data transmission. This check is particularly useful in the case of interactive input. Second, the output is more meaningful and self-explanatory when it contains a record of what input generated the output.

  Echo the input

- The output should be well labeled and easy to read. An output of

  Label the output

```
1800   6   1
Jones, Q.   223 2234.00 1088.19  N, J   Smith, T. 111
110.23 I,   Harris, V.   44   44000.00 22222.22
```

is more prone to misinterpretation than

```
CUSTOMER ACCOUNTS AS OF 1800 HOURS ON JUNE 1

Account status codes: N=new, J=joint, I=inactive

NAME            ACC#    CHECKING    SAVINGS     STATUS

Jones, Q.       223     $ 2234.00   $ 1088.19   N, J
Smith, T.       111     $  110.23   ---------   I
Harris, V.      44      $44000.00   $22222.22   ------
```

These characteristics of a good user interface are only the basics. Several more subtle points separate a program that is merely usable from one that is user friendly. Students tend to ignore a good user interface, but by investing a little extra time here, you can make a big difference: the difference between a good program and one that only solves the problem. For example, consider a

A good user interface is important

program that requires a user to enter a line of data in some fixed format, with exactly one blank between the items. A free-form input that allows any number of blanks between the items would be much more convenient for the user. It takes so little time to write code that skips blanks, so why require the user to follow an exact format? Once you have made this small additional effort, it is a permanent part of both your program and your library of techniques. The user of your program never has to think about input format.

Fail-Safe Programming

A fail-safe program is one that will perform reasonably no matter how anyone uses it. Unfortunately, this goal is usually unattainable. A more realistic goal is to anticipate the ways that people might misuse the program and to guard carefully against these abuses.

Check for errors in input

    This discussion considers two types of errors. The first type is an *error in input data*. For example, suppose that a program expects a nonnegative integer but reads −12. When a program encounters this type of problem, it should not produce incorrect results or abort with a vague error message. Instead, a fail-safe program provides a message such as

```
-12 is not a valid number of children.
Please enter this number again.
```

    The second type of error is an *error in the program logic*. Although a discussion of this type of error belongs in the debugging section at the end of this chapter, detecting errors in program logic is also an issue of fail-safe programming. A program that appears to have been running correctly may, at some point, behave unexpectedly, even if the data that it reads is valid. For example, the program may not have accounted for the particular data that elicited the surprise behavior, even though you tried your best to test the program's logic. Or perhaps you modified the program and that modification invalidated an assumption that you made in some other part of the program. Whatever the difficulty, a program should have built-in safeguards against these kinds of errors. It should monitor itself and be able to indicate that something is wrong and you should not trust the results.

Check for errors in logic

Guarding against errors in input data. Suppose that you are computing statistics about the people in income brackets between $10,000 and $100,000. The brackets are rounded to the nearest thousand dollars: $10,000, $11,000, and so on to $100,000. The raw data is a file of one or more lines of the form

    G N

where *N* is the number of people with an income that falls into the *G*-thousand-dollar group. If several people have compiled the data, several entries for the same value of *G* might occur. As the user enters data, the program must add up and record the number of people for each value of *G*. From the problem's context, it is clear that *G* is an integer in the range 10 to 100 inclusive, and *N* is a nonnegative integer.

As an example of how to guard against errors in input, consider an input method for this problem. The first attempt at writing this method will illustrate several common ways in which a program can fall short of the fail-safe ideal. Eventually you will see an input method that is much closer to the fail-safe ideal than the original solution.

A first attempt at the class and methods might be

```java
import java.util.Scanner;
public class IncomeStatistics {
  final static int LOW_END = 10;    // low end of incomes
  final static int HIGH_END = 100;  // high end of incomes
  final static int TABLE_SIZE = HIGH_END - LOW_END + 1;

  int[] incomeData;    // used to store the income data,
      // incomeData[G] stores the total number of
      // people that fall into the G-thousand-dollar
      // group

  public IncomeStatistics() {
    incomeData = new int[TABLE_SIZE];
  }  // end constructor

  public void readData() {
    // --------------------------------------------------------
    // Reads and organizes income statistics.
    // Precondition: The calling code gives directions and
    // prompts the user. Input data is error-free, and each
    // input line is in the form G N, where N is the number of
    // people with an income in the G-thousand-dollar group
    // and LOW_END <= G <= HIGH_END. An input line with values
    // of zero for both G and N terminates the input.
    // Postcondition: incomeData[G-LOW_END] = total number of
    // people with an income in the G-thousand-dollar group
    // for each G read. The values read are displayed.
    // --------------------------------------------------------
    int group, number;                        // input values
    Scanner input = new Scanner(System.in);

    for (group = LOW_END; group <= HIGH_END; ++group)  {
      // clear array
      incomeData[index(group)] = 0;
    }  // end for
```

This method is not fail-safe

```
            group = input.nextInt();
            number = input.nextInt();

            while ((group != 0) || (number != 0)) {
               System.out.println("Income group "+group+" contains " +
                                   number + " people.");
               incomeData[index(group)] += number;

               group = input.nextInt();
               number = input.nextInt();
            }  // end while
      }  // end readData

      private int index(int group) {
      // Returns the array index corresponding to group number.
         return group - LOW_END;
      }  // end index

// other methods for class IncomeStatistics would follow

} // end IncomeStatistics
```

The *readData* method has some problems. If an input line contains unexpected data, the program will not behave reasonably. Consider two specific possibilities:

■ The first integer on the input line, which the method assigns to *group*, is not in the range *LOW_END* to *HIGH_END*. The reference *income-Data[index(group)]* will then throw the exception *IndexOutOfBounds-Exception*.

■ The second number on the input line, which the method assigns to *number*, is negative. Although a negative value for *number* is invalid because you cannot have a negative number of people in an income group, the method will add *number* to the group's array entry. Thus, the array *incomeData* will be incorrect.

Test for invalid input data

After the method reads values for *group* and *number*, it must check to see whether *group* is in the range *LOW_END* to *HIGH_END* and whether *number* is positive. If either value is not in range, you must handle the input error.

Instead of checking *number*, you might think to check the value of *incomeData[index(group)]*, after adding *number*, to see whether it is positive. This approach is insufficient. First, notice that it is possible to add a negative value to an entry of *incomeData* without that entry becoming negative. For example, if *number* is −4,000 and the corresponding entry in *incomeData* is 10,000, the sum is 6,000. Thus, a negative value for *number* could remain undetected and invalidate the results of the rest of the program.

One possible course of action for the method to take when it detects invalid data is to raise an exception. If this is done when the bad input is detected, the exception is thrown to the point in the program where the method was called, and no further input is accepted from the user. Another possibility is for the method to set an error flag, ignore the bad input line, and continue taking input from the user. When the user has completed data entry, the method could either throw an exception back to the calling code, or simply return a Boolean value of false to indicate that an input error has occurred. If the input error is a rare event, using an exception would be a good way to handle this situation. But if the input errors are common, and it is acceptable to remove erroneous input from the results, the return of the Boolean value is a better choice.

The following *readData* method attempts to be as universally applicable as possible and to make the program that uses it as modifiable as possible. When the method encounters an error in input, it sets a flag, ignores the data line, and continues. By setting a flag and later returning its value, the method leaves it to the calling module to determine the appropriate action—such as abort or continue—when an input error occurs. Thus, you can use the same input method in many contexts and can easily modify the action taken upon encountering an error.

```
public boolean readData() {
   // --------------------------------------------------------
   // Reads and organizes income statistics.
   // Precondition: The calling code gives directions and
   // prompts the user. Each input line contains exactly two
   // integers in the form G N, where N is the number of
   // people with an income in the G-thousand-dollar group
   // and LOW_END <= G <= HIGH_END. An input line with
   // values of zero for both G and N terminates the input.
   // Postcondition: incomeData[G-LOW_END] = total number
   // of people with an income in the G-thousand-dollar
   // group. The values read are displayed. If either
   // G or N is erroneous (G and N are not both 0, and
   // either G < LOW_END, G > HIGH_END, or N <0),
   // the method prints a message indicating the line
   // will be ignored, sets the return value to false, and
   // continues. In this case, the calling code should take
   // action. The return value is true if the data is error
   // free.
   // --------------------------------------------------------
   int group, number;           // input values
   boolean dataCorrect = true;  // no data error found yet
   Scanner input = new Scanner(System.in);

   for (group = LOW_END; group <= HIGH_END; ++group)  {
      // clear array
      incomeData[index(group)] = 0;
   }  // end for
```

A method that includes fail-safe programming

```
    group = input.nextInt();
    number = input.nextInt();

    while ((group != 0) || (number != 0)) {
    // Invariant: group and number are not both 0
      System.out.print("Income group "+group+" contains " +
                            number + " people.  ");
      if ((group >= LOW_END) && (group <= HIGH_END) &&
                (number >=0)) {
        incomeData[index(group)] += number;
        System.out.println();
      }
      else {
        System.out.println("Data not valid - ignored.");
        dataCorrect = false;
      } // end if

      group = input.nextInt();
      number = input.nextInt();

    }  // end while
  return dataCorrect;
}  // end readData
```

Although this input method will behave gracefully in the face of most common input errors, it is not completely fail-safe. What happens if an input line contains only one integer? What happens if an input line contains a noninteger? The method would be more fail-safe if it read its input one line at a time, and verified that the line actually contains two integer values by using the *hasnextInt()* method from the *Scanner* class. In some contexts, this processing would be a bit extreme. However, if the people who enter the data frequently err by typing nonintegers, you could alter the input method easily because the method is an isolated module. In any case, the method's initial comments should include any assumptions it makes about the data and an indication of what might make the program abort abnormally.

Guarding against errors in program logic.   Now consider the second type of error that a program should guard against: errors in its own logic. These are errors that you may not have caught when you debugged the program or that you may have introduced through program modification.

Unfortunately, a program cannot reliably let you know when something is wrong with it. (Could you rely on a program to tell you that something is wrong with its mechanism for telling you that something is wrong?) You can, however, build into a program checks that ensure that certain conditions always hold when the program is correctly implementing its algorithm. As was mentioned earlier, such conditions are called invariants.

As a simple example of an invariant, consider again the previous example. *All integers in the array `incomeData` must be greater than or equal to zero.* Although the previous discussion argued that the method `readData` should not check the validity of the entries of `incomeData` instead of checking `number`, it could do so *in addition to* checking `number`. For example, if the method finds that an element in the array `incomeData` is outside some range of believability, it can signal a potential problem to its users.

Another general way in which you should make a program fail-safe is to make each method check its precondition. For example, consider the following method, `factorial`, which returns the factorial of an integer:

```java
public static int factorial(int n) {
// ------------------------------------------------------
// Computes the factorial of an integer.
// Precondition: n >= 0.
// Postcondition: Returns n * (n-1)*...*1, if n > 0;
// returns 1 if n = 0.
// ------------------------------------------------------
   int result = 1;

   for (int i = n; i > 1; --i) {
     result *= i;
   }  // end for
   return result;
} // end factorial
```

The initial comments in this method contain a precondition—information about what assumptions are made—as should always be the case. The value that this method returns is valid only if the precondition is met. If *n* is less than zero, the method will return the incorrect value of 1.

In the context of the program for which this method was written, it may be reasonable to make the assumption that *n* will never be negative. That is, if the rest of the program is working correctly, it will call `factorial` only with correct values of *n*. Ironically, this last observation gives you a good reason for `factorial` to check the value of *n*: If *n* is less than zero, the warning that results from the check indicates that something may be wrong elsewhere in the program.

Another reason the method `factorial` should check whether *n* is less than zero is that the method should be correct outside the context of its program. That is, if you borrow the method for use in another program, the method should warn you if you use it incorrectly by passing it an *n* that is negative. A stronger check than simply the statement of the precondition in a comment is desirable. Thus, *a method should state its assumptions and, when possible, check that its arguments conform to these assumptions.*

In this example, `factorial` could check the value of *n* and, if it is negative, return zero, since factorials are never zero. The program that uses `factorial` could then check for this unusual value.

Alternatively, `factorial` could abort execution if its argument was negative. Many programming languages, such as Java, support a mechanism for error handling called an exception. As discussed in Chapter 1, a module indicates that an error has occurred by throwing an exception. A module reacts to an exception that another module throws by catching the exception and executing code to deal with the error condition. Error handling is discussed further in the next section about programming style.

Style

This section considers the following five issues of personal style in programming:

KEY CONCEPTS

Five Issues of Style
1. Extensive use of methods
2. Use of private data fields
3. Error handling
4. Readability
5. Documentation

Admittedly, much of the following discussion reflects the personal taste of the authors; certainly other good programming styles are possible.

It is difficult
to overuse
methods

Extensive use of methods.   It is difficult to overuse methods. If a set of statements performs an identifiable, recurring task, it should be a method. However, a task need not be recurrent to justify the use of a method.

Although a program with all its code in-line runs faster than one that calls methods, programs without methods are not cheaper to use. The use of methods is cost-effective if you consider human time as a significant component of the program's cost. You have already seen the advantages of a modular program.

Use of private data fields.   Each object has a set of methods that represents the operations that can be performed on the object. The object also contains data fields to store information within the object. You should hide the exact representation of these data fields from modules that use the object by making all of the data fields private. Doing so supports the principle of information hiding. The details of the object's implementation are hidden from view, with methods providing the only mechanism to get information to and from the object. Even in a situation where the only operations involved with a particular data field are read and write, the object should provide a simple method—called an **accessor**—that returns the data field's value and another method—called a **mutator**—that sets the data field's value. For example, a `Person` object could provide access to the data field `theName` through the methods `getname()` to return the person's name and `setName()` to change the person's name.

Error handling.   A fail-safe program checks for errors in both its input and its logic and attempts to behave gracefully when it encounters them. A method should check for certain types of errors, such as invalid input or argument values. What action should a method take when it encounters an error? Depending on context, the appropriate action in the face of an error can range from ignoring erroneous data and continuing execution to terminating the program. The method `readData` in the income statistics program earlier in this chapter returned a boolean value to the calling module to indicate that it had encountered an invalid line of data. Thus, the method left it to the calling module to decide on the appropriate action. In general, methods should return a value or throw an exception instead of displaying a message when an error occurs.

> In case of an error, methods should return a value or throw an exception, but not display a message

In some situations, it is more appropriate for the method itself to take the action in case of an error. In the case of a fatal error that calls for termination of the program, Java provides a class `java.lang.Error`. The program will throw an object of type `java.lang.Error` when the error encountered in the program is too severe to warrant continued execution of the program. Dividing an integer by zero is a simple example of a situation that will cause the program to terminate abnormally in this manner.

Readability.   For a program to be easy to follow, it should have a good structure and design, a good choice of identifiers, good indentation and use of blank lines, and good documentation. Avoid clever programming tricks that save a little computer time at the expense of much human time. You will see examples of these points in programs throughout the book.

Choose identifiers that describe their purpose, that is, are self-documenting. Distinguish between keywords, such as `int`, and user-defined identifiers. This book uses the following conventions:

- Keywords are lowercase and appear in boldface.

- User-defined identifiers use both upper- and lowercase letters, as follows:

> Identifier style

  □ Class names are nouns, with each word in the identifier capitalized.

  □ Method names are verbs, with the first letter lowercase and subsequent internal words capitalized. Variables begin with a lowercase letter. Remaining words in multiple-word identifiers each begin with an uppercase letter.

  □ Named constants are entirely uppercase and use underscores to separate words.

Use a good indentation style to enhance the readability of a program. The layout of a program should make it easy for a reader to identify the program's modules. Use blank lines to offset each method. Also, within methods, you should indent individual blocks of code visibly and offset them with blank lines. These blocks are generally—but are not limited to—the actions performed within a control structure, such as a *while* loop or an *if* statement.

You can choose from among several good indentation styles. The five most important general requirements of an indentation style are as follows:

Guidelines for indentation style

- Blocks should be indented sufficiently so that they stand out clearly.

- Indentation should be consistent: Always indent the same type of construct in the same manner.

- The indentation style should provide a reasonable way to handle the problem of **rightward drift,** the problem of nested blocks bumping against the right-hand margin of the page.

- In a compound statement, the opening brace should be at the end of the line that begins the compound statement; the closing brace should line up with the beginning of the line that begins the compound statement:

```
while (i > 0) {
    statement(s)
}   // end while
```

- Braces are used around all statements, even single statements, when they are part of a control structure, such as an *if-else* or *for* statement. This makes it easier to add statements without accidentally introducing bugs due to forgetting to add braces.

Within these guidelines there is room for personal taste. Here is a summary of the style you will see in this book.

Indentation style in this book

- A *for* or *while* statement is written for a simple or compound action as

```
while (expression) {
    statement(s)
}   // end while
```

- A *do* statement is written for a simple or compound action as

```
do {
    statement(s)
} while (expression);
```

■ An *if* statement is written for simple or compound actions as

```
if (expression) {
    statement(s)
}
else {
    statement(s)
}  // end if
```

Nested *if* statements that choose among three or more different courses of action are written as

```
if (condition₁) {
    action₁
}
else if (condition₂) {
    action₂
}
else if (condition₃) {
    action₃
}  // end if
```

This indentation style better reflects the nature of the construct, which is like a generalized *switch* statement:

```
switch (expression) {
    case constant₁ : action₁; break;
    case constant₂ : action₂; break;
    case constant₃ : action₃; break;

}  // end switch
```

Documentation.   A program should be well documented so that others can read, use, and modify it easily. Many acceptable styles for documentation are in use today, and exactly what you should include often depends on the particular program or your individual circumstances. The following are the essential features of any program's documentation:

KEY CONCEPTS

Essential Features of Program Documentation

1. An initial comment for the program that includes
   a. Statement of purpose
   b. Author and date
   c. Description of the program's input and output
   d. Description of how to use the program
   e. Assumptions such as the type of data expected
   f. Statement of exceptions, that is, what could go wrong
   g. Brief description of the major classes
2. Initial comments in each class that state its purpose and describe the data contained in the class (constants and variables)
3. Initial comments in each method that state its purpose, preconditions, postconditions, and methods called
4. Comments in the body of each method to explain important features or subtle logic

---

Beginning programmers tend to downplay the importance of documentation because the computer does not read comments. By now, you should realize that people also read programs. Your comments must be clear enough for someone else to either use your method in a program or modify it. Thus, some of your comments are for people who want to use your method, while others are for people who will revise its implementation. You should distinguish between different kinds of comments.

Consider who will read your comments when you write them

Beginners have a tendency to document programs as a last step. You should, however, write documentation as you develop the program. Since the task of writing a large program might extend over a period of several weeks, you may find that the method that seemed so obvious when you wrote it seems confusing when you try to revise it a week later. Why not benefit from your own documentation by writing it now, while it's fresh in your mind?

You benefit from your own documentation by writing it now instead of later

Debugging

No matter how much care you take in writing a program, it will contain errors that you need to track down. Fortunately, programs that are modular, clear, and well documented are generally amenable to debugging. Fail-safe techniques, which guard against certain errors and report them when they are encountered, are also a great aid in debugging.

Many students seem to be totally baffled by errors in their programs and have no idea how to proceed. These students simply have not learned to track down errors systematically. Without a systematic approach, finding a small mistake in a large program can indeed be a difficult task.

The difficulty that many people have in debugging a program is perhaps due in part to a desire to believe that their program is really doing what it is supposed to do. For example, on receiving an execution-time error message at line 1098, a student might say, "That's impossible. The statement at line 1098 was not even executed, because it is in the *else* clause, and I am positive that it was not executed." This student must do more than simply protest. The proper approach is either to trace the program's execution by using available debugging facilities or to add *System.out.println* statements that show which part of the *if* statement was executed. By doing so, you verify the value of the expression in the *if* statement. If the expression is 0 when you expect it to be 1, the next step is to determine how it became 0.

How can you find the point in a program where something becomes other than what it should be? Typically, a programming environment allows you to trace a program's execution either by single-stepping through the statements in the program or by setting **breakpoints** at which execution will halt. You also can examine the contents of particular variables by either establishing **watches** or inserting temporary *System.out.println* statements. The key to debugging is simply to use these techniques to tell you what is going on. This may sound pretty mundane, but the real trick is to use these debugging aids in an effective manner. After all, you do not simply put breakpoints, watches, and *System.out.println* statements at random points in the program and have them report random information.

> Use either watches or temporary *System.out. println* statements to find logic

The main idea is systematically to locate the points of the program that cause the problem. A program's logic implies that certain conditions should be true at various points in the program. (Recall that these conditions are called invariants.) If the program's results differ from your expectations as stated in the invariants (you *did* write invariants, didn't you?), an error occurs. To correct the error, you must find the first point in the program at which this difference is evident. By inserting either breakpoints and watches or *System.out.println* statements at strategic locations of a program—such as at the entry and departure points of loops and methods—you can systematically isolate the error.

> Systematically check a program's logic to determine where an error occurs

These diagnostic techniques should inform you whether things start going wrong before or after a given point in the program. Thus, after you run the program with an initial set of diagnostics, you should be able to trap the error between two points. For example, suppose that things are fine before you call method M_1, but something is wrong by the time you call M_2. This kind of information allows you to focus your attention between these two points. You continue the process until eventually the search is limited to only a few statements. There is really no place in a program for an error to hide.

The ability to place breakpoints, watches, and *System.out.println* statements in appropriate locations and to have them report appropriate information comes in part from thinking logically about the problem and in part from experience. Here are a few general guidelines.

Debugging methods. You should examine the values of a method's arguments at its beginning and end by using either watches or *System.out.println* statements. Ideally, you should debug each major method separately before using it in your program.

Debugging loops. You should examine the values of key variables at the beginnings and ends of loops, as the comments in this example indicate:

```
// check values of start and stop before entering loop
for (index = start; index <= stop; ++index) {
  // check values of index and key variables
  // at beginning of iteration
     .
     .
     .

  // check values of index and key variables
  // at end of iteration
}  // end for
// check values of start and stop after exiting loop
```

Debugging *if* statements. Just before an *if* statement, you should examine the values of the variables within its expression. You can use either breakpoints or *System.out.println* statements to determine which branch the *if* statement takes, as this example indicates:

```
// check variables within expression before executing if
if (expression) {
  System.out.println("Value of expression is true");
  . . .
}
else {
  System.out.println("Value of expression is false");
  . . .
}  // end if
```

Using *System.out.println* statements. *System.out.println* statements can sometimes be more convenient than watches. Such statements should report both the values of key variables and the location in the program at which the variables have those values. You can use a comment to label the location, as follows:

```
// This is point A
System.out.println("At point A method compute:\n" +
                   "x = " + x + ", y = " + y );
```

Remember to either comment out or remove these statements when your program finally works.

Using special dump methods.   Often the variables whose values you wish to examine are arrays or other, more complex data structures. If so, you should write dump methods to display the data structures in a highly readable manner. You can easily move the single statement that calls each dump method from one point in the program to another as you track down an error. The time that you spend on these methods often proves to be worthwhile, as you can call them repeatedly while debugging different parts of the program.

Hopefully, this discussion has conveyed the importance of the *effective use of diagnostic aids in debugging*. Even the best programmers have to spend some time debugging. Thus, to be a truly good programmer, you must be a good debugger.

Summary

1. Software engineering is a branch of computer science that studies ways to facilitate the development of computer programs.

2. The life cycle of software consists of several phases: specifying the problem, designing the algorithm, analyzing the risks, verifying the algorithm, coding the programs, testing the programs, refining the solution, using the software, and maintaining the software.

3. A loop invariant is a property of an algorithm that is true before and after each iteration of a loop. Loop invariants are useful in developing iterative algorithms and establishing their correctness.

4. Java supports an `assert` statement that allows you to verify that a condition is true at a given point in a program.

5. When evaluating the quality of a solution, you must consider a diverse set of factors: the solution's correctness, its efficiency, the time that went into its development, its ease of use, and the cost of modifying and expanding it.

6. A combination of object-oriented and functional decomposition techniques will lead to a modular solution. For problems that primarily involve data management, encapsulate data with operations on that data by designing classes. The nouns in the problem statement can help you to identify appropriate classes. Break algorithmic tasks into independent subtasks that you gradually refine. In all cases, practice abstraction; that is, focus on what a module does instead of how it does it.

7. Take great care to ensure that your final solution is as easy to modify as possible. Generally, a modular program is easy to modify because changes in the problem's requirements frequently affect only a handful of the modules. Programs should not depend on the particular implementations of its modules.

8. A method should be as independent as possible and perform one well-defined task.

9. A method should always include an initial comment that states its purpose, its precondition—that is, the conditions that must exist at the beginning of a module—and its postcondition—the conditions at the end of a module.

10. A program should be as fail-safe as possible. For example, a program should guard against errors in input and errors in its own logic. By checking invariants—which are conditions that are true at certain points in a program—you can monitor correct program execution.

11. The effective use of available diagnostic aids is one of the keys to debugging. You should use watches or *System.out.println* statements to report the values of key variables at key locations. These locations include the beginnings and ends of methods and loops, and the branches of selection statements.

12. To make it easier to examine the contents of arrays and other, more complex data structures while debugging, you should write dump methods that display the contents of the data structures. You can easily move calls to such methods as you track down an error.

Cautions

1. Your programs should guard against errors. A fail-safe program checks that an input value is within some acceptable range and reports if it is not. An error in input should not cause a program to terminate before it clearly reports what the error was. A fail-safe program also attempts to detect errors in its own logic. For example, in many situations, methods should check that their arguments have valid values.

2. If you want to use the *assert* statement in a Java program, you must make sure that assertions are enabled when you compile the code.

3. You can write better, correct programs in less time if you pay attention to the following guidelines: Write precise specifications for the program. Use a modular design. Write pre- and postconditions for each method before you implement it. Use meaningful identifiers and consistent indentation. Write comments, including assertions and invariants.

Self-Test Exercises

The answers to all Self-Test Exercises are at the back of this book.

1. Think about the way that a cell phone manages a contact list.

   a. Write a specification for this problem. Be sure to account for the fact that there may be many different ways to contact a single person, including e-mail.

   b. Design a solution to this problem. Design at least two objects (no code here, we are in phase 2 of the software life cycle), one for each entry in the contact list, the other for the contact list itself. What are the data fields and methods for these objects? Also include preconditions and postconditions for the methods.

   c. Create a UML diagram that reflects your design in part b.

2. What is the loop invariant for the following?

```
int index = 0;
int sum = item[0];

while (index < n) {
  ++index;
  sum += item[index];
}   // end while
```

3. What is the loop invariant for the following? (Hint: Convert to a *while* loop first.)

```
for (int index = 0; index < n; index++) {
  sum += item[index];
}
```

4. Consider the following method, which interactively reads and writes the identification number, age, salary (in thousands of dollars), and name of each individual in a group of employees. How can you improve the program? Some of the issues are obvious, while others are more subtle. Try to keep in mind all the topics discussed in this chapter.

```
public static void main(String args[]) {
    int x1, x2, x3;
    String name;
    Scanner input = new Scanner(System.in);

    x1 = input.nextInt();
    x2 = input.nextInt();
    x3 = input.nextInt();

    while (x1 != 0) {
      name = input.next();
      System.out.println(x1 + " " + x2 + " " + x3 + name);

      x1 = input.nextInt();
      x2 = input.nextInt();
      x3 = input.nextInt();
    }   // end while

}   // end main
```

5. Suppose that, due to some severe error, you must abort a program from a location deep inside nested method calls, while loops, and if statements. Write a diagnostic method that you can call from anywhere in a program. This method should take an error code as an argument, display an appropriate error message, and terminate program execution.

Exercises

1. The greatest common divisor (GCD) of two integers is the largest positive integer that divides both numbers without a remainder. Write a specification for a method that computes the GCD of two integers Include a statement of purpose, the pre- and postconditions, and a description of the parameters.

2. The price of an item that you want to buy is given in dollars and cents. You pay for it in cash by giving the clerk *d* dollars and *c* cents. Write specifications for a method that computes the change, if any, that you should receive. Include a statement of purpose, the pre- and postconditions, and a description of the parameters.

3. The time of day consists of an hour, minute, second, and time zone. Integer values can be used to represent the hour (0-23) and minute (0-59). Seconds can be represented using a decimal value depending on how often the time is updated (for example, every millisecond). The time zone can be represented using a string. So for example, 2:30 p.m. Eastern time is 14 hours, 30 minutes with a time zone of "EDT." The seconds are not noted here, but will be a value between 0 and 60-for example, 03.120 is 3 seconds and 120 milliseconds.

   a. Write specifications for a method that advances any given date by one day. Include a statement of purpose, the pre- and postconditions, and a description of the parameters.

   b. Write a Java implementation of this method. Design and specify any other methods that you need. Include comments that will be helpful to someone who will maintain your implementation in the future.

4. The following program counts the number of occurrences of a given word in a file, but has many problems. It is written using poor style, and it contains syntax errors and even some logic errors. Identify and provide corrections for these problems so that the program follows the style guideline in this chapter and executes properly.

```java
import java.io.*;

public Class countWord {

    static final String
            prompt1 = "Enter the name of the text file: ";
    static final String
            PROMPT2 = "Enter the word to be counted in the file: ";

    public static void main(String args) {
        // Purpose: To count the number of occurrences of a word in a
        // text file. The user provides both the word and the text
        // file.

        Scanner input = new Scanner(System.out);

        String Filename = input.nextLine();
        System.out.print(prompt1);

        Scanner fileInput = null;
        try {
        fileInput = new Scanner(new File(Filename));
        } catch (FileNotFoundException e) {
        e.printStackTrace();
        }
        // Use anything but a letter as a delimiter
        fileInput.useDelimiter("[^a-zA-Z]+");
```

```
        String word = input.next();
        System.out.print(PROMPT2);

        while (fileInput.hasNext()) {
        String fileWord = fileInput.next();
        System.out.println(fileWord);
        int color = 0;
        if (Word.equalsIgnoreCase(fileWord)) {
        color++;
        }
        } // end while
        fileInput.close();
        System.out.println("The word " + word + "appeared "
                         + color + " times in the file" + Filename);
    }
} // end countWord
```

5. Social networking sites make it easy for people to stay in touch. Suppose you need to design a very simple social networking program that allows a user to post messages to all of his or her friends, so that when one of the user's friends logs into the program, the friend sees the message. Assume that friends must be confirmed, and that once a friendship is confirmed, each user is a friend of the other.

   a. Write a specification for this problem. Note that a person may have many friends.

   b. Design a solution to this problem. Determine what objects (with their data fields and methods) would be necessary to solve this problem.

   c. Draw a UML diagram that reflects your design in part b.

6. Draw a UML diagram for an `Automobile` class that could be used by a car rental company. The data members should include the make, model, year, license plate, mileage, amount of gasoline in the tank, and current location. When deciding on the operations to include, be aware that only some of these data members should be updateable, while others are read only.

7. Design a student registration system that manages student enrollment in courses. Each course can have many students enrolled in it, but only one instructor. Information stored on students and instructors is similar in that they all have a name, home address, and ID. Students also have their campus address and major stored, while instructors have department and salary. Courses have a title, course code, meeting time, and a list of the students enrolled in the class. Model this application using UML.

8. One way to compute the quotient and remainder of two numbers *num* and *den* is to use repeated subtraction as shown in the following code:

```
int q = 0;      // the quotient
int rem = num;  // the remainder

while (rem >= den) {
  rem = rem - den;
  q++;
} // end while
```

The invariant for this code is

```
rem >= 0 and
num = q * den + rem
```

For the values $num = 17$, $den = 4$, prove that the invariant is true before the loop begins, after each iteration (pass) of the loop, and when the loop terminates by completing the following table (you may not need all passes shown). The initial values are shown:

pass	q	rem	rem >= 0	num = q * den + rem
initially	0	17	true	17 = 0 * 17 + 17, true
1				
2				
3				
4				
5				

9. Write pre- and postconditions for the following methods:

   a. A method that takes an array of test scores and returns the average

   b. A method that computes a person's Body Mass Index (BMI), given the height in inches and the body weight in pounds

   c. A method that computes the monthly payment for a loan given the loan amount, the interest rate, and the loan term in months

10. Do you think that the assertion statement in Java can help you debug your program? Explain your answer.

11. What is the problem with the following code fragment?

```
num = 50;
while (num >= 0) {
    System.out.println (num);
    num = num + 1;
} // end while
```

12. The Fibonacci sequence is a sequence of integers, starting with 0 and 1, where every number is the sum of the previous two. Write a program to calculate and print the first twenty numbers of the Fibonacci sequence.

13. This chapter stressed the importance of adding fail-safe checks to a program wherever possible. What can go wrong with the following method? How can you protect yourself?

```
public static double getAverage(double[] x, int numItems) {
    double sum = 0;
    for (int i=0; i<numItems; i++){
        sum += x[i];
    } // end for
    return sum/numItems;
} // end getAverage
```

14. Write the loop invariants for the code segments shown:

a.
```
int i = 10;
while (i < 100)
    i++;
```

b.
```
int product = 1;
for (int i = 2; i <= n; i++)
    product = product * (2 * i - 1);
```

c.
```
int c = 0;
int p = 1;
while (c < b) {
    p = p * a;
    c++;
} // end while
```

15. In the following code, assume that the array item has been initialized with random integer values. Write the loop invariant for the following:.

```
int index = 0;
while (index < item.length)
    if (item[index] > 0) {
        sum += item[index];
    } // end if
    ++index;
} // end while
```

16. Using a *for* loop, write a program that displays the squares of prime numbers greater than 0 and less than or equal to a given number *n*.

17. The following code is supposed to compute the **floor** of the square root of its input value x. (The floor of a number *n* is the largest integer less than or equal to *n*.)

```
// Computes and writes floor(sqrt(x)) for
// an input value x >= 0.
public static void main(String args[]) {
    int x;  // input value
    Scanner input = new Scanner(System.in);

    // initialize
    int result = 0;  // will equal floor of sqrt(x)
    int temp1 = 1;
    int temp2 = 1;

    // read input
    x = input.nextInt();

    // compute floor
    while (temp1 < x) {
        ++result;
        temp2 += 2;
        temp1 += temp2;
    }  // end while
    System.out.println("The floor of the square root of "
                    + x + " is " + result);

}  // end main
```

This program contains an error.

   a. What output does the program produce when $x = 64$?

   b. Run the program and remove the error. Describe the steps that you took to find the error.

   c. How can you make the program more user friendly and fail-safe?

18. Create a class where one method reads and writes, through the terminal, the values of an array of any dimension chosen by the user. Another method of the same class performs the addition and multiplication of two arrays. Your program should have guard against errors.

19. Using a for loop, write a program that prints the following triangle

```
1
0 1
0 1 0
1 0 1 0
1 0 1 0 1
0 1 0 1 0 1
```

Programming Problems

1. Consider a program that will read student information into an array of objects, sort the array by student identification number, write out the sorted array, and compute various statistics on the data, such as the average GPA of a student. Write complete UML specifications for this problem that reflect an object-oriented solution. What classes and methods did you identify during the design of your solution? Write specifications, including preconditions and postconditions, for each method.

2. Write a program that sorts and evaluates bridge hands.
   The input is a stream of character pairs that represent playing cards. For example,

```
2C   QD   TC   AD   6C   3D   TD   3H   5H   7H   AS   JH   KH
```

represents the 2 of clubs, queen of diamonds, 10 of clubs, ace of diamonds, and so on. Each pair consists of a rank followed by a suit, where rank is A, 2, . . . , 9, T, J, Q, or K, and suit is C, D, H, or S. You can assume that each input line represents exactly 13 cards and is error-free. Input is terminated by an end-of-file.
   For each line of input, form a hand of 13 cards. Display each hand in a readable form arranged both by suits and by rank within suit (aces are high). Then evaluate the hand by using the following standard bridge values:
   Aces count 4
   Kings count 3
   Queens count 2
   Jacks count 1
   Voids (no cards in a suit) count 3
   Singletons (one card in a suit) count 2
   Doubletons (two cards in a suit) count 1
   Long suits with more than 5 cards in the suit
   count 1 for each card over 5 in number

For example, for the previous sample input line, the program should produce the output

```
CLUBS        10    6    2
DIAMONDS     A     Q    10    3
HEARTS       K     J    7     5    3
SPADES       A
Points = 16
```

because there are 2 aces, 1 king, 1 queen, 1 jack, 1 singleton, no doubletons, and no long suits. (The singleton ace of spades counts as both an ace and a singleton.)

Optional: See how much more flexible and fail-safe you can make your program. That is, try to remove as many of the previous assumptions in input as you can.

3. A *polynomial* of a single variable x with integer coefficients is an expression of the form

$$p(x) = c_0 + c_1 x + c_2 x^2 + \ldots + c_n x^n,$$

where c_i, $i = 0, 1, \ldots, n$, are integers.

Create a class for polynomials up to the nth degree. A specification of the methods for this class is provided next:

- **public** Polynomial(**int** maxDegree)

  Constructs a new polynomial of degree *maxDegree* with all of the coefficients set to zero

- **public** Polynomial(**int**[] coef)

  Constructs a new polynomial with the corresponding coefficients passed in the *coef* array, with the highest degree as *coef[0]* and the constant term in *coef[coef.length-1]*. So the array {3, 2, 1} creates the polynomial $3x^2 + 2x + 1$.

- **public int** getCoefficient(**int** power)

  Returns an integer representing the coefficient of the x^{power} term

- **public void** setCoefficient(**int** coef, **int** power)

  Sets the coefficient of the x^{power} term to coef

- **public** String toString()

  Returns the *String* representation of the polynomial. For example, $3x^2 + 2x + 1$ would be returned as 3 * x^2 + 2 * x + 1 or, more simply, 3x^2 + 2x + 1. Any term whose coefficient is zero should not appear in the string unless the polynomial has only a single constant term of zero.

- **public double** evaluate(**double** x)

  Evaluates the polynomial for the value x and returns the result p(x)

- **public static** Polynomial derivative(Polynomial p)

  Returns a *Polynomial* representing the derivative of the polynomial p

- **public double** bisection(**double** a, **double** b)
                throws java.lang.IllegalArgumentException

  Returns a *double* representing the root of the *Polynomial* using the Bisection Method. The bisection method requires two initial points a and b such that p(x) and p(x) have opposite signs; if they do not, then java.lang.IllegalArgumentException should be thrown. Though there could be multiple roots between a and b, the method will return the first root it finds such that evaluating the polynomial at $p(root) < 0.000001$.

One method that can be used to easily evaluate a polynomial is based upon Horner's rule. Note that the fourth degree polynomial $2x^4 + x^3 - 4x^2 + 3x + 5$ can be evaluated as

```
result = (((((((2 * x) + 1) * x) - 4) * x) + 3) * x) + 5
```

or, in more general terms

```
result = (((((((c₄ * x) + c₃) * x) + c₂) * x) + c₁) * x) + c₀
```

To find the derivative of a polynomial, you simply find the derivative of each term in the polynomial. The derivative of a term $c_i x^i$ is $(i * c_i)x^{i-1}$. So for example, the derivative of

$p(x) = 4x^2 + 3x + 1$ is

$p'(x) = 8x + 3$

To test the `Polynomial` class, create a second class called `TestPolynomial`. This class should support the following interaction with the user (user input is shaded):

```
Please enter the polynomial you wish to work with. You will be
prompted to enter the coefficient for each term in the
polynomial. You may enter zero if the term is absent from the
polynomial.

What degree polynomial would you like to create? 4

Please enter the coefficients:
   Coefficient for x^4: 2
   Coefficient for x^3: 1
   Coefficient for x^2: -4
   Coefficient for x^1: 3
   Coefficient for x^0: 5

 p(x) = 2x^4 + x^3 - x^2 + 3x + 5

What would you like to do with this polynomial?
  (E/e) Evaluate it for a particular value of x
  (D/d) Get the derivative of the polynomial
  (R/r) Find the root of the polynomial

Enter option: e

For what value of x would you like to evaluate the polynomial?
2.5
p(2.5) = 81.25

Would you like to select another option? (y/n) y

What would you like to do with this polynomial?
  (E/e) Evaluate it for a particular value of x
  (D/d) Get the derivative of the polynomial
  (R/r) Find the root of the polynomial
```

```
Enter option: d
p'(x) = 8 x^3 + 3 x^2 - 8 x + 3

Would you like to select another option? (y/n) n
Would you like to enter another polynomial? (y/n) n
```

4. Java provides a class `java.lang.BigInteger` that can be used to handle very large integers. Implement a similar class, called `BigInt`, that can be used to do simple calculations with very large nonnegative integers. Design this class carefully. You will need the following:

   ■ A data structure to represent large numbers: for example, a string or an array for the digits in a number.

   ■ **public** BigInt(String val)

   A constructor that uses a string representation of the integer for initialization. The string may contain leading zeros. Do not forget that zero is a valid number.

   ■ **public** String toString()

   Returns the *String* representation of this *BigInt*. It should not include leading zeros, but if the number consists of all zeros, it should return a String with a single zero.

   ■ **public** BigInt max(BigInt val)

   A method that returns a **BigInt** whose value is the maximum of *val* and the instance of *BigInt* that invokes *max*.

   ■ **public** BigInt min(BigInt val)

   A method that returns a **BigInt** whose value is the minimum of *val* and the instance of *BigInt* that invokes *min*.

   ■ **public** BigInt add(BigInt val)

   A method that returns a *BigInt* whose value is the sum of *val* and the instance of *BigInt* that invokes *add*.

   ■ **public** BigInt multiply(BigInt val)

   A method that returns a *BigInt* whose value is the product of *val* and the instance of *BigInt* that invokes *multiply*.

   Write a program that acts as an interactive calculator capable of handling very large nonnegative integers that uses the *BigInt* class. This calculator need perform only the operations of addition and multiplication.

   In this program each input line is of the form

   num_1 *op* num_2

   and should produce output such as

   num_1
   op num_2
   ----
        num_3

   where num_1 and num_2 are (possibly very large) nonnegative integers, *op* is the single character + or *, and num_3 is the integer that results from the desired calculation. Be sure your interface is user friendly.

   Optional: Allow signed integers (negative as well as positive integers), and write a method for subtraction.

CHAPTER 3

Recursion: The Mirrors

The goal of this chapter is to ensure that you have a basic understanding of recursion, which is one of the most powerful techniques of solution available to the computer scientist. This chapter assumes that you have had little or no previous introduction to recursion. If, however, you already have studied recursion, you can review this chapter as necessary.

By presenting several relatively simple problems, the chapter demonstrates the thought processes that lead to recursive solutions. These problems are diverse and include examples of counting, searching, and organizing data. In addition to presenting recursion from a conceptual viewpoint, this chapter discusses techniques that will help you to understand the mechanics of recursion. These techniques are particularly useful for tracing and debugging recursive methods.

Some recursive solutions are far more elegant and concise than the best of their nonrecursive counterparts. For example, the classic Towers of Hanoi problem appears to be quite difficult, yet it has an extremely simple recursive solution. On the other hand, some recursive solutions are terribly inefficient, as you will see, and should not be used.

Chapter 6 continues the formal discussion of recursion by examining more-difficult problems. Recursion will play a major role in many of the solutions that appear throughout the remainder of this book.

3.1 Recursive Solutions

Recursion is an extremely powerful problem-solving technique. Problems that at first appear to be quite difficult often have simple recursive solutions. Like top-down design, recursion breaks a problem into several smaller problems. What is striking about recursion is that these smaller problems are of *exactly the same type* as the original problem—mirror images, so to speak.

Did you ever hold a mirror in front of another mirror so that the two mirrors face each other? You will see many images of yourself, each behind and slightly smaller than the other. Recursion is like these mirror images. That is, a recursive solution solves a problem by solving a smaller instance of the same problem! It solves this new problem by solving an even smaller instance of the same problem. Eventually, the new problem will be so small that its solution will be either obvious or known. This solution will lead to the solution of the original problem.

For example, suppose that you could solve problem P_1 if you had the solution to problem P_2, which is a smaller instance of P_1. Suppose further that you could solve problem P_2 if you had the solution to problem P_3, which is a smaller instance of P_2. If you knew the solution to P_3 because it was small enough to be trivial, you would be able to solve P_2. You could then use the solution to P_2 to solve the original problem P_1.

Recursion can seem like magic, especially at first, but as you will see, it is a very real and important problem-solving approach that is an alternative to **iteration.** An iterative solution involves loops. You should know at the outset that not all recursive solutions are better than iterative solutions. In fact, some recursive solutions are impractical because they are so inefficient. Recursion, however, can provide elegantly simple solutions to problems of great complexity.

As an illustration of the elements in a recursive solution, consider the problem of looking up a word in a dictionary. Suppose you wanted to look up the word "vademecum." Imagine starting at the beginning of the dictionary and looking at every word in order until you found "vademecum." That is precisely what a **sequential search** does, and, for obvious reasons, you want a faster way to perform the search.

One such method is the **binary search,** which in spirit is similar to the way in which you actually use a dictionary. You open the dictionary—probably to a point near its middle—and by glancing at the page, determine which "half" of the dictionary contains the desired word. The following pseudocode is a first attempt to formalize this process:

Recursion breaks a problem into smaller identical problems

Some recursion solutions are inefficient and impractical

Complex problems can have simple recursive solutions

A binary search of a dictionary

```
// Search a dictionary for a word by using a recursive
// binary search

   if (the dictionary contains only one page) {
     Scan the page for the word
   }
   else {
     Open the dictionary to a point near the middle
     Determine which half of the dictionary contains the
        word
```

```
if (the word is in the first half of the dictionary) {
   Search the first half of the dictionary for the word
}
else {
   Search the second half of the dictionary for the word
} // end if
} // end if
```

Parts of this solution are intentionally vague: How do you scan a single page? How do you find the middle of the dictionary? Once the middle is found, how do you determine which half contains the word? The answers to these questions are not difficult, but they will only obscure the solution strategy right now.

The previous search strategy reduces the problem of searching the dictionary for a word to a problem of searching half of the dictionary for the word, as Figure 3-1 illustrates. Notice two important points. First, once you have divided the dictionary in half, you already know how to search the appropriate half: You can use exactly the same strategy that you employed to search the original dictionary. Second, note that there is a special case that is different from all the other cases: After you have divided the dictionary so many times that you are left with only a single page, the halving ceases. At this point, the problem is sufficiently small that you can solve it directly by scanning the single page that remains for the word. This special case is called the **base case** (or **basis** or **degenerate case**).

> A base case is a special case whose solution you know

This strategy is one of **divide and conquer.** You solve the dictionary search problem by first *dividing* the dictionary into two halves and then *conquering* the appropriate half. You solve the smaller problem by using the same divide-and-conquer strategy. The dividing continues until you reach the base case. As you will see, this strategy is inherent in many recursive solutions.

> A binary search uses a divide-and-conquer strategy

To further explore the nature of the solution to the dictionary problem, consider a slightly more rigorous formulation.

```
search(in theDictionary:Dictionary, in aWord: string)

   if (theDictionary is one page in size) {
      Scan the page for aWord
```

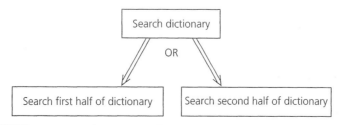

FIGURE 3-1

A recursive solution

```
    }
    else {
      Open theDictionary to a point near the middle
      Determine which half of theDictionary contains aWord

      if (aWord is in the first half of theDictionary) {
        search(first half of theDictionary, aWord)
      }
      else {
        search(second half of theDictionary, aWord)
      }  // end if
    }  // end if
```

Writing the solution as a method allows several important observations:

A recursive method
calls itself

1. One of the actions of the method is to call itself; that is, the method `search` calls the method `search`. This action is what makes the solution recursive. The solution strategy is to split `theDictionary` in half, determine which half contains `aWord`, and apply the same strategy to the appropriate half.

Each recursive call
solves an identical,
but smaller, problem

2. Each call to the method `search` made from within the method `search` passes a dictionary that is one-half the size of the previous dictionary. That is, at each successive call to `search (theDictionary, aWord)`, the size of `theDictionary` is cut in half. The method solves the search problem by solving another search problem that is identical in nature but smaller in size.

A test for the base
case enables the
recursive calls
to stop

3. There is one search problem that you handle differently from all of the others. When `theDictionary` contains only a single page, you use another technique: You scan the page directly. Searching a one-page dictionary is the base case of the search problem. When you reach the base case, the recursive calls stop and you solve the problem directly.

Eventually, one of
the smaller prob-
lems must be the
base case

4. The manner in which the size of the problem diminishes ensures that you will eventually reach the base case.

These facts describe the general form of a recursive solution. Though not all recursive solutions fit these criteria as nicely as this solution does, the similarities are far greater than the differences. As you attempt to construct a new recursive solution, you should keep in mind the following four questions:

KEY CONCEPTS

Four Questions for Constructing Recursive Solutions

1. How can you define the problem in terms of a smaller problem of the same type?

2. How does each recursive call diminish the size of the problem?

3. What instance of the problem can serve as the base case?

4. As the problem size diminishes, will you reach this base case?

Now consider two relatively simple problems: computing the factorial of a number and writing a string backward. Their recursive solutions further illustrate the points raised by the solution to the dictionary search problem. These examples also illustrate the difference between a recursive valued method and a recursive *void* method.

A Recursive Valued Method: The Factorial of n

Consider a recursive solution to the problem of computing the factorial of an integer n. This problem is a good first example because its recursive solution is easy to understand and neatly fits the mold described earlier. However, because the problem has a simple and efficient iterative solution, you should not use the recursive solution in practice.

Do not use recursion if a problem has a simple, efficient iterative solution

To begin, consider the familiar iterative definition of *factorial*(n) (more commonly written $n!$):

$$factorial(n) = n * (n-1) * (n-2) * \cdots * 1 \text{ for any integer } n > 0$$

$$factorial(0) = 1$$

An iterative definition of factorial

The factorial of a negative integer is undefined. You should have no trouble writing an iterative factorial method based on this definition.

To define *factorial(n)* recursively, you first need to define *factorial(n)* in terms of the factorial of a smaller number. To do so, simply observe that the factorial of n is equal to the factorial of $(n-1)$ multiplied by n; that is,

$$factorial(n) = n * [(n-1) * (n-2) * \cdots * 1]$$

$$= n * factorial(n-1)$$

A recurrence relation

The definition of *factorial(n)* in terms of *factorial(n − 1)*, which is an example of a **recurrence relation,** implies that you can also define *factorial(n − 1)* in terms of *factorial(n − 2)*, and so on. This process is analogous to the dictionary search solution, in which you search a dictionary by searching a smaller dictionary in exactly the same way.

The definition of *factorial(n)* lacks one key element: the base case. As was done in the dictionary search solution, here you must define one case differently from all the others, or else the recursion will never stop. The base case for the factorial method is *factorial(0)*, which you know is 1. Because n originally is greater than or equal to zero and each call to *factorial* decrements n by 1, you will always reach the base case. With the addition of the base case, the complete recursive definition of the factorial method is

$$factorial(n) \; = \; \begin{cases} 1 & \text{if } n = 0 \\ n * factorial(n-1) & \text{if } n > 0 \end{cases}$$

A recursive definition of factorial

To be sure that you understand this recursive definition, apply it to the computation of *factorial*(4). Since 4 > 0, the recursive definition states that

$$factorial(4) = 4 * factorial(3)$$

Similarly,

$$factorial(3) = 3 * factorial(2)$$

$$factorial(2) = 2 * factorial(1)$$

$$factorial(1) = 1 * factorial(0)$$

You have reached the base case, and the definition directly states that

$$factorial(0) = 1$$

At this point, the application of the recursive definition stops and you still do not know the answer to the original question: What is *factorial*(4)? However, the information to answer this question is now available:

Since $factorial(0) = 1$, then $factorial(1) = 1 * 1 = 1$

Since $factorial(1) = 1$, then $factorial(2) = 2 * 1 = 2$

Since $factorial(2) = 2$, then $factorial(3) = 3 * 2 = 6$

Since $factorial(3) = 6$, then $factorial(4) = 4 * 6 = 24$

You can think of recursion as a process that divides a problem into a task that you can do and a task that a friend can do for you. For example, if I ask you to compute *factorial*(4), you could first determine whether you know the answer immediately. You know immediately that *factorial*(0) is 1—that is, you know the base case—but you do not know the value of *factorial*(4) immediately. However, if your friend computes *factorial*(3) for you, you could compute *factorial*(4) by multiplying *factorial*(3) by 4. Thus, your task will be to do this multiplication, and your friend's task will be to compute *factorial*(3).

Your friend now uses the same process to compute *factorial*(3) as you are using to compute *factorial*(4). Thus, your friend determines that *factorial*(3) is not the base case, and so asks another friend to compute *factorial*(2). Knowing *factorial*(2) enables your friend to compute *factorial*(3), and when you learn the value of *factorial*(3) from your friend, you can compute *factorial*(4).

Notice that the recursive definition of *factorial*(4) yields the same result as the iterative definition, which gives 4 * 3 * 2 * 1 = 24. To prove that the two definitions of *factorial* are equivalent for all nonnegative integers, you would use **mathematical induction.** (See Appendix D.) Chapter 5 discusses the close tie between recursion and mathematical induction.

The recursive definition of the factorial method has illustrated two points: (1) *Intuitively,* you can define *factorial*(*n*) in terms of *factorial*(*n* − 1), and (2) *mechanically,* you can apply the definition to determine the value of a given factorial. Even in this simple example, applying the recursive definition required quite a bit of work. That, of course, is where the computer comes in.

Once you have a recursive definition of *factorial*(*n*), it is easy to construct a Java method that implements the definition:

```
public static int fact(int n) {
// ------------------------------------------------------
// Computes the factorial of a nonnegative integer.
// Precondition: n must be greater than or equal to 0.
// Postcondition: Returns the factorial of n.
// ------------------------------------------------------
   if (n == 0) {
     return 1;
   }
   else {
     return n * fact(n-1);
   }  // end if
}  // end fact
```

Suppose that you use the statement

```
System.out.println(fact(3));
```

to call the method. Figure 3-2 depicts the sequence of computations that this call would require.

Note that the *fact* method is defined as **static.** This means that *fact* is a class method; it is invoked independently of any instance of the class that contains *fact*. Instances of the class share the *fact* method, and if the static method is

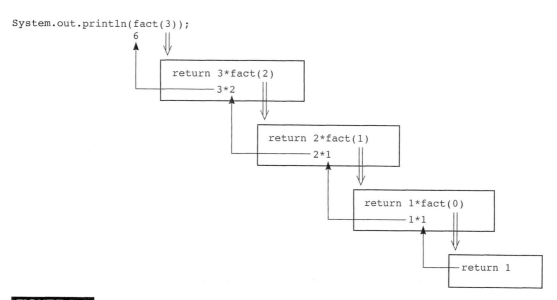

FIGURE 3-2

fact(3)

public, other objects can access it through the class name. For example, `java.lang.Math.sqrt` provides access to the static method `sqrt` contained in the class `java.lang.Math`. Methods that don't need access to instance variables and are self-contained (except for parameter input) are good candidates to be designated as static methods. For this reason, all of the recursive methods in this chapter are declared `static`.

The `fact` method fits the model of a recursive solution given earlier in this chapter as follows:

1. One action of `fact` is to *call itself*.

`fact` satisfies the
four criteria of a
recursive solution

2. At each recursive call to `fact`, the integer whose factorial you need to compute is *diminished by 1*.

3. The method handles the factorial of 0 differently from all the other factorials: It does not generate a recursive call. Rather, you know that `fact(0)` is 1. Thus, the *base case* occurs when *n* is 0.

4. Given that *n* is nonnegative, item 2 of this list assures you that you will always *reach the base case*.

At an intuitive level, it should be clear that the method `fact` implements the recursive definition of *factorial*. Now consider the mechanics of executing this recursive method. The logic of `fact` is straightforward except perhaps for the expression in the `else` clause. This expression has the following effect:

1. Each operand of the product $n * fact(n-1)$ is evaluated.

2. The second operand—`fact(n-1)`—is a call to the method `fact`. Although this is a recursive call (the method `fact` calls the method `fact`), there really is nothing special about it. Imagine substituting a call to another method— the Java API method `java.lang.Math.abs`, for example—for the recursive call to `fact`. The principle is the same: Simply evaluate the method.

In theory, evaluating a recursive method is no more difficult than evaluating a nonrecursive method. In practice, however, the bookkeeping can quickly get out of hand. The **box trace** is a systematic way to trace the actions of a recursive method. You can use the box trace both to help you to understand recursion and to debug recursive methods. However, such a mechanical device is no substitute for an intuitive understanding of recursion. The box trace illustrates how compilers frequently implement recursion. As you read the following description of the method, realize that each box roughly corresponds to an **activation record,** which a compiler typically uses in its implementation of a method call. Chapter 7 will discuss this implementation further.

An activation record
is created for each
method call

The box trace.   The box trace is illustrated here for the recursive method `fact`. As you will see in the next section, this trace is somewhat simpler for a *void* method, as no value needs to be returned.

1. Label each recursive call in the body of the recursive method. Several recursive calls might occur within a method, and it will be important to distin-

guish among them. These labels help you to keep track of the correct place to which you must return after a method call completes. For example, mark the expression `fact(n-1)` within the body of the method with the letter A:

```
if (n == 0) {
    return 1;
}
else {
    return n * fact(n-1);
}  // end if       (A)
```

Label each recursive call in the method

You return to point A after each recursive call, substitute the computed value for `fact(n-1)`, and continue execution by evaluating the expression `n * fact(n-1)`.

2. Represent each call to the method during the course of execution by a new box in which you note the method's **local environment.** More specifically, each box will contain

Each time a method is called, a new box represents its local environment

a. The values of the references and primitive types of the method's arguments.

b. The method's local variables.

c. A placeholder for the value returned by each recursive call from the current box. Label this placeholder to correspond to the labeling in Step 1.

d. The value of the method itself.

When you first create a box, you will know only the values of the input arguments. You fill in the values of the other items as you determine them from the method's execution. For example, you would create the box in Figure 3-3 for the call `fact(3)`. (You will see in later examples that you must handle reference arguments [objects] somewhat differently from value arguments [primitive types] and local variables.)

3. Draw an arrow from the statement that initiates the recursive process to the first box. Then, when you create a new box after a recursive call, as described in Step 2, you draw an arrow from the box that makes the call to the newly created box. Label each arrow to correspond to the label (from Step 1) of the recursive call; this label indicates exactly where to return after the call completes. For example, Figure 3-4 shows the first two boxes generated by the call to `fact` in the statement `System.out.println(fact(3))`.

```
n = 3
A: fact(n-1) = ?
return ?
```

FIGURE 3-3

A box

```
System.out.println(fact(3));
```

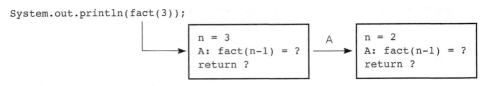

FIGURE 3-4

The beginning of the box trace

4. After you create the new box and arrow as described in Steps 2 and 3, start executing the body of the method. Each reference to an item in the method's local environment references the corresponding value in the current box, regardless of how you generated the current box.

5. On exiting the method, cross off the current box and follow its arrow back to the box that called the method. This box now becomes the current box, and the label on the arrow specifies the exact location at which execution of the method should continue. Substitute the value returned by the just-terminated method call into the appropriate item in the current box.

Figure 3-5 is a complete box trace for the call *fact(3)*. In the sequence of diagrams in this figure, the current box is the deepest along the path of arrows and is shaded, whereas crossed-off boxes have a dashed outline.

The initial call is made, and method `fact` begins execution:

```
n = 3
A: fact(n-1)=?
return ?
```

At point A a recursive call is made, and the new invocation of the method `fact` begins execution:

```
n = 3              n = 2
A: fact(n-1)=?  A  A: fact(n-1)=?
return ?           return ?
```

At point A a recursive call is made, and the new invocation of the method `fact` begins execution:

```
n = 3              n = 2              n = 1
A: fact(n-1)=?  A  A: fact(n-1)=?  A  A: fact(n-1)=?
return ?           return ?           return ?
```

At point A a recursive call is made, and the new invocation of the method `fact` begins execution:

```
n = 3              n = 2              n = 1              n = 0
A: fact(n-1)=?  A  A: fact(n-1)=?  A  A: fact(n-1)=?  A
return ?           return ?           return ?          return ?
```

FIGURE 3-5

Box trace of *fact(3)*   (continues)

FIGURE 3-5

(continued)

This is the base case, so this invocation of `fact` completes:

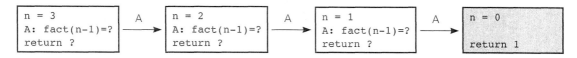

```
n = 3          A    n = 2          A    n = 1          A    n = 0
A: fact(n-1)=?  →   A: fact(n-1)=?  →   A: fact(n-1)=?  →
return ?            return ?            return ?            return 1
```

The method value is returned to the calling box, which continues execution:

```
n = 3          A    n = 2          A    n= 1               n = 0
A: fact(n-1)=?  →   A: fact(n-1)=?  →   A: fact(n-1)=1
return ?            return ?            return ?            return 1
```

The current invocation of `fact` completes:

```
n = 3          A    n = 2          A    n = 1              n = 0
A: fact(n-1)=?  →   A: fact(n-1)=?  →   A: fact(n-1)=1
return ?            return ?            return 1            return 1
```

The method value is returned to the calling box, which continues execution:

```
n = 3          A    n = 2              n = 1              n = 0
A: fact(n-1)=?  →   A: fact(n-1)=1     A: fact(n-1)=1
return ?            return ?            return 1            return 1
```

The current invocation of `fact` completes:

```
n = 3          A    n = 2              n = 1              n = 0
A: fact(n-1)=?  →   A: fact(n-1)=1     A: fact(n-1)=1
return ?            return 2            return 1            return 1
```

The method value is returned to the calling box, which continues execution:

```
n = 3              n = 2              n = 1              n = 0
A: fact(n-1)=2     A: fact(n-1)=1     A: fact(n-1)=1
return ?            return 2            return 1            return 1
```

The current invocation of `fact` completes:

```
n = 3              n = 2              n = 1              n = 0
A: fact(n-1)=2     A: fact(n-1)=1     A: fact(n-1)=1
return 6            return 2            return 1            return 1
```

The value 6 is returned to the initial call.

Invariants. Writing invariants for recursive methods is as important as writing them for iterative methods, and is often simpler. For example, consider the recursive method *fact*:

```
public static int fact(int n) {
// Precondition: n must be greater than or equal to 0.
// Postcondition: Returns the factorial of n.
  if (n == 0) {
  return 1;
  }
  else { // Invariant: n > 0, so n-1 >= 0.
        // Thus, fact(n-1) returns (n-1)!
    return n * fact(n-1);  // n * (n-1)! is n!
  } // end if
}  // end fact
```

Expect a recursive call's postcondition to be true if the precondition is true

The method requires as its precondition a nonnegative value of n. At the time of the recursive call *fact(n-1)*, n is positive, so $n - 1$ is nonnegative. Since the recursive call satisfies *fact*'s precondition, you can expect from the postcondition that *fact(n-1)* will return the factorial of $n - 1$. Therefore, n * *fact(n-1)* is the factorial of n. Chapter 6 uses mathematical induction to prove formally that *fact(n)* returns the factorial of n.

*Violating **fact**'s precondition causes "infinite" recursion*

If you ever violated *fact*'s precondition, the method would not behave correctly. That is, if the calling program ever passed a negative value to *fact*, an infinite sequence of recursive calls, terminated only by a system-defined limit, would occur because the method would never reach the base case. For example, *fact(-4)* would call *fact(-5)*, which would call *fact(-6)*, and so on.

The method ideally should protect itself by testing for a negative n. If $n < 0$, the method could, for example, either return zero to indicate an error or throw an exception. Chapter 2 discussed error checking in the two sections "Fail-Safe Programming" and "Style"; you might want to review that discussion at this time.

A Recursive *void* Method: Writing a String Backward

Now consider a problem that is slightly more difficult: Given a string of characters, write it in reverse order. For example, write the string "cat" as "tac". To construct a recursive solution, you should ask the four questions in the Key Concepts box on page 164.

You can construct a solution to the problem of writing a string of length *n* backward in terms of the problem of writing a string of length $n - 1$ backward. That is, each recursive step of the solution diminishes by 1 the length of the string to be written backward. The fact that the strings get shorter and shorter suggests that the problem of writing some very short strings backward can serve as the base case. One very short string is the empty string, the string of length zero. Thus, you can choose for the base case the problem

The base case

Write the empty string backward

The solution to this problem is to do nothing at all—a very straightforward solution indeed! (Alternatively, you could use the string of length 1 as the base case.)

Exactly how can you use the solution to the problem of writing a string of length $n - 1$ backward to solve the problem of writing a string of length n backward? This approach is analogous to the one used to construct the solution to the factorial problem, where you specified how to use *factorial*$(n - 1)$ in the computation of *factorial*(n). Unlike the factorial problem, however, the string problem does not suggest an immediately clear way to proceed. Obviously, not any string of length $n - 1$ will do. For example, there is no relation between writing "apple" (a string of length 5) backward and writing "pear" (a string of length 4) backward. You must choose the smaller problem carefully so that you can use its solution in the solution to the original problem.

> How can you write an *n*-character string backward, if you can write an (*n* – 1)-character string backward?

The string of length $n - 1$ that you choose must be a substring (part) of the original string. Suppose that you strip away one character from the original string, leaving a substring of length $n - 1$. For the recursive solution to be valid, the ability to write the substring backward, combined with the ability to perform some minor task, must result in the ability to write the original string backward. Compare this approach with the way you computed *factorial* recursively: The ability to compute *factorial*$(n - 1)$, combined with the ability to multiply this value by n, resulted in the ability to compute *factorial*(n).

You need to decide which character to strip away and which minor task to perform. Consider the minor task first. Since you are writing characters, a likely candidate for the minor task is writing a single character. As for the character that you should strip away from the string, there are several possible alternatives. Two of the more intuitive alternatives are

```
Strip away the last character
```

or

```
Strip away the first character
```

Consider the first of these alternatives, stripping away the last character, as Figure 3-6 illustrates.

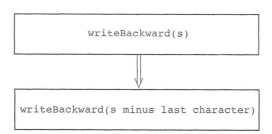

FIGURE 3-6

A recursive solution

For the solution to be valid, you must write the last character in the string first. Therefore, you must write the last character before you write the remainder of the string backward. A high-level recursive solution, given the string *s*, is

writeBackward
writes a string
backward

```
writeBackward(in s:string)

    if (the string s is empty) {
        Do nothing -- this is the base case
    }
    else {
        Write the last character of s
        writeBackward(s minus its last character)
    }  // end if
```

This solution to the problem is conceptual. To obtain a Java method, you must resolve a few implementation issues. Suppose that the method will receive one argument: a string *s* to be written backward. Note that the string begins at position 0 and ends at position *s.length()* − 1. That is, all characters, including blanks, in that range are part of the string. The Java method *writeBackward* appears as follows:

```
public static void writeBackward(String s) {
// ----------------------------------------------------
// Writes a character string backward.
// Precondition: None.
// Postcondition: The string is written backward
// ----------------------------------------------------
   if (s.length() > 0) {
     // write the last character
     System.out.println(s.substring(s.charAt(s.length()-1)));

     // write the rest of the string backward,
     // s minus the last character
     writeBackward(s.substring(0, s.length()-1));  // Point A
   }  // end if
   // size == 0 is the base case - do nothing
}  // end writeBackward
```

Notice that the recursive calls to *writeBackward* use successively smaller strings. Each recursive call has the effect of stripping away the last character of the string, which ensures that the base case will be reached.

You can trace the execution of *writeBackward* by using the box trace. As was true for the method *fact*, each box contains the local environment of the recursive call—in this case, the input argument. The trace will differ somewhat from the trace of *fact* shown in Figure 3-5 because, as a *void* method, *writeBackward*

writeBackward
does not return a
computed value

does not use a *return* statement to return a computed value. Figure 3-7 traces the call to the method *writeBackward* with the string "cat".

Now consider a slightly different approach to the problem. Recall the two alternatives for the character that you could strip away from the string: the last character or the first character. The solution just given strips away the last character of the string. It will now be interesting to construct a solution based on the second alternative:

Strip away the first character

To begin, consider a simple modification of the previous pseudocode solution that replaces each occurrence of "last" with "first." Thus, the method writes the first character rather than the last and then recursively writes the remainder of the string backward.

```
writeBackward1(in s:string)

    if (the string s is empty) {
      Do nothing -- this is the base case
    }
    else {
      Write the first character of s
      writeBackward1(s minus its first character)
    }  // end if
```

Does this solution do what you want it to? If you think about this method, you will realize that it writes the string in its normal left-to-right direction instead of backward. After all, the steps in the pseudocode are

```
Write the first character of s
Write the rest of s
```

These steps simply write the string s. Naming the method *writeBackward1* does not guarantee that it will actually write the string backward—recursion really is not magic!

You can write s backward correctly by using the following recursive formulation:

```
Write string s minus its first character backward
Write the first character of string s
```

In other words, you write the first character of s only *after* you have written the rest of s backward. This approach leads to the following pseudocode solution:

```
writeBackward2(in s:string)
```

writeBackward2 writes a string backward

The initial call is made, and the method begins execution:

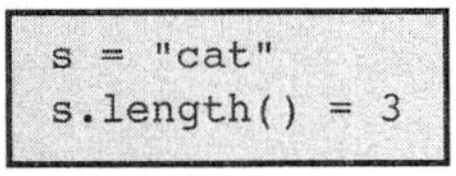

```
s = "cat"
s.length() = 3
```

Output line: **t**

Point A (writeBackward(s)) is reached, and the recursive call is made.

The new invocation begins execution:

```
s = "cat"          A    s = "ca"
s.length() = 3   ────►  s.length() = 2
```

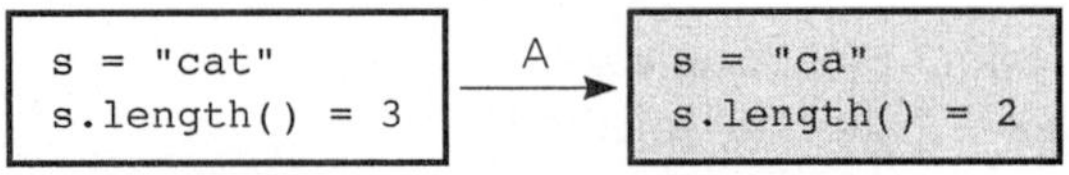

Output line: **ta**

Point A is reached, and the recursive call is made.

The new invocation begins execution:

```
s = "cat"          A    s = "ca"          A    s = "c"
s.length() = 3   ────►  s.length() = 2   ────►  s.length() = 1
```

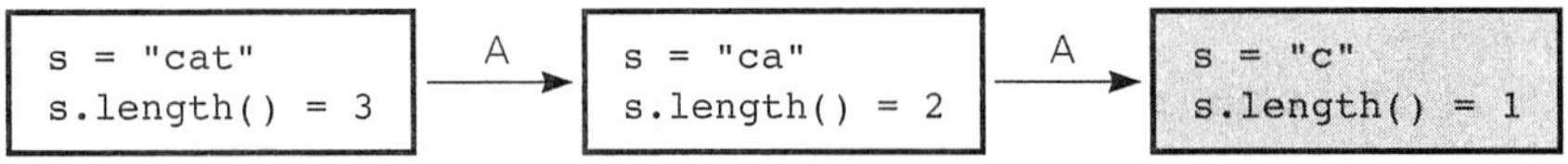

Output line: **tac**

Point A is reached, and the recursive call is made.

The new invocation begins execution:

```
s = "cat"      A   s = "ca"      A   s = "c"      A   s = ""
s.length() = 3 ──► s.length() = 2 ──► s.length() = 1 ──► s.length() = 0
```

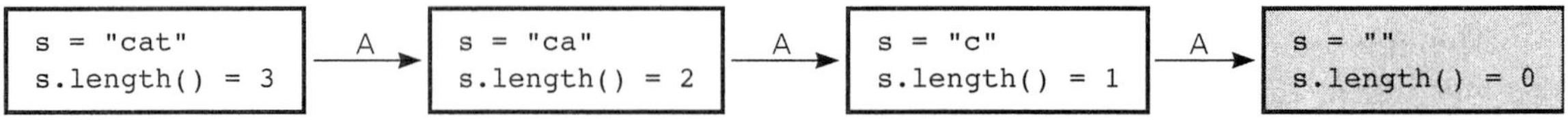

This is the base case, so this invocation completes.

Control returns to the calling box, which continues execution:

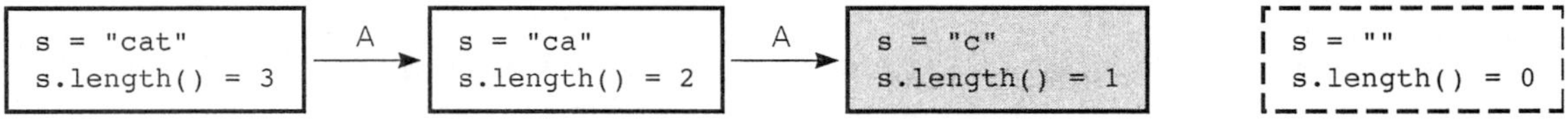

```
s = "cat"      A   s = "ca"      A   s = "c"         s = ""
s.length() = 3 ──► s.length() = 2 ──► s.length() = 1   s.length() = 0
```

This invocation completes. Control returns to the calling box, which continues execution:

```
s = "cat"      A   s = "ca"         s = "c"         s = ""
s.length() = 3 ──► s.length() = 2   s.length() = 1   s.length() = 0
```

This invocation completes. Control returns to the calling box, which continues execution:

```
s = "cat"         s = "ca"         s = "c"         s = ""
s.length() = 3    s.length() = 2   s.length() = 1   s.length() = 0
```

This invocation completes. Control returns to the statement following the initial call.

FIGURE 3-7

Box trace of **writeBackward("cat")**

```
if (the string s is empty) {
   Do nothing -- this is the base case
}
else {
   writeBackward2(s minus its first character)
   Write the first character of s
} // end if
```

The translation of *writeBackward2* into Java is similar to that of the original *writeBackward* method and is left as an exercise.

It is instructive to carefully trace the actions of the two pseudocode methods *writeBackward* and *writeBackward2*. First, add statements to each method to provide output that is useful to the trace, as follows:

writeBackward(in s:string)

```
System.out.println("Enter writeBackward, string: " + s );
if (the string s is empty) {
  Do nothing -- this is the base case
}
else {
  System.out.println("About to write last character of " +
                     "string: " + s);
  Write the last character of s
  writeBackward(s minus its last character)  // Point A
} // end if
System.out.println("Leave writeBackward, string: " + s);
```

Output statements can help you trace the logic of a recursive method

writeBackward2(in s:string)

```
System.out.println("Enter writeBackward2, string: " + s);
if (the string s is empty) {
  Do nothing -- this is the base case
}
else {
  writeBackward2(s minus its first character) // Point A
  System.out.println("About to write first character of" +
                     "string: " + s);
  Write the first character of s
} // end if
System.out.println("Leave writeBackward2, string: " + s);
```

Figures 3-8 and 3-9 show the output of the revised pseudocode methods *writeBackward* and *writeBackward2*, when initially given the string "cat".

You need to be comfortable with the differences between these two methods. The recursive calls that the two methods make generate a different sequence

The initial call is made, and the method begins execution:

```
s = "cat"
```

Output stream:

```
Enter writeBackward, string: cat
About to write last character of string: cat
t
```

Point A is reached, and the recursive call is made. The new invocation begins execution:

```
s = "cat"   A→   s = "ca"
```

Output stream:

```
Enter writeBackward, string: cat
About to write last character of string: cat
t
Enter writeBackward, string: ca
About to write last character of string: ca
a
```

Point A is reached, and the recursive call is made. The new invocation begins execution:

```
s = "cat"   A→   s = "ca"   A→   s = "c"
```

Output stream:

```
Enter writeBackward, string: cat
About to write last character of string: cat
t
Enter writeBackward, string: ca
About to write last character of string: ca
a
Enter writeBackward, string: c
About to write last character of string: c
c
```

Point A is reached, and the recursive call is made. The new invocation begins execution:

```
s = "cat"   A→   s = "ca"   A→   s = "c"   A→   s = " "
```

This invocation completes execution, and a return is made.

Output stream:

```
Enter writeBackward, string: cat
About to write last character of string: cat
t
```

FIGURE 3-8

Box trace of **writeBackward("cat")** in pseudocode

```
Enter writeBackward, string: ca
About to write last character of string: ca
a
Enter writeBackward, string: c
About to write last character of string: c
c
Enter writeBackward, string:
Leave writeBackward, string:
```

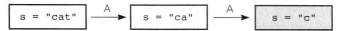

This invocation completes execution, and a return is made.

Output stream:

```
Enter writeBackward, string: cat
About to write last character of string: cat
t
Enter writeBackward, string: ca
About to write last character of string: ca
a
Enter writeBackward, string: c
About to write last character of string: c
c
Enter writeBackward, string:
Leave writeBackward, string:
Leave writeBackward, string: c
```

This invocation completes execution, and a return is made.

Output stream:

```
Enter writeBackward, string: cat
About to write last character of string: cat
t
Enter writeBackward, string: ca
About to write last character of string: ca
a
Enter writeBackward, string: c
About to write last character of string: c
c
Enter writeBackward, string:
Leave writeBackward, string:
Leave writeBackward, string: c
Leave writeBackward, string: ca
```

This invocation completes execution, and a return is made.

(continues)

FIGURE 3-8

(continued)

Output stream:

```
Enter writeBackward, string: cat
About to write last character of string: cat
t
Enter writeBackward, string: ca
About to write last character of string: ca
a
Enter writeBackward, string: c
About to write last character of string: c
c
Enter writeBackward, string:
Leave writeBackward, string:
Leave writeBackward, string: c
Leave writeBackward, string: ca
Leave writeBackward, string: cat
```

The initial call is made, and the method begins execution:

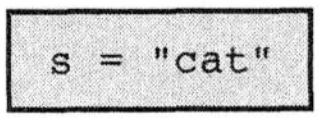

```
s = "cat"
```

Output stream:

```
Enter writeBackward2, string: cat
```

Point A is reached, and the recursive call is made. The new invocation begins execution:

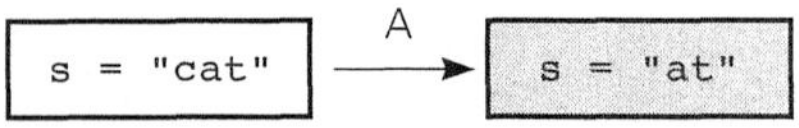

```
s = "cat"  ─A→  s = "at"
```

Output stream:

```
Enter writeBackward2, string: cat
Enter writeBackward2, string: at
```

Point A is reached, and the recursive call is made. The new invocation begins execution:

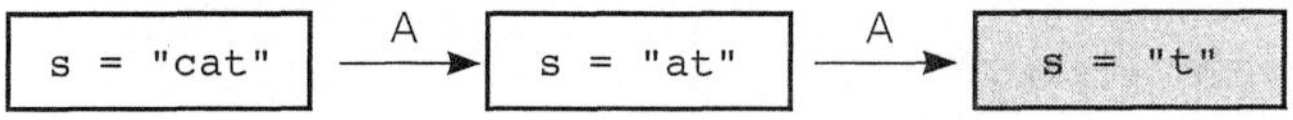

```
s = "cat"  ─A→  s = "at"  ─A→  s = "t"
```

Output stream:

```
Enter writeBackward2, string: cat
Enter writeBackward2, string: at
Enter writeBackward2, string: t
```

FIGURE 3-9

Box trace of *writeBackward2("cat")* in pseudocode

Point A is reached, and the recursive call is made. The new invocation begins execution:

This invocation completes execution, and a return is made.

Output stream:

```
Enter writeBackward2, string: cat
Enter writeBackward2, string: at
Enter writeBackward2, string: t
Enter writeBackward2, string:
Leave writeBackward2, string:
```

This invocation completes execution, and a return is made.

Output stream:

```
Enter writeBackward2, string: cat
Enter writeBackward2, string: at
Enter writeBackward2, string: t
Enter writeBackward2, string:
Leave writeBackward2, string:
About to write first character of string: t
t
Leave writeBackward2, string: t
```

This invocation completes execution, and a return is made.

Output stream:

```
Enter writeBackward2, string: cat
Enter writeBackward2, string: at
Enter writeBackward2, string: t
Enter writeBackward2, string:
Leave writeBackward2, string:
About to write first character of string: t
t
Leave writeBackward2, string: t
About to write first character of string: at
a
Leave writeBackward2, string: at
```

(continues)

FIGURE 3-9

(continued)

```
┌─────────────┐   ┌─────────────┐   ┌─────────────┐   ┌─────────────┐
│ s = "cat"   │   │ s = "at"    │   │ s = "t"     │   │ s = " "     │
└─────────────┘   └─ ─ ─ ─ ─ ─ ─┘   └─ ─ ─ ─ ─ ─ ─┘   └─ ─ ─ ─ ─ ─ ─┘
```

This invocation completes execution, and a return is made.

Output stream:

```
Enter writeBackward2, string: cat
Enter writeBackward2, string: at
Enter writeBackward2, string: t
Enter writeBackward2, string:
Leave writeBackward2, string:
About to write first character of string: t
t
Leave writeBackward2, string: t
About to write first character of string: at
a
Leave writeBackward2, string: at
About to write first character of string: cat
c
Leave writeBackward2, string: cat
```

of values for the argument *s*. Despite this fact, both methods correctly write the string argument backward. They compensate for the difference in the sequence of values for *s* by writing different characters in the string at different times relative to the recursive calls. In terms of the box traces in Figures 3-8 and 3-9, *writeBackward* writes a character just before generating a new box (just before a new recursive call), whereas *writeBackward2* writes a character just after crossing off a box (just after returning from a recursive call). When these differences are put together, the result is two methods that employ different strategies to accomplish the same task.

This example also illustrates the value of the box trace, combined with well-placed *System.out.println* statements, in debugging recursive methods. The *System.out.println* statements at the beginning, interior, and end of the recursive methods report the value of the argument *s*. In general, when debugging a recursive method, you should also report both the values of local variables and the point in the method where each recursive call occurred, as in this example:

Well-placed but temporary *System.out.println* statements can help you to debug a recursive method

```
abc(...)


  System.out.println("Calling abc from point A.");
  abc(...)   // this is point A


  System.out.println("Calling abc from point B.");
  abc(... )   // this is point B
```

Realize that the `System.out.println` statements do not belong in the final version of the method.

Remove **System.out.println** statements after you have debugged the method

3.2 Counting Things

The next three problems require you to count certain events or combinations of events or things. They are good examples of problems with more than one base case. They also provide good examples of tremendously inefficient recursive solutions. Do not let this inefficiency discourage you. Your goal right now is to understand recursion by examining simple problems. Soon you will see useful and efficient recursive solutions.

Multiplying Rabbits (The Fibonacci Sequence)

Rabbits are very prolific breeders. If rabbits did not die, their population would quickly get out of hand. Suppose we assume the following "facts," which were obtained in a recent survey of randomly selected rabbits:

- Rabbits never die.

- A rabbit reaches sexual maturity exactly two months after birth, that is, at the beginning of its third month of life.

- Rabbits are always born in male-female pairs. At the beginning of every month, each sexually mature male-female pair gives birth to exactly one male-female pair.

Suppose you started with a single newborn male-female pair. How many pairs would there be in month 6, counting the births that took place at the beginning of month 6? Since 6 is a relatively small number, you can figure out the solution easily:

Month 1:	1 pair, the original rabbits.
Month 2:	1 pair still, since it is not yet sexually mature.
Month 3:	2 pairs; the original pair has reached sexual maturity and has given birth to a second pair.
Month 4:	3 pairs; the original pair has given birth again, but the pair born at the beginning of month 3 is not yet sexually mature.
Month 5:	5 pairs; all rabbits alive in month 3 (2 pairs) are now sexually mature. Add their offspring to those pairs alive in month 4 (3 pairs) to yield 5 pairs.
Month 6:	8 pairs; 3 newborn pairs from the pairs alive in month 4 plus 5 pairs alive in month 5.

You can now construct a recursive solution for computing *rabbit*(*n*), the number of pairs alive in month *n*. You must determine how you can use *rab-*

bit(n − 1) to compute *rabbit*(n). Observe that *rabbit*(n) is the sum of the number of pairs alive just prior to the start of month n and the number of pairs born at the start of month n. Just prior to the start of month n, there are *rab-bit*(n − 1) pairs of rabbits. Not all of these rabbits are sexually mature at the start of month n. Only those who were alive in month n − 2 are ready to reproduce at the start of month n. That is, the number of pairs born at the start of month n is *rabbit*(n − 2). Therefore, you have the recurrence relation

$$rabbit(n) = rabbit(n − 1) + rabbit(n − 2)$$

Figure 3-10 illustrates this relationship.

This recurrence relation introduces a new point. In some cases, you solve a problem by solving more than one smaller problem of the same type. This change does not add much conceptual difficulty, but you must be very careful when selecting the base case. The temptation is simply to say that *rabbit*(1) should be the base case because its value is 1 according to the problem's statement. But what about *rabbit*(2)? Applying the recursive definition to *rabbit*(2) would yield

$$rabbit(2) = rabbit(1) + rabbit(0)$$

Thus, the recursive definition would need to specify the number of pairs alive in month 0—an undefined quantity.

Two base cases are necessary because there are two smaller problems of the same type

One possible solution is to define *rabbit*(0) to be 0, but this approach seems artificial. A slightly more attractive alternative is to treat *rabbit*(2) itself as a special case with the value of 1. Thus, the recursive definition has two base cases, *rabbit*(2) and *rabbit*(1). The recursive definition becomes

$$rabbit(n) = \begin{cases} 1 & \text{if } n \text{ is 1 or 2} \\ rabbit(n − 1) + rabbit(n − 2) & \text{if } n > 2 \end{cases}$$

Incidentally, the series of numbers *rabbit*(1), *rabbit*(2), *rabbit*(3), and so on is known as the **Fibonacci sequence,** which models many naturally occurring phenomena.

A Java method to compute *rabbit*(n) is easy to write from the previous definition:

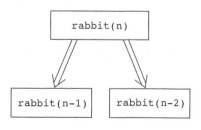

Recursive solution to the rabbit problem

```
public static int rabbit(int n) {
// ------------------------------------------------------
// Computes a term in the Fibonacci sequence.
// Precondition: n is a positive integer.
// Postcondition: Returns the nth Fibonacci number.
// ------------------------------------------------------
   if (n <= 2) {
      return 1;
   }
   else  { // n > 2, so n-1 > 0 and n-2 > 0
      return rabbit(n-1) + rabbit(n-2);
   }  // end if
}  // end rabbit
```

rabbit computes the Fibonacci sequence but does so inefficiently

Should you actually use this method? Figure 3-11 illustrates the recursive calls that *rabbit(7)* generates. Think about the number of recursive calls that *rabbit(10)* generates. At best, the method *rabbit* is inefficient. Thus, its use is not feasible for large values of *n*. This problem is discussed in more detail at the end of this chapter, at which time you will see some techniques for generating a more efficient solution from this same recursive relationship.

Organizing a Parade

You have been asked to organize the Fourth of July parade, which will consist of bands and floats in a single line. Last year, adjacent bands tried to outplay each other. To avoid this problem, the sponsors have asked you never to place one band immediately after another. In how many ways can you organize a parade of length n?

Assume that you have at least n marching bands and n floats from which to choose. When counting the number of ways to organize the parade, assume that the sequences *band-float* and *float-band*, for example, are different entities and count as two ways.

The parade can end with either a float or a band. The number of ways to organize the parade is simply the sum of the number of parades of each type. That is, let

$P(n)$ be the number of ways to organize a parade of length n

$F(n)$ be the number of parades of length n that end with a float

$B(n)$ be the number of parades of length n that end with a band

Then

$$P(n) = F(n) + B(n)$$

First, consider $F(n)$. You will have a parade of length n that ends with a float simply by placing a float at the end of *any* acceptable parade of length $n - 1$.

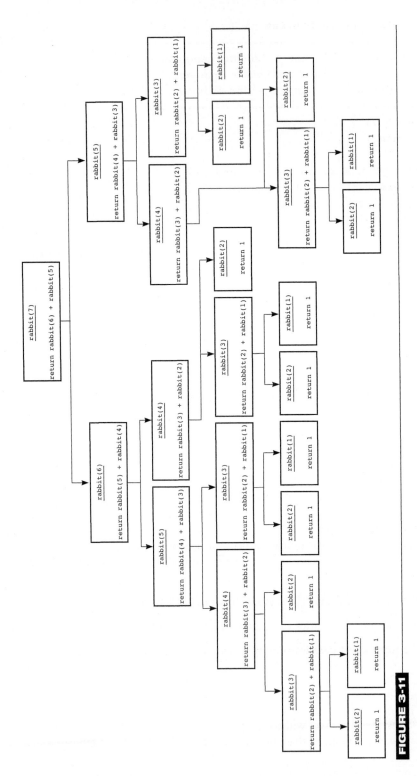

FIGURE 3-11

The recursive calls that `rabbit(7)` generates

Hence, the number of acceptable parades of length n that end with a float is precisely equal to the total number of acceptable parades of length $n - 1$; that is,

$$F(n) = P(n - 1)$$

The number of acceptable parades of length n that end with a float

Next, consider $B(n)$. The only way a parade can end with a band is if the unit just before the end is a float. (If it is a band, you will have two adjacent bands.) Thus, the only way to organize an acceptable parade of length n that ends with a band is first to organize a parade of length $n - 1$ that ends with a float and then add a band to the end. Therefore, the number of acceptable parades of length n that end with a band is precisely equal to the number of acceptable parades of length $n - 1$ that end with a float:

The number of acceptable parades of length n that end with a band

$$B(n) = F(n - 1)$$

You use the earlier fact that $F(n) = P(n - 1)$ to obtain

$$B(n) = P(n - 2)$$

Thus, you have solved $F(n)$ and $B(n)$ in terms of the smaller problems $P(n - 1)$ and $P(n - 2)$, respectively. You then use

$$P(n) = F(n) + B(n)$$

to obtain

$$P(n) = P(n - 1) + P(n - 2)$$

The number of acceptable parades of length n

The form of this recurrence relation is identical to the solution for the multiplying rabbits problem.

As you saw in the rabbit problem, two base cases are necessary because the recurrence relation defines a problem in terms of two smaller problems. As you did for the rabbit problem, you can choose $n = 1$ and $n = 2$ for the base cases. Although both problems use the same n's for their base cases, there is no reason to expect that they use the same values for these base cases. That is, there is no reason to expect that $rabbit(1)$ is equal to $P(1)$ and that $rabbit(2)$ is equal to $P(2)$.

A little thought reveals that for the parade problem,

Two base cases are necessary because there are two smaller problems of the same type

$P(1) = 2$ (The parades of length 1 are *float* and *band*.)

$P(2) = 3$ (The parades of length 2 are *float-float*, *band-float*, and *float-band*.)

In summary, the solution to this problem is

$P(1) = 2$

A recursive solution

$P(2) = 3$

$P(n) = P(n - 1) + P(n - 2)$ for $n > 2$

This example demonstrates the following points about recursion:

- Sometimes you can solve a problem by breaking it up into cases—for example, parades that end with a float and parades that end with a band.

- The values that you use for the base cases are extremely important. Although the recurrence relations for P and *rabbit* are the same, the different values for their base cases ($n = 1$ or 2) cause different values for larger values of n. For example, *rabbit*$(20) = 6,765$, while $P(20) = 17,711$. The larger the value of n, the larger the discrepancy. You should think about why this is so.

Mr. Spock's Dilemma (Choosing k out of n Things)

The five-year mission of the *U.S.S. Enterprise* is to explore new worlds. The five years are almost up, but the *Enterprise* has just entered an unexplored solar system that contains n planets. Unfortunately, time will allow for visits to only k planets. Mr. Spock begins to ponder how many different choices are possible for exploring k planets out of the n planets in the solar system. Because time is short, he does not care about the order in which he visits the same k planets.

Mr. Spock is especially fascinated by one particular planet, Planet X. He begins to think—in terms of Planet X—about how to pick k planets out of the n. "There are two possibilities: Either we visit Planet X, or we do not visit Planet X. If we do visit Planet X, I will have to choose $k - 1$ other planets to visit from the $n - 1$ remaining planets. On the other hand, if we do not visit Planet X, I will have to choose k planets to visit from the remaining $n - 1$ planets."

Mr. Spock is on his way to a recursive method of counting how many groups of k planets he can possibly choose out of n. Let $c(n, k)$ be the number of groups of k planets chosen from n. Then, in terms of Planet X, Mr. Spock deduces that

$$c(n, k) = \text{(the number of groups of } k \text{ planets that include Planet } X)$$

$$+$$

$$\text{(the number of groups of } k \text{ planets that do not include Planet } X)$$

But Mr. Spock has already reasoned that the number of groups that include Planet X is $c(n - 1, k - 1)$, and the number of groups that do not include Planet X is $c(n - 1, k)$. Mr. Spock has figured out a way to solve his counting problem in terms of two smaller counting problems of the same type:

$$c(n, k) = c(n - 1, k - 1) + c(n - 1, k)$$

The number of ways to choose k out of n things is the sum of the number of ways to choose $k - 1$ out of $n - 1$ things and the number of ways to choose k out of $n - 1$ things

Mr. Spock now has to worry about the base case(s). He also needs to demonstrate that each of the two smaller problems eventually reaches a base case. First, what selection problem does he immediately know the answer to? If the *Enterprise* had time to visit all the planets (that is, if $k = n$), no decision would be necessary; there is only one group of all the planets. Thus, the first base case is

$$c(k, k) = 1$$

If $k < n$, it is easy to see that the second term in the recursive definition, $c(n - 1, k)$, is "closer" to the base case $c(k, k)$ than is $c(n, k)$. However, the first term, $c(n - 1, k - 1)$, is not closer to $c(k, k)$ than is $c(n, k)$—they are the same "distance" apart. *When you solve a problem by solving two (or more) smaller problems, each of the smaller problems must be closer to a base case than the original problem.*

Mr. Spock realizes that the first term does, in fact, approach another trivial selection problem. This problem is the counterpart of his first base case, $c(k, k)$. Just as there is only one group of all the planets ($k = n$), there is also only one group of zero planets ($k = 0$). When there is no time to visit any of the planets, the *Enterprise* must head home without any exploration. Thus, the second base case is

$$c(n, 0) = 1$$

This base case does indeed have the property that $c(n - 1, k - 1)$ is closer to it than is $c(n, k)$. (Alternatively, you could define the second base case to be $c(n, 1) = n$.)

Mr. Spock adds one final part to his solution:

$$c(n, k) = 0 \quad \text{if } k > n$$

Although k could not be greater than n in the context of this problem, the addition of this case makes the recursive solution more generally applicable.

To summarize, the following recursive solution solves the problem of choosing k out of n things:

$$c(n, k) = \begin{cases} 1 & \text{if } k = 0 \\ 1 & \text{if } k = n \\ 0 & \text{if } k > n \\ c(n - 1, k - 1) + c(n - 1, k) & \text{if } 0 < k < n \end{cases}$$

You can easily derive the following method from this recursive definition:

```
public static int c(int n, int k) {
// ----------------------------------------------------
// Computes the number of groups of k out of n things.
// Precondition: n and k are nonnegative integers.
// Postcondition: Returns c(n, k).
// ----------------------------------------------------
   if ( (k == 0) || (k == n) ) {
      return 1;
   }
```

```
    else if (k > n) {
        return 0;
    }
    else {
        return c(n-1, k-1) + c(n-1, k);
    }  // end if
}  // end c
```

Like the *rabbit* method, this method is inefficient and not practical to use. Figure 3-12 shows the number of recursive calls that the computation of *c(4, 2)* requires.

3.3 Searching an Array

Searching is an important task that occurs frequently. This chapter began with an intuitive approach to a binary search algorithm. This section develops the binary search and examines other searching problems that have recursive solutions. The goal is to develop further your notion of recursion.

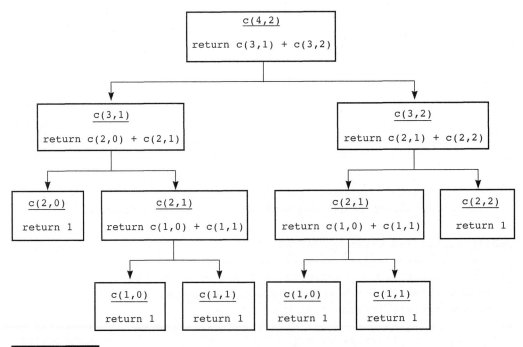

FIGURE 3-12

The recursive calls that *c(4, 2)* generates

Finding the Largest Item in an Array

Suppose that you have an array *anArray* of integers and you want to find the largest one. You could construct an iterative solution without too much difficulty, but instead consider a recursive formulation:

```
if (anArray has only one item) {
   maxArray(anArray) is the item in anArray
}
else if (anArray has more than one item) {
   maxArray(anArray) is the maximum of
      maxArray(left half of anArray) and
      maxArray(right half of anArray)
}  // end if
```

Notice that this strategy fits the divide-and-conquer model that the binary search algorithm used at the beginning of this chapter. That is, the algorithm proceeds by dividing the problem and conquering the subproblems, as Figure 3-13 illustrates. However, there is a difference between this algorithm and the binary search algorithm. While the binary search algorithm conquers only one of its subproblems at each step, *maxArray* conquers both. In addition, after *maxArray* conquers the subproblems, it must reconcile the two solutions—that is, it must find the maximum of the two maximums. Figure 3-14 illustrates the computations that are necessary to find the largest integer in the array that contains 1, 6, 8, and 3 (denoted here by <1, 6, 8, 3>).

You should develop a recursive solution based on this strategy. In so doing, you may stumble on several subtle programming issues. The binary search problem that follows raises virtually all of these issues, but this is a good opportunity for you to get some practice implementing a recursive solution.

maxArray conquers both of its subproblems at each step

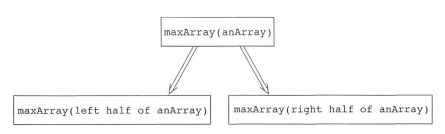

FIGURE 3-13

Recursive solution to the largest-item problem

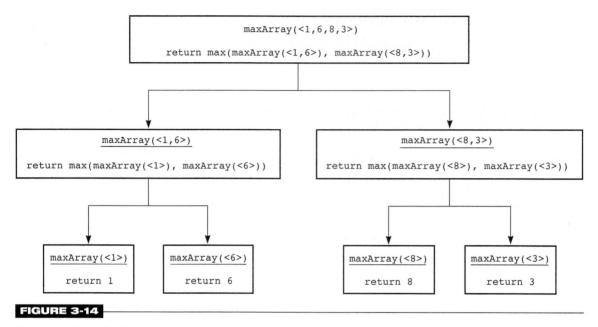

FIGURE 3-14

The recursive calls that *maxArray(<1,6,8,3>)* generates

Binary Search

The beginning of this chapter presented—at a high level—a recursive binary
search algorithm for finding a word in a dictionary. We now develop this algorithm fully and illustrate some important programming issues.

Recall the earlier solution to the dictionary problem:

```
search(in theDictionary:Dictionary, in aWord: string)
  if (theDictionary is one page in size) {
    Scan the page for aWord
  }
  else {
    Open theDictionary to a point near the middle
    Determine which half of theDictionary contains
        aWord
    if (aWord is in first half of theDictionary) {
      search(first half of theDictionary, aWord)
    }
    else {
      search(second half of theDictionary, aWord)
    }  // end if
  }  // end if
```

Now alter the problem slightly by searching an array *anArray* of integers for a given value. The array, like the dictionary, must be sorted, or else a binary search is not applicable. Hence, assume that

```
anArray[0] ≤ anArray[1] ≤ anArray[2] ≤ · · · ≤ anArray[size-1]
```

An array must be sorted before you can apply a binary search to it

where *size* is the size of the array. A high-level binary search for the array problem is

```
binarySearch(in anArray:ArrayType, in value:ItemType)

  if (anArray is of size 1) {
    Determine if anArray's item is equal to value
  }
  else {
    Find the midpoint of anArray
    Determine which half of anArray contains value
    if (value is in the first half of anArray) {
      binarySearch(first half of anArray, value)
    }
    else {
      binarySearch(second half of anArray, value)
    }  // end if
  }  // end if
```

Although the solution is conceptually sound, you must consider several details before you can implement the algorithm:

1. **How will you pass "half of *anArray*" to the recursive calls to *binarySearch*?** You can pass the entire array at each call but have *binarySearch* search only *anArray[first..last]*,[1] that is, the portion *anArray[first]* through *anArray[last]*. Thus, you would also pass the integers *first* and *last* to *binarySearch*:

   ```
   binarySearch(anArray, first, last, value)
   ```

   With this convention, the new midpoint is given by

   ```
   mid = (first + last)/2
   ```

   Then *binarySearch(first half of anArray, value)* becomes

   ```
   binarySearch(anArray, first, mid-1, value)
   ```

The array halves are *anArray [first..mid-1]* and *anArray [mid+1..last]*; neither half contains *anArray[mid]*

---

1. You will see this notation in the rest of the book to represent a portion of an array.

and *binarySearch(second half of anArray, value)* becomes

binarySearch(anArray, mid+1, last, value)

2. **How do you determine which half of the array contains `value`?** One possible implementation of

if (value is in the first half of anArray)

is

if (value < anArray[mid])

However, there is no test for equality between *value* and *anArray[mid]*. This omission can cause the algorithm to miss *value*. After the previous halving algorithm splits *anArray* into halves, *anArray[mid]* is not in either half of the array. (In this case, two halves do not make a whole!) Therefore, you must determine whether *anArray[mid]* is the value you seek *now* because later it will not be in the remaining half of the array. The interaction between the halving criterion and the termination condition (the base case) is subtle and is often a source of error. We need to rethink the base case.

Determine whether `anArray[mid]` is the value you seek

3. **What should the base case(s) be?** As it is written, *binarySearch* terminates only when an array of size 1 occurs; this is the only base case. By changing the halving process so that *anArray[mid] remains in one of the halves,* it is possible to implement the binary search correctly so that it has only this single base case. However, it can be clearer to have two distinct base cases as follows:

Two base cases

    a. *first > last.* You will reach this base case when *value* is not in the original array.

    b. *value == anArray[mid].* You will reach this base case when *value* is in the original array.

These base cases are a bit different from any you have encountered previously. In a sense, the algorithm determines the answer to the problem from the base case it reaches. Many search problems have this flavor.

4. **How will `binarySearch` indicate the result of the search?** If *binarySearch* successfully locates *value* in the array, it could return the index of the array item that is equal to *value*. Since this index would never be negative, *binarySearch* could return a negative value if it does not find *value* in the array.

The Java method *binarySearch* that follows implements these ideas. The two recursive calls to *binarySearch* are labeled as X and Y for use in a later box trace of this method.

```java
public static int binarySearch(int anArray[], int first,
                               int last, int value) {
// Searches the array items anArray[first] through
// anArray[last] for value by using a binary search.
// Precondition: 0 <= first, last <= SIZE-1, where
// SIZE is the maximum size of the array, and
// anArray[first] <= anArray[first+1] <= ... <=
// anArray[last].
// Postcondition: If value is in the array, the method
// returns the index of the array item that equals value;
// otherwise the method returns -1.
  int index;
  if (first > last) {
    index = -1;       // value not in original array
  }
  else {
    // Invariant: If value is in anArray,
    //            anArray[first] <= value <= anArray[last]
    int mid = (first + last)/2;
    if (value == anArray[mid]) {
      index = mid;  // value found at anArray[mid]
    }
    else if (value < anArray[mid]) {
     // point X
      index = binarySearch(anArray, first, mid-1, value);
    }
    else {
     // point Y
      index = binarySearch(anArray, mid+1, last, value);
    }  // end if
  }  // end if

  return index;
}  // end binarySearch
```

Notice that *binarySearch* has the following invariant: If *value* occurs in the array, then *anArray[first]* ≤ *value* ≤ *anArray[last]*.

Figure 3-15 shows box traces of *binarySearch* when it searches the array containing 1, 5, 9, 12, 15, 21, 29, and 31. Notice how the labels *X* and *Y* of the two recursive calls to *binarySearch* appear in the diagram. Exercise 16 at the end of this chapter asks you to perform other box traces with this method.

There is another implementation issue—one that deals specifically with Java—to consider. Recall that an array is an object, and when the method *binarySearch* is called, only the reference to the array is copied to the method, not the entire array contents. This aspect of Java is particularly useful in a recursive method such as *binarySearch*. If the array *anArray* is large,

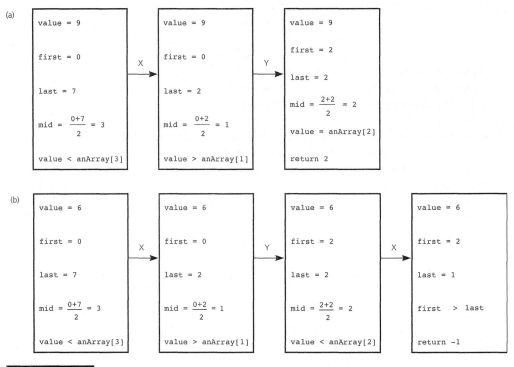

FIGURE 3-15

Box traces of *binarySearch* with *anArray* = *<1,5,9,12,15,21,29,31>*:
(a) a successful search for 9; (b) an unsuccessful search for 6

many recursive calls to *binarySearch* may be necessary. If each call copied *anArray*, much memory and time would be wasted.

A box trace of a recursive method that has an array argument requires a new consideration. Because only the reference to *anArray* is passed and it is not a local variable, the contents of the array are not a part of the method's local environment and should not appear within each box. Therefore, as Figure 3-16 shows, you represent *anArray* outside the boxes, and all references to *anArray* affect this single representation.

Finding the kth Smallest Item in an Array

Our discussion of searching concludes with a more difficult problem. Although you could skip this example now, Chapter 10 uses aspects of it in a sorting algorithm.

The previous two examples presented recursive methods for finding the largest item in an arbitrary array and for finding an arbitrary item in a sorted array. This example describes a recursive solution for finding the kth smallest item in an arbitrary array *anArray*. Would you ever be interested in such an

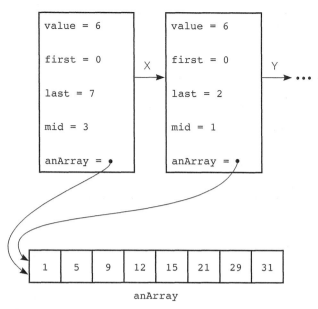

FIGURE 3-16

Box trace with a reference to an array

item? Statisticians often want the median value in a collection of data. The median value in an ordered collection of data occurs in the middle of the collection. In an unordered collection of data, there are about the same number of values smaller than the median value as there are larger values. Thus, if you have 49 items, the 25th smallest item is the median value.

Obviously, you could solve this problem by sorting the array. Then the kth smallest item would be *anArray[k-1]*. Although this approach is a legitimate solution, it does more than the problem requires; a more efficient solution is possible. The solution outlined here finds the kth smallest item without completely sorting the array.

By now, you know that you solve a problem recursively by writing its solution in terms of one or more smaller problems of the same type in such a way that this notion of *smaller* ensures that you will always reach a base case. For all of the earlier recursive solutions, the reduction in problem size between recursive calls is *predictable*. For example, the factorial method always decreases the problem size by 1; the binary search always halves the problem size. In addition, the base cases for all the previous problems except the binary search have a static, predefined size. Thus, by knowing only the size of the original problem, you can determine the number of recursive calls that are necessary before you reach the base case.

The solution that you are about to see for finding the kth smallest item departs from these traditions. Although you solve the problem in terms of a smaller problem, just how much smaller this problem is depends on the items in the array and cannot be predicted in advance. Also, the size of the base

For all previous examples, you know the amount of reduction made in the problem size by each recursive call

You cannot predict in advance the size of either the smaller problems or the base case in the recursive solution to the kth smallest item problem

case depends on the items in the array, as it did for the binary search. (Recall that you reach a base case for a binary search when the middle item is the one sought.)

This "unpredictable" type of solution is caused by the nature of the problem: The relationship between the rankings of the items in any predetermined parts of the array and the ranking of the items in the entire array is not strong enough to determine the kth smallest item. For example, suppose that `anArray` contains the items shown in Figure 3-17. Notice that 6, which is in `anArray[3]`, is the third smallest item in the first half of `anArray` and that 8, which is in `anArray[4]`, is the third smallest item in the second half of `anArray`. Can you conclude from these observations anything about the location of the third smallest item in all of `anArray`? The answer is no; these facts about parts of the array do not allow you to draw any useful conclusions about the entire array. You should experiment with other fixed splitting schemes as well.

The recursive solution proceeds by

1. Selecting a **pivot item** in the array

2. Cleverly arranging, or **partitioning,** the items in the array about this pivot item

3. Recursively applying the strategy to *one* of the partitions

Consider the details of the recursive solution: You want to find the kth smallest item in the array segment `anArray[first..last]`. Let the pivot p be any item of the array segment. (For now, ignore how to choose p.) You can partition the items of `anArray[first..last]` into three regions: S_1, which contains the items less than p; the pivot p itself; and S_2, which contains the items greater than or equal to p. This partition implies that all the items in S_1 are smaller than all the items in S_2. Figure 3-18 illustrates this partition.

> Partition *anArray* into three parts: items < *p*, *p*, and items ≥ *p*

All items in `anArray[first..pivotIndex-1]`, in terms of array subscripts, are less than p, and all items in `anArray[pivotIndex+1..last]` are greater than or equal to p. Notice that the sizes of the regions S_1 and S_2 depend on both p and the other items of `anArray[first..last]`.

This partition induces three "smaller problems," such that the solution to one of the problems will solve the original problem:

1. If S_1 contains k or more items, S_1 contains the k smallest items of the array segment `anArray[first..last]`. In this case, the kth smallest item must

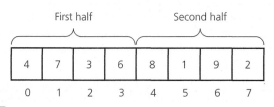

FIGURE 3-17

A sample array

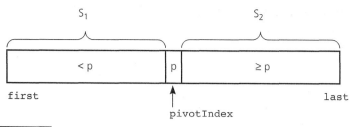

FIGURE 3-18

A partition about a pivot

be in S_1. Since S_1 is the array segment `anArray [first..pivotIndex−1]`, this case occurs if $k < $ `pivotIndex − first` + 1.

2. If S_1 contains $k − 1$ items, the kth smallest item must be the pivot p. This is the base case; it occurs if $k = $ `pivotIndex − first` + 1.

3. If S_1 contains fewer than $k − 1$ items, the kth smallest item in `anArray[first..last]` must be in S_2. Because S_1 contains `pivotIndex − first` items, the kth smallest item in `anArray [first..last]` is the $(k − ($`pivotIndex − first` $+ 1))^{th}$ smallest item in S_2. This case occurs if $k > $ `pivotIndex − first` + 1.

A recursive definition can summarize this discussion. Let

```
kSmall(k, anArray, first, last) =
```
k^{th} smallest item in `anArray[first..last]`

After you select the pivot item p and partition `anArray[first..last]` into S_1 and S_2, you have that

```
kSmall(k, anArray, first, last)
```

$$
= \begin{cases}
\texttt{kSmall(k, anArray, first, pivotIndex-1)} \\
\qquad\qquad \text{if } k < \texttt{pivotIndex} - \texttt{first} + 1 \\
p \qquad\qquad\ \text{if } k = \texttt{pivotIndex} - \texttt{first} + 1 \\
\texttt{kSmall(k-(pivotIndex-first+1), anArray,} \\
\qquad \texttt{pivotIndex+1, last)} \quad \text{if } k > \texttt{pivotIndex} - \texttt{first} + 1
\end{cases}
$$

The kth smallest item in `anArray [first..last]`

There is always a pivot, and since it is not part of either S_1 or S_2, the size of the array segment to be searched decreases by at least 1 at each step. Thus, you will eventually reach the base case: The desired item is a pivot. A high-level pseudocode solution is as follows:

```
kSmall(in k:integer, in anArray:ArrayType, in first:integer,
       in last:integer)
// Returns the kth smallest value in anArray[first..last].

   Choose a pivot item p from anArray[first..last]
   Partition the items of anArray[first..last] about p
```

```
if (k < pivotIndex - first + 1) {
   return kSmall(k, anArray, first, pivotIndex-1)
}
else if (k == pivotIndex - first + 1) {
   return p
}
else {
   return kSmall(k-(pivotIndex-first+1), anArray,
                 pivotIndex+1, last)
}  // end if
```

This pseudocode is not far from a Java method. The only questions that remain are how to choose the pivot item p and how to partition the array about the chosen p. The choice of p is arbitrary. Any p in the array will work, although the sequence of choices will affect how soon you reach the base case. Chapter 10 gives an algorithm for partitioning the items about p. There you will see how to turn the method *kSmall* into a sorting algorithm.

3.4 Organizing Data

Given some data organized in one way, you might need to organize the data in another way. Thus, you will actually change some aspect of the data and not, for example, simply search it. The problem in this section is called the Towers of Hanoi. Although this classic problem probably has no direct real-world application, we consider it because its solution so well illustrates the use of recursion.

The Towers of Hanoi

Many, many years ago, in a distant part of the Orient—in the Vietnamese city of Hanoi—the Emperor's wiseperson passed on to join his ancestors. The Emperor needed a replacement wiseperson. Being a rather wise person himself, the Emperor devised a puzzle, declaring that its solver could have the job of wiseperson.

The Emperor's puzzle consisted of n disks (he didn't say exactly how many) and three poles: A (the source), B (the destination), and C (the spare). The disks were of different sizes and had holes in the middle so that they could fit on the poles. Because of their great weight, the disks could be placed only on top of disks larger than themselves. Initially, all the disks were on pole A, as shown in Figure 3-19a. The puzzle was to move the disks, one by one, from pole A to pole B. A person could also use pole C in the course of the transfer, but again a disk could be placed only on top of a disk larger than itself.

As the position of wiseperson was generally known to be a soft job, there were many applicants. Scholars and peasants alike brought the Emperor their solutions. Many solutions were thousands of steps long, and many contained *goto*'s. "I can't understand these solutions," bellowed the Emperor. "There must be an easy way to solve this puzzle."

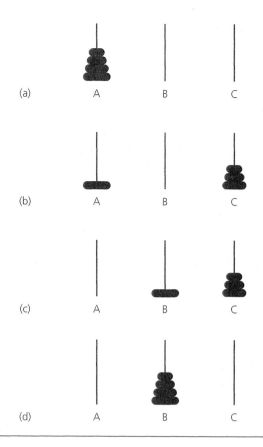

(a)   A   B   C

(b)   A   B   C

(c)   A   B   C

(d)   A   B   C

FIGURE 3-19
_____

(a) The initial state; (b) move $n - 1$ disks from A to C; (c) move one disk from A to B; (d) move $n - 1$ disks from C to B

And indeed there was. A great Buddhist monk came out of the mountains to see the Emperor. "My son," he said, "the puzzle is so easy, it almost solves itself." The Emperor's security chief wanted to throw this strange person out, but the Emperor let him continue.

"If you have only one disk (that is, $n = 1$), move it from pole A to pole B." So far, so good, but even the village idiot got that part right. "If you have more than one disk (that is, $n > 1$), simply

1. "Ignore the bottom disk and solve the problem for $n - 1$ disks, with the small modification that pole C is the destination and pole B is the spare." (See Figure 3-19b.)

2. "After you have done this, $n - 1$ disks will be on pole C, and the largest disk will remain on pole A. So solve the problem for $n = 1$ (recall that even the village idiot could do this) by moving the large disk from A to B." (See Figure 3-19c.)

3. "Now all you have to do is move the $n - 1$ disks from pole C to pole B; that is, solve the problem with pole C as the source, pole B as the destination, and pole A as the spare." (See Figure 3-19d.)

There was silence for a few moments, and finally the Emperor said impatiently, "Well, are you going to tell us your solution or not?" The monk simply gave an all-knowing smile and vanished.

The Emperor obviously was not a recursive thinker, but you should realize that the monk's solution is perfectly correct. The key to the solution is the observation that you can solve the Towers problem of n disks by solving three smaller—in the sense of number of disks—Towers problems. Let `towers(count, source, destination, spare)` denote the problem of moving `count` disks from pole `source` to pole `destination`, using pole `spare` as a spare. Notice that this definition makes sense even if there are more than `count` disks on pole `source`; in this case, you concern yourself with only the top `count` disks and ignore the others. Similarly, the poles `destination` and `spare` might have disks on them before you begin; you ignore these, too, except that you may place only smaller disks on top of them.

The problem statement

You can restate the Emperor's problem as follows: Beginning with n disks on pole A and 0 disks on poles B and C, solve `towers(n, A, B, C)`. You can state the monk's solution as follows:

The solution

Step 1.   Starting in the initial state—with all the disks on pole A—solve the problem

`towers(n-1, A, C, B)`

That is, ignore the bottom (largest) disk and move the top $n - 1$ disks from pole A to pole C, using pole B as a spare. When you are finished, the largest disk will remain on pole A, and all the other disks will be on pole C.

Step 2.   Now, with the largest disk on pole A and all others on pole C, solve the problem

`towers(1, A, B, C)`

That is, move the largest disk from pole A to pole B. Because this disk is larger than the disks already on the spare pole C, you really could not use the spare. However, fortunately—and obviously—you do not need to use the spare in this base case. When you are done, the largest disk will be on pole B and all other disks will remain on pole C.

Step 3.   Finally, with the largest disk on pole B and all the other disks on pole C, solve the problem

`towers(n-1, C, B, A)`

That is, move the $n - 1$ disks from pole C to pole B, using A as a spare. Notice that the destination pole B already has the largest disk, which you ignore. When you are done, you will have solved the original problem: All the disks will be on pole B.

The problem *towers(count, source, destination, spare)* has the following pseudocode solution:

```
solveTowers(in count:integer, in source:Pole,
            in destination:Pole, in spare:Pole)

  if (count is 1) {
     Move a disk directly from source to destination
  }
   else {
     solveTowers(count-1, source, spare, destination)
     solveTowers(1, source, destination, spare)
     solveTowers(count-1, spare, destination, source)
   } // end if
```

This recursive solution follows the same basic pattern as the recursive solutions you saw earlier in this chapter:

1. You solve a Towers problem by solving other Towers problems.

2. These other Towers problems are smaller than the original problem; they have fewer disks to move. In particular, the number of disks decreases by 1 at each recursive call.

3. When a problem has only one disk—the base case—the solution is easy to solve directly.

4. The way that the problems become smaller ensures that you will reach a base case.

The solution to the Towers problem satisfies the four criteria of a recursive solution

Solving the Towers problem requires you to solve many smaller Towers problems recursively. Figure 3-20 illustrates the resulting recursive calls and their order when you solve the problem for three disks.

Now consider a Java implementation of this algorithm. Notice that since most computers do not have arms (at the time of this writing), the method moves a disk by giving directions to a human. Thus, the formal parameters that represent the poles are of type *char*, and the corresponding actual arguments could be *'A'*, *'B'*, and *'C'*. The call *solveTowers(3, 'A', 'B', 'C')* produces this output:

```
Move top disk from pole A to pole B
Move top disk from pole A to pole C
Move top disk from pole B to pole C
Move top disk from pole A to pole B
Move top disk from pole C to pole A
Move top disk from pole C to pole B
Move top disk from pole A to pole B
```

The solution for three disks

The Java method follows:

```java
public static void solveTowers(int count, char source,
                               char destination, char spare) {
  if (count == 1) {
    System.out.println("Move top disk from pole " + source +
                       " to pole " + destination);
  }
  else {
    solveTowers(count-1, source, spare, destination); // X
    solveTowers(1, source, destination, spare);       // Y
    solveTowers(count-1, spare, destination, source); // Z
  }  // end if
}  // end solveTowers
```

The three recursive calls in the method are labeled *X*, *Y*, and *Z*. These labels appear in the box trace of *solveTowers(3, 'A', 'B', 'C')* in Figure 3-21. The recursive calls are also numbered to correspond to the numbers used in Figure 3-20. (Figure 3-21 abbreviates *destination* as *dest* to save space.)

3.5 Recursion and Efficiency

Recursion is a powerful problem-solving technique that often produces very clean solutions to even the most complex problems. Recursive solutions can be easier to understand and to describe than iterative solutions. By using recursion, you can often write simple, short implementations of your solution.

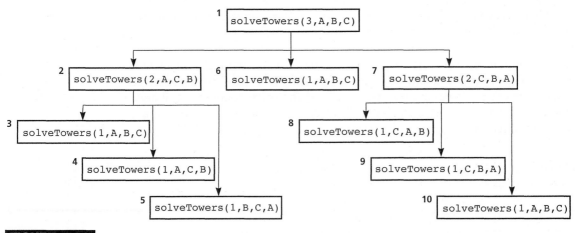

FIGURE 3-20

The order of recursive calls that results from *solveTowers(3, A, B, C)*

The initial call 1 is made, and `solveTowers` begins execution:

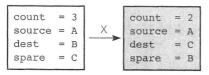

```
count  = 3
source = A
dest   = B
spare  = C
```

At point X, recursive call 2 is made, and the new invocation of the method begins execution:

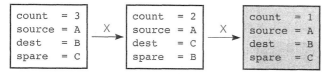

```
count  = 3          count  = 2
source = A      X   source = A
dest   = B     -->  dest   = C
spare  = C          spare  = B
```

At point X, recursive call 3 is made, and the new invocation of the method begins execution:

```
count  = 3          count  = 2          count  = 1
source = A      X   source = A      X   source = A
dest   = B     -->  dest   = C     -->  dest   = B
spare  = C          spare  = B          spare  = C
```

This is the base case, so a disk is moved, the return is made, and the method continues execution.

```
count  = 3          count  = 2          count  = 1
source = A      X   source = A          source = A
dest   = B     -->  dest   = C          dest   = B
spare  = C          spare  = B          spare  = C
```

At point Y, recursive call 4 is made, and the new invocation of the method begins execution:

```
count  = 3          count  = 2          count  = 1
source = A      X   source = A      Y   source = A
dest   = B     -->  dest   = C     -->  dest   = C
spare  = C          spare  = B          spare  = B
```

This is the base case, so a disk is moved, the return is made, and the method continues execution.

```
count  = 3          count  = 2          count  = 1
source = A      X   source = A          source = A
dest   = B     -->  dest   = C          dest   = C
spare  = C          spare  = B          spare  = B
```

At point Z, recursive call 5 is made, and the new invocation of the method begins execution:

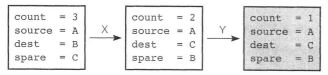

```
count  = 3          count  = 2          count  = 1
source = A      X   source = A      Z   source = B
dest   = B     -->  dest   = C     -->  dest   = C
spare  = C          spare  = B          spare  = A
```

FIGURE 3-21

Box trace of *solveTowers(3, 'A', 'B', 'C')*   (continues)

(continued)

This is the base case, so a disk is moved, the return is made, and the method continues execution.

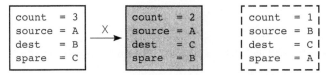

This invocation completes, the return is made, and the method continues execution.

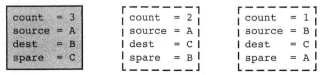

At point Y, recursive call 6 is made, and the new invocation of the method begins execution:

```
count   = 3          count   = 1
source = A      Y    source = A
dest    = B          dest    = B
spare   = C          spare   = C
```

This is the base case, so a disk is moved, the return is made, and the method continues execution.

```
count   = 3          count   = 1
source = A           source = A
dest    = B          dest    = B
spare   = C          spare   = C
```

At point Z, recursive call 7 is made, and the new invocation of the method begins execution:

```
count   = 3          count   = 2
source = A      Z    source = C
dest    = B          dest    = B
spare   = C          spare   = A
```

At point X, recursive call 8 is made, and the new invocation of the method begins execution:

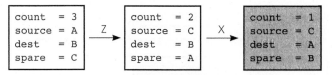

This is the base case, so a disk is moved, the return is made, and the method continues execution.

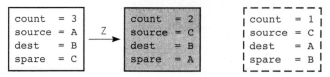

At point Y, recursive call 9 is made, and the new invocation of the method begins execution:

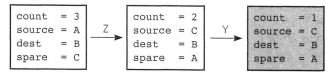

This is the base case, so a disk is moved, the return is made, and the method continues execution.

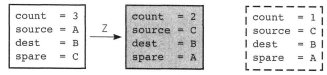

At point Z, recursive call 10 is made, and the new invocation of the method begins execution:

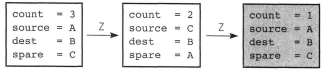

This is the base case, so a disk is moved, the return is made, and the method continues execution.

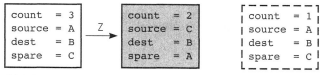

This invocation completes, the return is made, and the method continues execution.

count	= 3		spare	= 2		count	= 1
source	= A		source	= C		source	= A
dest	= B		dest	= B		dest	= B
spare	= C		spare	= A		spare	= C

FIGURE 3-21

The overriding concern of this chapter has been to give you a solid under-standing of recursion so that you will be able to construct recursive solutions on your own. Most of our examples, therefore, have been simple. Unfortu-nately, many of the recursive solutions in this chapter are so inefficient that you should not use them. The recursive methods *binarySearch* and *solveTowers* are the notable exceptions, as they are quite efficient.[2]

Two factors contribute to the inefficiency of some recursive solutions:

- The overhead associated with method calls

- The inherent inefficiency of some recursive algorithms

Factors that contribute to the inefficiency of some recursive solutions

---

2. Chapters 6 and 10 present other practical, efficient applications of recursion.

The first of these factors does not pertain specifically to recursive methods but is true of methods in general. In most implementations of Java and other high-level programming languages, a method call incurs a bookkeeping overhead. As was mentioned earlier, each method call produces an activation record, which is analogous to a box in the box trace. Recursive methods magnify this overhead because a single initial call to the method can generate a large number of recursive calls. For example, the call *fact(n)* generates *n* recursive calls.

How the parameters are passed to a recursive method can also increase the amount of overhead. Look at the implementation of *writeBackward* that was presented earlier in the chapter. In each recursive call, a new string was generated that was one character shorter than the previous string, and sent as a parameter to the next recursive call. An alternative way to implement *writeBackward* is to include a second parameter *size*, which indicates the size of the string stored in *s* to write backward:

```
public static void writeBackward(String s, int size) {
  if (size > 0) {
    // write the last character
    System.out.println(s.charAt(size-1));
    // write the rest of the string backward
    writeBackward(s, size-1);
  } // end if
  // size == 0 is the base case - do nothing
} // end writeBackward
```

Note that, in this implementation, just the reference to the string *s* is sent to the next recursive call—not another string object. Hence, this reduces the overhead associated with each recursive call. This technique was also employed by many of the recursive algorithms in this chapter that involved arrays.

Recursion can clarify complex solutions

Note that the use of recursion, as is true with modularity in general, can greatly clarify complex programs. This clarification frequently more than compensates for the additional overhead. Thus, the use of recursion is often consistent with the multidimensional view of the cost of a computer program, as Chapter 2 describes.

Do not use a recursive solution if it is inefficient and you have a clear, efficient iterative solution

However, you should not use recursion just for the sake of using recursion. For example, you probably should not use the recursive factorial method in practice. You easily can write an iterative factorial method given the iterative definition that was stated earlier in this chapter. The iterative method is almost as clear as the recursive one and is more efficient. There is no reason to incur the overhead of recursion when its use does not gain anything. *Recursion is truly valuable when a problem has no simple iterative solutions.*

The second point about recursion and efficiency is that some recursive algorithms are inherently inefficient. This inefficiency is a very different issue than that of overhead. It has nothing to do with how a compiler happens to implement a recursive method but rather is related to the method of solution that the algorithm employs.

As an example, recall the recursive solution for the multiplying rabbits problem that you saw earlier in this chapter:

$$rabbit(n) = \begin{cases} 1 & \text{if } n \text{ is 1 or 2} \\ rabbit(n-1) + rabbit(n-2) & \text{if } n > 2 \end{cases}$$

The recursive version of **rabbit** is inherently inefficient

The diagram in Figure 3-11 illustrated the computation of *rabbit(7)*. Earlier, you were asked to think about what the diagram would look like for *rabbit(10)*. If you thought about this question, you may have come to the conclusion that such a diagram would fill up most of this chapter. The diagram for *rabbit(100)* would fill up most of this universe!

The fundamental problem with *rabbit* is that it computes the same values over and over again. For example, in the diagram for *rabbit(7)*, you can see that *rabbit(3)* is computed five times. When *n* is moderately large, many of the values are recomputed literally trillions of times. This enormous number of computations makes the solution infeasible, even if each computation required only a trivial amount of work (for example, if you could perform 100 million of these computations per second).

However, do not conclude that the recurrence relation is of no use. One way to solve the rabbit problem is to construct an iterative solution based on this same recurrence relation. The iterative solution goes forward instead of backward and computes each value only once. You can use the following iterative method to compute *rabbit(n)* even for very large values of *n*.

You can use **rabbit**'s recurrence relation to construct an efficient iterative solution

```java
public static int iterativeRabbit(int n) {
// Iterative solution to the rabbit problem.
  // initialize base cases:
  int previous = 1;    // initially rabbit(1)
  int current = 1;     // initially rabbit(2)
  int next = 1;        // result when n is 1 or 2

  // compute next rabbit values when n >= 3
  for (int i = 3; i <= n; i++) {
    // current is rabbit(i-1), previous is rabbit(i-2)
    next = current + previous;  // rabbit(i)

    previous = current;         // get ready for
    current = next;             // next iteration
  }  // end for

  return next;
}  // end iterativeRabbit
```

Convert from recursion to iteration if it is easier to discover a recursive solution but more efficient to use an iterative solution

Thus, an iterative solution can be more efficient than a recursive solution. In certain cases, however, it may be easier to discover a recursive solution than an iterative solution. Therefore, you may need to convert a recursive solution to an iterative solution. This conversion process is easier if your recursive method calls itself once, instead of several times. Be careful when deciding whether your method calls itself more than once. Although the method *rabbit* calls itself twice, the method *binarySearch* calls itself once, even though you see two calls in the Java code. Those two calls appear within an *if* statement; only one of them will be executed.

A tail-recursive method

Converting a recursive solution to an iterative solution is even easier when the solitary recursive call is the last *action* that the method takes. This situation is called **tail recursion.** For example, the method *writeBackward* exhibits tail recursion because its recursive call is the last action that the method takes. Before you conclude that this is obvious, consider the method *fact*. Although its recursive call appears last in the method definition, *fact*'s last action is the multiplication. Thus, *fact* is not tail recursive.

Recall the definition of *writeBackward* presented earlier in this section:

```java
public static void writeBackward(String s, int size) {
  if (size > 0) {
    // write the last character
    System.out.println(s.substring(size-1, size));
    writeBackward(s, size - 1);      // write rest
  }  // end if
}  // end writeBackward
```

Removing tail recursion is often straightforward

Because this method is tail recursive, its last recursive call simply repeats the method's action with altered arguments. You can perform this repetitive action by using an iteration that will be straightforward and often more efficient. For example, the following definition of *writeBackward* is iterative:

```java
public static void writeBackward(String s, int size) {
// Iterative version.
  while (size > 0) {
    System.out.println(s.substring(size-1, size));
    --size;
  }  // end while
}  // end writeBackward
```

Because tail-recursive methods are often less efficient than their iterative counterparts and because the conversion of a tail-recursive method to an equivalent iterative method is rather mechanical, some compilers automatically replace tail recursion with iteration. Eliminating other forms of recursion is usually more complex, as you will see in Chapter 7, and is a task that *you* would need to undertake, if necessary.

Some recursive algorithms, such as *rabbit*, are inherently inefficient, while other recursive algorithms, such as the binary search,[3] are extremely efficient. You will learn how to determine the relative efficiency of a recursive algorithm in more advanced courses concerned with the analysis of algorithms. Chapter 10 introduces some of these techniques briefly.

Chapter 6 will continue the discussion of recursion by examining several difficult problems that have straightforward recursive solutions. Other chapters in this book use recursion as a matter of course.

Summary

1. Recursion is a technique that solves a problem by solving a smaller problem of the same type.

2. When constructing a recursive solution, keep the following four questions in mind:

   a. How can you define the problem in terms of a smaller problem of the same type?

   b. How does each recursive call diminish the size of the problem?

   c. What instance of the problem can serve as the base case?

   d. As the problem size diminishes, will you reach this base case?

3. When constructing a recursive solution, you should assume that a recursive call's postcondition is true if its precondition is true.

4. You can use the box trace to trace the actions of a recursive method. These boxes resemble activation records, which many compilers use to implement recursion. (Chapter 6 discusses implementing recursion further.) Although the box trace is useful, it cannot replace an intuitive understanding of recursion.

5. Recursion allows you to solve problems—such as the Towers of Hanoi—whose iterative solutions are difficult to conceptualize. Even the most complex problems often have straightforward recursive solutions. Such solutions can be easier to understand, describe, and implement than iterative solutions.

6. Some recursive solutions are much less efficient than a corresponding iterative solution, due to their inherently inefficient algorithms and the overhead of method calls. In such cases, the iterative solution can be preferable. You can use the recursive solution, however, to derive the iterative solution.

7. If you can easily, clearly, and efficiently solve a problem by using iteration, you should do so.

Cautions

1. A recursive algorithm must have a base case, whose solution you know directly without making any recursive calls. Without a base case, a recursive method will

---

3. The binary search algorithm also has an iterative formulation.

generate an infinite sequence of calls. When a recursive method contains more than one recursive call, you will often need more than one base case.

2. A recursive solution must involve one or more smaller problems that are each closer to a base case than is the original problem. You must be sure that these smaller problems eventually reach the base case. Failure to do so could result in an algorithm that does not terminate.

3. When developing a recursive solution, you must be sure that the solutions to the smaller problems really do give you a solution to the original problem. For example, *binarySearch* works because each smaller array is sorted and the value sought is between its first and last items.

4. The box trace, together with well-placed *System.out.println* statements, can be a good aid in debugging recursive methods. Such statements should report the point in the program from which each recursive call occurs as well as the values of input arguments and local variables at both entry to and exit from the methods. Be sure to remove these statements from the final version of the method.

5. A recursive solution that recomputes certain values frequently can be quite inefficient. In such cases, iteration may be preferable to recursion.

Self-Test Exercises

1. The following method computes the sum of the first $n \geq 1$ real numbers in an array. Show how this method satisfies the properties of a recursive method.

```
public static double sum(double anArray[], int n) {
// Precondition: 1 <= n <= max size of anArray.
// Postcondition: Returns the sum of the first n
// items in anArray; anArray is unchanged.
  if (n == 1) {
    return anArray[0];
  }
  else {
    return anArray[n-1] + sum(anArray, n-1);
  }  // end if
}  // end product
```

2. Given an integer $n > 0$, write a recursive method *count* that writes the integers 1, 2, ..., $n - 1$, n. *Hint*: What task can you do and what task can you ask a friend to do for you?

3. Write a recursive method that computes the product of the items in the array *anArray[first..last]*.

4. Of the following recursive methods that you saw in this chapter, identify those that exhibit tail recursion: *fact*, *writeBackward*, *writeBackward2*, *rabbit*, *c* in the Spock problem, *p* in the parade problem, *maxArray*, *binarySearch*, and *kSmall*. Are the methods in Self-Test Exercises 1 through 3 tail recursive?

5. Compute *c(5,1)* in the Spock problem.

6. Trace the execution of the method *solveTowers* to solve the Towers of Hanoi problem for *solveTowers(3, 'C', 'A', 'B')*. So in this case, 'C' is the original source, 'A' is the destination, and 'B' is the spare.

Exercises

1. The following recursive method *getNumberEqual* searches the array *x* of *n* integers for occurrences of the integer *val*. It returns the number of integers in *x* that are equal to *val*. For example, if *x* contains the 9 integers 1, 2, 4, 4, 5, 6, 7, 8, and 9, then *getNumberEqual(x, 9, 4)* returns the value 2 because 4 occurs twice in *x*.

```
public static int getNumberEqual(int x[], int n, int val) {
  if (n <= 0) {
    return 0;
  }
  else {
    if (x[n-1] == val) {
      return getNumberEqual(x, n-1, val) + 1;
    }
    else {
      return getNumberEqual(x, n-1, val);
    } // end if
  } // end if
} // end getNumberEqual
```

   Demonstrate that this method is recursive by listing the criteria of a recursive solution and stating how the method meets each criterion.

2. Perform a box trace of the following calls to recursive methods that appear in this chapter. Clearly indicate each subsequent recursive call.

   a. *rabbit(4)*

   b. *writeBackward("loop")* (Use the version that strips the last character.)

   c. *maxArray* Find the maximum element in the array {4, 10, 12, 1, 8, 3, 6, 9}

   d. *kSmall* Search for the 3rd smallest element in the array {4, 10, 12, 1, 8, 3, 6, 9}

3. Write a recursive algorithm that converts a string of characters representing numbers to its numerical equivalent. For example, the string "1234" should convert to the number 1234.

4. A palindrome is a word that has the same spelling forwards and backwards, like "MADAM". Write a recursive Java method to check if a string is a palindrome.

5. Add output code to the Spock method *c(n, k)* that shows the actual sequence of calls that are made and the value that they will return when the method is executed. For example, *c(3, 2)* outputs the following:

```
c(3, 2) = c(2, 1) + c(2, 2)
c(2, 1) = c(1, 0) + c(1, 1)
c(1, 0) = 1
c(1, 1) = 1
c(2, 2) = 1
```

   Use your modified version to run *c(4,2)* to show the actual order that the methods are called in Figure 3-12.

6. Given the following recursive method, answer each of the following questions.

```
public static void countDownByTwo(int n) {
  if (n != 1) {
    System.out.println(n + " ");
    countDownByTwo(n-2);
  } // end if
}   // end countDownByTwo
```

a. What happens when you execute the method with $n = 7$?

b. What happens when you execute the method with $n = 6$?

c. Answer the four questions for constructive recursive solutions to prove or disprove the correctness of this recursive solution.

d. If the answer to one or more of the questions in part c. indicates that this solution is incorrect, how would you change the method in such a way as to fix the problem?

7. Write a program which will read any string from the keyboard and then print it on the monitor in reverse order.

8. Write a program that reads a string from the keyboard, and includes a method that removes the character 'm' from that string recursively.

9. Write a recursive method that converts an integer to a hexadecimal number.

10. a. Write a recursive Java method *writeLine* that writes a character repeatedly to form a line of *n* characters. For example, *writeLine('*', 5)* produces the line *****.

    b. Now write a recursive method *writeBlock* that uses *writeLine* to write *m* lines of *n* characters each. For example, *writeBlock('*', 5, 3)* produces the output

    ```
    *****
    *****
    *****
    ```

11. What output does the following program produce?

```
import java.util.Arrays;
public class Exercise11 {

  public static int guess(int[] c, int x) {
    if (c.length==1) {
      System.out.printf("z(%d) = %d\n", c.length-1, c[0]);
      return c[0];
    }
    else {
      System.out.printf("z(%d) = %d * z(%d) + %d\n",
                        c.length-1, x, c.length-2, c[0]);
      return
        x*guess(Arrays.copyOfRange(c, 1, c.length), x) + c[0];
    } // end if
  }  // end guess
```

```
   public static void main(String[] args) {
     int[] x = {2, 4, 1};
     System.out.println(guess(x, 5));
   } // end main
 } // end Exercise11
```

12. What output does the following program produce? Try running it with a couple of different values for *n*. Can you guess what this computes?

```
public class Exercise12 {

  private static int search(int a, int b, int n) {
    int returnValue;

    int mid = (a + b)/2;
    System.out.printf("Enter: a = %2d, b = %2d, mid = %2d\n",
                      a, b, mid);
    if ((mid * mid <= n) && (n < (mid+1) * (mid+1))) {
      returnValue = mid;
    }
    else if (mid * mid > n) {
      returnValue = search(a, mid-1, n);
    }
    else {
      returnValue = search(mid+1, b, n);
    }  // end if
    System.out.printf("Leave: a = %2d, b = %2d, mid = %2d\n",
                      a, b, mid);
    return returnValue;
  }  // end search

  public static void main(String[] args) {
    int n = 64;
    System.out.printf("For n = %2d, the result is %d\n",
                      n, search(1, n, n));
  }  // end main
}  //end Exercise12
```

13. Consider the following method that converts a positive decimal number to base 8 and displays the result.

```
public static void displayOctal(int n) {
  if (n > 0) {
    if (n/8 > 0) {
      displayOctal(n/8);
    }  // end if
    System.out.println(n%8);
  }  // end if
}  // end displayOctal
```

a. Trace the method with *n* = 88.

b. Describe how this method answers the four questions for constructing a recursive solution.

14. Consider the following program:

```
public class Exercise14 {

    public static int f(int n) {
    // Precondition: n >= 0.
        System.out.printf("Enter f: n = %d\n", n);
        switch (n) {
          case 1: case 2: case 3:
            return n + 1;
          default:
            return f(n-1) * f(n-3);
        }  // end switch
    }  // end f

    public static void main(String[] args) {
        System.out.println("f(8) is equal to " + f(8));
    } // end main
} // end Exercise14
```

Show the exact output of the program. What argument values, if any, could you pass to the method *f* to cause the program to run forever?

15. Consider the following method

```
int  CallMe ( int a , int b )
{
    If ( a< b)
    return 6;
    else
    return ( CallMe (a+5, b+6-a));
}
```

What would be the value returned if the call is

a. `CallMe (6,7)`?

b. `CallMe (6-2,6)`?

c. `CallMe (6-1, -5)`?

16. Perform a box trace of the recursive method *binarySearch*, which appears in the section "Binary Search," with the array 2, 4, 5, 8, 9, 12, 15, 16, 20 for each of the following search values:
    a. 5   b. 21   c. 32

17. Imagine that you have 101 dalmatians; no two dalmatians have the same number of spots. Suppose that you create an array of 101 integers: The first integer is the number of spots on the first dalmatian, the second integer is the number of spots on the second dalmatian, and so on.
    Your friend wants to know whether you have a dalmatian with 99 spots. Thus, you need to determine whether the array contains the integer 99.

    a. If you plan to use a binary search to look for the 99, what, if anything, would you do to the array before searching it?

    b. What is the index of the integer in the array that a binary search would examine first?

    c. If all your dalmatians have more than 99 spots, exactly how many comparisons will a binary search require to determine that 99 is not in the array?

18. This problem considers several ways to compute x^n for some $n \geq 0$.

    a. Write an iterative method *power1* to compute x^n for $n \geq 0$.

    b. Write a recursive method *power2* to compute x^n by using the following recursive formulation:

$$x^0 = 1$$
$$x^n = x * x^{n-1} \text{ if } n > 0$$

    c. Write a recursive method *power3* to compute x^n by using the following recursive formulation:

$$x^0 = 1$$
$$x^n = (x^{n/2})^2 \text{ if } n > 0 \text{ and } n \text{ is even}$$
$$x^n = x * (x^{n/2})^2 \text{ if } n > 0 \text{ and } n \text{ is odd}$$

    d. How many multiplications will each of the methods *power1*, *power2*, and *power3* perform when computing 3^{32}? 3^{19}?

    e. How many recursive calls will *power2* and *power3* make when computing 3^{32}? 3^{19}?

19. Modify the recursive *rabbit* method so that it is visually easy to follow the flow of execution. Instead of just adding "Enter" and "Leave" messages, indent the trace messages according to how "deep" the current recursive call is. For example, the call *rabbit (4)* should produce the output

```
Enter rabbit:    n = 4
   Enter rabbit:    n = 3
      Enter rabbit:    n = 2
      Leave rabbit:    n = 2    value = 1
      Enter rabbit:    n = 1
      Leave rabbit:    n = 1    value = 1
   Leave rabbit:    n = 3    value = 2
   Enter rabbit:    n = 2
   Leave rabbit:    n = 2    value = 1
Leave rabbit:    n = 4    value = 3
```

Note how this output corresponds to figures such as Figure 3-11.

20. Consider the following recurrence relation:

$f(1) = 1; f(2) = 2; f(3) = 3; f(4) = 2; f(5) = 4;$
$f(n) = 2 * f(n-1) + f(n-5)$ for all $n > 5$.

    a. Compute $f(n)$ for the following values of n: 6, 7, 10, 12.

b. If you were careful, rather than computing $f(15)$ from scratch (the way a recursive Java method would compute it), you would have computed $f(6)$, then $f(7)$, then $f(8)$, and so on up to $f(15)$, recording the values as you computed them. This ordering would have saved you the effort of ever computing the same value more than once. (Recall the nonrecursive version of the `rabbit` method discussed at the end of this chapter.)

Note that during the computation, you never need to remember all the previously computed values—only the last five. By taking advantage of these observations, write a Java method that computes $f(n)$ for arbitrary values of n.

21. Write a recursive function that calculates the number of occurrences of a specific character within a given string.

22. Write a recursive program that will read ten integers from the command line and then store the corresponding octal values into a file octal.txt.

* 23. Consider the problem of finding the **greatest common divisor (gcd)** of two positive integers a and b. The algorithm presented here is a variation of Euclid's algorithm, which is based on the following theorem:[4]

THEOREM. If a and b are positive integers with $a > b$ such that b is not a divisor of a, then $gcd(a, b) = gcd(b, a \bmod b)$.

This relationship between $gcd(a, b)$ and $gcd(b, a \bmod b)$ is the heart of the recursive solution. It specifies how you can solve the problem of computing $gcd(a, b)$ in terms of another problem of the same type. Also, if b does divide a, then $b = gcd(a, b)$, so an appropriate choice for the base case is $(a \bmod b) = 0$.

This theorem leads to the following recursive definition:

$$gcd(a, b) = \begin{cases} b & \text{if } (a \bmod b) = 0 \\ gcd(b, a \bmod b) & \text{otherwise} \end{cases}$$

The following method implements this recursive algorithm:

```
public static int gcd(int a, int b) {
    if (a % b == 0) { // base case
        return b;
    }
    else {
        return gcd(b, a % b);
    }  // end if
}  // end gcd
```

a. Prove the theorem.

b. What happens if $b > a$?

c. How is the problem getting smaller? (That is, do you always approach a base case?) Why is the base case appropriate?

* 24. Let $C(n)$ be the number of different groups of integers that can be chosen from the integers 1 through $n - 1$ so that the integers in each group add up to n (for

---

4. This book uses mod as an abbreviation for the mathematical operation modulo. In Java, the modulo operator is %.

example, $4 = 1 + 1 + 1 + 1 = 1 + 1 + 2 = 2 + 2 \ldots$). Write recursive definitions for $C(n)$ under the following variations:

a. You count permutations. For example, 1, 2, 1 and 1, 1, 2 are two groups that each add up to 4.

b. You ignore permutations.

25. Consider the following recursive definition:

$$Acker(m, n) = \begin{cases} n + 1 & \text{if } m = 0 \\ Acker(m - 1, 1) & \text{if } n = 0 \\ Acker(m - 1, Acker(m, n - 1)) & \text{otherwise} \end{cases}$$

This function, called **Ackermann's function**, is of interest because it grows rapidly with respect to the sizes of m and n. What is $Acker(1, 2)$? Implement the function as a method in Java and do a box trace of $Acker(1, 2)$. (*Caution:* Even for modest values of m and n, Ackermann's function requires *many* recursive calls.)

Programming Problems

1. Write a program that will first accept an integer from the user and then compute the sum of the digits using the recursive method.

2. You have been offered a one month job that pays as follows: On the first day of the month, you are paid 1 cent. On the second day, 2 cents, on the third, 4 cents, and so forth; the amount doubles every day. Write a recursive method that, given the day number, computes the amount of money paid that day. Would you want this job?

3. Implement `maxArray`, discussed in the section "Finding the Largest Item in an Array," as a Java method. What other recursive definitions of `maxArray` can you describe?

4. Implement the `binarySearch` algorithm presented in this chapter for an array of strings.

5. Implement `kSmall`, discussed in the section "Finding the kth Smallest Item in an Array," as a Java method. Use the first item of the array as the pivot.

CHAPTER 4

Data Abstraction:
The Walls

This chapter elaborates on data abstraction, which was introduced in Chapter 2 as a technique for increasing the modularity of a program—for building "walls" between a program and its data structures. During the design of a solution, you will discover that you need to support several operations on the data and therefore need to define abstract data types (ADTs). This chapter introduces some simple abstract data types and uses them to demonstrate the advantages of abstract data types in general. In Part Two of this book, you will see several other important ADTs.

Only after you have clearly specified the operations of an abstract data type should you consider data structures for implementing it. This chapter explores implementation issues and introduces Java classes as a way to hide the implementation of an ADT from its users.

4.1 Abstract Data Types

Modularity is a technique that keeps the complexity of a large program manageable by systematically controlling the interaction of its components. You can focus on one task at a time in a modular program without other distractions. Thus, a modular program is easier to write, read, and modify. Modularity also isolates errors and eliminates redundancies.

You can develop modular programs by piecing together existing software components with methods that have yet to be written. In doing so, you should focus on *what* a module does and not on *how* it does it. To use existing software, you need a clear set of specifications that details how the modules behave. To write new methods, you need to decide what you would like them to do and proceed under the assumption that they exist and work. In this way you can write the methods in relative isolation from one another, knowing what each one will do but not necessarily *how* each will eventually do it. That is, you should practice **procedural abstraction.**

While writing a module's specifications, you must identify details that you can hide within the module. The principle of **information hiding** involves not only hiding these details, but also making them *inaccessible* from outside a module. One way to understand information hiding is to imagine **walls** around the various tasks a program performs. These walls prevent the tasks from becoming entangled. The wall around each task T prevents the other tasks from "seeing" how T is performed. Thus, if task Q uses task T, and if the method for performing task T changes, task Q will not be affected. As Figure 4-1 illustrates, the wall prevents task Q's method of solution from depending on task T's method of solution.

A modular program is easier to write, read, and modify

Write specifications for each module before implementing it

Isolate the implementation details of a module from other modules

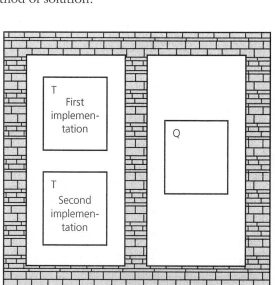

FIGURE 4-1

Isolated tasks: the implementation of task T does not affect task Q

The isolation of the modules cannot be total, however. Although task Q does not know *how* task T is performed, it must know *what* task T is and how to initiate it. For example, suppose that a program needs to operate on a sorted array of names. The program may, for instance, need to search the array for a given name or display the names in alphabetical order. The program thus needs a method S that sorts an array of names. Although the rest of the program knows that method S will sort an array, it should not care how S accomplishes its task. Thus, imagine a tiny slit in each wall, as Figure 4-2 illustrates. The slit is not large enough to allow the outside world to see the method's inner workings, but things can pass through the slit into and out of the method. For example, you can pass the array into the sort method, and the method can pass the sorted array out to you. What goes in and comes out is governed by the terms of the method's specifications, or **contract:** *If you use the method in this way, this is exactly what it will do for you.*

Often the solution to a problem requires operations on data. Such operations are broadly described in one of three ways:

- **Add** data to a data collection.

- **Remove** data from a data collection.

- **Ask questions** about the data in a data collection.

Typical operations on data

The details of the operations, of course, vary from application to application, but the overall theme is the management of data. Realize, however, that not all problems use or require these operations.

Data abstraction asks that you think in terms of *what* you can do to a collection of data independently of *how* you do it. Data abstraction is a technique that allows you to develop each data structure in relative isolation from the rest of the solution. The other modules of the solution will "know" what operations they can perform on the data, but they should not depend on how the data is stored or how the operations are performed. Again, the terms of the

Both procedural and data abstraction ask you to think "what," not "how"

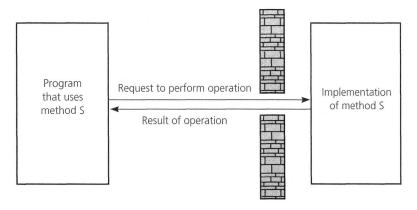

Program that uses method S

Request to perform operation

Result of operation

Implementation of method S

FIGURE 4-2

A slit in the wall

contract are *what* and not *how*. Thus, data abstraction is a natural extension of procedural abstraction.

A collection of data together with a set of operations on that data are called an **abstract data type,** or **ADT.** For example, suppose that you need to store a collection of names in a manner that allows you to search rapidly for a given name. The binary search algorithm described in Chapter 3 enables you to search an array efficiently, if the array is sorted. Thus, one solution to this problem is to store the names sorted in an array and to use a binary search algorithm to search the array for a specified name. You can view the *sorted array together with the binary search algorithm* as an ADT that solves this problem.

The description of an ADT's operations must be rigorous enough to specify completely their effect on the data, yet it must not specify how to store the data nor how to carry out the operations. For example, the ADT operations should not specify whether to store the data in consecutive memory locations or in disjoint memory locations. You choose a particular **data structure** when you **implement** an ADT.

Recall that a data structure is a construct that you can define within a programming language to store a collection of data. For example, arrays, which are built into Java, are data structures. However, you can invent other data structures. For example, suppose that you wanted a data structure to store both the names and salaries of a group of employees. You could use the following Java statements:

```
final int MAX_NUMBER = 500;
String[] names = new String[MAX_NUMBER];
double[] salaries = new double[MAX_NUMBER];
```

Here the employee *names[i]* has a salary of *salaries[i]*. The two arrays *names* and *salaries* together form a data structure, yet Java has no single data type to describe it.

When a program must perform data operations that are not directly supported by the language, you should first design an abstract data type and carefully specify what the ADT operations are to do (the contract). Then—*and only then*—should you implement the operations with a data structure. If you implement the operations properly, the rest of the program will be able to assume that the operations perform as specified—that is, that the terms of the contract are honored. However, the program must not depend on a particular approach for supporting the operations.

An abstract data type is not another name for a data structure.

To give you a better idea of the conceptual difference between an ADT and a data structure, consider a refrigerator's ice dispenser, as Figure 4-3 illustrates. It has water as input and produces as output either chilled water, crushed ice, or ice cubes, according to which one of the three buttons you push. It also has an indicator that lights when no ice is presently available. The dispenser is analogous to an abstract data type. The water is analogous to data; the operations are *chill, crush, cube,* and *isEmpty.* At this level of design, you are not concerned with how the dispenser will perform its operations, only that it

An ADT is a collection of data and a set of operations on that data

Specifications indicate what ADT operations do, but not how to implement them

Data structures are part of an ADT's implementation

Carefully specify an ADT's operations before you implement them

ADTs and data structures are not the same

KEY CONCEPTS

ADTs Versus Data Structures

▪ An abstract data type is a collection of data and a set of operations on that data.

▪ A data structure is a construct within a programming language that stores a collection of data.

---

performs them. If you want crushed ice, do you really care how the dispenser accomplishes its task as long as it does so correctly? Thus, after you have specified the dispenser's methods, you can design many uses for crushed ice without knowing how the dispenser accomplishes its tasks and without the distraction of engineering details.

Eventually, however, someone must build the dispenser. Exactly how will this machine produce crushed ice, for example? It could first make ice cubes and then either crush them between two steel rollers or smash them into small pieces by using hammers. Many other techniques are possible. The internal structure of the dispenser corresponds to the implementation of the ADT in a programming language—that is, to a data structure.

Although the owner of the dispenser does not care about its inner workings, he or she does want a design that is as efficient in its operation as possible. Similarly, the dispenser's manufacturer wants a design that is as easy and cheap to build as possible. You should have these same concerns when you choose a data structure to implement an ADT in Java. Even if you do not implement the ADT yourself, but instead use an already implemented ADT, you—like the person who buys a refrigerator—should care at least about the ADT's efficiency.

Notice that the dispenser is surrounded by steel walls. The only breaks in the walls accommodate the input (water) to the machine and its output (chilled water, crushed ice, or ice cubes). Thus, the machine's interior mechanisms are not only hidden from the user but also are inaccessible. In addition, the mechanism of one operation is hidden from and inaccessible to another operation.

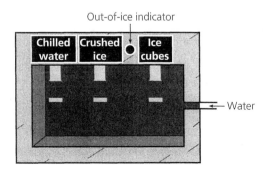

FIGURE 4-3

A dispenser of chilled water, crushed ice, and ice cubes

This modular design has benefits. For example, you can improve the operation *crush* by modifying its module without affecting the other modules. You could also add an operation by adding another module to the machine without affecting the original three operations. Thus, both abstraction and information hiding are at work here.

A program should not depend on the details of an ADT's implementation

To summarize, data abstraction results in a wall of ADT operations between data structures and the program that accesses the data within these data structures, as Figure 4-4 illustrates. If you are on the program's side of the wall, you will see an **interface** that enables you to communicate with the data structure. That is, you request the ADT operations to manipulate the data in the data structure, and they pass the results of these manipulations back to you.

Using an ADT is like using a vending machine

This process is analogous to using a vending machine. You press buttons to communicate with the machine and obtain something in return. The machine's external design dictates how you use it, much as an ADT's specifications govern what its operations are and what they do. As long as you use a vending machine according to its design, you can ignore its inner technology. As long as you agree to access data only by using ADT operations, your program can be oblivious to any change in the data structures that implement the ADT.

The following pages describe how to use an abstract data type to realize data abstraction's goal of separating the operations on data from the implementation of these operations. In doing so, we will look at several examples of ADTs.

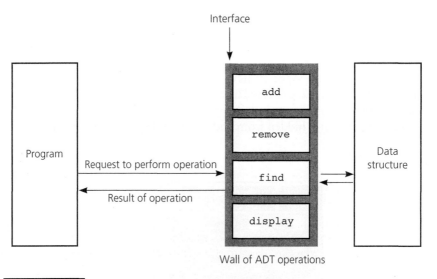

FIGURE 4-4

A wall of ADT operations isolates a data structure from the program that uses it

4.2 Specifying ADTs

To elaborate on the notion of an abstract data type, consider a list that you might encounter, such as a list of chores, a list of important dates, a list of addresses, or the grocery list pictured in Figure 4-5. As you write a grocery list, where do you put new items? Assuming that you write a neat one-column list, you probably add new items to the end of the list. You could just as well add items to the beginning of the list or add them so that your list is sorted alphabetically. Regardless, the items on a list appear in a sequence. The list has one first item and one last item. Except for the first and last items, each item has a unique **predecessor** and a unique **successor.** The first item—the **head** or **front** of the list—does not have a predecessor, and the last item—the **tail** or **end** of the list—does not have a successor.

Lists contain items of the same type: You can have a list of grocery items or a list of phone numbers. What can you do to the items on a list? You might count the items to determine the length of the list, add an item to the list, remove an item from the list, or look at (**retrieve**) an item. The items on a list, together with operations that you can perform on the items, form an abstract data type. You must specify the behavior of the ADT's operations on its data, that is, the list items. It is important that you focus only on specifying the operations and not on how you will implement them. In other words, do not bring to this discussion any preconceived notion of a data structure that the term "list" might suggest.

Where do you add a new item and which item do you want to look at? The various answers to these questions lead to several kinds of lists. You might decide to add, delete, and retrieve items only at the end of the list or only at the front of the list or at both the front and end of the list. The specifications of these lists are left as an exercise; next we will discuss a more general list.

FIGURE 4-5

A grocery list

The ADT List

Once again, consider the grocery list pictured in Figure 4-5. The previously described lists, which manipulate items at one or both ends of the list, are not really adequate for an actual grocery list. You would probably want to access items anywhere on the list. That is, you might look at the item at position i, delete the item at position i, or insert an item at position i on the list. Such operations are part of the ADT **list.**

Note that it is customary to include an initialization operation that creates an empty list. Other operations that determine whether the list is empty or the length of the list are also useful.

Although the six items on the list in Figure 4-5 have a sequential order, they are not necessarily sorted by name. Perhaps the items appear in the order in which they occur on the grocer's shelves, but more likely they appear in the order in which they occurred to you as you wrote the list. The ADT list is simply an ordered collection of items that you reference by position number. But to make this ADT list more like other built-in ADTs you will find in Java, the position number will start at zero. Note this is similar to the way that Java indexes an array, the subscript of the first element in an array is zero.

You reference list items by their position within the list

KEY CONCEPTS

ADT List Operations
1. Create an empty list.
2. Determine whether a list is empty.
3. Determine the number of items on a list.
4. Add an item at a given position in the list.
5. Remove the item at a given position in the list.
6. Remove all the items from the list.
7. Retrieve (get) the item at a given position in the list.

The following pseudocode specifies the operations for the ADT list in more detail. Figure 4-6 shows the UML diagram for this ADT.

To get a more precise idea of how the operations work, apply them to the grocery list

milk, eggs, butter, apples, bread, chicken

where milk is the first item on the list and chicken is the last item. To begin, consider how you can construct this list by using the operations of the ADT

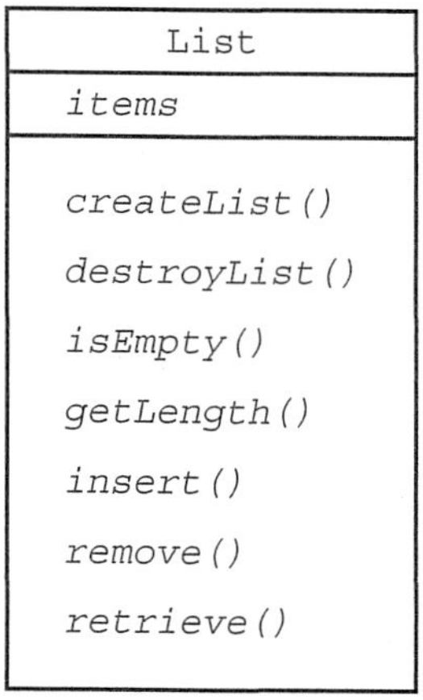

```
┌─────────────────────────────┐
│            List             │
├─────────────────────────────┤
│  items                      │
├─────────────────────────────┤
│  createList()               │
│                             │
│  destroyList()              │
│                             │
│  isEmpty()                  │
│                             │
│  getLength()                │
│                             │
│  insert()                   │
│                             │
│  remove()                   │
│                             │
│  retrieve()                 │
└─────────────────────────────┘
```

FIGURE 4-6

UML diagram for ADT `List`

list. One way is first to create an empty list `aList` and then use a series of insertion operations to append successively the items to the list as follows:

```
aList.createList()
aList.add(0, milk)
aList.add(1, eggs)
aList.add(2, butter)
aList.add(3, apple)
aList.add(4, bread)
aList.add(5, chicken)
```

The notation[1] `aList.O` indicates that an operation `O` applies to the list `aList`.

Notice that the list's insertion operation can insert new items into any position of the list, not just at its front or end. According to `add`'s specification, if a new item is inserted into position i, the position of each item that was at a position of i or greater is increased by 1. Thus, for example, if you start with the previous grocery list and you perform the operation

```
aList.add(3, nuts)
```

the list `aList` becomes

milk, eggs, butter, nuts, apples, bread, chicken

----

1. This notation is similar to the Java implementation of the ADT.

KEY CONCEPTS

Pseudocode for the ADT List Operations

```
+createList()
// Creates an empty list.

+isEmpty():boolean {query}
// Determines whether a list is empty.

+size():integer {query}
// Returns the number of items that are in a list.

+add(in index:integer, in item:ListItemType)
// Inserts item at position index of a list, if
// 0 <= index <= size().
// If index < size(), items are renumbered as
// follows: The item at index becomes the item at
// index+1, the item at index+1 becomes the
// item at index+2, and so on.
// Throws an exception when index is out of range or if
// the item cannot be placed on the list (list full).

+remove(in index:integer)
// Removes the item at position index of a list, if
// 0 <= index < size(). If index < size()-1, items are
// renumbered as follows: The item at index+1 becomes
// the item at index, the item at index+2 becomes the
// item at index+1, and so on.
// Throws an exception when index is out of range or if
// the list is empty.

+removeAll()
// Removes all the items in the list.

+get(index):ListItemType {query}
// Returns the item at position index of a list
// if 0 <= index < size(). The list is
// left unchanged by this operation.
// Throws an exception if index is out of range.
```

All items that had position numbers greater than or equal to 3 before the insertion now have their position numbers increased by 1 after the insertion.

Similarly, the deletion operation specifies that if an item is deleted from position i, the position of each item that was at a position greater than i is decreased by 1. Thus, for example, if `aList` is the list

milk, eggs, butter, nuts, apples, bread, chicken

and you perform the operation

`aList.remove(4)`

the list becomes

milk, eggs, butter, nuts, bread, chicken

All items that had position numbers greater than 4 before the deletion now have their position numbers decreased by 1 after the deletion.

These examples illustrate that an ADT can specify the effects of its operations without having to indicate how to store the data. The specifications of the seven operations are the sole terms of the contract for the ADT list: *If you request that these operations be performed, this is what will happen.* The specifications contain no mention of how to store the list or how to perform the operations; they tell you only what you can do to the list. It is of fundamental importance that the specification of an ADT *not* include implementation issues. This restriction on the specification of an ADT is what allows you to build a wall between an implementation of an ADT and the program that uses it. (Such a program is called a **client.**) The behavior of the operations is the only thing on which a program should depend.

> An ADT specification should not include implementation issues

Note that the insertion, deletion, and retrieval operations throw an exception when the argument *index* is out of range. This technique provides the ADT with a simple mechanism to communicate operation failure to its client. For example, if you try to delete the tenth item from a five-item list, `remove` can throw an exception indicating that *index* is out of range. Exceptions enable the client to handle error situations in an implementation-independent way.

> A program should depend only on the behavior of the ADT

What does the specification of the ADT list tell you about its behavior? It is apparent that the list operations fall into the three broad categories presented earlier in this chapter.

- The operation *add* **adds** data to a data collection.

- The operations *remove* and *removeAll* **remove** data from a data collection.

- The operations *isEmpty*, *size*, and *get* **ask questions** about the data in a data collection.

Once you have satisfactorily specified the behavior of an ADT, you can design applications that access and manipulate the ADT's data solely in terms of its operations and without regard for its implementation. As a simple example, suppose that you want to display the items in a list. Even though the wall between the implementation of the ADT list and the rest of the program prevents you from knowing how the list is stored, you can write a method *displayList* in terms of the operations that define the ADT list. The pseudocode for such a method follows:[2]

An implementation-independent application of the ADT list

```
displayList(in aList:List)
// Displays the items on the list aList.

    for (index = 0 through aList.size()-1) {
        dataItem = aList.get(index)
        Display dataItem
    }  // end for
```

Notice that as long as the ADT list is implemented correctly, the *displayList* method will perform its task. In this case, *get* successfully retrieves each list item, because *index*'s value is always valid.

The method *displayList* does not depend on *how* you implement the list. That is, the method will work regardless of whether you use an array or some other data structure to store the list's data. This feature is a definite advantage of abstract data types. In addition, by thinking in terms of the available ADT operations, you will not be distracted by implementation details. Figure 4-7 illustrates the wall between *displayList* and the implementation of the ADT list.

As another application of the ADT operations, suppose that you want a method *replace* that replaces the item in position i with a new item. If the ith item exists, *replace* deletes the item and inserts the new item at position i, as follows:

```
replace(in aList:List, in i:integer,
        in newItem:ListItemType
// Replaces the iᵗʰ item on the list aList with
// newItem.

    if (i >=0 and i < aList.size()) {
        aList.remove(i)
        aList.add(i, newItem)
    }  // end if
```

You can use ADT operations in an application without the distraction of implementation details

In both of the preceding examples, notice how you can focus on the task at hand without the distraction of implementation details such as arrays. With less to worry about, you are less likely to make an error in your logic when you use the ADT operations in applications such as *displayList* and *replace*. Likewise, when you finally implement the ADT operations in Java, you will not be distracted by these applications. In addition, because *displayList* and *replace* do not depend on any implementation decisions that you make for

---

2. In this example, *displayList* is not an ADT operation, so a procedural notation that specifies *aList* as a parameter is used.

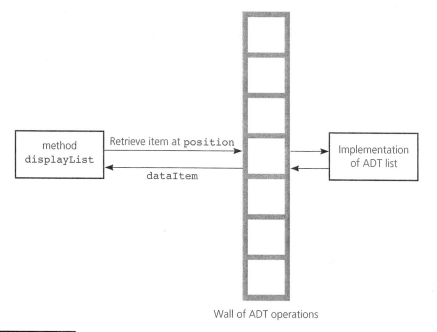

Wall of ADT operations

FIGURE 4-7

The wall between *displayList* and the implementation of the ADT list

the ADT list, they are not altered by your decisions. These assertions assume that you do not change the specifications of the ADT operations when you implement them. However, as Chapter 2 pointed out, developing software is not a linear process. You may realize during implementation that you need to refine your specifications. Clearly, changes to the specification of any module affect any already-designed uses of that module.

To summarize, you can specify the behavior of an ADT independently of its implementation. Given such a specification, and without any knowledge of how the ADT will be implemented, you can design applications that use the ADT's operations to access its data.

The ADT Sorted List

One of the most frequently performed computing tasks is the maintenance, in some *specified* order, of a collection of data. Many examples immediately come to mind: students placed in order by their names, baseball players listed in order by their batting averages, and corporations listed in order by their assets. These orders are called **sorted**. In contrast, the items on a grocery list might be ordered—the order in which they appear on the grocer's shelves, for example—but they are probably not sorted by name.

The problem of *maintaining* sorted data requires more than simply sorting the data. Often you need to insert some new data item into its proper, sorted place. Similarly, you often need to delete some data item. For example,

The ADT sorted list maintains items in sorted order

suppose your university maintains an alphabetical list of the students who are currently enrolled. The registrar must insert names into and delete names from this list because students constantly enroll in and leave school. These operations should preserve the sorted order of the data.

The following specifications define the operations for the ADT **sorted list.**

KEY CONCEPTS

Pseudocode for the ADT Sorted List Operations

```
+createSortedList()
// Creates an empty sorted list.


+sortedIsEmpty():boolean {query}
// Determines whether a sorted list is empty.


+sortedSize():integer {query}
// Returns the number of items that are in a sorted list.


+sortedAdd(in item:ListItemType)
// Inserts item into its proper sorted position in a
// sorted list. Throws an exception if the item
// cannot be placed on the list (list full).


+sortedRemove(in item:ListItemType)
// Deletes item from a sorted list.
// Throws an exception if the item is not found.


+sortedGet(in index:integer)
// Returns the item at position index of a
// sorted list, if 0 <= index < sortedSize().
// The list is left unchanged by this operation.
// Throws an exception if the index is out of range.


+locateIndex(in item:ListItemType):integer {query}
// Returns the position where item belongs or
// exists in a sorted list; item and the list are
// unchanged.
```

The ADT sorted list differs from the ADT list in that a sorted list inserts and deletes items by their values and not by their positions. For example, *sortedAdd* determines the proper position for *item* according to its value. Also, *locateIndex*—which determines the position of any item, given its value—is a sorted list operation but not a list operation. However, *sortedGet* is like list's *get*: Both operations retrieve an item, given its position. The method *sortedGet* enables you, for example, to retrieve and then display each item in a sorted list.

Designing an ADT

The design of an abstract data type should evolve naturally during the problem-solving process. As an example of how this process might occur, suppose that you want to determine the dates of all the holidays in a given year. One way to do this is to examine a calendar. That is, you could consider each day in the year and ascertain whether that day is a holiday. The following pseudocode is thus a possible solution to this problem:

```
listHolidays(in year:integer)
// Displays the dates of all holidays in a given year.

   date = date of first day of year
   while (date is before the first day of year+1) {
      if (date is a holiday) {
         write (date + " is a holiday")
      } // end if
      date = date of next day
   } // end while
```

What data is involved here? Clearly, this problem operates on dates, where a date consists of a month, day, and year. What operations will you need to solve the holiday problem? Your ADT must specify and restrict the legal operations on the dates just as the fundamental data type *int* restricts you to operations such as addition and comparison. You can see from the previous pseudocode that you must

What data does a problem require?

- Determine the date of the first day of a given year
- Determine whether a date is before another date
- Determine whether a date is a holiday
- Determine the date of the day that follows a given date

What operations does a problem require?

Thus, you could define the following operations for your ADT:

```
+firstDay(in year:integer):Date {query}
// Returns the date of the first day of a given year.

+isBefore(in date1:Date,
          in date2:Date) : boolean {query}
// Returns true if date1 is before date2,
// otherwise returns false.

+isHoliday(in aDate:Date) : boolean {query}
// Returns true if date is a holiday,
// otherwise returns false.
```

```
+nextDay(in aDate:Date) : Date
// Returns the date of the day after a given date.
```

The `listHolidays` pseudocode now appears as follows:

```
listHolidays(in year:integer)
// Displays the dates of all holidays in a given year.

  date = firstDay(year)
  while (isBefore(date, firstDay(year+1))) {
    if (isHoliday(date)) {
      write (date + " is a holiday ")
    } // end if
    date = nextDay(date)
  } // end while
```

Thus, you can design an ADT by identifying data and choosing operations that are suitable to your problem. After specifying the operations, you use them to solve your problem independently of the implementation details of the ADT.

An appointment book. As another example of an ADT design, imagine that you want to create a computerized appointment book that spans a one-year period. Suppose that you make appointments only on the hour and half hour between 8 A.M. and 5 P.M. For simplicity, assume that all appointments are 30 minutes in duration. You want your system to store a brief notation about the nature of each appointment along with the date and time.

To solve this problem, you can define an ADT appointment book. The data items in this ADT are the appointments, where an appointment consists of a date, time, and purpose. What are the operations? Two obvious operations are

- Make an appointment for a certain date, time, and purpose. (You will want to be careful that you do not make an appointment at an already occupied time.)

- Cancel the appointment for a certain date and time.

In addition to these operations, it is likely that you will want to

- Ask whether you have an appointment at a given time.

- Determine the nature of your appointment at a given time.

Finally, ADTs typically have initialization operations.

Thus, the ADT appointment book can have the following operations:

```
+createAppointmentBook()
// Creates an empty appointment book.

+isAppointment(in apptDate:Date,
               in apptTime:Time):boolean {query}
// Returns true if an appointment exists for the date
```

```
// and time specified; otherwise returns false.

+makeAppointment(in apptDate:Date, in apptTime:Time,
                 in purpose:string):boolean
// Inserts the appointment for the date, time, and purpose
// specified as long as it does not conflict with an
// existing appointment.
// Returns true if successful, false otherwise.

+cancelAppointment(in apptDate:Date,
                   in apptTime:Time):boolean
// Deletes the appointment for the date and time specified.
// Returns true if successful, false otherwise.

+checkAppointment(in apptDate:Date,
                  in apptTime:Time):string {query}
// Returns the purpose of the appointment at
// the given date/time, if one exists. Otherwise, returns
// null.
```

You can use these ADT operations to design other operations on the appointments. For example, suppose that you want to change the date or time of a particular appointment within the existing appointment book *apptBook*. The following pseudocode indicates how to accomplish this task by using the previous ADT operations:

```
// change the date or time of an appointment

read (oldDate, oldTime, newDate, newTime)
// get purpose of appointment
purpose = apptBook.checkAppointment(oldDate, oldTime)
if (purpose exists) {
  // see if new date/time is available
  if (apptBook.isAppointment(newDate, newTime)) {
    // new date/time is booked
    write ("You already have an appointment at " + newTime +
           " on " + newDate)
  }
  else  { // new date/time is available
    apptBook.cancelAppointment(oldDate, oldTime))
    if (apptBook.makeAppointment(newDate, newTime,
        purpose)){
      write ("Your appointment has been rescheduled to" +
             newTime + " on " + newDate)
    } //end if
  } // end if
}
```

```
else {
   write ("You do not have an appointment at " + oldTime +
         " on " + oldDate)
}  // end if
```

You can use an ADT
without knowledge
of its implementation

Again notice that you can design applications of ADT operations without knowing how the ADT is implemented. The exercises at the end of this chapter provide examples of other tasks that you can perform with this ADT.

ADTs that suggest other ADTs.   Both of the previous examples require you to represent a date; the appointment book example also requires you to represent the time. Java has a *java.util.Date* class that you can use to represent the date and time. You can also design ADTs to represent these items. It is not unusual for the design of one ADT to suggest other ADTs. In fact, you can use one ADT to implement another ADT. The programming problems at the end of this chapter ask you to design and implement the simple ADTs date and time.

You can use an
ADT to implement
another ADT

This final example also describes an ADT that suggests other ADTs for its implementation. Suppose that you want to design a database of recipes. You could think of this database as an ADT: The recipes are the data items, and some typical operations on the recipes could include the following:

```
+insertRecipe(in aRecipe:Recipe)
// Inserts recipe into the database.
```

```
+deleteRecipe(in aRecipe:Recipe)
// Deletes recipe from the database.
```

```
+retrieveRecipe(in name:string):Recipe {query}
// Retrieves the named recipe from the database.
```

This level of the design does not indicate such details as where *insertRecipe* will place a recipe into the database.

Now imagine that you want to write a method that scales a recipe retrieved from the database: If the recipe is for n people, you want to revise it so that it will serve m people. Suppose that the recipe contains measurements such as $2\frac{1}{2}$ cups, 1 tablespoon, and $\frac{1}{4}$ teaspoon. That is, the quantities are given as mixed numbers—integers and fractions—in units of cups, tablespoons, and teaspoons.

This problem suggests another ADT—measurement—with the following operations:

```
+getMeasure():Measurement {query}
// Returns the measure.
```

```
+setMeasure(in m:Measurement)
// Sets the measure.
```

```
+scaleMeasure(in scaleFactor: float):Measurement
// Multiplies measure by a fractional scaleFactor, which
// has no units, and returns the result.

+convertMeasure(in oldUnits:MeasureUnit,
                in newUnits:MeasureUnit):Measurement {query}
// Converts measure from its old units to a measure in
// new units, and returns the result.
```

Suppose that you want the ADT measurement to perform exact fractional arithmetic. Because our planned implementation language Java does not have a data type for fractions and floating-point arithmetic is not exact, another ADT called fraction is in order. Its operations could include addition, subtraction, multiplication, and division of fractions. For example, you could specify addition as

```
addFractions(in first:Fraction, in second:Fraction):Fraction
// Adds two fractions and returns the sum reduced to lowest
// terms.
```

Moreover, you could include operations to convert a mixed number to a fraction and to convert a fraction to a mixed number when feasible.

When you finally implement the ADT measurement, you can use the ADT fraction. That is, you can use one ADT to implement another ADT.

Axioms (Optional)

The previous specifications for ADT operations have been stated rather informally. For example, they rely on your intuition to know the meaning of "an item is at position i" in an ADT list. This notion is simple, and most people will understand its intentions. However, some abstract data types are much more complex and less intuitive than a list. For such ADTs, you should use a more rigorous method of defining the behavior of their operations: You must supply a set of mathematical rules—called **axioms**—that precisely specify the behavior of each ADT operation.

An axiom is a mathematical rule

An axiom is actually an invariant—a true statement—for an ADT operation. For example, you are familiar with axioms for algebraic operations; in particular, you know the following rules for multiplication:

$$(a \times b) \times c = a \times (b \times c)$$

$$a \times b = b \times a$$

$$a \times 1 = a$$

$$a \times 0 = 0$$

Axioms for multiplication

These rules, or axioms, are true for any numeric values of a, b, and c, and they describe the behavior of the multiplication operator $\times$.

Axioms specify
the behavior
of an ADT

In a similar fashion, you can write a set of axioms that completely describes the behavior of the operations for the ADT list. For example,

A newly created list is empty

is an axiom since it is true for all newly created lists. You can state this axiom succinctly in terms of the operations of the ADT list as follows:

```
(aList.createList()).isEmpty() is true
```

That is, the list `aList` is empty.

The statement

If you insert an item x into the ith position of an ADT list, retrieving the ith item will result in x

is true for all lists, and so it is an axiom. You can state this axiom in terms of the operations of the ADT list as follows:[3]

```
(aList.add(i, x)).get(i) = x
```

That is, `get` retrieves from position *i* of list `aList` the item *x* that `add` has put there.

The following axioms formally define the ADT list:

KEY CONCEPTS

Axioms for the ADT List

1. `(aList.createList()).size() = 0`
2. `(aList.add(i, x)).size() = aList.size() + 1`
3. `(aList.remove(i)).size() = aList.size() - 1`
4. `(aList.createList()).isEmpty() = true`
5. `(aList.add(i, item)).isEmpty() = false`
6. `(aList.createList()).remove(i) = error`
7. `(aList.add(i, x)).remove(i) = aList`
8. `(aList.createList()).get(i) = error`
9. `(aList.add(i, x)).get(i) = x`
10. `aList.get(i) = (aList.add(i, x)).get(i+1)`
11. `aList.get(i+1) = (aList.remove(i)).get(i)`

---

3. The = notation within these axioms denotes algebraic equality.

A set of axioms does not make the pre- and postconditions for an ADT's operations unnecessary. For example, the previous axioms do not describe add's behavior when you try to insert an item into position 50 of a list of 2 items. One way to handle this situation is to include the restriction

```
0 <= index <= size()
```

in *add*'s precondition. Another way—which you will see when we implement the ADT list later in this chapter—does not restrict *index*, but rather throws an exception if *index* is outside the previous range. Thus, you need both a set of axioms and a set of pre- and postconditions to define the behavior of an ADT's operations completely.

You can use axioms to determine the outcome of a sequence of ADT operations. For example, if aList is a list of characters, how does the sequence of operations

Use axioms to determine the effect of a sequence of ADT operations

```
aList.add(0, b)
aList.add(0, a)
```

affect aList? We will show that a is the first item in this list and that b is the second item by using *get* to retrieve these items.

You can write the previous sequence of operations in another way as

```
(aList.add(0, b)).add(0, a)
```

or

```
tempList.add(0, a)
```

where tempList represents aList.add(0, b). Now retrieve the first and second items in the list tempList.add(0, a), as follows:

```
(tempList.add(0, a)).get(0) = a    by axiom 9
```

and

```
(tempList.add(0, a)).get(1)
    = tempList.get(0)              by axiom 10
    = (aList.add(0, b)).get(0)     by definition of tempList
    = b                            by axiom 9
```

Thus, a is the first item in the list and b is the second item.

Axioms are treated further in exercises in the rest of the book.

4.3 Implementing ADTs

The previous sections emphasized the specification of an abstract data type. When you design an ADT, you concentrate on what its operations do, but you ignore how you will implement them. The result should be a set of clearly specified ADT operations.

How do you implement an ADT once its operations are clearly specified? That is, how do you store the ADT's data and carry out its operations? Earlier in this chapter you learned that when implementing an ADT, you choose data structures to represent the ADT's data. Thus, your first reaction to the implementation question might be to choose a data structure and then to write methods that access it in accordance with the ADT operations. Although this point of view is not incorrect, hopefully you have learned not to jump right into code. In general, you should refine an ADT through successive levels of abstraction. That is, you should use a top-down approach to designing an algorithm for each of the ADT operations. You can view each of the successively more concrete descriptions of the ADT as implementing its more abstract predecessors. The refinement process stops when you reach data structures that are available in your programming language. The more primitive your language, the more levels of implementation you will require.

The choices that you make at each level of the implementation can affect its efficiency. For now, our analyses will be intuitive, but Chapter 10 will introduce you to quantitative techniques that you can use to weigh the trade-offs involved.

Recall that the program that uses the ADT should see only a wall of available operations that act on data. Figure 4-8 illustrates this wall once again. Both the data structure that you choose to contain the data and the implementations of the ADT operations are hidden behind the wall. By now, you should realize the advantage of this wall.

In a non-object-oriented implementation, both the data structure and the ADT operations are distinct pieces. The client agrees to honor the wall by

Data structures are part of an ADT's implementation

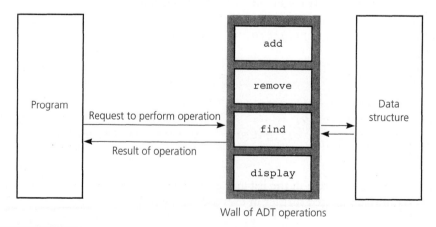

Wall of ADT operations

FIGURE 4-8

ADT operations provide access to a data structure

using only the ADT operations to access the data structure. Unfortunately, the data structure is hidden only if the client does not look over the wall! Thus, the client can violate the wall—either intentionally or accidentally—by accessing the data structure directly, as Figure 4-9 illustrates. Why is such an action undesirable? Later, this chapter will use an array *items* to store an ADT list's items. In a program that uses such a list, you might, for example, accidentally access the first item in the list by writing

```
firstItem = items[0];
```

instead of by invoking the list operation *get*. If you changed to another implementation of the list, your program would be incorrect. To correct your program, you would need to locate and change all occurrences of *items[0]*—but first you would have to realize that *items[0]* is in error!

Object-oriented languages such as Java provide a way for you to enforce the wall of an ADT, thereby preventing access of the data structure in any way other than by using the ADT operations. We will spend some time now exploring this aspect of Java by discussing classes, interfaces, and exceptions.

Java Classes Revisited

Recall from Chapter 2 that object-oriented programming, or OOP, views a program not as a sequence of actions but as a collection of components called objects. Encapsulation—one of OOP's three fundamental principles[4]—enables

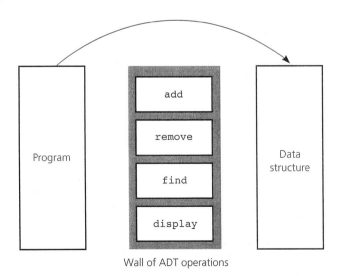

Wall of ADT operations

FIGURE 4-9

Violating the wall of ADT operations

4. The other principles are inheritance and polymorphism, which Chapter 9 will discuss

you to enforce the walls of an ADT. It is, therefore, essential to an ADT's implementation and our main focus here.

Encapsulation combines an ADT's data with its operations—called **methods**—to form an **object.** Rather than thinking of the many components of the ADT in Figure 4-8, you can think at a higher level of abstraction when you consider the object in Figure 4-10 because it is a single entity. The object hides its inner detail from the programmer who uses it. Thus, an ADT's operations become an object's behaviors.

Encapsulation hides implementation details

We could use a ball as an example of an object. Because thinking of a basketball, volleyball, tennis ball, or soccer ball probably suggests images of the game rather than the object itself, let's abstract the notion of a ball by picturing a sphere. A sphere of a given radius has attributes such as volume and surface area. A sphere as an object should be able to report its radius, volume, surface area, and so on. That is, the sphere object has methods that return such values. This section will develop the notion of a sphere as an object. Later, in Chapter 9, you will see how to derive a ball from a sphere.

A Java class defines a new data type

In Java, a class is a new data type whose instances are objects. A class contains **data fields** and **methods,** collectively known as class members. Methods typically act on the data fields. By default, all members in a class are **private**—they are not directly accessible by your program—unless you designate them as **public.** The implementations of a class's methods, however, can use any private members of that class.

An object is an instance of a class

You should almost always declare a class's data fields as private. Typically, as was mentioned in Chapter 2, you provide methods—such as *setDataField* and *getDataField*—to access the data fields. In this way, you control how and whether the rest of the program can access the data fields. This design principle should lead to programs that not only are easier to debug, but also have fewer logical errors from the beginning.

A class's data fields should be private

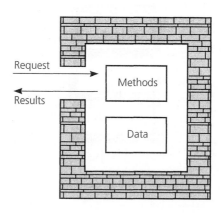

FIGURE 4-10

An object's data and methods are encapsulated

You should also distinguish between a class's data fields and any local variables that the implementation of a method requires. In Java, data fields are variables that are shared by all of the methods in the class. Data fields have initial default values, based on their type, and thus do not need to be explicitly initialized. But it is considered to be good programming practice to explicitly initialize data fields in the constructors when necessary. Local variables are used only within a single method and must be initialized explicitly before they are used.

The ADTs that you saw earlier had an operation for their creation. Classes have such methods, called **constructors.** A constructor creates and initializes new instances of a class. A typical class has several constructors. A constructor has the same name as the class. Constructors have no return type—not even *void*—and cannot use *return* to return a value. They can, however, have parameters. We will discuss constructors in more detail shortly, after we look at an example of a class definition.

A constructor creates and initializes an object

Java has a garbage collection mechanism to destroy objects that a program no longer needs. When a program no longer references an object, the Java runtime environment marks it for garbage collection. Periodically, the Java runtime environment executes a method that returns the memory used by these marked objects to the system for future use. Sometimes when an object is destroyed, other tasks beyond memory deallocation are necessary. In these cases, you define a *finalize* method for the object.

Java destroys objects that a program no longer references

Java Interfaces

Often it is convenient to be able to specify a set of methods that you might want to provide in many different classes. One way to do this is to define a superclass that contains these methods and then use inheritance to create the different classes that need to provide those methods. This could pose a problem, however, if the subclass also needs to extend another superclass. Java allows only one class to appear in the *extends* clause.

To address this situation, Java provides interfaces. An **interface** provides a way to specify methods and constants, but supplies no implementation details for the methods. Interfaces enable you to specify some desired common behavior that may be useful over many different types of objects. You can then design a method to work with a variety of object types that exhibit this common behavior by specifying the interface as the parameter type for the method, instead of a class. This allows the method to use the common behavior in its implementation, as long as the arguments to the method have implemented the interface.

An interface specifies methods and constants but supplies no implementations

The Java API has many predefined interfaces. For example, *java.util. Collection* is an interface that provides methods for managing a collection of objects. Here are two of the methods specified in the *Collection* interface:

```
public boolean add(Object o);
public boolean contains(Object o);
```

If you want to have your class provide the methods in this interface, you must indicate your intent to implement the interface by including an **implements** clause in your class definition and provide implementations of the methods:

A class that implements an interface

```
public class CardCollection
                        implements java.util.Collection {
   ...
  public boolean add(Object o) {
    // implementation of add method
  } // end add

  public boolean contains(Object o) {
    // implementation of contains method
  }  // end contains

  // and so on...
}  // end CardCollection
```

Suppose there is a *print(Collection c)* method. Instances of *CardCollection* are now eligible to be used as arguments to this method, since *CardCollection* implements the interface *Collection*.

To define your own interface, you use the keyword *interface* instead of *class*, and you provide only method specifications and constants in the interface definition. For example,

An example of an interface

```
public interface MyInterface {
  public final int f1 = 0;
  public void method1();
  public int method2(int a, int b);
}  // end MyInterface
```

This defines an interface *MyInterface* that has one constant *f1* and two methods *method1* and *method2*. Note that the name of the interface ends with *Interface*. This is another coding convention that we will use throughout this text.

Interfaces will be used to specify the ADTs that are developed in this text. The implementation of the ADT *list* presented later in this chapter will provide a more complete example of a user-defined interface and how it can be used.

Object Comparison. Earlier we saw the use of the *equals* method to determine the equality of two objects. Sometimes it is useful to also be able to determine not only the equality of objects, but if one object is greater or less than another object.

When comparing objects in this way, the determination of what makes one object "less" than another object can be specified by implementing the `java.lang.Comparable` interface. This interface contains one method, *compareTo*, that returns a negative integer, zero, or a positive integer if the current object is less than, equal to, or greater than the specified object. Here is an example showing the *SimpleSphere* class implementing the *Comparable* interface:

```
class SimpleSphere implements java.lang.Comparable<Object> {

  // same methods as before

  public int compareTo(Object rhs){
  // Compares rhs object with this object
  // Precondition: The object rhs should be a Sphere object
  // Postcondition: If this sphere has the same radius as the
  // rhs sphere, returns zero. If this sphere has a larger
  // radius than the rhs sphere, a positive integer is
  // returned. If this sphere has a smaller radius than the
  // rhs sphere, a negative integer is returned.
  // Throws: ClassCastException if the rhs object is not a
  // Sphere object.

    // Throws ClassCastException if rhs cannot be cast to
    // Sphere
    Sphere other = (Sphere)rhs;

    if (radius == other.radius) {
       return 0;   //Equal
    } else if (radius < other.radius) {
       return -1;
    } else {   // radius > other.radius
       return 1;
    }
  } // end compareTo
} // end SimpleSphere class
```

In this example, the criterion for comparison is based solely in the radius of the sphere. Spheres with a smaller radius value are considered "less than" spheres with a larger radius. Sometimes, the criterion used to compare objects depends on multiple values. For example, suppose you want to compare the names of people, consisting of a first name and a last name. Simply examining the last name might be sufficient unless you have two people with the same last name, then you would resort to comparing the two first names. The following example defines a *FullName* class, and demonstrates how such a comparison could be defined:

```
public class FullName implements java.lang.Comparable<Object> {
  private String firstName;
  private String lastName;
```

```
public FullName(String first, String last) {
  firstName = first;
  lastName = last;
} // end constructor

public int compareTo(Object rhs) {
// Precondition: The object rhs should be a Fullname object
// Postcondition: Returns 0 if all fields match
//    if lastName equals rhs.lastName and
//    firstName is greater than rhs.firstName.
// Returns -1 if lastName is less than rhs.lastName or
//    if lastName equals rhs.lastName and
//    firstName is less than rhs.firstName
// Throws: ClassCastException if the rhs object is not a Fullname
// object.

  // Throws ClassCastException if rhs cannot be cast to Fullname
  FullName other = (FullName)rhs;

  if (lastName.compareTo(((FullName)other).lastName)==0){
    return firstName.compareTo(((FullName)other).firstName);
  }
  else {
    return lastName.compareTo(((FullName)other).lastName);
  } // end if
} // end compareTo
} // end class FullName
```

Java Packages

Java **packages** provide a way to group related classes together. To create a package, you place a *package* statement at the top of each class file that is part of the package. For example, Java source files that are part of a drawing package would include the following line at the top of the file (Java package names usually begin with a lowercase letter):

To include a class in a package, begin the class's source file with a *package* statement

Place the files that contain a package's classes in the same directory

```
package drawingPackage;
```

Just as you must use the same name for both a Java class and the file that contains the class, you must use the same name for a package and the directory that contains all the classes in the package. Thus, the source files for the drawing package must be contained in a directory called *drawingPackage*.

When declaring classes within a package, the keyword *public* must appear in front of the *class* keyword to make the class available to clients of the package. If the drawing package contains a class *Palette*, the source file for *Palette* begins as follows:

```
package drawingPackage;
public class Palette {
  ...
```

Omitting the keyword *public* will make the class available only to other classes within the package. Sometimes, such restricted access is desirable.

When a class is publicly available within a package, it can also be used as a superclass for any new class, even those appearing in other packages. This is actually done often within the Java API. For example, the exception class *java.lang.RuntimeException* is the superclass for the class *java.util.NoSuchElementException*.

A package can contain other packages as well. If *shapePackage* is a package in *drawingPackage*, the directory for *shapePackage* must be a subdirectory of the *drawingPackage* directory. The package name consists of the hierarchy of package names, separated by periods. For example, if the Java source file for the class *Sphere* is part of *shapePackage*, the following line must appear at the top of the file *Sphere.java*:

```
package drawingPackage.shapePackage;
```

You already use packages in your programs when you place an *import* statement in your code. When you write a statement such as

```
import java.io.*;
```

you indicate to the compiler that you want to use classes in the package *java.io*. The * is a way to indicate that you might use any class in *java.io*, but if you know the specific class from the *java.io* package that you plan to use, you replace the * with the name of that class. For example, the statement

```
import java.io.DataStream;
```

indicates that you will use the class *DataStream* from the package *java.io*.

If you omit the package declaration from the source file for a class, the class is added to a default, unnamed package. If all the classes in a group are declared this way, they are all considered to be within this same unnamed package and hence do not require an *import* statement. But if you are developing a package, and you want to use a class that is contained in the unnamed package, you will need to import the class. In this case, since the package has no name, the class name itself is sufficient in the *import* statement.

Access to a package's classes can be public or restricted

Using a package

An Array-Based Implementation of the ADT List

We will now implement the ADT list as a class. Recall that the ADT list operations are

```
+createList()
+isEmpty():boolean
+size():integer
+add(in index:integer, in newItem:ListItemType)
+remove(in index:integer)
+removeAll()
+get(in index:integer):ListItemType
```

You need to represent the items in the ADT list and its length. Your first thought is probably to store the list's items in an array *items*. In fact, you might believe that the list is simply a fancy name for an array. This belief is not quite true, however. An **array-based implementation** is a natural choice because both an array and a list identify their items by number. However, the ADT list has operations such as *removeAll* that an array does not. In the next chapter you will see another implementation of the ADT list that does not use an array.

In any case, you can store a list's k^{th} item in *items[k]*. How much of the array will the list occupy? Possibly all of it, but probably not. That is, you need to keep track of the array elements that you have assigned to the list and those that are available for use in the future. The maximum length of the array—its **physical size**—is a known, fixed value such as *MAX_LIST*. You can keep track of the current number of items in the list—that is, the list's length or **logical size**—in a variable *numItems*. An obvious benefit of this approach is that implementing the operation *size* will be easy. Thus, we could use the following statements to implement a list of integers:

```
private final int MAX_LIST = 100; // max length of list
private int items[MAX_LIST];      // array of list items
private int numItems;             // length of list
```

Shift array elements to insert an item

Figure 4-11 illustrates the data fields for an array-based implementation of an ADT list of integers. To insert a new item at a given position in the array of list items, you must shift to the right the items from this position on, and insert the new item in the newly created opening. Figure 4-12 depicts this insertion.

Now consider how to delete an item from the list. You could blank it out, but this strategy can lead to gaps in the array, as Figure 4-13a illustrates. An array that is full of gaps has three significant problems:

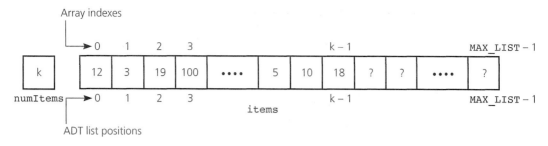

FIGURE 4-11

An array-based implementation of the ADT list

- *numItems − 1* is no longer the index of the last item in the array. You need another variable, *lastPosition*, to contain this index.

- Because the items are spread out, the method *get* might have to look at every cell of the array even when only a few items are present.

- When *items[MAX_LIST - 1]* is occupied, the list could appear full, even when fewer than *MAX_LIST* items are present.

Thus, what you really need to do is shift the elements of the array to fill the gap left by the deleted item, as shown in Figure 4-13b.

You should implement each ADT operation as a method of a class. Each operation will require access to both the array *items* and the list's length *numItems*, so make *items* and *numItems* data fields of the class. To hide *items* and *numItems* from the clients of the class, make these data fields private.

If one of the operations is provided an index value that is out of range, an exception should be thrown. Here is a definition of an exception that can be used for an out-of-bounds list index called *ListIndexOutOfBoundsException*. It is based upon the more general *IndexOutOfBoundsException* from the Java API:

Shift array elements to delete an item

Implement the ADT list as a class

items and *numItems* are private data fields

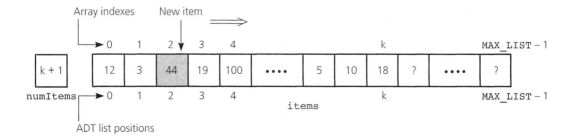

FIGURE 4-12

Shifting items for insertion at position 3

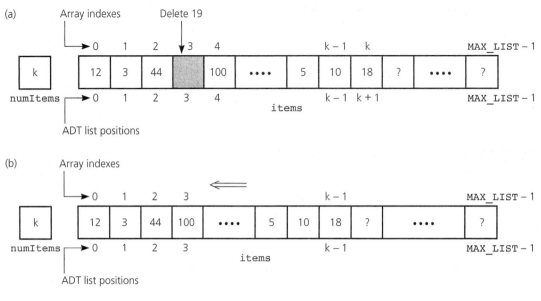

FIGURE 4-13

(a) Deletion causes a gap; (b) fill gap by shifting

```
public class ListIndexOutOfBoundsException
            extends IndexOutOfBoundsException {
  public ListIndexOutOfBoundsException(String s) {
    super(s);
  } // end constructor
} // end ListIndexOutOfBoundsException
```

Also, the exception *ListException* is needed when the array storing the list becomes full. Here is the exception *ListException*:

```
public class ListException extends RuntimeException {
  public ListException(String s) {
    super(s);
  } // end constructor
} // end ListException
```

The following interface *IntegerListInterface* provides the specifications for the list operations. The ADT operation *createList* does not appear in the interface because it will be implemented as a constructor.

Interface for a list
of integers

```
// ************************************************************
// Interface IntegerListInterface for the ADT list.
// ************************************************************
```

```java
public interface IntegerListInterface {
    public boolean isEmpty();
    // Determines whether a list is empty.
    // Precondition: None.
    // Postcondition: Returns true if the list is empty,
    // otherwise returns false.
    // Throws: None.

    public int size();
    // Determines the length of a list.
    // Precondition: None.
    // Postcondition: Returns the number of items that are
    // currently in the list.
    // Throws: None.

    public void removeAll();
    // Deletes all the items from the list.
    // Precondition: None.
    // Postcondition: The list is empty.
    // Throws: None.

    public void add(int index, int item)
            throws ListIndexOutOfBoundsException,
                ListException;
    // Adds an item to the list at position index.
    // Precondition: index indicates the position at which
    // the item should be inserted in the list.
    // Postcondition: If insertion is successful, item is
    // at position index in the list, and other items are
    // renumbered accordingly.
    // Throws: ListIndexOutOfBoundsException if index < 0 or
    // index > size().
    // Throws: ListException if item cannot be placed on
    // the list.

    public int get(int index) throws
        ListIndexOutOfBoundsException;
    // Retrieves a list item by position.
    // Precondition: index is the number of the item to be
    // retrieved.
    // Postcondition: If 0 <= index < size(), the item at
    // position index in the list is returned.
    // Throws: ListIndexOutOfBoundsException if index < 0 or
    // index > size()-1.

    public void remove(int index)
            throws ListIndexOutOfBoundsException;
```

```
// Deletes an item from the list at a given position.
// Precondition: index indicates where the deletion
// should occur.
// Postcondition: If 0 <= index < size(), the item at
// position index in the list is deleted, and other items
// are renumbered accordingly.
// Throws: ListIndexOutOfBoundsException if index < 0 or
// index > size()-1.

} // end IntegerListInterface
```

The notion of a list and of the operations that you perform on the list are really independent of the type of items that are stored in the list. The definition just given is very limiting in that it will support only a list of integers. If you use the class *Object* as the type for the list's elements, the specification will be far more flexible. Every class in Java is ultimately derived from the class *Object* through inheritance. This means that any class created in Java could be used as an item in the list class that implements the new list interface.

Use **Object** as the type of list elements

What happens if you want to have a list of integers? If the list item type is *Object*, you can no longer use the primitive type *int* as the item type, since *int* is not derived from the class *Object*. In cases where you want a list to contain items of a primitive type, you will need to use a corresponding wrapper class from the Java API. For example, instead of using items of type *int* in the list, the items would be of the type *java.lang.Integer*, a subclass of *Object*.

Here is a revised version, called *ListInterface*, that uses the class *Object* for the list elements. The comments, which are the same as those in *IntegerListInterface*, are left out to save space:

Interface for a list of objects

```
// ********************************************************
// Interface ListInterface for the ADT list.
// ********************************************************
public interface ListInterface {
  public boolean isEmpty();
  public int size();
  public void add(int index, Object item)
                    throws ListIndexOutOfBoundsException,
                           ListException;
  public Object get(int index)
                      throws ListIndexOutOfBoundsException;
  public void remove(int index)
                        throws ListIndexOutOfBoundsException;
  public void removeAll();
} // end ListInterface
```

The following class implements the interface *ListInterface*, using arrays.

```java
// ***********************************************************
// Array-based implementation of the ADT list.
// ***********************************************************
public class ListArrayBased implements ListInterface {            Implementation file
  private static final int MAX_LIST = 50;
  private Object items[];  // an array of list items
  private int numItems;  // number of items in list

  public ListArrayBased() {
    items = new Object[MAX_LIST];
    numItems = 0;
  }  // end default constructor

  public boolean isEmpty() {
    return (numItems == 0);
  } // end isEmpty

  public int size() {
    return numItems;
  }  // end size

  public void removeAll() {
    // Creates a new array; marks old array for
    // garbage collection.
    items = new Object[MAX_LIST];
    numItems = 0;
  } // end removeAll

  public void add(int index, Object item)
                  throws  ListIndexOutOfBoundsException {
    if (numItems > MAX_LIST) {
      throw new ListException("ListException on add");
    }  // end if
    if (index >= 0 && index <= numItems) {
      // make room for new element by shifting all items at
      // positions >= index toward the end of the
      // list (no shift if index == numItems+1)
      for (int pos = numItems; pos >= index; pos--) {
          items[pos+1] = items[pos];
      } // end for
      // insert new item
      items[index] = item;
      numItems++;
    }
    else {  // index out of range
      throw new ListIndexOutOfBoundsException(
        "ListIndexOutOfBoundsException on add");
```

```java
    }   // end if
  } //end add

  public Object get(int index)
                   throws ListIndexOutOfBoundsException {
    if (index >= 0 && index < numItems) {
      return items[index];
    }
    else {   // index out of range
      throw new ListIndexOutOfBoundsException(
        "ListIndexOutOfBoundsException on get");
    }   // end if
  } // end get

  public void remove(int index)
                   throws ListIndexOutOfBoundsException {
    if (index >= 0 && index < numItems) {
      // delete item by shifting all items at
      // positions > index toward the beginning of the list
      // (no shift if index == size)
      for (int pos = index+1; pos <= size(); pos++) {
        items[pos-1] = items[pos];
      }   // end for
      numItems--;
    }
    else {   // index out of range
        throw new ListIndexOutOfBoundsException(
        "ListIndexOutOfBoundsException on remove");
    }   // end if
  } // end remove

}   // end ListArrayBased
```

The following program segment demonstrates the use of *ListArrayBased*:

```java
static public void main(String args[]) {
  . . .
  ListArrayBased aList = new ListArrayBased();
  String dataItem;

  aList.add(0, "Cathryn");
  . . .
  dataItem = (String)aList.get(0);
  . . .
```

Note that references within this program such as *aList.numItems* and *aList.items[4]* would be illegal because *numItems* and *items* are private members of the class.

> A client of the class cannot access the class's private members directly

In summary, to implement an ADT, given implementation-independent specifications of the ADT operations, you first must choose a data structure to contain the data. Next, you define and implement a class within a Java source file. The ADT operations are public methods within the class, and the ADT data is represented as data fields that are typically private. You then implement the class's methods within an implementation file. The program that uses the class will be able to access the data only by using the ADT operations.

Summary

1. Data abstraction is a technique for controlling the interaction between a program and its data structures. It builds walls around a program's data structures, just as other aspects of modularity build walls around a program's algorithms. Such walls make programs easier to design, implement, read, and modify.

2. The specification of a set of data-management operations together with the data values upon which they operate define an abstract data type (ADT).

3. The formal mathematical study of ADTs uses systems of axioms to specify the behavior of ADT operations.

4. Only after you have fully defined an ADT should you think about how to implement it. The proper choice of a data structure to implement an ADT depends both on the details of the ADT operations and on the context in which you will use the operations.

5. Even after you have selected a data structure as an implementation for an ADT, the remainder of the program should not depend on your particular choice. That is, you should access the data structure by using only the ADT operations. Thus, you hide the implementation behind a wall of ADT operations. To enforce the wall within Java, you define the ADT as a class, thus hiding the ADT's implementation from the program that uses the ADT.

6. An object encapsulates both data and operations on that data. In Java, objects are instances of a class, which is a programmer-defined data type.

Cautions

1. After you design a class, try writing some code that uses your class before you commit to your design. Not only will you see whether your design works for the problem at hand, but you will also test your understanding of your own design and check the comments that document your specifications.

2. When you implement a class, you might discover problems with either your class design or your specifications. If these problems occur, change your design and

specifications, try using the class again, and continue implementing. These comments are consistent with the discussion of software life cycle in Chapter 1.

3. A program should not depend upon the particular implementations of its ADTs. By using a class to implement an ADT, you encapsulate the ADT's data and operations. In this way, you can hide implementation details from the program that uses the ADT. In particular, by making the class's data fields private, you can change the class's implementation without affecting the client.

4. By making a class's data fields private, you make it easier to locate errors in a program's logic. An ADT—and hence a class—is responsible for maintaining its data. If an error occurs, you look at the class's implementation for the source of the error. If the client could manipulate this data directly because the data was public, you would not know where to look for errors.

5. Variables that are local to a method's implementation should not be data fields of the class.

6. An array-based implementation of an ADT restricts the number of items that you can store. Chapter 5 will discuss a way to avoid this problem.

Self-Test Exercises

1. What is the significance of "wall" and "contract"? Why do these notions help you to become a better problem solver?

2. Write a pseudocode method *swap(aList, i, j)* that interchanges the items currently in positions *i* and *j* of a list. Define the method in terms of the operations of the ADT list, so that it is independent of any particular implementation of the list. Assume that the list, in fact, has items at positions *i* and *j*. What impact does this assumption have on your solution? (See Exercise 2.)

3. What grocery list results from the following sequence of ADT list operations?

```
aList.createList()
aList.add(0, butter)
aList.add(1, eggs)
aList.add(0, cereal)
aList.add(1, milk)
aList.add(0, coffee)
aList.add(1, bread)
```

4. Write specifications for a list whose insertion, deletion, and retrieval operations are at the beginning of the list.

5. In mathematics, a **set** is a group of distinct items. Specify an ADT *Set* that includes operations such as equality, subset, union, and intersection. Can you think of any other operations?

6. Write a pseudocode method that creates a sorted list *sortedList* from the list *aList* by using the operations of the ADTs list and sorted list.

7. The specifications of the ADTs list and sorted list do not mention the case in which two or more items have the same value. Are these specifications sufficient to cover this case, or must they be revised?

8. Specify operations that are a part of the ADT character string. Include typical operations such as length computation and concatenation (appending one string to another).

Exercises

1. Write an ADT for a library management system which stores the title (string), author (string), ISBN (string), list price (positive integers), edition (numbers), and publisher (string).

2. Implement the method `swap`, as described in Self-Test Exercise 2, but remove the assumption that the ith and j^{th} items in the list exist. Throw an exception `ListIndexOutOfBoundsException` if i or j is out of range.

3. Explain what, if any, the difference is between the algorithm of an application program and the algorithm of any abstract data type.

4. The section "The ADT List" describes the methods `displayList` and `replace`. As given in this chapter, these operations exist outside of the ADT; that is, they are not operations of the ADT list. Instead, their implementations are written in terms of the ADT list's operations.

   a. What is an advantage and a disadvantage of the way that `displayList` and `replace` are implemented?

   b. What is an advantage and a disadvantage of adding the operations `displayList` and `replace` to the ADT list?

5. The ADT `Bag` is a group of items, much like what you might have with a bag of groceries. Note that the items in the bag are in no particular order and that the bag may contain duplicate items. Specify operations to put an item in the bag, remove the last item put in the bag, remove a random item from the bag, check how many items are in the bag, check to see if the bag is full or empty, and completely empty the bag.

6. Design and implement an ADT that represents a credit card. The data of the ADT should include the customer name, the account number, the next due date, the reward points, and the account balance. The initialization operation should set the data to client-supplied values. Include operations for a credit card charge, a cash advance, a payment, the addition of interest to the balance, and the display of the statistics of the account.

7. Specify operations that are a part of the ADT fraction. Include typical operations such as addition, subtraction, and reduce (reduce fraction to lowest terms).

8. Suppose you want to write a program to play the card game War. Create an ADT for a card, a second ADT for a deck of cards, and a third ADT for a hand. What operations will you need on each of these ADTs to play the game of War? Note that in the game of War, you must be able to determine the higher card (Ace is high), and the winner wins all of the cards in that round and places those cards at the bottom of his or her hand. When there is a tie, a "war" is dealt with three cards face down, then the fourth face up, and again the winner wins all the cards. If there is a tie again, "war" is played again until the tie is broken. If a player runs out of cards in his or her hand, that last card is always played face up, even if it is in the middle of a "war."

9. Write pseudocode implementations of the operations of an ADT that represents a trapezoid. Include typical operations, such as setting and retrieving the dimensions of the trapezoid, finding the area and the perimeter of the trapezoid, and displaying the statistics of the trapezoid.

10. Write the ADT constructive specification for storing a student's name (string), address (string), phone number (integers), and test score (positive decimal integers).

11. Write a pseudocode method in terms of the ADT appointment book, described in the section "Designing an ADT," for each of the following tasks:

    a. Change the purpose of the appointment at a given date and time.

    b. Display all the appointments for a given date.

    Do you need to add operations to the ADT to perform these tasks?

12. Consider the ADT polynomial—in a single variable x—whose operations include the following:

```
+degree():integer {query}
// Returns the degree of a polynomial.
+getCoefficient(in power:integer):integer
// Returns the coefficient of the x^power term.
+changeCoefficient(in newCoef:integer,
                   in power:integer)
// Replaces the coefficient of the x^power term
// with newCoef.
```

For this problem, consider only polynomials whose exponents are nonnegative integers. For example,

$p = 4x^5 + 7x^3 - x^2 + 9$

The following examples demonstrate the ADT operations on this polynomial.

`p.degree()` is 5 (the highest power of a term with a nonzero coefficient)

`p.getCoefficient(3)` is 7 (the coefficient of the x^3 term)

`p.getCoefficient(4)` is 0 (the coefficient of a missing term is implicitly 0)

`p.changeCoefficient(-3, 7)` produces the polynomial

$p = -3x^7 + 4x^5 + 7x^3 - x^2 + 9$

Using only the ADT operations provided, write statements to perform the following tasks:

    a. Display the constant term (the coefficient for the x^0 term).

    b. Change each coefficient in the polynomial by multiplying them by 5.

    c. For a given polynomial such as $p = -3x^7 + 4x^5 + 7x^3 - x^2 + 9$, display the expression in the form $- 3x^7 + 4x^5 + 7x^3 - 1x^2 + 9$.

    d. Change the polynomial to its derivative—for example, $p = -3x^7 + 4x^5 + 7x^3 - x^2 + 9$ becomes $p = -21x^6 + 20x^4 + 21x^2 - 2x^1$.

13. Design and implement an ADT for a *Playing Card* and a *Deck* of playing cards. Each *Playing Card* must keep track of its suit (heart, diamond, club, spade), rank (2, 3, 4, 5, 6, 7, 8, 9, 10, Jack, Queen, King, Ace), and value (2 through 10 are face value, Jack is 11, Queen is 12, King is 13, and Ace is 14). The *Deck* of cards is all 52 cards—assume no Jokers will be used. The *Deck* ADT should initialize the 52 cards by suit (hearts, diamonds, clubs, spades) and within each suit as 2 through Ace. Operations for the Deck ADT should minimally include shuffling the deck and dealing a card from the deck.

14. Imagine an unknown implementation of an ADT sorted list of integers. This ADT organizes its items into ascending order. Suppose that you have just read N integers into a one-dimensional array of integers called `data`. Write some Java statements that use the operations of the ADT sorted list to sort the array into ascending order.

15. Use the axioms for the ADT list, as given in this chapter in the section "Axioms," to prove that the sequence of operations

    ```
    Insert A into position 2
    Insert B into position 3
    Insert C into position 2
    ```

    has the same effect on a nonempty list of characters as the sequence

    ```
    Insert B into position 2
    Insert A into position 2
    Insert C into position 2
    ```

16. Define a set of axioms for the ADT sorted list and use them to prove that the sorted list of characters, which is defined by the sequence of operations

    ```
    Create an empty sorted list
    Insert S
    Insert T
    Insert R
    Delete T
    ```

    is exactly the same as the sorted list defined by the sequence

    ```
    Create an empty sorted list
    Insert T
    Insert R
    Delete T
    Insert S
    ```

17. An organisation wishes to increase every employee's wages by 30%. Write a pseudo code algorithm for calculating this increase on every salary entered.

18. Write a pseudo code algorithm that builds a frequency array of data values in the range of 5 bits and then prints their histogram. The data has to be read from the command line.

Programming Problems

1. Design and implement an ADT that represents a triangle. The data for the ADT should include the three sides of the triangle but could also include the triangle's three angles. This data should be declared private in the class that implements the ADT.

   Include at least two initialization operations: One that provides default values for the ADT's data (in this case a 3, 4, 5 right triangle), and another that sets this data to client-supplied values. These operations are the class's constructors.

   The ADT also should include operations that look at the values of the ADT's data; change the values of the ADT's data; compute the triangle's area; and determine whether the triangle is a right triangle, an equilateral triangle, or an isosceles triangle.

2. Design and implement an ADT that represents the time of day. Represent the time as hours, minutes, and seconds on a 24-hour clock. The hours, minutes, and seconds are the private data fields of the class that implements the ADT.

   Include at least two initialization operations: One that provides a default value for the time (midnight, all fields zero), and another that sets the time to a client-supplied value. These operations are the class's constructors.

   Include operations that set the time, increase the time by 1 second, return the number of seconds between the time and a given time, increase the present time by a number of minutes, and two operations to display the time in 12-hour and 24-hour notations.

3. Design and implement an ADT that represents a calendar date. You can represent a date's month, day, and year as integers (for example, 5/15/2011). Include operations that advance the date by one day and provide two operations to display the date by using either numbers (05/16/2011) or words for the months (May 16, 2011). As an enhancement, include the name of the day.

4. Design and implement an ADT that represents a price in U.S. currency as dollars and cents. After you complete the implementation, write a client method that computes the change due a customer who pays *x* for an item whose price is *y*.

5. Define a class for an array-based implementation of the ADT sorted list. Consider a recursive implementation for *locateIndex*. Should *sortedAdd* and *sortedRemove* call *locateIndex*?

6. Write recursive array-based implementations of the insertion, deletion, and retrieval operations for the ADTs list and sorted list.

7. Implement the ADT bag that you specified in Exercise 5 by using only arrays and simple variables.

8. Implement the ADT character string that you specified in Self-Test Exercise 8.

9. Write a program to play the card game *War*. Use the Playing Card and Card Deck ADTs developed in Exercise 13. You will also need to create an ADT for the player's cards that keeps track of the cards in the player's hand.

   The game begins by evenly dividing the deck between two players and creating a hand for each player, which they hold face down. Then, each player shows a card. The player whose card has a higher point value (as provided by the Playing Card ADT) wins both cards and has them added to the "bottom" of his or her hand. If the two cards have the same point value, then it is "war": Each player plays three cards face down, with a fourth card face up. In this case, the player whose card has a higher point value wins all 10 cards (the 2 original cards in the tie, plus the 6 face down cards, and the last 2 face up cards), and again, adds them to the bottom of his or her hand. Should a player "run out" of cards in the midst of a "war," his or her last card is the face up card. If there is a tie in a "war," then another "war" is played, with the winner taking all of the cards and adding them to the bottom of his or her hand. Play continues as long as a player has cards in his or her hand—once they run out, the other player is declared the winner.

10. Implement the ADT appointment book, described in the section "Designing an ADT." Add operations as necessary. For example, you should add operations to read and write appointments.

11. a. Implement the ADT fraction that you specified in Exercise 7. Provide operations that read, write, add, subtract, multiply, and divide fractions. The results of all arithmetic operations should be in lowest terms, so include a private method *reduceToLowestTerms*. Exercise 23 in Chapter 3 will help you with the details of this method. (Should your read and write operations call *reduceToLowestTerms*?) To simplify the determination of a fraction's sign, you should maintain the denominator of the fraction as a positive value, and keep the sign on the numerator.

    b. Specify and implement an ADT for mixed numbers, each of which contains an integer portion and a fractional portion in lowest terms. Assume the existence of the ADT fraction (see part a). Provide operations that read, write, add, subtract, multiply, and divide mixed numbers. The results of all arithmetic operations should have fractional portions that are in lowest terms. Also include an operation that converts a fraction to a mixed number.

12. Implement the recipe database as described in the section "Designing an ADT" and, in doing so, also implement the ADTs recipe and measurement. A recipe has a title, a list of ingredients with measurements, and a list of directions. Add operations as necessary. For example, you should add operations to the ADT recipe database to read, write, and scale recipes.

13. Implement a program based on the UML specification in Programming Problem 1 of Chapter 2.

14. In mathematics, a set is a group of distinct items. Design and implement (using an array) an ADT *Set* that supports the following operations:

```
+createSet()
// creates an empty set

+isEmpty():boolean {query}
// Determines whether a set is empty

+size():integer {query}
// Returns the number of elements in this set (its
// cardinality)

+add(in item:integer)
// Adds the specified element to this set if it is not already
// present

+contains(in item:integer):boolean {query}
```

```
// Determines if this set contains the specified item

+union(in other:Set):Set
// Creates a new set containing all of the elements of this
// set and the other set (no duplicates) and returns the
// resulting set

+intersection(in other:Set):Set
// Creates a new set of elements that appear in both this set
// and the other set and returns the resulting set

+removeAll()
// Removes all of the items in the set
```

CHAPTER 5

Linked Lists

This chapter reviews Java references and introduces you to the data structure linked list. You will see algorithms for fundamental linked list operations such as insertion and deletion. The chapter also describes several variations of the basic linked list. As you will see, you can use a linked list and its variations when implementing many of the ADTs that appear throughout the remainder of this book. The material in this chapter is thus essential to much of the presentation in the following chapters.

5.1 Preliminaries

The ADT list, as described in the previous chapter, has operations to insert, delete, and retrieve items, given their positions within the list. A close examination of the array-based implementation of the ADT list reveals that an array is not always the best data structure to use to maintain a collection of data. An array has a **fixed size**—at least in most commonly used programming languages—but the ADT list can have an arbitrary length. Thus, in the strict sense, you cannot use an array to implement a list because it is certainly possible for the number of items in the list to exceed the fixed size of the array. When developing implementations for ADTs, you often are confronted with this fixed-size problem. In many contexts, you must reject an implementation that has a fixed size in favor of one that can grow dynamically.

In addition, although the most intuitive means of imposing an order on data is to sequence it physically, this approach has its disadvantages. In a physical ordering, the successor of an item x is the next data item in sequence after x, that is, the item "to the right" of x. An array orders its items physically and, as you saw in the previous chapter, when you use an array to implement a list, you must shift data when you insert or delete an item at a specified position. Shifting data can be a time-consuming process that you should avoid, if possible. What alternatives to shifting data are available?

To get a conceptual notion of a list implementation that does not involve shifting, consider Figure 5-1. This figure should help free you from the notion that the only way to maintain a given order of data is to store the data in that order. In these diagrams, each item of the list is actually *linked to* the next item. Thus, if you know where an item is, you can determine its successor, which can be anywhere physically. This flexibility not only allows you to insert and delete data items without shifting data, but it also allows you to increase the size of the list easily. If you need to insert a new item, you simply find its place in the list and set two **links.** Similarly, to delete an item, you find the item and change a link to bypass the item.

An item in a linked list references its successor

Because the items in this data structure are *linked* to one another, it is called a **linked list.** As you will see shortly, *a linked list is able to grow as needed*, whereas an array can hold only a fixed number of data items. In many applications, this flexibility gives a linked list a significant advantage.

Before we examine linked lists and their use in the implementation of an ADT, we will examine how Java references can be used to implement a linked list. Like many programming languages, Java allows one object to reference another, and you can use this ability to build a linked list. The next section reviews the mechanics of these references.

Object References

A reference contains the address of an object

When you declare a variable that refers to an object of a given class, you are creating a reference to the object. Note that an object of that class does not come into existence until you apply the *new* operator. A **reference variable,** or simply a **reference,** contains the location, or **address** in memory, of an object.

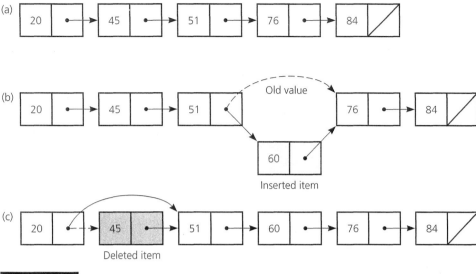

FIGURE 5-1

(a) A linked list of integers; (b) insertion; (c) deletion

By using a reference to a particular object, you can locate the object and, for example, access the object's public members.

Let's look at an example using the class *java.lang.Integer* to help us visualize this scenario:

```
Integer intRef;
intRef = new Integer(5);
```

intRef references the newly instantiated ***Integer*** object

The first line declares a reference variable *intRef* that can be used to locate an *Integer* object. The second line actually instantiates an *Integer* object and assigns its location to *intRef*. Figure 5-2 illustrates that there are now two separate entities in our program: an *Integer* object and a reference variable *intRef* that provides the location of that *Integer* object.

When you declare a reference variable as a data field within a class but do not instantiate an object for it in a constructor, it is initialized to *null*. You can use this constant *null* as the value of a reference to any type of object. This use indicates that the reference variable does not currently reference any object. For example, if *intRef* is declared as a data field, and you attempt to use it before you instantiate an *Integer* object for it, the exception *java.lang.NullPointerException* will be thrown at runtime. This exception indicates that you attempted to access an object by using a reference variable that contains a *null* value.

A reference variable as a data field of a class has the default value ***null***

When you declare a reference variable to be local to a method, no default value is provided. For example, let *p* be declared as a reference to an *Integer* object. If you attempt to use *p* to access an object before *p* is initialized, the compiler will give you the error message "*variable p may not have been initialized.*"

A local reference variable has no default value

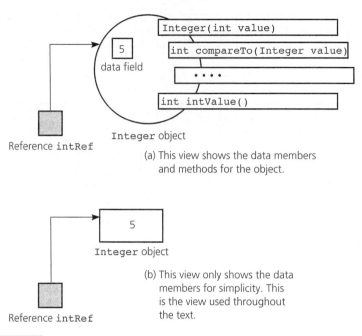

Reference intRef

Integer object

(a) This view shows the data members
and methods for the object.

Integer object

Reference intRef

(b) This view only shows the data
members for simplicity. This
is the view used throughout
the text.

FIGURE 5-2

A reference to an *Integer* object

 When one reference variable is assigned to another reference variable, both references then refer to the same object. For example,

```
Integer p, q;
p = new Integer(6);
q = p;
```

Figure 5-3d illustrates the result of this assignment. Now the *Integer* object has two references to it, *p* and *q*. The effect of the assignment operator is to cause the reference variable on the left side of the assignment to reference the same object as referenced by the right side of the assignment operator. Alternatively, you could let *q* reference a new object, as Figure 5-3e shows.

 Suppose that you no longer need the value in a reference variable. That is, you do not want the reference variable to locate any particular object. You can explicitly assign the constant value *null*, discussed earlier, to a reference variable to indicate that it no longer references any object. When you remove all references to an object, the system marks the object for garbage collection, as shown in Figures 5-3c and 5-3f. The Java runtime environment will periodically run a method that returns the memory allocated to the marked objects back to the system for future use. In other programming languages, such as C++, the programmer must explicitly deallocate memory using special language constructs.

The system marks
unreferenced
objects for garbage
collection

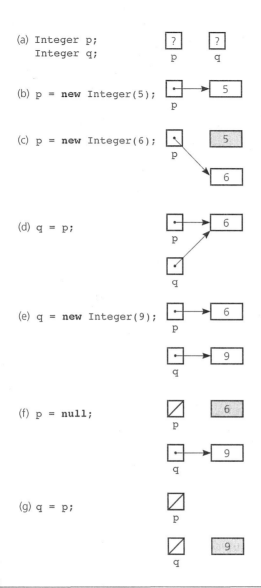

FIGURE 5-3

(a) Declaring reference variables; (b) allocating an object; (c) allocating another object, with the dereferenced object marked for garbage collection; (d) assigning a reference; (e) allocating an object; (f) assigning *null* to a reference variable; (g) assigning a reference with a *null* value

When you declare an array of objects and apply the *new* operator, an array of references is actually created, not an array of objects. For example,

```
Integer[] scores = new Integer[30];
```

An array of objects is actually an array of references to the objects

creates an array of 30 references for *Integer* objects. You must instantiate actual *Integer* objects for each of the array references. For example, you might instantiate objects for the array just created as follows:

```
scores[0] = new Integer(7);
scores[1] = new Integer(9); // and so on ...
```

Equality operators compare values of reference variables, not the objects that they reference

When you use the equality operators (== and !=), you are actually comparing the values of the reference variables, not the objects that they reference. Suppose that you have the following class definition:

```
public class MyNumber {
  private int num;

  public MyNumber(int n) {
    num = n;
  } // end constructor

  public String toString() {
    return "My number is " + num;
  } // end toString
} // end class MyNumber
```

and you declare the following:

```
MyNumber x = new MyNumber(9);
MyNumber y = new MyNumber(9);
MyNumber z = x;
```

Although objects *x* and *y* contain the same data, the == operator returns *false*, since *x* and *y* refer to different objects. The expression *x* == *z* is *true* because the assignment statement *z* = *x* causes *z* to refer to the same object that *x* references. If you need to be able to compare objects field by field, you must redefine the *equals* method for the class, as discussed in Chapter 1.

When you pass an object to a method as an argument, the reference to the object is copied to the method's formal parameter

Parameter passing in Java can also be discussed in terms of reference variables. When a method is called and has parameters that are objects, the reference value of the actual argument is copied to a formal parameter reference variable. During the execution of the method, the object is accessed through the formal parameter reference variable. This provides the same result as if the original reference was used. Upon completion of the method, the references stored in these formal parameters are discarded, although the objects that the parameters reference may be retained.

This method of parameter passing helps to explain why the use of the *new* operator with a formal parameter in a method can produce unexpected results. For example, suppose you have the following method *changeNumber*, which uses the *MyNumber* class:

```
public void changeNumber(MyNumber n) {
  n = new MyNumber(5);
} // end changeNumber
```

and the following Java statements:

```
MyNumber x = new MyNumber(9);
changeNumber(x); // attempts to assign 5 to x
System.out.println(x);
```

The output is "My number is 9". Figure 5-4 demonstrates why this is the case. When the *changeNumber* method is invoked, the reference to object *x* is copied to the formal parameter reference *n* of *changeNumber*. During the execution of *changeNumber*, a new object is created for *n* to reference. But when the *change-Number* method completes execution, the reference variable *n* is discarded. This causes the newly created object containing 5 to be marked for garbage collection. The value of the reference variable *x* remains unchanged; it still references the same object (containing 9) that it did before the *changeNumber* method was executed.

Note that ADT implementations and data structures that use Java references are said to be **reference based.**

KEY CONCEPTS

Java Reference Variables

1. The declaration

```
Integer intRef;
```

statically allocates a reference variable *intRef* whose value is *null*. When a reference variable contains *null*, it does not reference anything.

2. *intRef* can reference an *Integer* object. The statement

```
intRef = new Integer(5);
```

dynamically allocates an *Integer* object referenced by *intRef*. (However, see item 3 on this list.)

3. If, for some reason, *new* cannot instantiate an object of the class represented, it may throw a *java.lang.InstantiationException* or a *java.lang.IllegalAccessException*. Thus, you can place the following statement within a *try* block to test whether memory was successfully allocated:

```
intRef = new Integer(5);
```

4. When the last reference to an object is removed, the object is marked for garbage collection.

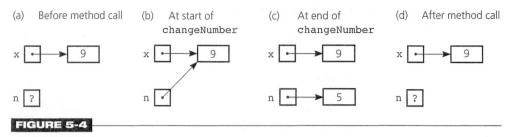

FIGURE 5-4

The value of a parameter does not affect the argument's value

Resizeable Arrays

When you declare an array in Java by using statements such as

The number of references in a Java array is of a fixed size

```
final int MAX_SIZE = 50;
double[] myArray = new double[MAX_SIZE];
```

the Java runtime environment reserves a specific number—*MAX_SIZE*, in this case—of references for the array. Once the array has been instantiated, it has a fixed size for the remainder of its lifetime. We have already discussed the problem this fixed-size data structure causes when your program has more than *MAX_SIZE* items to place into the array.

You can create the illusion of a resizeable array—an array that grows and shrinks as the program executes—by using an allocate and copy strategy with fixed-size arrays. If the array that you are currently using in the program reaches its capacity, you allocate a larger array and copy the references stored in the original array to the larger array. How much larger should the new array be? The increment size can be a fixed number of elements or a multiple of the current array size. The following statements demonstrate how you could accomplish this task for an array *myArray*:

Allocate a larger array

Copy the original array to the new larger array

```
if (capacityIncrement == 0) {
  capacity *= 2;
}
else {
  capacity += capacityIncrement;
}
// now create a new array using the updated
// capacity value
double [] newArray = new double[capacity];
// copy the contents of the original array
// to the new array
for (int i = 0; i < myArray.length; i++) {
  newArray[i] = myArray[i];
} // end for
```

```
// now change the reference to the original array
// to the new array
myArray = newArray;
```

In this example, `capacity` and `capacityIncrement` represent the capacity of the array and the size of the increment, respectively. Once you exceed the capacity of `myArray`, you allocate a larger array `newArray` according to the value of `capacityIncrement`. Note that if the `capacityIncrement` is zero, the array capacity doubles instead of increasing by a fixed amount. You must copy the values from the original array to the new array and then change the original array reference to reference the new array.

The classes `java.util.Vector` and `java.util.ArrayList` use a similar technique to implement a growable array of objects. The underlying implementation of `java.util.Vector` uses a fixed array of size `capacity` and has a `capacityIncrement` that you can change to suit your needs. Exercise 20 asks you to explore the `java.util.Vector` class to determine when resizing the underlying array will occur.

Subsequent discussion in this book will refer to both fixed-sized and resizeable arrays. Our array-based ADT implementations will use fixed-sized arrays for simplicity. The programming problems will ask you to create array-based implementations that use resizeable arrays.

Reference-Based Linked Lists

A linked list, such as the one in Figure 5-1, contains components that are linked to one another. Each component—usually called a **node**—contains both data and a "link" to the next item. Typically, such links are Java reference variables; another possibility is mentioned at the end of this section. Although you have seen most of the mechanics of references, using references to implement a linked list is probably not yet completely clear to you. Consider now how you can set up such a linked list.

Each node of the list can be implemented as an object. For example, if you want to create a linked list of integers, you could use the following class definition, as Figure 5-5 illustrates:

A node in a linked list is an object

A node definition that is not desirable because its data fields are public

```
public class IntegerNode {
  public int item;
  public IntegerNode next;
} // end class IntegerNode
```

However, this type of definition violates our rule that data fields must be declared private, especially in public classes. But what if the `IntegerNode` class is not declared `public`, and is only used as a building block in the actual list implementation? In Java, classes can be declared as public using the access modifier `public`, or as package-private if no access modifier is used. Hence, it is possible to make a class available only for other classes within the same package by declaring it package-private. This effectively prevents the user of the package from gaining access to the underlying implementation. Should the

item   next

FIGURE 5-5

A node

underlying implementation be changed, no code outside of the package will be affected. So, we could rewrite the *IntegerNode* class as follows:

A node for a linked list of integers

```
package IntegerList;
class IntegerNode {
   int item;
   IntegerNode next;
} // end class IntegerNode
```

and use this class as follows:

Defining a reference to a node

```
IntegerNode n1 = new IntegerNode();
IntegerNode n2 = new IntegerNode();
n1.item = 5; // set item in first node
n2.item = 9; // set item in second node
n1.next = n2; // link the nodes
```

This scenario is depicted in Figure 5-6. The *item* field is initialized for each node. The *next* field for the node *n1* is then set to *n2*, which in effect links the nodes by making the first node reference the second. Exercise 8 will ask you to explore the declaration of a node class with private data fields.

We could improve this class by adding constructors, as follows:

```
package IntegerList;
class IntegerNode {
   int item;
   IntegerNode next;
```

Constructors

```
   IntegerNode(int newItem) {
      item = newItem;
      next = null;
   } // end constructor
```

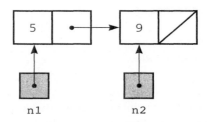

n1   n2

FIGURE 5-6

The result of linking two instances of *IntegerNode*

```
IntegerNode(int newItem, IntegerNode nextNode) {
    item = newItem;
    next = nextNode;
  } // end constructor
}    // end class IntegerNode
```

This definition of a node restricts the data to a single integer field. Since we would like to have this class be as reusable as possible, it would be better to change the data field to be of type *Object*. Recall that every class in Java is ultimately derived from the class *Object* through inheritance. This means that any class created in Java could use this node definition for storing objects. Let's first examine the revised class, using objects for data:

```
package List;

class Node {
  Object item;
  Node next;

  Node(Object newItem) {
    item = newItem;
    next = null;
  } // end constructor

  Node(Object newItem, Node nextNode) {
    item = newItem;
    next = nextNode;
  } // end constructor
} // end class Node
```

A node for a linked list of objects

You can use this class as follows:

```
Node n = new Node(new Integer(6));
Node first = new Node(new Integer(9), n);
```

Figure 5-7 illustrates this scenario. The constructors are used to initialize the data field and a link value that is either *null* or provided as an argument. Although the data portion of each node in a linked list can reference an instance of any class, the figure illustrates data items that are instances of the class *java.lang.Integer*.

To complete our general description of the linked list, we must consider two other issues. First, what is the value of the data field *next* in the last node in the list? By setting this field to *null*, you can easily detect when you are at the end of the linked list.

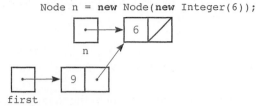

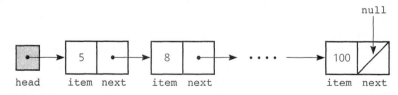

Node n = **new** Node(**new** Integer(6));

Node first = **new** Node(**new** Integer(9), n);

FIGURE 5-7

Using the **Node** constructor to initialize a data field and a link value

Second, nothing so far references the beginning of the linked list. If you cannot get to the beginning of the list, you cannot get to the second node in the list, and if you cannot get to the second node in the list, you cannot get to the third node in the list, and so on. The solution is to have an additional reference variable whose sole purpose is to locate the first node in the linked list. Such a variable is often called **head.**

The head of a linked list references the list's first node

Observe in Figure 5-8 that the reference variable *head* is different from the other reference variables in the diagram in that it is not within one of the nodes. Rather, it is a simple reference variable that is external to the linked list, whereas the *next* data fields are internal reference variables within the nodes of the list. The variable *head* simply enables you to access the list's beginning. Also, note that *head* always exists, even at times when there are no nodes in the linked list. The statement

Node head = **null**;

creates the variable *head*, whose value is initially *null*. This indicates that *head* does not reference anything, and therefore that this list is empty.

It is a common mistake to think that before you can assign *head* a value, you must execute the statement *head = new Node()*. This misconception is rooted in the belief that the variable *head* does not exist unless you create a new node. This is not at all true; *head* is a reference variable waiting to be

FIGURE 5-8

A *head* reference to a linked list

assigned a value. Thus, for example, you can assign *null* to *head* without first using *new*. In fact, the sequence

```
head = new Node();  // Don't really need to use new here
head = null;   // since we lose the new Node object here
```

A common misconception

destroys the contents of the only reference—*head*—to the newly created node, as Figure 5-9 illustrates. Thus, you have needlessly created a new node and then made it inaccessible. Remember that when you remove the last reference from a node, the system marks it for garbage collection.

As was mentioned earlier, you do not need references to implement a linked list. Programming Problem 10 at the end of this chapter discusses an implementation that uses an array to represent the items in a linked list. Although sometimes useful, such implementations are unusual.

5.2 Programming with Linked Lists

The previous section illustrated how you can use reference variables to implement a linked list. This section begins by developing algorithms for displaying the data portions of such a linked list and for inserting items into and deleting items from a linked list. These linked list operations are the basis of many of the data structures that appear throughout the remainder of the book. Thus, the material in this section is essential to much of the discussion in the following chapters.

Displaying the Contents of a Linked List

Suppose now that you have a linked list, as was pictured in Figure 5-8, and that you want to display the data in the list. A high-level pseudocode solution is

```
Let a variable curr reference the first node in
    the linked list
while (the curr reference is not null) {
  Display the data portion of the current node
  Set the curr reference to the next field of the
     current node
}  // end while
```

```
head = new Node(new Integer(5));   head = null;
```

FIGURE 5-9

A lost node

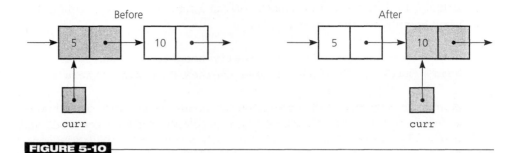

FIGURE 5-10

The effect of the assignment **curr = curr.next**

This solution requires that you keep track of the current position within the linked list. Thus, you need a reference variable *curr* that references the current node. Initially, *curr* must reference the first node. Since *head* references the first node, simply copy *head* into *curr* by writing

```
Node curr = head;
```

To display the data portion of the current node, you can use the statement[1]

```
System.out.println(curr.item);
```

Finally, to advance the current position to the next node, you write

```
curr = curr.next;
```

    Figure 5-10 illustrates this action. If the previous assignment statement is not clear, consider

```
temp = curr.next;
curr = temp;
```

and then convince yourself that the intermediate variable *temp* is not necessary.
    These ideas lead to the following loop in Java:

```
// Display the data in a linked list that head
// references.
// Loop invariant: curr references the next node to be
// displayed
```

---

1. See Chapter 1 for a discussion of *System.out.println* with object parameters.

```
for (Node curr = head; curr != null; curr = curr.next) {
   System.out.println(curr.item);
} // end for
```

The variable *curr* references each node in a nonempty linked list during the course of the *for* loop's execution, and so the data portion of each node is displayed. After the last node is displayed, *curr* becomes *null* and the *for* loop terminates. When the list is empty—that is, when *head* is *null*—the *for* loop is correctly skipped.

A common error in the *for* statement is to compare *curr.next* instead of *curr* with *null*. When *curr* references the last node of a nonempty linked list, *curr.next* is *null*, and so the *for* loop would terminate before displaying the data in the last node. In addition, when the list is empty—that is, when *head* and therefore *curr* are *null*—*curr.next* will throw a *NullPointerException*. Such references are incorrect and should be avoided.

Displaying a linked list is an example of a common operation, **list traversal.** A traversal sequentially **visits** each node in the list until it reaches the end of the list. Our example displays the data portion of each node when it visits the node. Later in this book, you will see that you can do other useful things to a node during a visit.

> A traverse operation visits each node in the linked list

Displaying a linked list does not alter it; you will now see operations that modify a linked list by deleting and inserting nodes. These operations assume that the linked list has already been created. Ultimately, you will see how to build a linked list by inserting nodes into an initially empty list.

Deleting a Specified Node from a Linked List

So that you can focus on how to delete a particular node from a linked list, assume that the linked list shown in Figure 5-11 already exists. Notice that, in addition to *head*, the diagram includes two external reference variables, *curr* and *prev*. The task is to delete the node that *curr* references. As you soon will see, you also need *prev* to complete the deletion. For the moment, do not worry about how to establish *curr* and *prev*.

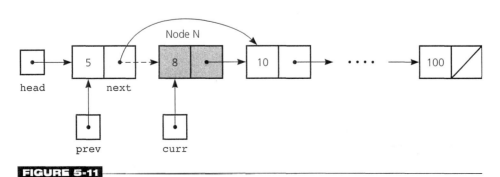

FIGURE 5-11

Deleting a node from a linked list

As Figure 5-11 indicates, you can delete a node *N,* which `curr` references, by altering the value of the reference *next* in the node that precedes *N.* You need to set this data field to reference the node that follows *N,* thus bypassing *N* on the chain. (The dashed line indicates the old reference value.) Notice that this reference change does not directly affect node *N.* Since `curr` still references node *N,* the node remains in existence, and it references the same node that it referenced before the deletion. However, the node has effectively been deleted from the linked list. For example, the method `display-List` from the previous section would not display the contents of node *N.* If `curr` is the only reference to node *N,* when we change `curr` to reference another node or set it equal to `null`, node *N* is marked for garbage collection.

To accomplish this deletion, notice first that if only the reference `curr` points to *N,* you would have no direct way to access the node that precedes *N.* After all, you cannot follow the links in the list backward. However, notice that the reference variable *prev* in Figure 5-11 references the node that precedes *N* and makes it possible for you to alter that node's *next* data field. Doing so deletes node *N* from the linked list. The following assignment statement is all that you need to delete the node that `curr` references:

Deleting an interior node

```
prev.next = curr.next;
```

A question comes to mind at this point:

■ Does the previous method work for any node *N,* regardless of where in the linked list it appears?

No, the method does not work if the node to be deleted is the *first* node in the list, because it certainly does not make sense to assert that *prev* references the node that precedes this node! Thus, *deletion of the first node in a linked list is a special case,* as Figure 5-12 depicts. In this case, `curr` references the first node and *prev* is `null`.

When you delete the first node of the list, you must change the value of *head* to reflect the fact that, after the deletion, the list has a new first node.

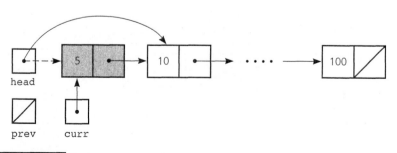

FIGURE 5-12

Deleting the first node

That is, the node that was second prior to the deletion is now first. You make this change to *head* by using the assignment statement

```
head = head.next;
```

Deleting the first node is a special case

As was the case for the deletion of an interior node, the *head* reference now bypasses the old first node. Notice also that if the node to be deleted is the *only* node in the list—and thus it is both the first node and the last node—the previous assignment statement assigns the value *null* to the variable *head*. Recall that the value *null* in *head* indicates an empty list, and so this assignment statement handles the deletion of the only node in a list correctly.

If the node *N* is no longer needed, you should change the *next* data field of the node *N* to *null* and also the value of *curr* to *null*, as the following statements show:

```
curr.next = null;
curr = null;
```

This serves two purposes. First, the reference variables *curr* and *next* (in node *N*) can't be inadvertently followed, leading to subtle errors later in the program. Second, the system can now use this returned memory and possibly even reallocate it to your program as a result of the *new* operator.

So far, we have deleted the node *N* that *curr* references, given a reference variable *prev* to the node that precedes *N*. However, another question remains:

- How did the variables *curr* and *prev* come to reference the appropriate nodes?

To answer this question, consider the context in which you might expect to delete a node. In one common situation, you need to delete a node that you specify by position. Such is the case if you use a linked list to implement an ADT list. In another situation, you need to delete a node that contains a particular data value. Such is the case if you use a linked list to implement an ADT sorted list. In both of these situations, you do not pass the values of *curr* and *prev* to the deletion method, but instead the method establishes these values as its first step by searching the linked list for the node *N* that either is at a specified position or contains the data value to be deleted. Once the method finds the node *N*—and the node that precedes *N*—the deletion of *N* proceeds as described previously. The details of determining *curr* and *prev* for deletion are actually the same as for insertion, and they appear in the next section.

To summarize, the deletion process has three high-level steps:

Three steps to delete a node from a linked list

1. Locate the node that you want to delete.

2. Disconnect this node from the linked list by changing references.

3. Return the node to the system.

Later in this chapter, we will incorporate this deletion process into the implementation of the ADT list.

Inserting a Node into a Specified Position of a Linked List

Figure 5-13 illustrates the technique of inserting a new node into a specified position of a linked list. You insert the new node, which the reference variable *newNode* references, between the two nodes that *prev* and *curr* reference. As the diagram suggests, you can accomplish the insertion by using the following pair of assignment statements:

Inserting a node between nodes

```
newNode.next = curr;
prev.next = newNode;
```

The following two questions are analogous to those previously asked about the deletion of a node:

- How did the variables *newNode*, *curr*, and *prev* come to reference the appropriate nodes?

- Does the method work for inserting a node into any position of a linked list?

The answer to the first question, like the answer to the analogous question for deletion, is found by considering the context in which you will use the insertion operation. You establish the values of *curr* and *prev* by traversing the linked list until you find the proper position for the new item.

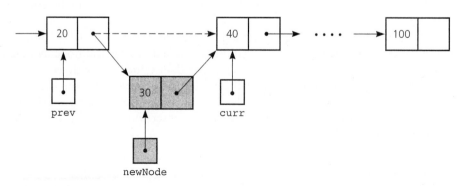

FIGURE 5-13

Inserting a new node into a linked list

You then use the *new* operator to create a new node that references the item as follows:

```
newNode = new Node(item);
```

Creating a node for the new item

You can now insert the node into the list, as was just described.

The answer to the second question is that *insertion, like deletion, must account for special cases.* First, consider the insertion of a node at the beginning of the linked list, as shown in Figure 5-14. You must make *head* reference the new node, and the new node must reference the node that had been at the beginning of the list. You accomplish this by using these statements:

```
newNode.next = head;
head = newNode;
```

Inserting a node at the beginning of a linked list

Observe that if the list is empty before the insertion, *head* is *null*, so the *next* reference of the new item is set to *null*. This step is correct because the new item is the last item—as well as the first item—on the list.

Figure 5-15 shows the insertion of a new node at the end of a linked list. This insertion is potentially a special case because the intention of the pair of assignment statements

```
newNode.next = curr;
prev.next = newNode;
```

If **curr** is **null**, inserting at the end of a linked list is not a special case

is to insert the new node *between* the node that *curr* references and the node that *prev* references. If you are to insert the new node at the end of the list, what node should *curr* reference? In this situation, it makes sense to view the value of *curr* as *null* because, as you traverse the list, *curr* becomes *null* as it moves past the end of the list. Observe that if *curr* has the value *null* and

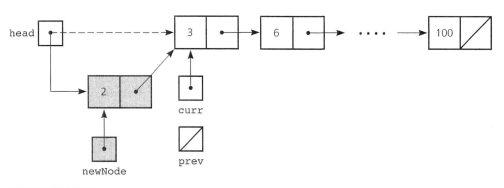

FIGURE 5-14

Inserting at the beginning of a linked list

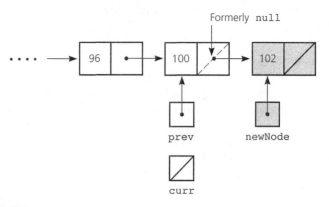

Inserting at the end of a linked list

prev references the last node on the list, the previous pair of assignment statements will indeed insert the new node at the end of the list. Thus, insertion at the end of a linked list is not a special case.

To summarize, the insertion process requires three high-level steps:

Three steps to insert a new node into a linked list

1. Determine the point of insertion.

2. Create a new node and store the new data in it.

3. Connect the new node to the linked list by changing references.

Determining *curr* and *prev*.   Let us now examine in more detail how to determine the references *curr* and *prev* for the insertion operation just described. As was mentioned, this determination depends on the context in which you will insert a node. As an example, consider a linked list of integers that are sorted into ascending order using the *IntegerNode* class in the previous section. To simplify the discussion, assume that the integers are distinct; that is, no duplicates are present in the list.

To determine the point at which the value *newValue* should be inserted into a sorted linked list, you must traverse the list from its beginning until you find the appropriate place for *newValue*. This appropriate place is just before the node that contains the first data item greater than *newValue*. You know that you will need a reference *curr* to the node that is to follow the new node; that is, *curr* references the node that contains the first data item greater than *newValue*. You also need a reference *prev* to the node that is to precede the new node; that is, *prev* references the node that contains the last data item smaller than *newValue*. Thus, as you traverse the linked list, you keep both a current reference *curr* and a *trailing* reference *prev*. When you reach the node that contains the first value larger than *newValue*, the trailing reference *prev* references the previous node. At this time, you can insert the new node between the two nodes that *prev* and *curr* reference, as was described earlier.

A first attempt at some pseudocode follows:

A first attempt at a solution

```
// determine the point of insertion into a sorted
// linked list
// initialize prev and curr to start the traversal
// from the beginning of the list
prev = null
curr = head

// advance prev and curr as long as
// newValue > the current data item
// Loop invariant: newValue > data items in all
// nodes at and before the node that prev references
while (newValue > curr.item) { // causes a problem!
  prev = curr
  curr = curr.next
}  // end while
```

Unfortunately, the *while* loop causes a problem when the new value is greater than all the values in the list, that is, when the insertion will be at the end of the linked list (or when the linked list is empty). Eventually, the *while* statement compares *newValue* to the value in the last node. During that execution of the loop, *curr* is assigned the value *null*. After this iteration, *newValue* is again compared to *curr.item*, which, when *curr* is *null*, will throw the exception *NullPointerException*.

To solve this problem, you need another test in the termination condition of the *while* statement so that the loop exits when *curr* becomes *null*. Thus, you replace the *while* statement with

```
while (curr != null && newValue > curr.item)
```

The revised pseudocode is

The correct solution

```
// determine the point of insertion into a sorted
// linked list
// initialize prev and curr to start the traversal
// from the beginning of the list
prev = null
curr = head

// advance prev and curr as long as newValue > the
// current data item; do not go beyond end of list
// Loop invariant: newValue > data items in all
// nodes at and before the node that prev references
while (curr != null && newValue > curr.item) {
  prev = curr
  curr = curr.next
}  // end while
```

Notice how the `while` statement also solves the problem of inserting a node at the end of the linked list. In the case where `newValue` is greater than all the values in the list, `prev` references the last node in the list and `curr` becomes `null`, thus terminating the `while` loop. (See Figure 5-16.) Therefore, as you saw earlier, you can insert the new node at the end of the list by using the standard pair of assignment statements

Insertion at the end of a linked list is not a special case

```
newNode.next = curr;
prev.next = newNode;
```

Now consider the insertion of a node at the beginning of the linked list. This situation arises when the value to be inserted is *smaller* than all the values currently in the list. In this case, the `while` loop in the previous pseudocode is never entered, so `prev` and `curr` maintain their original values, as Figure 5-17 illustrates. In particular, `prev` maintains its original value of `null`. This is the only situation in which the value of `prev` is equal to `null` after execution of the `while` loop ends. Thus, you can detect an insertion at the beginning of the list by comparing `prev` to `null`.

When _prev_ is _null_, insertion will be at the beginning of the linked list

Observe that the solution also correctly handles insertion into an empty linked list as an insertion at the beginning of the list. When the list is empty, the statement `curr = head` assigns `curr` an initial value of `null`, and thus the `while` loop is never entered. Therefore, `prev` maintains its original value of `null`, indicating an insertion at the beginning of the list.

Insertion into an empty linked list is really an insertion at the beginning of the list

A little thought should convince you that the solution that determines the point of insertion also works for deletion. If you want to delete a given integer from a linked list of sorted integers, you obviously want to traverse the list until you find the node that contains the value sought. The previous pseudocode will do just that: `curr` will reference the desired node and `prev` either will reference the preceding node or, if the desired node is first on the list, will be `null`, as shown in Figure 5-17.

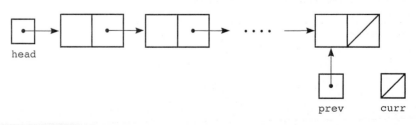

head

prev   curr

FIGURE 5-16

When *prev* references the last node and *curr* is *null*, insertion will be at the end of the linked list

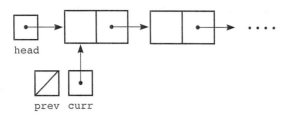

FIGURE 5-17

When **prev** is **null** and **curr** references the first node, insertion or deletion will be at the beginning of the linked list

The following Java statements implement the previous pseudocode:

```
// determine the point of insertion or deletion
// for a sorted linked list
// Loop invariant: newValue > data items in all
// nodes at and before the node that prev references
for ( prev = null, curr = head;
     (curr != null) && (newValue > curr.item);
     prev = curr, curr = curr.next ) {
  // no statements in loop body
} // end for
```

A Java solution for the point of insertion or deletion

Recall that the *&&* (*and*) operator in Java does not evaluate its second operand if its first operand is *false*. Thus, when *curr* becomes *null*, the loop exits without attempting to evaluate *curr.item*. It is, therefore, essential that *curr != null* be first in the logical expression.

Notice that this implementation relies on the ability to compare one value to another by using the built-in greater than (>) operation for the primitive data type *int*. Suppose instead that the items in the list are of data type *Object*. As mentioned in Chapter 4, you can compare objects if they implement the interface *java.lang.Comparable* and have an implementation of the method *compareTo*.

You can then use the following code to find the location of the item *newValue* of type *Comparable* within the list:

```
// determine the point of insertion or deletion
// for a sorted linked list of objects
// Loop invariant: newValue > data items (using
// compareTo method) in all nodes at and before
// the node that prev references
for ( prev = null, curr = head;
     (curr != null ) &&
     (newValue.compareTo(curr.item) > 0);
     prev = curr, curr = curr.next ) {
} // end for
```

Determining the point of insertion or deletion for a sorted linked list of objects

Use **compareTo** to compare objects

The compareTo method defines the criteria to decide when objects are equal or when one object is less than or greater than another. This in turn can be used to create a sorted list of objects based upon the criteria defined by the new comparison method.

Determining the values of *curr* and *prev* is simpler when you insert or delete a node by position instead of by its value. This determination is necessary when you use a linked list to implement the ADT list, as you will see next.

A Reference-Based Implementation of the ADT List

This section considers how you can use Java references instead of an array to implement the ADT list. Unlike the array-based implementation, a reference-based implementation does not shift items during insertion and deletion operations. It also does not impose a fixed maximum length on the list—except, of course, as imposed by the storage limits of the system.

As in Chapter 4, and as we will do in the rest of the book, we will implement this ADT as a Java class. For the array-based implementation, we wrote declarations for public methods corresponding to the operation of the ADT list. These declarations will appear unchanged in the reference-based implementation.

You need to represent the items in the ADT list and its length. Figure 5-18 indicates one possible way to represent this data by using references. The variable *head* references a linked list of the items in the ADT list, where the first node in the linked list contains the first item in the ADT list and so on. The variable *numItems* is an integer that is the current number of items in the list. Both *head* and *numItems* will be private data fields of our class.

head and **numItems** are private data fields

As you saw previously, you use two references—*curr* and *prev*—to manipulate a linked list. These reference variables will be local to the methods that need them; they are not appropriate data fields of the class.

curr and **prev** should not be data fields of the class

Recall that the ADT list operations for insertion, deletion, and retrieval specify the position number i of the relevant item. Assume that position number 0 is the first node in the list, referenced by *head*. In an attempt to obtain values for *curr* and *prev* from i, suppose that you define a method *find(i)* that returns a reference to the ith node in the linked list. If *find* provides a reference *curr* to the ith node, how will you get a reference *prev* to the previous node, that is, to the $(i-1)^{th}$ node? You can get the value of *prev* by invoking *find(i-1)*. Instead of calling *find* twice, however, note that once you have *prev*, *curr* is simply *prev.next*. The only exception to using *find* in this way is for the first node, but you know immediately from i whether the

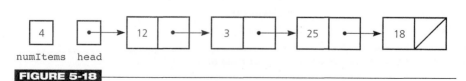

numItems   head

FIGURE 5-18

A reference-based implementation of the ADT list

operation involves the first node. If it does, you know the reference to the first node, namely *head*, without invoking *find*.

The method *find* is not an ADT operation. Because *find* returns a reference, you would not want any client to call it. Such clients should be able to use the ADT without knowledge of the references that the implementation uses. It is perfectly reasonable for the implementation of an ADT to define variables and methods that the rest of the program should not access. Therefore, *find* is a private method that only the implementations of the ADT operations call.

find is a private method

The following interface specification developed in Chapter 4 will be used for the reference-based implementation of the ADT list. The pre- and postconditions for the ADT list operations are the same as for the array-based implementation that you saw in Chapter 4; they are omitted here to save space.

```
package List;
// ***************************************************
// Interface for the ADT list
// ***************************************************
public interface ListInterface {
  // list operations:
  public boolean isEmpty();
  public int size();
  public void add(int index, Object item)
                       throws ListIndexOutOfBoundsException;
  public void remove(int index)
                       throws ListIndexOutOfBoundsException;
  public Object get(int index)
                       throws ListIndexOutOfBoundsException;
  public void removeAll();
} // end ListInterface
```

The implementation of the list begins as follows:

```
package List;
// ***************************************************
// Reference-based implementation of ADT list.
// ***************************************************
public class ListReferenceBased implements ListInterface {
  // reference to linked list of items
  private Node head;
  private int numItems; // number of items in list

  // definitions of constructors and methods
     . . .
```

You include the implementations of the class's methods at this point in the class as well as any private methods that may be needed. We now examine each of these implementations.

Default constructor. The default constructor simply initializes the data fields *numItems* and *head*:

Default constructor

```java
public ListReferenceBased() {
   numItems = 0;
   head = null;
}  // end default constructor
```

Since the variables *numItems* and *head* are initialized to these same values by default, this constructor is really not necessary. But if you have other constructors defined and you want to allow for a constructor without parameters, it must be defined explicitly. In general, it's a good idea to define all constructors explicitly.

List operations. The methods *isEmpty* and *size* have straightforward implementations:

```java
public boolean isEmpty() {
   return numItems == 0;
}  // end isEmpty

public int size() {
   return numItems;
}  // end size
```

Because a linked list does not provide direct access to a specified position, the retrieval, insertion, and deletion operations must all traverse the list from its beginning until the specified point is reached. The method *find* performs this traversal and has the following implementation:

Private method to locate a particular node

```java
private Node find(int index) {
// -----------------------------------------------
// Locates a specified node in a linked list.
// Precondition: index is the number of the desired
// node. Assumes that 1 <= index <= numItems+1
// Postcondition: Returns a reference to the desired
// node.
// -----------------------------------------------
   Node curr = head;
   for (int skip = 0; skip < index; skip++) {
      curr = curr.next;
   } // end for
   return curr;
} // end find
```

The precondition for *find* requires the *index* to be in the proper range. The *get* operation calls *find* to locate the desired node:

```
public Object get(int index)
              throws ListIndexOutOfBoundsException {
  if (index >= 0 && index < numItems) {
    // get reference to node, then data in node
    Node curr = find(index);
    Object dataItem = curr.item;
    return dataItem;
  }
  else {
    throw new ListIndexOutOfBoundsException(
                      "List index out of bounds on get");
  } // end if
} // end get
```

Retrieved by position

The reference-based implementations of the insertion and deletion operations use the linked list processing techniques developed earlier in this chapter. To insert an item after the first item of a list, you must first obtain a reference to the preceding item. Insertion into the first position of a list is a special case.

```
public void add(int index, Object item)
              throws ListIndexOutOfBoundsException {
  if (index >= 0 && index < numItems+1) {
    if (index == 0) {
      // insert the new node containing item at
      // beginning of list
      Node newNode = new Node(item, head);
      head = newNode;
    }
    else {
      Node prev = find(index-1);

      // insert the new node containing item after
      // the node that prev references
      Node newNode = new Node(item, prev.next);
      prev.next = newNode;
    } // end if
    numItems++;
  }
  else {
    throw new ListIndexOutOfBoundsException(
                      "List index out of bounds on add");
  } // end if
}  // end add
```

Insertion at a given position

The *remove* operation is analogous to insertion. To delete an item that occurs after the first item of a list, you must first obtain a reference to the item that precedes it. Removal from the first position of a list is a special case.

Deletion from a given position

```
public void remove(int index)
                      throws ListIndexOutOfBoundsException {
  if (index >= 0 && index < numItems) {
    if (index == 0) {
      // delete the first node from the list
      head = head.next;
    }
    else {
      Node prev = find(index-1);
      // delete the node after the node that prev
      // references, save reference to node
      Node curr = prev.next;
      prev.next = curr.next;
    } // end if
    numItems--;
  } // end if
  else {
    throw new ListIndexOutOfBoundsException(
            "List index out of bounds on remove");
  } // end if
}    // end remove
```

The *removeAll* operation simply sets the head reference to *null*, making the nodes in the list unreachable and thus marking them for garbage collection.

```
public void removeAll() {
  // setting head to null causes list to be
  // unreachable and thus marked for garbage
  // collection
  head = null;
  numItems = 0;
} // end removeAll
```

Comparing Array-Based and Reference-Based Implementations

Typically, the various implementations that a programmer contemplates for a particular ADT have advantages and disadvantages. When you must select an implementation, you should weigh these advantages and disadvantages before you make your choice. As you will see, the decision among possible implementations of an ADT is one that you must make time and time again. This section compares the two implementations of the ADT list that you have seen as an example of how you should proceed in general.

The array-based implementation that you saw in Chapter 4 appears to be a reasonable approach. An array behaves like a list, and arrays are easy to use. However, as was already mentioned, an array has a fixed size; it is possible for the number of items in the list to exceed this fixed size. In practice, when choosing among implementations of an ADT, you must ask the question, does the fixed-size restriction of an array-based implementation present a problem in the context of a particular application? The answer to this question depends on two factors. The obvious factor is whether or not, for a given application, you can predict in advance the maximum number of items in the ADT at any one time. If you cannot, it is quite possible that an operation—and hence the entire program—will fail because the ADT in the context of a particular application requires more storage than the array can provide.

Arrays are easy to use, but they have a fixed size

Can you predict the maximum number of items in the ADT?

On the other hand, if, for a given application, you can predict in advance the maximum number of items in the ADT list at any one time, you must explore a more subtle factor: Would you waste storage by declaring an array to be large enough to accommodate this maximum number of items? Consider a case in which the maximum number of items is large, but you suspect that this number rarely will be reached. For example, suppose that your list could contain as many as 10,000 items, but the actual number of items in the list rarely exceeds 50. If you declare 10,000 array locations at compilation time, at least 9,950 array locations will be wasted most of the time. In both of the previous cases, the array-based implementation given in Chapter 4 is not desirable.

Will an array waste storage?

What if you used a resizeable array? Because you would use the *new* operator to allocate a larger array dynamically, you would be able to provide as much storage as the list needs (within the bounds of the particular computer, of course). Thus, you would not have to predict the maximum size of the list. However, if you doubled the size of the array each time you reached the end of the array—which is a reasonable approach to enlarging the array—you still might have many unused array locations. In the example just given, you could allocate an array of 50 locations initially. If you actually have 10,000 items in your list, array doubling will eventually give you an array of 12,800 locations, 2,800 more than you need. Remember also that you waste time by copying the array each time you need more space.

Increasing the size of a resizeable array can waste storage and time

Now suppose that your list will never contain more than 25 items. You could allocate enough storage in the array for the list and know that you would waste little storage when the list contained only a few items. With respect to its size, an array-based implementation is perfectly acceptable in this case.

An array-based implementation is a good choice for a small list

A reference-based implementation can solve any difficulties related to the fixed size of an array-based implementation. You use the *new* operator to allocate storage dynamically, so you do not need to predict the maximum size of the list. Because you allocate memory one item at a time, the list will be allocated only as much storage as it needs. Thus, you will not waste storage.

Linked lists do not have a fixed size

There are other differences between the array-based and reference-based implementations. These differences affect both the time and memory

The item after an array item is implied; in a linked list, an item explicitly references the next item

An array-based implementation requires less memory than a reference-based implementation

You can access array items directly with equal access time

requirements of the implementations. Any time you store a collection of data in an array or a linked list, the data items become ordered; that is, there is a first item, a second item, and so on. This order implies that a typical item has a predecessor and a successor. In an array `anArray`, the location of the next item after the item in `anArray[i]` is *implicit*—it is in `anArray[i+1]`. In a linked list, however, you *explicitly* determine the location of the next item by using the reference in the current node. This notion of an implicit versus explicit next item is one of the primary differences between an array and a linked list. Therefore, an advantage of an array-based implementation is that it does not have to store explicit information about where to find the next data item, thus requiring less memory than a reference-based implementation.

Another, more important advantage of an array-based implementation is that it can provide **direct access** to a specified item. For example, if you use the array `items` to implement the ADT list, you know that the item associated with list position *i* is stored in `items[i-1]`. Accessing either `items[0]` or `items[49]` takes the same amount of time. That is, the **access time** is constant for an array.

You must traverse a linked list to access its ith node

The time to access the ith node in a linked list depends on *i*

On the other hand, if you use a linked list to implement the ADT list, you have no way of immediately accessing the node that contains the ith item. To get to the appropriate node, you use the *next* data fields to traverse the linked list from its beginning until you reach the ith node. That is, you access the first node and get the reference to the second node, access the second node and get the reference to the third node, and so on until you finally access the ith node. Clearly, the time it takes you to access the first node is less than the time it takes to access the 50th node. The access time for the ith node depends on *i*.

The type of implementation chosen will affect the efficiency of the operations of the ADT list. An array-based *get* is almost instantaneous, regardless of which list item you access. A reference-based retrieval operation like *get*, however, requires *i* steps to access the ith item in the list.

Insertion into and deletion from a linked list do not require you to shift data

You already know that the array-based implementation of the ADT list requires you to shift the data when you insert items into or delete items from the list. For example, if you delete the first item of a 20-item list, you must shift 19 items. In general, deleting the ith item of a list of *n* items requires *n* − *i* shifts. Thus, *remove* requires *n* − 1 shifts to delete the first item, but zero shifts to delete the last item. The list insertion operation *add* has similar requirements.

Insertion into and deletion from a linked list require a list traversal

In contrast, you do not need to shift the data when you insert items into or delete items from the linked list of a reference-based implementation. The methods *add* and *remove* require essentially the same effort, regardless of the length of the list or the position of the operation within the list, once you know the point of insertion or deletion. Finding this point, however, requires a list traversal, the time for which will vary depending on where in the list the operation will occur. Recall that the private method *find* performs this traversal. If you examine the definition of *find*, you will see that *find(i)* requires *i* assignment operations. Thus, *find*'s effort increases with *i*.

We will continue to compare various solutions to a problem throughout this book. Chapter 10 will introduce a more formal way to discuss the efficiency of algorithms. Until then, our discussions will be informal.

Passing a Linked List to a Method

How can a method access a linked list? It is sufficient for the method to have access to the list's head reference. From this variable alone, the method can access the entire linked list. In the reference-based implementation of the ADT list that you saw earlier in this chapter, the head reference *head* to the linked list that contains the ADT's items is a private data field of the class *ListReferenceBased*. The methods of this class use *head* directly to manipulate the linked list.

> A method with access to a linked list's **head** reference has access to the entire list

Would you ever want *head* to be an argument of a method? Certainly not for methods outside of the class, because such methods should not have access to the class's underlying data structure. Although on the surface, it would seem that you would never need to pass the head reference to a method, that is not the case. Recursive methods, for example, might need the head reference as an argument. You will see examples of such methods in the next section. Realize that these methods must not be public members of their class. If they were, clients could access the linked list directly, thereby violating the ADT's wall.

As Figure 5-19 illustrates, when *head* is an actual argument to a method, its value is copied into the corresponding formal parameter. The method then can access and alter the nodes in the list. However, the method cannot modify *head*'s value (recall our earlier example in Figure 5-4). This is fine for situations, such as a search method, that do not modify the list. But what should you do if you want to write a method that may need to modify the *head* reference? For example, a method that inserts a node at the beginning of the list will need to modify the *head* reference. One solution is for the return value of the method to be the new value for the *head* reference. Such an example will appear in the next section.

Processing Linked Lists Recursively

It is possible, and sometimes desirable, to process linked lists recursively. This section examines recursive traversal and insertion operations on a linked list. If

Actual argument
head

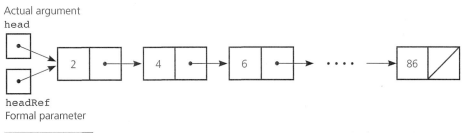

headRef
Formal parameter

FIGURE 5-19

A head reference as an argument

the recursive methods in this section are members of a class, they should not be public because they require the linked list's head reference as an argument.

Traversal. Suppose that you want to display the elements in a list referenced by *head*. That is, you want to write the objects in the order in which they appear in the linked list. The recursive strategy is simply

```
Write the first node of the list
Write the list minus its first node
```

The following Java method implements this strategy:

A recursive traversal method

```java
private static void writeList(Node nextNode) {
// -----------------------------------------------------------
// Writes a list of objects.
// Precondition: The linked list is referenced by nextNode.
// Postcondition: The list is displayed. The linked list
// and nextNode are unchanged.
// -----------------------------------------------------------
  if (nextNode != null) {
    // write the first data object
    System.out.println(nextNode.item);
    // write the list minus its first node
    writeList(nextNode.next);
  }  // end if
}  // end writeList
```

This method is uncomplicated. It requires that you have direct access only to the first node of the list. The linked list provides this direct access because the list's first node, referenced by *head*, contains the list's first data item. Furthermore, you can easily pass the list minus its first node to *writeList*. If *head* references the beginning of the list, *head.next* references the list minus its first node. You should compare *writeList* to the iterative technique that we used earlier in this chapter to display a linked list.

Compare the recursive *writeList* to the iterative technique on page 277

Now suppose that you want to display the list backward. Chapter 3 already developed two recursive strategies for writing a string *s* backward. Recall that the strategy of the method *writeBackward* is

writeBackward strategy

```
Write the last character of string s
Write string s minus its last character backward
```

The strategy of the method *writeBackward2* is

writeBackward2 strategy

```
Write string s minus its first character backward
Write the first character of string s
```

We can easily translate these strategies to linked lists. The method *writeBackward* translates to

Write the last node of the list
Write the list minus its last node backward

writeListBack-ward strategy

and the strategy of the method *writeBackward2* translates to

Write the list minus its first node backward
Write the first node of the list

writeListBack-ward2 strategy

You saw that these two strategies work equally well when an array is used. However, when a linked list is used, the first strategy is very difficult to implement: If *nextNode* references the node that contains the first node of the list, how do you get to the last node? Even if you had some way to get to the last node in the list quickly, it would be very difficult for you to move toward the front of the list at each recursive call. That is, it would be difficult for you to access the ends of the successively shorter lists that the recursive calls generate. (Later you will see a doubly linked list, which would solve this problem.)

This discussion illustrates one of the primary disadvantages of linked lists: Whereas an array provides direct access to any of its items, a linked list does not. Fortunately, however, the strategy of method *writeBackward2* requires that you have direct access only to the first character of the string. This access is the same that *writeListBackward2* requires: The list's head reference *nextNode* locates the first node in the list, and *nextNode.next* references the list minus the first node.

writeListBack-ward2 is much easier to implement recursively than *writeListBack-ward*

The following Java method implements the *writeListBackward2* strategy for a linked list:

```
private static void writeListBackward2(Node nextNode) {
// ----------------------------------------------------
// Writes a list of objects backwards.
// Precondition: The linked list is referenced by
// nextNode.
// Postcondition: The list is displayed backwards. The
// linked list and nextNode are unchanged.
// ----------------------------------------------------
   if (nextNode != null) {
     // write the list minus its first node backward
     writeListBackward2(nextNode.next);
     // write the data object in the first node
     System.out.println(nextNode.item);
   } // end if
}   // end writeListBackward2
```

Self-Test Exercise 8 asks you to trace this method. This trace will be similar to the box trace in Figure 3-9. Exercise 5 asks you to write an iterative version of this method. Which version is more efficient?

Insertion.   Now view the insertion of a node into a sorted linked list from a new perspective—that is, recursively. Later in this book you will need a recursive algorithm to perform an insertion into a linked structure. Interestingly, recursive insertion eliminates the need for both a trailing reference and a special case for inserting into the beginning of the list.

Consider the following recursive view of a sorted linked list: A linked list is sorted if its first data item is less than its second data item and the list that begins with the second data item is sorted. More formally, you can state this definition as follows:

The linked list that *head* references is a sorted linked list if

> *head* is *null* (the empty list is a sorted linked list)

or

> *head.next* is *null* (a list with a single node is a sorted linked list)

or

> *head.item* < *head.next.item*, and *head.next* references a sorted linked list

You can base a recursive insertion on this definition. Notice that the following method inserts the node at one of the base cases—either when the list is empty or when the new data item is smaller than all the data items in the list. In both cases, you need to insert the new data item at the beginning of the list.

```
private static Node insertRecursive(Node headNode,
                          java.lang.Comparable newItem) {
  if ( (headNode == null) ||
       (newItem.compareTo(headNode.item) < 0) ) {
    // base case: insert newItem at the beginning of the
    // linked list that nextNode references
    Node newNode = new Node(newItem, headNode);
    headNode = newNode;
  }
  else { //insert into rest of linked list
    Node nextNode = insertRecursive(headNode.next,newItem);
    headNode.next = nextNode;
  } // end if
  return headNode;
}  // end insertRecursive
```

First, consider the context for *insertRecursive*. Recall from Chapter 4 that the ADT operation *sortedAdd(newItem)* inserts *newItem* into its proper order in the sorted list. As a public method of the class, *sortedAdd* would call *insertRecursive* to do the insertion recursively. However, *insertRecursive* requires the linked list's head reference as an argument. Since the reference *head* is private and hidden from the client, you would not want *insertRecursive* to be an ADT operation. Thus, you would make it private.

To see how *insertRecursive* works, consider that *sortedAdd* will invoke *insertRecursive* by using the statement

```
head = insertRecursive(head, newItem);
```

Although *insertRecursive* does not maintain a trailing reference, inserting the new node is easy when the base case is reached. Note that within *insertRecursive*, *headNode* references the beginning of the sorted linked list. You use *headNode* to make the new node reference the first node in the original list and then change *headNode* so that it references the new node. Since *insertRecursive* returns *headNode*, *sortedAdd*'s assignment to *head* makes *head* reference the new node as required.

To understand the previous remarks, consider the case in which the new item is to be inserted at the beginning of the original list that has the external reference *head*. In this case, no recursive calls are made, and consequently when the base case is reached—that is, when *newItem.compareTo(headNode.item) < 0*—the actual argument that corresponds to *headNode* is *head*, as Figure 5-20a illustrates.

Insertion occurs at
the base case

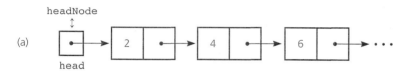

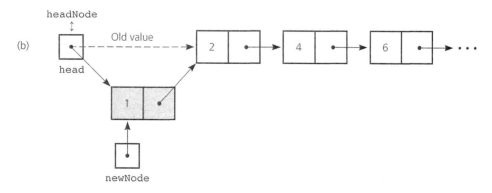

FIGURE 5-20

(a) A sorted linked list; (b) the assignment made for insertion at the beginning of the list

The assignment *headNode* = *newNode* then sets the method's return value to reference the new node. Upon return of *insertRecursive*, the statement

```
head = insertRecursive(head, newItem);
```

assigns the return value to *head*, as Figure 5-20b shows.

The general case in which the new item is inserted into the interior of the list that *head* references is similar. When *insertRecursive* is first called, the *else* clause of the *if* statement executes, making a recursive call to *insertRecursive*. When the base case is reached, what is the actual argument that corresponds to *headNode*? It is the *next* reference of the node that should precede the new node, as Figure 5-21 illustrates. Therefore, the base case returns a reference to the new node. The *else* clause assigns this reference to *nextNode*, and sets the next reference of the appropriate node to reference the new node.

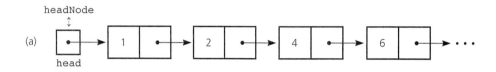

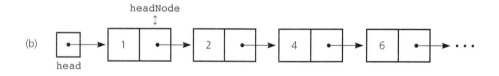

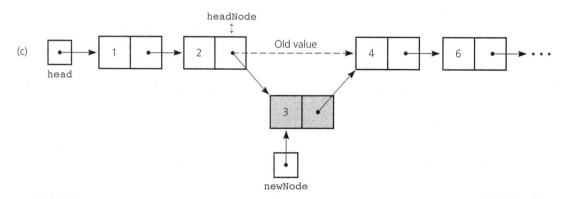

FIGURE 5-21

(a) The initial call *insertRecursive(head,newItem)*; (b) the first recursive call; (c) the second recursive call inserts at the beginning of the list that *headNode* references

When the original call to *insertRecursive* returns *headNode*, its value is unchanged from its original value of *head*. Thus, the assignment

```
head = insertRecursive(head, newItem);
```

leaves the value of *head* unchanged.

Although it could be argued that you should perform the operations on a sorted linked list recursively (after all, recursion does eliminate special cases and the need for a trailing reference), the primary purpose in presenting the recursive *insertRecursive* is to prepare you for the binary search tree algorithms to be presented in Chapter 11.

5.3 Variations of the Linked List

This section briefly introduces several variations of the linked list that you have just seen. These variations are often useful, and you will encounter them later in this text. Many of the implementation details are left as exercises. Note that in addition to the data structures discussed in this section, it is possible to have other data structures, such as arrays of references to linked lists and linked lists of linked lists. These data structures are also left as exercises.

Tail References

In many situations, you simply want to add an item to the end of a list. For example, maintaining a list of requests for a popular book at the local library would require that new requests for the book be placed at the end of a waiting list. You could use an ADT list called *waitingList* as follows:

```
waitingList.add(request, waitingList.size()+1);
```

This statement adds *request* to the end of *waitingList*. Recall that in implementing *add* to insert an item at the position indicated, we used the method *find* to traverse the list to that position. Note that this statement actually performs these four steps:

1. Allocate a new node for the linked list.

2. Set the reference in the last node in the list to reference the new node.

3. Put the new *request* in the new node.

4. Set the reference in the new node to *null*.

Each time you add a new request, you must get to the last node in the linked list. One way to accomplish this is to traverse the list each time you add a new request. A much more efficient method uses a **tail reference** *tail* to remember where the end of the linked list is—just as *head* remembers where the beginning of the list is. Like *head*, *tail* is external to the list. Figure 5-22 illustrates a linked list of integers that has both *head* and *tail* references.

*Use a **tail** reference to facilitate adding nodes to the end of a linked list*

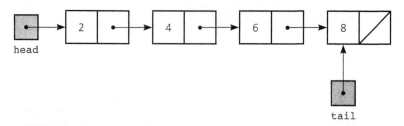

FIGURE 5-22

A linked list with *head* and *tail* references

With `tail` pointing to the end of the linked list, you can perform Steps 1 through 4 by using the single statement

```
tail.next = new Node(request, null);
```

This statement sets the *next* reference in the last node in the list to point to a newly allocated node. You then update `tail` so that it references the new last node by writing `tail = tail.next;`. You thus have an easy method for adding a new item to the end of the list. Initially, however, when you insert the first item into an empty linked list, `tail`—like `head`—is `null`. We leave the details of a solution as an exercise.

Treat the first insertion as a special case

Circular Linked Lists

When you use a computer that is part of a network, you share the services of another computer—called a **server**—with many other users. A similar sharing of resources occurs when you access a central computer by using a remote terminal. The system must organize the users so that only one user at a time has access to the shared computer. By ordering the users, the system can give each user a turn. Because users regularly enter and exit the system (by logging on or logging off), a linked list of user names allows the system to maintain order without shifting names when it makes insertions to and deletions from the list. Thus, the system can traverse the linked list from the beginning and give each user on the list a turn on the shared computer. What must the system do when it reaches the end of the list? It must return to the beginning of the list. However, the fact that the last node of a linked list does not reference another node can be an inconvenience.

If you want to access the first node of a linked list after accessing the last node, you must resort to the head reference. Suppose that you change the *next* portion of the list's last node so that, instead of containing *null*, it references the first node. The result is a **circular linked list,** as illustrated in Figure 5-23. In contrast, the linked list you saw earlier is said to be a **linear linked list.**

Every node in a circular linked list has a successor

Every node in a circular linked list references a successor, so you can start at any node and traverse the entire list. Although you could think of a circular

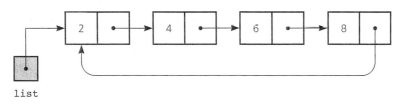

FIGURE 5-23

A circular linked list

list as not having either a beginning or an end, you still would have an external reference to one of the nodes in the list. Thus, it remains natural to think of both a first and a last node in a circular list. If the external reference locates the "first" node, you still would have to traverse the list to get to the last node. However, if the external reference—call it *list*—references the "last" node, as it does in Figure 5-24, you can access both the first and last nodes without a traversal, because *list.next* references the first node.

A *null* value in the external reference indicates an empty list, as it did for a linear list. However, no node in a circular list contains *null* in its *next* reference. Thus, you must alter the algorithm for detecting when you have traversed an entire list. By simply comparing the current reference *curr* to the external reference *list*, you can determine when you have traversed the entire circular list. For example, the following Java statements display the data portions of every node in a circular list, assuming that *list* references the "last" node:

No node in a circular linked list contains *null*

```
// display the data in a circular linked list;
// list references its last node
if (list != null) {
   // list is not empty
   Node first = list.next; // reference first node

   Node curr = first;         // start at first node
```

Write the data in a circular linked list

list

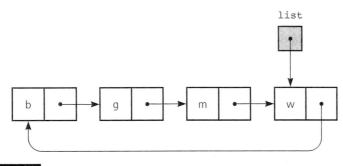

FIGURE 5-24

A circular linked list with an external reference to the last node

```
   // Loop invariant: curr references next node to display
   do {
     // write data portion
     System.out.println(curr.item);
     curr = curr.next;        // reference next node
   } while (curr != first);     // list traversed?
 }  // end if
```

Operations such as insertion into and deletion from a circular linked list are left as exercises.

Dummy Head Nodes

Both the insertion and deletion algorithms presented earlier for linear linked lists require a special case to handle action at the first position of a list. Many people prefer a method that eliminates the need for the special case. One such method is to add a **dummy head node**—as Figure 5-25 depicts—that is always present, even when the linked list is empty. In this way, the item at the first position of the list is actually in the second node. Also, the insertion and deletion algorithms initialize *prev* to reference the dummy head node, rather than *null*. Thus, for example, in the deletion algorithm, the statement

```
prev.next = curr.next;
```

deletes from the list the node that *curr* references, regardless of whether or not this node is the first element in the list.

Despite the fact that a dummy head node eliminates the need for a special case, handling the first list position separately can, in general, be less distracting than altering the list's structure by adding a dummy head node. However, dummy head nodes are useful with doubly linked lists, as you will see in the next section.

Doubly Linked Lists

Suppose that you wanted to delete a particular node from a linked list. If you were able to locate the node directly without a traversal, you would not have established a trailing reference to the node that precedes it in the list. Without a trailing reference, you would be unable to delete the node. You could overcome this

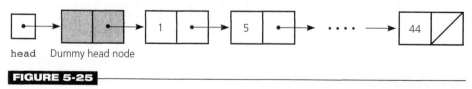

head   Dummy head node

FIGURE 5-25

A dummy head node

problem if you had a way to back up from the node that you wished to delete to the node that precedes it. A **doubly linked list** solves this problem because each of its nodes has references to both the next node and the previous node.

Each node in a doubly linked list references both its predecessor and its successor

Consider a sorted linked list of customer names such that each node contains, in addition to its data field, two reference variables, *preceding* and *next*. As usual, the *next* reference of node *N* references the node that follows *N* in the list. The *preceding* data field references the node that precedes *N* in the list. Figure 5-26 shows the form of this sorted linked list of customers.

Notice that if *curr* references a node *N*, you can get a reference to the node that precedes *N* in the list by using the assignment statement

```
prev = curr.preceding;
```

A doubly linked list thus allows you to delete a node without traversing the list to establish a trailing reference.

Because there are more references to set, the mechanics of inserting into and deleting from a doubly linked list are a bit more involved than for a singly linked list. In addition, the special cases at the beginning or the end of the list are more complicated. It is common to eliminate the special cases by using a dummy head node. Although dummy head nodes may not be worthwhile for singly linked lists, the more complicated special cases for doubly linked lists make them very attractive.

Dummy head nodes are useful in doubly linked lists

As Figure 5-27a shows, the external reference *listHead* always references the dummy head node. Notice that the dummy head node has the same data type as the other nodes in the list; thus it also contains *preceding* and *next* references. You can link the list so that it becomes a **circular doubly linked list.** The *next* reference of the dummy head node then references the first "real node"—for example, the first customer name—in the list, and the *preceding* reference of the first real node refers back to the dummy head node. Similarly, the *preceding* reference of the dummy head node references the last node in the list, and the *next* reference of the last node references the dummy head node. Note that the dummy head node is present even when the list is empty. In this case, both reference variables of the dummy head node reference the head node itself, as Figure 5-27b illustrates.

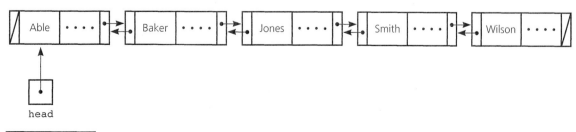

head

FIGURE 5-26

A doubly linked list

(a) `listHead`

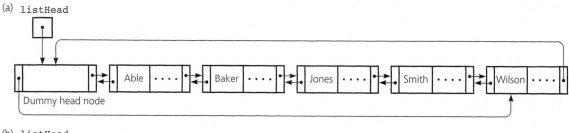

Dummy head node

(b) `listHead`

FIGURE 5-27

(a) A circular doubly linked list with a dummy head node; (b) an empty list with a dummy head node

A circular doubly linked list eliminates special cases for insertion and deletion

By using a circular doubly linked list, you can perform insertions and deletions without special cases: Inserting into and deleting from the first or last position is the same as for any other position. Consider, for example, how to delete the node *N* that `curr` references. As Figure 5-28 illustrates, you need to

1. Change the *next* reference of the node that precedes *N* so that it references the node that follows *N*.

2. Change the *preceding* reference of the node that follows *N* so that it references the node that precedes *N*.

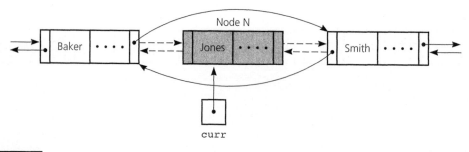

FIGURE 5-28

Reference changes for deletion

The following Java statements accomplish these two steps:

```
// delete the node that curr references
curr.preceding.next = curr.next;
curr.next.preceding = curr.preceding;
```

Deleting a node

You should convince yourself that these statements work even when the node to be deleted is the first, last, or only data (nonhead) node in the list.

Now consider how to insert a node into a circular doubly linked list. In general, the fact that the list is doubly linked does not mean that you avoid traversing the list to find the proper place for the new item. For example, if you insert a new customer name, you must find the proper place within the sorted linked list for the new node. The following pseudocode sets *curr* to reference the node that contains the first name greater than *newName*. Thus, *curr* will reference the node that is to follow the new node on the list:

```
// find the insertion point
curr = listHead.next // reference first node, if any
while (curr != listHead and newName > curr.item) {
   curr = curr.next
} // end while
```

Traverse the list to locate the insertion point

Notice that if you want to insert the new node either at the end of the list or into an empty list, the loop will set *curr* to reference the dummy head node.

As Figure 5-29 illustrates, once *curr* references the node that is to follow the new node, you need to

1. Set the *next* reference in the new node to reference the node that is to follow it.

2. Set the *preceding* reference in the new node to reference the node that is to precede it.

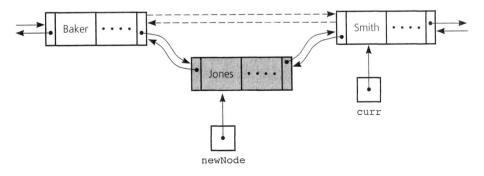

FIGURE 5-29

Reference changes for insertion

3. Set the *preceding* reference in the node that is to follow the new node so that it references the new node.

4. Set the *next* reference in the node that is to precede the new node so that it references the new node.

The following Java statements accomplish these four steps, assuming that *newNode* references the new node:

Inserting a node

```
// insert the new node that newNode references before
// the node referenced by curr
newNode.next = curr;
newNode.preceding = curr.preceding;
curr.preceding = newNode;
newNode.preceding.next = newNode;
```

You should convince yourself that these statements work even when you insert the node into the beginning of a list; at the end of a list, in which case *curr* references the head node; or into an empty list, in which case *curr* also references the head node.

5.4 Application: Maintaining an Inventory

Imagine that you have a part-time job at the local movie rental store. Realizing that you know a good deal about computers, the store owner asks you to write an interactive program that will maintain the store's inventory of DVDs that are for sale. The inventory consists of a list of movie titles and the following information associated with each title:

- **Have value:** number of DVDs currently in stock.

- **Want value:** number of DVDs that should be in stock. (When the have value is less than the want value, more DVDs are ordered.)

- **Wait list:** list of names of people waiting for the title if it is sold out.

Because the owner plans to turn off the power to the computer when the store is closed, your inventory program will not be running at all times. Therefore, the program must save the inventory in a file before execution terminates and later restore the inventory when it is run again.

Program input and output are as follows:

Input

- A file that contains a previously saved inventory.

- A file that contains information on an incoming shipment of DVDs. (See command D.)

- Single-letter commands—with arguments where necessary—that inquire about or modify the inventory and that the user will enter interactively.

Output

- A file that contains the updated inventory. (Note that you remove from the inventory all items whose have values and want values are zero and whose wait lists are empty. Thus, such items do not appear in the file.)

- Output as specified by the individual commands.

The program should be able to execute the following commands:

H	(help)	Provide a summary of the available commands.	Program commands
I *<title>*	(inquire)	Display the inventory information for a specified title.	
L	(list)	List the entire inventory (in alphabetical order by title).	
A *<title>*	(add)	Add a new title to the inventory. Prompt for initial want value.	
M *<title>*	(modify)	Modify the want value for a specified title.	
D	(delivery)	Take delivery of a shipment of DVDs, assuming that the clerk has entered the shipment information (titles and counts) into a file. Read the file, reserve DVDs for the people on the wait list, and update the have values in the inventory accordingly. Note that the program must add an item to the inventory if a delivered title is not present in the current inventory.	
O	(order)	Write a purchase order for additional DVDs based on a comparison of the have and want values in the inventory, so that the have value is brought up to the want value.	
R	(return)	Write a return order based on a comparison of the have and want values in the inventory and decrease the have values accordingly (make the return). The purpose is to reduce the have value to the want value.	
S *<title>*	(sell)	Decrease the count for the specified title by 1. If the title is sold out, put a name on the wait list for the title.	
Q	(quit)	Save the inventory and wait lists in a file and terminate execution.	

The problem-solving process that starts with a statement of the problem and ends with a program that effectively solves the problem—that is, a program that meets its specification—has three main stages:

1. The design of a solution

2. The implementation of the solution

3. The final set of refinements to the program

Realize, however, that you cannot complete one stage in total isolation from the others. Also realize that at many steps in the development of a solution, you must make choices. Although the following discussion may give the impression that the choices are clear-cut, this is not always the case. In reality, both the trade-offs between choices and the false starts (wrong choices considered) are often numerous.

This problem primarily involves data management and requires certain program commands. These commands suggest the following operations on the inventory:

Operations on the
inventory

- List the inventory in alphabetical order by title (L command).

- Find the inventory item associated with a title (I, M, D, O, and S commands).

- Replace the inventory item associated with a title (M, D, R, and S commands).

- Insert new inventory items (A and D commands).

Recall that each title might have an associated wait list of people who are waiting for that title. You must be able to

- Add new people to the end of the wait list when they want a DVD that is sold out (S command).

- Delete people from the beginning of the wait list when new DVDs are delivered (D command).

- Display the names on a wait list for a particular title (I and L commands).

In addition, you must be able to

- Save the current inventory and associated wait lists when program execution terminates (Q command).

- Restore the current inventory and associated wait lists when program execution begins again.

You could think of these operations as part of an ADT inventory. Your next step should be to specify each of the operations fully. Since this chapter is about linked lists and implementation issues, the completion of the specifications will be left as an exercise. We will turn our attention to a data structure that could implement the inventory.

Each data item in the ADT inventory represents a movie and contains a title, the number of DVDs in stock (a *have* value), the number desired (a *want* value), and a wait list. How will you represent the wait list? First, you need to decide what information you want to store in the wait list. For example, you might want to keep track of the full name and phone number of each person, and create a class `Customer` containing data fields for the first and last names along with the telephone number of the person. This class might be structured as follows:

A customer in the
wait list

```
public class Customer {
    private String lastName;
```

```
private String firstName;
private String phone;

public Customer(String first, String last, String phone) {
  // to be implemented
  . . .
} // end constructor

public String toString() {
  // to be implemented
  . . .
} // end toString
} // end class Customer
```

This definition contains the minimum number of methods required to use instances of the *Customer* class in our inventory problem. You may also decide that you want to keep additional information about a person, such as their address. The *toString* method is provided for printing purposes.

Now that you have decided what information to keep in the wait list, how will you implement the wait list itself in the ADT inventory? Could you use any of the implementations of the ADT list we developed previously? To make this decision, you must review the requirements of the wait list as stated in the inventory problem and then see if the ADT list will be able to meet these requirements. The inventory problem requires you to be able to add to the end of the wait list and delete from the beginning of the wait list. Clearly, removing an item from the beginning of the list is easy: You can simply use the ADT list operation *remove* with an index value of 1. Adding an item to the end of the list is also fairly easy. You know the size of the list from the ADT list operation *size()*, and you could use the ADT list operation *add* with an index value of *size()* + 1 to place an item at the end of the wait list.

One of the requirements of the inventory problem is that the L command list the inventory in alphabetical order by movie title. Will you be able to use the ADT list in a way that will support this requirement? Not easily, since the ADT list is based on index position, not on a sorted order. A better choice is the ADT sorted list. Not only does it maintain the data in a sorted order for us, but it also provides an operation *locateIndex(item)* that can be used to search for an item in the sorted list.

The ADT list is not the best choice for data that must be in alphabetical order

If the ADT sorted list is not yet implemented, should you use an array-based implementation or a reference-based implementation? If you use an array to contain the items, you can use a binary search. Inserting and deleting items, however, requires you to shift array elements. Using a linked list for the items avoids these data shifts but makes a binary search impractical. (How do you quickly locate the middle item in a linked list?) Weighing these trade-offs, we choose a linked list to implement the ADT sorted list.

To summarize, we have made the following choices:

A sorted list represents the inventory

- The inventory is a sorted list of data items (the ADT sorted list implemented as a linked list of data items), sorted by the title that each item represents.

- Each inventory item contains a title, a have value, a want value, and a list of customers (the wait list).

Figure 5-30 and the following Java statements summarize these choices:

```java
public class StockItem implements java.lang.Comparable {
    private String title;
    private int have, want;
    private ListReferenceBased waitingList;

    // various constructors for StockItem
    . . .
```

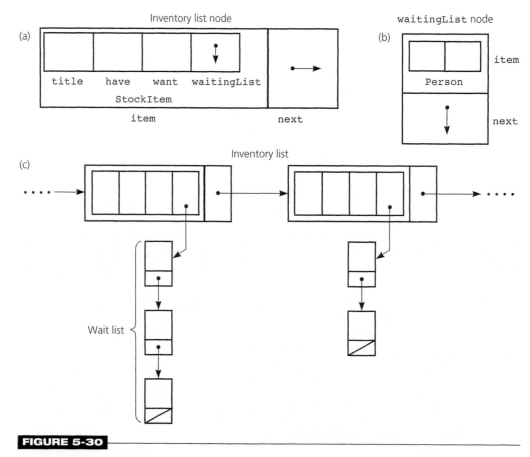

FIGURE 5-30

(a) Inventory list node; (b) wait list node; (c) orthogonal structure for the inventory

```
public void addToWaitingList(String lastName,
                            String firstName, String phone) {
// add a person to the waiting list
  waitingList.addSorted(
             new Customer(lastName, firstName, phone);
} // end addToWaitingList

public String toString() {
  // for displaying StockItem instances
  . . .
} // end toString

public int compareTo(Object rhs) {
// define how StockItems are compared, only by title
   return title.compareTo(((StockItem)rhs).title);
} // end compareTo

// mutator and accessor methods for other data fields
  . . .


} // end class StockItem
```

You declare the inventory as follows:

```
SortedList inventory = new SortedList();
```

Before you can proceed with the implementation, you must consider how you will save the inventory in a file. Java provides **object serialization,** a process that transforms an object into a stream of bytes that you can save and restore from a file. The most powerful aspect of object serialization is that when you write any object to a file, any other objects that are referenced by that object are also written to the file. As mentioned in Chapter 1, to enable this feature, you place an *implements Serializable* clause in each class that has instances that will be written to the file. Thus, to write the inventory successfully, you would include the clause in the classes *ListReferenceBased*, *Node*, *SortedList*, *StockItem*, and *Customer*. Then, when you write an inventory object to a file, all of the stock items in the inventory list and their wait lists are also be placed in the file. Here is the code that accomplishes that task:

```
try {
  FileOutputStream fos = new
                    FileOutputStream("inventory.dat");
  ObjectOutputStream oos = new ObjectOutputStream(fos);
  oos.writeObject(inventory);
  fos.close();
} // end try
catch (Exception e) {
```

```
    System.out.println(e);
} // end catch
```

Restoring the inventory is also straightforward:

```
ListReferenceBased restoredInventory;
try {
  FileInputStream fis = new
                      FileInputStream("inventory.dat");
  ObjectInputStream ois = new ObjectInputStream(fis);
  Object o = ois.readObject();
  restoredInventory = (ListReferencedBased) o;
  System.out.println(restoredInventory);
} // end try
catch (Exception e) {
  System.out.println(e);
} // end catch
```

The completion of this solution is left as an exercise.

5.5 The Java Collections Framework

The Java Collections Framework (JCF) provides classes for common ADTs

Many modern programming languages, such as Java, provide classes that implement many of the more commonly used ADTs. In Java, many of these classes are defined in the Java Collections Framework or JCF. The JCF contains a number of classes and interfaces that can be applied to nearly any type of data.

Many of the ADTs that are presented in this text have a corresponding class or interface in the JCF. For example, a *List* interface is defined in the JCF that is similar to the *ListInterface* specification presented earlier in this chapter. You may be wondering why we spend so much time developing ADTs in this text if they are already provided in the JCF. There are many reasons for doing so; here are just a few:

- Developing simple ADTs provides a foundation for learning other ADTs.

- You may find yourself working in a language that does not provide any predefined ADTs. You need to have the ability to develop ADTs on your own, and hence understand the process.

- If the ADTs defined by the language you are using are not sufficient, you may need to develop your own or enhance existing ones.

A collections framework includes interfaces, implementations, and algorithms

A collections framework is a unified architecture for representing and manipulating collections. It includes *interfaces,* or ADTs representing collections; *implementations,* or concrete implementations of collection interfaces; and *algorithms,* or methods that perform useful computations, such as sorting and searching, on objects that implement collection interfaces. These algorithms are *polymorphic* because the same method can be used on many different implementations of the appropriate collections interface.

The JCF also contains iterators. Iterators provide a way to cycle through the contents of a collection. Before we can discuss the JCF further, we will give a brief overview of generics and iterators.

Generics

The JCF relies heavily on Java generics. Generics allow you to develop classes and interfaces and defer certain data-type information until you are actually ready to use the class or interface. For example, our list interface was developed independently from the type of the list items by using the `Object` class. With generics, this data type is left as a data-type parameter in the definition of the class or interface. The start of the definition of the class or interface is followed by `<E>`, where the data-type parameter `E` represents the data type that the client code will specify. Here is an example of a simple generic class:

Generic classes allow data-type information to be deferred

```
public class MyClass<E> {
   private E theData;
   private int n;

   public MyClass() {
      n = 0;
   } // end constructor

   public MyClass(E initData, int num) {
      n = num;
      theData = initData;
   } // end constructor

   public void setData(E newData) {
      theData = newData;
   } // end setData

   public E getData() {
      return theData;
   } // end get Data

   public int getNum() {
      return n;
   } // end getNum
} // end MyClass
```

Chapter 9 describes in more detail how to create your own generics.

When you (the client) declare instances of the class, you specify the actual data type that the parameter represents. This data type cannot be a primitive type, only object types are allowed. For example, a simple program that uses this generic class could begin as follows:

Only object types are allowed for data type parameters

```
static public void main(String[] args) {
  MyClass<String> a = new MyClass<String>();
  Double d = new Double(6.4);
  MyClass<Double> b = new MyClass<Double>(d, 51);

  a.setData("Sarah");
  System.out.println(a.getData() + ", " + b.getData());
  System.out.println(a.getNum() + ", " + b.getNum());
```

Notice how the declarations of *a* and *b* specify the data type of *MyClass*'s data member *theData*. Also note that when we previously used *Object* as the return type, we often had to cast the result back to the desired type that is no longer required when using generics.

Iterators

An **iterator** is an object that gives you the ability to cycle through the items in a collection in much the same way that we used a reference to traverse a linked list. If you have an iterator call *iter*, you can access the next item in the collection by using the notation *iter.next()*.

The JFC provides two primary iterator interfaces, *java.util.Iterator* and *java.util.ListIterator*. Note that all interface methods are implicitly public, so the *Iterator* interface is defined as follows:

```
public interface Iterator<E> {
  boolean hasNext();
    // Returns true if the iteration has more elements.

  E next();
    // Returns the next element in the iteration.

  void remove() throws UnsupportedOperationException,
                       IllegalStateException;
    // Removes from the underlying collection the last
    // element returned by the iterator (optional
    // operation).
} // end Iterator
```

The method next is used to return the next element in the collection. When an iterator is initially created, it is positioned so that the first call to *next* on the iterator object will return the initial element in the collection. The method *hasNext* can be used to determine if another element is available in the collection.

Notice that one of the operations, *remove*, can throw the exception *UnsupportedOperationException*. The expectation is that the *remove* operation will simply throw this exception if the operation is not available in the class that implements the interface.

Iterators are an integral part of all of the classes and interfaces used for representing collections in the JCF. Note that just as you can use inheritance to derive new classes, you can use inheritance to derive new interfaces, often called **subinterfaces.** The basis for the ADT collections in the JCF is the interface `java.util.Iterable`, with the subinterface `java.util.Collection`:

```java
public interface Iterable<E> {
  Iterator<E> iterator();
  // Returns an iterator over the elements in this collection
} // end Iterable
public interface Collection<E> extends Iterable<E> {
  // Only a portion of the Collection interface is shown here.
  // See the J2SE documentation for a complete listing of
  // methods

  boolean add(E o);
    // Ensures that this collection contains the specified
    // element (optional operation).

  boolean remove(Object o);
    // Removes a single instance of the specified element from
    // this collection, if it is present (optional operation).

  void clear();
    // Removes all of the elements from this collection
    // (optional operation).

  boolean contains(Object o);
    // Returns true if this collection contains the specified
    // element.

  boolean equals(Object o);
    // Compares the specified object with this collection for
    // equality.

  boolean isEmpty()
    // Returns true if this collection contains no elements.

  int size();
    // Returns the number of elements in this collection.

  Object[] toArray();
    //Returns an array containing all of the elements in this
    // collection.
} // end Collection
```

Thus, every ADT collection in the JCF will have a method to return an iterator object for the underlying collection. The following example shows how an iterator can be used with the JCF list class *LinkedList*:

```
import java.util.LinkedList;
import java.util.Iterator;

public class TestLinkedList {
  static public void main(String[] args) {
    LinkedList<Integer> myList = new LinkedList<Integer>();

    Iterator iter = myList.iterator();
    if (!iter.hasNext()) {
      System.out.println("The list is empty");
    } // end if

    for (int i=1; i <= 5; i++) {
      myList.add(new Integer(i));
    } // end for

    iter = myList.iterator();
    while (iter.hasNext()) {
      System.out.println(iter.next());
    } // end while
  } // end main
} // end TestLinkedList
```

The behavior of an iterator is unspecified if the underlying collection is modified while the iteration is in progress in any way other than by calling the *remove* method.

Another example of a subinterface in the JCF is *java.util.ListIterator*, derived from the *java.util.Iterator interface*:

```
public interface ListIterator<E> extends Iterator<E> {

  void add(E o);
    // Inserts the specified element into the list (optional
    // operation).

  boolean hasNext();
    // Returns true if this list iterator has more elements when
    // traversing the list in the forward direction.

  boolean hasPrevious();
    // Returns true if this list iterator has more elements when
    // traversing the list in the reverse direction.
```

```
   E next();
     // Returns the next element in the list.

   int nextIndex();
     // Returns the index of the element that would be returned
     // by a subsequent call to next.

   E previous();
     // Returns the previous element in the list.

   int previousIndex();
     // Returns the index of the element that would be returned
     // by a subsequent call to previous.

   void remove();
     // Removes from the list the last element that was
     // returned by next or previous (optional operation).

   void set(E o);
     // Replaces the last element returned by next or previous
     // with the specified element (optional operation).
} // end ListIterator
```

The *ListIterator* interface extends *Iterator* by providing support for **bidirectional** access to the collection as well as adding or changing elements in the collection. A bidirectional iterator enables you to move to either the next or previous element in the collection.

Bidirectional iterators allow you to move forward or back through a collection

Chapter 9 describes how to create your own iterator.

The Java Collection's Framework *List* Interface

The JCF provides an interface *java.util.List* that is quite similar to the list interface created in Chapter 4. The JCF *List* interface supports an ordered collection, also known as a sequence. Like the *ListInterface* presented in this text, users can specify by position (integer index) where elements are added to and removed from the list, and the position numbering starts at zero (as in *ListInterface*). Though the interface provides methods based upon positional access to the elements, the time to execute these methods may be proportional to the index value, depending on the implementing class. As such, it is usually preferable to use an iterator instead of index access when possible to locate and process elements in a list.

The JCF *List* interface supports an ordered collection

Declarations for all the methods in the *List* interface are shown here, even the ones inherited from the *Collection* interface. Notice that the methods *iterator*, *add*, *remove*, and *equals* place additional stipulations beyond those specified in the *Collection* interface. The *List* interface also provides other methods not shown here that allow multiple elements to be inserted and removed at any point in the list.

The *List* interface inherits methods from the *Collection* interface

Notice that the *List* interface provides a *ListIterator* that allows bidirectional access in addition to the normal operations that the *Iterator* interface provides. There is also a method to obtain a list iterator that starts at a specified position in the list.

The JCF *List* interface is derived from the JCF *Collection* interface:

```
public interface List<E> extends Collection<E>
  // Only a portion of the List interface is shown here.
  // See the J2SE documentation for a complete listing of
  // methods

  boolean add(E o);
    // Appends the specified element to the end of this list
    // (optional operation).

  void add(int index, E element);
    // Inserts the specified element at the specified position in
    // this list (optional operation).

  void clear();
    // Removes all of the elements from this list (optional
    // operation).

  boolean contains(Object o);
    // Returns true if this list contains the specified element.

  boolean equals(Object o);
    // Compares the specified object with this list for equality.

  E get(int index);
    // Returns the element at the specified position in this
    // list.

  int indexOf(Object o);
    // Returns the index in this list of the first occurrence of
    // the specified element, or -1 if this list does not contain
    // this element.

  boolean isEmpty();
    // Returns true if this list contains no elements.

  Iterator<E> iterator();
    // Returns an iterator over the elements in this list in
    // proper sequence.

  ListIterator<E> listIterator();
    // Returns a list iterator of the elements in this list (in
    // proper sequence).
```

```java
ListIterator<E> listIterator(int index);
  // Returns a list iterator of the elements in this list (in
  // proper sequence), starting at the specified position in
  // this list.

E remove(int index);
  // Removes the element at the specified position in this list
  // (optional operation).

boolean remove(Object o);
  // Removes the first occurrence in this list of the specified
  // element (optional operation).

E set(int index, E element);
  // Replaces the element at the specified position in this
  // list with the specified element (optional operation).

int size();
  // Returns the number of elements in this list.

List<E> subList(int fromIndex, int toIndex);
  // Returns a view of the portion of this list between the
  // specified fromIndex, inclusive, and toIndex,
  // exclusive.

Object[] toArray();
  // Returns an array containing all of the elements in this
  // list in proper sequence.
} // end List
```

The JCF provides numerous classes that implement the *List* interface, including *LinkedList*, *ArrayList*, and *Vector*. Here is an example of how the JCF class *ArrayList* is used to maintain a grocery list:

```java
import java.util.ArrayList;
import java.util.Iterator;

public class GroceryList {

  static public void main(String[] args) {
    ArrayList<String> groceryList = new ArrayList<String>();
    Iterator<String> iter;

    groceryList.add("apples");
    groceryList.add("bread");
    groceryList.add("juice");
```

```
        groceryList.add("carrots");
        groceryList.add("ice cream");

        System.out.println("Number of items on my grocery list: "
                            + groceryList.size());
        System.out.println("Items are: ");
        iter = groceryList.listIterator();
        while (iter.hasNext()) {
          String nextItem = iter.next();
          System.out.println(groceryList.indexOf(nextItem)+") "
                             + nextItem);
        } // end while

     } // end main

} // end GroceryList
```

The output of this program is

```
Number of items on my grocery list: 5
Items are:
0) apples
1) bread
2) juice
3) carrots
4) ice cream
```

Clearly it is more efficient to use a counter to number the items than to use the method *indexOf*; it was done for illustrative purposes.

Summary

1. You can use reference variables to implement the data structure known as a linked list by using a class definition such as the following:

```
package List;

class Node {
  Object item;
  Node next;

  Node(Object newItem) {
    item = newItem;
    next = null;
  } // end constructor
```

```
Node (Object newItem, Node nextNode) {
   item = newItem;
   next = nextNode;
} // end constructor
} // end class Node
```

2. Each reference in a linked list is a reference to the next node in the list. For example, if *nodeRef* is a variable of type *Node* that references a node in this linked list,

   ■ *nodeRef.item* is the data portion of the node.

   ■ *nodeRef.next* references the next node.

3. Algorithms for inserting data into and deleting data from a linked list both involve these steps: Traverse the list from the beginning until you reach the appropriate position; perform reference changes to alter the structure of the list. In addition, you use the *new* operator to dynamically allocate a new node for insertion. When all references to a node are removed, the node is automatically marked for garbage collection.

4. Inserting a new node at the beginning of a linked list or deleting the first node of a linked list are cases that you treat differently from insertions and deletions anywhere else in the list.

5. An array-based implementation uses an implicit ordering scheme—for example, the item that follows *anArray[i]* is stored in *anArray[i+1]*. A reference-based implementation uses an explicit ordering scheme—for example, to find the item that follows the one in node N, you follow node N's reference.

6. You can access any element of an array directly, but you must traverse a linked list to access a particular node. Therefore, the access time for an array is constant, whereas the access time for a linked list depends upon the location of the node within the list.

7. You can insert items into and delete items from a reference-based linked list without shifting data. This characteristic is an important advantage of a linked list over an array.

8. Although you can use the *new* operator to allocate memory dynamically for either an array or a linked list, you can increase the size of a linked list one node at a time more efficiently than an array. When you increase the size of a resizeable array, you must copy the original array elements into the new array and then deallocate the original array.

9. A binary search of a linked list is impractical because you cannot quickly locate its middle item.

10. You can use recursion to perform operations on a linked list. Such use will eliminate special cases and the need for a trailing reference.

11. The recursive insertion algorithm for a sorted linked list works because each smaller linked list is also sorted. When the algorithm makes an insertion at the beginning of one of these lists, the inserted node will be in the proper position in the original list. The algorithm is guaranteed to terminate because each smaller list contains one fewer node than the preceding list and because the empty list is a base case.

12. A tail reference can be used to facilitate locating the end of a list. This is especially useful when an append operation is required.

13. In a circular linked list, the last node references the first node, so that every node has a successor. If the list's external reference references the last node instead of the first node, you can access both the last node and the first node without traversing the list.

14. Dummy head nodes provide a method for eliminating the special cases for insertion into and deletion from the beginning of a linked list. The use of dummy head nodes is a matter of personal taste for singly linked lists, but it is helpful for a doubly linked list.

15. A doubly linked list allows you to traverse the list in either direction. Each node references its successor as well as its predecessor. Because insertions and deletions with a doubly linked list are more involved than with a singly linked list, it is convenient to use both a dummy head node and a circular organization to eliminate complicated special cases for the beginning and end of the list.

16. If you plan on storing the data contained in a linked list to a file, be sure to place the implements *Serializable* clause in each class that has instances that will be written to the file.

17. A generic class or interface enables you to defer the choice of certain data-type information until its use.

18. The Java Collections Framework contains interfaces, implementations, and algorithms for many common ADTs.

19. A collection is an object that holds other objects. An iterator cycles through the contents of a collection.

Cautions

1. An uninitialized reference variable has the value *null*. Attempting to use a reference with a value of *null* will cause a *NullPointerException* to be thrown.

2. The sequence

```
Integer intRef = new Integer(5);
intRef = null;
```

allocates a memory cell and then destroys the only means of accessing it. Do not use *new* when you simply want to assign a value to a reference.

3. Insertions into and deletions from the beginning of a linked list are special cases unless you use a dummy head node. Failure to recognize this fact can result in a *null* reference being used, causing a *NullPointerException* to be thrown.

4. When traversing a linked list by using the reference variable *curr*, you must be careful not to reference *curr* after it has "passed" the last node in the list, because it will have the value *null* at that point. For example, the loop

```
while (value > curr.item)
   curr = curr.next;
```

is incorrect if *value* is greater than all the data values in the linked list, because *curr* becomes *null*. Instead, you should write

```
while ((curr != null) && (value > curr.item))
   curr = curr.next;
```

Because Java uses short-circuit evaluation of logical expressions, if *curr* becomes *null*, the expression *curr.item* is not evaluated.

5. A doubly linked list is a data structure that programmers tend to overuse. However, a doubly linked list is appropriate to use when you have direct access to a node. In such cases, you would not have traversed the list from its beginning. If the list were singly linked, you would not have a reference to the preceding node. Because doubly linking the list provides an easy way to get to the node's predecessor as well as its successor, you can, for example, delete the node readily.

Self-Test Exercises

1. Given the following declarations, and the list shown, draw a picture which shows the result of each sequence of statements given below. If something illegal is done (as noted by the compiler), circle the offending statement and explain why it is illegal. Assume they all begin with this list:

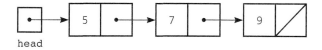

head

```
package IntegerList;

class IntegerNode {
  int item;
  IntegerNode next;

  Node (Object newItem) {
    item = newItem;
    next = null;
  } // end constructor

  Node(Object newItem, Node nextNode) {
    item = newItem;
    next = nextNode;
  } // end constructor

} // end IntegerNode
```

```
IntegerNode head, p, q;
int x;
```

a. p = new IntegerNode();	b. p = new IntegerNode(1, head);

c. p = new IntegerNode(1);
  q = new IntegerNode(3, p);
  p.next = head;
  head = q;
	d. x = 3;
	  p = new IntegerNode(x, head);
	  q = new IntegerNode(p);
	  head = q;

e. IntegerNode curr = head;
  while (curr != null) {
    curr.item++;
    curr = curr.next;
  }
	f. x = 3;
	  p = new IntegerNode(x,
	  head.next);
	  head = p;

2. Consider the algorithm for deleting a node from a linked list that this chapter describes.

   a. Is the deletion of the first node of a linked list a special case? Explain.

   b. Is deletion of the last node of a linked list a special case? Explain.

   c. Is deletion of the only node of a one-node linked list a special case? Explain.

   d. Does deleting the first node take more effort than deleting the last node? Explain.

3. a. Write Java statements that create the linked list pictured in Figure 5-31, as follows. Beginning with an empty linked list, first create and attach a node for K, then create and attach a node for M, and finally create and attach a node for S.

   b. Repeat Part *a*, but instead create and attach nodes in the order B, E, J.

4. Consider the sorted linked list of single characters in Figure 5-31. Suppose that *prev* references the first node in this list and *curr* references the second node.

   a. Write Java statements that delete the second node. (*Hint:* First modify Figure 5-31.)

   b. Now assume that *curr* references the first node of the remaining two nodes of the original list. Write Java statements that delete the last node.

   c. Now *head* references the only node that is left in the list. Write Java statements that insert a new node that contains J into the list so that the list remains sorted.

   d. Revise Figure 5-31 so that your new diagram reflects the results of the previous deletions and insertion.

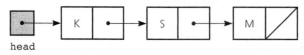

head

FIGURE 5-31

Linked list for Self-Test Exercises 3, 4, and 7

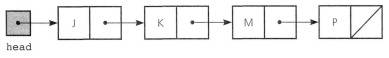

head

FIGURE 5-32

Linked list for Exercise 1

5. There were many types of linked lists discussed in the chapter. What was common in the nodes used in all of these classes?

6. How many assignment operations does the method that you wrote for Self-Test Exercise 5 require?

7. Do a box trace of *writeBackwards2(head)*, where *head* references the linked list of characters pictured in Figure 5-31. Show which node *head* points to in each recursive call. The method *writebackwards2* appears on page 297 of this chapter.

Exercises

1. For each of the following, write the Java statements that perform the requested operation on the list shown in Figure 5-32. Also draw a picture of the status of the list after each operation is complete. When you delete a node from the list, make sure it will eventually be returned to the system. All insertions into the list should maintain the list's sorted order. Do not use any of the methods that were presented in this chapter.

   a. Assume that *prev* references the first node and *curr* references the second node. Insert L into the list.

   b. Assume that *prev* references the second node and that *curr* references the third node of the list after you revised it in Part *a*. Delete the last node of the list.

   c. Assume that *prev* references the last node of the list after you revised it in Part *b*, and assume that *curr* is *null*. Insert Q into the list.

2. Consider a linked list of items that are in no particular order.

   a. Write a method that inserts a node at the beginning of the linked list and a method that deletes the first node of the linked list.

   b. Repeat Part *a*, but this time perform the insertion and deletion at the end of the list instead of at the beginning. Assume the list has only a head reference.

   c. Repeat Part *b*, but this time assume that the list has a tail reference as well as a head reference.

3. Write a method that randomly removes and returns an item from a linked list. Write the method such that

   a. the method uses only the ADT List operations; that is, it is independent of the list's implementation.

b. the method assumes and uses the reference-based implementation of the ADT List.

c. the method assumes and uses the array-based implementation of the ADT List.

4. Given the following `Student` class:

```
class Student {
  private String name;
  private int age;

  public Student(String n, int a) {
    name = n;
    age = a;
  } // end constructor

  public String getName() {
    return name;
  } // end getName

  public int getAge() {
    return age;
  } // end getAge
} // end Student
```

Write a Java method that displays only the name of the ith student in a linked list of students. Assume that $i \geq 0$ and that the linked list contains at least i nodes.

5. Using the `Student` class in Exercise 4, write a recursive version of the method that displays only the name of the ith student in a linked list of students. Assume that $i \geq 1$ and that the linked list contains at least i nodes. (Hint: If $i = 0$, print the name of the first student in the list; otherwise, print the $(i-1)^{th}$ student name from the rest of the list.)

6. The section "Processing Linked Lists Recursively" discussed the traversal of a linked list.

a. Compare the efficiencies of an iterative method that displays a linked list with the method `writeList`.

b. Write an iterative method that displays a linked list backward. Compare the efficiencies of your method with the method `writeListBackward2`.

7. Write a method to merge two linked lists of integers that are sorted into descending order. The result should be a third linked list that is the sorted combination of the original lists. Do not destroy the original lists.

8. The `Node` class presented in this chapter assumed that it would be declared package-private; hence, the data fields were declared for package access only.

a. Suppose that the data fields were declared `private`. Write accessor and mutator methods for both the `item` and `next` fields.

b. Give at least three different examples of how the code in the `ListReferenceBased` implementation would have to be changed.

9. Assume that the reference `list` references the last node of a circular linked list like the one in Figure 5-24. Write a loop that searches for an item in the list and if

found, returns its position. If it is not found, return −1. Assume that the node referenced by `list.next` is the node in the first position.

10. A polynomial is stored in a linked list. Write a method that adds two such polynomials and calculates the final polynomial.

11. Write a method `L.reverse()`, which reverses the order of node list `L1`. For example, if `L1=(BRZ, ARG, SPAIN)`, executing `L.reverse()` changes `L1` to be `(SPAIN, ARG, BRZ)`.

12. The following method has been written to find the last node of a list `L` and return a reference to it. What is the problem with it?

```
public List lastNode( )
{
  List N = firstNode;
  If (N != null)
  {
    do {
      N= N.link;
      }while (N.link !=null);
  }
  return N;
}
```

13. Write a method that traverses a linked list and deletes all duplicate data entries in the list.

14. Write a program that implements a two dimensional array using a linked list.

15. Imagine a circular linked list of integers that are sorted into ascending order, as Figure 5-33a illustrates. The external reference `list` references the last node, which contains the largest integer. Write a method that revises the list so that its data elements are sorted into descending order, as Figure 5-33b illustrates. Do not allocate new nodes.

(a)

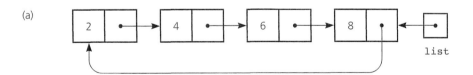

(b)

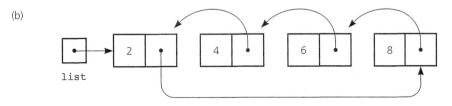

FIGURE 5-33

Two circular linked lists

16. Write a program that merges two ordered doubly linked lists into a single doubly linked list.

17. Write a program that creates a database of all your friends' telephone numbers and full names using a linked list. Write a method for the addition, modification and deletion of numbers, and a searching procedure that uses the first name.

18. Consider the sorted doubly linked list shown in Figure 5-27. This list is a circular doubly linked list and has a dummy head node. Write methods for the following operation for a sorted list:

    ```
    +sortedAdd(in item:ListItemType)
    // Inserts item into its proper sorted position in a
    // sorted list.

    +sortedRemove(in item:ListItemType)
    // Deletes item from a sorted list.
    // Throws an exception if the item is not found.
    ```

19. Repeat Exercise 18 for the sorted doubly linked list shown in Figure 5-26. This list is not circular and does not have a dummy head node. Watch out for the special cases at the beginning and end of the list.

20. You can have a linked list of linked lists, as Figure 5-30 indicates. Assume the Java definitions on page 288-289. Suppose that *curr* references a desired stock item (node) in the inventory list. Write some Java statements that add yourself as a customer to the end of the wait list associated with the node referenced by *curr*.

21. Write a method that sorts a double linked list in descending order.

22. Write a method to interchange the second last and the last elements of a list.

Programming Problems

1. Chapter 4 introduced the ADT sorted list, which maintains its data in sorted order. For example, a sorted list of names would be maintained in alphabetical order, and a sorted list of numbers would be maintained in either increasing or decreasing order. The operations for a sorted list are summarized on page 234.

   Some operations—*sortedIsEmpty*, *sortedSize*, and *sortedGet*, for example—are just like those for the ADT list. Insertion and deletion operations, however, are by value, not by position as they are for a list. For example, when you insert an item into a sorted list, you do not specify where in the list the item belongs. Instead, the insertion operation determines the correct position of the item by comparing its value with those of the existing items on the list. A new operation, *locateIndex*, determines from the value of an item its numerical position within the sorted list.

   Note that the specifications given in Chapter 4 do not say anything about duplicate entries in the sorted list. Depending on your application, you might allow duplicates, or you might want to prevent duplicates from entering the list. For example, a sorted list of Social Security numbers probably should disallow duplicate entries. In this example, an attempt to insert a Social Security number that already exists in the sorted list would fail.

Write a nonrecursive, reference-based implementation of the ADT sorted list of objects as a Java class *SortedListRefBased* such that

a. Duplicates are allowed

b. Duplicates are not allowed, and operations must prevent duplicates from entering the list

2. Repeat Programming Problem 1, but write a recursive, reference-based implementation instead. Recall from this chapter that the recursive methods must be in the private section of the class.

3. Write an implementation of the ADT list interface *ListInterface* that uses the JFC *Vector* class to represent the list items.

4. Write a reference-based implementation of the ADT two-ended list, which has insertion and deletion operations at both ends of the list,

a. Without a tail reference

b. With a tail reference

5. Implement the node structure, including the constructors, for a circular doubly linked list with a dummy head node, assuming it will be package-private. Write an implementation of the ListInterface using a circular doubly linked list. Note that the section "Doubly Linked Lists" has a discussion on how to insert and delete nodes from such a list.

6. Implement the ADT character string as the class *LinkedString* by using a linked list of characters. Include the following *LinkedString* constructors and methods:

LinkedString(**char[]** value)

Allocates a new character linked list so that it represents the sequence of characters currently contained in the character array argument.

LinkedString(String original)

Initializes a new character linked list so that it represents the same sequence of characters as the argument.

char charAt(**int** index)

Returns the char value at the specified index. The first character in the linked character string is in position zero.

LinkedString concat(LinkedStringstr)

Concatenates the specified linked character string to the end of this linked character string.

boolean isEmpty()

Returns true if, and only if, length() is 0.

int length()

Returns the length of this linked character string.

`LinkedString substring(int beginIndex, int endIndex)`

Returns a new linked character string that is a substring of this linked character string.

Implement `LinkedString` so that it is consistent with the `String` class. For example, character positions start at zero. Also, keep track of the number of characters in the string; the length should be determined without traversing the linked list and counting.

7. A *polynomial* of a single variable x with integer coefficients is an expression of the form

$$p(x) = c_0 + c_1 x + c_2 x^2 + \ldots + c_n x^n,$$

where c_i, $i = 0, 1, \ldots, n$, are integers.

Consider a sparse implementation of the ADT polynomials up to the nth degree that stores only the terms with nonzero coefficients. For example, the polynomial

$$p = -3x^7 + 4x^5 + 7x^3 - x^2 + 9$$

can be represented using the linked list shown in Figure 5-35. Complete the class `Polynomial` based on this sparse implementation. Assume `Polynomial` has the following methods:

`Polynomial()`

Constructs a new polynomial of degree zero.

`int getCoefficient(int power)`

Returns an integer representing the coefficient of the x^{power} term.

`void setCoefficient(int coef, int power)`

Sets the coefficient of the x^{power} term to `coef`.

`String toString()`

Returns the `String` representation of the polynomial. For example, $3x^2 + 2x + 1$ would be returned as `3 * x^2 + 2 * x + 1` or, more simply, `3x^2 + 2x + 1`. Any term whose coefficient is zero should not appear in the string unless the polynomial has only a single constant term of zero.

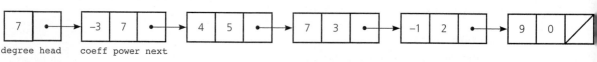

FIGURE 5-34

A sparse polynomial

`double` evaluate(`double` x)

Evaluates the polynomial for the value x and returns the result $p(x)$.

Polynomial **double** add(Polynomial other)

Add to this polynomial the polynomial other and return the resulting polynomial.

8. Round-robin (RR) is a simple scheduling algorithm for processes using the CPU. Each process is given a slice of time on the CPU in equal portions and in circular order. The algorithm assumes that we know the burst time for each process—this is the amount of time that the process needs the CPU before the next I/O request.

   a. Design an ADT to represent a process. Each process has an id and keeps track of the burst time.

   b. Design an ADT that keeps track of a group of processes using the CPU with round-robin scheduling. Use a circular linked list as the data structure that keeps track of the processes wanting to use the CPU. Run the schedule by traversing through the list, simulating each process getting a slice of the CPU, assuming that the process gets a 100 millisecond time slice, and that its burst time is then reduced by 100 milliseconds. Each time the process has the CPU, print to the console the process id and burst time remaining after the process uses the CPU. If a process completes execution (on its last time slice it has 100 milliseconds or less), remove it from the list. When the list of processes is empty, the schedule is complete.

   c. Write a test program that demonstrates your ADT completely. Your program should try many different scenarios—for example, the process with the shortest burst time first, all the processes with the same burst time, and processes with burst times that are not multiples of 100 milliseconds.

9. Occasionally, a linked structure that does not use references is useful. One such structure uses an array whose items are "linked" by array indexes. Figure 5-35a illustrates an array of nodes that represents the linked list in Figure 5-31. Each node has two data fields, *item* and *next*. The *next* data field is an integer index to the array element that contains the next node in the linked list. Note that the *next* data field of the last node contains –1. The integer variable *head* contains the index of the first node in the list.

   The array elements that currently are not a part of the linked list make up a **free list** of available nodes. These nodes form another linked list, with the integer variable *free* containing the index of the first free node. To insert an item into the original linked list, you take a free node from the beginning of the free list and insert it into the linked list (Figure 5-35b). When you delete an item from the linked list, you insert the node into the beginning of the free list (Figure 5-35c). In this way, you can avoid shifting data items.

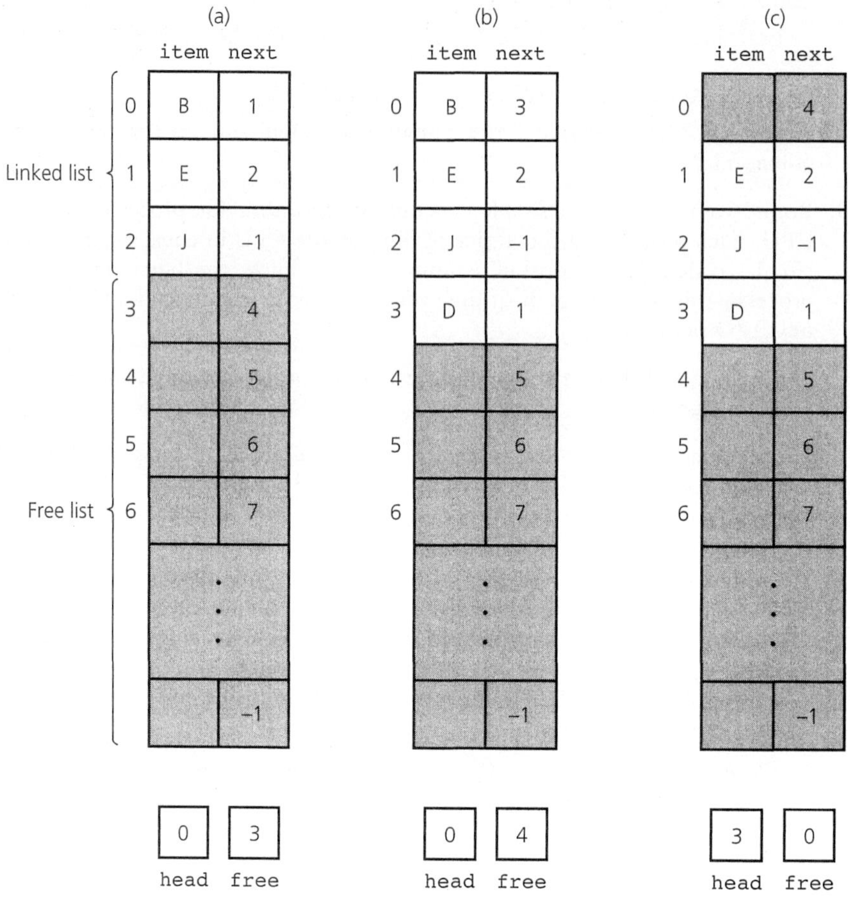

FIGURE 5-35

(a) An array-based implementation of the linked list in Figure 5-31; (b) after inserting D in sorted order; (c) after deleting B

Implement the ADT list by using this array-based linked list.

10. Write the program for the DVD inventory problem that this chapter describes.

11. Modify and expand the inventory program that you wrote for the previous programming problem. Here are a few suggestions:

   a. Add the ability to manipulate more than one inventory with the single program.

   b. Add the ability to keep various statistics about each of the inventory items (such as the average number sold per week for the last 10 weeks).

c. Add the ability to modify the have value for an inventory item (for example, when a DVD is damaged or returned by a customer). Consider the implications for maintaining the relationship between a have value and the size of the corresponding wait list.

d. Make the wait lists more sophisticated. For example, keep names and addresses; mail letters automatically when a DVD comes in.

e. Make the ordering mechanism more sophisticated. For instance, do not order DVDs that have already been ordered but have not yet been delivered.

PART TWO

Problem Solving with Abstract Data Types

Part One of this book reviewed aspects of problem solving that are closely related to programming issues, presented data abstraction as a technique for solution design that permeates our approach to problem solving, introduced Java classes as a way to hide a solution's implementation details and to increase its modularity, introduced the linked list as a data structure that you will see throughout this book, and developed recursion as a problem-solving technique that is useful in the construction of algorithms. The primary concerns of the remainder of this book are the aspects of problem solving that involve the *management of data*—that is, the identification and implementation of some of the more common data-management operations.

You saw in Part One that you can organize data either by position—as in the ADT list—or by value—as in the ADT sorted list. In general, these organizations are appropriate for applications of rather different natures. For example, if an application needs to ask a question about the first person in a line, you should organize the data by position. On the other hand, if an application needs to ask a question about the employee named Smith, you should organize the data by value. In Part Two, you will see other ADTs that use these two data organizations.

Our study of data management has three goals. The first is to identify useful sets of operations—that is, to identify abstract data types. The second goal is to examine applications that use these abstract data types. The third goal is to construct implementations for the abstract data types—that is, to develop data structures and classes. As you will discover, the nature of the operations of an abstract data type, along with the application in which you will use it, greatly influences the choice of its implementation.

CHAPTER 6

Recursion as a Problem-Solving Technique

Chapter 3 presented the basic concepts of recursion, and now this chapter moves on to some extremely useful and somewhat complex applications in computer science. The recursive solutions to the problems you will see are far more elegant and concise than the best of their non-recursive counterparts.

This chapter introduces two new concepts, backtracking and formal grammars. Backtracking is a problem-solving technique that involves guesses at a solution. Formal grammars enable you to define, for example, syntactically correct algebraic expressions. The chapter concludes with a discussion of the close relationship between recursion and mathematical induction; you will learn how to use mathematical induction to study properties of algorithms.

More applications of recursion appear in subsequent chapters.

6.1 Backtracking

This section considers an organized way to make successive guesses at a solution. If a particular guess leads to a dead end, you back up to that guess and replace it with a different guess. This strategy of retracing steps in reverse order and then trying a new sequence of steps is called **backtracking.** You can combine recursion and backtracking to solve the problem that follows.

Backtracking is a strategy for guessing at a solution and backing up when an impasse is reached

The Eight Queens Problem

A chessboard contains 64 squares that form 8 rows and 8 columns. The most powerful piece in the game of chess is the queen because it can attack any other piece within its row, within its column, or along its diagonal. The Eight Queens problem asks you to place eight queens on the chessboard so that no queen can attack any other queen.

Place eight queens on the chessboard so that no queen can attack any other queen

One strategy is to guess at a solution. However, there are $c(64,8) = 4,426,165,368$ ways to arrange 8 queens on a chessboard of 64 squares—so many ways that it would be exhausting to check all of them for a solution to this problem. Nevertheless, a simple observation eliminates many arrangements from consideration: No queen can reside in a row or a column that contains another queen. In other words, each row and column can contain exactly one queen. Thus, attacks along rows or columns are eliminated, leaving only $8! = 40,320$ arrangements of queens to be checked for attacks along diagonals. A solution now appears more feasible.

Place queens one column at a time

Suppose that you provide some organization for the guessing strategy by placing one queen per column, beginning with the first square of column 1. When you consider column 2, you eliminate its first square because row 1 contains a queen, you eliminate its second square because of a diagonal attack, and you finally place a queen in the third square of column 2. Figure 6-1a shows the placement of five queens as a result of this procedure. The dots in the figure indicate squares that are rejected because a queen in that square is subject to attack by another queen in an earlier column.

If you reach an impasse, backtrack to the previous column

Notice that the five queens in Figure 6-1a can attack any square in column 6. Therefore, you cannot place a queen in column 6, so you must back up to column 5 and move its queen. As Figure 6-1b indicates, the next possible square in column 5 is in the last row. When you consider column 6 once again, there are still no choices for a queen in that column. As you have exhausted the possibilities in column 5, you must back up to column 4. The next possible square in column 4 is in row 7, as Figure 6-1c indicates. You then consider column 5 again and place a queen in row 2.

How can you use recursion in the solution that was just described? Consider an algorithm that places a queen in a column, given that you have placed queens correctly in the preceding columns. First, if there are no more columns to consider, you are finished; this is the base case. Otherwise, after you successfully place a queen in the current column, you need to consider the next column. That is, you need to solve the same problem with one fewer column; this is the recursive step. Thus, you begin with eight columns, consider smaller

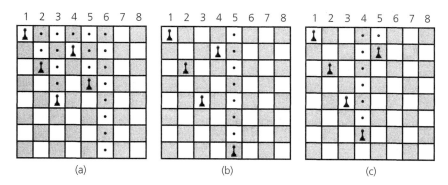

FIGURE 6-1

(a) Five queens that cannot attack each other, but that can attack all of column 6; (b) backtracking to column 5 to try another square for the queen; (c) backtracking to column 4 to try another square for the queen and then considering column 5 again

problems that decrease in size by one column at each recursive step, and reach the base case when you have a problem with no columns.

This solution appears to satisfy the criteria for a recursive solution. However, you do not know whether you can successfully place a queen in the current column. If you can, you recursively consider the next column. If you cannot place a queen in the current column, you need to backtrack, as has already been described. The following pseudocode describes the algorithm for placing queens in columns, given that the previous columns contain queens that cannot attack one another:

```
placeQueens(in currColumn:integer)
// Places queens in columns numbered currColumn through 8.

  if (currColumn > 8) {
    The problem is solved
  }
  else {
    while ( unconsidered squares exist in currColumn
            and the problem is unsolved ) {
      Determine the next square in column currColumn that
          is not under attack by a queen in an earlier
          column
      if (such a square exists) {
        Place a queen in the square
        placeQueens(currColumn+1)  // try next column
        if (no queen is possible in column currColumn+1) {
          Remove queen from column currColumn and consider
              the next square in that column
```

The solution combines recursion with backtracking

```
            }  // end if
          }  // end if
        }  // end while
      }  // end if
```

The method *placeQueens* is used in the following context:

Using **placeQueens**

```
Clear all squares on the board
placeQueens(1)              // begin with the first
                            // column
if (a solution exists) {
  Display solution
}
else {
  Display message          // no solution found
}  // end if
```

This context suggests the following class. For simplicity, the class uses a two-dimensional array to represent the board. Each square on the board either contains a queen or is empty.

```java
public class Queens {
  // squares per row or column
  public static final int BOARD_SIZE = 8;

  // used to indicate an empty square
  public static final int EMPTY = 0;

  // used to indicate square contains a queen
  public static final int QUEEN = 1;

  private int board[][]; // chess board
  public Queens() {
  // -------------------------------------------------
  // Constructor: Creates an empty square board.
  // -------------------------------------------------
    board = new int[BOARD_SIZE][BOARD_SIZE];
  }  // end constructor

  public void clearBoard() {
  // -------------------------------------------------
  // Clears the board.
  // Precondition: None.
  // Postcondition: Sets all squares to EMPTY.
  // -------------------------------------------------
    // To be implemented in Programming Problem 1
  }  // end clearBoard
```

```
public void displayBoard() {
// ------------------------------------------------
// Displays the board.
// Precondition: None.
// Postcondition: Board is written to standard
// output; zero is an EMPTY square, one is a square
// containing a queen (QUEEN).
// ------------------------------------------------
   // To be implemented in Programming Problem 1
} // end displayBoard

public boolean placeQueens(int column) {
// ------------------------------------------------
// Places queens in columns of the board beginning
// at the column specified.
// Precondition: Queens are placed correctly in
// columns 1 through column-1.
// Postcondition: If a solution is found, each
// column of the board contains one queen and method
// returns true; otherwise, returns false (no
// solution exists for a queen anywhere in column
// specified).
// ------------------------------------------------
  if (column > BOARD_SIZE) {
    return true;  // base case
  }
  else {
    boolean queenPlaced = false;
    int row = 1;  // number of square in column

    while ( !queenPlaced && (row <= BOARD_SIZE) ) {
      // if square can be attacked
      if (isUnderAttack(row, column)) {
        ++row;  // consider next square in column
      } // end if
      else { // place queen and consider next column
        setQueen(row, column);
        queenPlaced = placeQueens(column+1);
        // if no queen is possible in next column,
        if (!queenPlaced) {
          // backtrack: remove queen placed earlier
          // and try next square in column
          removeQueen(row, column);
          ++row;
        } // end if
      } // end if
    } // end while
```

```
      return queenPlaced;
   } // end if
} // end placeQueens


private void setQueen(int row, int column) {
// -----------------------------------------------------
// Sets a queen at square indicated by row and
// column.
// Precondition: None.
// Postcondition: Sets the square on the board in a
// given row and column to QUEEN.
// -----------------------------------------------------
   // To be implemented in Programming Problem 1
}  // end setQueen


private void removeQueen(int row, int column) {
// -----------------------------------------------------
// Removes a queen at square indicated by row and
// column.
// Precondition: None.
// Postcondition: Sets the square on the board in a
// given row and column to EMPTY.
// -----------------------------------------------------
   // To be implemented in Programming Problem 1
}  // end removeQueen


private boolean isUnderAttack(int row, int column) {
// -----------------------------------------------------
// Determines whether the square on the board at a
// given row and column is under attack by any queens
// in the columns 1 through column-1.
// Precondition: Each column between 1 and column-1
// has a queen placed in a square at a specific row.
// None of these queens can be attacked by any other
// queen.
// Postcondition: If the designated square is under
// attack, returns true; otherwise, returns false.
// -----------------------------------------------------
   // To be implemented in Programming Problem 1
}  // end isUnderAttack


private int index(int number) {
// -----------------------------------------------------
// Returns the array index that corresponds to
// a row or column number.
// Precondition: 1 <= number <= BOARD_SIZE.
// Postcondition: Returns adjusted index value.
```

```
// -----------------------------------------------
   // To be implemented in Programming Problem 1
} // end index
} // end Queens
```

Figure 6-2 indicates the solution that the previous algorithm finds.

By modifying how you use *placeQueens*, you can discover other solutions to the Eight Queens problem. You can also improve this algorithm. Although we used an 8-by-8 array to represent the board because it simplified the implementation, such an array wastes space; after all, only 8 squares out of 64 are used. The programming problems at the end of this chapter consider modifications and improvements to this algorithm.

6.2 Defining Languages

English and Java are two languages with which you are familiar. A **language** is nothing more than a set of strings of symbols from a finite alphabet. For example, if you view a Java program as one long string of characters, you can define the set of all syntactically correct Java programs. This set is the language

JavaPrograms = {strings w : w is a syntactically correct Java program}

Notice that whereas all programs are strings, not all strings are programs. A Java compiler is a program that, among other things, determines whether a given string is a member of the language *JavaPrograms;* that is, the compiler determines whether the string is a syntactically correct Java program. Of course, this definition of *JavaPrograms* is not descriptive enough to allow the construction of a compiler. The definition specifies a characteristic of the strings in the set *JavaPrograms*: The strings are syntactically correct Java programs. However, this definition does not give the rules for determining

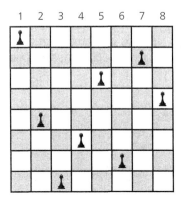

FIGURE 6-2

A solution to the Eight Queens problem

whether a string is in the set or not; that is, the definition does not specify what is meant by a syntactically correct Java program.

The word "language" does not necessarily mean a programming language or a communication language. For example, the set of algebraic expressions forms a language

$$AlgebraicExpressions = \{w : w \text{ is an algebraic expression}\}$$

The language *AlgebraicExpressions* is the set of strings that meets certain rules of syntax; however, the set's definition does not give these rules.

In both examples, the rules for forming a string within the language are missing. A **grammar** states the rules of a language. The grammars that you will see in this chapter are recursive in nature. One of the great benefits of using such a grammar to define a language is that you can often write a straightforward recursive algorithm, based on the grammar, that determines whether a given string is in the language. Such an algorithm is called a **recognition algorithm** for the language.

A grammar states the rules for forming the strings in a language

As it is a complex task to present a grammar for the set *JavaPrograms*, we instead will look at grammars for some simpler languages, including several common languages of algebraic expressions.

The Basics of Grammars

A grammar uses several special symbols:

Symbols that grammars use

■ $x \mid y$ means x or y.

■ $x\ y$ means x followed by y. (When the context requires clarification, the notation $x \cdot y$ will be used. The symbol • means concatenate, or append.)

■ < *word* > means any instance of *word* that the definition defines.

A grammar for the language

$$JavaIds = \{w : w \text{ is a legal Java identifier}\}$$

is simple, so we begin with it. As you know, a legal Java identifier begins with a letter and is followed by zero or more letters and digits. In this context, the underscore (_) and dollar sign ($) are letters. One way to represent this definition of an identifier is with a syntax diagram, as shown in Figure 6-3.

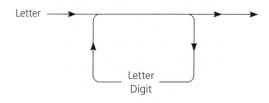

FIGURE 6-3

A syntax diagram for Java identifiers

A syntax diagram is convenient for people to use, but a grammar is a better starting point if you want to write a method that will recognize an identifier. A grammar for the language *JavaIds* is

$< identifier > = < letter > | < identifier > < letter > | < identifier > < digit > |$
$\quad\quad \$<identifier> | \_<identifier>$
$< letter > =$ a | b | $\cdots$ | z | A | B | $\cdots$ | Z
$< digit > = 0 | 1 | \cdots | 9$

A grammar for the language of Java identifiers

The definition reads as follows:

> *An identifier is a letter, or an identifier followed by a letter, or an identifier followed by a digit.*

The most striking aspect of this definition is that *identifier* appears in its own definition: This grammar is recursive, as are many grammars.

Many grammars are recursive

Given a string *w*, you can determine whether it is in the language *JavaIds* by using the grammar to construct the following recognition algorithm: If *w* is of length 1, it is in the language if the character is a letter. (This statement is the base case, so to speak.) If *w* is of length greater than 1, it is in the language if the last character of *w* is either a letter or a digit, and *w* minus its last character is an identifier.

The pseudocode for a recursive valued method that determines whether a string is in *JavaIds* follows:

A recognition algorithm for Java identifiers

```
isId(in w:string):boolean
// Returns true if w is a legal Java identifier;
// otherwise returns false.
  if (w is of length 1)  { // base case
    if (w is a letter) {
      return true
    }
    else {
      return false
    }  // end if
  }
  else if (the last character of w is a letter or a digit) {
    return isId(w minus its last character)  // Point X
  }
  else  {
    return false
  } // end if
```

Figure 6-4 contains a trace of this method for the string *A2B*.

Two Simple Languages

Now consider two more simple examples of languages, their grammars, and resulting recognition algorithms.

The initial call is made and the method begins execution.

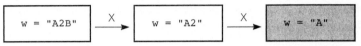

At point X, a recursive call is made and the new invocation of `isId` begins execution:

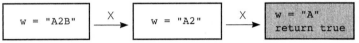

At point X, a recursive call is made and the new invocation of `isId` begins execution:

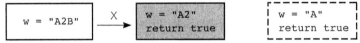

This is the base case, so this invocation of `isId` completes:

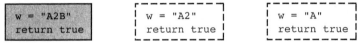

The value is returned to the calling method, which completes execution:

The value is returned to the calling method, which completes execution:

FIGURE 6-4

Trace of *isId("A2B")*

Palindromes.   A palindrome is a string that reads the same from left to right as it does from right to left. For example, "radar" and "deed" are both palindromes. You can define the language of palindromes as follows:

Palindromes = {*w* : *w* reads the same left to right as right to left}

How can you use a grammar to define the language *Palindromes*? You need to devise a rule that allows you to determine whether a given string *w* is a palindrome. In the spirit of recursive definitions, you should state this rule in terms of determining whether a *smaller string* is a palindrome. Your first instinct might be to choose *w* minus its last (or first) character for the smaller string. However, this does not work because there is no relationship between the statements

w is a palindrome

and

w minus its last character is a palindrome

That is, *w* might be a palindrome, although *w* minus its last character is not, as is the case for "deed." Similarly, *w* minus its last character might be a palindrome, although *w* is not, as is the case for "deeds."

A little thought reveals that you must consider characters in pairs: There *is* a relationship between the statements

w is a palindrome

and

w minus its first and last characters is a palindrome

Specifically, *w* is a palindrome if and only if

■ The first and last characters of *w* are the same

A recursive description of a palindrome

and

■ *w* minus its first and last characters is a palindrome

You need a base case that you will reach after stripping away enough pairs of characters. If *w* has an even number of characters, you will eventually be left with two characters, and then, after you strip away another pair, you will be left with zero characters. A string of length zero is called the **empty string** and is a palindrome. If *w* has an odd number of characters, you will eventually be left with one character, after which you cannot strip away another pair. Hence, you must have a second base case: A string of length 1 is a palindrome.

Strings of length 0 or 1 are the base cases

This discussion leads to the following grammar for the language *Palindromes*:

$$< pal > = \text{empty string} \mid < ch > \mid \text{a} < pal > \text{a} \mid \text{b} < pal > \text{b} \mid \cdots$$
$$\mid \text{Z} < pal > \text{Z}$$

A grammar for the language of palindromes

$$< ch > = \text{a} \mid \text{b} \mid \cdots \mid \text{z} \mid \text{A} \mid \text{B} \mid \cdots \mid \text{Z}$$

Based on this grammar, you can construct a recursive valued method for recognizing palindromes. The pseudocode for such a method follows:

```
isPal(in w:string):boolean
// Returns true if the string w of letters is a palindrome;
// otherwise returns false.

   if (w is the empty string or w is of length 1) {
     return true
   }
   else if (w's first and last characters are the same
            letter) {
     return isPal(w minus its first and last characters)
   }
   else {
     return false
   } // end if
```

A recognition algorithm for palindromes

Strings of the form $A^n B^n$. The symbol $A^n B^n$ is standard notation for the string that consists of n consecutive A's followed by n consecutive B's. Another simple language consists of such strings:

$$L = \{w : w \text{ is of the form } A^n B^n \text{ for some } n \geq 0\}$$

The grammar for this language is actually very similar to the grammar for palindromes. You must strip away both the first and last characters and check to see that the first character is an A and the last character is a B. Thus, the grammar is

A grammar for the language of strings $A^n B^n$

$$< legal\text{-}word > = \text{empty string} \mid A < legal\text{-}word > B$$

The pseudocode for a recognition method for this language follows:

A recognition algorithm for strings $A^n B^n$

```
isAnBn(in w:string):boolean
// Returns true if w is of the form A^nB^n;
// otherwise returns false.

  if (the length of w is zero) {
    return true
  }
  else if (w begins with the character A and ends with the
            character B) {
    return isAnBn(w minus its first and last characters)
  }
  else {
    return false
  }  // end if
```

Algebraic Expressions

One of the tasks a compiler must perform is to recognize and evaluate algebraic expressions. For example, consider the Java assignment statement

```
y = x + z * (w/k + z * (7 * 6));
```

A Java compiler must determine whether the right side is a syntactically legal algebraic expression; if so, the compiler must then indicate how to compute the expression's value.

There are several common definitions for a "syntactically legal" algebraic expression. Some definitions force an expression to be *fully parenthesized*, that is, to have parentheses around each pair of operands together with their operator. Thus, you would have to write *((a * b) * c)* rather than *a * b * c*. In general, the stricter a definition, the easier it is to recognize a syntactically legal expression. On the other hand, conforming to overly strict rules of syntax is an inconvenience for programmers.

This section presents three different languages for algebraic expressions. The expressions in these languages are easy to recognize and evaluate but are generally inconvenient to use. However, these languages provide us with good, nontrivial applications of grammars. We will see other languages of algebraic expressions whose members are difficult to recognize and evaluate but are convenient to use. To avoid unnecessary complications, assume that you have only the binary operators +, −, *, and / (no unary operators or exponentiation). Also, assume that all operands in the expression are single-letter identifiers.

Infix, prefix, and postfix expressions.   The algebraic expressions you learned about in school are called infix expressions. The term "infix" indicates that every binary operator appears *between* its operands. For example, in the expression

$$a + b$$

the operator + is between its operands a and b. This convention necessitates associativity rules, precedence rules, and the use of parentheses to avoid ambiguity. For example, the expression

$$a + b * c$$

is ambiguous. What is the second operand of the +? Is it b or is it $(b * c)$? Similarly, the first operand of the * could be either b or $(a + b)$. The rule that * has higher precedence than + removes the ambiguity by specifying that b is the first operand of the * and that $(b * c)$ is the second operand of the +. If you want another interpretation, you must use parentheses:

$$(a + b) * c$$

Even with precedence rules, an expression like

$$a / b * c$$

is ambiguous. Typically, / and * have equal precedence, so you could interpret the expression either as $(a / b) * c$ or as $a / (b * c)$. The common practice is to *associate from left to right*, thus yielding the first interpretation.

Two alternatives to the traditional infix convention are **prefix** and **postfix.** Under these conventions, an operator appears either before its operands (prefix) or after its operands (postfix). Thus, the infix expression

$$a + b$$

is written in prefix form as

$$+ \, a \, b$$

and in postfix form as

$$a \, b \, +$$

To further illustrate the conventions, consider the two interpretations of the infix expression $a + b * c$ just considered. You write the expression

$$a + (b * c)$$

in prefix form as

$$+ \, a * b \, c$$

In a prefix expression, an operator precedes its operands

In a postfix expression, an operator follows its operands

The + appears before its operands a and ($*$ b c), and the $*$ appears before its operands b and c. The same expression is written in postfix form as

   $a\ b\ c\ *\ +$

The $*$ appears after its operands b and c, and the + appears after its operands a and (b c $*$).

Similarly, you write the expression

   $(a + b) * c$

in prefix form as

   $*\ +\ a\ b\ c$

The $*$ appears before its operands (+ a b) and c, and the + appears before its operands a and b. The same expression is written in postfix form as

   $a\ b\ +\ c\ *$

The + appears after its operands a and b, and the $*$ appears after its operands (a b +) and c.

If the infix expression is fully parenthesized, converting it to either prefix or postfix form is straightforward. Because each operator then corresponds to a pair of parentheses, you simply move the operator to the position marked by either the "(" if you want to convert to prefix form or the ")" if you want to convert to postfix form. This position either precedes or follows the operands of the operator. All parentheses would then be removed.

For example, consider the fully parenthesized infix expression

   $((a + b) * c)$

To convert this expression to prefix form, you first move each operator to the position marked by its corresponding open parenthesis:

Converting to prefix
form $(\ (\ a\ b\ )\ c\ )$

   $*\ +$

Next, you remove the parentheses to get the desired prefix expression:

   $*\ +\ a\ b\ c$

Similarly, to convert the infix expression to postfix form, you move each operator to the position marked by its corresponding closing parenthesis:

Converting to postfix
form $(\ (\ a\ b\ )\ c\ )$

         $+$ $*$

Then you remove the parentheses:

   $a\ b\ +\ c\ *$

When an infix expression is not fully parenthesized, these conversions are more complex. Chapter 7 discusses the general case of converting an infix expression to postfix form.

The advantage of prefix and postfix expressions is that they never need precedence rules, association rules, and parentheses. Therefore, the grammars for prefix and postfix expressions are quite simple. In addition, the algorithms that recognize and evaluate these expressions are relatively straightforward.

Prefix and postfix expressions never need precedence rules, association rules, and parentheses

Prefix expressions.   A grammar that defines the language of all prefix expressions is

< *prefix* > = < *identifier* > | < *operator* > < *prefix* > < *prefix* >

< *operator* > = + | − | * | /

< *identifier* > = a | b | · · · | z

From this grammar you can construct a recursive algorithm that recognizes prefix expressions. Suppose that you treat the expression in question as a substring of a String variable *strExp*, from index *first* through *last*. If the expression is of length 1, it is a prefix expression if and only if *strExp* is a single lowercase letter. Expressions of length 1 can be the base case. If the length of the expression is greater than 1, then for it to be a legal prefix expression, it must be of the form

< *operator* > < *prefix* > < *prefix* >

Thus, the algorithm must check to see that

- The first character of *strExp* is an operator

and

- The remainder of *strExp* (index *first* + 1 through *last*) consists of two consecutive prefix expressions

The first task is trivial, but the second is a bit tricky. How can you determine whether you are looking at two consecutive prefix expressions? A key observation is that if you add *any* string of nonblank characters to the end of a prefix expression, you will no longer have a prefix expression. That is, if *E* is a prefix expression and *Y* is any nonempty string of nonblank characters, then *E Y* cannot be a prefix expression. This is a subtle point; Exercise 17 at the end of this chapter asks you to prove it.

If *E* is a prefix expression, *E Y* cannot be

Given this observation, you can begin to determine whether the substring of *strExp* starting after the operator consists of two consecutive prefix expressions by identifying a first prefix expression. If you cannot find one, the original string itself is not a prefix expression. If you do find one, you need to know where it ends. Notice that the previous observation implies that only one endpoint is possible for this first expression: Given that the substring of *strExp* from index *first* + 1 through *end1* is a prefix expression, no other prefix expression can begin at position *first* + 1. That is, it is not possible that another substring of *strExp* from index *first* + 1 through *end2* is a prefix expression for any *end2* not equal to *end1*.

If you find that the first prefix expression ends at position *end1*, you then attempt to find a second prefix expression beginning at position *end1* + 1 and ending at or before position `last`. If you find the second expression, you must check that you are at the end of the string in question.

By using these ideas, you can show, for example, that +/*ab–cd* is a prefix expression. For +/*ab–cd* to be a prefix expression, it must be of the form +$E_1 E_2$, where E_1 and E_2 are prefix expressions. Now you can write

$$E_1 = /E_3 E_4 \text{ where}$$

$$E_3 = a$$

$$E_4 = b$$

Since E_3 and E_4 are prefix expressions, E_1 is a prefix expression. Similarly, you can write

$$E_2 = -E_5 E_6 \text{ where}$$

$$E_5 = c$$

$$E_6 = d$$

and see that E_2 is a prefix expression.

If we assume that the class for prefix expressions has a private data field *strExp*, you can write a method in the same class to determine whether the expression is a prefix expression. First, you construct a recursive valued method *endPre(first, last)* that returns either the index of the end of the prefix expression *strExp* or the value –1, which signals that no prefix expression begins at *strExp*. The method appears in pseudocode as follows:

endPre determines the end of a prefix expression

```
endPre(in first:integer, in second:integer):integer
// Finds the end of a prefix expression, if one exists.
// Precondition: The substring of strExp from index first
// through last contains no blank characters.
// Postcondition: Returns the index of the last character
// in strExp that begins at index first, if one exists, or
// returns -1 if no such prefix expression exists.

  if (first < 0 or first > last) {
     return -1
  }  // end if
  ch = character at position first of strExp
  if (ch is an identifier) {
     // index of last character in simple prefix expression
     return first
  }
  else if (ch is an operator) {
     // find the end of the first prefix expression
     firstEnd = endPre(first + 1, last)          // Point X

     // if the end of the first expression was found
     // find the end of the second prefix expression
```

```
  if (firstEnd > -1) {
    return endPre(firstEnd + 1, last)          // Point Y
  }
  else {
    return -1
  } // end if
}
else {
  return -1
} // end if
```

Figure 6-5 contains a trace of *endPre* when the initial expression is *+/ab−cd*.

The initial call is made and **endPre** begins execution:

first character of **strExp** is +, so at point X, a recursive call is made and the new invocation of **endPre** begins execution:

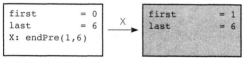

Next character of **strExp** is /, so at point X, a recursive call is made and the new invocation of **endPre** begins execution:

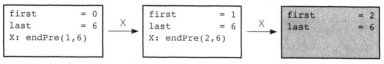

Next character of **strExp** is a, which is a base case. The current invocation of **endPre** completes execution and returns its value:

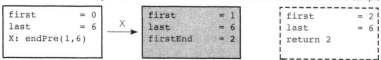

Because **firstEnd** > —1, a recursive call is made from point Y and the new invocation of **endPre** begins execution:

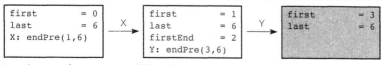

Next character of **strExp** is b, which is a base case. The current invocation of **endPre** completes execution and returns its value:

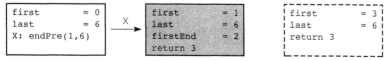

FIGURE 6-5

Trace of **endPre(first, last)**, where **strExp** is +/ab-cd

(continues)

FIGURE 6-5

(continued)

The current invocation of `endPre` completes execution and returns its value:

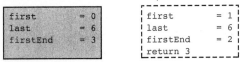

Because `firstEnd > —1`, a recursive call is made from point Y and the new invocation of `endPre` begins execution:

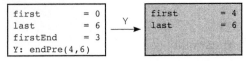

Next character of `strExp` is -, so at point X, a recursive call is made and the new invocation of `endPre` begins execution:

Next character of `strExp` is c, which is a base case. The current invocation of `endPre` completes execution and returns its value:

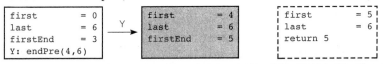

Because `firstEnd > —1`, a recursive call is made from point Y and the new invocation of `endPre` begins execution:

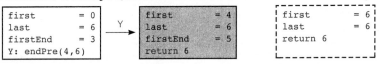

Next character of `strExp` is d, which is a base case. The current invocation of `endPre` completes execution and returns its value:

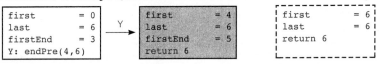

The current invocation of `endPre` completes execution and returns its value:

The current invocation of `endPre` completes execution and returns its value to the original call to `endPre`:

A recognition algorithm for prefix expressions

Now you can use the method *endPre* to determine whether the data field *strExp* is a prefix expression as follows:

```
isPre():boolean
// Determines whether the string expression in this class
// is a prefix expression.
```

```
// Precondition: The class has a data field strExp that
// has been initialized with a string expression that
// contains no blank characters.
// Postcondition: Returns true if the expression is in
// prefix form; otherwise returns false.

  size = length of expression strExp
  lastChar = endPre(0, size - 1)

  if (lastChar >= 0 and lastChar == size-1) {
    return true
  }
  else {
    return false
  }  // end if
```

Having determined that your string is a prefix expression, how can you evaluate it? Since each operator is followed by its two operands, you can look ahead in the expression for them. However, such operands can themselves be prefix expressions, which you must evaluate first. These prefix expressions are subexpressions of the original expression and must therefore be "smaller." A recursive solution to this problem seems natural.

The following method, which appears in pseudocode, evaluates a prefix expression. This algorithm is simpler than one that evaluates infix expressions.

```
evaluatePrefix(in strExp:string):float
// Evaluates the prefix expression strExp.
// Precondition: strExp is a string consisting of a valid
// prefix expression containing no blanks.
// Postcondition: Returns the value of the prefix
// expression.
  ch = first character of expression strExp
  Delete first character from strExp
  if (ch is an identifier) {
    // base case - single identifier
    return value of the identifier
  }
  else if (ch is an operator named op) {
    operand1 = evaluatePrefix(strExp)
    operand2 = evaluatePrefix(strExp)
    return operand1 op operand2
  } // end if
```

An algorithm to evaluate a prefix expression

Notice that each recursive call to *evaluatePrefix* removes from *strExp* the most recently evaluated prefix expression. The resulting substring is then used in the next recursive call of *evaluatePrefix*. To implement this method in Java requires that the parameter of `evaluatePrefix` be a mutable string type such as `java.lang.StringBuffer`. (See Appendix A for a discussion of mutable strings.)

Postfix expressions.   A grammar that defines the language of all postfix expressions is

< *postfix* > = < *identifier* > | < *postfix* > < *postfix* > < *operator* >

< *operator* > = + | − | * | /

< *identifier* > = a | b | · · · | z

Some calculators require that you enter two numbers before you enter the operation that you want to perform. Such calculators, in fact, require you to enter postfix expressions.

Here we will develop an algorithm for converting a prefix expression to a postfix expression. Chapter 7 presents a nonrecursive algorithm for evaluating postfix expressions. Together these two algorithms give you another method for evaluating a prefix expression. To simplify the conversion algorithm, assume that the prefix recognition algorithm has identified this as a syntactically correct prefix expression.

If you think recursively, the conversion from prefix form to postfix form is straightforward. If the prefix expression *exp* is a single letter, then

$$postfix(exp) = exp$$

Otherwise *exp* must be of the form

< *operator* > < *prefix*1 > < *prefix*2 >

The corresponding postfix expression is then

< *postfix1* > < *postfix2* > < *operator* >

where < *prefix1* > converts to < *postfix1* > and < *prefix2* > converts to < *postfix2* >. Therefore,

$$postfix(exp) = postfix(prefix1) + postfix(prefix2) + operator$$

Thus, at a high level, the conversion algorithm is

An algorithm that converts a prefix expression to postfix form

```
if (exp is a single letter) {
   return exp
}
else {
   return postfix(prefix1) + postfix(prefix2) + operator

} // end if
```

The following pseudocode method *convert* refines this algorithm. As in *evaluatePrefix*, the parameter *pre* should be a mutable string type.

```
convert(in pre:string):string
// Converts a prefix expression pre to postfix form.
// Precondition: The expression in the string pre is a
// valid prefix expression.
// Postcondition: Returns the equivalent postfix expression
// as a string.

    // check the first character of the given string
    ch = first character of pre        // get first character
    Delete first character of pre
    if (ch is a lowercase letter) {  // check character
        // base case - single identifier expression
        return ch as a string
    }
    else  { // ch is an operator
        // do the conversion recursively
        postfix1 = convert(pre)
        postfix2 = convert(pre)
        return postfix1 + postfix2 + ch  // concatenate operator
    }  // end if
```

A recursive algorithm that converts a prefix expression to postfix form

Fully parenthesized expressions. Most programmers would object to using prefix or postfix notation for their algebraic expressions, so most programming languages use infix notation. However, infix notation requires precedence rules, rules for association, and parentheses to avoid ambiguity within the expressions.

You can make precedence and association rules unnecessary by placing parentheses around each pair of operands together with their operator, thereby avoiding any ambiguity. A grammar for the language of all fully parenthesized infix expressions is

$$< infix > = < identifier > \mid (< infix > < operator > < infix >)$$

$$< operator > = + \mid - \mid * \mid /$$

$$< identifier > = a \mid b \mid \cdots \mid z$$

A grammar for the language of fully parenthesized algebraic expressions

Although the grammar is simple, the language is rather inconvenient for programmers.

Therefore, most programming languages support a definition of algebraic expressions that includes both precedence rules for the operators and rules of association so that fully parenthesized expressions are not required. However, the grammars for defining such languages are more involved, and the algorithms for recognizing and evaluating their expressions are more difficult than those you have seen in this section. Programming Problem 7 at the end of this chapter describes such a grammar without left-to-right association rules and asks you to write a recognition algorithm. Chapter 7 presents a nonrecursive evaluation algorithm for algebraic expressions that follows both precedence and left-to-right association rules.

6.3 The Relationship Between Recursion and Mathematical Induction

A very strong relationship exists between recursion and mathematical induction. Recursion solves a problem by specifying a solution to one or more base cases and then demonstrating how to derive the solution to a problem of an arbitrary size from the solutions to smaller problems of the same type. Similarly, mathematical induction proves a property about the natural numbers by proving the property about a base case—usually 0 or 1—and then proving that the property must be true for an arbitrary natural number N if it is true for the natural numbers smaller than N.

Given the similarities between recursion and mathematical induction, it should not be surprising that induction is often employed to prove properties about recursive algorithms. What types of properties? You can, for example, prove that an algorithm actually performs the task that you intended. As an illustration, we will prove that the recursive *factorial* algorithm of Chapter 3 does indeed compute the factorial of its argument. Another use of mathematical induction is to prove that a recursive algorithm performs a certain amount of work. For example, we will prove that the solution to the Towers of Hanoi problem—also from Chapter 3—makes exactly $2^N - 1$ moves when it starts with N disks.

You can use induction to prove that a recursive algorithm either is correct or performs a certain amount of work

The Correctness of the Recursive Factorial Method

The following pseudocode describes a recursive method that computes the factorial of a nonnegative integer *n:*

```
fact(in n:integer):integer

  if (n is 0) {
    return 1
  }
  else {
    return n * fact(n - 1)
  }  // end if
```

You can prove that the method *fact* returns the values

$fact(0)$ $= 0! = 1$

$fact(n)$ $= n! = n * (n - 1) * (n - 2) * \cdots * 1$ if $n > 0$

The proof is by induction on n.

Basis. *Show that the property is true for n = 0.* That is, you must show that *fact(0)* returns 1. But this result is simply the base case of the method: *fact(0)* returns 1 by its definition.

You now must establish that

property is true for an arbitrary k $\Rightarrow$ property is true for k + 1

Inductive hypothesis. *Assume that the property is true for n = k.* That is, assume that

$$fact(k) = k * (k-1) * (k-2) * \cdots * 2 * 1$$

Inductive conclusion. *Show that the property is true for n = k + 1.* That is, you must show that $fact(k + 1)$ returns the value

$$(k+1) * k * (k-1) * (k-2) * \cdots * 2 * 1$$

By definition of the method $fact$, $fact(k + 1)$ returns the value

$$(k+1) * fact(k)$$

But by the inductive hypothesis, $fact(k)$ returns the value

$$k * (k-1) * (k-2) * \cdots * 2 * 1$$

Thus, $fact(k + 1)$ returns the value

$$(k+1) * k * (k-1) * (k-2) * \cdots * 2 * 1$$

which is what you needed to show to establish that

property is true for an arbitrary k $\Rightarrow$ property is true for k + 1

The inductive proof is thus complete.

The Cost of Towers of Hanoi

In Chapter 3, you saw the following solution to the Towers of Hanoi problem:

```
solveTowers(in count:integer, in source:Pole,
            in destination:Pole, in spare:Pole)

  if (count is 1) {
    Move a disk directly from source to destination
  }
  else {
    solveTowers(count-1, source, spare, destination)
    solveTowers(1, source, destination, spare)
    solveTowers(count-1, spare, destination, source)
  } // end if
```

We now pose the following question: If you begin with N disks, how many moves does $solveTowers$ make to solve the problem?

Let $moves(N)$ be the number of moves made starting with N disks. When $N = 1$, the answer is easy:

$$moves(1) = 1$$

When $N > 1$, the value of $moves(N)$ is not so apparent. An inspection of the $solveTowers$ algorithm, however, reveals three recursive calls. Therefore, if you knew how many moves *solveTowers* made starting with $N - 1$ disks, you could figure out how many moves it made starting with N disks; that is,

$$moves(N) = moves(N - 1) + moves(1) + moves(N - 1)$$

Thus, you have a recurrence relation for the number of moves required for N disks:

A recurrence relation for the number of moves that **solveTowers** requires for *N* disks

$$moves(1) = 1$$

$$moves(N) = 2 * moves(N - 1) + 1 \qquad \text{if } N > 1$$

For example, you can determine $moves(3)$ as follows:

$$
\begin{aligned}
moves(3) \;&= 2 * moves(2) + 1 \\
&= 2 * (2 * moves(1) + 1) + 1 \\
&= 2 * (2 * 1 + 1) + 1 \\
&= 7
\end{aligned}
$$

Although the recurrence relation gives you a way to compute $moves(N)$, a **closed-form formula**—such as an algebraic expression—would be more satisfactory because you could substitute any given value for N and obtain the number of moves made. However, the recurrence relation is useful because there are techniques for obtaining a closed-form formula from it. Since these techniques are not relevant to us right now, we simply pull the formula out of the blue and use mathematical induction to prove that it is correct.

A closed-form formula for the number of moves that **solveTowers** requires for *N* disks

The solution to the previous recurrence relation is

$$moves(N) = 2^N - 1, \text{ for all } N \geq 1$$

Notice that $2^3 - 1$ agrees with the value 7 that was just computed for $moves(3)$.

The proof that $moves(N) = 2^N - 1$ is by induction on N.

Basis. *Show that the property is true for N = 1.* Here, $2^1 - 1 = 1$, which is consistent with the recurrence relation's specification that $moves(1) = 1$.

You now must establish that

property is true for an arbitrary k $\Rightarrow$ property is true for k + 1

Inductive hypothesis. *Assume that the property is true for N = k.* That is, assume

$$moves(k) = 2^k - 1$$

Inductive conclusion. *Show that the property is true for N = k + 1.* That is, you must show that $moves(k + 1) = 2^{k+1} - 1$. Now

$$
\begin{aligned}
moves(k + 1) \;&= 2 * moves(k) + 1 \qquad \text{from the recurrence relation} \\
&= 2 * (2^k - 1) + 1 \qquad \text{by the inductive hypothesis} \\
&= 2^{k+1} - 1
\end{aligned}
$$

which is what you needed to show to establish that

property is true for an arbitrary k ⇒ property is true for k + 1

The inductive proof is thus complete.

Do not get the false impression that proving properties of programs is an easy matter. These two proofs are about as easy as any will be. However, well-structured programs are far more amenable to these techniques than are poorly structured programs.

Appendix D provides more information about mathematical induction.

Summary

1. Backtracking is a solution strategy that involves both recursion and a sequence of guesses that ultimately lead to a solution. If a particular guess leads to an impasse, you retrace your steps in reverse order, replace that guess, and try to complete the solution again.

2. A grammar is a device for defining a language, which is a set of strings of symbols. By using a grammar to define a language, you often can construct a recognition algorithm that is directly based on the grammar. Grammars are frequently recursive, thus allowing you to describe vast languages concisely.

3. To illustrate the use of grammars, we defined several different languages of algebraic expressions. These different languages have their relative advantages and disadvantages. Prefix and postfix expressions, while difficult for people to use, have simple grammars and eliminate problems of ambiguity. On the other hand, infix expressions are easier for people to use but require parentheses, precedence rules, and rules of association to eliminate ambiguity. Therefore, the grammar for infix expressions is more involved.

4. A close relationship between mathematical induction and recursion exists. You can use induction to prove properties about a recursive algorithm. For example, you can prove that a recursive algorithm is correct, and you can derive the amount of work it requires.

Cautions

1. The subproblems that a recursive solution generates eventually must reach a base case. Failure to do so could result in an algorithm that does not terminate. Solutions that involve backtracking are particularly subject to this kind of error.

2. Grammars, like recursive algorithms, must have carefully chosen base cases. You must ensure that when a string is decomposed far enough, it will always reach the form of one of the grammar's base cases.

3. The subtleties of some of the algorithms you encountered in this chapter indicate the need for mathematical techniques to prove their correctness. The application of these techniques during the design of the various components of a solution can help to eliminate errors in logic before they appear in the program. One such technique is mathematical induction; another is the use of loop invariants, which we discussed in Chapter 2 and will discuss again in subsequent chapters.

Self-Test Exercises

1. Consider a Four Queens problem, which has the same rules as the Eight Queens problem but uses a 4-by-4 board. Find all solutions to this new problem by applying backtracking by hand.

2. Write a recursive grammar for the language of octal numbers in Java. Recall that an octal number starts with a zero.

3. A number 12345 would be written in scientific notation as 1.2345E+4. Note that the number has a coefficient of 1.2345 (a decimal number greater than or equal to 1 and less than 10), followed by E, followed by a signed number for the exponent of 10. Write a recursive grammar for the language of numbers in scientific notation.

4. Consider the language of these strings: $, cc$d, cccc$dd, cccccc$ddd, and so on. Write a recursive grammar for this language.

5. For the following infix expression, write the equivalent prefix and postfix expressions:
   $(a*b-c)/d*e-(f-g)$

6. Write the infix and postfix expressions that represent the following prefix expression: $--a/b+c*def$

7. Is the following string a prefix expression? $+-/abc*+def*gh$

8. Use mathematical induction to show that the recurrence relation $f(n) = 2n + f(n-1)$ has the closed-form solution $f(n) = n(n-1)$.

Exercises

1. Trace the following recursive methods:

   a. *isPal* with the string "abccda"

   b. *isAnBn* with the string "AAAB"

   c. *endPre* where *strExp* = "*+ab-cd"

2. Write a Java program that implements this factorial using stacks.

   $$\text{Fact}(n) \begin{cases} 1 & : \text{if } n = 0 \ \& \ n > 0 \\ n * \text{fact}(n-1) & : \text{if } n > 1 \end{cases}$$

3. Write a program that checks whether the given parentheses are right or wrong.

   (A + B) / ((C * D) + (E / F) * D + C

4. What is the postfix expression for the following infix: $(a + b*(c - a) - d)$

   a. $d\,b\,c\,a - *\,a + -$

   b. $a\,b\,c\,a\,d - - *+$

   c. $a\,b\,c\,a - *+d -$

   d. None of the above.

5. Here is an infix expression: *4+3*(6*3-12)*. Suppose that the usual stack algorithm is used to convert the expression from an infix to postfix notation. What is the maximum number of symbols that will appear on the stack at one time during the conversion of this expression?

   a. 1

   b. 2

   c. 3

   d. 4

   e. 5

6. Consider a language of words, where each word is a string of dots and dashes. The following grammar describes this language:

   < *word* > = < *dot* > | < *dash* > < *word* > | < *word* > < *dot* >

   < *dot* > = •

   < *dash* > = −

   a. Write all three-character strings that are in this language.

   b. Is the string • • • − − in this language? Explain.

   c. Write a seven-character string that contains more dashes than dots and is in the language. Show how you know that your answer is correct.

   d. Write pseudocode for a recursive recognition method *isIn(str)* that returns *true* if the string *str* is in this language and returns *false* otherwise.

7. What is the value of the postfix expression |2|3|2|4|+| - | * |

   a. Something between -15 and -100

   b. Something between -5 and -15

   c. Something between 5 and -5

   d. Something between 5 and 15

   e. Something between 15 and 100

8. Consider a language that the following grammar defines:

   <*G*> = empty string | <*E*> | <*V*> <*E*> | <*E*> <*G*> <*V*>

   <*E*> = & | #

   <*V*> = W | A

   a. Write pseudocode for a recursive method that determines whether the string w is in this language.

   b. Is the string &W#W in this language?

9. Let *L* be the language

   $L = \{S : S \text{ is of the form } A^{2n} B^n, \text{ for some } n > 0\}$

Thus, a string is in *L* if and only if it starts with a sequence of A's and is followed by a sequence of half as many B's. For example, AAAABB is in *L*, but ABBB, BAABAA, and the empty string are not.

   a. Give a grammar for the language *L*.

   b. Write a recursive method that determines whether the string `str` is in *L*.

10. Consider the language that the following grammar defines:

$< S > \, = \, < L > \, | \, < S > < S > < D >$

$< L > \, = \, A \, | \, B$

$< D > \, = \, 1 \, | \, 2$

   a. Write all four-character strings that are in this language.

   b. Write one string in this language that contains more than four characters.

11. Consider a language of the following strings: The letter A, the letter B, the letter C preceded by a string that is in the language, the letter D preceded by a string in the language. For example, these strings are in this language: A, AC, ACC, ACD, B, BC, BCC, BD, BCDC.

   a. Write a grammar for this language.

   b. Is BAC in this language? Explain.

   c. Write a recursive recognition algorithm for this language.

12. Consider the language that the following grammar defines:

$< word > \, = \, \$ \, | \, a < word > a \, | \, b < word > b \, | \cdots | \, y < word > y \, | \, z < word > z$

Equivalently,

$L = \{ w \$ reverse(w) : w \text{ is a string of letters of length} \geq 0 \}$

Note that this language is very similar to the language of palindromes, but there is a special middle character here.

    The algorithm that this chapter gave for recognizing palindromes can be adapted easily to this language. The algorithm, which is recursive and processes the string `str` from both ends toward the middle, is based on the following facts:

■ A string with no characters is not in the language.

■ A string with exactly one character is in the language if the character is a $.

■ A longer string is in the language if the ends are identical letters and the inner substring (from the second character to the next to the last character of `str`) is in the language.

    Describe a recursive recognition algorithm that processes the string from left to right, reading one character at a time and not explicitly saving the string for future reference. Write a Java method that implements your algorithm.

13. Write a Java program that resolves the following postfix expression: *8416+*122/-*

14. Is *abc*+*def/gh-** a postfix expression? Explain in terms of the grammar for postfix expressions.

15. Prove the following for single-letter operands: If E is a prefix expression and Υ is a nonempty string of nonblank characters, then $E\,\Upsilon$ cannot be a legal prefix expression. (*Hint:* Use a proof by induction on the length of E.)

16. Consider the following recursive method:

```
public static int p(int x) {
   if (x < 3) {
      return x;
   }
   else {
      return p(x-1) * p(x-3);
   }  // end if
}  // end p
```

Let $m(x)$ be the number of multiplication operations that the execution of $p(x)$ performs.

   a. Write a recursive definition of $m(x)$.

   b. Prove that your answer to Part a is correct by using mathematical induction.

17. Consider numeric palindromes that consist only of digits, such as 34943 and 1001, but not 1121, 1A1, or "abba." Let $p(n)$ be the number of numeric palindromes of length n.

   a. Write a recursive definition of $p(n)$.

   b. Prove that your answer to Part a is correct by using mathematical induction.

18. Suppose we have the following recurrence relation for $f(n)$:

$f(0) = 0$ for $n = 0$;

$f(n) = f(n-1) + 3n$ for $n > 0$;

Prove by induction on n that the following is a closed-form formula for f:

$f(n) = 3n(n+1)/2$

19. Suppose we have the following recurrence relation for $f(n)$:

$f(0) = 1$ for $n = 0$;

$f(n) = 2f(n-1) + 3$ for $n > 0$;

Prove by induction on n that the following is a closed-form formula for f:

$f(n) = 2^{n+2} - 3$

20. Chapter 3 gave the following definition for $c(n, k)$, where n and k are assumed to be nonnegative integers:

$$c(n, k) = \begin{cases} 1 & \text{if } k = 0 \\ 1 & \text{if } k = n \\ 0 & \text{if } k > n \\ c(n-1, k-1) + c(n-1, k) & \text{if } 0 < k < n \end{cases}$$

Prove by induction on n that the following is a closed form for $c(n, k)$:

$$c(n, k) = \frac{n!}{(n-k)!\,k!}$$

Programming Problems

1. Complete the program that solves the Eight Queens problem.

2. Revise the program that you just wrote for the Eight Queens problem so that it answers the following questions:

    a. How many backtracks occur? That is, how many times does the program remove a queen from the board?

    b. How many calls to *isUnderAttack* are there?

    c. How many recursive calls to *placeQueens* are there?

    d. Can you make *isUnderAttack* more efficient? For example, as soon as you detect that a queen can attack a given square, do you still look for another queen?

* 3. You can begin the Eight Queens problem by placing a queen in the second square of the first column instead of the first square. You can then call *placeQueens* to begin with the second column. This revision should lead you to a new solution. Write a program that finds all solutions to the Eight Queens problem.

4. Instead of using an 8-by-8 array to represent the board in the Eight Queens program, you can use a one-dimensional array to represent only the squares that contain a queen. Let *col* be an array of eight integers such that

    col[k] = row index of the queen in column $k + 1$

    For example, if *col[2]* is 3, then a queen is in the fourth row (square) of the third column—that is, in *board[3][2]*. Thus, you use *col[k]* to represent a queen instead of *board[col[k]][k]*.

    This scheme requires that you also store information about whether each queen is subject to attack. Because only one queen per column is permitted, you do not have to check columns. To check for a row attack, define an array *rowAttack* such that *rowAttack[k]* is nonzero if the queen in column $k + 1$ can be attacked by a queen in its row.

    To check for diagonal attacks, observe that diagonals have either a positive slope or a negative slope. Those with a positive slope are parallel to the diagonal that runs from the lower left corner of the board to the upper right corner. Diagonals with a negative slope are parallel to the diagonal that runs from the upper left corner to the lower right corner. Convince yourself that if *board[i][j]* represents a square, then $i + j$ is constant for squares that are in a diagonal with a positive slope, and $i - j$ is constant for squares that are in a diagonal with a negative slope. You will find that $i + j$ ranges from 0 to 14 and that $i - j$ ranges from –7 to +7. Thus, define arrays *posDiagonal* and *negDiagonal* such that

    posDiagonal[k] is true if the queen in column $k + 1$ can be attacked by a queen in its positive-sloped diagonal, and

    negDiagonal[k] is true if the queen in column $k + 1$ can be attacked by a queen in its negative-sloped diagonal.

    Use these ideas to write a program that solves the Eight Queens problem.

5. Do you know how to find your way through a maze? After you write this program, you will never be lost again!

Assume that a maze is a rectangular array of squares, some of which are blocked to represent walls. The maze has one entrance and one exit. For example, if x's represent the walls, a maze could appear as:

```
xxxxxxxxxxxxxxxxxx x
x       x      xxxx x
x xxxxx xxxxx   xx x
x xxxxx xxxxxxx xx x
x x          xx xx x
x xxxxxxxxxx xx    x
xxxxxxxxxxxxxoxxxxxx
```

A creature, indicated in the previous diagram by o, sits just inside the maze at the entrance. Assume that the creature can move in only four directions: north, south, east, and west. In the diagram, north is up, south is down, east is to the right, and west is to the left. The problem is to move the creature through the maze from the entrance to the exit, if possible. As the creature moves, it should mark its path. At the conclusion of the trip through the maze, you should see both the correct path and incorrect attempts.

Squares in the maze have one of several states: CLEAR (the square is clear), WALL (the square is blocked and represents part of the wall), PATH (the square lies on the path to the exit), and VISITED (the square was visited, but going that way led to an impasse).

This problem uses two ADTs that must interact. The ADT creature represents the creature's current position and contains operations that move the creature. The creature should be able to move north, south, east, and west one square at a time. It should also be able to report its position and mark its trail.

The ADT maze represents the maze itself, which is a two-dimensional rectangular arrangement of squares. Suppose that we number the rows of squares from the top beginning with zero, and we number the columns of squares from the left beginning with zero. Thus, you can use a row number and a column number to identify uniquely any square within the maze. The ADT clearly needs a data structure to represent the maze. It also needs such data as the height and width of the maze, given in numbers of squares; the length of a side of a square; and the row and column coordinates of both the entrance to and the exit from the maze.

The ADT maze should also contain, for example, operations that create a specific maze, given a text file of data; display a maze; determine whether a particular square is part of the wall; determine whether a particular square is part of the path; and so on.

The text file that you will use to represent a maze is simple. An example of how this can be done for the previously given maze is:

```
20   7 width and height of maze in squares
0   18 row  and column coordinate of maze exit
6   12 row  and column coordinate of maze entrance
xxxxxxxxxxxxxxxxxx x
x       x      xxxx x
x xxxxx xxxxx   xx x
x xxxxx xxxxxxx xx x
x x          xx xx x
```

```
x xxxxxxxxxx xx     x
xxxxxxxxxxxx xxxxxxx
```

Each line in the file corresponds to a row in the maze; each character in a line corresponds to a column in the maze. X's indicate blocked squares (the walls), and blanks indicate clear squares. This notation is convenient because you can see what the maze looks like as you design it.

If you are at the maze's entrance, you can systematically find your way out of the maze by using the following search algorithm. It involves backtracking—that is, retracing your steps when you reach an impasse.

1. First, check whether you are at the exit. If you are, you're done (a very simple maze); if you are not, go to Step 2.

2. Try to move to the square directly to the north by calling the method *goNorth* (described later).

3. If *goNorth* was successful, you are done. If it was unsuccessful, try to move to the square directly to the west by calling the method *goWest* (described later).

4. If *goWest* was successful, you are done. If it was unsuccessful, try to move to the square directly to the south by calling the method *goSouth* (described later).

5. If *goSouth* was successful, you are done. If it was unsuccessful, try to move to the square directly to the east by calling the method *goEast* (described later).

6. If *goEast* was successful, you are done. If it was unsuccessful, you are still done, because no path exists from the entrance to the exit.

The method *goNorth* will examine all the paths that start at the square to the north of the present square as follows. If the square directly to the north is clear, is inside the maze, and has not been visited before, move into this square and mark it as part of the path. (Note that you are moving from the south.) Check whether you are at the exit. If you are, you're done. Otherwise, try to find a path to the exit from here by trying all paths leaving this square except the one going south (going south would put you back in the square from which you just came) as follows. Call *goNorth*; if it is not successful, call *goWest* and, if it is not successful, call *goEast*. If *goEast* is not successful, mark this square as visited, move back into the square to the south, and return.

The following pseudocode describes the *goNorth* algorithm:

```
goNorth(maze, creature)

  if (the square to the north is clear,
      inside the maze, and unvisited) {
    Move to the north
    Mark the square as part of the path
    if (at exit) {
      success = true
    }
    else {
      success = goNorth(maze, creature)
      if (!success) {
        success = goWest(maze, creature)
        if (!success) {
          success = goEast(maze, creature)
          if (!success) {
```

```
        Mark square visited
        Backtrack south
      } // end if
    } // end if
   } // end if
  } // end if
 }
 else {
   success = false
 }  // end if
 return success
```

The *goWest* method will examine all the paths that start at the square to the west of the present square as follows. If the square directly to the west is clear, is inside the maze, and has not been visited before, move into this square and mark it as part of the path. (Note that you are moving from the east.) Check whether you are at the exit. If you are, you're done. Otherwise, try to find a path to the exit from here by trying all paths leaving this square except the one going east (this would put you back in the square from which you just came) as follows. Call *goNorth*; if it is not successful, call *goWest* and, if it is not successful, call *goSouth*. If *goSouth* is not successful, mark this square as visited, move back into the square to the east, and return.

The methods *goEast* and *goSouth* are analogous to the methods just described.

6. You may have heard of a puzzle where you must fill in squares for a 9x9 grid with the digits one through nine using the following rules. The digits can appear only once in each row and column. Furthermore, the 9x9 grid is divided into nine regions of 3x3 grids, and the digits can only appear once in each region. Given the following puzzle, write a recursive solution using backtracking that solves such a puzzle.

		3			8		2	
6			3					9
	9		7			1		4
9			2			5	4	3
	8		4		1			
4	6	2			7			1
1		6			3		9	
8					9	3		6
	3		6			7		

7. Write a program that gives all of the permutations of characters stored in an array. For example:

```
char[] charArr = {'A', 'B', 'C'};
findPermuations(charArr);
```

produces the following result:

```
[A, B, C]
[A, C, B]
```

```
[B, A, C]
[B, C, A]
[C, A, B]
[C, B, A]
```

Note that the strategy here is to start with an array of n items, and solve this problem in terms of permuting *n-1* items—so notice that the program starts by finding permutations that start with A, leaving the problem of finding permutations of B and C. Once that is completed, you must go back and start again with B, and find permutations of A and C, and so on until each element in the array has been used as the first element. So the problem starts to look like this:

p({A, B, C}) =	A + p({B, C}) producing	[A, B, C]
		[A, C, B]
	B + p({A, C}) producing	[B, A, C]
		[B, C, A]
	C + p({A, B})producing	[C, A, B]
		[C, B, A]

Rather than trying to work with a portion of the array, it will be helpful to include an index that keeps track of which element you are working on. For example, the initial call should include a parameter 0 (representing the fact that you are starting with the first element), and subsequent calls increment this index, so now we have

p({A, B, C}, 0) =	p({A, B, C}, 1) producing	[A, B, C]
		[A, C, B]
	p({B, A, C}, 1) producing	[B, A, C]
		[B, C, A]
	p({C, A, B}, 1) producing	[C, A, B]
		[C, B, A]

Since each subsequent call needs to change the order of the elements, you should make a copy of the array and use that in the recursive call. Also, think about what would be the base case—and when it is reached, print the array using `ArraytoString`.

8. Write a program that implements the tower of Hanoi using 3 stacks. Consider three rods and a number of disks of different sizes which can be slide onto any rod. The puzzle starts with the disks in a stack, in ascending order of size on one rod, the smallest at the top, thus making a conical shape. Hint: In programming, the disks are replaced by numbers.

9. The following is a grammar that allows you to omit parentheses in infix algebraic expressions when the precedence rules remove ambiguity. For example, $a + b * c$ means $a + (b * c)$. However, the grammar requires parentheses when ambiguity would otherwise result. That is, the grammar does not permit left-to-right association when several operators have the same precedence. For example, $a/b * c$ is illegal. Notice that the definitions introduce factors and terms.

< expression > = < term > | < term > + < term > | < term > − < term >

*< term > = < factor > | < factor > * < factor > | < factor > / < factor >*

< *factor* > = < *letter* > | (< *expression* >)

< *letter* > = a | b | · · · | z

The recognition algorithm is based on a recursive chain of subtasks: *find an expression* → *find a term* → *find a factor.* What makes this a recursive chain is that *find an expression* uses *find a term*, which in turn uses *find a factor. Find a factor* either detects a base case or uses *find an expression*, thus forming the recursive chain.

The pseudocode for the recognition algorithm follows:

```
FIND AN EXPRESSION
// The grammar specifies that an expression is either
// a single term or a term followed by a + or a -,
// which then must be followed by a second term.

  Find a term
  if (the next symbol is a + or a -) {
    Find a term
  }  // end if

FIND A TERM
// The grammar specifies that a term is either a
// single factor or a factor followed by a * or a /,
// which must then be followed by a second factor.

  Find a factor
  if (the next symbol is a * or a /) {
    Find a factor
  }  // end if

FIND A FACTOR
// The grammar specifies that a factor is either a
// single letter (the base case) or an
// expression enclosed in parentheses.

  if (the first symbol is a letter) {
    Done
  }
  else if (the first symbol is a '(') {
    Find an expression starting at character after '('
    Check for ')'
  }
  else {
    No factor exists
  }  // end if
```

Design and implement a class of infix expressions, as described by the given grammar. Include a method to recognize a legal infix expression.

CHAPTER 7

Stacks

This chapter introduces a well-known ADT called a stack and presents both its applications and implementations. You will see how the operations on a stack give it a last-in, first-out behavior. Two of the several applications of a stack that the chapter considers are evaluating algebraic expressions and searching for a path between two points. Finally, the chapter discusses the important relationship between stacks and recursion.

7.1 The Abstract Data Type Stack

The specification of an abstract data type that you can use to solve a particular problem can emerge during the design of the problem's solution. The ADT developed in the following example happens to be an important one: the ADT stack.

Developing an ADT During the Design of a Solution

When you type a line of text on a keyboard, you are likely to make mistakes. If you use the backspace key to correct these mistakes, each backspace erases the previous character entered. Consecutive backspaces are applied in sequence and so erase several characters. For instance, if you type the line

```
abcc←ddde←←←ef←fg
```

where ← represents the backspace character, the corrected input would be

```
abcdefg
```

How can a program read the original line and get the correct input? In designing a solution to this problem, you eventually must decide how to store the input line. In accordance with the ADT approach, you should postpone this decision until you have a better idea of what operations you will need to perform on the data.

A first attempt at a solution leads to the following pseudocode:

Initial draft of a solution

```
// read the line, correcting mistakes along the way
while (not end of line) {
  Read a new character ch
  if (ch is not a '←') {
    Add ch to the ADT
  }
  else {
    Remove from the ADT the item added most recently
  } // end if
} // end while
```

This solution calls to attention two of the operations that the ADT will have to include:

Two ADT operations that are required

- Add a new item to the ADT.
- Remove from the ADT the item that was added most recently.

Notice that potential trouble lurks if you type a ← when the ADT is empty, that is, when the ADT contains no characters. If this situation should occur, you have two options: (1) have the program terminate and write an error message, or (2) have the program ignore the ← and continue. Either option is reasonable, so let's suppose that you decide to ignore the ← and continue. Therefore, the algorithm becomes

```
// read the line, correcting mistakes along the way
while (not end of line) {
  Read a new character ch
  if (ch is not a '←') {
    Add ch to the ADT
  }
  else if (the ADT is not empty) {
    Remove from the ADT the item added most recently
  }
  else {
    Ignore the '←'
  }  // end if
}  // end while
```

The "read and correct" algorithm

From this pseudocode you can identify a third operation required by the ADT:

- Determine whether the ADT is empty.

Another required ADT operation

This solution places the corrected input line in the ADT. Now suppose that you want to display the line. At first, it appears that you can accomplish this task by using the ADT operations already identified, as follows:

```
// write the line
while (the ADT is not empty) {
  Remove from the ADT the item added most recently
  Write .....Uh-oh!
}  // end while
```

A false start at writing the line

This pseudocode is incorrect for two reasons:

1. When you remove an item from the ADT, the item is gone, so you cannot write it. What you should have done was to *retrieve* from the ADT the item that was added most recently. A retrieval operation means to *look at, but leave unchanged*. Only after retrieving and writing the item should you remove it from the ADT.

Reasons why the attempted solution is incorrect

2. The most recently added item is the last character of the input line. You certainly do not want to write it first. The resolution of this particular difficulty is left to you as an exercise.

If we address only the first difficulty, the following pseudocode writes the input line in reversed order:

```
// write the line in reversed order
while (the ADT is not empty) {
  Retrieve from the ADT the item that was
      added most recently and put it in ch
  Write ch
  Remove from the ADT the item added most recently
}  // end while
```

The write-backward algorithm

Thus, a fourth operation is required by the ADT:

Another required
ADT operation

■ Retrieve from the ADT the item that was added most recently.

Although you have yet to think about an implementation of the ADT, you know that you must be able to perform four specific operations.[1] These operations define the required ADT, which happens to be well known: It is usually called a **stack.** As you saw in Chapter 4, it is customary to include initialization operations in an ADT. Thus, the following operations define the ADT stack.

KEY CONCEPTS

ADT Stack Operations

1. Create an empty stack.

2. Determine whether a stack is empty.

3. Add a new item to the stack.

4. Remove from the stack the item that was added most recently.

5. Remove all the items from the stack.

6. Retrieve from the stack the item that was added most recently.

The term "stack" is intended to conjure up visions of things encountered in daily life, such as a stack of dishes in the school cafeteria, a stack of books on your desk, or a stack of assignments waiting for you to work on them. In common English usage, "stack of" and "pile of" are synonymous. To computer scientists, however, a stack is not just any old pile. A stack has the property that the last item placed on the stack will be the first item removed. This property is commonly referred to as **last-in, first-out,** or simply **LIFO.**

Last-in, first-out

A stack of dishes in a cafeteria makes a very good analogy of the abstract data type stack, as Figure 7-1 illustrates. As new dishes are added, the old dishes drop farther into the well beneath the surface. At any particular time, only the dish last placed on the stack is above the surface and visible. This dish is at the **top** of the stack and is the one that must be removed next. In general, the dishes are removed in exactly the opposite order from that in which they were added.

The LIFO property of stacks seems inherently unfair. Think of the poor person who finally gets the last dish on the cafeteria's stack, a dish that may have been placed there six years ago. Or how would you like to be the first person to arrive on the stack for a movie—as opposed to the line for a movie.

---

1. As you will learn if you complete Exercise 8 at the end of this chapter, the final algorithm to write the line correctly instead of in reversed order does not require additional ADT operations.

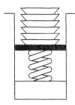

FIGURE 7-1

Stack of cafeteria dishes

You would be the last person allowed in! These examples demonstrate the reason that stacks are not especially prevalent in everyday life. The property that we usually desire in our daily lives is **first in, first out,** or **FIFO. A queue,** which you will study in the next chapter, is the abstract data type with the FIFO property. Most people would much prefer to wait in a movie *queue*—as a line is called in Britain—than in a movie *stack*. However, while the LIFO property of stacks is not appropriate for very many day-to-day situations, it is precisely what is needed for a large number of problems that arise in computer science.

Notice how well the analogy holds between the abstract data type stack and the stack of cafeteria dishes. The operations that manipulate data in the ADT stack are the *only* such operations, and they correspond to the only things that you can do to a stack of dishes. You can determine whether the stack of dishes is empty but not how many dishes are on the stack; you can inspect the top dish but no other dish; you can place a dish on top of the stack but at no other position; and you can remove a dish from the top of the stack but from no other position. If any of these operations was not available, or if you were permitted to perform any other operations, the ADT would not be a stack.

Although the stack of cafeteria dishes suggests that, as you add or remove dishes, the other dishes move, do not have this expectation of the ADT stack. The stack operations involve only the top item and imply only that the other items in the stack remain in sequence. Implementations of the ADT stack operations might or might not move the stack's items. The implementations given in this chapter do not move data items.

Refining the definition of the ADT stack.   Before we specify the details of the stack operations, consider the removal and retrieval operations more carefully. The current definition enables you to remove the stack's top without inspecting it, or to inspect the stack's top without removing it. Both tasks are reasonable and occur in practice. However, if you wanted to inspect *and* remove the top item of a stack—a task that is not unusual—you would need the sequence of operations

- Retrieve from the stack the item that was added most recently.

- Remove from the stack the item that was added most recently.

An operation that retrieves and then removes the top of a stack would allow you to perform this common task in one operation.

The following pseudocode specifies the operations for the ADT stack in more detail, and includes a combined retrieval and removal operation. The names given here for the operations that add and remove items are conventional for stacks. Figure 7-2 shows a UML diagram for the class *Stack*.

Recall that Chapter 2 urged you to focus on the specification of a module before you considered its implementation. After specifying an ADT's operations in pseudocode, you should try to use them as a check of your design. Such a test can highlight any deficiencies in your specifications or design. For example, you can use the previous stack operations to refine the algorithms developed earlier in this chapter.

Using the ADT stack in a solution. You now can refine the algorithms developed earlier in this chapter by using the stack operations:

The refined
algorithms

```
+displayBackward(in aStack:Stack)
// Displays the input line in reversed order by
```

KEY CONCEPTS

Pseudocode for the ADT Stack Operations

```
// StackItemType is the type of the items stored in the stack.

+createStack()
// Creates an empty stack.

+isEmpty():boolean {query}
// Determines whether a stack is empty.

+push(in newItem:StackItemType) throws StackException
// Adds newItem to the top of the stack. Throws
// StackException if the insertion is not successful.

+pop():StackItemType throws StackException
// Retrieves and then removes the top of the stack (the
// item that was added most recently). Throws
// StackException if the deletion is not successful.

+popAll()
// Removes all items from the stack.

+peek():StackItemType {query} throws StackException
// Retrieves the top of the stack. That is, peek
// retrieves the item that was added most recently.
// Retrieval does not change the stack. Throws
// StackException if the retrieval is not successful.
```

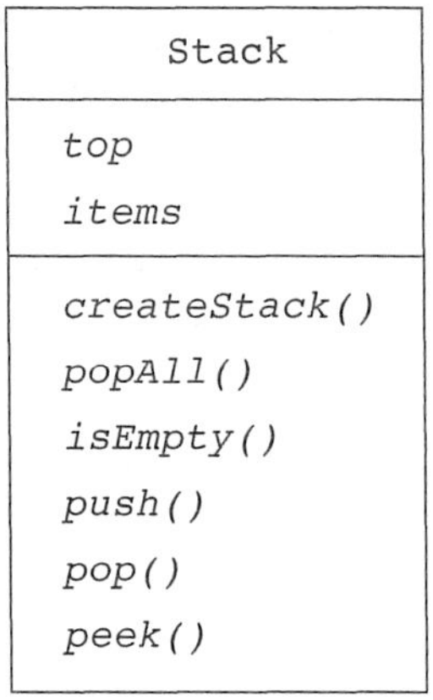

Stack

top
items

createStack()
popAll()
isEmpty()
push()
pop()
peek()

FIGURE 7-2

UML diagram for the class *Stack*

```
// writing the contents of stack.
        aStack = readAndCorrect()

  while (!aStack.isEmpty()) {
    newChar = aStack.pop()
    Write newChar
  }  // end while

  Advance to new line



+readAndCorrect():Stack
// Reads the input line and returns the corrected
// version as a stack. For each character read,
// either enters it into the stack or, if it
// is '←', corrects the contents of stack.

  aStack.createStack()²
  Read newChar
  while (newChar is not the end-of-line symbol) {
    if (newChar is not '←') {
      aStack.push(newChar)
    }
    else if (!aStack.isEmpty()) {
      oldChar = aStack.pop()
```

---

2. You implement the step *aStack.createStack()* in Java by declaring *aStack* as an instance of the stack class, since *createStack* is implemented as the class's constructor.

```
    } // end if
    Read newChar
  } // end while
return aStack
```

We have used the stack operations without knowing their implementations or even what a stack looks like. Because the ADT approach builds a wall around the implementation of the stack, your program can use a stack independently of the stack's implementation. As long as the program correctly uses the ADT operations—that is, as long as it honors the contract—it will work regardless of how you implement the ADT.

The contract, therefore, must be written precisely. That is, before you implement any ADT operations, you should specify both their preconditions and their postconditions. Realize, however, that during program design, the first attempt at specification is often informal and is only later made precise by the writing of preconditions and postconditions.

Axioms (*optional*). As Chapter 4 noted, intuitive specifications, such as those given previously for the stack operations, are not really sufficient to define an ADT formally. For example, to capture formally the intuitive notion that the last item inserted into *aStack* is the first item to be removed, you could write an axiom such as

An example of an axiom

```
(aStack.push(newItem)).pop() = aStack
```

That is, if you push *newItem* onto *aStack* and then pop it, you are left with the original stack *aStack*. Exercise 16 at the end of this chapter discusses the axioms for a stack further.

7.2 Simple Applications of the ADT Stack

This section presents two rather simple examples for which the LIFO property of stacks is appropriate. Note that we will be using the operations of the ADT stack, even though we have not discussed their implementations yet.

Checking for Balanced Braces

Java uses curly braces, "{" and "}", to delimit groups of statements. For example, braces begin and end a method's body. If you treat a Java program as a string of characters, you can use a stack to verify that a program contains balanced braces. For example, the braces in the string

```
abc{defg{ijk}{l{mn}}op}qr
```

are balanced, while the braces in the string

```
abc{def}}{ghij{kl}m
```

are not balanced. You can check whether a string contains balanced braces by traversing it from left to right. As you move from left to right, you match each successive close brace "}" with the most recently encountered unmatched open brace "{"; that is, the "{" must be to the left of the current "}". The braces are balanced if

1. Each time you encounter a "}", it matches an already encountered "{"

2. When you reach the end of the string, you have matched each "{"

Requirements for balanced braces

The solution requires that you keep track of each unmatched "{" and discard one each time you encounter a "}". One way to perform this task is to push each "{" encountered onto a stack and pop one off each time you encounter a "}". Thus, a first-draft pseudocode solution is

```
while (not at the end of the string) {
  if (the next character is a '{') {
    aStack.push('{')
  }
  else if (the character is a '}') {
    openBrace = aStack.pop()
  } // end if
} // end while
```

Initial draft of a solution

Although this solution correctly keeps track of braces, missing from it are the checks that conditions 1 and 2 are met—that is, that the braces are indeed balanced. To verify condition 1 when a "}" is encountered, you must check to see whether the stack is empty before popping from it. If it is empty, you terminate the loop and report that the string is not balanced. To verify condition 2, you must check that the stack is empty when the end of the string is reached.

Thus, the pseudocode solution to check for balanced braces in *aString* becomes

```
aStack.createStack()
balancedSoFar = true
i = 0

while (balancedSoFar and i < length of aString) {
  ch = character at position i in aString
  ++i
  // push an open brace
  if (ch is '{') {
    aStack.push('{')
  }
  // close brace
  else if (ch is '}') {
    if (!aStack.isEmpty()) {
```

A detailed pseudocode solution to check a string for balanced braces

```
        openBrace = aStack.pop()    // pop a matching open brace
      }
      else {                        // no matching open brace
        balancedSoFar = false
      }  // end if
    }  // end if
    // ignore all characters other than braces
  }  // end while


  if (balancedSoFar and aStack.isEmpty()) {
    aString has balanced braces
  }
  else {
    aString does not have balanced braces
  }  // end if
```

Figure 7-3 shows the stacks that result when this algorithm is applied to several simple examples.

It may have occurred to you that a simpler solution to this problem is possible. You need only keep a count of the current number of unmatched open braces.[3] You need not actually store the open braces in a stack. However, the

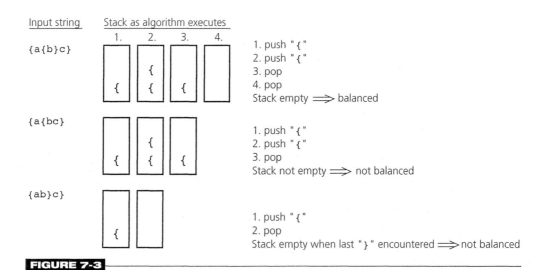

FIGURE 7-3

Traces of the algorithm that checks for balanced braces

---

3. Each time you encounter an open brace, you increment the count; each time you encounter a close brace, you decrement the count. If this count ever falls below zero or if it is greater than zero when the end of the string is reached, the string is unbalanced.

stack-based solution is conceptually useful as it previews more legitimate uses of stacks. For example, Exercise 9 at the end of this chapter asks you to extend the algorithm given here to check for balanced parentheses and square brackets in addition to braces.

The exception `StackException`. Although the previous algorithm—in its present state of refinement—ignores the exception `StackException`, a Java implementation should not. The implementation either should take precautions to avoid an exception or should provide `try` and `catch` blocks to handle a possible exception. Suppose that *push* or *pop* throws `StackException`. Exactly how should you interpret this event?

The informality of the ADT specifications given earlier complicates the interpretation of `StackException`. For example, as it is specified, `StackException` is thrown if *pop* is not successful. Later, this chapter will clarify this particular specification: *pop* will be unsuccessful if it tries to delete an item from an empty stack. Under this assumption, you can refine the pseudocode

```
// close brace
else if (ch is '}') {
  if (!aStack.isEmpty()) {
    openBrace = aStack.pop()  // pop open brace
  }
  else {                      // no open brace
    balancedSoFar = false
  }  // end if
}  // end if
```

This section of the previous algorithm ignores **StackException**

in the previous algorithm to

```
// close brace
else if (ch is '}') {
  try {
    // try to pop open brace
    openBrace = aStack.pop()
  }  // end try
  catch (StackException e) {
    balancedSoFar = false  // no open brace
  }  // end catch
}  // end if
```

Revision that makes use of **StackException**

The *push* operation can fail for implementation-dependent reasons. For example, *push* throws `StackException` if the array in an array-based implementation is full. In the spirit of fail-safe programming, a method that implements this balanced-braces algorithm should check for a thrown `StackException` after *push* and report an unsuccessful insertion.

Recognizing Strings in a Language

Consider the problem of recognizing whether a particular string is in the language

$$L = \{w\$w' : w \text{ is a possibly empty string of characters other than } \$,$$
$$w' = \text{reverse } (w) \}$$

For example, the strings AA, ABCCBA, and $ are in L, but AB$AB and ABC$CB are not. (Exercise 14 in Chapter 6 introduced a similar language.) This language is like the language of palindromes that you saw in Chapter 6, but strings in this language have a special middle character.

A stack is useful in determining whether a given string is in L. Suppose you traverse the first half of the string and push each character onto a stack. When you reach the $, you can undo the process: For each character in the second half of the string, you pop a character off the stack. However, you must match the popped character with the current character in the string to ensure that the second half of the string is the reverse of the first half. The stack must be empty when—and only when—you reach the end of the string; otherwise, one "half" of the string is longer than the other, and so the string is not in L.

The following algorithm uses this strategy. To avoid unnecessary complications, assume that *aString* contains exactly one $.

A pseudocode recognition algorithm for the language L

```
aStack.createStack()

// push the characters before $, that is, the
// characters in w, onto the stack
i = 0
ch = character at position i in aString
while (ch is not '$') {
  aStack.push(ch)
  ++i
  ch = character at position i in aString
}  // end while

// skip the $
++i

// match the reverse of w
inLanguage = true  // assume string is in language
while (inLanguage and i < length of aString) {
  ch = character at position i in aString
  try {
    stackTop = aStack.pop()
    if (stackTop equals ch) {
      ++i  // characters match
    }
    else {
```

```
         //  top of stack is not ch (characters do not match)
         inLanguage = false  // reject string
      }  // end if
   }  // end try
   catch (StackException e) {
      // aStack.pop() failed, aStack is empty (first half of
      // string is shorter than second half)
      inLanguage = false
   }  // end catch
}  // end while

if (inLanguage and aStack.isEmpty()) {
   aString is in language
}
else {
   aString is not in language
}  // end if
```

Notice that the two algorithms presented in this section depend only on the specifications of the stack operations and not on their implementations.

7.3 Implementations of the ADT Stack

This section develops three Java implementations of the ADT stack. The first implementation uses an array to represent the stack, the second uses a linked list, and the third uses the ADT list. Figure 7-4 illustrates these three implementations. The following interface *StackInterface* is used to provide a common specification for the three implementations.

```
public interface StackInterface {
  public boolean isEmpty();
  // Determines whether the stack is empty.
  // Precondition: None.
  // Postcondition: Returns true if the stack is empty;
  // otherwise returns false.

  public void popAll();
  // Removes all the items from the stack.
  // Precondition: None.
  // Postcondition: Stack is empty.

  public void push(Object newItem) throws StackException;
  // Adds an item to the top of a stack.
  // Precondition: newItem is the item to be added.
  // Postcondition: If insertion is successful, newItem
  // is on the top of the stack.
```

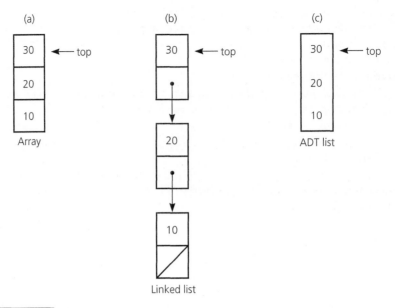

FIGURE 7-4

Implementations of the ADT stack that use (a) an array; (b) a linked list; (c) an ADT list

```
    // Exception: Some implementations may throw
    // StackException when newItem cannot be placed on
    // the stack.

    public Object pop() throws StackException;
    // Removes the top of a stack.
    // Precondition: None.
    // Postcondition: If the stack is not empty, the item
    // that was added most recently is removed from the
    // stack and returned.
    // Exception: Throws StackException if the stack is
    // empty.

    public Object peek() throws StackException;
    // Retrieves the top of a stack.
    // Precondition: None.
    // Postcondition: If the stack is not empty, the item
    // that was added most recently is returned. The
    // stack is unchanged.
    // Exception: Throws StackException if the stack is
    // empty.
}   // end StackInterface
```

Here is the class *StackException* that is used in *StackInterface*:

```
public class StackException
            extends java.lang.RuntimeException {
  public StackException(String s) {
    super(s);
  }  // end constructor
}  // end StackException
```

Note that *StackException* extends *java.lang.RuntimeException*, so that the calls to methods that throw *StackException* do not have to be enclosed in *try* blocks. This is a reasonable choice for the operations *pop* and *peek*, since you can avoid the exception by checking to see whether the stack is empty before calling these operations. But *push* can also throw *StackException* in an array-based implementation when a fixed-size array is used and becomes full. You can avoid this exception in an array-based implementation by providing a method *isFull* that determines whether the stack is full; you call *isFull* before you call *push*.

In a reference-based implementation, this *isFull* method would not be necessary. Also, although the *push* method throws *StackException* in the interface specification, the *throws* clause could be omitted in a reference-based implementation of *push*.

An Array-Based Implementation of the ADT Stack

Figure 7-5 suggests that you use an array of *Objects* called *items* to represent the items in a stack and an index *top* such that *items[top]* is the stack's top. We want to define a class whose instances are stacks and whose private data fields are *items* and *top*.

The following class is an array-based implementation of the ADT stack. The default constructor for this class corresponds to and replaces the ADT operation *createStack*. Note that the preconditions and postconditions given earlier in *StackInterface* apply here as well, and so are omitted to save space.

```
public class StackArrayBased implements StackInterface {
  final int MAX_STACK = 50;   // maximum size of stack
  private Object items[];
  private int top;
```

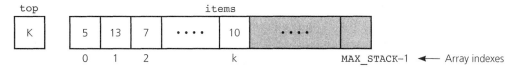

FIGURE 7-5

An array-based implementation

```java
public StackArrayBased() {
  items = new Object[MAX_STACK];
  top = -1;
}  // end default constructor

public boolean isEmpty() {
  return top < 0;
}  // end isEmpty

public boolean isFull() {
  return top == MAX_STACK-1;
}  // end isFull

public void push(Object newItem) throws StackException {
  if (!isFull()) {
    items[++top] = newItem;
  }
  else {
    throw new StackException("StackException on " +
                             "push: stack full");
  }  // end if
}  // end push

public void popAll() {
  items = new Object[MAX_STACK];
  top = -1;
}  // end popAll

public Object pop() throws StackException {
  if (!isEmpty()) {
    return items[top--];
  }
  else {
    throw new StackException("StackException on " +
                             "pop: stack empty");
  }  // end if
}  // end pop

public Object peek() throws StackException {
  if (!isEmpty()) {
    return items[top];
  }
  else {
    throw new StackException("Stack exception on " +
                             "peek - stack empty");
  }  // end if
```

```
  }  // end peek
}  // end StackArrayBased
```

A program that uses a stack could begin as follows:

```
public class StackTest {
  public static final int MAX_ITEMS = 15;

  public static void main(String[] args) {
    StackArrayBased stack = new StackArrayBased();
    Integer items[] = new Integer[MAX_ITEMS];
    for (int i=0; i<MAX_ITEMS; i++) {
      items[i] = new Integer(i);
      if (!stack.isFull()) {
        stack.push(items[i]);
      }  // end if
    }  // end for
    while (!stack.isEmpty()) {
      // cast result of pop to Integer
      System.out.println((Integer)(stack.pop()));
    }  // end while
    ...
```

By implementing the stack as a class, and by declaring *items* and *top* as private, you ensure that the client cannot violate the ADT's walls. If you did not hide your implementation within a class, or if you made the array *items* public, the client could access the elements in *items* directly instead of by using the operations of the ADT stack. Thus, the client could access any elements in the stack, not just its top element. You might find this capability attractive, but in fact it violates the specifications of the ADT stack. If you truly need to access all the items of your ADT randomly, do not use a stack!

Again, note that *StackException* provides a simple way for the implementer to indicate to the stack's client unusual circumstances, such as an attempted insertion into a full stack or a deletion from an empty stack.

Finally, note that instances of *StackArrayBased* cannot contain items of a primitive type such as *int*, because *int* is not derived from *Object*. If you need a stack of integers, for example, you will have to use the corresponding wrapper class, which in this case is *Integer*. Finally, *pop* and *peek* return an item that is an instance of *Object*. You must cast this item back to the subtype of *Object* that you pushed onto the stack. Otherwise, methods available for the subtype will not be accessible.

A Reference-Based Implementation of the ADT Stack

Many applications require a reference based implementation of a stack so that the stack can grow and shrink dynamically. Figure 7-6 illustrates a reference-based

Private data fields are hidden from the client

StackException *provides a simple way to indicate unusual events*

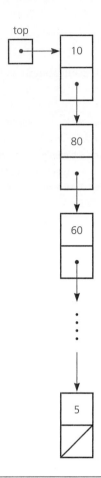

FIGURE 7-6

A reference-based implementation

implementation of a stack where *top* is a reference to the head of a linked list of items. The implementation uses the same node class developed for the linked list in Chapter 5.

Note that the preconditions and postconditions given earlier in *Stack-Interface* apply here as well, and so are omitted to save space.

```java
public class StackReferenceBased
                  implements StackInterface {
  private Node top;

  public StackReferenceBased() {
    top = null;
  }  // end default constructor

  public boolean isEmpty() {
```

```
      return top ==  null;
   }  // end isEmpty

   public void push(Object newItem) {
     top = new Node(newItem, top);
   }  // end push

   public Object pop() throws StackException {
     if (!isEmpty()) {
       Node temp = top;
       top = top.next;
       return temp.item;
     }
     else {
       throw new StackException("StackException on " +
                               "pop: stack empty");
     }  // end if
   }  // end pop

   public void popAll() {
     top = null;
   }  // end popAll

   public Object peek() throws StackException {
     if (!isEmpty()) {
       return top.item;
     }
     else {
       throw new StackException("StackException on " +
                               "peek: stack empty");
     }  // end if
   }  // end peek
}  // end StackReferenceBased
```

An Implementation That Uses the ADT List

You can use the ADT list to represent the items in a stack, as Figure 7-7 illustrates. If the item in position 0 of a list represents the top of the stack, you can implement the stack operation *push(newItem)* as *add(0, newItem)*. Similarly, you can implement the stack operation *pop()* using *get(0)* and *remove(0)* and the stack operation *peek()* as *get(0)*.

Recall that Chapter 5 presented the ADT list as the class *List-ReferenceBased*. (See page 289.) The following class for the ADT stack uses an instance of *ListReferenceBased* to represent the stack.

```
public class StackListBased implements StackInterface {
  private ListInterface list;
```

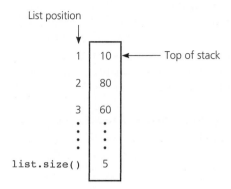

List position

1	10	◄──── Top of stack
2	80
3	60
.	.
.	.
.	.
list.size()	5

FIGURE 7-7

An implementation that uses the ADT list

```
public StackListBased() {
  list = new ListReferenceBased();
}  // end default constructor

public boolean isEmpty() {
  return list.isEmpty();
}  // end isEmpty

public void push(Object newItem) {
  list.add(0, newItem);
}  // end push

public Object pop() throws StackException {
  if (!list.isEmpty()) {
    Object temp = list.get(0);
    list.remove(0);
    return temp;
  }
  else {
    throw new StackException("StackException on " +
                             "pop: stack empty");
  }  // end if
}  // end pop

public void popAll() {
  list.removeAll();
}  // end popAll

public Object peek() throws StackException {
  if (!isEmpty()) {
    return list.get(0);
  }
```

```
    else {
      throw new StackException("StackException on " +
                               "peek: stack empty");
    }  // end if
  }  // end peek
}  // end StackListBased
```

The data field `list` is an instance of the class `ListReferenceBased`. Also, the class `ListReferenceBased`'s constructor is called by `StackList-Based`'s constructor.

Comparing Implementations

You have seen implementations of the ADT stack that use an array, a linked list, and the ADT list to represent the items in a stack. We have treated the array and linked list as data structures, but the list is an ADT that we have implemented by using either an array or a linked list. Thus, all our implementations of the ADT stack are ultimately array based or reference based.

Once again the reasons for making the choice between array-based and reference-based implementations are the same as those discussed in earlier chapters. The array-based implementation given in this chapter uses fixed-sized arrays. As such, it prevents the *push* operation from adding an item to the stack if the stack's size limit, which is the size of the array, has been reached. If this restriction is not acceptable, you must use either a resizeable array or a reference-based implementation. For the problem that reads·and corrects an input line, for example, the fixed-size restriction might not present a difficulty: If the system allows a line length of only 80 characters, you could reasonably use a statically allocated array to represent the stack.

Fixed size versus dynamic size

Suppose that you decide to use a reference-based implementation. Should you choose the implementation that uses a linked list or the one that uses a reference-based implementation of the ADT list? Because a linked list actually represents the items on the ADT list, you might feel that using an ADT list to represent a stack is not as efficient as using a linked list directly. You would be right, but notice that the ADT list approach is much simpler to write. If you have battled references to produce a correct reference-based implementation of the ADT list, why do so again when you can *reuse* your work in the implementation of the stack? Which approach would you choose to produce a correct implementation of the stack in the least time? Chapter 9 discusses further the reuse of previously written classes.

Reuse of an already implemented class saves you time

The Java Collections Framework Class *Stack*

Chapter 5 introduced the Java Collections Framework (JCF) and the interface `List` that was used for the implementation of JCF list classes such as `LinkedList` and `ArrayList`. The JCF also contains an implementation of a stack class called `Stack`. Like many of the classes and interfaces we have seen so far from the JCF, the `Stack` class is a generic class.

The *Stack* class is derived from the class *Vector*—a growable array of objects. It extends the *Vector* class with five methods that allow for a LIFO stack of objects. Most of these methods are quite similar to the ones presented in this chapter: *push*, *pop*, *empty*, and *peek*. An additional method, called *search*, allows you to determine how far an item is from the top of the stack. Here is the specification for the JCF *Stack* collection as it is derived from *Vector*, only the method headings are shown:

```java
public class Stack<E> extends Vector<E> {

  public Stack()
  // Creates an empty Stack

  public boolean empty()
  // Tests if this stack is empty.

  public E peek() throws EmptyStackException
  // Looks at the object at the top of this stack without
  // removing it from the stack.

  public E pop() throws EmptyStackException
  // Removes the object at the top of this stack and
  // returns that object as the value of this function.

  public E push(E item)
  // Pushes an item onto the top of this stack.

  public int search(Object o)
  // Returns the 1-based position where an object is on this
  // stack. The topmost item on the stack is considered to be
  // at distance 1.

} // end Stack
```

Note that the *Stack* has one data-type parameter for the items contained in the stack. Here is an example of how the JCF *Stack* is used:

```java
import java.util.Stack;

public class TestStack {

  static public void main(String[] args) {
    Stack<Integer> aStack = new Stack<Integer>();
    if (aStack.empty()) {
      System.out.println("The stack is empty");
    } // end if
```

```
    for (int i = 0; i < 5; i++) {
      aStack.push(i); // With autoboxing, this is the same
                      // as aStack.push(new Integer(i))
    } // end for

    while (!aStack.empty()) {
      System.out.print(aStack.pop()+ " ");
    } // end while
    System.out.println();

  } // end main

} // end TestStack
```

The output of this program is

```
The stack is empty
4 3 2 1 0
```

7.4 Application: Algebraic Expressions

This section contains two more problems that you can solve neatly by using the ADT stack. Keep in mind throughout that you are using the ADT stack to solve the problems. You can use the stack operations, but you may not assume any particular implementation. You choose a specific implementation only as a last step.

Chapter 6 presented recursive grammars that specified the syntax of algebraic expressions. Recall that prefix and postfix expressions avoid the ambiguity inherent in the evaluation of infix expressions. We will now consider stack-based solutions to the problems of evaluating infix and postfix expressions. To avoid distracting programming issues, we will allow only the binary operators $*, /, +,$ and $-$, and disallow exponentiation and unary operators.

Your use of an ADT's operations should not depend on its implementation

The strategy we shall adopt here is first to develop an algorithm for evaluating postfix expressions and then to develop an algorithm for transforming an infix expression into an equivalent postfix expression. Taken together, these two algorithms provide a way to evaluate infix expressions. This strategy eliminates the need for an algorithm that directly evaluates infix expressions, a somewhat more difficult problem that Programming Problem 7 at the end of this chapter considers.

To evaluate an infix expression, first convert it to postfix form and then evaluate the postfix expression

Evaluating Postfix Expressions

As we mentioned in Chapter 6, some calculators require you to enter postfix expressions. For example, to compute the value of

2 * (3 + 4)

by using a postfix calculator, you would enter the sequence 2, 3, 4, +, *, which corresponds to the postfix expression

2 3 4 + *

Recall that an operator in a postfix expression applies to the two operands that immediately precede it. Thus, the calculator must be able to retrieve the operands entered most recently. The ADT stack provides this capability. In fact, each time you enter an operand, the calculator pushes it onto a stack. When you enter an operator, the calculator applies it to the top two operands on the stack, pops the operands from the stack, and pushes the result of the operation onto the stack. Figure 7-8 shows the action of the calculator for the previous sequence of operands and operators. The final result, 14, is on the top of the stack.

You can formalize the action of the calculator to obtain an algorithm that evaluates a postfix expression, which is entered as a string of characters. To avoid issues that cloud the algorithm with programming details, assume that

Simplifying assumptions

- The string is a syntactically correct postfix expression

- No unary operators are present

- No exponentiation operators are present

- Operands are single lowercase letters that represent integer values

The pseudocode algorithm is then

A pseudocode algorithm that evaluates postfix expressions

```
for (each character ch in the string) {
  if (ch is an operand) {
    Push value that operand ch represents onto stack
  }
```

Key entered	Calculator action		Stack (bottom to top)
2	push 2		2
3	push 3		2 3
4	push 4		2 3 4
+	operand2 = pop stack	(4)	2 3
	operand1 = pop stack	(3)	2
	result = operand1 + operand2	(7)	2
	push result		2 7
*	operand2 = pop stack	(7)	2
	operand1 = pop stack	(2)	
	result = operand1 * operand2	(14)	
	push result		14

FIGURE 7-8

The action of a postfix calculator when evaluating the expression
2 * (3 + 4)

```
else {  // ch is an operator named op
  // evaluate and push the result
  operand2 = Pop the top of the stack
  operand1 = Pop the top of the stack
  result = operand1 op operand2
  Push result onto stack
}  // end if
} // end for
```

Upon termination of the algorithm, the value of the expression will be on the top of the stack. Programming Problem 4 at the end of this chapter asks you to implement this algorithm.

Converting Infix Expressions to Equivalent Postfix Expressions

Now that you know how to evaluate a postfix expression, you will be able to evaluate an infix expression, if you first can convert it into an equivalent postfix expression. The infix expressions here are the familiar ones, such as $(a + b) * c / d - e$. They allow parentheses, operator precedence, and left-to-right association.

Will you ever want to evaluate an infix expression? Certainly, you have written such expressions in programs. The compiler that translated your programs had to generate machine instructions to evaluate the expressions. To do so, the compiler first transformed each infix expression into postfix form. Knowing how to convert an expression from infix to postfix notation not only will lead to an algorithm to evaluate infix expressions, but also will give you some insight into the compilation process.

If you manually convert a few infix expressions to postfix form, you will discover three important facts:

- The operands always stay in the same order with respect to one another.

- An operator will move only "to the right" with respect to the operands; that is, if, in the infix expression, the operand x precedes the operator op, it is also true that in the postfix expression, the operand x precedes the operator op.

- All parentheses are removed.

Facts about converting from infix to postfix

As a consequence of these three facts, the primary task of the conversion algorithm is determining where to place each operator.

The following pseudocode describes a first attempt at converting an infix expression to an equivalent postfix expression *postfixExp*:

```
Initialize postfixExp to the null string
for (each character ch in the infix expression) {
  switch (ch) {
```

First draft of an algorithm to convert an infix expression to postfix form

```
    case ch is an operand:
      Append ch to the end of postfixExp
      break
    case ch is an operator:
      Store ch until you know where to place it
      break
    case ch is '(' or ')':
      Discard ch
      break
  } // end switch
} // end for
```

You may have guessed that you really do not want to simply discard the parentheses, as they play an important role in determining the placement of the operators. In any infix expression, a set of matching parentheses defines an isolated subexpression that consists of an operator and its two operands. Therefore, the algorithm must evaluate the subexpression independently of the rest of the expression. Regardless of what the rest of the expression looks like, the operator within the subexpression belongs with the operands in that subexpression. The parentheses tell the rest of the expression

You can have the value of this subexpression after it is evaluated; simply ignore everything inside.

Parentheses, operator precedence, and left-to-right association determine where to place operators in the postfix expression

Parentheses are thus one of the factors that determine the placement of the operators in the postfix expression. The other factors are precedence and left-to-right association.

In Chapter 6, you saw a simple way to convert a fully parenthesized infix expression to postfix form. Because each operator corresponded to a pair of parentheses, you simply moved each operator to the position marked by its closing parenthesis, and finally removed the parentheses.

The actual problem is more difficult, however, because the infix expression is not always fully parenthesized. Instead, the problem allows precedence and left-to-right association, and therefore requires a more complex algorithm. The following is a high-level description of what you must do when you encounter each character as you read the infix string from left to right.

Five steps in the process to convert from infix to postfix form

1. When you encounter an operand, append it to the output string *postfixExp*. *Justification*: The order of the operands in the postfix expression is the same as the order in the infix expression, and the operands that appear to the left of an operator in the infix expression also appear to its left in the postfix expression.

2. Push each " (" onto the stack.

3. When you encounter an operator, if the stack is empty, push the operator onto the stack. However, if the stack is not empty, pop operators of greater or equal precedence from the stack and append them to *postfixExp*. You stop when you encounter either a " (" or an operator of lower precedence

ch	stack (bottom to top)	postfixExp	
a		a	
−	−	a	
(	− (	a	
b	− (	ab	
+	− (+	ab	
c	− (+	abc	
*	− (+ *	abc	
d	− (+ *	abcd	
)	− (+	abcd*	Move operators
	− (	abcd*+	from stack to
	−	abcd*+	postfixExp until " ("
/	− /	abcd*+	
e	− /	abcd*+e	Copy operators from
		abcd*+e/−	stack to postfixExp

FIGURE 7-9

A trace of the algorithm that converts the infix expression $a - (b + c * d)/e$ to postfix form

or when the stack becomes empty. You then push the new operator onto the stack. Thus, this step orders the operators by precedence and in accordance with left-to-right association. Notice that you continue popping from the stack until you encounter an operator of strictly lower precedence than the current operator in the infix expression. You do not stop on equality, because the left-to-right association rule says that in case of a tie in precedence, the leftmost operator is applied first—and this operator is the one that is already on the stack.

4. When you encounter a ")", pop operators off the stack and append them to the end of *postfixExp* until you encounter the matching "(". *Justification:* Within a pair of parentheses, precedence and left-to-right association determine the order of the operators, and Step 3 has already ordered the operators in accordance with these rules.

5. When you reach the end of the string, you append the remaining contents of the stack to *postfixExp*.

For example, Figure 7-9 traces the action of the algorithm on the infix expression $a - (b + c * d)/e$, assuming that the stack and the string *postfixExp* are initially empty. At the end of the algorithm, *postfixExp* contains the resulting postfix expression $abcd*+e/-$.

You can use the previous five-step description of the algorithm to develop a fairly concise pseudocode solution, which follows. The symbol + means concatenate (append), so *postfixExp* + x means concatenate the string currently in *postfixExp* and the character x—that is, follow the string in *postfixExp* with the character x. Both the stack *stack* and the postfix expression *postfixExp* are initially empty.

A pseudocode algorithm that converts an infix expression to postfix form

```
for (each character ch in the infix expression) {
  switch (ch) {
    case operand:  // append operand to end of postfixExp
      postfixExp = postfixExp + ch
      break
    case '(':       // save '(' on stack
      aStack.push(ch)
      break
    case ')':       // pop stack until matching '('
      while (top of stack is not '(') {
        postfixExp = postfixExp + aStack.pop()
      } // end while
      openParen = aStack.pop() // remove the open parenthesis
      break
    case operator:                // process stack operators of
                                  // greater precedence
      while ( !aStack.isEmpty() and
              top of stack is not '(' and
              precedence(ch) <= precedence(top of stack) ) {
        postfixExp = postfixExp + aStack.pop()
      }  // end while

      aStack.push(ch)  // save new operator
      break
  }  // end switch
} // end for
// append to postfixExp the operators remaining in the stack
while (!aStack.isEmpty()) {
  postfixExp = postfixExp + aStack.pop()
}  // end while
```

Because this algorithm assumes that the given infix expression is syntactically correct, it can ignore the possibility of a *StackException* on *pop*. Programming Problem 6 at the end of this chapter asks you to remove this assumption. In doing so, you will find that you must provide *try* and *catch* blocks for the stack operations.

7.5 Application: A Search Problem

This final application of stacks will introduce you to a general type of **search problem**. In this particular problem, you must find a path from some point of origin to some destination point. We will solve this problem first by using stacks and then by using recursion. The recursive solution will bring to light the close relationship between stacks and recursion.

The High Planes Airline Company (HPAir) wants a program to process customer requests to fly from some origin city to some destination city. So that you can focus on the issue at hand—the use of stacks during problem solving—we will simplify the problem: For each customer request, just indicate whether a sequence of HPAir flights exists from the origin city to the destination city. The more realistic problem of actually producing an itinerary—that is, the sequence of flights—is considered in Programming Problem 12 at the end of this chapter.

Determine whether HPAir flies from one city to another

Imagine three input text files that specify all of the flight information for the airline as follows:

- The names of the cities that HPAir serves

- Pairs of city names; each pair represents the origin and destination of one of HPAir's flights

- Pairs of city names; each pair represents a request to fly from some origin to some destination

The program should then produce output such as

```
Request is to fly from Providence to San Francisco.
HPAir flies from Providence to San Francisco.

Request is to fly from Philadelphia to Albuquerque.
Sorry. HPAir does not fly from Philadelphia to Albuquerque.

Request is to fly from Salt Lake City to Paris.
Sorry. HPAir does not serve Paris.
```

Representing the flight data. The flight map in Figure 7-10 represents the routes that HPAir flies. An arrow from city C_1 to city C_2 indicates a flight from C_1 to C_2. In this case C_2 is **adjacent** to C_1 and the path from C_1 to C_2 is called a **directed path**. Notice that if C_2 is adjacent to C_1, it does not follow that C_1 is adjacent to C_2. For example, in Figure 7-10, there is a flight from city R to city X, but not from city X to city R. As you will see in Chapter 14, the map in Figure 7-10 is called a **directed graph**.

C_2 is adjacent to C_1 if there is a directed path from C_1 to C_2

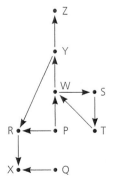

FIGURE 7-10

Flight map for HPAir

A Nonrecursive Solution That Uses a Stack

When processing a customer's request to fly from some origin city to some destination city, you must determine from the flight map whether there is a route from the origin to the destination. For example, by examining the flight map in Figure 7-10, you can see that a customer could fly from city P to city Z by flying first to city W, then to city Y, and finally to city Z; that is, there is a directed path from P to Z: $P \rightarrow W$, $W \rightarrow Y$, $Y \rightarrow Z$. Thus, you must develop an algorithm that searches the flight map for a directed path from the origin city to the destination city. Such a path might involve either a single flight or a

Use a stack to orga-
nize an exhaustive
search

sequence of flights. The solution developed here performs an **exhaustive search.** That is, beginning at the origin city, the solution will try every possible sequence of flights until either it finds a sequence that gets to the destination city or it determines that no such sequence exists. You will see that the ADT stack is useful in organizing this search.

First consider how you might perform the search by hand. One approach is to start at the origin city C_0 and select an arbitrary path to travel—that is, select an arbitrary flight departing from the origin city. This flight will lead you to a new city, C_1. If city C_1 happens to be the destination city, you are done; otherwise, you must attempt to get from C_1 to the destination city. To do this, you select a path to travel out of C_1. This path will lead you to a city C_2. If C_2 is the destination, you are done; otherwise, you must attempt to get from C_2 to the destination city, and so on.

Consider the possible outcomes of applying the previous strategy:

Possible outcomes
of the exhaustive
search strategy

1. You eventually reach the destination city and can conclude that it is possible to fly from the origin to the destination.

2. You reach a city C from which there are no departing flights.

3. You go around in circles. For example, from C_1 you go to C_2, from C_2 you go to C_3, and from C_3 you go back to C_1. You might continue this tour of the three cities forever; that is, the algorithm might enter an infinite loop.

If you always obtained the first outcome, everyone would be happy. However, because HPAir does not fly between all pairs of cities, you certainly cannot expect that the algorithm will always find a path from the origin city to the destination. For example, if city P in Figure 7-10 is the origin city and city Q is the destination city, the algorithm could not possibly find a path from city P to city Q.

Even if there were a sequence of flights from the origin city to the destination, it would take a bit of luck for the previous strategy to discover it—the algorithm would have to select a "correct" flight at each step. For example, even though there is a way to get from city P to city Z in Figure 7-10, the algorithm might not find it and instead might reach outcome 2 or 3. That is, suppose that from city P the algorithm chose to go to city R. From city R, the algorithm would have to go to city X, from which there are no flights out (outcome 2). On the other hand, suppose that the algorithm chose to go to city W

from city P. From city W, the algorithm might choose to go to city S. It would then have to go to city T and then back to W. From W it might once again choose to go to city S and continue to go around in circles (outcome 3).

You thus need to make the algorithm more sophisticated, so that it always finds a path from the origin to the destination, if such a path exists, and otherwise terminates with the conclusion that there is no such path. Suppose that the earlier strategy results in outcome 2: You reach a city C from which there are no departing flights. This certainly does not imply that there is no way to get from the origin to the destination; it implies only that there is no way to get from city C to the destination. In other words, it was a mistake to go to city C. After discovering such a mistake, the algorithm can retrace its steps, or *backtrack*, to the city C' that was visited just before city C was visited. Once back at city C', the algorithm can select a flight to some city other than C. Notice that it is possible that there are no other flights out of city C'. If this were the case, it would mean that it was a mistake to visit city C', and thus you would want to backtrack again, this time to the city that was visited just before city C'.

Use backtracking to recover from a wrong choice

For example, you saw that, in trying to get from city P to city Z in Figure 7-10, the algorithm might first choose to go from city P to city R and then on to city X. As there are no departing flights from city X, the algorithm must backtrack to city R, the city visited before city X. Once back at city R, the algorithm would attempt to go to some city other than city X, but would discover that this is not possible. The algorithm would thus backtrack once more, this time to city P, which was visited just before city R. From city P, the algorithm would choose to go to city W, which is a step in the right direction!

For the algorithm to implement this new strategy, it must maintain information about the order in which it visits the cities. First notice that when the algorithm backtracks from a city C, it must retreat to the city that it visited most recently before C. This observation suggests that you maintain the sequence of visited cities in a stack. That is, each time you decide to visit a city, you push its name onto the stack, as parts a, b, and c of Figure 7-11 illustrate for the flights from P to R to X in the previous example. You select the next city to visit from those adjacent to the city on the top of the stack. When you need to backtrack from the city C at the top of the stack (for example, because there are no flights out of the city), you simply pop a city from the stack, as shown in Figure 7-11d. After the pop, the city on the top of the stack is the city on the current path that you visited most recently before C. Parts e and f of Figure 7-11 illustrate the backtrack to city P and the subsequent flight to W.

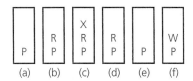

(a) (b) (c) (d) (e) (f)

FIGURE 7-11

The stack of cities as you travel (a) from P; (b) to R; (c) to X; (d) back to R; (e) back to P; (f) to W

The algorithm, as developed so far, is

```
aStack.createStack()

aStack.push(originCity)   // push origin city onto stack

while (a sequence of flights from the origin to the
                         destination has not been found){
  if (you need to backtrack from the city on the
         top of the stack) {
     temp = aStack.pop()
  }
   else {
      Select a destination city C for a flight from
      the city on the top of the stack
      aStack.push(C)
   }  // end if
}  // end while
```

Notice that at any point in the algorithm, the contents of the stack correspond to the sequence of flights currently under consideration. The city on the top of the stack is the city you are visiting currently, directly "below" it is the city visited previously, and so forth down to the bottom city, which is the first city visited in the sequence, or the origin city. In other words, an invariant of the *while* loop is that

The stack contains a directed path from the origin city at the bottom of the stack to the city at the top of the stack.

You can therefore always retrace your steps as far back through the sequence as needed.

Now consider the question of when to

`Backtrack from the city on the top of the stack.`

You have already seen one case when backtracking is necessary. You must backtrack from the city on the top of the stack when there are no flights out of that city. Another time when you need to backtrack is related to the problem of going around in circles, described previously as the third possible outcome of the original strategy.

A key observation that will tell you when to backtrack is, *you never want to visit a city that the search has already visited.* As a consequence, you must backtrack from a city whenever there are no more unvisited cities to fly to. To see why you never want to visit a city a second time, consider two cases:

Two reasons for not
visiting a city more
than once

- If you have visited city C and it is still somewhere in the stack—that is, it is part of the sequence of cities that you are exploring currently—you do not want to visit C again. Any sequence that goes from C through C_1, C_2, ..., C_k, back to C, and then to C' might just as well skip the intermediate cities and go from C directly to C'.

For example, suppose that the algorithm starts at *P* in Figure 7-10 and, in trying to find a path to *Y*, visits *W*, *S*, and *T*. There is now no reason for the algorithm to consider the flight from *T* to *W* because *W* is already in the stack. Anywhere you could fly to by going from *W* to *S*, from *S* to *T*, and then back to *W*, such as city *Y*, you could fly to directly from *W* without first going through *S* and *T*. Because you do not allow the algorithm to visit *W* a second time, it will backtrack from *S* and *T* to *W* and then go from *W* directly to *Y*. Figure 7-12 shows how the stack would appear if revisits were allowed and how it looks after backtracking when revisits are not allowed. Notice that backtracking to *W* is very different from visiting *W* for a second time.

■ If you have visited city *C*, but it is no longer in the stack—because you backtracked from it and popped it from the stack—you do not want to visit *C* again. This situation is subtle; consider two cases that depend on why you backtracked from the city.

If you backtracked from *C* because there were no flights out of it, then you certainly do not ever want to try going through *C* again. For example, if, starting at *P* in Figure 7-10, the algorithm goes to *R* and then to *X*, it will backtrack from *X* to *R*. At this point, although *X* is no longer in the stack, you certainly do not want to visit it again, because you know there are no flights out of *X*.

Now suppose that you backtracked from city *C* because all cities adjacent to it had been visited. This situation implies that you have already tried all possible flights from *C* and have failed to find a way to get to the destination city. There is thus no reason to go to *C* again. For example, suppose that starting from *P* in Figure 7-10, the algorithm executes the following sequence: Visit *R*, visit *X*, backtrack to *R* (because there are no flights out of *X*), backtrack to *P* (because there are no more unvisited cities

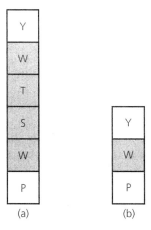

(a)   (b)

FIGURE 7-12

The stack of cities (a) allowing revisits and (b) after backtracking when revisits are not allowed

adjacent to *R*), visit *W*, visit *Y*. At this point the stack contains *P-W-Y*, with *Y* on top, as Figure 7-12b shows. You need to choose a flight out of *Y*. You do not want to fly from *Y* to *R*, because you have visited *R* already and tried all possible flights out of *R*.

In both cases, visiting a city a second time does not gain you anything, and in fact it may cause you to go around in circles.

Mark the visited cities

To implement the rule of not visiting a city more than once, you simply mark a city when it has been visited. When choosing the next city to visit, you restrict consideration to unmarked cities adjacent to the city on the top of the stack. The algorithm thus becomes

Next draft of the search algorithm

```
aStack.createStack()
Clear marks on all cities
aStack.push(originCity)  // push origin city onto stack
Mark the origin as visited
while (a sequence of flights from the origin to the
                        destination has not been found) {
   // loop invariant: The stack contains a directed path
   // from the origin city at the bottom of the stack to
   // the city at the top of the stack
   if (no flights exist from the city on the
         top of the stack to unvisited cities) {
      temp = aStack.pop()  // backtrack
   }
   else {
      Select an unvisited destination city C for a
        flight from the city on the top of the stack
      aStack.push(C)
      Mark C as visited
   }  // end if
}  // end while
```

Finally, you need to refine the condition in the *while* statement. That is, you need to refine the algorithm's final determination of whether a path exists from the origin to the destination. The loop invariant, which states that the stack contains a directed path from the origin city to the city on the top of the stack, implies that the algorithm can reach an affirmative conclusion if the city at the top of the stack is the destination city. On the other hand, the algorithm can reach a negative conclusion only after it has exhausted all possibilities— that is, after the algorithm has backtracked to the origin and there remain no unvisited cities to fly to from the origin. At that point, the algorithm will pop the origin city from the stack and the stack will become empty.

With this refinement, the algorithm appears as follows:

The final version of the search algorithm

```
+searchS(in originCity:City, in destinationCity:City)
// Searches for a sequence of flights from
```

```
// originCity to destinationCity

  aStack.createStack()
  Clear marks on all cities

  aStack.push(originCity)   // push origin onto stack
  Mark the origin as visited

  while (!aStack.isEmpty() and
         destinationCity is not at the top of the stack) {
    // Loop invariant: The stack contains a directed path
    // from the origin city at the bottom of the stack to
    // the city at the top of the stack
    if (no flights exist from the city on the
            top of the stack to unvisited cities) {
      temp = aStack.pop()   // backtrack
    }
    else {
      Select an unvisited destination city C for a
          flight from the city on the top of the stack
      aStack.push(C)
      Mark C as visited
    }  // end if
  }  // end while

  if (aStack.isEmpty()) {
    return false  // no path exists
  }
  else {
    return true    // path exists
  }  // end if
```

Notice that the algorithm does not specify the order of selection for the unvisited cities. It really does not matter what selection criteria the algorithm uses, because the choice will not affect the final outcome: Either a sequence of flights exists or it does not. The choice, however, will affect the specific flights that the algorithm considers. For example, suppose that the algorithm always flies to the alphabetically earliest unvisited city from the city on the top of the stack. Under this assumption, Figure 7-13 contains a trace of the algorithm's action, given the map in Figure 7-10, with P as the origin city and Z as the destination city. The algorithm terminates with success.

Now consider the operations that the search algorithm must perform on the flight map. The algorithm marks cities as it visits them, determines whether a city has been visited, and determines which cities are adjacent to a given city. You can treat the flight map as an ADT that has at least these operations, in addition to the search operation itself. Other desirable operations include placing data into the flight map, inserting a city adjacent to another city,

Action	Reason	Contents of stack (bottom to top)
Push P	Initialize	P
Push R	Next unvisited adjacent city	P R
Push X	Next unvisited adjacent city	P R X
Pop X	No unvisited adjacent city	P R
Pop R	No unvisited adjacent city	P
Push W	Next unvisited adjacent city	P W
Push S	Next unvisited adjacent city	P W S
Push T	Next unvisited adjacent city	P W S T
Pop T	No unvisited adjacent city	P W S
Pop S	No unvisited adjacent city	P W
Push Y	Next unvisited adjacent city	P W Y
Push Z	Next unvisited adjacent city	P W Y Z

FIGURE 7-13

A trace of the search algorithm, given the flight map in Figure 7-10

displaying the flight map, displaying a list of all cities, and displaying all cities that are adjacent to a given city. Thus, the ADT flight map could include the following operations:

ADT flight map operations

```
+createFlightMap()
// Creates an empty flight map.

+readFlightMap(in cityFileName:string,
              in flightFileName:string)
// Reads flight information into the flight map.

+displayFlightMap() {query}
// Displays flight information.

+displayAllCities() {query}
// Displays the names of all cities that HPAir serves.

+displayAdjacentCities(in aCity:City) {query}
// Displays all cities that are adjacent to a given city.

+markVisited(in aCity:City)
// Marks a city as visited.

+unvisitAll()
// Clears marks on all cities.

+isVisited(in aCity:City):boolean {query}
// Determines whether a city was visited.

+insertAdjacent(in aCity:City, in adjCity:City)
// Inserts a city adjacent to another city in a
// flight map.
```

```
+getNextCity(in fromCity:City)
// Returns the next unvisited city, if any, that
// is adjacent to a given city.  Returns null if no
// unvisited adjacent city was found.

+isPath(in originCity:City, in destinationCity:City)
// Determines whether a sequence of flights between
// two cities exists.
```

The following Java method implements the *isPath* operation by using the *searchS* algorithm. It assumes that the class *StackReferenceBased* implements the stack operations and the class *Map* implements the ADT flight map operations just described. Notice that you must represent the cities by creating a class *City* that implements the *java.lang.Comparable* interface.

```
public boolean isPath(City originCity,
                      City destinationCity) {
// ----------------------------------------------------
// Determines whether a sequence of flights between two cities
// exists. Nonrecursive stack version.
// Precondition: originCity and destinationCity are the origin
// and destination cities, respectively.
// Postcondition: Returns true if a sequence of flights exists
// from originCity to destinationCity, otherwise returns
// false. Cities visited during the search are marked as
// visited in the flight map.
// Implementation notes: Uses a stack for the cities of a
// potential path. Calls unvisitAll, markVisited, and
// getNextCity.
// ----------------------------------------------------
   StackReferenceBased stack = new StackReferenceBased();

   City topCity, nextCity;
   unvisitAll();  // clear marks on all cities

   // push origin city onto stack, mark it visited
   stack.push(originCity);
   markVisited(originCity);

   topCity = (City)(stack.peek());
   while (!stack.isEmpty() &&
          (topCity.compareTo(destinationCity) != 0)) {
      // loop invariant: stack contains a directed path
      // from the origin city at the bottom of the stack
      // to the city at the top of the stack

      // find an unvisited city adjacent to the city on
      // the top of the stack
```

Java implementation of **searchS**

```
    nextCity = getNextCity(topCity);

    if (nextCity == null) {
      stack.pop();  // no city found; backtrack
    }
    else {                      // visit city
      stack.push(nextCity);
      markVisited(nextCity);
    }  // end if
    topCity = (City)stack.peek();
  }  // end while
  if (stack.isEmpty()) {
    return false;  // no path exists
  }
  else {
    return true;   // path exists
  }  // end if
}  // end isPath
```

Programming Problem 10 at the end of this chapter provides implementation details that will enable you to complete the solution to the HPAir problem.

A Recursive Solution

Recall the initial attempt at a solution to the HPAir problem of searching for a sequence of flights from some origin city to some destination city. Consider how you might perform the search "by hand." One approach is to start at the origin city and select an arbitrary flight that departs from the origin city. This flight will lead you to a new city, C_1. If city C_1 happens to be the destination city, you are done; otherwise, you must attempt to get from C_1 to the destination city by selecting a flight out of C_1. This flight will lead you to city C_2. If C_2 is the destination, you are done; otherwise, you must attempt to get from C_2 to the destination city, and so on. There is a distinct recursive flavor to this search strategy, which can be restated as follows:

A recursive search strategy

```
To fly from the origin to the destination:
  Select a city C adjacent to the origin
  Fly from the origin to city C
  if (C is the destination city) {
    Terminate -- the destination is reached
  }
  else {
    Fly from city C to the destination
  }  // end if
```

This statement of the search strategy makes its recursive nature very apparent. The first step in flying from the origin city to the destination city is to fly from the origin city to city *C*. Once at city *C*, you are confronted with another problem of the same type—you now must fly from city *C* to the destination.

This recursive formulation is nothing more than a restatement of the initial (incomplete) strategy developed previously. As such it has the same three possible outcomes:

1. You eventually reach the destination city and can conclude that it is possible to fly from the origin to the destination.

2. You reach a city *C* from which there are no departing flights.

3. You go around in circles.

Possible outcomes of the recursive search strategy

The first of these outcomes corresponds to a base case of the recursive algorithm. If you ever reach the destination city, no additional problems of the form "fly from city *C* to the destination" are generated, and the algorithm terminates. However, as was observed previously, the algorithm might not produce this outcome; that is, it might not reach this base case. The algorithm might reach a city *C* that has no departing flights. (Notice that the algorithm does not specify what to do in this case—in this sense the algorithm is incomplete.) Or the algorithm might repeatedly cycle through the same sequence of cities and thus never terminate.

You can resolve these problems by mirroring what you did in the previous solution. Consider the following refinement, in which you mark visited cities and never fly to a city that has been visited already:

A refinement of the recursive search algorithm

```
+searchR(in originCity:City, in destinationCity:City):boolean
// Searches for a sequence of flights from
// originCity to destinationCity.

  Mark originCity as visited

  if (originCity is destinationCity) {
    Terminate -- the destination is reached
  }
  else {
    for (each unvisited city C adjacent to originCity) {
      searchR(C, destinationCity)
    }  // end for
  }  // end if
```

Now consider what happens when the algorithm reaches a city that has no unvisited city adjacent to it. For example, consider the piece of a flight map in Figure 7-14. When *searchR* reaches city *X*—that is, when the parameter *originCity* has the value *X*—the *for* loop will not be entered, because no unvisited cities are adjacent to *X*. Hence, the method *searchR* returns. This return has the effect of backtracking to city *W*, from which the flight to *X* originated. In terms of the previous pseudocode, the return is made to the point from which the call *searchR(X, destinationCity)* occurred. This point is within

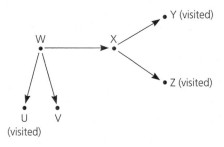

FIGURE 7-14

A piece of a flight map

the `for` loop, which iterates through the unvisited cities adjacent to *W*; that is, the parameter `originCity` has the value *W*.

After backtracking from *X* to *W*, the `for` loop will again execute. This time the loop chooses city *V*, resulting in the recursive call `searchR(V, destinationCity)`. From this point, the algorithm either will eventually reach the destination city and terminate, or it will backtrack once again to city *W*. If it backtracks to *W*, the `for` loop will terminate because there are no more unvisited cities adjacent to *W*, and a return from `searchR` will occur. The effect is to backtrack to the city where the flight to *W* originated. If the algorithm ever backtracks to the origin city and no remaining unvisited cities are adjacent to it, the algorithm will terminate, and you can conclude that no sequence of flights from the origin to the destination exists. Notice that the algorithm will always terminate in one way or another, because it will either reach the destination city or run out of unvisited cities to try.

The following Java method implements the `searchR` algorithm:

Java implementation of **searchR**

```
public boolean isPath(City originCity,
                      City destinationCity) {
   City  nextCity;
   boolean done;

   // mark the current city as visited
   markVisited(originCity);

   // base case: the destination is reached
   if (originCity.compareTo(destinationCity) == 0) {
     return true;
   }
   else { // try a flight to each unvisited city
     done = false;
     nextCity = getNextCity(originCity);

     while (nextCity != null && !done) {
       done = isPath(nextCity, destinationCity);
```

```
      if (!done) {
         nextCity = getNextCity(originCity);
      }  // end if
   }  // end while

   return done;
  }  // end if
} // end isPath
```

You have probably noticed a close parallel between this recursive algorithm and the earlier stack-based algorithm `searchS`. In fact, the two algorithms simply employ different techniques to implement the identical search strategy. The next section will elaborate on the relationship between the two algorithms.

7.6 The Relationship Between Stacks and Recursion

The previous section solved the HPAir problem once by using the ADT stack and again by using recursion. The goal of this section is to relate the way that the stack organizes the search for a sequence of flights to the way a recursive algorithm organizes the search. You will see that the ADT stack has a hidden presence in the concept of recursion and, in fact, that stacks have an active role in most computer implementations of recursion.

Consider how the two search algorithms implement three key aspects of their common strategy.

- **Visiting a new city.** The recursive algorithm `searchR` visits a new city C by calling `searchR(C, destinationCity)`. The algorithm `searchS` visits city C by pushing C onto a stack. Notice that if you were to use the box trace to trace the execution of `searchR`, the call `searchR(C, destinationCity)` would generate a box in which the city C is associated with the formal parameter `originCity` of `searchR`.

  For example, Figure 7-15 shows both the state of the box trace for `searchR` and the stack for `searchS` at corresponding points of their search for a path from city P to city Z in Figure 7-10.

A comparison of key aspects of two search algorithms

- **Backtracking.** Both search algorithms attempt to visit an unvisited city that is adjacent to the current city. Notice that this current city is the value associated with the formal parameter `originCity` in the deepest (rightmost) box of `searchR`'s box trace. Similarly, the current city is on the top of `searchS`'s stack. In Figure 7-15, this current city is X. If no unvisited cities are adjacent to the current city, the algorithms must backtrack to the previous city. The algorithm `searchR` backtracks by returning from the current recursive call. You represent this action in the box trace by crossing off the deepest box. The algorithm `searchS` backtracks by explicitly popping from its stack. For example, from the state depicted in Figure 7-15, both algorithms backtrack to city R and then to city P, as Figure 7-16 illustrates.

■ **Termination.** The search algorithms terminate either when they reach the destination city or when they exhaust all possibilities. All possibilities are exhausted when, after backtracking to the origin city, no unvisited adjacent cities remain. This situation occurs for *searchR* when all boxes have been crossed off in the box trace and a return occurs to the point of the original call to the method. For *searchS*, no unvisited cities are adjacent to the origin when the stack becomes empty.

Thus, the two search algorithms really do perform the identical action. In fact, provided that they use the same rule to select an unvisited city—for example, traverse the current city's list of adjacent cities alphabetically—they will always visit the identical cities in the identical order. The similarities between the algorithms are far more than coincidence. In fact, it is always possible to capture the actions of a recursive method by using a stack.

An important context in which the close tie between stacks and recursion is explicitly utilized is a compiler's implementation of a recursive method. It is common for a compiler to use a stack to implement a recursive method in a manner that greatly resembles the box trace. When a recursive call to a method occurs, the implementation must remember certain information. This information consists essentially of the same local environment that you place in the boxes—values of both parameters and local variables, and a reference to the point from which the recursive call was made.

Typically, stacks are used to implement recursive methods

(a) Box trace:

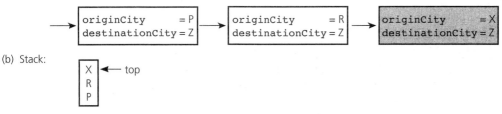

(b) Stack:

FIGURE 7-15

Visiting city *P*, then *R*, then *X*: (a) box trace versus (b) stack

(a) Box trace:

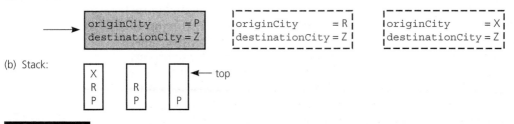

(b) Stack:

FIGURE 7-16

Backtracking from city *X* to *R* to *P*: (a) box trace versus (b) stack

During execution, the compiled program must manage these boxes of information, or **activation records,** just as you must manage them on paper. As the HPAir example has indicated, the operations needed to manage the activation records are those that a stack provides. When a recursive call occurs, a new activation record is created and pushed onto a stack. This action corresponds to the creation of a new box at the deepest point in the sequence. When a return is made from a recursive call, the stack is popped, bringing the activation record that contains the appropriate local environment to the top of the stack. This action corresponds to crossing off the deepest box and following the arrow back to the preceding box. Although we have greatly simplified the process, most implementations of recursion are based on stacks of activation records.

Each recursive call generates an activation record that is pushed onto a stack

You can use a similar strategy to implement a nonrecursive version of a recursive algorithm. You might need to recast a recursive algorithm into a nonrecursive form to make it more efficient, as mentioned in Chapter 3. The previous discussion should give you a taste of the techniques for removing recursion from a program. You will encounter recursion removal as a formal topic in more advanced courses, such as compiler construction.

You can use stacks when implementing a nonrecursive version of a recursive algorithm

Summary

1. The ADT stack operations have a last-in, first-out (LIFO) behavior.

2. Algorithms that operate on algebraic expressions are an important application of stacks. The LIFO nature of stacks is exactly what the algorithm that evaluates postfix expressions needs to organize the operands. Similarly, the algorithm that transforms infix expressions to postfix form uses a stack to organize the operators in accordance with precedence rules and left-to-right association.

3. You can use a stack to determine whether a sequence of flights exists between two cities. The stack keeps track of the sequence of visited cities and enables the search algorithm to backtrack easily. However, displaying the sequence of cities in their normal order from origin to destination is awkward, because the origin city is at the bottom of the stack and the destination is at the top.

4. A strong relationship between recursion and stacks exists. Most implementations of recursion maintain a stack of activation records in a manner that resembles the box trace.

Cautions

1. Operations such as *peek* and *pop* must take reasonable action when the stack is empty. One possibility is to ignore the operation and throw an exception *Stack-Exception*.

2. Algorithms that evaluate an infix expression or transform one to postfix form must determine which operands apply to a given operator. Doing so allows for precedence and left-to-right association so that you can omit parentheses.

3. When searching for a sequence of flights between cities, you must take into account the possibility that the algorithm will make wrong choices. For example,

the algorithm must be able to backtrack when it hits a dead end, and you must eliminate the possibility that the algorithm will cycle.

Self-Test Exercises

1. If you push the letters W, Y, X, Z, and V in order onto a stack of characters and then pop them, in what order will they be deleted from the stack?

2. What do the initially empty stacks *stack1* and *stack2* "look like" after the following sequence of operations?

   ```
   stack1.push(23)
   stack1.push(17)
   stack1.push(50)
   stack2.push(42)
   top1 = stack1.pop()
   top2 = stack2.peek()
   stack2.push(top1)
   stack1.push(top2)
   stack1.push(13)
   top2 = stack2.pop()
   stack2.push(49)
   ```

   Compare these results with Self-Test Exercise 2.

3. The algorithms that appear in the section "Simple Applications of the ADT Stack" involve strings. Under what conditions would you choose an array-based implementation for the stack in these algorithms? Under what conditions would you choose a reference-based implementation?

4. Describe the difference between the *peek* operation and the *pop* operations in an ADT stack.

5. For each of the following strings, trace the execution of the balanced-braces algorithm and show the contents of the stack at each step.

   a. x{{{y}z}

   b. {x{y{z}}}

   c. {xy{z}}}

6. Use the stack algorithms in this chapter to evaluate the postfix expression $ab-c+$. Assume the following values for the identifiers: $a = 7$; $b = 3$; $c = -2$. Show the status of the stack after each step.

7. Use the stack algorithms in this chapter to convert the infix expression $a/b*c$ to postfix form. Be sure to account for left-to-right association. Show the status of the stack after each step.

8. Explain the significance of the precedence tests in the infix-to-postfix conversion algorithm. Why is a $\geq$ test used rather than a $>$ test?

9. Execute the HPAir algorithm with the map in Figure 7-17 for the following requests. Show the state of the stack after each step.

   a. Fly from *F* to *I*.

   b. Fly from *F* to *C*.

   c. Fly from *H* to *C*.

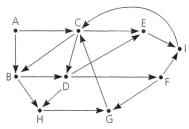

FIGURE 7-17

Flight map for Self-Test Exercise 9 and Exercise 15

Exercises

1. What makes a linked list a good choice for implementing a stack?

2. Write a Java program to implement two stacks in a single array.
   (*Hint:* There should be only one stack, with two different top references.)

3. Suppose that you have a stack *aStack* and an empty auxiliary stack *auxStack*. Show how you can do each of the following tasks by using only the operations of the ADT stack:

   a. Display the contents of *aStack* in reverse order; that is, display the top last.

   b. Count the number of items in *aStack*, leaving *aStack* unchanged.

   c. Delete every occurrence of a specified item from *aStack*, leaving the order of the remaining items unchanged.

4. Recall the search method from the JCF class *Stack*:

```
public int search(Object o)
// Returns the 1-based position where an object is on this
// stack. The topmost item on the stack is considered to be at
// distance 1.
```

   a. Add this method to the *StackListBased* implementation given in this chapter.

   b. Add this method to the *StackArrayBased* implementation given in this chapter.

   c. Add this method to the *StackReferenceBased* implementation given in this chapter.

5. Which of the following stack operations could result in stack underflow?

   a. `is_empty ()`

   b. `push ()`

   c. `pop ()`

   d. Two or more of the above answers

6. Another operation that could be added to the ADT Stack is one that removes and discards the user specified number of elements from the top of the stack. Assume this operation is called *popAndDiscard* and that it does not return a value and accepts a parameter called count of data type *int*.

   a. Add this operation to the `StackListBased` implementation given in this chapter.

   b. Add this operation to the `StackArrayBased` implementation given in this chapter.

   c. Add this operation to the `StackReferenceBased` implementation given in this chapter.

7. The diagram of a railroad switching system in Figure 7-18 is commonly used to illustrate the notion of a stack. Identify three stacks in the figure and show how they relate to one another. Suppose you had four train cars arrive in the order shown: A followed by B, then C, then D.

   a. How could you use the railroad switch to change the order so that A is still first, B is still second, but D is third, and C is fourth?

   b. How could you use the railroad switch to change the order of the cars so that B is first, D is second, A is third and C is fourth?

   c. Can any possible permutation of railroad cars be achieved with this switch? Justify your answer.

8. Suppose you have a stack in which the values 1 through 5 must be pushed on the stack in that order, but that an item on the stack can be popped and printed at any time. So for example, the operations

```
s.push(1)
s.push(2)
print s.pop()
```

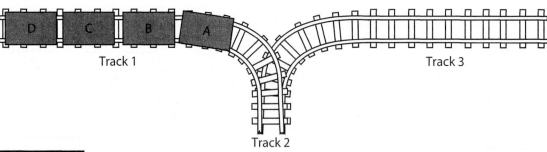

FIGURE 7-18

Railroad switching system for Exercise 4

```
s.push(3)
s.push(4)
print s.pop()
s.push(5)
print s.pop()
print s.pop()
print s.pop()
```

produce the sequence 2 4 5 3 1. Based on the constraints mentioned above, give the list of operations that would produce each of the following sequences. If it is not possible, state so.

a. 1 3 5 4 2

b. 2 3 4 5 1

c. 1 4 3 5 2

d. 1 5 4 2 3

e. Are there sequences that cannot occur? Explain why or why not.

9. What is the output of the following code for n = 15? n = 65? What does this program appear to do?

```
public static void mystery(int n) {
   StackInterface s = new StackReferenceBased();
   while (n > 0) {
      s.push(n % 8);
      n = n / 8;
   }
   while (!s.isEmpty())
      System.out.print(stack.pop());
   System.out.println();
} // end mystery
```

10. Write a Java program that reads a string from the console and pushes any capital letter in the string into a stack called CAP, then pops those letters from CAP and counts the number of vowels in the stack.

11. The section "Developing an ADT During the Design of a Solution" described an algorithm readAndCorrect that reads a string of characters, correcting mistakes along the way.

a. For the following input line, trace the execution of readAndCorrect and show the contents of the stack at each step:

ab←cde←←fgh←i

b. The nature of the stack-based algorithm makes it simple to display the string in reverse order (as was done in displayBackward), but somewhat harder to display it in its correct order. Write a pseudocode algorithm called displayForward that displays the string in its correct forward order.

c. Implement readAndCorrect and displayForward as Java methods.

12. Write a Java program that converts a given decimal number into a hexadecimal number using a stack. (Remember, numbers 10 to 15 are represented as A to F in the hexadecimal format.)

13. Consider the following code:

```
MyStack s = new MyStack ( );
s.push('A');
s.push('B');
s.push('C');
System.out.println(s.pop( ));
```

Suppose that the stack is represented by a linked list. The 'Head' reference of the stack will track the top element in the stack.

Now draw the state of the stack after each operation given in the above code. What will be the output of "`System.out.println(s.pop( ))`   " ?

14. Write a pseudocode method that uses a stack to determine whether a string is in the language L, where

    a. $L = \{w : w$ contains equal numbers of A's and B's in any order$\}$

    b. $L = \{w : w$ is of the form $A^{2n}B^n$ for some $n \geq 0\}$

15. Write a method that uses a stack to determine whether a string is in the language L, where:

    $L = \{ww' : w$ is a string of characters
    $w' = reverse\ (w) \}$
    Note: The empty string, a string with less than 2 characters, or a string with an odd number of characters will not be in the language.

16. Evaluate the following postfix expressions by using the algorithm given in this chapter. Show the status of the stack after each step of the algorithm. Assume that division is integer division as in Java, and the identifiers have the following values: $a = 7$; $b = 3$; $c = 12$; $d = -5$; $e = 1$.

    a. $ab* d+ -$

    b. $abcd+-*$

    c. $ab/c+d*e-$

17. Consider the following pseudocode:

```
declare a stack of characters
while ( there are more characters in the word to read )
{
read a character
push the character on the stack
}
while ( the stack is not empty )
{
write the stack's top character to the screen
pop a character off the stack
}
```

What is the output in the console for the input: "MORNING"?

a. MMOORRNNIINNGG

    b. GIRM

    c. MORNING

    d. GNINROM

18. Execute the HPAir algorithm with the map in Figure 7-17 (see Self-Test Exercise 9) for the following requests. Assume that the algorithm always flies to the alphabetically earliest unvisited city from the city on the top of the stack. Show the state of the stack after each step and indicate whether the flight is possible or not possible.

    a. Fly from A to I.

    b. Fly from G to A.

    c. Fly from H to I.

    d. Fly from F to I.

    e. Fly from I to G.

19. As Chapter 4 pointed out, you can define ADT operations in a mathematically formal way by using axioms. For example, the following axioms formally define the ADT stack, where *stack* is an arbitrary stack and *item* is an arbitrary stack item.

```
(aStack.createStack()).isEmpty() = true
(aStack.push(item)).isEmpty() = false
(aStack.createStack()).pop() = error
(aStack.push(item)).pop() = aStack
(aStack.createStack()).peek() = error
(aStack.push(item)).peek() = item
```

    You can use these axioms, for example, to prove that the stack defined by the sequence of operations

```
Create an empty stack
Push a 5
Push a 7
Push a 3
Pop (the 3)
Push a 9
Push a 4
Pop (the 4)
```

which you can write as

```
((((((aStack.createStack()).push(5)).push(7)).push(3)).
  pop()).push(9)).push(4)).pop()
```

is exactly the same as the stack defined by the sequence

```
Create an empty stack
Push a 5
Push a 7
Push a 9
```

which you can write as

```
(((aStack.createStack()).push(5)).push(7)).push(9)
```

Similarly, you can use the axioms to show that

```
(((((((aStack.createStack()).push(1)).push(2)).pop()).
  push(3)).pop()).pop()).isEmpty()
```

is true.

a. The following representation of a stack as a sequence of *push* operations without any *pop* operations is called a **canonical form:**

```
(...(aStack.createStack()).push()).push()... ).push()
```

Prove that any stack is equal to a stack that is in canonical form.

b. Prove that the canonical form is unique. That is, a stack is equal to exactly one stack that is in canonical form.

c. Use the axioms to show formally that

```
((((((((((aStack.createStack()).push(6)).push(9)).
  pop()).pop()).push(2)).pop()).push(3)).push(1)).
  pop()).peek()
```

equals 3.

Programming Problems

1. Write a Java program using stack ADT, which will read the following values in the given order: USA, INDIA, CANADA, CHINA, BRAZIL, UK, JAPAN. Now write a separate function that can replace any value from the given list depending upon the user.

2. Write a program that uses a stack to read an integer and prints all its prime divisors in descending order. (For example, for the integer 39, the output should be 13,3).

3. Two different stacks contain the following characters:

```
Stack 1: 'A', 'X', 'T', 'U', 'R'.
Stack 2: 'R', 'F', 'H', 'B', 'X'.
```

Write a program that merges the above two stacks to create the merged stack 'A', 'X', 'T', 'U', 'R', 'R', 'F', 'H', 'B', 'X'.

4. Design and implement a class of postfix calculators. Use the algorithm given in this chapter to evaluate postfix expressions, as entered into the calculator. Use only the operators +, −, *, %, and /. Assume that the postfix expressions have single digit numbers in the expression and are syntactically correct.

5. The postfix calculator in Programming Problem 4 assumed single digit operands. Modify the calculator so that operators and operands may be separated by any number of spaces and

a. the operands may be multi-digit integers.

b. the operands may be multi-digit numbers with a decimal point.

6. Consider simple infix expressions that consist of single-digit operands; the operators +, −, *, %, and /; and parentheses. Assume that unary operators are illegal and
   that the expression contains no embedded spaces.

   Design and implement a class for an infix calculator. Use the algorithms given in
   this chapter to convert the infix expression to postfix form and to evaluate the resulting postfix expression. Note that if the methods *evaluate* and *getPostfix* are called
   before the *convertPostfix* method, then the exception *IllegalStateException*
   should be thrown by these methods.

   ```
   class Calculator {
       public Calculator(String exp)     // initializes infix expression
       public String toString()          // returns infix expression
       private boolean convertPostfix()  // creates postfix expression
                                         // returns true if successful

       // The following methods should throw IllegalStateException if
       // they are called before convertPostfix

       // returns the resulting postfix expression
       public String getPostfix() throws IllegalStateException


       // evaluates the expression
       public int evaluate() throws IllegalStateException
   } //end Calculator
   ```

7. The infix-to-postfix conversion algorithm described in this chapter assumes single
   digit operands and that the given infix expression is syntactically correct. Repeat
   Programming Problem 6 with the following enhancements. If the expression has
   one of the errors mentioned, print out an appropriate error message, and where
   possible, indicate where the error occurred in the expression. If the expression is
   syntactically correct, evaluate the expression.

   a. Allow for any type of spacing between operands, operators, and parentheses.

   b. Allow for multi-digit integer operands. Even better, allow for multi-digit oper-
      ands with a decimal point.

   c. The algorithms in the text assume that the given infix expression is syntactically
      correct. Watch for errors in the infix expression. Here are some examples:
      i. a + 4 (Illegal character a)
      ii. 4 + 5 3 (Space between 5 and 3, a missing operator)
      iii. 4 + * 5 − 2 (Missing operand)
      iv.) 2+3 ((Improperly nested parenthesis)
      v. (2 + 3) * 5) (Mismatched parentheses-right or left)

      If an error is detected during the method *convertPostfix*, it should return false,
      but first print a message that identifies the error and, when possible, indicate where
      the error occurred in the expression. If the expression is not successfully converted, a
      call to *evaluate* or *getPostfix* should throw *IllegalStateException*.

8. Repeat Programming Problem 5, but use the following algorithm to evaluate an
   infix expression *infixExp*. The algorithm uses two stacks: One stack, *opStack*,
   contains operators, and the other stack, *valStack*, contains values of operands and
   intermediate results. Note that the algorithm treats parentheses as operators with
   the lowest precedence.

```
for (each character ch in infixExp) {
  switch (ch) {
    case ch is an operand, that is, a digit
      valStack.push(ch)
      break
    case ch is '('
      opStack.push(ch)
      break
    case ch is an operator
      if (opStack.isEmpty()) {
        opStack.push(ch)
      }
      else if (precedence(ch) >
                  precedence(top of opStack)) {
        opStack.push(ch)
      }
      else {
        while (!opStack.isEmpty() and
          precedence(ch) <= precedence(top of opStack)) {
          Execute
        }  // end while
        opStack.push(ch)
      }  // end if
      break

    case ch is ')'
      while (top of opStack is not '(') {
        Execute
      }  // end while
      opStack.pop()
      break
  }  // end switch
}  // end for

while (!opStack.isEmpty()) {
  Execute
}  // end while
result = valStack.peek()
```

Note that *Execute* means

```
operand2 = valStack.pop()
operand1 = valStack.pop()
op = opStack.pop()
result = operand1 op operand2
valStack.push(result)
```

9. In the chapter, we examined one strategy to evaluate an infix expression—first convert the infix expression to a postfix expression, then evaluate the resulting postfix expression. An alternative strategy would be to convert the infix expression to prefix, and then evaluate the resulting prefix expression.

The following pseudocode algorithm for converting an infix expression to prefix is similar to, but not quite the same as, the infix to postfix conversion algorithm:

```
Initialize the string temp to the null string
Reverse the characters in the infix expression
```

```
for (each character ch in the reversed infix expression) {
  switch(ch) {
    case ch is an operand:
      Append ch to the end of temp expression
    case ch is ')':
      Push ch on the stack
    case ch is '(':
      Pop stack and append item to output expression until the
        matching ')' is popped off the stack
    case ch is an operator:
      Pop operators off stack and append to temp expression as
        appropriate (similar to postfix conversion)
      Push ch on the stack
  } // end switch
} // end for
// append remaining stack contents to output expression
while (stack is not empty) {
  Pop stack and append to temp expression
} // end while
Reverse temp expression to produce prefix expression
```

Also note that evaluating a prefix expression is almost the same as evaluating a postfix expression, with one small change—with prefix expressions, you start at the end of the expression. For example:

```
Postfix : 3 5 +
```

You start at the beginning of the expression, moving forward through the expression, pushing operands, and popping the operands when the operators appear, then pushing the result.

```
Prefix: + 3 5
```

You start at the end of the expression, moving backward through the expression, pushing operands, and popping the operands when the operators appear, then pushing the result.

Design and implement a class (as shown next) for an infix calculator based on prefix expressions. Use the algorithms given above to convert the infix expression to prefix form and to evaluate the resulting prefix expression. Note that if the methods *evaluate* and *getPrefix* are called before the *convertPrefix* method, then the exception *IllegalStateException* should be thrown by these methods.

```
class Calculator {
  public Calculator(String exp)   // initializes infix expression
  public String toString()        // returns infix expression
  private boolean convertPrefix() // creates prefix expression
                                  // returns true if successful

  // The following methods should throw IllegalStateException if
  // they are called before convertPrefix

  // returns the resulting prefix expression
  public String getPretix() throws IllegalStateException
```

```
        // evaluates the expression
        public int evaluate() throws IllegalStateException
} //end Calculator
```

10. Using stacks, write a nonrecursive version of the method *solveTowers*, as defined in Chapter 3.

11. Complete the solution to the HPAir problem. The input to the program consists of three text files, as follows:

cityFile   Each line contains the name of a city that HPAir serves. The names are in alphabetical order.

flightFile   Each line contains a pair of city names that represents the origin and destination of one of HPAir's flights.

requestFile   Each line contains a pair of city names that represents a request to fly from some origin to some destination.

You can make the following assumptions:

- Each city name contains at most 15 characters. Pairs of city names are separated by a comma.
- HPAir serves at most 20 cities.
- The input data is correct.

For example, the input files could appear as

```
    cityFile:       Albuquerque
                    Chicago
                    San Diego

    flightFile:     Chicago,        San Diego
                    Chicago,        Albuquerque
                    Albuquerque,    Chicago

    requestFile:    Albuquerque,    San Diego
                    Albuquerque,    Paris
                    San Diego,      Chicago
```

For this input, the program should produce the following output:

```
    Request is to fly from Albuquerque to San Diego.
    HPAir flies from Albuquerque to San Diego.

    Request is to fly from Albuquerque to Paris.
    Sorry. HPAir does not serve Paris.

    Request is to fly from San Diego to Chicago.
    Sorry. HPAir does not fly from San Diego to Chicago.
```

Begin by implementing the ADT flight map as the Java class *Map*. Use the nonrecursive version of *isPath*. Since *getNextCity* is the primary operation that the search algorithm performs on the flight map, you should choose an implementation that will efficiently determine which cities are adjacent to a given city. If there are *N* cities, you can use *N* linked lists to represent the flight map. You place a node on list *i* for city *j* if and only if there is a directed path from city *i* to city *j*. Such a data structure is called an **adjacency list;** Figure 7-19 illustrates an adjacency list for the flight map in Figure 7-10. Chapter 14 discusses adjacency lists further when it presents ways to represent graphs. At that time, you will learn why an adjacency list is a good choice for the present program.

Although you can implement the adjacency list from scratch, you should also consider using *N* instances of *ListReferenceBased*, which has a reference-based implementation.

You must also create a class *City* that implements the *java.lang.Comparable* interface to store the city name. The class *City* and the previously described adjacency list are the underlying data structures for the ADT flight map.

To simplify reading the input text files, define a class that includes the following methods:

```
+getName():String
// Gets a name from the next line in a text file.

+getNamePair():String
// Returns a string containing the two names from the next
// line in a text file.
```

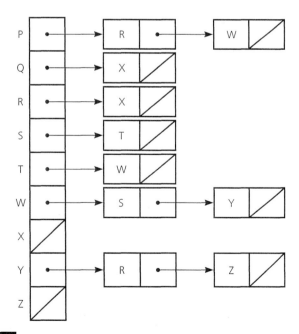

FIGURE 7-19

Adjacency list for the flight map in Figure 7-10

12. In the implementation of the HPAir problem (see Programming Problem 10), the search for the next unvisited city adjacent to a city i always starts at the beginning of the ith linked list in the adjacency list. This approach is actually a bit inefficient, because once the search visits a city, the city can never become unvisited. Modify the program so that the search for the next city begins where the last search left off. That is, maintain an array of *tryNext* references into the adjacency list.

13. Implement an expanded version of the HPAir problem. In addition to the "from" and "to" cities, each line of input contains a flight number (an integer) and the cost of the flight (an integer). Modify the HPAir program so that it will produce a complete itinerary for each request, including the flight number of each flight, the cost of each flight, and the total cost of the trip.

    For example, the input files could appear as

    ```
    cityFile:        Albuquerque
                     Chicago
                     San Diego

    flightFile:      Chicago,      San Diego    703   325
                     Chicago,      Albuquerque  111   250
                     Albuquerque,  Chicago      178   250

    requestFile:     Albuquerque,  San Diego
                     Albuquerque,  Paris
                     San Diego,    Chicago
    ```

    For this input, the program should produce the following output:

    ```
    Request is to fly from Albuquerque to San Diego.
    Flight #178 from Albuquerque to Chicago     Cost: $250
    Flight #703 from Chicago to San Diego       Cost: $325
    Total Cost ............  $575
    Request is to fly from Albuquerque to Paris.
    Sorry. HPAir does not serve Paris.
    Request is to fly from San Diego to Chicago.
    Sorry. HPAir does not fly from San Diego to Chicago.
    ```

    When the nonrecursive *isPath* method finds a sequence of flights from the origin city to the destination city, its stack contains the corresponding path of cities. The stumbling block to reporting this path is that the cities appear in the stack in reverse order; that is, the destination city is at the top of the stack and the origin city is at the bottom. For example, if you use the program to find a path from city P to city Z in Figure 7-10, the final contents of the stack will be P-W-Y-Z, with Z on top. You want to display the origin city P first, but it is at the bottom of the stack. If you restrict yourself to the stack operations, the only way that you can write the path in its correct order is first to reverse the stack by popping it onto a temporary stack and then to write the cities as you pop them off the temporary stack. Note that this approach requires that you process each city on the path twice.

    Evidently a stack is not the appropriate ADT for the problem of writing the path of cities in the correct order; the appropriate ADT is a **traversable stack.** In addition to the standard stack operations, *isEmpty*, *push*, *pop*, and *peek*, a traversable stack includes the operation *traverse*. This operation begins at one end of the stack and *visits* each item in the stack until it reaches the other end of the stack. For this project, you want *traverse* to begin at the bottom of the stack and move toward the top.

14. Write a Java program that read strings from a given file, then, using stack ADT, reverses the string and writes again on to another file.

CHAPTER 8

Queues

Whereas a stack's behavior is characterized as last-in, first-out, a queue's behavior is characterized as first-in, first-out. This chapter defines the queue's operations and discusses strategies for implementing them. As you will see, queues are common in everyday life. Their first-in, first-out behavior makes them appropriate ADTs for situations that involve waiting. Queues are also important in simulation, a technique for analyzing the behavior of complex systems. This chapter uses a queue to model the behavior of people in a line.

8.1 The Abstract Data Type Queue

A **queue** is like a line of people. The first person to join a line is the first person served and is thus the first to leave the line. New items enter a queue at its **back,** or **rear,** and items leave a queue from its **front.** Operations on a queue occur only at its two ends. This characteristic gives a queue its **first-in, first-out (FIFO)** behavior. In contrast, you can think of a stack as having only one end, because all operations are performed at the top of the stack. This characteristic gives a stack its last-in, first-out behavior.

FIFO: The first item inserted into a queue is the first item out

As an abstract data type, the queue has the following operations:

KEY CONCEPTS

ADT Queue Operations
1. Create an empty queue.
2. Determine whether a queue is empty.
3. Add a new item to the queue.
4. Remove from the queue the item that was added earliest.
5. Remove all the items from the queue.
6. Retrieve from the queue the item that was added earliest.

Queues occur in everyday life

Queues are appropriate for many real-world situations. You wait in a queue—that is, a line—to buy a movie ticket, to check out at the book store, or to use an automatic teller machine. The person at the front of the queue is served, while new people join the queue at its back. Even when you call an airline to make a reservation, your call actually enters a queue while you wait for the next available agent.

Queues have applications in computer science

Queues also have applications in computer science. When you print an essay, the computer sends lines faster than the printer can print them. The lines are held in a queue for the printer, which removes them in FIFO order. If you share the printer with other computers, your request to print enters a queue to wait its turn.

Since all of these applications involve waiting, people study them to see how to reduce the wait. Such studies are called **simulations,** and they typically use queues. Later, this chapter examines a simulation of a line of customers at a bank.

The following pseudocode describes the operations for the ADT queue in more detail, and Figure 8-1 shows a UML diagram for the class *Queue*. As we did for the ADT stack, we specify that the remove operation both retrieves and then removes the item at the front of the queue.

Figure 8-2 illustrates these operations with a queue of integers. Notice that *enqueue* inserts an item at the back of the queue and that *peek* looks at the item at the front of the queue, whereas *dequeue* deletes the item at the front of the queue.

KEY CONCEPTS

Pseudocode for the ADT Queue Operations

```
//QueueItemType is the type of the items stored in the queue
+createQueue()
// Creates an empty queue.
+isEmpty():boolean {query}
// Determines whether a queue is empty.
+enqueue(in newItem:QueueItemType) throws QueueException
// Adds NewItem at the back of a queue. Throws
// QueueException if the operation is not successful.
+dequeue():QueueItemType throws QueueException
// Retrieves and removes the front of a queue—the
// item that was added earliest. Throws QueueException
// if the operation is not successful.
+dequeueAll()
// Removes all items from a queue
+peek():QueueItemType {query} throws QueueException
// Retrieves the front of a queue. That is,
// retrieves the item that was added earliest.
// Throws QueueException if the retrieval is not
// successful. The queue is unchanged.
```

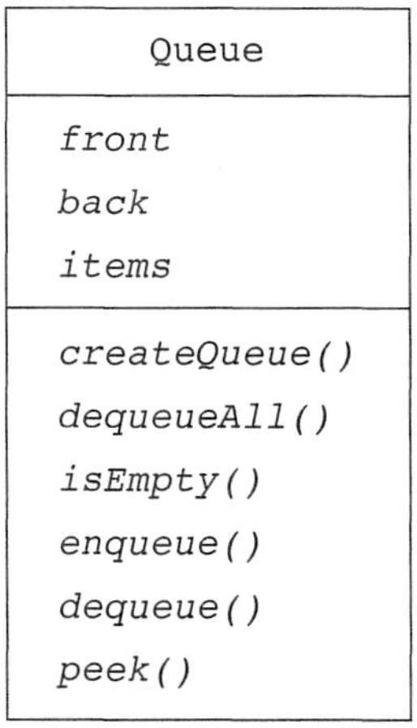

Queue
front
back
items
createQueue()
dequeueAll()
isEmpty()
enqueue()
dequeue()
peek()

FIGURE 8-1

UML diagram for the class *Queue*

Operation	Queue after operation
	┌─────────── Front
queue.createQueue()	↓
queue.enqueue(5)	5
queue.enqueue(2)	5 2
queue.enqueue(7)	5 2 7
queueFront = queue.peek()	5 2 7 (queueFront is 5)
queueFront = queue.dequeue()	5 2 7 (queueFront is 5)
queueFront = queue.dequeue()	2 7 (queueFront is 2)

FIGURE 8-2

Some queue operations

8.2 Simple Applications of the ADT Queue

This section presents two simple applications of the ADT queue. The applications use the operations of the ADT queue independently of their implementations.

Reading a String of Characters

When you enter characters at a keyboard, the system must retain them in the order in which you typed them. It could use a queue for this purpose, as the following pseudocode indicates:

A queue can retain characters in the order in which you type them

```
// read a string of characters from a
// single line of input into a queue
aQueue.createQueue()
while (not end of line) {
   Read a new character ch
   aQueue.enqueue(ch)
}  // end while
```

Once the characters are in a queue, the system can process them as necessary. For example, if you had typed an integer—without any mistakes, but possibly preceded or followed by blanks—the queue would contain digits and possibly blanks. If the digits are 2, 4, and 7, the system could convert them into the decimal value 247 by computing

$$10 * (10 * 2 + 4) + 7$$

The following pseudocode performs this conversion in general:

```
// convert digits in queue aQueue into a decimal integer n

// get first digit, ignoring any leading blanks
do  {
  ch = aQueue.dequeue()
}  while (ch is blank)
```

```
// Assertion: ch contains first digit
// compute n from digits in queue
n = 0
done = false
do  {
  n = 10 * n + integer that ch represents
  if (!aQueue.isEmpty()) {
    ch = aQueue.dequeue()
  }
  else {
    done = true
  }  // end if
}  while (!done and ch is a digit)
// Assertion: n is result
```

Recognizing Palindromes

Recall from Chapter 6 that a palindrome is a string of characters that reads the same from left to right as it does from right to left. In the previous chapter, you learned that you can use a stack to reverse the order of occurrences. You should realize by now that you can use a queue to preserve the order of occurrences. Thus, you can use both a queue and a stack to determine whether a string is a palindrome.

You can use a queue in conjunction with a stack to recognize palindromes

As you traverse the character string from left to right, you can insert each character into both a queue and a stack. Figure 8-3 illustrates the result of this action for the string abcbd, which is not a palindrome. You can see that the first character in the string is at the front of the queue and the last character in the string is at the top of the stack. Thus, characters removed from the queue

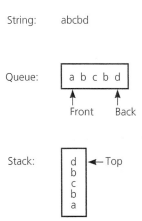

FIGURE 8-3

The results of inserting a string into both a queue and a stack will occur in the order in which they appear in the string; characters removed from the stack will occur in the opposite order.

Knowing this, you can compare the characters at the front of the queue and the top of the stack. If the characters are the same, you can delete them. You repeat this process until either the ADTs become empty, in which case the original string is a palindrome, or the two characters are not the same, in which case the string is not a palindrome.

The following is a pseudocode version of a nonrecursive recognition algorithm for the language of palindromes:

A nonrecursive recognition algorithm for palindromes

```
+isPal(in str:String):boolean
// Determines whether str is a palindrome.

    // create an empty queue and an empty stack
    aQueue.createQueue()
    aStack.createStack()

    // insert each character of the string into both
    // the queue and the stack
    length = the length of str
    for (i = 1 through length) {
        nextChar = iᵗʰ character of str
        aQueue.enqueue(nextChar)
        aStack.push(nextChar)
    }  // end for

    // compare the queue characters with the stack
    // characters
    charactersAreEqual = true
    while (aQueue is not empty and charactersAreEqual is true) {
        queueFront = aQueue.dequeue()
        stackTop = aStack.pop()
        if (queueFront not equal to stackTop) {
            charactersAreEqual = false
        }  // end if
    }  // end while
    return charactersAreEqual
```

8.3 Implementations of the ADT Queue

This section develops three Java implementations of the ADT queue. The first uses a linked list to represent the queue, the second uses an array, and the third uses the ADT list. The following interface *QueueInterface* is used to provide a common specification for the three implementations. Note that *enqueue*, *dequeue*, and *peek* may throw *QueueException*.

The *QueueException* class, which is similar to the *StackException* class developed in Chapter 7, appears next.

```java
public interface QueueInterface {

  public boolean isEmpty();
  // Determines whether a queue is empty.
  // Precondition: None.
  // Postcondition: Returns true if the queue is empty;
  // otherwise returns false.

  public void enqueue(Object newItem) throws QueueException;
  // Adds an item at the back of a queue.
  // Precondition: newItem is the item to be inserted.
  // Postcondition: If the operation was successful, newItem
  // is at the back of the queue. Some implementations may
  // throw QueueException if newItem cannot be added to the
  // queue.

  public Object dequeue() throws QueueException;
  // Retrieves and removes the front of a queue.
  // Precondition: None.
  // Postcondition: If the queue is not empty, the item
  // that was added to the queue earliest is returned and
  // the item is removed. If the queue is empty, the
  // operation is impossible and QueueException is thrown.

  public void dequeueAll();
  // Removes all items of a queue.
  // Precondition: None.
  // Postcondition: The queue is empty.

  public Object peek() throws QueueException;
  // Retrieves the item at the front of a queue.
  // Precondition: None.
  // Postcondition: If the queue is not empty, the item
  // that was added to the queue earliest is returned.
  // If the queue is empty, the operation is impossible
  // and QueueException is thrown.
}  // end QueueInterface
```

The *QueueException* class, which is similar to the *StackException* class developed in Chapter 7, appears next.

```java
public class QueueException extends RuntimeException {

  public QueueException(String s) {
    super(s);
  }  // end constructor
}  // end QueueException
```

For queues, the reference-based implementation is a bit more straightfor-ward than the array-based one, so we start with it.

A Reference-Based Implementation

A reference-based implementation of a queue could use a linear linked list with two external references, one to the front and one to the back, as Figure 8-4a illustrates.[1] However, as Figure 8-4b shows, you can actually get by with a single external reference—to the back—if you make the linked list circular.

A circular linked list can represent a queue

When a circular linked list represents a queue, the node at the back of the queue references the node at the front. Thus,

lastNode references the node at the back of the queue, and

lastNode.next references the node at the front

Insertion at the back and deletion from the front are straightforward. Figure 8-5 illustrates the addition of an item to a nonempty queue. Inserting the new node, which *newNode* references, at the back of the queue requires three reference changes: the next reference in the new node, the next reference in the back node, and the external reference *lastNode*. Figure 8-5 depicts

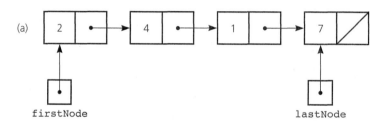

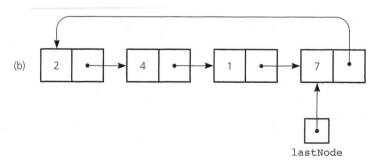

FIGURE 8-4

A reference-based implementation of a queue: (a) a linear linked list with two external references; (b) a circular linear linked list with one external reference

1. Programming Problem 1 asks you consider the details of this implementation.

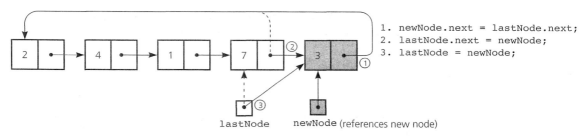

FIGURE 8-5

Inserting an item into a nonempty queue

these changes and indicates the order in which they must occur. (The dashed lines indicate reference values before the changes.) The addition of an item to an empty queue is a special case, as Figure 8-6 illustrates.

Deletion from the front of the queue is simpler than insertion at the back. Figure 8-7 illustrates the removal of the front item of a queue that contains more than one item. Notice that you need to change only one reference within the queue. Deletion from a queue of one item is a special case that sets the external reference *lastNode* to *null*.

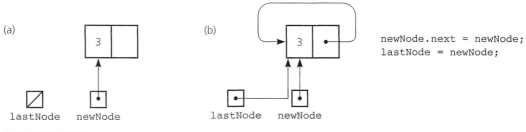

FIGURE 8-6

Inserting an item into an empty queue: (a) before insertion; (b) after insertion

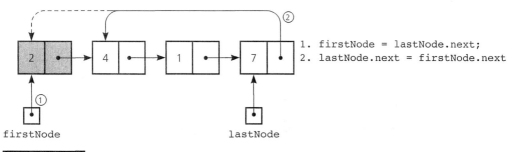

FIGURE 8-7

Deleting an item from a queue of more than one item

The following class is a reference-based implementation of the ADT queue. The implementation uses the *Node* class developed in Chapter 5.

```java
public class QueueReferenceBased implements QueueInterface {
  private Node lastNode;

  public QueueReferenceBased() {
    lastNode = null;
  }  // end default constructor

  // queue operations:
  public boolean isEmpty() {
    return lastNode == null;
  }  // end isEmpty

  public void dequeueAll() {
    lastNode = null;
  }  // end dequeueAll

  public void enqueue(Object newItem) {
    Node newNode = new Node(newItem);

    // insert the new node
    if (isEmpty()) {
      // insertion into empty queue
      newNode.next = newNode;
    }
    else {
      // insertion into nonempty queue
      newNode.next = lastNode.next;
      lastNode.next = newNode;
    }  // end if

    lastNode = newNode;   // new node is at back
  }  // end enqueue

  public Object dequeue() throws QueueException {
    if (!isEmpty()) {
      // queue is not empty; remove front
      Node firstNode = lastNode.next;
      if (firstNode == lastNode) { // special case?
        lastNode = null;               // yes, one node in queue
      }
      else {
        lastNode.next = firstNode.next;
      }  // end if
```

```
      return firstNode.item;
    }
    else {
      throw new QueueException("QueueException on dequeue:"
                                + "queue empty");
    }  // end if
  }  // end dequeue

  public Object peek() throws QueueException {
    if (!isEmpty()) {
      // queue is not empty; retrieve front
      Node firstNode = lastNode.next;
      return firstNode.item;
    }
    else {
      throw new QueueException("QueueException on peek:"
                                + "queue empty");
    }  // end if
  }  // end peek

} // end QueueReferenceBased
```

A program that uses this implementation could begin as follows:

```
    public class QueueTest {
      public static void main(String[] args) {
        QueueReferenceBased aQueue =
                                new QueueReferenceBased();
        for (int i = 0; i < 9; i++) {
          aQueue.enqueue(new Integer(i));
        }  // end for
        . . .
      }  // end main
    }  // end QueueTest
```

An Array-Based Implementation

For applications in which a fixed-sized queue does not present a problem, you can use an array to represent a queue. As Figure 8-8a illustrates, a naive array-based implementation of a queue might include the following definitions:

```
final int MAX_QUEUE = maximum-size-of-queue;

Object[] items;
int      front;
int      back;
```

A naive array-based implementation of a queue

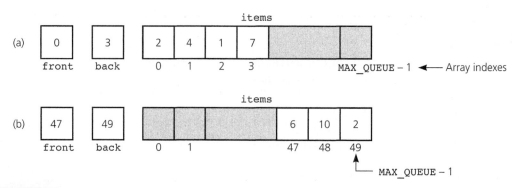

(a) A naive array-based implementation of a queue; (b) rightward drift can cause the queue to appear full

The indexes of the front and back items in the queue are, respectively, *front* and *back*. Initially, *front* is 0 and *back* is −1. To insert a new item into the queue, you increment *back* and place the item in *items[back]*. To delete an item, you simply increment *front*. The queue is empty whenever *back* is less than *front*. The queue is full when *back* equals *MAX_QUEUE* − 1.

Rightward drift can cause a queue-full condition even though the queue contains few entries

Shifting elements to compensate for rightward drift is

The problem with this strategy is **rightward drift**—that is, after a sequence of additions and removals, the items in the queue will drift toward the end of the array, and *back* could equal *MAX_QUEUE* − 1 even when the queue contains only a few items. Figure 8-8b illustrates this situation.

One possible solution to this problem is to shift array elements to the left, either after each deletion or whenever *back* equals *MAX_QUEUE* − 1. This solution guarantees that the queue can always contain up to *MAX_QUEUE* items. Shifting is not really satisfactory, however, as it would dominate the cost of the implementation.

A circular array eliminates rightward drift

A much more elegant solution is possible by viewing the array as circular, as Figure 8-9 illustrates. You advance the queue indexes *front* (to delete an item) and *back* (to insert an item) by moving them clockwise around the array. Figure 8-10 illustrates the effect of a sequence of three queue operations on

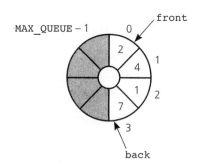

A circular implementation of a queue

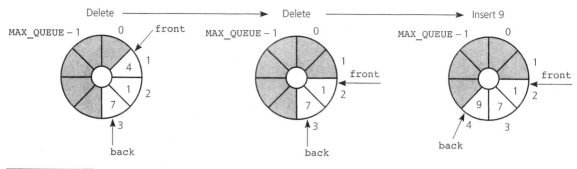

FIGURE 8-10

The effect of some operations on the queue in Figure 8-9

front, *back*, and the array. When either *front* or *back* advances past
MAX_QUEUE – 1, it wraps around to 0. This wraparound eliminates the problem
of rightward drift, which occurred in the previous implementation, because
here the circular array has no end.

The only difficulty with this scheme involves detecting the queue-empty
and queue-full conditions. It seems reasonable to select as the queue-empty
condition

front is one slot ahead of *back*

since this appears to indicate that *front* "passes" *back* when the queue
becomes empty, as Figure 8-11a depicts. However, it is also possible that this
condition signals a full queue: Because the queue is circular, *back* might in fact
"catch up" with *front* as the queue becomes full; Figure 8-11b illustrates this
situation.

> **front** and **back**
> cannot be used to
> distinguish between
> queue-full and
> queue-empty
> conditions

Obviously, you need a way to distinguish between the two situations. One
such way is to keep a count of the number of items in the queue. Before inserting into the queue, you check to see if the count is equal to MAX_QUEUE; if it is,
the queue is full. Before deleting an item from the queue, you check to see if
the count is equal to zero; if it is, the queue is empty.

> By counting queue
> items, you can
> detect queue-full
> and queue-empty
> conditions

To initialize the queue, you set *front* to 0, *back* to MAX_QUEUE – 1, and
count to 0. You obtain the wraparound effect of a circular queue by using
modulo arithmetic (that is, the Java % operator) when incrementing *front* and
back. For example, you can insert *newItem* into the queue by using the statements

> Initialize **front**,
> **back**, and **count**

```
back = (back+1) % MAX_QUEUE;
items[back] = newItem;
++count;
```

> Inserting into a
> queue

Notice that if *back* equaled MAX_QUEUE – 1 before the insertion of *newItem*,
the first statement, *back = (back+1) % MAX_QUEUE*, would have the effect of
wrapping *back* around to location 0.

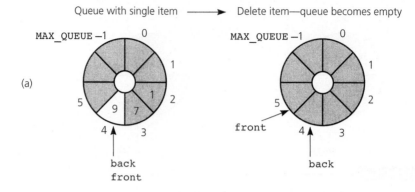

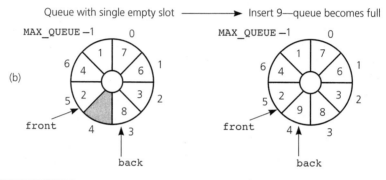

FIGURE 8-11

(a) *front* passes *back* when the queue becomes empty; (b) *back* catches up to *front* when the queue becomes full

Similarly, you can delete the item at the front of the queue by using the statements

Deleting from a queue

```
front = (front+1) % MAX_QUEUE;
--count;
```

The following Java class is an array-based implementation of the ADT queue that uses a circular array as just described. Preconditions and postconditions have been omitted to save space but are the same as those given in the *QueueInterface* specification.

```
public class QueueArrayBased implements QueueInterface {
  private final int MAX_QUEUE = 50; // maximum size of queue
  private Object[] items;
  private int front, back, count;

  public QueueArrayBased() {
    items = new Object[MAX_QUEUE];
```

```java
      front = 0;
      back = MAX_QUEUE-1;
      count = 0;
   }  // end default constructor

// queue operations:
public boolean isEmpty() {
   return count == 0;
}  // end isEmpty

public boolean isFull() {
   return count == MAX_QUEUE;
}  // end isFull

public void enqueue(Object newItem) throws QueueException {
   if (!isFull()) {
      back = (back+1) % (MAX_QUEUE);
      items[back] = newItem;
      ++count;
   }
   else {
      throw new QueueException("QueueException on enqueue: "
                              + "Queue full");
   }  // end if
}  // end enqueue
public Object dequeue() throws QueueException {
   if (!isEmpty()) {
      // queue is not empty; remove front
      Object queueFront = items[front];
      front = (front+1) % (MAX_QUEUE);
      --count;
      return queueFront;
   }
   else {
      throw new QueueException("QueueException on dequeue: "
                              + "Queue empty");
   }    // end if
}  // end dequeue
public void dequeueAll() {
   items = new Object[MAX_QUEUE];
   front = 0;
   back = MAX_QUEUE-1;
   count = 0;
}  // end dequeueAll

public Object peek() throws QueueException {
   if (!isEmpty()) {
```

```
      // queue is not empty; retrieve front
      return items[front];
   }
   else {
      throw new QueueException("Queue exception on peek: " +
                                  + "Queue empty");
   }  // end if
}  // end peek

} // end QueueArrayBased
```

A **full** flag can replace the counter

Several commonly used variations of this implementation do not require a count of the number of items in the queue. One approach uses a flag *full* to distinguish between the full and empty conditions. The expense of maintaining a *full* flag is about the same as that of maintaining a counter, however. A faster implementation declares *MAX_QUEUE* + 1 locations for the array *items*, but uses only *MAX_QUEUE* of them for queue items. You sacrifice one array location and make *front* the index of the location before the front of the queue. As Figure 8-12 illustrates, the queue is full if

front equals *(back+1) % (MAX_QUEUE+1)*

but the queue is empty if

front equals *back*

Using an extra array location is more time-efficient

This implementation does not have the overhead of maintaining a counter or flag, and so is more efficient time-wise. For the standard data types, the implementation requires the same space as either the counter or the flag implementation (why?). Programming Problems 3 and 4 discuss these two alternate implementations further.

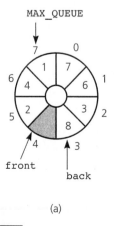

(a)

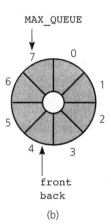

(b)

FIGURE 8-12

A more efficient circular implementation: (a) a full queue; (b) an empty queue

An Implementation That Uses the ADT List

You can use the ADT list to represent the items in a queue, as Figure 8-13 illustrates. If the item in position 1 of a list represents the front of the queue, you can implement the operation *dequeue()* as the list operation *remove(0)* and the operation *peek()* as *get(0)*. Similarly, if you let the item at the end of the list represent the back of the queue, you can implement the operation *enqueue(newItem)* as the list operation *add(size(), newItem)*.

Recall that Chapters 4 and 5 presented the ADT list as an implementation of the interface *ListInterface*. (See, for example, page 255.) The following class for the ADT queue uses an instance of the reference-based implementation *ListReferenceBased* to represent the queue. Preconditions and postconditions are omitted to save space but are the same as those given earlier in this chapter.

```
public class QueueListBased implements QueueInterface {
  private ListInterface aList;

  public QueueListBased() {
    aList = new ListReferenceBased();
  }  // end default constructor

  // queue operations:
  public boolean isEmpty() {
    return aList.isEmpty();
  }  // end isEmpty

  public void enqueue(Object newItem) {
    aList.add(aList.size(), newItem);
  }  // end enqueue

  public Object dequeue() throws QueueException {
    if (!isEmpty()) {
      // queue is not empty; remove front
      Object queueFront = aList.get(0);
      aList.remove(0);
      return queueFront;
    }
```

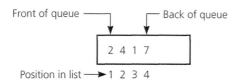

FIGURE 8-13

An implementation that uses the ADT list

```
          else {
            throw new QueueException("Queue exception on dequeue: "
                                   + " queue empty");
          }  // end if
      }  // end dequeue

      public void dequeueAll() {
        aList.removeAll();
      }  // end dequeueAll

      public Object peek() throws QueueException {
        if (!isEmpty()) {
          // queue is not empty; retrieve front
          return aList.get(0);
        }
        else {
          throw new QueueException("Queue exception on peek "
                                 + "queue empty");
        }  // end if
      }  // end peek

    }  // end QueueListBased
```

As was true for the analogous implementation of the ADT stack in Chapter 7, implementing the queue is simple once you have implemented the ADT list. Exercise 6 at the end of this chapter asks you to consider the efficiency of this implementation.

The JCF Interfaces *Queue* and *Deque*

The Java Collections Framework (JCF) contains two interfaces for queues: *Queue* and *Deque* (usually pronounced "deck"). Like the *List* interface, *Queue* is derived from the interface *Collection*, and thus inherits all of the methods defined in *Collection*. The *Deque* interface is derived from the *Queue* interface and is for collections that support element insertion and removal at both ends. The name *Deque* is short for "double ended queue."

The *Queue* Interface.   The *Queue* interface extends *Collection* with the following methods:

```
public interface Queue<E> extends Collection<E> {

  E element() throws NoSuchElementException;
    // Retrieves, but does not remove, the head of this queue.
    // If this queue is empty, throws NoSuchElementException.

  boolean offer(E o);
    // Inserts the specified element into this queue, if
    // possible.
```

```
E peek();
   // Retrieves, but does not remove, the head of this queue,
   // returning null if this queue is empty.

E poll();
   // Retrieves and removes the head of this queue, or null
   // if this queue is empty.

E remove() throws NoSuchElementException;
   // Retrieves and removes the head of this queue,
   // or throws NoSuchElementException if this queue
   // is empty.
} // end Queue
```

Note that the *Queue* has one data-type parameter for the items contained in the queue.

Queues are often used to hold elements before processing. In this chapter, the ADT queue that we studied ordered elements in the queue in a FIFO manner. But as you will see later in Chapter 12 when we discuss priority queues, other orderings are possible. Priority queues use a priority level to determine the ordering of the elements in the queue, usually so that the elements with a higher priority will get processed first. Another example is a stack; sometimes you will see a stack referred to as a LIFO queue.

Regardless of the ordering used, the head of the queue is always removed first by a call to *remove* or *poll*. Both methods retrieve and remove an element from the queue, but if the queue is empty, *poll* returns *null*, whereas *remove* will raise *NoSuchElementException*. Similarly, *element* and *peek* can be used to retrieve an element from the queue, with element raising *NoSuchElementException* and *peek* returning *null* if the queue is empty.

Note that *Queue* implementations may allow the insertion of *null* elements. But this makes it difficult to determine if methods such as *poll* and *remove* are returning *null* as an element or *null* meaning that a queue is empty. For this reason, the use of *null* elements is discouraged in queues based on the *Queue* interface.

When adding an element to the queue there are also two methods available: the method *add* (inherited from the interface *Collection*), and the method *offer*. Both methods provide a way to add an element to the queue (based upon the ordering in effect), but differ when adding an element to the queue fails; the add method will return an unchecked exception whereas the *offer* method will return *false*.

The *Queue* interface does not specify the ordering of the elements, it is the responsibility of the class that implements the *Queue* interface to specify its ordering properties through the implementations of the queue interface methods.

The *Deque* Interface.   The *Deque* interface extends the *Queue* interface with the following methods (not all of the methods are shown here, see the Java documentation on the *Deque* class for a complete list):

```
public interface Deque<E> extends Queue<E>

  // Three methods for adding an element, if no space is
  // available, they throw IllegalStateException.

  boolean add(E e) throws IllegalStateException;
    // Inserts the specified element into the queue
    // represented by this deque (in other words, at the
    // tail of this deque).

  void addFirst(E e) throws IllegalStateException;
    // Inserts the specified element at the front of this
    // deque.

  void addLast(E e) throws IllegalStateException;
    // Inserts the specified element at the end of this deque.

  // These three methods also add an element, but rather than
  // throw an exception, they return true upon success and
  // false if no space is currently available.

  boolean offer(E e)
    // Inserts the specified element into the queue
    // represented by this deque (in other words, at the
    // tail of this deque), returning true upon success and
    // false if no space is currently available.

  boolean offerFirst(E e)
    // Inserts the specified element at the front of this
    // deque, returning true upon success and false if no
    // space is currently available.

  boolean offerLast(E e)
    // Inserts the specified element at the end of this deque,
    // returning true upon success and false if no space is
    // currently available.

  // Three methods for retrieving but not removing an element,
  // if the deque is empty, they throw NoSuchElementException.

  E element() throws NoSuchElementException;
    // Retrieves, but does not remove, the head of the queue
    // represented by this deque (in other words, the first
    // element of this deque).
```

```
E getFirst() throws NoSuchElementException;
   // Retrieves, but does not remove, the first element of
   // this deque.

E getLast() throws NoSuchElementException;
   // Retrieves, but does not remove, the last element of
   // this deque.

// These three methods also retrieve but do not removing an
// element, but if the deque is empty, they return null.

E peek()
   // Retrieves, but does not remove, the head of the queue
   // represented by this deque (in other words, the first
   // element of this deque).

E peekFirst()
   // Retrieves, but does not remove, the first element of
   // this deque.

E peekLast()
   // Retrieves, but does not remove, the last element of
   // this deque.

// Three methods for retrieving and removing an element,
// if the deque is empty, they throw NoSuchElementException.

E remove() throws NoSuchElementException;
   // Retrieves and removes the head of the queue represented
   // by this deque (in other words, the first element of
   // this deque).

E removeFirst()throws NoSuchElementException;
   // Retrieves and removes the first element of this deque.

E removeLast()throws NoSuchElementException;
   // Retrieves and removes the last element of this deque.

   // These three methods also retrieve and remove an
   // element, but if the deque is empty, they return null.

E poll()
   // Retrieves and removes the head of the queue represented
   // by this deque (in other words, the first element of
   // this deque).
```

```
E pollFirst()
   // Retrieves and removes the first element of this deque.

E pollLast()
   // Retrieves and removes the last element of this deque.

   // Miscellaneous methods

boolean contains(Object o)
   // Returns true if this deque contains the specified
   // element.

int size()
   // Returns the number of elements in this deque.
} // end Deque
```

Note that, as with the `Queue` interface, many of the methods exist in two forms: one that throws an exception if the operation fails, the other that returns a special value (either *null* or *false*, depending on the operation). We would only expect an insert operation to fail if the implementation is based upon a capacity-restricted data structure, as in our array-based implementation of a queue presented in this chapter. Figure 8-14 and Figure 8-15 summarize the behavior of the various methods for insertions to a deque as well as removal and retrieval from a deque.

Operation	Condition	Throws Exception	No Exception	Return Value
Insert	*Full deque*	addFirst(e)	offerFirst(e)	*false*
Remove	*Empty deque*	removeFirst()	pollFirst()	*null*
Examine	*Empty deque*	getFirst()	peekFirst()	*null*

FIGURE 8-14

Summary of Operations on First Element of Deque

Operation	Condition	Throws Exception	No Exception	Return Value
Insert	*Full deque*	addLast(e)	offerLast(e)	*false*
Remove	*Empty deque*	removeLast()	pollLast()	*null*
Examine	*Empty deque*	getLast()	peekLast()	*null*

FIGURE 8-15

Summary of Operations on Last Element of Deque

Note that a deque can be used as either a stack or a queue depending on the set of methods that are used. When a deque is used as a queue, FIFO (First-In-First-Out) behavior results. A summary of the methods for queues is presented in Figure 8-16. Deques can also be used as LIFO (Last-In-First-Out) stacks. When a deque is used as a stack, elements are pushed and popped from the beginning of the deque. A summary of the methods for stacks is presented in Figure 8-17.
Like the JCF *Queue* interface discussed earlier, use of the value *null* is discouraged in deques based on implementations of the *Deque* interface.

***Queue* and *Deque* Implementations.**   The JCF provides numerous implementations of the *Queue* and *Deque* interfaces. Given that the *Deque* interface is based on the *Queue* interface, there are classes such as *LinkedList* and *ArrayDeque* that implement both interfaces. There are also classes that implement only the *Queue* interface, such as *PriorityQueue*. The *LinkedList* implementation is the one that most closely resembles the queue presented in this chapter. Here is an example of how the JCF *LinkedList* is used as a queue:

```
import java.util.LinkedList;
public class TestQueue {

   static public void main(String[] args) {
      LinkedList<Integer> aQueue = new LinkedList<Integer>();
      boolean ok = true;
      Integer item;
```

ADT Queue	JCF Queue	JCF Deque
enqueue(e)	add(e)	addLast(e)
	offer(e)	offerLast(e)
dequeue()	remove()	removeFirst()
	poll()	pollFirst()
peek()	peek()	peekFirst()
	element()	getFirst()

FIGURE 8-16

Summary of Queue Operations

ADT Stack	JCF Stack	JCF Deque
push(e)	push(e)	addFirst(e)
pop()	pop()	removeFirst()
peek()	peek()	peekFirst()

FIGURE 8-17

Summary of Operations on Last Element of Deque

```
    if (aQueue.isEmpty()) {
      System.out.println("The queue is empty");
    } // end if

    for (int i = 0; i < 5; i++) {
      aQueue.add(i); // With autoboxing, this is the same as
                     // aQueue.add(new Integer(i))
    } // end for

    while (!aQueue.isEmpty()) {
      System.out.print(aQueue.peek()+ " ");
      item = aQueue.remove();
    } // end while
    System.out.println();

  } // end main

} // end TestQueue
```

The output of this program is

```
The queue is empty
0 1 2 3 4
```

Comparing Implementations

We have suggested implementations of the ADT queue that use either a linear linked list, a circular linked list, an array, a circular array, or the ADT list to represent the items in a queue. You have seen the details of three of these implementations. All of our implementations of the ADT queue are ultimately either array based or reference based.

The reasons for making the choice between array-based and reference-based implementations are the same as those discussed in earlier chapters. The discussion here is similar to the one in Chapter 7 in the section "Comparing Implementations." We repeat the highlights here in the context of queues.

Fixed size versus dynamic size

An implementation based on a statically allocated array prevents the *enqueue* operation from adding an item to the queue if the array is full. If this restriction is not acceptable, you must use either a resizeable array or a reference-based implementation.

Suppose you decide to use a reference-based implementation. Should you choose the implementation that uses a linked list, or should you choose a reference-based implementation of the ADT list? Because a linked list actually represents the items on the ADT list, using the ADT list to represent a queue is not as efficient as using a linked list directly. However, the ADT list approach is much simpler to write.

Reuse of an already implemented class saves you time

If you decide to use a linked list instead of the ADT list to represent the queue, should you use a linear linked list or a circular linked list? We leave this question for you to answer in Programming Problem 1.

8.4 A Summary of Position-Oriented ADTs

So far, we have seen three abstract data types—the list, the stack, and the queue—that have a common theme: All of their operations are defined in terms of the positions of their data items. Stacks and queues greatly restrict the positions that their operations can affect; only their end positions can be accessed. The list removes this restriction.

Stacks are really quite similar to queues. This similarity becomes apparent if you pair off their operations, as follows:

Operations for the ADTs list, stack, and queue reference the position of items

- *createStack* and *createQueue*. These operations create an empty ADT of the appropriate type.

A comparison of stack and queue operations

- Stack *isEmpty* and queue *isEmpty*. These operations determine whether any items exist in the ADT.

- *push* and *enqueue*. These operations insert a new item into one end (the top and back, respectively) of the ADT.

- *pop* and *dequeue*. The *pop* operation deletes the most recent item, which is at the top of the stack, and *dequeue* deletes the first item, which is at the front of the queue.

- Stack *peek* and queue *peek*. Stack *peek* retrieves the most recent item, which is at the top of the stack, and queue *peek* retrieves the first item, which is at the front of the queue.

The ADT list, introduced in Chapter 4, allows you to insert into, delete from, and inspect the item at any position of the list. Thus, it has the most flexible operations of the three **position-oriented** ADTs. You can view the list operations as general versions of the stack and queue operations, as follows:

- *length*. If you remove the restriction that the stack and queue versions of *isEmpty* can tell only when an item is present, you obtain an operation that can count the number of items that are present.

ADT list operations generalize stack and queue operations

- *add*. If you remove the restriction that *push* and *enqueue* can insert new items into only one position, you obtain an operation that can insert a new item into any position of the list.

- *remove*. If you remove the restriction that *pop* and *dequeue* can delete items from only one position, you obtain an operation that can delete an item from any position of the list.

■ *get*. If you remove the restriction that the stack and queue versions of *peek* can retrieve items from only one position, you obtain an operation that can retrieve the item from any position of the list.

Because each of these three ADTs defines its operations in terms of an item's position in the ADT, this book has presented implementations for them that can provide easy access to specified positions. For example, the stack implementations allow the first position (top) to be accessed quickly, while the queue implementations allow the first position (front) and the last position (back) to be accessed quickly.

8.5 Application: Simulation

Simulation—a major application area for computers—is a technique for modeling the behavior of both natural and human-made systems. Generally, the goal of a simulation is to generate statistics that summarize the performance of an existing system or to predict the performance of a proposed system. In this section, we will consider a simple example that illustrates one important type of simulation.

Simulation models the behavior of systems

Consider the following problem. Ms. Simpson, president of the First City Bank of Springfield, has heard her customers complain about how long they have to wait for service. Because she fears that they may move their accounts to another bank, she is considering whether to hire a second teller.

Before Ms. Simpson hires another teller, she would like an approximation of the average time that a customer has to wait for service from First City's only teller. How can Ms. Simpson obtain this information? She could stand with a stopwatch in the bank's lobby all day, but she does not find this prospect particularly exciting. Besides, she would like to use a method that also allows her to predict how much improvement she could expect if the bank hired a given number of additional tellers. She certainly does not want to hire the tellers on a trial basis and monitor the bank's performance before making a final decision.

Ms. Simpson concludes that the best way to obtain the information she wants is to use a computer model to simulate the behavior of her bank. The first step in simulating a system such as a bank is to construct a mathematical model that captures the relevant information about the system. For example, how many tellers does the bank employ? How often do customers arrive? If the model accurately describes the real-world system, a simulation can derive accurate predictions about the system's overall performance. For example, a simulation could predict the average time a customer has to wait before receiving service. A simulation can also evaluate proposed changes to the real-world system. For example, it could predict the effect of hiring more tellers in the bank. A large decrease in the time predicted for the average wait of a customer might justify the cost of hiring additional tellers.

Simulated time

Central to a simulation is the concept of simulated time. Envision a stopwatch that measures time elapsed during a simulation. For example, suppose that the model of the bank specifies only one teller. At time 0, which is the start of the banking day, the simulated system would be in its initial state with no customers. As the simulation runs, the stopwatch ticks away units of time—perhaps minutes—and certain events occur. At time 12, the bank's first customer arrives. Since there is no line, the customer goes directly to the teller and begins her transaction. At time 20, a second customer arrives. Because the first customer has not yet completed her transaction, the second customer must wait in line. At time 38, the first customer completes her transaction and the second customer can begin his. Figure 8-18 illustrates these four times in the simulation.

To gather the information you need, you run this simulation for a specified period of simulated time. During the course of the run, you need to keep track of certain statistics, such as the average time a customer has to wait for service. Notice that in the small example of Figure 8-18, the first customer had to wait 0 minutes to begin a transaction and the second customer had to wait 18 minutes to begin a transaction—an average wait of 9 minutes.

One point not addressed in the previous discussion is how to determine when certain events occur. For example, why did we say that the first customer arrived at time 12 and the second at time 20? By studying real-world systems like our bank, mathematicians have learned to model events such as the arrival of people, using techniques from probability theory. This statistical information is incorporated into the mathematical model of the system and is used to generate events in a way that reflects the real world. The simulation uses these events and is thus called an **event-driven simulation.** Note that the goal is to reflect the long-term average behavior of the system rather than to predict occurrences of specific events. This goal is sufficient for the needs of the simulation.

Although the techniques for generating events to reflect the real world are interesting and important, they require a good deal of mathematical sophistication. Therefore, simply assume that you already have a list of events available for your use. In particular, for the bank problem, assume that a file contains the time of each customer's arrival—an **arrival event**—and the duration of that customer's transaction once the customer reaches the teller. For example, the data

20	5
22	4
23	2
30	3

Sample arrival and transaction times

indicates that the first customer arrives 20 minutes into the simulation and that the transaction—once begun—requires 5 minutes; the second customer arrives 22 minutes into the simulation and the transaction requires 4 minutes; and so on. Assume that the input file is ordered by arrival time.

Notice that the file does not contain **departure events;** the data does not specify when a customer will complete the transaction and leave. Instead, the simulation must determine when departures occur. By using the arrival time

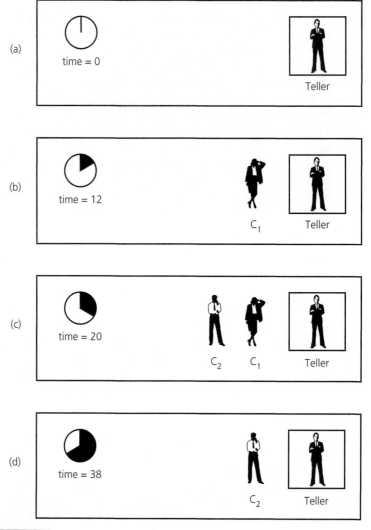

FIGURE 8-18

A bank line at time (a) 0; (b) 12; (c) 20; (d) 38

and the transaction length, the simulation can easily determine the time at which a customer departs. To see how to make this determination, you can conduct a simulation by hand with the previous data as follows:

The results of a simulation

Time	Event
20	Customer 1 enters bank and begins transaction
22	Customer 2 enters bank and stands at end of line

23	Customer 3 enters bank and stands at end of line
25	Customer 1 departs; customer 2 begins transaction
29	Customer 2 departs; customer 3 begins transaction
30	Customer 4 enters bank and stands at end of line
31	Customer 3 departs; customer 4 begins transaction
34	Customer 4 departs

A customer's wait time is the elapsed time between arrival in the bank and the start of the transaction. The average of this wait time over all the customers is the statistic that you want to obtain.

To summarize, this simulation is concerned with two types of events:

- **Arrival events.** These events indicate the arrival at the bank of a new customer. The input file specifies the times at which the arrival events occur. As such, they are **external events.** When a customer arrives at the bank, one of two things happens. If the teller is idle when the customer arrives, the customer enters the line and begins the transaction immediately. If the teller is busy, the new customer must stand at the end of the line and wait for service.

- **Departure events.** These events indicate the departure from the bank of a customer who has completed a transaction. The simulation determines the times at which the departure events occur. As such, they are **internal events.** When a customer completes the transaction, he or she departs and the next person in line—if there is one—begins a transaction.

The main tasks of an algorithm that performs the simulation are to determine the times at which the events occur and to process the events when they do occur. The algorithm is stated at a high level as follows:

```
// initialize
currentTime = 0
Initialize the line to "no customers"

while (currentTime ≤ time of the final event) {

  if (an arrival event occurs at time currentTime) {
    Process the arrival event
  }  // end if
  if (a departure event occurs at time currentTime) {
    Process the departure event
  }  // end if
  // when an arrival event and departure event
  // occur at the same time, arbitrarily process
  // the arrival event first
```

A first attempt at a
simulation algorithm

```
    ++currentTime
}   // end while
```

But do you really want to increment `currentTime` by 1? You would for a **time-driven simulation,** where you would determine arrival and departure times at random and compare those times to `currentTime`. In such a case, you would increment `currentTime` by 1 to simulate the ticking of a clock. Recall, however, that this simulation is event driven, so you have a file of arrival times and transaction times. Because you are interested only in those times at which arrival and departure events occur and because no action is required between events, you can advance `currentTime` from the time of one event directly to the time of the next.

A time-driven simulation simulates the ticking of a clock

An event-driven simulation considers only times of certain events, in this case, arrivals and departures

Thus, you can revise the pseudocode solution as follows:

First revision of the simulation algorithm

```
// initialize the line to "no customers"

while (events remain to be processed) {
  currentTime = time of next event
  if (event is an arrival event) {
    Process the arrival event
  }
  else {
    Process the departure event
  } // end if
  // when an arrival event and departure event
  // occur at the same time, arbitrarily process
  // the arrival event first
} // end while
```

You must determine the time of the next arrival or departure event so that you can implement the statement

```
currentTime = time of next event
```

To make this determination, you must maintain an **event list.** An event list contains all arrival and departure events that will occur but have not occurred yet. The times of the events in the event list are in ascending order, and thus the next event to be processed is always at the beginning of the list. The algorithm simply gets the event from the beginning of the list, advances to the time specified, and processes the event. The difficulty, then, lies in successfully managing the event list.

An event list contains all future events

Since each arrival event generates exactly one departure event, you might think that you should read the entire input file and create an event list of all arrival and departure events sorted by time. Self-Test Exercise 5 asks you to explain why this approach is impractical. As you will see, you can instead manage the event list for this particular problem so that it always contains at most one event of each kind.

This event list contains at most one arrival event and one departure event

Recall that the arrival events are specified in the input file in ascending time order. You thus never need to worry about an arrival event until you have processed all the arrival events that precede it in the file. You simply keep the earliest unprocessed arrival event in the event list. When you eventually process this event—that is, when it is time for this customer to arrive—you replace it in the event list with the next unprocessed arrival event, which is the next item in the input file.

Similarly, you need to place only the next departure event to occur on the event list. But how can you determine the times for the departure events? Observe that the next departure event always corresponds to the customer that the teller is currently serving. As soon as a customer begins service, the time of his or her departure is simply

time of next departure = time service begins + length of transaction

Recall that the length of the customer's transaction is in the input file, along with the arrival time. Thus, as soon as a customer begins service, you place a departure event corresponding to this customer in the event list. Figure 8-19 illustrates a typical instance of the event list for this simulation.

Now consider how you can process an event when it is time for the event to occur. You must perform two general types of actions:

- **Update the line:** Add or remove customers.

- **Update the event list:** Add or remove events.

Two tasks are required to process each event

As customers arrive, they go to the back of the line. The current customer, who is at the front of the line, is being served, and it is this customer that you remove from the system next. It is thus natural to use a queue to represent the line of customers in the bank. For this problem, the only information that you

A queue represents the customers in line

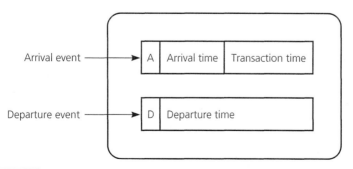

FIGURE 8-19

A typical instance of the event list

must store in the queue about each customer is the time of arrival and the length of the transaction. The event list, since it is sorted by time, is not a queue. We will examine it in more detail shortly.

The event list is not a queue

To summarize, you process an event as follows:

The algorithm for arrival events

TO PROCESS AN ARRIVAL EVENT

```
// Update the event list
Delete the arrival event for customer C from
    the event list

if (new customer C begins transaction immediately) {
   Insert a departure event for customer C into the
       event list (time of event = current time +
       transaction length)
}  // end if
if (not at the end of the input file) {
   Read a new arrival event and add it to the event list
       (time of event = time specified in file)
}  // end if
```

A new customer always enters the queue and is served while at the queue's front

Because a customer is served while at the front of the queue, a new customer always enters the queue, even if the queue is empty. You then delete the arrival event for the new customer from the event list. If the new customer is served immediately, you insert a departure event into the event list. Finally, you read a new arrival event into the event list. This arrival event can occur either before or after the departure event.

The algorithm for departure events

TO PROCESS A DEPARTURE EVENT

```
// Update the line
Delete the customer at the front of the queue
if (the queue is not empty) {
   The current front customer begins transaction
}  // end if

// Update the event list
Delete the departure event from the event list
if (the queue is not empty) {
   Insert into the event list the departure event for
       the customer now at the front of the queue
       (time of event = current time + transaction length)
}  // end if
```

After processing the departure event, you do not read another arrival event from the file. Assuming that the file has not been read completely, the event list will contain an arrival event whose time is earlier than any arrival still in the input file.

Examining the event list more closely will help explain the workings of the algorithm. There is no typical form that an event list takes. For this simulation, however, the event list has four possible configurations:

Four configurations of the event list for this simulation

- Initially, the event list contains an arrival event A after you read the first arrival event from the input file but before you process it:

  Event list: A (initial state)

- Generally, the event list for this simulation contains exactly two events: one arrival event A and one departure event D. Either the departure event is first or the arrival event is first as follows:

  Event list: $D\ A$ (general case—next event is a departure)

  or

  Event list: $A\ D$ (general case—next event is an arrival)

- If the departure event is first and that event leaves the teller's line empty, a new departure event does not replace the just-processed event. Thus, in this case, the event list appears as

  Event list: A (a departure leaves the teller's line empty)

  Notice that this instance of the event list is the same as its initial state.

- If the arrival event is first and if, after it is processed, you are at the end of the input file, the event list contains only a departure event:

  Event list: D (the input has been exhausted)

Other situations result in an event list that has one of the previous four configurations.

You insert new events either at the beginning of the event list or at the end, depending on the relative times of the new event and the event currently in the event list. For example, suppose that the event list contains only an arrival event A and that another customer is now at the front of the line and beginning a transaction. You need to generate a departure event D for this customer. If the customer's departure time is before the time of the arrival event A, you must insert the departure event D before the event A in the event list. However, if the departure time is after the time of the arrival event, you must insert the departure event D after the arrival event A. In the case of a tie, you need a rule to determine which event should take precedence. In this solution, we arbitrarily choose to place the departure event after the arrival event.

You can now combine and refine the pieces of the solution into an algorithm that performs the simulation by using the ADT queue operations to manage the bank line:

The final pseudo-
code for the event-
driven simulation

```
+simulate()
// Performs the simulation.

   Create an empty queue bankQueue to represent the bank line
   Create an empty event list eventList

   Get the first arrival event from the input file
   Place the arrival event in the event list

   while (the event list is not empty) {
     newEvent = the first event in the event list

     if (newEvent is an arrival event) {
       processArrival(newEvent, arrivalFile,
                      eventList, bankQueue)
     }
     else {
       processDeparture(newEvent, eventList, bankQueue)
     }  // end if
   }  // end while

+processArrival(in arrivalEvent:Event,
               in arrivalFile:File,
               inout anEventList:EventList,
               inout bankQueue:Queue)
// Processes an arrival event.

   atFront = bankQueue.isEmpty()  // present queue status

   // update the bankQueue by inserting the customer, as
   // described in arrivalEvent, into the queue
   bankQueue.enqueue(arrivalEvent)

   // update the event list
   Delete arrivalEvent from anEventList

   if (atFront) {
     // the line was empty, so new customer is at front
     // of line and begins transaction immediately
     Insert into the anEventList a departure event that
         corresponds to the new customer and has
     currentTime = currentTime + transaction length
   }  // end if

   if (not at end of input file) {
     Get the next arrival event from arrivalFile
     Add the event -- with time as specified in the input
```

```
          file -- to anEventList
  }   // end if

+processDeparture(in departureEvent:Event,
                  in anEventList:EventList,
                  inout bankQueue:Queue)
// Processes a departure event.

  // update the line by deleting the front customer
  bankQueue.dequeue()

  // update the event list
  Delete departureEvent from anEventList
  if (!bankQueue.isEmpty())
    // customer at front of line begins transaction
    Insert into anEventList a departure event that
        corresponds to the customer now at the front of the
        line and has currentTime = currentTime
        + transaction length
  }   // end if
```

Figure 8-20 begins a trace of this algorithm for the data on page 460 and shows the changes to the queue and event list. Self-Test Exercise 6 at the end of this chapter asks you to complete the trace.

The event list is, in fact, an ADT. By examining the previous pseudocode, you can see that this ADT must include at least the following operations:

```
+createEventList()
// Creates an empty event list.

+isEmpty():boolean {query}
// Determines whether an event list is empty.

+insert(in anEvent:Event)
// Inserts anEvent into an event list so that events
// are ordered by time. If an arrival event and a
// departure event have the same time, the arrival
// event precedes the departure event.

+delete()
// Deletes the first event from an event list.

+retrieve():Event
// Retrieves the first event in an event list.
```

ADT event list
operations

Time	Action	bankQueue (front to back)	anEventList (beginning to end)
0	Read file, place event in `anEventList`	*(empty)*	A 20 5
20	Update `anEventList` and `bankQueue`: Customer 1 enters bank	20 5	*(empty)*
	Customer 1 begins transaction, create departure event	20 5	D 25
	Read file, place event in `anEventList`	20 5	A 22 4 — D 25
22	Update `anEventList` and `bankQueue`: Customer 2 enters bank	20 5 — 22 4	D 25
	Read file, place event in `anEventList`	20 5 — 22 4	A 23 2 — D 25
23	Update `anEventList` and `bankQueue`: Customer 3 enters bank	20 5 — 22 4 — 23 2	D 25
	Read file, place event in `anEventList`	20 5 — 22 4 — 23 2	D 25 — A 30 3
25	Update `anEventList` and `bankQueue`: Customer 1 departs Customer 2 begins transaction, create departure event	22 4 — 23 2	A 30 3
		22 4 — 23 2	D 29 — A 30 3

Self-Test Exercise 6 asks you to complete this trace.

FIGURE 8-20

A partial trace of the bank simulation algorithm for the data
   20 5
   22 4
   23 2
   30 3

Programming Problem 8 at the end of this chapter asks you to complete the implementation of this simulation.

Summary

1. The definition of the queue operations gives the ADT queue first-in, first-out (FIFO) behavior.

2. The insertion and deletion operations for a queue require efficient access to both ends of the queue. Therefore, a reference-based implementation of a queue uses either a circular linked list or a linear linked list that has both a head reference and a tail reference.

3. An array-based implementation of a queue is prone to rightward drift. This phenomenon can make a queue look full when it really is not. Shifting the items in the array is one way to compensate for rightward drift. A more efficient solution uses a circular array.

4. If you use a circular array to implement a queue, you must be able to distinguish between the queue-full and queue-empty conditions. You can make this distinction

by either counting the number of items in the queue, using a *full* flag, or leaving one array location empty.

5. Models of real-world systems often use queues. The event-driven simulation in this chapter uses a queue to model a line of customers in a bank.

6. Central to a simulation is the notion of simulated time. In a time-driven simulation, simulated time is advanced by a single time unit, whereas in an event-driven simulation, simulated time is advanced to the time of the next event. To implement an event-driven simulation, you maintain an event list that contains events that have not yet occurred. The event list is ordered by the time of the events so that the next event to occur is always at the head of the list.

Cautions

1. If you use a linear linked list with only a head reference to implement a queue, the insertion operation will be inefficient. Each insertion requires a traversal to the end of the linked list. As the queue increases in length, the traversal time—and hence the insertion time—will increase.

2. The management of an event list in an event-driven simulation is typically more difficult than it was in the example presented in this chapter. For instance, if the bank had more than one teller line, the structure of the event list would be much more complex.

Self-Test Exercises

1. If you add the letters W, Y, X, Z, and V in sequence to a queue of characters and then remove them, in what order will they be deleted from the queue?

2. What do the initially empty queues *queue1* and *queue2* "look like" after the following sequence of operations?

```
queue1.enqueue(23)
queue1.enqueue(17)
queue1.enqueue(50)
queue2.enqueue(42)
qFront1 = queue1.dequeue()
qFront2 = queue2.peek()
queue2.enqueue(top1)
queue1.enqueue(top2)
queue1.enqueue(13)
qFront2 = queue2.pop()
queue2.enqueue(49)
```

Compare these results with Self-Test Exercise 2 in Chapter 7.

3. Trace the palindrome-recognition algorithm described in the section "Simple Applications of the ADT Queue" for each of the following strings:

   a. abracadabra   c. rotator

   b. radar   d. xyzzy

4. For each of the following situations, which of these ADTs (1 through 4) would be most appropriate: (1) a queue; (2) a stack; (3) a list; (4) none of these?

   a. The customers at a deli counter who take numbers to mark their turn

   b. An alphabetic list of names

   c. Integers that need to be sorted

   d. The boxes in a box trace of a recursive method

   e. A grocery list ordered by the occurrence of the items in the store

   f. The items on a cash register tape

   g. A word processor that allows you to correct typing errors by using the back-space key

   h. A program that uses backtracking

   i. A list of ideas in chronological order

   j. Airplanes that stack above a busy airport, waiting to land

   k. People who are put on hold when they call an airline to make reservations

   l. An employer who fires the most recently hired person

   m. People who go to a store on Black Friday hoping to get the best holiday buys

5. In the bank simulation problem that this chapter discusses, why is it impractical to read the entire input file and create a list of all the arrival and departure events before the simulation begins?

6. Complete the hand trace of the bank-line simulation that Figure 8-20 began with the data given on page 460. Show the state of the queue and the event list at each step.

Exercises

1. Write a Java program that replaces the uppercase characters in a string with lower-case characters. Use the ADT queue to replace the uppercase characters.

2. Write a Java program to insert an item into a circular queue. Now write another Java function that prints the elements of the circular queue in reverse order.

3. Suppose you have a queue in which the values 1 through 5 must be enqueued on the queue in that order, but that an item on the queue can be dequeued and printed at any time. Based on these constraints, give the list of operations that would produce each of the following sequences. If it is not possible, state so.

   a. 1 3 5 4 2

   b. 1 2 3 4 5

   c. Are there sequences that cannot occur? Explain why or why not.

4. Implement the pseudocode conversion algorithm that converts a sequence of character digits in a queue to an integer (it is in the section "Reading a String of Characters"). Assume that you are using a queue to read in a series of characters that represent a correct postfix expression. The postfix expression has operators and multi-digit integers separated by single blanks. When the conversion method is called, the next item in the queue should be a character digit followed by zero or more character digits. The digits should be read until a non-digit character is found, and the resulting integer returned.

5. Consider the palindrome-recognition algorithm described in the section "Simple Applications of the ADT Queue." Is it necessary for the algorithm to look at the entire queue and stack? That is, can you reduce the number of times that the loop must execute?

6. Consider the language

L = {w\$$w'$: w is a possibly empty string of characters other than \$,
         w' = *reverse*(w)}

as defined in Chapter 7. Write a recognition algorithm for this language that uses both a queue and a stack. Thus, as you traverse the input string, you insert each character of w into a queue and each character of w' into a stack. Assume that each input string contains exactly one \$.

7. What is output by the following code section?

```
QueueInterface aQueue = new QueueReferenceBased();
int num1, num2;
for (int i = 1; i <= 5; i++) {
  aQueue.enqueue(i);
} // end for

for (int i = 1; i <= 5; i++) {
  num1 = (Integer)aQueue.dequeue();
  num2 = (Integer)aQueue.dequeue();
  aQueue.enqueue(num1 + num2);
  aQueue.enqueue(num2 - num1);
} // end for

while(!aQueue.isEmpty()) {
  System.out.print(aQueue.dequeue() + " ");
} // end for
```

8. Assume you have a queue q that has already been populated with data. What does the following code fragment do to the queue q?

```
Stack s = new Stack();
while (!q.isEmpty())
    s.push(q.dequeue());
while (!ss.isEmpty())
    q.enqueue(s.pop());
```

9. Another operation that could be added to the ADT Queue is one that removes and discards the user-specified number of elements from the front of the queue.

Assume this operation is called *dequeueAndDiscard* and that it does not return a value and accepts a parameter called *count* of data type int.

a. Add this operation to the *QueueListBased* implementation given in this chapter.

b. Add this operation to the *QueueArrayBased* implementation given in this chapter.

c. Add this operation to the *QueueReferenceBased* implementation given in this chapter.

10. The JCF class *Deque* had a method called *contains* that would return true if an *Object* was in the deque. For a queue, the method could be specified as follows:

```
public boolean contains(Object o)
// Returns true if this queue contains the specified element.
```

a. Add this method to the *QueueListBased* implementation given in this chapter.

b. Add this method to the *QueueArrayBased* implementation given in this chapter.

c. Add this method to the *QueueReferenceBased* implementation given in this chapter.

11. Write a Java program that merges the contents of two different queues into a single queue.

12. Consider the queue implementation that uses the ADT list to represent the items in the queue. Discuss the efficiency of the queue's insertion and deletion operations when the ADT list's implementation is

a. Array based

b. Reference based

13. An operation that displays the contents of a queue can be useful during program debugging. Add a *display* operation to the ADT queue such that

a. *display* uses only ADT queue operations, so it is independent of the queue's implementation

b. *display* assumes and uses the reference-based implementation of the ADT queue

14. Write a Java program that removes all blank spaces from a given string. To remove the spaces, store the non-space characters in a queue. When you reach the end of the string, extract all elements from the queue to get the output.

15. The Java Collections Framework provides a class called *ArrayDeque* that is an implementation of the *Deque* interface presented in this chapter. Use the class *ArrayDeque* to solve the read-and-correct problem presented in the "Developing an ADT During the Design of a Solution" section of Chapter 7. In that problem, you enter text at a keyboard and correct typing mistakes by using the backspace key. Each backspace erases the most recently entered character. Your solution should provide a corrected string of characters in the order in which they were entered at the keyboard.

16. With the following data, hand-trace the execution of the bank-line simulation that this chapter describes. Each line of data contains an arrival time and a transaction time. Show the state of the queue and the event list at each step.

5	5
7	9
8	4
23	6
30	5
33	4
38	6

Note that at time 23 there is a tie between the execution of an arrival event and a departure event.

17. A given queue already has values stored in it. Write a Java program that sorts the values of the queue and also indicates the second highest value in the queue.

18. Consider a queue maintained by a circular array $QUEUE$, with $n = 20$ rooms. Find the number of elements in $QUEUE$ if

   a. Front = 3 and Rear = 10;

   b. Front = 19 and Rear = 8;

   c. Front = 8 and Rear = 13;

19. As Chapter 4 pointed out, you can define ADT operations in a mathematically formal way by using axioms. Consider the following axioms for the ADT queue, where $queue$ is an arbitrary queue and $item$ is an arbitrary queue item.

```
(queue.createQueue()).isEmpty() = true
  (queue.enqueue(item)).isEmpty() = false
(queue.createQueue()).dequeue() = error
((queue.createQueue()).enqueue(item)).dequeue() =
                                 queue.createQueue()
queue.isEmpty() = false ⇒
    (queue.enqueue(item)).dequeue() =
                     (queue.dequeue()).enqueue(item)
(queue.createQueue()).peek() = error
((queue.createQueue()).enqueue(item)).peek() = item
queue.isEmpty() = false ⇒
    (queue.enqueue(item)).peek() = queue.peek()
```

   a. Note the recursive nature of the definition of $peek$. What is the base case? What is the recursive step? What is the significance of the $isEmpty$ test? Why is $peek$ recursive in nature while the operation $peek$ for the ADT stack is not?

   b. The representation of a stack as a sequence of $push$ operations without any pop operations was called a canonical form. (See Exercise 16a in Chapter 7.) Is there a canonical form for the ADT queue that uses only $enqueue$ operations? That is, is every queue equal to a queue that can be written with only $enqueues$? Prove your answer.

Programming Problems

1. Write a reference-based implementation of a queue that uses a linear linked list to represent the items in the queue. You will need both a head reference and a tail reference. When you are done, compare your implementation to the one given in this chapter that uses a circular linked list with one external reference. Which implementation is easier to write? Which is easier to understand? Which is more efficient?

2. Write a Java program that creates a queue from a given stack. The rear reference of the queue should point to the base of the stack and the front reference of the queue should point to the top of the stack. At the end of the code, the contents of the stack should be copied in the queue.

3. Consider the array-based implementation of a queue given in the text. Instead of counting the number of items in the queue, you could maintain a flag `full` to distinguish between the full and empty conditions. Revise the array-based implementation by using the `full` flag.

   a. Does this implementation have the same space requirements as the `count` or `full` implementations? Why?

   b. Implement this array-based approach.

4. This chapter described another array-based implementation of a queue that uses no special data field—such as `count` or `full` (see Programming Problem 3)—to distinguish between the full and empty conditions. In this implementation, you declare `MAX_QUEUE + 1` locations for the array `items`, but use only `MAX_QUEUE` of them for queue items. You sacrifice one array location by making `front` the index of the location before the front of the queue. The queue is full if `front` equals `(back+1) % (MAX_QUEUE+1)`, but the queue is empty if `front` equals `back`.

   a. Does this implementation have the same space requirements as the `count` or `full` implementations? Why?

   b. Implement this array-based approach.

5. Write a Java program that reads integer values from the terminal, then stores all negative values in one queue and all positive values in another queue.

6. Implement the recognition algorithm described in Exercise 5 using the JCF `Stack` and `LinkedList` classes.

7. As discussed in this chapter, the JCF provides an interface for a double ended queue that supports insertion and deletion of items from both the front and back of the data structure. Here is a simplified version of a deque interface:

```
public interface Deque {

  public boolean isEmpty();
    // Return true if the deque is empty, false otherwise.

  public boolean addFirst(Object item);
    // Insert the item at the front of the deque. Returns false
    // if the item cannot be added to the deque, true otherwise.
```

```
    public boolean addLast(Object item);
      // Insert the item at the back of the deque. Returns false if
      // the item cannot be added to the deque, true otherwise.

    public Object removeFirst();
      // Delete and return the first item in the deque if the deque
      // is not empty, otherwise return null (the deque was empty).

    public Object removeLast();
      // Delete and return the last item in the deque if the deque
      // is not empty, otherwise return null (the deque was empty).

    public Object peekFirst();
      // Return the first item in the deque if the deque is
      // not empty, leaving the deque unchanged. Otherwise return
      // null (the deque was empty).

    public Object peekLast();
      // Return the last item in the deque if the deque is
      // not empty, leaving the deque unchanged. Otherwise return
      // null (the deque was empty).
} // end Deque
```

a. Create a reference-based implementation of the *Deque* interface.

b. Create an array-based implementation of the *Deque* interface.

8. Implement the event-driven simulation of a bank that this chapter described. A queue of arrival events will represent the line of customers in the bank. Maintain the arrival events and departure events in an ADT event list, sorted by the time of the event. Use a reference-based implementation for the ADT event list.

   The input is a text file of arrival and transaction times. Each line of the file contains the arrival time and required transaction time for a customer. The arrival times are ordered by increasing time.

   Your program must count customers and keep track of their cumulative waiting time. These statistics are sufficient to compute the average waiting time after the last event has been processed.

   Display a trace of the events executed and a summary of the computed statistics (total number of arrivals and average time spent waiting in line). For example, the input file shown in the left columns of the following table should produce the output shown in the right column.

Input File   Output

```
1    5    Simulation Begins
2    5    Processing an arrival event at time:    1
4    5    Processing an arrival event at time:    2
20   5    Processing an arrival event at time:    4
22   5    Processing a departure event at time:   6
24   5    Processing a departure event at time:   11
26   5    Processing a departure event at time:   16
28   5    Processing an arrival event at time:    20
30   5    Processing an arrival event at time:    22
88   3    Processing an arrival event at time:    24
          Processing a departure event at time:   25
```

```
Processing an arrival event at time:    26
Processing an arrival event at time:    28
Processing an arrival event at time:    30
Processing a departure event at time:   30
Processing a departure event at time:   35
Processing a departure event at time:   40
Processing a departure event at time:   45
Processing a departure event at time:   50
Processing an arrival event at time:    88
Processing a departure event at time:   91
Simulation Ends

Final Statistics:
Total number of people processed: 10
Average amount of time spent waiting: 5.6
```

9. Modify and expand the event-driven simulation program that you wrote in Programming Problem 6. Here are a few suggestions:

   a. Add an operation that displays the event list, and use it to check your hand trace in Exercise 10.

   b. Add some statistics to the simulation. For example, compute the maximum wait in line, the average length of the line, and the maximum length of the line.

   c. Modify the simulation so that it accounts for three tellers, each with a distinct line. You should keep in mind that there should be

      ■ Three queues, one for each teller

      ■ A rule that chooses a line when processing an arrival event (for example, enter the shortest line)

      ■ Three distinct departure events, one for each line

      ■ Rules for breaking ties in the event list

      Run both this simulation and the original simulation on several sets of input data. How do the statistics compare?

   d. The bank is considering the following change: Instead of having three distinct lines (one for each teller), there will be a single line for the three tellers. The person at the front of the line will go to the first available teller. Modify the simulation of Part *c* to account for this variation. Run both simulations on several sets of input data. How do the various statistics compare (averages and maximums)? What can you conclude about having a single line as opposed to having distinct lines?

10. The people that run the Motor Vehicle Department (MVD) have a problem. They are concerned that people do not spend enough time waiting in lines to appreciate the privilege of owning and driving an automobile. The current arrangement is as follows:

    ■ When people walk in the door, they must wait in a line to sign in.

    ■ Once they have signed in, they are told either to stand in line for registration renewal or to wait until they are called for license renewal.

    ■ Once they have completed their desired transaction, they must go and wait in line for the cashier.

- When they finally get to the front of the cashier's line, if they expect to pay by check, they are told that all checks must get approved. To do this, it is necessary to go to the check-approver's table and then reenter the cashier's line at the end.

Write an event-driven simulation to help the Motor Vehicle Department gather statistics.

Each line of input will contain

- A desired transaction code (L for license renewal, R for registration renewal)
- A method-of-payment code ($ for cash, C for check)
- An arrival time (integer)
- A name

Write out the specifics of each event (when, who, what, and so on). Then display these final statistics:

- The total number of license renewals and the average time spent in MVD (arrival until completion of payment) to renew a license
- The total number of registration renewals and the average time spent in MVD (arrival until completion of payment) to renew a registration

Incorporate the following details into your program:

- Define the following events: arrive, sign in, renew license, renew registration, and interact with the cashier (make a payment or find out about check approval).
- In the case of a tie, let the order of events be determined by the list of events just given—that is, arrivals have the highest priority.
- Assume that the various transactions take the following amounts of time:

Sign in	10 seconds
Renew license	90 seconds
Register automobile	60 seconds
See cashier (payment)	30 seconds
See cashier (check not approved)	10 seconds

- As ridiculous as it may seem, the people waiting for license renewal are called in alphabetical order. Note, however, that people are not pushed back once their transactions have started.
- For the sake of this simulation, you can assume that checks are approved instantly. Therefore, the rule for arriving at the front of the cashier's line with a check that has not been approved is to go to the back of the cashier's line with a check that has been approved.

CHAPTER 9

Advanced Java Topics

Java classes provide a way to enforce the walls of data abstraction by encapsulating an abstract data type's data and operations. An object-oriented approach, however, goes well beyond encapsulation. Inheritance and polymorphism allow you to derive new classes from existing classes. This chapter describes techniques that make collections of reusable software components possible. It also discusses some of the useful components that exist in the Java API and how they can be used. Realize that much more can and should be said about these techniques. Consider this chapter as an introduction to this material.

9.1 Inheritance Revisited

When you think of inheritance, you might imagine a bequest of one million dollars from some long-lost wealthy relative. In the object-oriented world, however, **inheritance** describes the ability of a class to derive properties from a previously defined class. These properties are like the genetic characteristics you received from your parents: Some traits are the same, some are similar but different, and some are new.

A class can derive the behavior and structure of another class

Inheritance, in fact, is a relationship among classes. One class can derive the behavior and structure of another class. For example, Figure 9-1 illustrates some relationships among various timepieces. Digital clocks, for example, include the clock in the dashboard of your car, the clock on the sign of the downtown bank, and the clock on your microwave oven. All digital clocks have the same underlying structure and perform operations such as

```
Set the time
Advance the time
Display the time
```

A digital alarm clock is a digital clock

A digital alarm clock is a digital clock that also has alarm methods, such as

```
Set the alarm
Enable the alarm
Sound the alarm
Silence the alarm
```

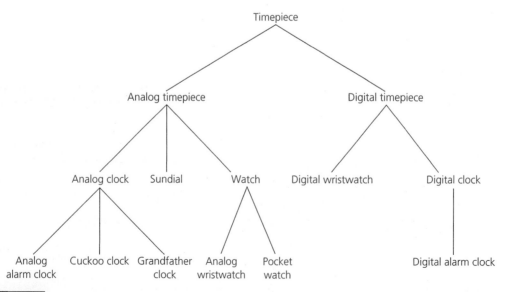

FIGURE 9-1

Inheritance: Relationships among timepieces

That is, a digital alarm clock has the structure and operations of a digital clock and, in addition, has an alarm and operations to manipulate the alarm.

You can think of the group of digital clocks and the group of digital alarm clocks as classes. The class of digital alarm clocks is a **subclass** or a **derived class** of the class of digital clocks. The class of digital clocks is a **superclass** or **base class** of the class of digital alarm clocks.

A subclass **inherits** all the members of its superclass, except the constructors. That is, a subclass has the data fields and methods of the superclass in addition to the data fields and methods it defines. A subclass can also have its own version of an inherited method. For example, according to Figure 9-1, a cuckoo clock is a **descendant,** or subclass, of an analog clock, like the one on a classroom wall. The cuckoo clock inherits the structure and behavior of the analog clock, but revises the way it reports the time each hour by adding a cuckoo.

> A subclass inherits the members of its superclass

Inheritance enables you to **reuse** software components when you define a new class. For example, you can reuse your design and implementation of an analog clock when you design a cuckoo clock. A simpler example will demonstrate the details of such reuse and show you how Java implements inheritance.

> Inheritance enables the reuse of existing classes

Chapter 4 spoke of volleyballs and soccer balls as objects. While designing a class of balls—*Ball*—you might decide that a ball is simply a sphere with a name. This realization is significant in that *Sphere*—the class of spheres— already exists. Thus, if you let *Sphere* be a superclass of *Ball*, you can implement *Ball* without reinventing the sphere. Toward that end, here is a definition of *Sphere* that is similar to the *SimpleSphere* class presented in Chapter 1:

> Inheritance reduces the effort necessary to add features to an existing object

```java
public class Sphere {
  private double radius;
  public static final double DEFAULT_RADIUS = 1.0;

  public Sphere() {
    setRadius(DEFAULT_RADIUS);
  } // end default constructor

  public Sphere(double initialRadius) {
    setRadius(initialRadius);
  } // end constructor

  public boolean equals(Object rhs) {
    return ((rhs instanceof Sphere) &&
            (radius == ((Sphere)rhs).radius));
  }  // end equals

  public void setRadius(double newRadius) {
    if (newRadius >= 0.0) {
      radius = newRadius;
    }  // end if
  } // end setRadius
```

```java
public double getRadius() {
  return radius;
} // end getRadius

public double diameter() {
  return 2.0 * radius;
} // end diameter

public double circumference() {
  return Math.PI * diameter();
} // end circumference

public double area() {
  return 4.0 * Math.PI * radius * radius;
} // end area

public double volume() {
  return (4.0*Math.PI * Math.pow(radius, 3.0)) / 3.0;
} // end volume

public void displayStatistics() {
  System.out.println("\nRadius = " + getRadius() +
              "\nDiameter = " + diameter() +
              "\nCircumference = " + circumference() +
              "\nArea = " + area() +
              "\nVolume = " + volume());
}  // end displayStatistics
} // end Sphere
```

The subclass *Ball* will inherit all the members of the class *Sphere*—except the constructor—and define additional methods and data fields. The *Ball* class could add:

- A data field that names the ball

A subclass can add new members to those it inherits

- Methods to access this name and set this name

- A method to alter an existing ball's radius and name

- A revised method *displayStatistics* to display the ball's name in addition to its statistics as a sphere

You can add as many new members to a subclass as you like. Although you cannot revise a superclass's private data fields and should not reuse their names, you can **override** methods in the superclass. A method in a subclass overrides a method in the superclass if the two methods have the same declarations. Here, the class *Ball* overrides *displayStatistics*. Figure 9-2 illustrates the relationship between *Sphere* and *Ball*.

A subclass can override an inherited method of its superclass

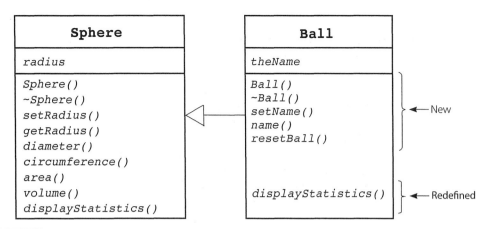

FIGURE 9-2
The subclass **Ball** inherits members of the superclass **Sphere** and overrides and adds methods

You can declare *Ball* as follows:

```
public class Ball extends Sphere {
  private String name;  // the ball's name

  // constructors:
  public Ball() {
  // Creates a ball with radius 1.0 and name "unknown."
    setName("unknown");
  }  // end default constructor

  public Ball(double initialRadius, String initialName) {
  // Creates a ball with radius initialRadius and
  // name initialName.
    super(initialRadius);
    setName(initialName);
  }  // end constructor

  // additional or revised operations:
  public boolean equals(Object rhs) {
    return ((rhs instanceof Ball) &&
            (getRadius() == ((Ball)rhs).getRadius()) &&
            (name.compareTo(((Ball)rhs).name)==0) );
  }  // end equals

  public String getName() {
  // Determines the name of a ball.
```

This constructor calls **Sphere**'s default constructor implicitly

This constructor calls another **Sphere** constructor explicitly

```
        return name;
    }  // end getName

    public void setName(String newName) {
    // Sets (alters) the name of an existing ball.
        name = newName;
    }  // end setName

    public void resetBall(double newRadius, String newName) {
    // Sets (alters) the radius and name of an existing
    // ball to newRadius and newName, respectively.
        setRadius(newRadius);
        setName(newName);
    }  // end resetBall

    public void displayStatistics() {
    // Displays the statistics of a ball.
        System.out.print("\nStatistics for a "+ name());
        super.displayStatistics();
    }  // end displayStatistics

}  // end Ball
```

Adding *extends Sphere* after *class Ball* indicates that *Sphere* is a superclass of *Ball* or, equivalently, that *Ball* is a subclass of *Sphere*.

An instance of *Ball* has two data fields—*radius*, which is inherited, and *name*, which is new. An instance of a subclass can invoke any public method in the superclass. Thus, an instance of *Ball* has all the methods that *Sphere* defines; new constructors; new methods *getName*, *setName*, and *resetBall*; and revised methods *equals* and *displayStatistics*.

An instance of a subclass has all the behaviors of its superclass

A subclass inherits private members from the super-class, but cannot access them directly

A subclass cannot access the private members of the superclass directly, even though they are inherited. Inheritance does not imply access. After all, you can inherit a locked vault but not be able to open it. In the current example, the data field *radius* of *Sphere* is private, so you can reference it only within the definition of *Sphere* and not within the definition of *Ball*. However, *Ball* can use *Sphere*'s public methods *setRadius* and *radius* to set or obtain the value of *radius* indirectly, as is done in the revised *equals* method in the *Ball* class.

A subclass's methods can call the superclass's public methods

Within the implementation of *Ball*, you can use the methods that *Ball* inherits from *Sphere*. For example, the new method *resetBall* calls the inherited method *setRadius*. Also, *Ball*'s *displayStatistics* calls the inherited version of *displayStatistics*, which you indicate by writing *super.displayStatistics()*. The word *super* represents the object reference for the superclass and is necessary to differentiate between the two versions of the method. Thus, you can access a superclass method, even though it has been overridden, by using the *super* reference.

In the version of *displayStatistics* in the *Ball* class, the subclass overrides the superclass version of the method. The subclass version calls the superclass version of the method and performs additional tasks as well.

Java **annotations** provides a mechanism for a programmer to explicitly notify the compiler that a method from the superclass is being overridden. Annotations have a number of uses including providing additional information to the compiler to detect errors, informing the compiler to suppress warnings, and warning of the use of deprecated elements. Of interest here is the annotation *@Override*—it is used to indicate that the annotated method is overriding a method in a super class. If a method with this annotation does not override its superclass's method because you misspell the method name or do not correctly match the parameters, the compiler will generate an error. It also makes your code easier to read and understand because the fact that you are overriding the method is explicitly stated in the code.

> The annotation *@Override* indicates that a method from the superclass is being overridden

To use the *@Override* annotation, simply place it on the line preceding the overriding method:

```
@Override
public void myMethod() {   }
```

So for example, in the *Ball* class, *displaystatistics* would now appear as follows:

```
@Override
public void displayStatistics() {
// Displays the statistics of a ball.
  System.out.print("\nStatistics for a "+ name());
  super.displayStatistics();
} // end displayStatistics
```

Clients of a subclass can invoke the public members of the superclass. For example, if you write

> Clients of a subclass can invoke the superclass's public methods

```
Ball myBall = new Ball(5.0, "Volleyball");
```

myBall.diameter() returns *myBall*'s diameter, 10.0 (2 times *myBall*'s radius), by using the method *diameter* that *Ball* inherits from *Sphere*. If a new method has the same name as a superclass method—*displayStatistics*, for example—instances of the new class will use the new method, while instances of the superclass will use the original method. Therefore, if *mySphere* is an instance of *Sphere*, the call *mySphere.displayStatistics()* will invoke *Sphere*'s *displayStatistics*, whereas *myBall.displayStatistics()* will invoke *Ball*'s *displayStatistics*, as Figure 9-3 illustrates.

Finally, note that before any constructor in the subclass is executed, the default constructor (the constructor with no parameters) of the superclass will be executed unless you've specified an alternative constructor from the superclass. To call an alternative constructor, invoke the method with the arguments for the

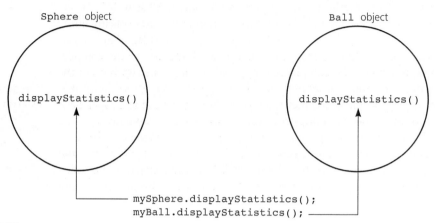

FIGURE 9-3

An object invokes the correct version of a method

superclass constructor you want to use. For example, the class *Ball* constructor *Ball(double initialRadius, String initialName)* calls the single-parameter constructor *Sphere(double initialRadius)* by using the statement *super(initialRadius)*. This call must appear as the first statement of the subclass's constructor.

Because the default constructor for the class *Ball* does not specify an alternative constructor, the *Sphere* constructor with no parameters is automatically called. Hence, if an instance of the class *Ball* is created using the following statement:

```
Ball myBall = new Ball();
```

myBall will have a radius of 1.0 and *"unknown"* as its name.

Java Access Modifiers

A class with no access modifier is available to other classes within the same package

The keywords *public* and *private* are called **access modifiers.** They are used to control the visibility of the members of a class. When no access modifier is specified on a member declaration, the member is visible only to classes in the same package. In addition to the *public* and *private* access modifiers, the *protected* access modifier allows a class designer to hide the members from a class's clients but make them available to a subclass or to another class within the same package. That is, a subclass can reference the protected members of its superclass directly, but clients of the superclass or subclass cannot. Also, classes within the same package can access protected members directly.

For example, *Sphere* has a private field *radius*, which the subclass *Ball* cannot reference directly. If, instead, you declared *radius* as protected, the class *Ball* would be able to access *radius* directly. Any other classes within the same package would also be able to access *radius* directly. Clients of *Ball* or *Sphere*, however, would not have direct access to *radius*. Figure 9-4

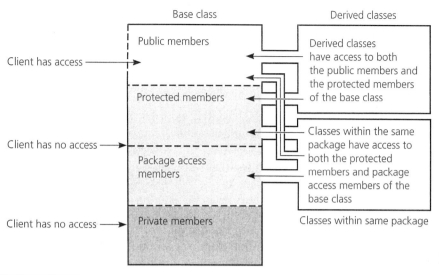

FIGURE 9-4

Access to public, protected, package access, and private members of a class by a client and a subclass

illustrates public, private, protected, and package (default) access for members of a class.

As a general stylistic guideline, you should make all data fields of a public class private and, if desired, provide indirect access to them by defining methods that are either public or protected. Although a class's public members are available to anyone, its protected members are available exclusively to either its own methods, members of other classes in the same package, or the methods of a subclass. The following summary distinguishes among the access modifiers for members of a class:

In general, a class's data fields should be private

KEY CONCEPTS

Membership Categories of a Class

1. Public members can be used by anyone.
2. Members declared without an access modifier (the default) are available to methods of the class and methods of other classes in the same package.
3. Private members can be used only by methods of the class.
4. Protected members can be used only by methods of the class, methods of other classes in the same package, and methods of the subclasses.

Is-a and Has-a Relationships

As you just saw, inheritance provides for superclass/subclass relationships among classes. Other relationships are also possible. When designing new classes from existing ones, it is important to identify their relationship so that you can determine whether to use inheritance. Two basic kinds of relationships are possible: *is-a* and *has-a*.

Is-a **relationships.**   Earlier in this chapter, we used inheritance to derive the class *Ball* from *Sphere*. You should use inheritance only when an *is-a* relationship exists between the superclass and the subclass. In this example, a ball *is a* sphere, as Figure 9-5 illustrates. That is, whatever is true of the superclass *Sphere* is also true of the subclass *Ball*. Wherever you can use an object of type *Sphere*, you can also use an object of type *Ball*. This feature is called **object type compatibility.** In general, a subclass is type-compatible with all of its superclasses. Thus, you can use an instance of a subclass instead of an instance of its superclass, but not the other way around.

The object type of an actual argument in a call to a method can be a subclass of the object type of the corresponding formal parameter. As you've seen in many of the implementations of ADTs presented earlier, you can use the class *Object* as the type of the formal parameter, and since all classes are derived from the *Object* class, you can use any object type as the actual argument.

As another example, suppose your program uses *Sphere* and *Ball* and contains the following static method:

```
public static void displayDiameter(Sphere aSphere) {
   System.out.println("The diameter is "
                      + aSphere.diameter() + ".");
}  // end displayDiameter
```

> Inheritance should imply an is-a relationship

> You can use an instance of a subclass anywhere you can use an instance of the superclass

FIGURE 9-5

A ball "is a" sphere

If you define *mySphere* and *myBall* as

```
Sphere mySphere = new Sphere(2.0);
Ball myBall = new Ball(5.0, "Volleyball");
```

the following calls to *displayDiameter* are legal:

```
displayDiameter(mySphere);   // mySphere's diameter
displayDiameter(myBall);     // myBall's diameter
```

The first call is unremarkable because both the actual argument *mySphere* and the formal parameter *aSphere* have the same data type. The second call is more interesting: The type of the actual argument *myBall* is a subclass of the data type of the formal parameter *aSphere*. Because a ball is a sphere, it can behave like a sphere. That is, *myBall* can perform sphere behaviors, so you can use *myBall* anywhere you can use *mySphere*.

> Since a ball is a sphere, you can use it anywhere you can use a sphere

***Has-a* relationships.**   A ball-point pen *has a* ball as its point, as Figure 9-6 illustrates. Although you would want to use *Ball* in your definition of a class *Pen*, you should not use inheritance, because a pen is not a ball. In fact, you do not use inheritance at all to implement a *has-a* relationship. Instead, you can define a data field *point*—whose type is *Ball*—within the class *Pen*, as follows:

> If the relationship between two classes is not is-a, you should not use inheritance

```
public class Pen {
   private Ball point;
   ...
}  // end Pen
```

class Pen

class Ball

FIGURE 9-6

A pen "has a" or "contains a" ball

An instance of *Pen* has, or *contains*, an instance of *Ball*. Thus, another name for the *has-a* relationship is **containment.**

You have already seen two other examples of the *has-a* relationship among classes in the preceding two chapters: Chapter 7 presented an implementation of *StackInterface* that used the ADT list to represent the items in a stack, while Chapter 8 used a similar implementation for the ADT queue. The class *StackListBased*, for example, contains a private data field *list* of type *ListReferenceBased*. That is, an instance of *StackListBased* has, or contains, an instance of *ListReferenceBased* that manages the stack's items.

The *has-a* relationship between two classes is possible when inheritance is inappropriate. Later, this chapter implements the ADT sorted list by using the two relationships just discussed.

9.2 Dynamic Binding and Abstract Classes

As you saw earlier, if *mySphere* is an instance of *Sphere* and *myBall* is an instance of *Ball*, *mySphere.displayStatistics()* invokes *Sphere*'s version of *displayStatistics*, whereas *myBall.displayStatistics()* invokes *Ball*'s version of *displayStatistics*. (See Figure 9-3.) Suppose, however, that the following statements are executed:

```
Ball myBall = new Ball(1.25, "golfball");
Sphere mySphere = myBall;
mySphere.displayStatistics();
```

Since *mySphere* actually references an instance of *Ball*, the *Ball* version of *displayStatistics* is executed. Thus, the appropriate version of a method is decided at execution time, instead of at compilation time, based on the type of object referenced. This situation is called **late binding,** or **dynamic binding,** and a method such as *displayStatistics* is called **polymorphic.** We also say that *Ball*'s version of *displayStatistics* **overrides** *Sphere*'s version.

A polymorphic method has multiple meanings

We will now examine a more subtle example of late binding. Suppose you wanted the class *Ball* to have a method *area* that behaved differently than *Sphere*'s *area*. Just as *Ball* overrides *displayStatistics*, it could override *area* to compute, for example, the ball's cross-sectional area, which is used to compute the drag on a ball. Thus, you would add the method

```
@Override
public double area() {  // cross-sectional area
    double r = getRadius()
    return Math.PI * r * r;  // Math.PI is a constant
}  // end area
```

as a public member of the class *Ball*, overriding *Sphere*'s *area*. Consider

```
public class Sphere {
   . . .       // everything as before
  public double area() {  // surface area
    return 4.0 * Math.PI * radius * radius;
  } // end area

  public void displayStatistics() {
    System.out.println("\nRadius = " + getRadius()
              + "\nDiameter = " + diameter()
              + "\nCircumference = " + circumference()
              + "\nArea = " + area()
              + "\nVolume = " + volume());
  } // end displayStatistics

  . . .
} // end Sphere

public class Ball extends Sphere {
   . . .  // everything as before, except
          // displayStatistics is omitted
          // and area is revised:
  @Override
  public double area() {
    double r = getRadius();
    return Math.PI * r * r;
  } // end area
  . . .
} // end Ball
```

Now when an instance of *Sphere* calls *displayStatistics*, *displayStatistics* will call *Sphere*'s *area* (Figure 9-7a), yet when an instance of *Ball* calls *displayStatistics*, *displayStatistics* will call *Ball*'s *area* (Figure 9-7b). Thus, the meaning of *displayStatistics* depends on the type of object that invokes it.

The designer of a superclass does have some control over whether a subclass is allowed to override a superclass method. If the field modifier *final* is specified in the method definition (typically after other field modifiers such as *public* and *static*), the method cannot be overridden by a subclass. On the other hand, the field modifier *abstract* requires the subclass to override the method. Abstract methods are discussed in more detail in the next section.

You can control whether a subclass can override a superclass method

When a method is defined as *final*, the compiler can determine which form of a method to use at compilation time—as opposed to at execution time. This situation is called **early binding,** or **static binding.** Methods declared *static* also use static binding, since only one version of the method is available for all classes.

Methods that are **final** or **static** use static binding

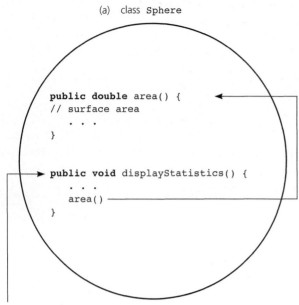

(a)   class `Sphere`

```
public double area() {
// surface area
    . . .
}

public void displayStatistics() {
    . . .
    area()
}
```

`mySphere.displayStatistics();`

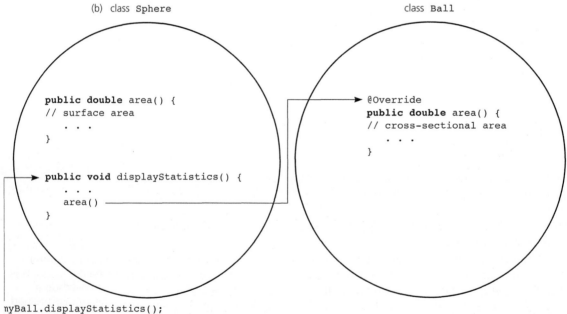

(b)   class `Sphere`   class `Ball`

```
public double area() {
// surface area
    . . .
}

public void displayStatistics() {
    . . .
    area()
}
```

```
@Override
public double area() {
// cross-sectional area
    . . .
}
```

`myBall.displayStatistics();`

FIGURE 9-7

`area` is overridden: (a) *mySphere.displayStatistics()* calls *area* in *Sphere*;
(b) *myBall.displayStatistics()* calls *area* in *Ball*

Overloading methods.   When you override a method, you create a method that has the same name and same set of parameters as the original method. Sometimes it is convenient to define another method with the same name as the first but with a different set of parameters. Such a method **overloads** the first method. Frequently you overload constructors so that each constructor has a different set of parameters. Often the choice of which constructor to use depends on the information available when you create an instance. Some of the constructors require fewer parameters and will set some of the data fields to default values.

For another example of overloading, consider the class *Ball* and the method *resetBall*, defined as follows:

```
public void resetBall(double newRadius, String newName) {
// Sets (alters) the radius and name of an existing
// ball to newRadius and newName, respectively.
   setRadius(newRadius);
   setName(newName);
}  // end resetBall
```

You could define two other methods to reset the data fields:

```
public void resetBall(double newRadius) {
// Sets (alters) the radius of an existing
// ball to newRadius.
   setRadius(newRadius);
}  // end resetBall
```

```
public void resetBall(String newName) {
// Sets (alters) the name of an existing
// ball to newName.
   setName(newName);
}  // end resetBall
```

All three methods have the same name but different sets of parameters. The arguments in each call to *resetBall* determine which version of the method will be used.

Abstract Classes

Suppose you have a CD player (CDRW) and a DVD player (DVDRW). Both devices share several characteristics. Each involve an optical disc. You can insert, remove, play, record, and stop such discs. Some of these operations are essentially the same for both devices, while others—in particular, the play and record methods—are different but similar.

If you were specifying both devices, you might begin by describing the common operations:

Disc transport operations

```
+insert()
// Inserts a disc into the player.

+remove()
// Removes a disc from the player.

+play()
// Plays the disc.

+record()
// Record the disc.

+stop()
// Stops playing the disc.

+skipForward()
// Skip ahead to another section of the disc.

+skipBackward()
// Skip back to an earlier section of the disc.
```

These operations could constitute a generic disc player (GDRW).

If GDRW, CDRW, and DVDRW were classes, GDRW could be the base class of CDRW and DVDRW, as Figure 9-8 illustrates. While GDRW could implement operations such as *insert* and *remove* that would be suitable for both a CDRW and a DVDRW, it could only indicate that these devices have a *play* and *record* operation. So CDRW, for example, inherits the operations

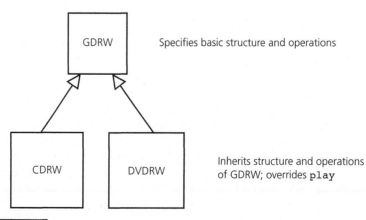

FIGURE 9-8

CDRW and DVDRW have an abstract base class GDRW

provided by GDRW but overrides the *play* and *record* operation to suit CDs, as Figure 9-9 illustrates. If necessary, CDRW could override any of GDRW's operations or define additional ones. We can make similar comments about DVDRW. Thus,

- A CDRW is a GDRW that plays sound.

- A DVDRW is a GDRW that plays sound and video.

Because GDRW cannot implement its play or record operations, we would not want instances of it. So GDRW is simply a class without instances that forms the basis of other classes. If a class never has instances, its methods need not be implemented. Such methods, however, must be abstract so that subclasses can supply their own implementations.

An **abstract class** has no instances and is used only as the basis of other classes. Thus, the general disc player is an abstract class. In Java, you declare an abstract class by including the keyword *abstract* in the class definition.

A class that contains at least one abstract method is an abstract class

An abstract class, like other classes, can contain both data fields and methods. Although an abstract class contains the methods and data fields common to all of its subclasses, some of its methods might have their implementations deferred to the subclasses. In these cases, you also declare the methods themselves to be abstract by including the field modifier *abstract* in the method definition. An abstract method does not have a body; instead, the method heading ends with a semicolon. For example, the following is a declaration for an abstract method:

```
public abstract void record();
```

Any class that contains at least one abstract method must itself be declared abstract. Any subclass that fails to implement all of the abstract methods in its superclass must also be declared as an abstract class.

An abstract class has subclasses but no instances

Another example. The previous classes *Sphere* and *Ball* describe points that are equidistant from the origin of a three-dimensional coordinate system. The

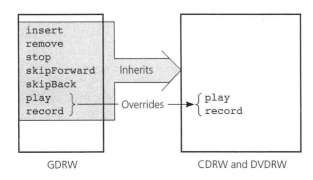

GDRW   CDRW and DVDRW

FIGURE 9-9

CDRW and DVDRW are subclasses of GDRW

following class, *EquidistantShape*, which declares operations to set and return the distance of a point from the origin, could be an abstract class of *Sphere*:

An abstract class of
Sphere

```java
public abstract class EquidistantShape {
  private double radius;
  public static final double DEFAULT_RADIUS = 1.0;

  public void setRadius(double newRadius) {
    if (newRadius >= 0.0) {
      radius = newRadius;
    }  // end if
  }  // end setRadius

  public double getRadius() {
    return radius;
  }  // end getRadius

  public abstract double area();
  public abstract void displayStatistics();
}  // end EquidistantShape
```

This class declares a private data field *radius* with the public methods *setRadius* and *getRadius* to access *radius*. The class also contains two abstract methods, *area* and *displayStatistics*.

Now you could define the class *Sphere* as a subclass of *EquidistantShape*:

```java
public class Sphere extends EquidistantShape {
  public Sphere() {
    setRadius(1.0);
  } // end default constructor

  public Sphere(double initialRadius) {
    setRadius(initialRadius);
  } // end constructor

  // Implementation of abstract methods

  @Override
  public double area() {
    double r = getRadius();
    return 4.0 * Math.PI * r * r;
  } // end area

  @Override
  public void displayStatistics...
```

```
   public void displayStatistics() {
     System.out.println("\nRadius = " + getRadius()
              + "\nDiameter = " + diameter()
              + "\nCircumference = " + circumference()
              + "\nArea = " + area()
              + "\nVolume = " + volume());
   }  // end displayStatistics

   // Remaining methods for class appear here
   . . .


} // end Sphere
```

By including the abstract method *displayStatistics* in the abstract class *EquidistantShape*, you force some subclass—like *Sphere*—to implement it. The class *Ball* can now be a subclass of *Sphere*, just as it appeared earlier in this chapter.

Note that *radius* is a private data field of *EquidistantShape* instead of *Sphere*. This means that subclasses of *Sphere* will be unable to access *radius* directly by name. Thus, the class *EquidistantShape* must contain the methods *setRadius* and *getRadius*, and you must provide default implementations for the subclasses to inherit. Alternatively, you could define *radius* to be a protected data field of *EquidistantShape*, enabling the subclass to both access *radius* directly and define *setRadius* and *getRadius*. Although data fields are generally private, a protected data field within an abstract class is reasonable, since the class is always a superclass of another class. That is, an abstract class has no other purpose but to form the basis of another class.

An abstract class can provide a constructor, but the constructors cannot be abstract. The key points about abstract classes are summarized as follows:

KEY CONCEPTS

Abstract Classes

1. An abstract class is used only as the basis for subclasses and thus defines a minimum set of methods and data fields for its subclasses.
2. An abstract class has no instances.
3. An abstract class should, in general, omit implementations except for the methods that provide access to private data fields or that express functionality common to all of the subclasses.
4. A class that contains at least one abstract method must be declared as an abstract class.
5. A subclass of an abstract class must be declared abstract if it does not provide implementations for all abstract methods in the superclass.

Java Interfaces Revisited

Inheritance is one way to have a common set of methods (or common behavior) available for a group of classes. Inheritance also allows the subclasses to inherit the structure of the superclass. In some instances, however, it is only the behavior that is of interest. Java interfaces provide another mechanism for specifying common behavior for a set of (perhaps unrelated) classes.

A Java interface specifies the common behavior of a set of classes

You have already seen how to use Java interfaces to specify the methods for a class. The methods were then implemented by using a variety of techniques, including array-based and reference-based implementations. Clients of the class could use one of these implementations. To facilitate moving from one implementation to another, you can declare references to the class by using the interface definition instead of the class definition. For example, the class *StackArrayBased* implements *StackInterface*. A client of the ADT stack could contain the following statement:

```
StackInterface stack = new StackArrayBased();
```

A client can reference a class's interface instead of the class itself

Since *stack* has the type *StackInterface*, you can use only methods that appear in the interface definition with *stack*—for example, *stack.pop()*. The interface definition should also be used whenever the stack appears as a formal parameter in a method. If you do this throughout the client, all you will need to do to move to the reference-based implementation will be to change the places where instances of the stack are created. For example, the previous definition of *stack* would change to

```
StackInterface stack = new StackReferenceBased();
```

and method calls that adhere to the interface, such as *stack.pop()*, would continue to work in the client.

An interface specifies behaviors that are common to a group of classes

As was mentioned earlier, another common use of interfaces is to specify behavior that is common to a group of unrelated classes. For example, you could define an interface called *AnimateInterface*, as follows:

```
public interface AnimateInterface {
   public void move(int x, int y);
   public void paint();
}  // end AnimateInterface
```

The intent is to provide a common set of methods needed for screen animation. Thus, many different classes, such as the class *Ball*, could implement this interface so that instances of *Ball* could be animated on the screen. If the class *Ball* does not implement all of the methods in the interface, with the intent that a subclass will implement the missing methods, the *Ball* class must be declared as abstract.

You can use inheritance to define a subinterface

As you saw in the discussion of the Java Collections Framework in Chapter 5, you can use inheritance to derive new interfaces, often called **subinterfaces.** In particular, the basis for the ADT collections in the JCF is the interface *java.util.Iterable*, with the subinterface *java.util.Collection*. This allowed the *Collection* interface to inherit a method called *Iterator* that returns an *Iterator* object for the collection. Later in the chapter, we will examine how to create an iterator for our own collection classes.

9.3 Java Generics

Generic Classes

The ADTs developed in this text thus far relied upon the use of the *Object* class as the data type for the elements. For example, the interface *List-Interface* in the previous section used *Object* as the data type for the list items. Because of polymorphism, we could use objects of any class as items in the list. But this approach has some issues:

- Though the ADTs were intended to be used as homogeneous data structures, in reality, items of any type could be added to the same ADT instance.

- To use objects returned from the ADT instance, we usually had to cast the object back to the actual type in use.

The second issue may lead to class-cast exceptions if the items removed from the ADT instance are not of the type expected.

You can avoid these issues by using Java generics to specify a class in terms of a data-type parameter. When you (the client) declare instances of the class, you specify the actual data type that the parameter represents. We have seen such declarations in our discussions of the Java Collections Framework.

Here is a simple generic class definition, where *T* is the formal data-type parameter:

A generic class describes a class in terms of a data-type parameter

```java
public class NewClass <T> {

  private int year;
  private T data = null;

  public NewClass() {
    year = 1970;
  }  // end constructor

  public NewClass(T initialData) {
    year = 1970;
    data = initialData;
  }  // end constructor

  public NewClass(T initialData, int year) {
    this.year = year;
    data = initialData;
  }  // end constructor
```

```
public void setData(T newData) {
  data = newData;
} // end setData

public T getData() {
  return data;
} // end getData

public String toString() {
  if (data != null) {
    return data.toString() + ", " + year;
  }
  else {
    return null + ", " + year;
  } // end if
} // end toString
} // end NewClass
```

You follow the class definition with the data-type parameter enclosed in < >. If there is more than one type to be parameterized, they are separated by commas. In the implementation of the class, you use the data-type parameter exactly as you would any other type.

A simple program that uses this generic class could begin as follows:

The client specifies an actual data type when declaring an instance of the class

```
static public void main(String[] args) {
  NewClass<String> first = new NewClass<String>("Wally", 2010);
  NewClass<Integer> second = new NewClass<Integer>(15);

  System.out.println("Contents of first => " + first);
  first.setData("Wood");
  System.out.println("After modifying first => " + first);
  System.out.println("Result of getData on second=> " +
                                       second.getData());

  . . .
} // end main
```

Primitive types are not allowed as type-parameters

Notice that the declarations of *first* and *second* specify the data type that the parameter *T* represents within the generic class. When using a generic class, the data-type parameters should always be included. Primitive types are not allowed as generic type-parameters.

The Java compiler will allow generic classes without data type parameters to be declared, but it is primarily for backward compatibility with code written prior to generics being included in the language. In the absence of a data type being specified, the compiler will generate warning messages when actual instances are used where instances of the data-type parameter are expected.

You must be careful about what you do with objects of the data-type parameter within the implementation of a generic class. For example, note the `toString` method in `NewClass`. It utilizes the `toString` method of `data` that has been declared of type `T`. This will use the definition for `toString` that exists for `T`, so if the `toString` method for that type does not override the one provided by the class `Object`, you will get the default string representation provided by the class `Object`, which includes the class name and hash code for the object.

Finally, Java does not allow generic types to be used in array declarations. When you declare an array with a generic type and attempt to instantiate it, you will get the following error message:

```
Error: generic array creation
  T[] test = new T[10];
```

The alternative is to use either the `ArrayList` or `Vector` class in the Java Collections Framework using the data-type parameter as follows:

```
Vector<T> test = new Vector<T>();
ArrayList<T> test2 = new ArrayList<T>();
```

Generic Wildcards

Note that when generic classes are instantiated, they are not necessarily related. For example, if we try to assign *second* to *first* in the above code, we get the following error message:

Instances of generic classes are not related

```
Error: incompatible types
     found   : NewClass<java.lang.Integer>
     required: NewClass<java.lang.String>
       first = second;
```

The instances *first* and *second* are considered to be of two different types. But there are situations where it would be convenient to write code that could handle both of these instances based upon the fact that they utilize the same generic class. This can be indicated by using the *?* wildcard as the data-type parameter, where the *?* stands for an unknown type. For example, the method:

```
public void process(NewClass<?> temp) {
   System.out.println("getData() => " + temp.getData());
}  // end process
```

can be used to process both the *first* and *second* instances.

Generic Classes and Inheritance

Generic classes can be used with inheritance

You can still use inheritance with a generic class or interface. You can specify actual data-types that should be used, or allow the subclass to maintain the same data-type parameter by utilizing the same name in the declaration. Additional data-type parameters may also be specified. For example, given the generic class *Book* defined as follows:

```
public class Book<T, S, R>
```

The following are legal subclasses of *Book*:

```
// Uses same generic parameters
public class RuleBook<T, S, R> extends Book<T, S, R>

// Specifies actual types for all of the type parameters
public class MyBook extends Book<Integer, String, String>

// Specifies the types for some of the type parameters and adds an
// additional one Q
public class TextBook<T, Q> extends Book<T, String, String>
```

Note that the rules of method overriding are in effect, a method (with the same name) defined in a subclass will override a method in the superclass if:

- you declare a method with the same parameters in the subclass, and

- the return type of the method is a subtype of all the methods it overrides.

The second point was introduced in Java 1.5.

To further our discussion of some of the other features of Java generics, assume that we have the class hierarchy shown in Figure 9-10. Note that the class *Object* is at the root of the hierarchy, *Person* is a subclass of *Object*, *Student* is a subclass of *Person*, and *UgradStudent* and *GradStudent* are subclasses of *Student*.

When specifying a generic class, it is sometimes useful to indicate that the data-type parameter should be constrained to a class or one of its subclasses or an implementation of a particular interface. To indicate this, you use the keyword *extends* to indicate that the type should be a subclass or an implementation of an interface. The following definition of the interface *Registration* restricts the generic parameter to *Student* or classes that extend *Student*:

```
public interface Registration <T extends Student> {

  public void register(T student, CourseID cid);
  public void drop(T student, CourseID cid);
  ...
} // end Registration
```

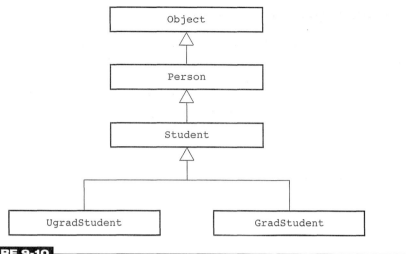

FIGURE 9-10

Sample class hierarchy

So the following declarations would be allowed:

```
Registration<Student> students = new Registration<Student>();
Registration<UpgradStudent> ugrads = new Registration<UgradStudent>();
Registration<GradStudent> grads = new Registration<GradStudent>();
```

Attempting to use a class that is not a subclass of *Student* will result in a compile-time error. For example:

```
Registration<Person> people = new Registration<Person>();
```

generates an error similar to this:

```
Error: type parameter Person is not within its bound
```

Hence, use of the *extends* clause is a way of constraining or placing an *upper bound* on the data-type parameter.

The *extends* clause can also be used to bound the *?* wildcard discussed earlier. For example, the following declaration could process any *ArrayList*:

The **extends** clause places an *upper bound* on the data-type parameter

```
public void process(ArrayList<?> list)
```

But you might want the method to be constrained to a list containing objects of type *Student* or one of its subclasses as follows:

```
public void process(ArrayList<? extends Student> stuList)
```

In this case, a call to the method *process* might look like this:

```
ArrayList<UgradStudent> ugList =
                            new ArrayList<UgradStudent>();
test1.process(ugList);
```

But if an attempt (similar to the following) to use a class that is not of type *Student* or one of its subclasses is made,

```
ArrayList<Person>pList = new ArrayList<Person>();
test1.process(pList);
```

an error message similar to the following will be generated by the compiler:

```
Error: process(java.util.ArrayList<? extends Student>) in Test
cannot be applied to (java.util.ArrayList<Person>)
```

Sometimes, the specification of a type can be too restrictive. One common scenario where this occurs is when the *Comparable* interface is involved. Let's assume that the *Student* class extends the *Comparable* interface as follows:

```
class Student extends Person implements Comparable<Student> {
  protected String id;
  ...

  public int compareTo(Student s) {
    return id.compareTo(s.id);
  } // end compareTo
  ...
} // end Student
```

Furthermore, assume that we have a class defined as follows:

```
import java.util.ArrayList;
class MyList <T extends Comparable<T>> {

  ArrayList<T> list = new ArrayList<T>();

  public void add(T x) {
    ...
    if ((list.get(i)).compareTo(list.get(j)) < 0) {
      ...
    } // end if
  } // end add
  ...
} // end MyList
```

Note that the following declaration compiles:

```
MyList<Student> it320 = new MyList<Student>();
```

But that the declaration:

```
MyList<UgradStudent> it321 = new MyList<UgradStudent>();
```

produces an error message similar to the following:

```
Error: type parameter UgradStudent is not within its bound
```

Note that the data-type parameter for *MyList* expects a class that implements the *Comparable* interface for *T*. The class *UgradStudent* does not implement this directly, it is inherited from the superclass *Student*. To allow the *UgradStudent* class as the parameter to the generic class *MyList*, the class must define the data-type parameter to allow for a superclass of *T* to implement the *Comparable* interface. This is done as follows:

```
class MyList <T extends Comparable<? super T>>
```

The clause `<? super T>` specifies a *lower bound* on the data-type parameter. In essence, it is a way to say that the class or one of its superclasses can be used as the actual data-type parameter.

The **super** clause places a *lower bound* on the data-type parameter

Generic Implementation of the Class List

The following files revise the reference-based list class—which appears in Chapter 5 and was discussed again earlier in this chapter—as a generic class. Differences between this generic version and the earlier version are shaded. The data-type parameter *T* is used instead of *Object*.

```
// ****************************************************
// Interface for the ADT list
// ****************************************************
public interface ListInterface<T> {

  public int size();
  public boolean isEmpty();
  public void removeAll();
  public void add(int index, T item)
                    throws ListIndexOutOfBoundsException;
  public void remove(int index)
                    throws ListIndexOutOfBoundsException;
  public T get(int index)
                    throws ListIndexOutOfBoundsException;
} // end ListInterface
```

```java
// ***************************************************
// Class Node used in the implementation of ADT list
// ***************************************************
class Node <T> {
  T item;
  Node<T> next;

  public Node(T newItem) {
    item = newItem;
    next = null;
  } // end constructor

  public Node(T newItem, Node<T> nextNode) {
    item = newItem;
    next = nextNode;
  } // end constructor

} // end class Node

// ***************************************************
// Reference-based implementation of ADT list.
// ***************************************************
public class ListReferenceBased<T> implements ListInterface<T> {
  // reference to linked list of items
  private Node<T> head;
  private int numItems; // number of items in list

  public ListReferenceBased() {
    numItems = 0;
    head = null;
  }  // end default constructor

  public boolean isEmpty() {
    return numItems == 0;
  }  // end isEmpty

  public int size() {
    return numItems;
  }  // end size

  private Node<T> find(int index) {
    Node<T> curr = head;
    for (int skip = 1; skip < index; skip++) {
      curr = curr.next;
    } // end for
    return curr;
  } // end find
```

```
// The methods get, add, and remove are omitted here — see
// Exercise 12.

public void removeAll() {
   // setting head to null causes list to be
   // unreachable and thus marked for garbage
   // collection
   head = null;
   numItems = 0;
} // end removeAll
} // end ListReferenceBased
```

Generic Methods

Just like class and interface declarations, method declarations can also be generic. Methods, both static and non-static, and constructors can have data-type parameters. Like classes and interfaces, the declaration of the formal data-type parameters appears within the < > brackets, immediately before the method's return type. For example, here is a method to sort an *ArrayList*, where the elements in the *ArrayList* must belong to a class that implements the *Comparable* interface:

```
class MyMethods {

   public static <T extends Comparable<? super T>>
         void sort(ArrayList<T> list) {
      // implementation of sort appears here
   } // end sort
} // end MyMethods
```

To invoke a generic method, you simply call the method just as you would a non-generic method. Generic methods are invoked like regular non-generic methods. The user doesn't need to explicitly specify the actual data-type parameters; the compiler automatically determines this by using the actual arguments provided in the method invocation. For example:

```
class TestMethod {
   public static void main (String[ ] args) {
      ArrayList<String> names = new ArrayList<String>();
      names.add("Janet");
      names.add("Andrew");
      names.add("Sarah");
      . . .

      MyMethods.sort(names);
   }  // end main
}  // end TestMethod
```

Since the names in the list are of type *String*, the compiler automatically determines that the actual data-type argument for *T* is *String*.

9.4 The ADTs List and Sorted List Revisited

Chapter 4 introduced the ADT list and the ADT sorted list. As you know, these lists have some characteristics and operations in common. For example, each ADT can determine its length, determine whether it is empty, and remove all items from the list. Both ADTs also provide a retrieval operation that returns an object at a given index position in the list. You can organize such commonalities into an interface, which can be the basis of these and other list operations. For example,

An interface for lists and sorted lists
```
public interface BasicADTInterface {
   public int size();
   public boolean isEmpty();
   public void removeAll();
}  // end BasicADTInterface
```

The designer of this interface wants all implementing classes to have the operations *size*, *isEmpty*, and *removeAll*.

Notice that the *BasicADTInterface* could be used as the interface for the three ADTs that we have studied thus far: list, stack, and queue. All of the ADTs had the methods *isEmpty* and *removeAll*, and they could easily have had the method *size* as well. Using *BasicADTInterface* would be a way to guarantee that all subinterfaces minimally will have these three methods. For example, here is a new interface definition based upon *BasicADTInterface*

An interface for a list
for the ADT list presented in section 9.3:

```
public interface ListInterface<T> extends BasicADTInterface {
   public void add(int index, T item)
         throws ListIndexOutOfBoundsException;
   public T get(int index)
         throws ListIndexOutOfBoundsException;
   public void remove(int index)
         throws ListIndexOutOfBoundsException;
}  // end ListInterface
```

The implementation of *ListReferenceBased<T>*, started in section 9.3, is consistent with this interface, so the implementation is omitted here.

Implementations of the ADT Sorted List That Use the ADT List

Now suppose you want to define and implement a class for the ADT sorted list, whose operations are

```
+createSortedList()
+isEmpty():boolean {query}
+size():integer {query}
+sortedAdd(in newItem:ListItemType) throw ListException
+sortedRemove(in anItem:ListItemType) throw ListException
+removeAll()
+get(in index:integer) throw ListIndexOutOfBoundsException
+locateIndex(in anItem:ListItemType):integer {query}
```

ADT sorted list operations

The method *createSortedList* is implemented as a constructor for the class. The methods *isEmpty*, *size*, and *removeAll* have already been specified in the interface *BasicADTInterface*. The interface definition for the ADT sorted list extends *BasicADTInterface* to include the other methods. The elements of the sorted list have one additional requirement: They must implement the *Comparable* interface, as discussed in Chapter 5, so that the sorted list can order the elements. Thus, we have

```
public interface
        SortedListInterface<T extends Comparable<? super T>>
        extends BasicADTInterface {
  public void sortedAdd(T newItem) throws ListException;
  public T get (int index)
          throws ListIndexOutOfBoundsException;
  public int locateIndex(T anItem);
  public void sortedRemove(T anItem) throws ListException;
}  // end SortedListInterface
```

You could, of course, use an array or a linked list to implement a sorted list, but such an approach would force you to repeat much of the corresponding implementations of *ListArrayBased* and *ListReferenceBased*. Fortunately, you can avoid this repetition by using one of the previously defined classes, *ListReferenceBased<T>*, to implement the class *SortedList*.

Two approaches are possible by using the *is-a* and *has-a* relationships between the new class *SortedList* and the existing class *ListReference-Based*. In most cases, one of the approaches will be best. However, we will use the sorted list to demonstrate both approaches.

You can reuse **ListArray-Based** *to implement* **SortedList**

A sorted list *is a* list. Chapter 4 stated that the ADT list is simply a list of items that you reference by position number. If you maintained those items in sorted order, would you have a sorted list? Ignoring name differences, most operations for the ADT list *are* the same as the corresponding operations for the ADT sorted list. The insertion and deletion operations differ, however, and the ADT sorted list has an additional operation, *locateIndex*.

You can insert an item into a sorted list by first using *locateIndex* to determine the position in the sorted list where the new item belongs. You then use *ListReferenceBased*'s *add* method to insert the item into that position in the list. You use a similar approach to delete an item from a sorted list.

An is-a relationship implies inheritance

Thus, a sorted list *is a* list, so you can use inheritance. That is, the class *SortedList* can be a subclass of the class *ListReferenceBased*, inheriting *ListReferenceBased*'s members and implementing the additional methods specified in the interface *SortedListInterface*. Thus, we have the following:

```java
public class SortedList<T extends Comparable<? super T>>
        extends ListReferenceBased<T>
        implements SortedListInterface<T> {

  public SortedList() {
    // invokes default constructor of superclass
  }  // end default constructor

  public void sortedAdd(T newItem) {
  // Adds an item to the list.
  // Precondition: None.
  // Postcondition: The item is added to the list in
  // sorted order.
    int newPosition = locateIndex(newItem);
    super.add(newPosition, newItem);
  }  // end sortedAdd

  public void sortedRemove(T anItem) throws ListException {
  // Removes an item from the list.
  // Precondition: None.
  // Postcondition: The item is removed from the list
  // and the sorted order maintained.
    int position = locateIndex(anItem);
    if ((anItem.compareTo(get(position))==0)) {
      super.remove(position);
    }
    else {
      throw new ListException("Sorted remove failed");
    }  // end if
  }  // end sortedRemove

  public int locateIndex(T anItem) {
  // Finds an item in the list.
  // Precondition: None.
  // Postcondition: If the item is in the list, its
  // index position in the list is returned.  If the
```

```
   // item is not in the list, the index of where it
   // belongs in the list is returned.
     int index = 0;
     // Loop invariant: anItem belongs after all the
     // elements up to the element referenced by index
     while ( (index < size()) &&
             (anItem.compareTo(get(index)) > 0 ) ) {
       ++index;
     }  // end while
     return index;
   }  // end locateIndex
}  // end SortedList
```

Note that by carefully designing the method implementations, especially *locateIndex*, we do not need access to any of the private data fields of the class *ListReferenceBased*. This means that we could just as easily have used a generic version of *ListArrayBased* as the superclass.

The class *SortedList* now has operations such as *isEmpty*, *size*, and *get*—which it inherits from *ListReferenceBased*—and *sortedAdd* and *sortedRemove*. Note also, however, that *SortedList* has also inherited the *add* and *remove* methods from *ListReferenceBased*. The availability of all of the methods from the superclass may or may not be desirable. In this case, the *add* method could potentially destroy the sorted list by making inappropriate insertions into the sorted list. In general, there are two techniques that you can use to solve this problem:

1. You can override the unwanted method with one that provides the correct semantics.

2. You can override the unwanted method with one that simply raises an exception indicating that the method is not supported.

In the present situation, the first technique does not provide a satisfactory solution. The *add* method in the superclass *ListReferenceBased* has a parameter that designates the position of the insertion, whereas the *add* method in the subclass *SortedList* does not. Even if we change the name *sortedAdd* to *add*, the subclass's *add* could not override the superclass's *add*, because the two *add* methods have different sets of parameters.

The second technique, however, does provide a solution. The subclass overrides the superclass's *add* method with a method that throws an *UnsupportedOperationException*. For example, the subclass could contain the following method:

```
public void add(int index, T item)
       throws UnsupportedOperationException {
   throw new UnsupportedOperationException();
}
```

When the *add* method is overridden in this way, the exception *UnsupportedOperationException* is thrown if an instance of *SortedList* invokes *add*.

A sorted list *has a* list as a member. If you do not have an *is-a* relationship between your new class and an existing class, inheritance is inappropriate. You may, however, be able to use an instance of the existing class to implement the new class. The following declaration of the class *SortedList has a* private data field that is an instance of *ListInterface* and that contains the items in the sorted list:

An instance of **ListInterface** can implement the sorted list

```java
public class SortedList<T extends Comparable<? super T>>
        implements SortedListInterface<T> {
  private ListInterface<T> aList;

// constructors:
  public sortedList() {
    aList = new ListReferenceBased<T>();
  }  // end default constructor

// sorted list operations:
  public boolean isEmpty() {
    // To be implemented in Programming Problem 1
  }  // end isEmpty

  public int size() {
    // To be implemented in Programming Problem 1
  }  // end size

  public void sortedAdd(T newItem) {
    int newPosition = locateIndex(newItem);
    aList.add(newPosition, newItem);
  }  // end sortedAdd

  public void sortedRemove(T anItem) {
    // To be implemented in Programming Problem 1
  }  // end sortedRemove

  public T get(int position) {
    // To be implemented in Programming Problem 1
  }  // end get

  public int locateIndex(T anItem) {
    // To be implemented in Programming Problem 1
  }  // end locateIndex
```

```
public void removeAll() {
    // to be implemented in Programming Problem 1
} // end removeAll
}  // end SortedList
```

The data field *aList* is an instance of *ListInterface* and is a member of *SortedList*. The constructor and the *sortedAdd* method are implemented. The notation *aList.add* indicates an invocation to the insertion operation of the ADT list.

Programming Problem 1 at the end of this chapter asks you to complete this implementation. In doing so, you will realize that *locateIndex* needs *get* to access items in *aList*; that is, *ListInterface*'s implementation is hidden from *SortedList*. Notice also that a client of *SortedList* cannot access *aList* and has only the sorted list operations available.

9.5 Iterators

Earlier discussions about the Java Collections Framework introduced iterators. An iterator is an object that can access a collection of objects one object at a time. That is, an iterator traverses the collection of objects. Recall the JCF generic interface *java.util.ListIterator*:

An iterator accesses a collection one item at a time

```
public interface ListIterator<E> extends Iterator<E> {

  void add(E o);
  // Inserts the specified element into the list (optional
  // operation). The element is inserted immediately before
  // the next element that would be returned by next, if any,
  // and after the next element that would be returned by
  // previous, if any. (If the list contains no elements, the
  // new element becomes the sole element on the list.) The
  // new element is inserted before the implicit cursor: a
  // subsequent call to next would be unaffected, and a
  // subsequent call to previous would return the new element.

  boolean hasNext();
  // Returns true if this list iterator has more elements when
  // traversing the list in the forward direction.

  boolean hasPrevious();
  // Returns true if this list iterator has more elements when
  // traversing the list in the reverse direction.
```

```
E next() throws NoSuchElementException;
// Returns the next element in the list. Throws
// NoSuchElementException if the iteration has no next
// element.

int nextIndex();
// Returns the index of the element that would be returned
// by a subsequent call to next. (Returns list size if the
// list iterator is at the end of the list.)

E previous()throws NoSuchElementException;
// Returns the previous element in the list. This method may
// be called repeatedly to iterate through the list
// backwards, or intermixed with calls to next to go back
// and forth. (Note that alternating calls to next and
// previous will return the same element repeatedly.) Throws
// NoSuchElementException if the iteration has no previous
// element.

int previousIndex()
// Returns the index of the element that would be returned
// by a subsequent call to previous. (Returns -1 if the list
// iterator is at the beginning of the list.)

void remove() throws UnsupportedOperationException,
                     IllegalStateException;
// Removes from the list the last element that was
// returned by next or previous (optional
// operation).

void set(E o) throws UnsupportedOperationException,
                     IllegalStateException;
// Replaces the last element returned by next or
// previous with the specified element (optional
// operation).
} // end ListIterator
```

Some iterator methods may not be supported

Notice that many of the operations, such as *remove*, can throw the exception *UnsupportedOperationException*. The expectation is that operations will simply throw this exception if the operation is not available in the class that implements the interface.

An iterator has an implicit cursor that keeps track of where you are in the ADT. It is best to think of this cursor as being either before the first item in the list, between two items in the list, or after the last item in the list. The *hasPrevious* and the *previous* operations refer to the element before the cursor, whereas the *hasNext* and *next* operations refer to the element after the cursor. The *previous*

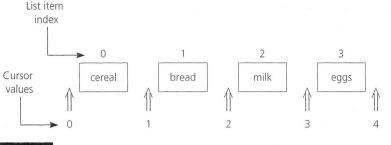

FIGURE 9-11

Relationship between iterator cursor and list elements

operation moves the cursor backward, whereas *next* moves it forward. Figure 9-11 shows the relationship between the iterator's cursor and the items in a `ListInterface` list. Note that the cursor value ranges from 0 to the size of the list.

So the implementation of an iterator must use some mechanism to keep track of the cursor. You also need to be able to identify the element that was extracted by the most recent call to *next* or *previous*. This is necessary for the implementation of the *remove* and *set* operations, which must operate on the last item returned by *previous* or *next*. And lastly, note that the operations *set* and *remove* may only be executed after a call to *previous* or *next*.

The implementation of an iterator can be approached in two ways. First, the iterator can be implemented using only the public methods available in the ADT. This leaves the iterator independent of the underlying implementation, but may not necessarily be the most efficient. So a second possibility is to implement the class as part of the ADT package, utilizing the underlying storage structure of the corresponding ADT to implement the iterator.

The following implementation is based upon the first approach, so it uses only the methods available in `ListInterface` to implement the `ListIterator` operations.

```java
public class MyListIterator<T>
        implements java.util.ListIterator<T> {

  private ListInterface<T> list;
  private int cursor;          // location of the cursor in list
  private int lastItemIndex;   // index of last item returned
                               // by previous or next

  public MyListIterator(ListInterface<T> list) {
    this.list = list;
    cursor = 0;
    lastItemIndex = -1;
  } // end constructor
```

```java
public void add(T item) {
  list.add(cursor+1, item);
  cursor++;
  lastItemIndex = -1;
} // end add

public boolean hasNext() {
  return (cursor < list.size());
} // end hasNext

public boolean hasPrevious() {
  return (cursor >= 0);
} // end hasPrevious

public T next() throws java.util.NoSuchElementException {
  try {
    T item = list.get(cursor + 1);
    lastItemIndex = cursor;
    cursor++;
    return item;
  } // end try
  catch (IndexOutOfBoundsException e){
    throw new java.util.NoSuchElementException();
  } // end catch
} // end next

public int nextIndex() {
  return cursor;
} // end nextIndex

public T previous()
      throws java.util.NoSuchElementException {
  try {
    T item = list.get(cursor);
    lastItemIndex = cursor;;
    cursor--;
    return item;
  } // end try
  catch(IndexOutOfBoundsException e) {
    throw new java.util.NoSuchElementException();
  } // catch
} // end previous

public int previousIndex() {
  return cursor - 1;
} // end previousIndex
```

```
public void remove() throws UnsupportedOperationException,
                            IllegalStateException {
  // See Programming Problem 10.
  throw new UnsupportedOperationException();
} // end remove

public void set(T item)
      throws UnsupportedOperationException {
  // See Programming Problem 10.
  throw new UnsupportedOperationException();
} // end set

} // end MyListIterator
```

Note that if this iterator implementation is used with a `ListReferenceBased` list, this will be quite inefficient (Exercise 16 will ask you to explore this). As such, Programming Problem 11 asks you to create an iterator for a generic doubly linked list.

Summary

1. Classes can have ancestor and descendant relationships. A subclass inherits all members of its previously defined superclass, but can access only the public and protected members. Private members of a class are accessible only by its methods. Protected members can be accessed by methods of both the class and any subclasses, but not by clients of these classes.

2. With inheritance, the public and protected members of the superclass remain, respectively, public and protected members of the subclass. Such a subclass is type-compatible with its superclass. That is, you can use an instance of a subclass wherever you can use an instance of its superclass. This relationship between superclasses and subclasses is an *is-a* relationship.

3. A method in a subclass overrides a method in the superclass if they have the same parameter declarations. The Java annotation `@Override` provides a mechanism for a programmer to explicitly notify the compiler that a method from the superclass is being overridden. If the superclass has defined the method to be **final**, the subclass cannot override the method.

4. An abstract method in a class is a method that you can override in a subclass. When a method is abstract, you can either implement it or defer it to a further subclass.

5. A subclass inherits the interface of each method that is in its superclass. A subclass also inherits the implementation of each nonabstract method that is in its superclass.

6. An abstract class specifies only the essential members necessary for its subclasses and, therefore, can serve as the superclass for a family of classes. A class with at least one abstract method must also be declared abstract and is referred to as an abstract superclass.

7. Early, or static, binding describes a situation whereby a compiler can determine at compilation time the correct method to invoke. Late, or dynamic, binding describes a situation whereby the system makes this determination at execution time.

8. When you invoke a method that is not declared *final*—for example, *mySphere.displayStatistics()*—the type of object is the determining factor under late binding.

9. Generic classes enable you to parameterize the type of a class's data.

10. Iterators provide an alternative way to cycle through a collection of items.

Cautions

1. If a method is abstract, and an implementation is not provided by the subclass, the subclass must also be declared abstract.

2. If a class fails to implement all of the methods in an interface, it must be declared abstract.

3. You should use inheritance only if the relationship between two classes is *is-a*.

Self-Test Exercises

Self-Test Exercises 1, 2, and 3 consider the classes *Sphere* and *Ball*, which this chapter describes in the section "Inheritance Revisited."

1. Write Java statements for the following tasks:

   a. Declare an instance *mySphere* of *Sphere* with a radius 2.

   b. Declare an instance *myBall* of *Ball* whose radius is 6 and whose name is *Beach ball*.

   c. Display the diameters of *mySphere* and *myBall*.

2. Define a class *Planet* that inherits *Ball*, as defined in this chapter. Your new class should have private data fields that specify a planet's mimimum and maximum distances from the sun and public methods that access or alter these distances.

3. a. Can *resetBall*, which is a method of *Ball*, access *Sphere*'s data field *radius* directly, or must *resetBall* call *Sphere*'s *setRadius*? Explain.

   b. Repeat Part *a*, but assume that *radius* is a protected data field instead of a private data field of the class *Sphere*.

4. Consider the interface *SortedListInterface*, as described in this chapter.

   a. When can a reference be declared as type *SortedListInterface*?

   b. When must a class that implements *SortedListInterface* be used?

   c. Show a legal declaration that uses the *SortedListInterface* with one of the *SortedList* implementations.

5. a. What are the similarities between abstract classes and interfaces?

    b. What are the differences between abstract classes and interfaces?

6. Why should a class's private methods never be abstract?

7. Given the generic class *NewClass* as described in the section "Generic Classes" write a statement that defines an instance *myClass* of *NewClass* for data declared as *Student*:

```
class Student {
  private String name;
  private double gpa;

  public Student(String name, double gpa) {
    this.name = name;
    this.gpa = gpa;
  }  // end constructor
  ...
}  // end Student
```

Exercises

1. Given the following:

```
class Test {
  public static Foo f = new Foo();
  public static Foo f2;
  public static Bar b = new Bar();

  public static void main(String [] args) {
    for (int x=0; x<6; x++) {
    f2 = getFoo(x);
    f2.react();
    }
  }

  static Foo getFoo(int y) {
    if ( 0 == y % 2 ) {
      return f;
    } else {
      return b;
    }
  }
}

class Bar extends Foo {
  void react() { System.out.print("Bar "); }
}

class Foo {
  void react() { System.out.print("Foo "); }
}
```

what is the output?

a. `Bar Bar Bar Bar Bar Bar`

b. `Foo Bar Foo Bar Foo Bar`

c. `Foo Foo Foo Foo Foo Foo`

d. Compilation fails.

e. An exception is thrown at runtime.

2. Define and implement a class `Pen` that has an instance of `Ball` as one of its data fields. Provide several members for the class `Pen`, such as the data field `color` and methods `isEmpty` and `write`.

3. Consider the following classes:

   `Clock` represents a device that keeps track of the time. Its public methods include `setTime` and `chime`.

   `AlarmClock` represents a clock that also has an alarm that can be set. Its public methods include `setSoundLevel` and `getAlarmTime`.

   a. Which of the methods mentioned above can the implementation of `setTime` invoke?

   b. Which of the methods mentioned above can the implementation of `getAlarmTime` invoke?

4. Assume the classes described in the previous question and consider a main method that contains the following statements:

   ```
   Clock wallClock;
   AlarmClock myAlarm;
   ```

   a. Which of these objects can correctly invoke the method `chime`?

   b. Which of these objects can correctly invoke the method `setSoundLevel`?

5. The `Node<T>` class used in the generic implementation of the class `ListReferencebased<T>` in this chapter assumed that it would be declared package-private; hence, the data fields were declared for package access only.

   a. Suppose that the data fields were declared private. Write accessor and mutator methods for both the `item` and `next` fields.

   b. Give at least three different examples of how the code in the `ListReferencebased<T>` implementation would have to be changed.

6. Given the following:

   ```
   class Foo {
   String doStuff(int x) { return "hello"; }
   }
   ```

which method would not be legal in a subclass of Foo?

a. `String doStuff(int x) { return "hello"; }`

b. `int doStuff(int x) { return 42; }`

c. `public String doStuff(int x) { return "Hello"; }`

d. `protected String doStuff(int x) { return "Hello"; }`

7. Consider the following classes:

   Expression represents algebraic expressions, including prefix, postfix, and infix expressions. Its public methods include *characterAt*. Its protected methods include *isOperator* and *isIdentifier*. It also has several private methods.

   InfixExpression is derived from *Expression* and represents infix expressions. Its public methods include *isLegal* and *evaluate*. It also has several protected and private methods.

   a. What methods can the implementation of *isIdentifier* invoke?

   b. What methods can the implementation of *isLegal* invoke?

8. Assume the classes described in the previous question and consider a main method that contains

   ```
   Expression algExp;
   InfixExpression infixExp;
   ```

   a. Which of these objects can correctly invoke the method *characterAt*?

   b. Which of these objects can correctly invoke the method *isOperator*?

   c. Which of these objects can correctly invoke the method *isLegal*?

9. Consider an ADT back list, which restricts insertions, deletions, and retrievals to the last item in the list.

   a. Define a generic interface *BackListInterface* that is a subclass of the interface *BasicListInterface*. Provide a reference-based implementation of the interface *BackListInterface* called *BackList*.

   b. Define and implement a class for the ADT stack that is a subclass of *BackList*.

10. Define an abstract class *Person* that describes a typical person. Include methods to retrieve the person's name, and to get or change his or her address. Next, define a subclass *Student* that describes a typical student. Include methods to retrieve his or her ID number, number of credits completed, and grade point average. Also include methods to get or change his or her campus address. Finally, derive from *Student* a class *UgradStudent* for a typical undergraduate student. Include methods for retrieving his or her degree and major.

11. Implement a generic version of *ListArrayBased* based on the generic *ListInterface* presented in this chapter. You will need to use the JFC *ArrayList* class instead of an array for the underlying implementation, since you cannot declare an array using a generic type in Java. Write a small test program as well to verify that your generic *ListArrayBased* class is working properly.

522 Chapter 9 Advanced Java Topics

12. Complete the implementation of the class `ListReferenceBased` presented in the section "Generic Implementation of the Class List." In particular, write the implementations of the methods `get`, `add`, and `remove`.

13. Given the following:

```
class Over {
int doStuff(int a, float b) {
return 7;
}
}
```

```
class Over2 extends Over {
line no 8:   // insert code here
}
```

which two methods, if inserted independently at line 8, will not compile? (Choose two.)

a. `public int doStuff(int x, float y) { return 4; }`

b. `protected int doStuff(int x, float y) {return 4; }`

c. `private int doStuff(int x, float y) {return 4; }`

d. `private int doStuff(int x, double y) { return 4; }`

e. `long doStuff(int x, float y) { return 4; }`

f. `int doStuff(float x, int y) { return 4; }`

14. Given the following:

```
class MySuper {
  public MySuper(int i) {
    System.out.println("super " + i);
  }
}
```

```
public class MySub extends MySuper {
  public MySub() {
    super(2);
    System.out.println("sub");
  }

  public static void main(String [] args) {
    MySuper sup = new MySub();
  }
}
```

what is the output?

a. sub
   super 2

b. super 2
   Sub

c. Compilation fails at line 2.

d. Compilation fails at line 8.

15. What is the output of the following code?

```
public  class A {
  public void print Value(){
  System.out.println("Val e-A ");
  }
}

public  class B  extends   A {
  public void printNameB(){
  System.out. println(" Name-B ");
  }
}

public  class C  extends   A {
  public void printNameC(){
  System.out.println (" Name-C ");
  }
}

public  class Test{
  public static void main (String[] args) {

  B  b = new B();
  C  c = new C();
  newPrint(b);
  newPrint(c);
  }

    public static void new Print(A a) {
    a.printValue();
    }
}
```

a. Value-A Name-B

b. Value-A Value-A

c. Value-A Name-C

d. Name-B Name-C

16. It was noted that the *MyListIterator* implementation presented in section 9.5 would be inefficient if it were used with a *ListReferenceBased* list. Explain why this is the case and give a specific example demonstrating this inefficiency.

17. Given the following:

```
public class TestPoly {
  public static void main(String [] args ){
  Parent p = new Child();
  }
}
class Parent {
  public Parent() {
    super();
    System.out.println("instantiate a parent");
  }
}
```

```
class Child extends Parent {
  public Child() {
  System.out.println("instantiate a child");
  super();
  }
}
```

what is the output?

a. instantiate a child

b. instantiate a parent

c. instantiate a child
   instantiate a parent

d. instantiate a parent
   instantiate a child

e. Compilation fails.

f. An exception is thrown at run time.

Programming Problems

1. Complete the implementation of *SortedList* that has a reference of type *List-Interface* as a data field, as described in the section "Implementations of the ADT Sorted List that Use the ADT List."

2. The interface *ListInterface*, as described in this chapter, does not contain a method *position* that returns the number of a particular item, given the item's value. Such a method enables you to pass the node's number to *remove*, for example, to delete the item.

   Define a subinterface of *ListInterface* that has *position* as a method as well as methods that insert, delete, and retrieve items by their values instead of their positions. Write a class that implements this interface. Always make insertions at the beginning of the list. Although the items in this list are not sorted, the new ADT is analogous to *SortedList*, which contains the method *locatePosition*.

3. Consider an ADT circular list, which is like the ADT list but treats its first item as being immediately after its last item. For example, if a circular list contains six items, retrieval or deletion of the eighth item actually involves the list's second item. Let insertion into a circular list, however, behave exactly like insertion into a list. Define and implement the ADT circular list as a subclass of *ListReferenceBased*, as described in Chapter 5.

4. Write a Java program for bank transactions by creating the Abstract Class: *BankAccount* and derive the classes *SavingsAccount* and *CurrentAccount*.

   There are five methods to be implemented in BankAccount:

   displayBalance () - Displays the balance in the account
   depositAccount () - Creates a deposit in the account (adds amount to the balance)
   withdrawAccount () - Withdraws money from the account (reduces the balance by amount withdrawn)

`calculateInterest ()` - Shows the interest for the current balance.
Interest Rates - Savings 5.5% Current 2%
This method is implemented as an abstract function in `BankAccount` Class and implemented in the child classes.

`displayCount()` - Displays the total number of transactions (deposits/withdrawals). The count should be the sum total of both Savings and Current Account transactions.

The first menu should ask the user to choose the type of account (Savings/Current) and process the further requests accordingly.

5. A company has been asked to set up a system to collect tolls from vehicles that use a particular bridge. The toll amount will vary depending on the type of vehicle that uses the bridge. The company needs a system that can determine the toll amount based on the type of vehicle. Following is the design to be implemented:

Create an abstract class `Vehicle` with the following attributes:

Number of wheels
Weight
Toll amount

Create the following methods in `Vehicle` class:
`displayVehicle()` - should display the first two attributes
Write the following pure virtual function:
`calculateToll()` - to be implemented in the derived classes

Derive two classes: `Truck` and `Car` from `Vehicle`.

In the class `Car`, implement the `calculateToll()` method as follows:

If number of wheels < 6 and weight < 1000 kg, then toll is number of wheels × 10
Else toll is number of wheels × 15

In the class `Truck`, implement `calculateToll()` as follows:

If number of wheels < 8 and weight < 5000 kg, then toll is number of wheels × 25
If number of wheels < 8 and weight > 5000 kg, then toll is number of wheels × 30
If number of wheels > 8 and weight < 10000 kg, then toll is number of wheels × 40
If number of wheels > 8 and weight > 10000 kg, then toll is number of wheels × 50

The system should ask the user to enter the number of wheels and the weight of the vehicle and then the system should print the toll.
Include exception handling to verify the input. For example, if a user enters an odd number for the number of wheels, it should throw up an exception and say *"Invalid Input - odd number of wheels"*.

6. Write a generic version of the class `Stack` presented in Chapter 7.

   a. Use the reference-based version as the basis of your implementation.

   b. Use the array-based version as the basis of your implementation, using an `ArrayList` for the array.

7. Write a generic version of the class `Queue` presented in Chapter 8.

   a. Use the reference-based version as the basis of your implementation.

   b. Use the array-based version as the basis of your implementation, using an `ArrayList` for the array.

8. Algebraic expressions are character strings, but since `String` is a `final` class, you cannot derive a class of expressions from `String`. Instead, define an abstract class `Expression` that can be the basis of other classes of algebraic expressions. Provide methods such as `characterAt`, `isOperator`, and `isIdentifier`. Next design and implement a class `InfixExpression` derived from the class `Expression`.

   Programming Problem 9 of Chapter 6 describes a grammar and a recognition algorithm for infix algebraic expressions. That grammar makes left-to-right association illegal when consecutive operators have the same precedence. Thus, $a/b*c$ is illegal, but both $a/(b*c)$ and $(a/b)*c$ are legal.

   Programming Problem 8 of Chapter 7 describes an algorithm to evaluate an infix expression that is syntactically correct by using two stacks.

   Include in the class `InfixExpression` an `isLegal` method—based on the recognition algorithm given in Chapter 6—and an `evaluate` method—based on the evaluation algorithm given in Chapter 7. Use one of the ADT stack implementations presented in Chapter 7.

9. Chapter 6 described the class `Queens` that was used in a solution to the Eight Queens problem. A two-dimensional array represented the chessboard and was a data field of the class. Programming Problem 1 of Chapter 6 asked you to write a program to solve the Eight Queens problem based on these ideas. Revise that program by replacing the two-dimensional array with a class that represents the chessboard.

10. Implement the methods `remove` and `set` for the class `MyListIterator`. These methods should behave as follows:

    public void remove( )

    Removes from the list the last element that was returned by `next` or `previous`. This call can be made only once per call to `next` or `previous`. It can be made only if the `add` method in `MyListIterator` has not been called after the last call to `next` or `previous`.

    Throws `IllegalStateException` if neither `next` or `previous` has been called, or if `remove` or `add` has been called after the last call to `next` or `previous`.

    public void set(T item)

    Replaces the last element returned by `next` or `previous` with the specified element. This call can be made only if neither `remove` nor `add` have been called after the last call to `next` or `previous`.

    Throws `IllegalStateException` if neither `next` nor `previous` has been called, or if `remove` or `add` has been called after the last call to `next` or `previous`.

    Note that `remove` and `set` require you to keep track of the state of the iterator; in other words, you must know whether or not `next` and `previous` are called immediately before the use of `remove` or `set`. You may also need to keep track of whether `previous` or `next` was called last to make sure that the correct element is deleted from or replaced in the list when *remove* and *set* are called. You may find it useful to use the variable *lastItemIndex* to determine if the last call made was to *next* or *previous*.

11. Implement a generic doubly linked list implementation called *DoubleRefBasedList* that implements the generic *ListInterface* presented in this chapter. In addition, create an iterator called *DListIterator* for the *DoubleRefBasedList* class. To make the implementation of *DListIterator* more efficient, you need to have access to the underlying doubly linked list in *DoubleRefBasedList*. The easiest way to accomplish this is to move the iterator class inside the list class. This inner class is then a member of the *DoubleRefBasedList* class and will have access to all of the members of that class. So the *DoubleRefBasedList* class with an inner *DListIterator* class will be structured as follows:

```
public class DoubleRefBasedList<T> implements ListInterface<T> {

    private DNode<T> head;
    // Assume Dnode has been defined as a node class with both
    // a next and previous reference.  It is used to implement
    // the doubly linked list.

    // Class members for ListInterface implementation appear here.

    // Inner class DListIterator
    private class DListIterator
            implements java.util.ListIterator<T> {

        private DNode<T> cursor = head;

        // Class members for ListIterator implementation appear here.
        // This inner class has access to members of the outer class.

    } // end DListIterator

    public java.util.ListIterator<T> listIterator() {
      return new DListIterator();
    } // end listIterator
} // end DoubleRefBasedList
```

The cursor declaration is shown to demonstrate how members of the outer class can be accessed from the inner class. When a call is made to the *DoubleRefBasedList* method *listIterator*, the cursor will be initialized to reference the first node in the list.

Also write a test class that tests that the operations for both the *DoubleRefBasedList* class and the *DListIterator* class are working properly.

12. Create a generic class for a circular doubly linked list as shown in Figure 5-29 of Chapter 5. Also define and implement a bidirectional iterator for this class.

CHAPTER 10

Algorithm Efficiency and Sorting

This chapter will show you how to analyze the efficiency of algorithms. The basic mathematical techniques for analyzing algorithms are central to more advanced topics in computer science and give you a way to formalize the notion that one algorithm is significantly more efficient than another. As examples, you will see analyses of some algorithms that you have studied before, including those that search data. In addition, this chapter examines the important topic of sorting data. You will study some simple algorithms, which you may have seen before, and some more-sophisticated recursive algorithms. Sorting algorithms provide varied and relatively easy examples of the analysis of efficiency.

10.1 Measuring the Efficiency of Algorithms

The comparison of algorithms is a topic that is central to computer science. Measuring an algorithm's efficiency is quite important because your choice of algorithm for a given application often has a great impact. Responsive word processors, grocery checkout systems, automatic teller machines, video games, and life support systems all depend on efficient algorithms.

Suppose two algorithms perform the same task, such as searching. What does it mean to compare the algorithms and conclude that one is better? Chapter 2 discussed the several components that contribute to the cost of a computer program. Some of these components involve the cost of human time—the time of the people who develop, maintain, and use the program. The other components involve the cost of program execution—that is, the program's efficiency—measured by the amount of computer time and space that the program requires to execute.

We have, up to this point, emphasized the human cost of a computer program. The early chapters of this book stressed style and readability. They pointed out that well-designed algorithms reduce the human costs of implementing the algorithm with a program, of maintaining the program, and of modifying the program. The primary concern has been to develop good problem-solving skills and programming style. Although we will continue to concentrate our efforts in that direction, the efficiency of algorithms is also important. Efficiency is one criterion that you should use when selecting an algorithm and its implementation. The solutions in this book, in addition to illustrating good programming style, are frequently based on relatively efficient algorithms.

Consider efficiency when selecting an algorithm

The **analysis of algorithms** is the area of computer science that provides tools for contrasting the efficiency of different methods of solution. Notice the use of the term *methods of solution* rather than *programs*; it is important to emphasize that the analysis concerns itself primarily with *significant* differences in efficiency—differences that you can usually obtain only through superior methods of solution and rarely through clever tricks in coding. Reductions in computing costs due to clever coding tricks are often more than offset by reduced program readability, which increases human costs. An analysis should focus on gross differences in the efficiency of algorithms that are likely to dominate the overall cost of a solution. To do otherwise could lead you to select an algorithm that runs a small fraction of a second faster than another algorithm yet requires many more hours of your time to implement and maintain.

A comparison of algorithms should focus on significant differences in efficiency

The efficient use of both time and memory is important. Computer scientists use similar techniques to analyze an algorithm's time and space efficiency. Since none of the algorithms covered in this text has significant space requirements, our focus will be primarily on time efficiency.

How do you compare the time efficiency of two algorithms that solve the same problem? One possible approach is to implement the two algorithms in Java and run the programs. This approach has at least three fundamental difficulties:

1. **How are the algorithms coded?** If algorithm A_1 runs faster than algorithm A_2, it could be the result of better programming. Thus, if you compare the running times of the programs, you are really comparing implementations of the algorithms rather than the algorithms themselves. You should not compare implementations, because they are sensitive to factors such as programming style that tend to cloud the issue of which algorithm is inherently more efficient.

2. **What computer should you use?** The particular computer on which the programs are run also obscures the issue of which algorithm is inherently more efficient. One computer may simply be much faster than the other, so clearly you should use the same computer for both programs. Which computer should you choose? The particular operations that the algorithms require can cause A_1 to run faster than A_2 on one computer, while the opposite is true on another computer. You should compare the efficiency of the algorithms independently of a particular computer.

3. **What data should the programs use?** Perhaps the most important difficulty on this list is the selection of the data for the programs to use. There is always the danger that you will select instances of the problem for which one of the algorithms runs uncharacteristically fast. For example, when comparing a sequential search and a binary search of a sorted array, you might search for an item that happens to be the smallest item in the array. In such a case, the sequential search will find the item more quickly than the binary search because the item is first in the array and so is the first item that the sequential search will examine. Any analysis of efficiency must be independent of specific data.

Three difficulties with comparing programs instead of algorithms

To overcome these difficulties, computer scientists employ mathematical techniques that analyze algorithms independently of specific implementations, computers, or data. You begin this analysis by counting the number of significant operations in a particular solution, as the next section describes.

Algorithm analysis should be independent of specific implementations, computers, and data

The Execution Time of Algorithms

Previous chapters have informally compared different solutions to a given problem by looking at the number of operations that each solution required. For example, Chapter 5 compared array-based and reference-based implementations of the ADT list and found that an array-based `list.get(n)` could access the nth item in a list directly in one step, because the item is stored in `items[n-1]`. A reference-based `list.get(n)`, however, must traverse the list from its beginning until the nth node is reached, and so would require n steps.

An algorithm's execution time is related to the number of operations it requires. Counting an algorithm's operations—if possible—is a way to assess its efficiency. Consider a few other examples.

Counting an algorithm's operations is a way to assess its efficiency

Traversal of a linked list. Recall from Chapter 5 that you can display the contents of a linked list that *head* references by using the following statements:[1]

```
Node curr = head;                    ← 1 assignment
while (curr != null) {               ← n+1 comparisons
   System.out.println(curr.item);    ← n writes
   curr = curr.next;                 ← n assignments
}   // end while
```

Assuming a linked list of n nodes, these statements require $n + 1$ assignments, $n + 1$ comparisons, and n write operations. If each assignment, comparison, and write operation requires, respectively, a, c, and w time units, the statements require $(n + 1) * (a + c) + n * w$ time units.[2] Thus, the time required to write n nodes is proportional to n. This conclusion makes sense intuitively: It takes longer to display, or traverse, a linked list of 100 items than it does a linked list of 10 items.

Displaying the data in a linked list of n nodes requires time proportional to n

The Towers of Hanoi. Chapter 6 proved recursively that the solution to the Towers of Hanoi problem with n disks requires $2^n - 1$ moves. If each move requires the same time m, the solution requires $(2^n - 1) * m$ time units. As you will soon see, this time requirement increases rapidly as the number of disks increases.

Nested loops. Consider an algorithm that contains nested loops of the following form:

```
for (i = 1 through n) {
  for (j = 1 through i) {
    for (k = 1 through 5) {
      Task T
    } // end for
  } // end for
} // end for
```

If task T requires t time units, the innermost loop on k requires $5 * t$ time units. The loop on j requires $5 * t * i$ time units, and the outermost loop on i requires

$$\sum_{i=1}^{n} (5 * t * i) = 5 * t * (1 + 2 + \cdots + n) = 5 * t * n * (n + 1)/2$$

time units.

---

1. Chapter 5 actually used a `for` statement. We use an equivalent `while` statement here to clarify the analysis.
2. Although omitting multiplication operators is common in algebra, we indicate them explicitly here to facilitate counting them.

Algorithm Growth Rates

As you can see, the previous examples derive an algorithm's time requirement as a function of the problem size. The way to measure a problem's size depends on the application—typical examples are the number of nodes in a linked list, the number of disks in the Tower of Hanoi problem, the size of an array, or the number of items in a stack. Thus, we reached conclusions such as

Algorithm A requires $n^2/5$ time units to solve a problem of size n

Algorithm B requires $5 * n$ time units to solve a problem of size n

The time units in these two statements must be the same before you can compare the efficiency of the two algorithms. Perhaps we should have written

Algorithm A requires $n^2/5$ seconds to solve a problem of size n

Our earlier discussion indicates the difficulties with such a statement: On what computer does the algorithm require $n^2/5$ seconds? What implementation of the algorithm requires $n^2/5$ seconds? What data caused the algorithm to require $n^2/5$ seconds?

What specifically do you want to know about the time requirement of an algorithm? The most important thing to learn is how quickly the algorithm's time requirement grows as a function of the problem size. Statements such as

Algorithm A requires time proportional to n^2

Algorithm B requires time proportional to n

each express an algorithm's proportional time requirement, or **growth rate,** and enable you to compare algorithm *A* with another algorithm *B*. Although you cannot determine the exact time requirement for either algorithm *A* or algorithm *B* from these statements, you can determine that for large problems, *B* will require significantly less time than *A*. That is, *B*'s time requirement—as a function of the problem size *n*—increases at a slower rate than *A*'s time requirement, because *n* increases at a slower rate than n^2. Even if *B* actually requires $5 * n$ seconds and *A* actually requires $n^2/5$ seconds, *B* eventually will require significantly less time than *A*, as *n* increases. Figure 10-1 illustrates this fact. Thus, an assertion like "*A* requires time proportional to n^2" is exactly the kind of statement that characterizes the inherent efficiency of an algorithm independently of such factors as particular computers and implementations.

Figure 10-1 also shows that *A*'s time requirement does not exceed *B*'s until *n* exceeds 25. Algorithm efficiency is typically a concern for large problems only. The time requirements for small problems are generally not large enough to matter. Thus, our analyses assume large values of *n*.

Order-of-Magnitude Analysis and Big O Notation

If

Algorithm A requires time proportional to $f(n)$

> Measure an algorithm's time requirement as a function of the problem size

> Compare algorithm efficiencies for large problems

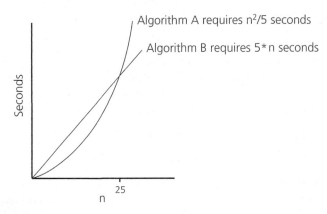

Time requirements as a function of the problem size *n*

Algorithm *A* is said to be **order $f(n)$**, which is denoted as **O($f(n)$)**. The function $f(n)$ is called the algorithm's **growth-rate function.** Because the notation uses the capital letter O to denote *order*, it is called the **Big O notation.** If a problem of size *n* requires time that is directly proportional to *n*, the problem is O(n)—that is, order *n*. If the time requirement is directly proportional to n^2, the problem is O(n^2), and so on.

The following definition formalizes these ideas:

KEY CONCEPTS

Definition of the Order of an Algorithm

Algorithm *A* is order $f(n)$—denoted O($f(n)$)—if constants k and n_0 exist such that *A* requires no more than $k * f(n)$ time units to solve a problem of size $n \geq n_0$.

The requirement $n \geq n_0$ in the definition of O($f(n)$) formalizes the notion of sufficiently large problems. In general, many values of k and n can satisfy the definition.

The following examples illustrate the definition:

■ Suppose that an algorithm requires $n^2 - 3 * n + 10$ seconds to solve a problem of size *n*. If constants k and n_0 exist such that

$$k * n^2 > n^2 - 3 * n + 10 \text{ for all } n \geq n_0$$

the algorithm is order n^2. In fact, if k is 3 and n_0 is 2,

$$3 * n^2 > n^2 - 3 * n + 10 \text{ for all } n \geq 2$$

as Figure 10 2 illustrates. Thus, the algorithm requires no more than $k * n^2$ time units for $n \geq n_0$, and so is O(n^2).

- Previously, we found that displaying a linked list's first n items requires $(n + 1) * (a + c) + n * w$ time units. Since $2 * n \geq n + 1$ for $n \geq 1$,

$$(2 * a + 2 * c + w) * n \geq (n + 1) * (a + c) + n * w \text{ for } n \geq 1$$

Thus, this task is O(n). Here, k is $2 * a + 2 * c + w$, and n_0 is 1.

- Similarly, the solution to the Towers of Hanoi problem requires $(2^n - 1) * m$ time units. Since

$$m * 2^n > (2^n - 1) * m \text{ for } n \geq 1$$

the solution is O(2^n).

The requirement $n \geq n_0$ in the definition of O($f(n)$) means that the time estimate is correct for sufficiently large problems. In other words, the time estimate is too small for at most a finite number of problem sizes. For example, the function log n takes on the value 0 when n is 1. Thus, the fact that $k * \log 1$ is 0 for all constants k implies an unrealistic time requirement; presumably, all algorithms require more than 0 time units even to solve a problem of size 1. Thus, you can discount problems of size $n = 1$ if $f(n)$ is log n.

To dramatize further the significance of an algorithm's proportional growth rate, consider the table and graph in Figure 10-3. The table (Figure 10-3a) gives, for various values of n, the approximate values of some common growth-rate functions, which are listed in order of growth:

$$O(1) < O(\log_2 n) < O(n) < O(n * \log_2 n) < O(n^2) < O(n^3) < O(2^n)$$

Order of growth of some common functions

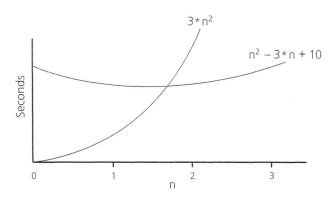

$3*n^2$

$n^2 - 3*n + 10$

Seconds

0   1   2   3

n

FIGURE 10-2

When $n \geq 2$, $3 * n^2$ exceeds $n^2 - 3 * n + 10$

The table demonstrates the relative speed at which the values of the functions grow. (Figure 10-3b represents the growth-rate functions graphically.[3])

(a)

Function	10	100	1,000	10,000	100,000	1,000,000
1	1	1	1	1	1	1
$\log_2 n$	3	6	9	13	16	19
n	10	10^2	10^3	10^4	10^5	10^6
$n * \log_2 n$	30	664	9,965	10^5	10^6	10^7
n^2	10^2	10^4	10^6	10^8	10^{10}	10^{12}
n^3	10^3	10^6	10^9	10^{12}	10^{15}	10^{18}
2^n	10^3	10^{30}	10^{301}	$10^{3,010}$	$10^{30,103}$	$10^{301,030}$

(b)

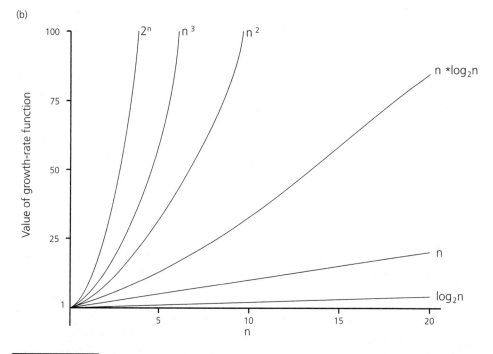

FIGURE 10-3

A comparison of growth-rate functions: (a) in tabular form; (b) in graphical form

---

3. The graph of $f(n) = 1$ is omitted because the scale of the figure makes it difficult to draw. It would, however, be a straight line parallel to the x axis through $y = 1$.

These growth-rate functions have the following intuitive interpretations:

1

A growth-rate function of 1 implies a problem whose time requirement is constant and, therefore, independent of the problem's size n.

Intuitive interpretations of growth-rate functions

$\log_2 n$

The time requirement for a **logarithmic** algorithm increases slowly as the problem size increases. If you square the problem size, you only double its time requirement. Later you will see that the recursive binary search algorithm that you studied in Chapter 3 has this behavior. Recall that a binary search halves an array and then searches one of the halves. Typical logarithmic algorithms solve a problem by solving a smaller constant fraction of the problem.

The base of the log does not affect a logarithmic growth rate, so you can omit it in a growth-rate function. Exercise 6 at the end of this chapter asks you to show why this is true.

n

The time requirement for a **linear** algorithm increases directly with the size of the problem. If you square the problem size, you also square its time requirement.

$n * \log_2 n$

The time requirement for an $n * \log_2 n$ algorithm increases more rapidly than a linear algorithm. Such algorithms usually divide a problem into smaller problems that are each solved separately. You will see an example of such an algorithm—the mergesort—later in this chapter.

n^2

The time requirement for a **quadratic** algorithm increases rapidly with the size of the problem. Algorithms that use two nested loops are often quadratic. Such algorithms are practical only for small problems. Later in this chapter, you will study several quadratic sorting algorithms.

n^3

The time requirement for a **cubic** algorithm increases more rapidly with the size of the problem than the time requirement for a quadratic algorithm. Algorithms that use three nested loops are often cubic, and are practical only for small problems.

2^n

As the size of a problem increases, the time requirement for an **exponential** algorithm usually increases too rapidly to be practical.

If algorithm A requires time that is proportional to function f and algorithm B requires time that is proportional to a slower-growing function g, it is apparent that B will always be significantly more efficient than A for large enough problems. For large problems, the proportional growth rate dominates all other factors in determining an algorithm's efficiency.

Several mathematical properties of Big O notation help to simplify the analysis of an algorithm. As we discuss these properties, you should keep in mind that $O(f(n))$ means "is of order $f(n)$" or "has order $f(n)$." O is not a function.

Some properties of growth-rate functions

1. **You can ignore low-order terms in an algorithm's growth-rate function.** For example, if an algorithm is $O(n^3 + 4 * n^2 + 3 * n)$, it is also $O(n^3)$. By examining the table in Figure 10-3a, you can see that the n^3 term is significantly larger than either $4 * n^2$ or $3 * n$, particularly for large values of n. For large n, the growth rate of $n^3 + 4 * n^2 + 3 * n$ is the same as the growth rate of n^3. It is the growth rate of $f(n)$, not the value of $f(n)$, that is important here. Thus, even if an algorithm is $O(n^3 + 4 * n^2 + 3 * n)$, we say that it is simply $O(n^3)$. In general, you can usually conclude that an algorithm is $O(f(n))$, where f is a function similar to the ones listed in Figure 10-3.

2. **You can ignore a multiplicative constant in the high-order term of an algorithm's growth-rate function.** For example, if an algorithm is $O(5 * n^3)$, it is also $O(n^3)$. This observation follows from the definition of $O(f(n))$, if you let $k = 5$.

3. **$O(f(n)) + O(g(n)) = O(f(n) + g(n))$.** You can combine growth-rate functions. For example, if an algorithm is $O(n^2) + O(n)$, it is also $O(n^2 + n)$, which you write simply as $O(n^2)$ by applying property 1. Analogous rules hold for multiplication.

These properties imply that you need only an estimate of the time requirement to obtain an algorithm's growth rate; you do not need an exact statement of an algorithm's time requirement, which is fortunate because deriving the exact time requirement is often difficult and sometimes impossible.

An algorithm can require different times to solve different problems of the same size

Worst-case and average-case analyses. A particular algorithm might require different times to solve different problems of the same size. For example, the time that an algorithm requires to search n items might depend on the nature of the items. Usually you consider the maximum amount of time that an algorithm can require to solve a problem of size n—that is, the worst case. **Worst-case analysis** concludes that algorithm A is $O(f(n))$ if, in the worst case, A requires no more than $k * f(n)$ time units to solve a problem of size n for all but a finite number of values of n. Although a worst-case analysis can produce a pessimistic time estimate, such an estimate does not mean that your algorithm will always be slow. Instead, you have shown that the algorithm will never be slower than your estimate. Realize, however, that an algorithm's worst case might happen rarely, if at all, in practice.

An **average-case analysis** attempts to determine the average amount of time that an algorithm requires to solve problems of size n. In an average-case analysis, A is O($f(n)$) if the average amount of time that A requires to solve a problem of size n is no more than $k * f(n)$ time units for all but a finite number of values of n. Average-case analysis is, in general, far more difficult to perform than worst-case analysis. One difficulty is determining the relative probabilities of encountering various problems of a given size; another is determining the distributions of various data values. Worst-case analysis is easier to calculate and is thus more common.

Keeping Your Perspective

Before continuing with additional order-of-magnitude analyses of specific algorithms, a few words about perspective are appropriate. For example, consider an ADT list of n items. You saw earlier that an array-based `list.get(n)` operation can access the nth item in the list directly. This access is independent of n; `get` takes the same time to access the hundredth item as it does to access the first item in the list. Thus, the array-based implementation of the retrieval operation is O(1). However, the reference-based implementation of `get` in the class `ListReferenceBased` requires n steps to traverse the list until it reaches the nth item, and so is O(n).

An array-based **get** is O(1)

A reference-based **get** is O(n)

Throughout the course of an analysis, you should always keep in mind that you are interested only in *significant* differences in efficiency. Is the difference in efficiency for the two implementations of `get` significant? As the size of the list grows, the reference-based implementation might require more time to retrieve the desired node, because the node can be farther away from the beginning of the list. In contrast, regardless of how large the list is, the array-based implementation always requires the same constant amount of time to retrieve any particular item. Thus, no matter what your notion of a significant difference in time is, you will reach this time difference if the list is large enough. In this example, observe that the difference in efficiency for the two implementations is worth considering only when the problem is large enough. If the list never has more than 25 items, for example, the difference in the implementations is not significant at all.

Now consider an application—such as a word processor's spelling checker—that frequently retrieves items from a list but rarely inserts or deletes an item. Since an array-based `get` is faster than a reference-based `get`, you should choose an array-based implementation of the list for the application. On the other hand, if an application requires frequent insertions and deletions but rarely retrieves an item, you should choose a reference-based implementation of the list. The most appropriate implementation of an ADT for a given application strongly depends on how frequently the application will perform the operations. You will see more examples of this point in the next chapter.

When choosing an ADT's implementation, consider how frequently particular ADT operations occur in a given application

The response time of some ADT operations, however, can be crucial, even if you seldom use them. For example, an air traffic control system could include an emergency operation to resolve the impending collision of two airplanes. Clearly,

Some seldom-used but critical operations must be efficient

this operation must occur quickly, even if it is rarely used. Thus, before you choose an implementation for an ADT, you should know what operations a particular application requires, approximately how often the application will perform each operation, and the response times that the application requires of each operation.

Soon we will compare a searching algorithm that is $O(n)$ with one that is $O(\log_2 n)$. While it is true that an $O(\log_2 n)$ searching algorithm requires significantly less time on large arrays than an $O(n)$ algorithm requires, on small arrays—say, $n < 25$—the time requirements might not be significantly different at all. In fact, it is entirely possible that, because of factors such as the size of the constant k in the definition of Big O, the $O(n)$ algorithm will run faster on small problems. It is only on large problems that the slower growth rate of an algorithm necessarily gives it a significant advantage. Figure 10-1 illustrated this phenomenon.

If the problem size is always small, you can probably ignore an algorithm's efficiency

Thus, in general, if the maximum size of a given problem is small, the time requirements of any two solutions for that problem likely will not differ significantly. If you know that your problem size will always be small, do not overanalyze; simply choose the algorithm that is easiest to understand, verify, and code.

Weigh the trade-offs between an algorithm's time requirements and its memory requirements

Frequently, when evaluating an algorithm's efficiency, you have to weigh carefully the trade-offs between a solution's execution time requirements and its memory requirements. You are rarely able to make a statement as strong as "This method is the best one for performing the task." A solution that requires a relatively small amount of computer time often also requires a relatively large amount of memory. It may not even be possible to say that one solution requires less time than another. Solution A may perform some components of the task faster than solution B, while solution B performs other components of the task faster than solution A. Often you must analyze the solutions in light of a particular application.

Compare algorithms for both style and efficiency

In summary, it is important to examine an algorithm for both style and efficiency. The analysis should focus only on gross differences in efficiency and not reward coding tricks that save milliseconds. Any finer differences in efficiency are likely to interact with coding issues, which you should not allow to interfere with the development of your programming style. If you find a method of solution that is significantly more efficient than others, you should select it, unless you know that the maximum problem size is quite small. If you will be solving only small problems, it is possible that a less efficient algorithm would be more appropriate. That is, other factors, such as the simplicity of the algorithm, could become more significant than minor differences in efficiency.

Order-of-magnitude analysis focuses on large problems

In fact, performing an order-of-magnitude analysis implicitly assumes that an algorithm will be used to solve large problems. This assumption allows you to focus on growth rates because, regardless of other factors, an algorithm with a slow growth rate will require less time than an algorithm with a fast growth rate, provided that the problems to be solved are sufficiently large.

The Efficiency of Searching Algorithms

As another example of order-of-magnitude analysis, consider the efficiency of two search algorithms: the sequential search and the binary search of an array.

Sequential search.   In a sequential search of an array of n items, you look at each item in turn, beginning with the first one, until either you find the desired item or you reach the end of the data collection. In the best case, the desired item is the first one that you examine, so only one comparison is necessary. Thus, in the best case, a sequential search is $O(1)$. In the worst case, the desired item is the last one you examine, so n comparisons are necessary. Thus, in the worst case, the algorithm is $O(n)$. In the average case, you would find the desired item in the middle of the collection, making $n/2$ comparisons. Thus, the algorithm is $O(n)$ in the average case.

Sequential search. Worst case: $O(n)$; average case: $O(n)$; best case: $O(1)$

     What is the algorithm's order when you do not find the desired item? Does the algorithm's order depend on whether or not the initial data is sorted? These questions are left for you in Self-Test Exercise 4 at the end of this chapter.

Binary search.   Is a binary search of an array more efficient than a sequential search? The binary search algorithm, which Chapter 3 presents, searches a sorted array for a particular item by repeatedly dividing the array in half. The algorithm determines which half the item must be in—if it is indeed present—and discards the other half. Thus, the binary search algorithm searches successively smaller arrays: The size of a given array is approximately one-half the size of the array previously searched.

     At each division, the algorithm makes a comparison. How many comparisons does the algorithm make when it searches an array of n items? The exact answer depends, of course, on where the sought-for item resides in the array. However, you can compute the maximum number of comparisons that a binary search requires—that is, the worst case. The number of comparisons is equal to the number of times that the algorithm divides the array in half. Suppose that $n = 2^k$ for some k. The search requires the following steps:

1. Inspect the middle item of an array of size n.

2. Inspect the middle item of an array of size $n/2$.

3. Inspect the middle item of an array of size $n/2^2$, and so on.

To inspect the middle item of an array, you must first divide the array in half. If you divide an array of n items in half, then divide one of those halves in half, and continue dividing halves until only one item remains, you will have performed k divisions. This is true because $n/2^k = 1$. (Remember, we assumed that $n = 2^k$.) In the worst case, the algorithm performs k divisions and, therefore, k comparisons. Because $n = 2^k$,

$$k = \log_2 n$$

Thus, the algorithm is $O(\log_2 n)$ in the worst case when $n = 2^k$.

What if n is not a power of 2? You can easily find the smallest k such that

$$2^{k-1} < n < 2^k$$

(For example, if n is 30, then $k = 5$, because $2^4 = 16 < 30 < 32 = 2^5$.) The algorithm still requires at most k divisions to obtain a subarray with one item. Now it follows that

$$k - 1 < \log_2 n < k$$

$$k < 1 + \log_2 n < k + 1$$

$$k = 1 + \log_2 n \text{ rounded down}$$

Binary search is $O(\log_2 n)$ in the worst case

Thus, the algorithm is still $O(\log_2 n)$ in the worst case when $n \neq 2^k$. In general, the algorithm is $O(\log_2 n)$ in the worst case for any n.

Is a binary search better than a sequential search? Much better! For example $\log_2 1{,}000{,}000 = 19$, so a sequential search of one million sorted items can require one million comparisons, but a binary search of the same items will require at most 20 comparisons. For large arrays, the binary search has an enormous advantage over a sequential search.

Realize, however, that maintaining the array in sorted order requires an overhead cost, which can be substantial. The next section examines the cost of sorting an array.

10.2 Sorting Algorithms and Their Efficiency

Sorting is a process that organizes a collection of data into either ascending[4] or descending order. The need for sorting arises in many situations. You may simply want to sort a collection of data before including it in a report. Often, however, you must perform a sort as an initialization step for certain algorithms. For example, searching for data is one of the most common tasks performed by computers. When the collection of data to be searched is large, an efficient method for searching—such as the binary search algorithm—is desirable. However, the binary search algorithm requires that the data be sorted. Thus, sorting the data is a step that must precede a binary search on a collection of data that is not already sorted. Good sorting algorithms, therefore, are quite valuable.

The sorts in this chapter are internal sorts

You can organize sorting algorithms into two categories. An **internal sort** requires that the collection of data fit entirely in the computer's main memory. The algorithms in this chapter are internal sorting algorithms. You use an

---

4. To allow for duplicate data items, "ascending" is used here to mean nondecreasing and "descending" to mean nonincreasing.

external sort when the collection of data will not fit in the computer's main memory all at once but must reside in secondary storage, such as on a disk.

The data items to be sorted might be integers, character strings, or even objects. It is easy to imagine the results of sorting a collection of integers or character strings, but consider a collection of objects. If each object contains only one data field, sorting the objects is really no different than sorting a collection of integers. However, when each object contains several data fields, you must know which data field determines the order of the entire object within the collection of data. This data field is called the **sort key**. For example, if the objects represent people, you might want to sort on their names, their ages, or their zip codes. Regardless of your choice of sort key, the sorting algorithm orders entire objects based on only one data field, the sort key.

For simplicity, this chapter assumes that the data items are instances of a class that has implemented the *Comparable* interface. The *Comparable* interface method *compareTo* returns either a negative integer, zero, or a positive integer based upon whether the sort key is less than, equal to, or greater than the sort key of the specified object. All algorithms in this chapter sort the data into ascending order. Modifying these algorithms to sort data into descending order is simple. Finally, each example assumes that the data resides in an array.

Selection Sort

Imagine some data that you can examine all at once. To sort it, you could select the largest item and put it in its place, select the next largest and put it in its place, and so on. For a card player, this process is analogous to looking at an entire hand of cards and ordering it by selecting cards one at a time in their proper order. The **selection sort** formalizes these intuitive notions. To sort an array into ascending order, you first search it for the largest item. Because you want the largest item to be in the last position of the array, you swap the last item with the largest item, even if these items happen to be identical. Now, ignoring the last—and largest—item of the array, you search the rest of the array for its largest item and swap it with its last item, which is the next-to-last item in the original array. You continue until you have selected and swapped $n - 1$ of the n items in the array. The remaining item, which is now in the first position of the array, is in its proper order, so it is not considered further.

Select the largest item

Figure 10-4 provides an example of a selection sort. Beginning with five integers, you select the largest—37—and swap it with the last integer—13. (As the items in this figure are ordered, they appear in boldface. This convention will be used throughout this chapter.) Next you select the largest integer—29—from among the first four integers in the array and swap it with the next-to-last integer in the array—13. Notice that the next selection—14—is already in its proper position, but the algorithm ignores this fact and performs a swap of 14 with itself. It is more efficient in general to occasionally perform an unnecessary swap than it is to continually ask whether the swap is necessary.

Shaded elements are selected;
boldface elements are in order.

Initial array:

| 29 | 10 | 14 | 37 | 13 |

After 1st swap:

| 29 | 10 | 14 | 13 | **37** |

After 2nd swap:

| 13 | 10 | 14 | **29** | **37** |

After 3rd swap:

| 13 | 10 | **14** | **29** | **37** |

After 4th swap:

| **10** | **13** | **14** | **29** | **37** |

FIGURE 10-4

A selection sort of an array of five integers

Finally, you select the 13 and swap it with the item in the second position of the array—10. The array is now sorted into ascending order.

A Java method that performs a selection sort on an array called *theArray* with n items follows:

```
public static <T extends Comparable<? super T>>
      void selectionSort(T[] theArray, int n) {
// ------------------------------------------------------
// Sorts the items in an array into ascending order.
// Precondition: theArray is an array of n items.
// Postcondition: theArray is sorted into
// ascending order.
// Calls: indexOfLargest.
// ------------------------------------------------------
  // last = index of the last item in the subarray of
  //        items yet to be sorted
  // largest = index of the largest item found

  for (int last = n-1; last >= 1; last--) {
    // Invariant: theArray[last+1..n-1] is sorted
    // and > theArray[0..last]

    // select largest item in theArray[0..last]
    int largest = indexOfLargest(theArray, last+1);

    // swap largest item theArray[largest] with
    // theArray[last]
    T temp = theArray[largest];
```

```
      theArray[largest] = theArray[last];
      theArray[last] = temp;
   }  // end for
}  // end selectionSort
```

The *selectionSort* method calls the following method:

```
private static <T extends Comparable<? super T>>
        int indexOfLargest(T[] theArray, int size) {
// --------------------------------------------------
// Finds the largest item in an array.
// Precondition: theArray is an array of size items;
// size >= 1.
// Postcondition: Returns the index of the largest
// item in the array.
// --------------------------------------------------
   int indexSoFar = 0; // index of largest item found so far

   // Invariant: theArray[indexSoFar]>=theArray[0..currIndex-1]
   for (int currIndex = 1; currIndex < size; ++currIndex) {
     if (theArray[currIndex].compareTo(theArray[indexSoFar])>0) {
        indexSoFar = currIndex;
     }  // end if
   } // end for

   return indexSoFar;  // index of largest item
}  // end indexOfLargest
```

Analysis.   As you can see from the previous algorithm, sorting in general compares, exchanges, or moves items. Depending on the programming language and implementation used for storing the data, the cost associated with each of these operations varies. For example, in Java, an array stores references to objects, not the objects themselves. Thus, moving or exchanging data is not expensive in Java, because only the references are moved or exchanged, rather than entire objects. Other languages, however, such as C++, could use an implementation in which the actual objects are stored in an array. In this case, moving and exchanging data becomes much more expensive since entire objects are actually moved around memory.

The comparison operation is typically more involved, since actual data values must be compared. In Java, one way to compare data values is through the implementation of the *java.util.Comparable* interface, and in particular, the *compareTo* method. In Java, the use of the *Comparable* interface provides what is referred to as the *natural ordering* for a class. Alternatively, you can create a class that implements the interface *java.util.Comparator*. It provides a method *compare* which imposes a *total ordering* on some collection of objects. These two approaches to implementing the element comparison are discussed later in this chapter. In either case, the comparison itself is usually based upon a portion of the object, that is, the sort key.

As a first step in analyzing sorting algorithms, you should count the move, exchange, and compare operations. In Java, the comparison operation is usually the most expensive and is thus often the only operation analyzed. However, since other programming languages may incur more expense in moving or exchanging data, we provide some analysis of these operations here. Generally, move, exchange, and compare operations are more expensive than the ones that control loops or manipulate array indexes, particularly when the data to be sorted is more complex than integers or characters. Thus, our approach ignores these less expensive operations. You should convince yourself that ignoring such operations does not affect our final result. (See Exercise 7.)

Clearly, the *for* loop in the method *selectionSort* executes $n - 1$ times. Thus, *selectionSort* calls the method *indexOfLargest* $n - 1$ times. Each call to *indexOfLargest* causes its loop to execute *last* times (that is, *size* $- 1$ times when *size* is *last* $+ 1$). Thus, the $n - 1$ calls to *indexOfLargest*, for values of *last* that range from $n - 1$ down to 1, cause the loop in *indexOfLargest* to execute a total of

$$(n - 1) + (n - 2) + \cdots + 1 = n * (n-1)/2$$

times. Because each execution of *indexOfLargest*'s loop performs one comparison, the calls to *indexOfLargest* require

$$n * (n-1)/2$$

comparisons.

At the end of the *for* loop in *selectionSort*, an exchange is performed between elements *theArray[largest]* and *theArray[last]*. Each exchange requires three assignments, or

$$3 * (n-1)$$

data moves.

Together, a selection sort of *n* items requires

$$n * (n-1)/2 + 3 * (n-1)$$

$$= n^2/2 + 5 * n/2 - 3$$

Selection sort is
$O(n^2)$

major operations. By applying the properties of growth-rate functions (see page 532), you can ignore low-order terms to get $O(n^2/2)$ and then ignore the multiplier $1/2$ to get $O(n^2)$. Thus, selection sort is $O(n^2)$.

Although a selection sort does not depend on the initial arrangement of the data, which is an advantage of this algorithm, it is appropriate only for small *n* because $O(n^2)$ grows rapidly. While the algorithm requires $O(n^2)$ comparisons, it requires only $O(n)$ data moves. A selection sort could be a good choice over other methods when data moves are costly but comparisons are not. As we mentioned earlier, there really is no such thing as an expensive data move in a normal sorting situation in Java, because it would surely be references, not entire objects, that are copied in the process of performing the move.

Bubble Sort

The next sorting algorithm is one that you may have seen already. That is precisely why it is analyzed here, because it is not a particularly good algorithm. The **bubble sort** compares adjacent items and exchanges them if they are out of order. This sort usually requires several passes over the data. During the first pass, you compare the first two items in the array. If they are out of order, you exchange them. You then compare the items in the next pair—that is, in positions 2 and 3 of the array. If they are out of order, you exchange them. You proceed, comparing and exchanging items two at a time until you reach the end of the array.

Figure 10-5a illustrates the first pass of a bubble sort of an array of five integers. You compare the items in the first pair—29 and 10—and exchange them because they are out of order. Next you consider the second pair—29 and 14—and exchange these items because they are out of order. The items in the third pair—29 and 37—are in order, and so you do not exchange them. Finally, you exchange the items in the last pair—37 and 13.

Although the array is not sorted after the first pass, the largest item has "bubbled" to its proper position at the end of the array. During the second pass of the bubble sort, you return to the beginning of the array and consider pairs of items in exactly the same manner as the first pass. You do not, however, include the last—and largest—item of the array. That is, the second pass considers the first $n - 1$ items of the array. After the second pass, the second largest item in the array will be in its proper place in the next-to-last position of the array, as Figure 10-5b illustrates. Now, ignoring the last two items, which are in order, you continue with subsequent passes until the array is sorted.

> When you order successive pairs of items, the largest item bubbles to the top (end) of the array

> Bubble sort usually requires several passes through the array

Although a bubble sort requires at most $n - 1$ passes to sort the array, fewer passes might be possible to sort a particular array. Thus, you could terminate the process if no exchanges occur during any pass. The following Java method *bubbleSort* uses a flag to signal when an exchange occurs during a particular pass.

(a) Pass 1   (b) Pass 2

Initial array:

29	10	14	37	13

10	14	29	13	37

10	29	14	37	13

10	14	29	13	37

10	14	29	37	13

10	14	29	13	37

10	14	29	37	13

10	14	13	29	37

10	14	29	13	37

FIGURE 10-5

The first two passes of a bubble sort of an array of five integers: (a) pass 1; (b) pass 2

```
public static <T extends Comparable<? super T>>
        void bubbleSort(T[] theArray, int n) {
// --------------------------------------------------
// Sorts the items in an array into ascending order.
// Precondition: theArray is an array of n items.
// Postcondition: theArray is sorted into ascending
// order.
// --------------------------------------------------
   boolean sorted = false;  // false when swaps occur

   for (int pass = 1; (pass < n) && !sorted; ++pass) {
     // Invariant: theArray[n+1-pass..n-1] is sorted
     //            and > theArray[0..n-pass]
     sorted = true;  // assume sorted
     for (int index = 0; index < n-pass; ++index) {
       // Invariant: theArray[0..index-1] <= theArray[index]
       int nextIndex = index + 1;
       if (theArray[index].compareTo(theArray[nextIndex]) > 0) {
         // exchange items
         T temp = theArray[index];
         theArray[index] = theArray[nextIndex];
         theArray[nextIndex] = temp;
         sorted = false;  // signal exchange
       } // end if
     } // end for

     // Assertion: theArray[0..n-pass-1] < theArray[n-pass]
   } // end for
} // end bubbleSort
```

Analysis. As was noted earlier, the bubble sort requires at most $n-1$ passes through the array. Pass 1 requires $n-1$ comparisons and at most $n-1$ exchanges; pass 2 requires $n-2$ comparisons and at most $n-2$ exchanges. In general, pass i requires $n-i$ comparisons and at most $n-i$ exchanges. Therefore, in the worst case, a bubble sort will require a total of

$$(n-1) + (n-2) + \cdots + 1 = n * (n-1)/2$$

comparisons and the same number of exchanges. Recall that each exchange requires three data moves. Thus, altogether there are

$$2 * n * (n-1) = 2 * n^2 - 2 * n$$

Bubble sort. Worst case: $O(n^2)$; best case: $O(n)$

major operations in the worst case. Therefore, the bubble sort algorithm is $O(n^2)$ in the worst case.

The best case occurs when the original data is already sorted: *bubbleSort* uses one pass, during which $n-1$ comparisons and no exchanges occur. Thus, the bubble sort is $O(n)$ in the best case.

Insertion Sort

Imagine once again arranging a hand of cards, but now you pick up one card at a time and insert it into its proper position; in this case you are performing an **insertion sort.** Chapter 5 introduced the insertion sort algorithm in the context of a linked list: You can create a sorted linked list from a file of unsorted integers, for example, by repeatedly calling a method that inserts an integer into its proper sorted order in a linked list.

You can use the insertion sort strategy to sort items that reside in an array. This version of the insertion sort partitions the array into two regions: sorted and unsorted, as Figure 10-6 depicts. Initially, the entire array is the unsorted region, just as the cards dealt to you sit in an unsorted pile on the table. At each step, the insertion sort takes the first item of the unsorted region and places it into its correct position in the sorted region. This step is analogous to taking a card from the table and inserting it into its proper position in your hand. The first step, however, is trivial: Moving *theArray[0]* from the unsorted region to the sorted region really does not require moving data. Therefore, you can omit this first step by considering the initial sorted region to be *theArray[0]* and the initial unsorted region to be *theArray[1..n-1]*. The fact that the items in the sorted region are sorted among themselves is an invariant of the algorithm. Because at each step the size of the sorted region grows by 1 and the size of the unsorted region shrinks by 1, the entire array will be sorted when the algorithm terminates.

Take each item from the unsorted region and insert it into its correct order in the sorted region

Figure 10-7 illustrates an insertion sort of an array of five integers. Initially, the sorted region is *theArray[0]*, which is 29, and the unsorted region is the rest of the array. You take the first item in the unsorted region—the 10—and insert it into its proper position in the sorted region. This insertion requires you to shift array items to make room for the inserted item. You then take the first item in the new unsorted region—the 14—and insert it into its proper position in the sorted region, and so on.

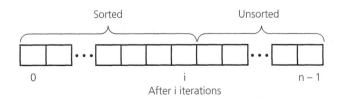

FIGURE 10-6

An insertion sort partitions the array into two regions

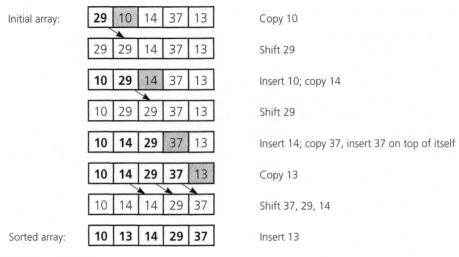

Initial array:

| 29 | 10 | 14 | 37 | 13 |

Copy 10

| 29 | 29 | 14 | 37 | 13 |

Shift 29

| 10 | 29 | 14 | 37 | 13 |

Insert 10; copy 14

| 10 | 29 | 29 | 37 | 13 |

Shift 29

| 10 | 14 | 29 | 37 | 13 |

Insert 14; copy 37, insert 37 on top of itself

| 10 | 14 | 29 | 37 | 13 |

Copy 13

| 10 | 14 | 14 | 29 | 37 |

Shift 37, 29, 14

Sorted array:

| 10 | 13 | 14 | 29 | 37 |

Insert 13

FIGURE 10-7

An insertion sort of an array of five integers

A Java method that performs an insertion sort on an array of *n* items follows:

```java
public static <T extends Comparable<? super T>>
       void insertionSort(T[] theArray, int n) {
// ----------------------------------------------------
// Sorts the items in an array into ascending order.
// Precondition: theArray is an array of n items.
// Postcondition: theArray is sorted into ascending
// order.
// ----------------------------------------------------
   // unsorted = first index of the unsorted region,
   // loc = index of insertion in the sorted region,
   // nextItem = next item in the unsorted region

   // initially, sorted region is theArray[0],
   //            unsorted region is theArray[1..n-1];
   // in general, sorted region is theArray[0..unsorted-1],
   //            unsorted region is theArray[unsorted..n-1]

   for (int unsorted = 1; unsorted < n; ++unsorted) {
     // Invariant: theArray[0..unsorted-1] is sorted

     // find the right position (loc) in
     // theArray[0..unsorted] for theArray[unsorted],
     // which is the first item in the unsorted
     // region; shift, if necessary, to make room
     T nextItem = theArray[unsorted];
```

```
    int loc = unsorted;

    while ((loc > 0) &&
           (theArray[loc-1].compareTo(nextItem) > 0)) {
      // shift theArray[loc-1] to the right
      theArray[loc] = theArray[loc-1];
      loc--;
    } // end while
    // Assertion: theArray[loc] is where nextItem belongs
    // insert nextItem into sorted region
    theArray[loc] = nextItem;
  } // end for
} // end insertionSort
```

Analysis.   The outer *for* loop in the method *insertionSort* executes $n - 1$ times. This loop contains an inner *for* loop that executes at most *unsorted* times for values of *unsorted* that range from 1 to $n - 1$. Thus, in the worst case, the algorithm's comparison occurs

$$1 + 2 + \cdots + (n - 1) = n * (n - 1)/2$$

times. In addition, the inner loop moves data items at most the same number of times.

The outer loop moves data items twice per iteration, or $2 * (n - 1)$ times. Together, there are

$$n * (n - 1) + 2 * (n - 1) = n^2 + n - 2$$

major operations in the worst case.

Therefore, the insertion sort algorithm is $O(n^2)$ in the worst case. For small arrays—say, fewer than 25 items—the simplicity of the insertion sort makes it an appropriate choice. For large arrays, however, an insertion sort can be prohibitively inefficient.

> Insertion sort is $O(n^2)$ in the worst case

Mergesort

Two important divide-and-conquer sorting algorithms, mergesort and quick-sort, have elegant recursive formulations and are highly efficient. The presentations here are in the context of sorting arrays, but note that mergesort generalizes to external files. It will be convenient to express the algorithms in terms of the array *theArray[first..last]*.

> Divide and conquer

Mergesort is a recursive sorting algorithm that always gives the same performance, regardless of the initial order of the array items. Suppose that you divide the array into halves, sort each half, and then **merge** the sorted halves into one sorted array, as Figure 10-8 illustrates. In the figure, the halves <1, 4, 8> and <2, 3> are merged to form the array <1, 2, 3, 4, 8>. This merge step compares an item in one half of the array with an item in the other half and moves the smaller item to a temporary array. This process continues until there are no more items to consider in one half. At that time, you simply

> Halve the array, recursively sort its halves, and then merge the halves

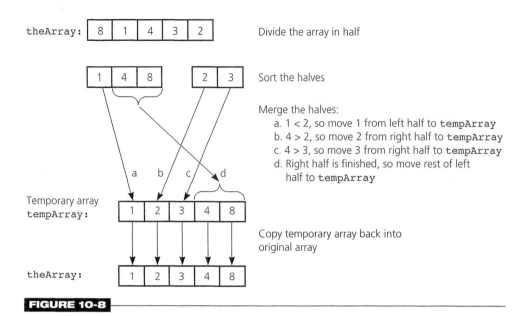

theArray: Divide the array in half

Sort the halves

Merge the halves:
a. 1 < 2, so move 1 from left half to `tempArray`
b. 4 > 2, so move 2 from right half to `tempArray`
c. 4 > 3, so move 3 from right half to `tempArray`
d. Right half is finished, so move rest of left half to `tempArray`

Temporary array tempArray:

Copy temporary array back into original array

theArray:

FIGURE 10-8

A mergesort with an auxiliary temporary array

move the remaining items to the temporary array. Finally, you copy the temporary array back into the original array.

Although the merge step of mergesort produces a sorted array, how do you sort the array halves prior to the merge step? Mergesort sorts the array halves by using mergesort—that is, by calling itself recursively. Thus, the pseudocode for mergesort is

```
+mergesort(inout theArray:ItemArray,
           in first:integer, in last:integer)
// Sorts theArray[first..last] by
//    1. sorting the first half of the array
//    2. sorting the second half of the array
//    3. merging the two sorted halves

  if (first < last) {
    mid = (first + last)/2    // get midpoint
    // sort theArray[first..mid]
    mergesort(theArray, first, mid)
    // sort theArray[mid+1..last]
    mergesort(theArray, mid + 1, last)
    // merge sorted halves theArray[first..mid]
    // and theArray[mid+1..last]
    merge(theArray, first, mid, last)
  } // end if
  // if first >= last, there is nothing to do
```

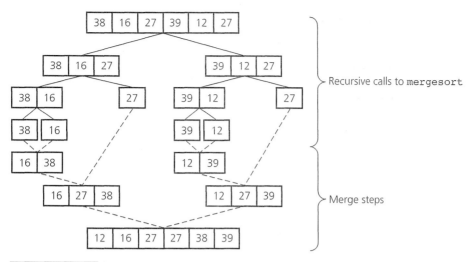

FIGURE 10-9

A mergesort of an array of six integers

Clearly, most of the effort in the mergesort algorithm is in the merge step, but does this algorithm actually sort? The recursive calls continue dividing the array into pieces until each piece contains only one item; obviously an array of one item is sorted. The algorithm then merges these small pieces into larger sorted pieces until one sorted array results. Figure 10-9 illustrates both the recursive calls and the merge steps in a mergesort of an array of six integers.

The following Java methods implement the mergesort algorithm. To sort an array *theArray* of *n* items, you would invoke the method *mergesort* by writing *mergesort(theArray)*. Notice that this method creates a reusable temporary array that can be used later on for the merge. It then calls the recursive function *mergesort(theArray, tempArray, 0, theArray.length-1)* with this temporary array to actually complete the sort.

```
public static<T extends Comparable<? super T>>
       void mergesort(T[ ] theArray) {
// Declare temporary array used for merge, must do
// unchecked cast from Comparable<?>[] to T[]

  T[] tempArray = (T[])new Comparable<?>[theArray.length];
  mergesort(theArray, tempArray, 0, theArray.length - 1 );
} // end mergesort

private static<T extends Comparable<? super T>>
        void merge(T[] theArray, T[] tempArray,
                  int first, int mid, int last) {
```

```
// ------------------------------------------------------------
// Merges two sorted array segments theArray[first..mid] and
// theArray[mid+1..last] into one sorted array.
// Precondition: first <= mid <= last. The subarrays
// theArray[first..mid] and theArray[mid+1..last] are
// each sorted in increasing order.
// Postcondition: theArray[first..last] is sorted.
// Implementation note: This method merges the two
// subarrays into a temporary array and copies the result
// into the original array theArray.
// ------------------------------------------------------------

  // initialize the local indexes to indicate the subarrays
  int first1 = first;    // beginning of first subarray
  int last1  = mid;      // end of first subarray
  int first2 = mid + 1;  // beginning of second subarray
  int last2  = last;     // end of second subarray
  // while both subarrays are not empty, copy the
  // smaller item into the temporary array
  int index = first1;    // next available location in
                         // tempArray

 while ((first1 <= last1) && (first2 <= last2)) {
   // Invariant: tempArray[first1..index-1] is in order
   if (theArray[first1].compareTo(theArray[first2])<0) {
     tempArray[index] = theArray[first1];
     first1++;
   }
   else {
     tempArray[index] = theArray[first2];
     first2++;
   }  // end if
   index++;
 }  // end while

 // finish off the nonempty subarray

 // finish off the first subarray, if necessary
 while (first1 <= last1) {
   // Invariant: tempArray[first1..index-1] is in order
   tempArray[index] = theArray[first1];
   first1++;
   index++;
 }  // end while
```

```
    // finish off the second subarray, if necessary
    while (first2 <= last2) {
      // Invariant: tempArray[first1..index-1] is in order
      tempArray[index] = theArray[first2];
      first2++;
      index++;
    }  // end while

    // copy the result back into the original array
    for (index = first; index <= last; ++index) {
      theArray[index] = tempArray[index];
    }  // end for
  }  // end merge

public static <T extends Comparable<? super T>>
        void mergesort(T[] theArray, T[] tempArray,
                   int first, int last) {
// -------------------------------------------------------
// Sorts the items in an array into ascending order.
// Precondition: theArray[first..last] is an array.
// Postcondition: theArray[first..last] is sorted in
// ascending order.
// Calls: merge.
// -------------------------------------------------------
  if (first < last) {
    // sort each half
    int mid = (first + last)/2;    // index of midpoint
    // sort left half theArray[first..mid]
    mergesort(theArray, tempArray, first, mid);
    // sort right half theArray[mid+1..last]
    mergesort(theArray, tempArray, mid+1, last);

    // merge the two halves
    merge(theArray, tempArray, first, mid, last);
  }  // end if
}  // end mergesort
```

Analysis.   Because the merge step of the algorithm requires the most effort, let's begin the analysis there. Each merge step merges *theArray[first..mid]* and *theArray[mid+1..last]*. Figure 10-10 provides an example of a merge step that requires the maximum number of comparisons. If the total number of items in the two array segments to be merged is n, then merging the segments requires at most $n-1$ comparisons. (For example, in Figure 10-10 there are six items in the segments and five comparisons.) In addition, there are n moves from the original array to the temporary array, and n moves from the temporary array back to the original array. Thus, each merge step requires $3 * n - 1$ major operations.

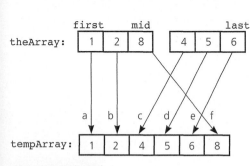

Merge the halves:

a. 1 < 4, so move 1 from `theArray[first..mid]` to `tempArray`
b. 2 < 4, so move 2 from `theArray[first..mid]` to `tempArray`
c. 8 > 4, so move 4 from `theArray[mid+1..last]` to `tempArray`
d. 8 > 5, so move 5 from `theArray[mid+1..last]` to `tempArray`
e. 8 > 6, so move 6 from `theArray[mid+1..last]` to `tempArray`
f. `theArray[mid+1..last]` is finished, so move 8 to `tempArray`

FIGURE 10-10

A worst-case instance of the merge step in *mergesort*

Each call to `mergesort` recursively calls itself twice. As Figure 10-11 illustrates, if the original call to `mergesort` is at level 0, two calls to `mergesort` occur at level 1 of the recursion. Each of these calls then calls `mergesort` twice, so four calls to `mergesort` occur at level 2 of the recursion, and so on. How many levels of recursion are there? We can count them as follows.

Each call to `mergesort` halves the array. Halving the array the first time produces two pieces. The next recursive calls to `mergesort` halve each of these two pieces to produce four pieces of the original array; the next recursive calls halve each of these four pieces to produce eight pieces, and so on. The recursive calls continue until the array pieces each contain one item—that is, until there are n pieces, where n is the number of items in the original array. If n is a power of $2(n = 2^k)$, then the recursion goes $k = \log_2 n$ levels deep. For example, in Figure 10-11, there are three levels of recursive calls to `mergesort` because the original array contains eight items, and $8 = 2^3$. If n is not a power of 2, there are $1 + \log_2 n$ (rounded down) levels of recursive calls to `mergesort`.

The original call to `mergesort` (at level 0) calls `merge` once. When called, `merge` merges all n items and requires $3 * n - 1$ operations, as was shown earlier. At level 1 of the recursion, two calls to `mergesort`, and hence to `merge`,

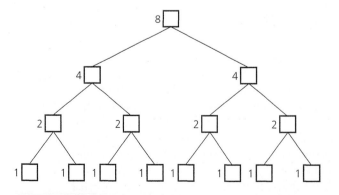

Level 0: mergesort 8 items

Level 1: 2 calls to mergesort with 4 items each

Level 2: 4 calls to mergesort with 2 items each

Level 3: 8 calls to mergesort with 1 item each

FIGURE 10-11

Levels of recursive calls to *mergesort*, given an array of eight items occur. Each of these two calls to `merge` merges $n/2$ items and requires $3 * (n/2) - 1$ operations. Together these two calls to `merge` require $2 * (3 * (n/2) - 1)$, or $3 * n - 2$ operations. At level m of the recursion, 2^m calls to `merge` occur; each of these calls merges $n/2^m$ items and so requires $3 * (n/2^m) - 1$ operations. Together the 2^m calls to `merge` require $3 * n - 2^m$ operations. Thus, each level of the recursion requires $O(n)$ operations. Because there are either $\log_2 n$ or $1 + \log_2 n$ levels, `mergesort` is $O(n * \log_2 n)$ in both the worst and average cases. You should look at Figure 10-3 again to convince yourself that $O(n * \log_2 n)$ is significantly faster than $O(n^2)$.

Mergesort is $O(n * \log_2 n)$

Although mergesort is an extremely efficient algorithm with respect to time, it does have one drawback: To perform the step

```
Merge sorted halves theArray[first..mid]
    and theArray[mid+1..last]
```

the algorithm requires an auxiliary array whose size equals the size of the original array. In Java, this auxiliary array is simply an array of references and hence has little impact. Other programming languages, however, such as C++, actually store the data items in the array. With such languages, this requirement might not be acceptable in situations where storage is limited.

Mergesort requires a second array as large as the original array

Quicksort

Consider the first two steps of the solution to the problem of finding the kth smallest item of the array `theArray[first..last]` that was discussed in Chapter 3:

Another divide-and-conquer algorithm

```
Choose a pivot item p from theArray[first..last]
Partition the items of theArray[first..last] about p
```

Recall that this partition, which is pictured again in Figure 10-12, has the property that all items in S_1 = `theArray[first..pivotIndex-1]` are less than the pivot p, and all items in S_2 = `theArray[pivotIndex+1..last]` are greater than or equal to p. Although this property does not imply that the array is sorted, it does imply an extremely useful fact: The items in positions `first` through `pivotIndex` $-$ 1 remain in positions `first` through `pivotIndex` $-$ 1

Quicksort partitions an array into items that are less than the pivot and those that are greater than or equal to the pivot

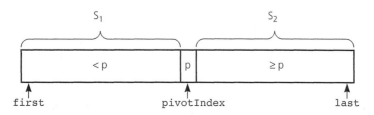

FIGURE 10-12

A partition about a pivot

when the array is properly sorted, although their positions relative to one another may change. Similarly, the items in positions *pivotIndex* + 1 through *last* will remain in positions *pivotIndex* + 1 through *last* when the array is sorted, although their relative positions may change. Finally, the pivot item remains in its position in the final, sorted array.

Partitioning places the pivot in its correct position within the array

The partition induces relationships among the array items that are the ingredients of a recursive solution. Arranging the array items around the pivot p generates two smaller sorting problems—sort the left section of the array (S_1), and sort the right section of the array (S_2). The relationships between the pivot and the array items imply that once you solve the left and right sorting problems, you will have solved the original sorting problem. That is, partitioning the array before making the recursive calls places the pivot in its correct position and ensures that when the smaller array segments are sorted, their items will be in the proper relation to the rest of the array. Also, the quicksort algorithm will eventually terminate: The left and right sorting problems are indeed smaller problems and are each closer than the original sorting problem to the base case—which is an array containing one item—because the pivot is not part of either S_1 or S_2.

The pseudocode for the quicksort algorithm follows:

```
+quicksort(inout theArray:ItemArray,
          in first:integer, in last:integer)
// Sorts theArray[first..last].

  if (first < last) {
    Choose a pivot item p from theArray[first..last]
    Partition the items of theArray[first..last] about p
    // the partition is theArray[first..pivotIndex..last]

    // sort S₁
    quicksort(theArray, first, pivotIndex-1)
    // sort S₂
    quicksort(theArray, pivotIndex+1, last)
  }  // end if
  // if first >= last, there is nothing to do
```

It is worth contrasting *quicksort* with the pseudocode method given for the kth smallest integer problem in Chapter 3:

```
+kSmall(in k:integer, in theArray:ItemArray,
        in first:integer, in last:integer):ItemType
// Returns the kᵗʰ smallest value in theArray[first..last].

  Choose a pivot item p from theArray[first..last]
  Partition the items of theArray[first..last] about p
  if (k < pivotIndex - first + 1) {
    return kSmall(k, theArray, first, pivotIndex-1)
  }
```

```
else if (k == pivotIndex - first + 1) {
  return p
}
else {
  return kSmall(k-(pivotIndex-first+1),
              theArray, pivotIndex+1, last)
}  // end if
```

Note that *kSmall* is called recursively only on the section of the array that contains the desired item, and it is not called at all if the desired item is the pivot. On the other hand, *quicksort* is called recursively on both unsorted sections of the array. Figure 10-13 illustrates this difference.

Difference between
kSmall and
quicksort

Using an invariant to develop a partition algorithm. Now consider the partition method that both *kSmall* and *quicksort* must call. Partitioning an array section about a pivot item is actually the most difficult part of these two problems.

The partition method will receive an array segment *theArray [first..last]* as an argument. The method must arrange the items of the array segment into two regions: S_1, the set of items less than the pivot, and S_2, the set of items greater than or equal to the pivot. The method arranges the array so that S_1 is *theArray[first..pivotIndex-1]* and S_2 is *theArray [pivotIndex+1..last]*, as you saw in Figure 10-12.

What pivot should you use? If the items in the array are arranged randomly, you can choose a pivot at random. For example, you can choose *theArray[first]* as the pivot. (The choice of pivot will be discussed in more detail later.) While you are

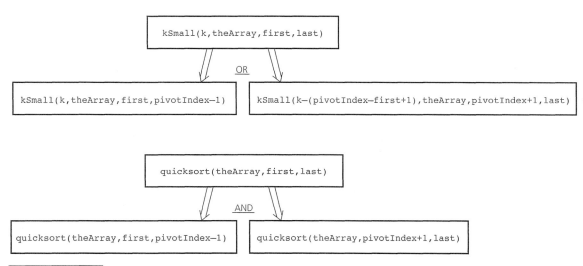

FIGURE 10-13

kSmall versus *quicksort*

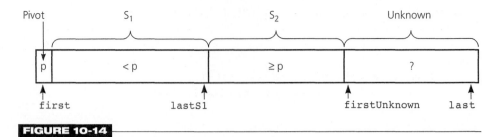

FIGURE 10-14

Invariant for the partition algorithm

Place your choice of pivot in **theArray[first]** before partitioning

developing the partition, it is convenient to place the pivot in the `theArray[first]` position, regardless of which pivot you choose.

The items that await placement into either S_1 or S_2 are in another region of the array, called the unknown region. Thus, you should view the array as shown in Figure 10-14. The array indexes `first`, `lastS₁`, `firstUnknown`, and `last` divide the array as just described. The relationships between the pivot and the items in the unknown region—which is `theArray[firstUnknown..last]`—are, simply, unknown!

Throughout the entire partitioning process, the following is true:

Invariant for the partition algorithm

The items in the region S_1 are all less than the pivot, and those in S_2 are all greater than or equal to the pivot.

This statement is the invariant for the partition algorithm. For the invariant to be true at the start of the partition algorithm, the array's indexes must be initialized as follows so that the unknown region spans all of the array segment to be partitioned except the pivot:

Initially, all items except the pivot **theArray[first]** constitute the unknown region

```
lastS₁ = first
firstUnknown = first + 1
```

Figure 10-15 shows the initial status of the array.

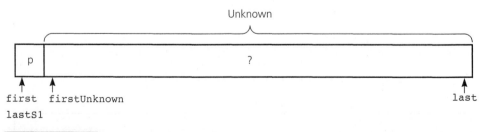

FIGURE 10-15

Initial state of the array

At each step of the partition algorithm, you examine one item of the unknown region, determine in which of the two regions, S_1 or S_2, it belongs, and place it there. Thus, the size of the unknown region decreases by 1 at each step. The algorithm terminates when the size of the unknown region reaches 0—that is, when *firstUnknown > last*.

The following pseudocode describes the partitioning algorithm:

```
+partition(inout theArray:ItemArray,
          in first:integer, in last:integer)
// Returns the index of the pivot element after
// partitioning theArray[first..last].

  // initialize
  Choose the pivot and swap it with theArray[first]
  p = theArray[first]        // p is the pivot
  lastS₁ = first             // set S₁ and S₂ to empty
  firstUnknown = first + 1   // set unknown region
                             // to theArray[first+1..last]
  // determine the regions S₁ and S₂
  while (firstUnknown <= last) {
    // consider the placement of the "leftmost"
    // item in the unknown region
    if (theArray[firstUnknown] < p) {
      Move theArray[firstUnknown] into S₁
    }
    else {
      Move theArray[firstUnknown] into S₂
    }  // end if
  }  // end while
  // place pivot in proper position between
  // S₁ and S₂, and mark its new location
  Swap theArray[first] with theArray[lastS₁]
  return lastS₁ // the index of the pivot element
```

The partition
algorithm

The algorithm is straightforward enough, but its move operations need clarifying. Consider the two possible actions that you need to take at each iteration of the *while* loop:

Move *theArray[firstUnknown]* into S_1. S_1 and the unknown region are, in general, not adjacent: S_2 is between the two regions. However, you can perform the required move efficiently. You swap *theArray[firstUnknown]* with the first item of S_2—which is *theArray[lastS₁ + 1]*, as Figure 10-16 illustrates. Then you increment *lastS₁* by 1. The item that was in *theArray [firstUnknown]* will then be at the rightmost position of S_1. What about the item of S_2 that was moved to *theArray[firstUnknown]*? If you increment *firstUnknown* by 1, that item becomes the rightmost member of S_2. Thus, you should perform the following steps to move *theArray[firstUnknown]* into S_1:

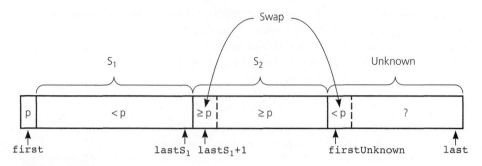

FIGURE 10-16

Moving `theArray[firstUnknown]` into S_1 by swapping it with `theArray[lastS1+1]` and by incrementing both `lastS1` and `firstUnknown`

```
Swap theArray[firstUnknown] with theArray[lastS₁+1]
Increment lastS₁
Increment firstUnknown
```

This strategy works even when S_2 is empty. In that case, $lastS_1 + 1$ equals `firstUnknown`, and thus the swap simply exchanges an item with itself. *This move preserves the invariant.*

Move `theArray[firstUnknown]` into S_2. This move is simple to accomplish. Recall that the rightmost boundary of the region S_2 is at position `firstUnknown` − 1; that is, regions S_2 and the unknown region are adjacent, as Figure 10-17 illustrates. Thus, to move `theArray[firstUnknown]` into S_2, simply increment `firstUnknown` by 1: S_2 expands to the right. *This move preserves the invariant.*

After you have moved all items from the unknown region into S_1 and S_2, one final task remains. You must place the pivot between the segments S_1 and S_2. Observe that `theArray[lastS₁]` is the rightmost item in S_1. By interchanging this item with the pivot, which is `theArray[first]`, you will place the pivot in its correct location. Then the statement

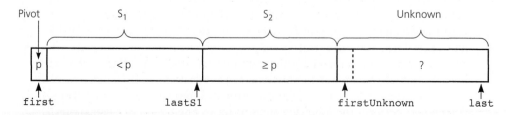

FIGURE 10-17

Moving `theArray[firstUnknown]` into S_2 by incrementing `firstUnknown`

return lastS₁

returns the location of the pivot. You can use this index to determine the boundaries of S_1 and S_2. Figure 10-18 traces the partition algorithm for an array of six integers when the pivot is the first item.

Before continuing the implementation of quicksort, we will establish the correctness of the partition algorithm by using invariants. Again, the loop invariant for the algorithm is

> *All items in S_1 (theArray[first+1..lastS₁]) are less than the pivot, and all items in S_2 (theArray[lastS₁+1..firstUnknown-1]) are greater than or equal to the pivot.*

Recall that when you use invariants to establish the correctness of an iterative algorithm, a four-step process is required:

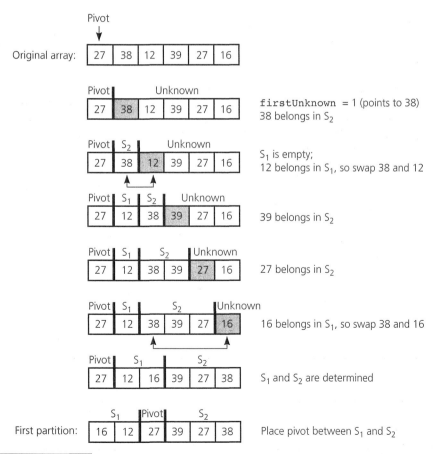

FIGURE 10-18

Developing the first partition of an array when the pivot is the first item

The proof that the partition algorithm is correct uses an invariant and requires four steps

1. The invariant must be true initially, before the loop begins execution. In the partition algorithm, before the loop that swaps array items is entered, the pivot is `theArray[first]`, the unknown region is `theArray[first+1..last]`, and S_1 and S_2 are empty. The invariant is clearly true initially.

2. An execution of the loop must preserve the invariant. That is, if the invariant is true before any given iteration of the loop, you must show that it is true after the iteration. In the partition algorithm, at each iteration of the loop a single item moves from the unknown region into either S_1 or S_2, depending on whether or not the item is less than the pivot. Thus, if the invariant was true before the move, it will remain true after the move.

3. The invariant must capture the correctness of the algorithm. That is, you must show that if the invariant is true when the loop terminates, the algorithm is correct. In the partition algorithm, the termination condition is that the unknown region is empty. But if the unknown region is empty, each item of `theArray[first+1..last]` must be in either S_1 or S_2—in which case the invariant implies that the partition algorithm has done what it was supposed to do.

4. The loop must terminate. That is, you must show that the loop will terminate after a finite number of iterations. In the partition algorithm, the size of the unknown region decreases by 1 at each iteration. Therefore, the unknown region becomes empty after a finite number of iterations, and thus the termination condition for the loop will be met.

The following Java methods implement the quicksort algorithm. The method *choosePivot* enables you to try various pivots easily. To sort an array *theArray* of *n* items, you invoke the method *quicksort* by writing `quicksort(theArray, 0, n-1)`.

```
private static <T extends Comparable<? super T>>
        void choosePivot(T[] theArray, int first, int last) {
// ---------------------------------------------------------
// Chooses a pivot for quicksort's partition algorithm and
// swaps it with the first item in an array.
// Precondition: theArray[first..last] where first <= last.
// Postcondition: theArray[first] is the pivot.
// ---------------------------------------------------------
// Implementation left as an exercise.
}  // end choosePivot
```

```
private static <T extends Comparable<? super T>>
        int partition(T[] theArray, int first, int last) {
// ------------------------------------------------------------
// Partitions an array for quicksort.
// Precondition: theArray[first..last] where first <= last.
// Postcondition: Returns the index of the pivot element of
// theArray[first..last]. Upon completion of the method,
// this will be the index value lastS1 such that
//     S1 = theArray[first..lastS1-1] <  pivot
//          theArray[lastS1]          == pivot
//     S2 = theArray[lastS1+1..last]  >= pivot
// Calls: choosePivot.
// ------------------------------------------------------------
  // tempItem is used to swap elements in the array
  T tempItem;
  // place pivot in theArray[first]
  choosePivot(theArray, first, last);
  T pivot = theArray[first];   // reference pivot

  // initially, everything but pivot is in unknown
  int lastS1 = first;          // index of last item in S1

  // move one item at a time until unknown region is empty
  // firstUnknown is the index of first item in unknown region

  for (int firstUnknown = first + 1; firstUnknown <= last;
                              ++firstUnknown) {
    // Invariant: theArray[first+1..lastS1] < pivot
    //            theArray[lastS1+1..firstUnknown-1] >= pivot
    // move item from unknown to proper region
    if (theArray[firstUnknown].compareTo(pivot) < 0) {
      // item from unknown belongs in S1
      ++lastS1;
      tempItem = theArray[firstUnknown];
      theArray[firstUnknown] = theArray[lastS1];
      theArray[lastS1] = tempItem;
    }  // end if
  // else item from unknown belongs in S2
  }  // end for

  // place pivot in proper position and mark its location
  tempItem = theArray[first];
  theArray[first] = theArray[lastS1];
  theArray[lastS1] = tempItem;
  return lastS1;
}  // end partition
```

```
public static <T extends Comparable<? super T>>
        void quickSort(T[] theArray, int first, int last) {

// -----------------------------------------------------------
// Sorts the items in an array into ascending order.
// Precondition: theArray[first..last] is an array.
// Postcondition: theArray[first..last] is sorted.
// Calls: partition.
// -----------------------------------------------------------

  int pivotIndex;

  if (first < last) {
    // create the partition: S1, Pivot, S2
    pivotIndex = partition(theArray, first, last);

    // sort regions S1 and S2
    quickSort(theArray, first, pivotIndex-1);
    quickSort(theArray, pivotIndex+1, last);
  }  // end if
}  // end quickSort
```

In the analysis to follow, you will learn that it is desirable to avoid a pivot that makes either S_1 or S_2 empty. A good choice of pivot is one that is near the median of the array items. Exercise 20 at the end of this chapter considers this choice of pivot.

As you can see, *quicksort* and *mergesort* are similar in spirit, but whereas *quicksort* does its work before its recursive calls, *mergesort* does its work after its recursive calls. That is, while *quicksort* has the form

```
+quicksort(inout theArray:ItemArray,
        in first:integer, in last:integer)

  if (first < last) {
    Prepare theArray for recursive calls
    quicksort(S₁ region of theArray)
    quicksort(S₂ region of theArray)
        }  // end if
```

mergesort has the general form

```
+mergesort(inout theArray:ItemArray,
        in first:integer, in last:integer)
```

```
if (first < last) {
  mergesort(Left half of theArray)
  mergesort(Right half of theArray)
  Tidy up array after the recursive calls
}  // end if
```

The preparation in `quicksort` is to partition the array into regions S_1 and S_2. The algorithm then sorts S_1 and S_2 independently, because every item in S_1 belongs to the left of every item in S_2. In `mergesort`, on the other hand, no work is done before the recursive calls: The algorithm sorts each half of the array with respect to itself. However, the algorithm must still deal with the interaction between the items in the two halves. That is, the algorithm must merge the two halves of the array after the recursive calls.

Analysis.   The major effort in the `quicksort` method occurs during the partitioning step. As you consider each item in the unknown region, you compare `theArray[firstUnknown]` with the pivot and move `theArray[firstUnknown]` into either S_1 or S_2. It is possible for one of S_1 or S_2 to remain empty. For example, if the pivot is the smallest item in the array segment, S_1 will remain empty. This occurrence is the worst case because S_2 decreases in size by only 1 at each recursive call to `quicksort`. Thus, the maximum number of recursive calls to `quicksort` will occur.

Notice what happens when the array is already sorted into ascending order and you choose the first array item as the pivot. Figure 10-19 shows the results of the first call to `partition` for this situation. The pivot is the smallest item in the

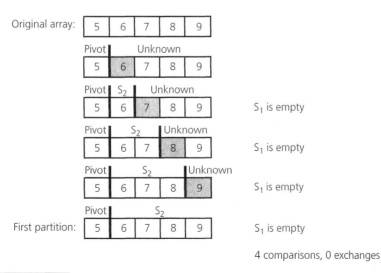

4 comparisons, 0 exchanges

FIGURE 10-19

A worst-case partitioning with `quicksort`

quicksort is slow when the array is already sorted and you choose the smallest item as the pivot

array, and S_1 remains empty. In this case, *partition* requires $n - 1$ comparisons to partition the n items in this array. On the next recursive call to *quicksort*, *partition* is passed $n - 1$ items, so it will require $n - 2$ comparisons to partition them. Again, S_1, will remain empty. Because the array segment that *quicksort* considers at each level of recursion decreases in size by only 1, $n - 1$ levels of recursion are required. Therefore, *quicksort* requires

$$1 + 2 + \cdots + (n - 1) = n * (n - 1)/2$$

comparisons. However, recall that a move into S_2 does not require an exchange of array items; it requires only a change in the index *firstUnknown*.

Similarly, if S_2 remains empty at each recursive call, $n * (n - 1)/2$ comparisons are required. In addition, however, an exchange is necessary to move each unknown item to S_1. Thus, $n * (n - 1)/2$ exchanges are necessary. (Again, each exchange requires three data moves.) Thus, you can conclude that *quicksort* is $O(n^2)$ in the worst case.

In contrast, Figure 10-20 shows an example in which S_1 and S_2 contain the same number of items. In the average case, when S_1 and S_2 contain the same—or nearly the same—number of items arranged at random, fewer recursive calls to *quicksort* occur. As in the previous analysis of *mergesort,* you can conclude that there are either $\log_2 n$ or $1 + \log_2 n$ levels of recursive calls to *quicksort*. Each call to *quicksort* involves m comparisons and at most m exchanges, where m is the number of items in the subarray to be sorted. Clearly $m \leq n - 1$.

Quicksort. Worst case: $O(n^2)$; average case: $O(n * \log_2 n)$

A formal analysis of *quicksort's* average-case behavior would show that it is $O(n * \log_2 n)$. Thus, on large arrays you can expect *quicksort* to run significantly faster than *insertionSort*, although in its worst case, *quicksort* will require roughly the same amount of time as *insertionSort*.

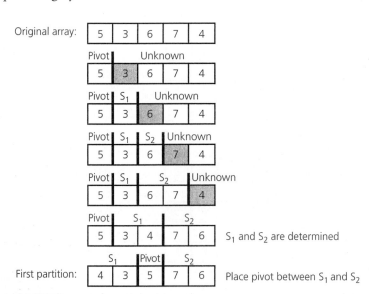

FIGURE 10-20

An average-case partitioning with *quicksort*

It might seem surprising, then, that `quicksort` is often used to sort large arrays. The reason for `quicksort`'s popularity is that it is usually extremely fast in practice, despite its unimpressive theoretical worst-case behavior. Although a worst-case situation is not typical, even if the worst case occurs, `quicksort`'s performance is acceptable for moderately large arrays.

The fact that `quicksort`'s average-case behavior is far better than its worst-case behavior distinguishes it from the other sorting algorithms considered in this chapter. If the original arrangement of data in the array is "random," `quicksort` performs at least as well as any known sorting algorithm that involves comparisons. Unless the array is already ordered, `quicksort` is best.

The efficiency of `mergesort` is somewhere between the possibilities for `quicksort:` Sometimes `quicksort` is faster, and sometimes `mergesort` is faster. While the worst-case behavior of `mergesort` is of the same order of magnitude as `quicksort`'s average-case behavior, in most situations `quicksort` will run somewhat faster than `mergesort`. However, in its worst case, `quicksort` will be significantly slower than `mergesort`.

Radix Sort

The final sorting algorithm in this chapter is included here because it is quite different from the others.

Imagine one last time that you are sorting a hand of cards. This time you pick up the cards one at a time and arrange them by rank into 13 possible groups in this order: 2, 3, . . . , 10, J, Q, K, A. Combine these groups and place the cards face down on the table so that the 2s are on top and the aces are on the bottom. Now pick up the cards one at a time and arrange them by suit into four possible groups in this order: clubs, diamonds, hearts, and spades. When taken together, the groups result in a sorted hand of cards.

A **radix sort** uses this idea of forming groups and then combining them to sort a collection of data. The sort treats each data item as a character string. As a first simple example of a radix sort, consider this collection of three-letter strings:

ABC, XYZ, BWZ, AAC, RLT, JBX, RDT, KLT, AEO, TLJ

The sort begins by organizing the data according to their rightmost (least significant) letters. Although none of the strings ends in A or B, two strings end in C. Place those two strings into a group. Continuing through the alphabet, you form the following groups:

(ABC, AAC) (TLJ) (AEO) (RLT, RDT, KLT) (JBX) (XYZ, BWZ)   Group strings by rightmost letter

The strings in each group end with the same letter, and the groups are ordered by that letter. The strings within each group retain their relative order from the original list of strings.

Now combine the groups into one as follows. Take the items in the first group in their present order, follow them with the items in the second group in their present order, and so on. The following group results:

ABC, AAC, TLJ, AEO, RLT, RDT, KLT, JBX, XYZ, BWZ   Combine groups

Next, form new groups as you did before, but this time use the middle letter of each string instead of the last letter:

Group strings by middle letter

(AAC) (ABC, JBX) (RDT) (AEO) (TLJ, RLT, KLT) (BWZ) (XYZ)

Now the strings in each group have the same middle letter, and the groups are ordered by that letter. As before, the strings within each group retain their relative order from the previous group of all strings.

Combine these groups into one group, again preserving the relative order of the items within each group:

Combine groups

AAC, ABC, JBX, RDT, AEO, TLJ, RLT, KLT, BWZ, XYZ

Now form new groups according to the first letter of each string:

Group strings by first letter

(AAC, ABC, AEO) (BWZ) (JBX) (KLT) (RDT, RLT) (TLJ) (XYZ)

Finally, combine the groups, again maintaining the relative order within each group:

Sorted strings

AAC, ABC, AEO, BWZ, JBX, KLT, RDT, RLT, TLJ, XYZ

The strings are now in sorted order.

In the previous example, all character strings had the same length. If the character strings have varying lengths, you can treat them as if they were the same length by padding them on the right with blanks as necessary.

To sort numeric data, the radix sort treats a number as a character string. You can treat numbers as if they were padded on the left with zeros, making them all appear to be the same length. You then form groups according to the rightmost digits, combine the groups, form groups according to the next-to-last digits, combine them, and so on, just as you did in the previous example. Figure 10-21 shows a radix sort of eight integers.

0123, 2154, 0222, 0004, 0283, 1560, 1061, 2150	Original integers
(1560, 2150) (1061) (0222) (0123, 0283) (2154, 0004)	Grouped by fourth digit
1560, 2150, 1061, 0222, 0123, 0283, 2154, 0004	Combined
(0004) (0222, 0123) (2150, 2154) (1560, 1061) (0283)	Grouped by third digit
0004, 0222, 0123, 2150, 2154, 1560, 1061, 0283	Combined
(0004, 1061) (0123, 2150, 2154) (0222, 0283) (1560)	Grouped by second digit
0004, 1061, 0123, 2150, 2154, 0222, 0283, 1560	Combined
(0004, 0123, 0222, 0283) (1061, 1560) (2150, 2154)	Grouped by first digit
0004, 0123, 0222, 0283, 1061, 1560, 2150, 2154	Combined (sorted)

FIGURE 10-21

A radix sort of eight integers

The following pseudocode describes the algorithm for a radix sort of n decimal integers of d digits each:

```
+radixSort(inout theArray:ItemArray,
           in n:integer, in d:integer)
// Sorts n d-digit integers in the array theArray.

  for (j = d down to 1) {
    Initialize 10 groups to empty
    Initialize a counter for each group to 0
    for (i = 0 through n-1) {
      k = jth digit of theArray[i]
      Place theArray[i] at the end of group k
      Increase kth counter by 1
    }   // end for i

    Replace the items in theArray with all the
        items in group 0, followed by all the items
        in group 1, and so on.
  }   // end for j
```

Analysis.   From the pseudocode for the radix sort, you can see that this algorithm requires n moves each time it forms groups and n moves to combine them again into one group. The algorithm performs these $2 * n$ moves d times. Therefore, the radix sort requires $2 * n * d$ moves to sort n strings of d characters each. However, notice that no comparisons are necessary. Thus, radix sort is $O(n)$.

A Comparison of Sorting Algorithms

Figure 10-22 summarizes the worst-case and average-case orders of magnitude for the sorting algorithms that appear in this chapter. For reference purposes, two other algorithms—treesort and heapsort—are

	Worst case	Average case
Selection sort	n^2	n^2
Bubble sort	n^2	n^2
Insertion sort	n^2	n^2
Mergesort	$n * \log n$	$n * \log n$
Quicksort	n^2	$n * \log n$
Radix sort	n	n
Treesort	n^2	$n * \log n$
Heapsort	$n * \log n$	$n * \log n$

FIGURE 10-22

Approximate growth rates of time required for eight sorting algorithms

included here, even though you will not study them until Chapters 11 and 12, respectively.

The Java Collections Framework Sort Algorithm

The Java Collections Framework provides numerous polymorphic algorithms. These algorithms appear in the class *java.util.Collections*. Note that this is a different class than the *Collection* class used as the root interface in the collection hierarchy. The *Collections* class provides only static methods that operate on or return collections.

Typically, these static methods take an argument that is the collection on which the method is to be performed. Many of the methods have a parameter that is of type *Collection* or *List*.

The sort algorithm used in the JCF is a slightly optimized version of the *mergesort* algorithm. As we have seen in our analysis of *mergesort*, it is guaranteed to run in $n*log(n)$ time. Also note that *mergesort* is stable; the elements with the same value are guaranteed to remain in the same relative order. This can be important if you are sorting the same list repeatedly on different attributes. For example, if a threaded discussion is sorted by date and then sorted by sender, the user expects the now-contiguous list of messages from a given sender will still be sorted by date. This will only happen if the algorithm used for the second sort is stable.

There are actually two sort methods provided in the *Collections* class:

```
static <T extends Comparable<? super T>> void sort(List<T> list)
   // Sorts the specified list into ascending order, according
   // to the natural ordering of its elements.

static <T> void sort(List<T> list, Comparator<? super T> c)
   // Sorts the specified list according to the order induced
   // by the specified comparator.
```

The first form takes a *List<T>*, where *T* or one of its super classes should implement the *Comparable* interface. It sorts the items into ascending order based upon the natural ordering of the elements. Here is a simple program that demonstrates how to use this sort to alphabetically order a list of names:

```
public static void main(String args[]) {
   String[] names = {"Janet", "Michael", "Andrew", "Kate",
                     "Sarah", "Regina", "Rachael", "Allie"};
   List<String> l = Arrays.asList(names);
   Collections.sort(l);
   System.out.println(l);
} // end main
```

The method `Arrays.asList` takes an array argument and returns it as a serializable `List` that is subsequently sent to the `Collections.sort` method. This program produces the following output:

```
[Allie, Andrew, Janet, Kate, Michael, Rachael, Regina, Sarah]
```

The second form of sort takes two parameters, the first is a `List<T>`, this time with no restrictions on `T`, and a second parameter that is a `Comparator` object. Note the `Comparator` interface is defined as follows:

```
public interface Comparator<T> {

   int compare(T o1, T o2);
      // Compares its two arguments for order.

   boolean equals(Object obj);
      // Indicates whether some other object is "equal to" this
      // Comparator.
} // end Comparator
```

As mentioned earlier in the chapter, use of the `Comparator` object imposes a total ordering on some collection of objects. This may be the same as the natural ordering that is usually implemented using the `Comparable` interface. To utilize the `sort` method with a `Comparator` object requires an implementation of the `Comparator` interface for the data type of the objects in the collection.

For example, suppose we have a simple collection of `Person` objects, where each object contains the name and age for a person as follows:

```
class Person implements Serializable {
   private String name;
   private int age;

   public Person(String name, int age) {
      this.name = name;
      this.age = age;
   } // end constructor
```

```
  public String getName() {
    return name;
  } // end getName

  public int getAge() {
    return age;
  } // end getAge

  public String toString() {
   return name + " - " + age;
  } // end toString
} //end Person
```

The *Person* class implements the *Serializable* interface since we plan to use the *Arrays.asList* method again to create a list. We will demonstrate two different comparators for the *Person* class, one to compare by name, the other by age. The *Comparator* class is a generic class, so when we implement it, the data type *Person* will be provided as the generic parameter. Each comparator requires the definition of a *compare* method and an *equals* method. The *compare* method is implemented to impose and ordering on two *Person* objects based upon some criteria, name or age. The *equals* method is intended to allow you to determine if you have two comparators that are the same. The implementation shown here simply checks to see if the comparator objects are the same object, not the same type of object. Other interpretations are possible.

Here is the definition of the *NameComparator* class; the compare method is based solely on the *name* field of the *Person* object:

```
import java.util.Comparator;
import java.io.Serializable;

class NameComparator implements Comparator<Person>, Serializable {

  public int compare(Person o1, Person o2) {
    // Compares its two arguments for order by name.
    return o1.getName().compareTo(o2.getName());
  } // end compare

  public boolean equals(Object obj) {
    // Simply checks to see if we have the same object
    return this==obj;
  } // end equals

} // end NameComparator
```

The definition of the *AgeComparator* class is quite similar, but the compare method is based solely on the *age* field of the *Person* object:

```java
import java.util.Comparator;
import java.io.Serializable;

class AgeComparator implements Comparator<Person>, Serializable {
  public int compare(Person o1, Person o2) {
    // Returns the difference:
    // if positive, age of o1 person is greater than o2 person
    // if zero, the ages are equal
    // if negative, age of o1 person is less than o2 person
    return o1.getAge() - o2.getAge();
  } // end compare

  public boolean equals(Object obj) {
    // Simply checks to see if we have the same object
    return this==obj;
  } // end equals
} // end AgeComparator
```

Note that the comparators implement the *Serializable* interface. It is considered good programming practice to do this as it is quite possible that these comparator objects may be part of other serializable data structures.

Now that these comparator classes exist, comparator objects are instantiated for use in the sort method. For example:

```java
public static void main(String args[]) {
  NameComparator nameComp = new NameComparator();
  AgeComparator ageComp = new AgeComparator();

  Person[] p = new Person[5];
  p[0] = new Person("Michael", 45);
  p[1] = new Person("Janet", 39);
  p[2] = new Person("Sarah", 17);
  p[3] = new Person("Kate", 20);
  p[4] = new Person("Andrew", 20);
  List<Person> list = Arrays.asList(p);

  System.out.println("Sorting by age:");
  Collections.sort(list, ageComp);
  System.out.println(list);

  System.out.println("Sorting by name:");
  Collections.sort(list, nameComp);
  System.out.println(list);
```

```
    System.out.println("Now sorting by age, after sorting by name:");
    Collections.sort(list, ageComp);
    System.out.println(list);
} // end main
```

This program produces the following output:

```
Sorting by age:
[Sarah - 17, Kate - 20, Andrew - 20, Janet - 39, Michael - 45]
Sorting by name:
[Andrew - 20, Janet - 39, Kate - 20, Michael - 45, Sarah - 17]
Now sorting by age, after sorting by name:
[Sarah - 17, Andrew - 20, Kate - 20, Janet - 39, Michael - 45]
```

Note that the sort is stable—it maintains the order of equal elements. This is evident by observing that the first sort by age kept the names with the same age in their original order. After sorting by name first, then by age, the names are now displayed by age with the names in alphabetical order.

Summary

1. Order-of-magnitude analysis and Big O notation measure an algorithm's time requirement as a function of the problem size by using a growth-rate function. This approach enables you to analyze the efficiency of an algorithm without regard for such factors as computer speed and programming skill that are beyond your control.

2. When you compare the inherent efficiency of algorithms, you examine their growth-rate functions when the problems are large. Only significant differences in growth-rate functions are meaningful.

3. Worst-case analysis considers the maximum amount of work an algorithm will require on a problem of a given size, while average-case analysis considers the expected amount of work that it will require.

4. You can use order-of-magnitude analysis to help you choose an implementation for an abstract data type. If your application frequently uses particular ADT operations, your implementation should be efficient for at least those operations.

5. Selection sort, bubble sort, and insertion sort are all $O(n^2)$ algorithms. Although, in a particular case, one might be faster than another, for large problems they all are slow.

6. Quicksort and mergesort are two very efficient recursive sorting algorithms. In the "average" case, quicksort is among the fastest known sorting algorithms. However, quicksort's worst-case behavior is significantly slower than mergesort's. Fortunately, quicksort's worst case rarely occurs in practice. Actual execution time for mergesort is not quite as fast as quicksort in the average case, even though they have the same order. However, mergesort's performance is consistently good in all cases. Mergesort has the disadvantage of requiring extra storage equal to the size of the array to be sorted.

Cautions

1. In general, you should avoid analyzing an algorithm solely by studying the running times of a specific implementation. Running times are influenced by such factors as programming style, the particular computer, and the data on which the program is run.

2. When comparing the efficiency of various solutions, look only at significant differences. This rule is consistent with the multidimensional view of the cost of a computer program.

3. While manipulating the Big O notation, remember that $O(f(n))$ represents an inequality. It is not a function but simply a notation that means "is of order $f(n)$" or "has order $f(n)$".

4. If a problem is small, do not overanalyze it. In such a situation, the primary concern should be simplicity. For example, if you are sorting an array that contains only a small number of items—say, fewer than 25—a simple $O(n^2)$ algorithm such as an insertion sort is appropriate.

5. If you are sorting a very large array, an $O(n^2)$ algorithm is probably too inefficient to use.

6. Quicksort is appropriate when you are confident that the data in the array to be sorted is arranged randomly. Although quicksort's worst-case behavior is $O(n^2)$, the worst case rarely occurs in practice.

Self-Test Exercises

1. How many comparisons of array items do the following loops contain?

```
int temp;
for (j = 1; j <= n-1; ++j) {
  i = j + 1;
  do {
    if (theArray[i] < theArray[j]) {
      temp = theArray[i];
      theArray[i] = theArray[j];
      theArray[j] = temp;
    }  // end if
    ++i;
  } while (i <= n);
}  // end for
```

2. Repeat Self-Test Exercise 1, replacing the statement $i = j + 1$ with $i = j$.

3. What order is an algorithm that has as a growth-rate function
   a. $8 * n^3 - 9 * n^2$ b. $7 * \log_2 n + 20$ c. $7 * \log_2 n * n$

4. Consider a sequential search of n data items.

   a. If the data items are sorted into descending order, how can you determine that your desired item is not in the data collection without always making n comparisons?

b. What is the order of the sequential search algorithm when the desired item is not in the data collection? Do this for both sorted and unsorted data, and consider the best, average, and worst cases.

c. Show that if the sequential search algorithm finds the desired item in the data collection, the algorithm's order does not depend upon whether or not the data items are sorted.

5. Trace the selection sort as it sorts the following array into ascending order: 80 40 25 20 30 60.

6. Repeat Self-Test Exercise 5, but instead sort the array into descending order.

7. Trace the bubble sort as it sorts the following array into ascending order: 80 40 25 20 30 60.

8. Trace the insertion sort as it sorts the array in Self-Test Exercise 7 into ascending order.

9. Show that the mergesort algorithm satisfies the four criteria of recursion that Chapter 3 describes.

10. Trace quicksort's partitioning algorithm for an ascending sort as it partitions the following array. Use the first item as the pivot.

   39 12 16 38 40 27

11. Suppose that you sort a large array of integers by using mergesort. Next you use a binary search to determine whether a given integer occurs in the array. Finally, you display all the integers in the sorted array.

   a. Which algorithm is faster, in general: the mergesort or the binary search? Explain in terms of Big O notation.

   b. Which algorithm is faster, in general: the binary search or displaying the integers? Explain in terms of Big O notation.

Exercises

1. What is the order of each of the following tasks in the worst case?

   a. Computing the sum of the first half of an array of n items

   b. Initializing each element of an array `items` to 1

   c. Displaying every other integer in a linked list of n nodes

   d. Displaying all n names in a circular linked list

   e. Displaying the third element in a linked list

   f. Displaying the last integer in a linked list of n nodes

   g. Searching an array of n integers for a particular value by using a binary search

   h. Sorting an array of n integers into ascending order by using a mergesort

2. Why do we include the variable `sorted` in the implementation of the bubble sort?

3. For queues and stacks presented earlier in this text, three implementations were provided—a reference based implementation, an array based implementation, and a list based implementation. For each of these implementations, what is the order of each of the following tasks in the worst case?

   a. Adding an item to a stack of n items

   b. Adding an item to a queue of n items

4. Find an array that makes the bubble sort exhibit its worst behavior.

5. Suppose that your implementation of a particular algorithm appears in Java as

   ```
   for (int pass = 1; pass <= n; ++pass) {
     for (int index = 0; index < n; ++index) {
       for (int count = 1; count < 10; ++count) {
         . . .
       } // end for
     } // end for
   } // end for
   ```

   The previous code shows only the repetition in the algorithm, not the computations that occur within the loops. These computations, however, are independent of n. What is the order of the algorithm? Justify your answer.

6. Consider the following Java method f. Do not be concerned with f's purpose.

   ```
   public static void f(int[] theArray, int n) {
     int temp;
     for (int j = 0; j < n; ++j) {
       int i = 0;
       while (i <= j) {
         if (theArray[i] < (theArray[j])) {
           temp = theArray[i];
           theArray[i] = theArray[j];
           theArray[j] = temp;
         } // end if
         ++i;
       } // end while
     } // end for
   } // end f
   ```

   How many comparisons does f perform?

7. For large arrays and in the worst case, is selection sort faster than insertion sort? Explain.

8. In how many ways can 2 sorted arrays of combined size N be merged?

9. Show that for all constants $a, b > 1$, $f(n)$ is $O(\log_a n)$ if and only if $f(n)$ is $O(\log_b n)$. Thus, you can omit the base when you write $O(\log n)$. *Hint:* Use the identity $\log_a n = \log_b n / \log_b a$ for all constants $a, b > 1$.

10. This chapter's analysis of selection sort ignored operations that control loops or manipulate array indexes. Revise this analysis by counting *all* operations, and show that the algorithm is still $O(n^2)$.

11. Prove that sorting N elements with integer keys in the range $1 < \text{Key} < M$ takes $O(M+N)$ time using radix sort.

12. Trace the selection sort as it sorts the following array into ascending order:
    8 11 23 1 20 33

13. Trace the bubble sort as it sorts the following array into descending order:
    10 12 23 34 5

14. Here is an array which has just been partitioned by the first step of quick sort:
    $$2, 14, 40, 22, 44, 25, 58$$
    Which of these elements could be the pivot? (There may be more than one possibility)

15. When is insertion sort a good choice for sorting an array?

    a. Each component of the array requires a large amount of memory.

    b. Each component of the array requires a small amount of memory.

    c. The array has only a few items out of place.

    d. The processor speed is fast.

16. Write recursive versions of `selectionSort`, `bubbleSort`, and `insertionSort`.

17. One way computer speeds are measured is by the number of instructions they can perform per second. Assume that a comparison or a data move are each a single instruction. If the bubble sort is being used to sort 1,000,000 items in a worst case scenario, what is the approximate amount of time it takes to execute this sort on each of the following computers? Express your answer in days, hours, minutes, and seconds.

    a. An early computer that could only execute one thousand instructions per second

    b. A more recent computer that can execute one billion instructions per second

18. Here is an array of ten integers:
    $$35, 23, 18, 93, 51, 12, 64, 2, 45, 1$$
    Draw this array after the first iteration of the large loop in a selection sort (sorting from smallest to largest).

19. In case of a selection sort algorithm of n elements, how many times is the function swap called during the execution of the algorithm?

    a. 1

    b. $n - 1$

    c. $n \log n$

    d. n^2

20. Trace the quicksort algorithm as it sorts the following array into ascending order. List the calls to `quicksort` and to `partition` in the order in which they occur.
    80 40 25 20 30 60 15

21. Suppose that you remove the call to `merge` from the `mergesort` algorithm to obtain

```
+mystery(inout theArray:ItemArray,
         in first:integer, in last:integer)
// mystery algorithm for theArray[first..last].

   if (first < last) {
     mid = (first + last) / 2
     mystery(theArray, first, mid)
     mystery(theArray, mid+1, last)
   } // end if
```

   What does this new algorithm do?

22. You can choose any array item as the pivot for `quicksort`. You then interchange items so that your pivot is in `theArray[first]`.

    a. One way to choose a pivot is to take the middle value of the three values `theArray[first]`, `theArray[last]`, and `theArray [(first + last)/2]`. How many comparisons are necessary to sort an array of size n if you always choose the pivot in this way?

    b. If the actual median value could be chosen as the pivot at each step, how many comparisons are necessary to sort an array of size n?

23. Selection sort and quick sort both fall into the same category of sorting algorithms. What is this category?

    a. O(n log n) sorts

    b. Divide-and-conquer sorts

    c. Interchange sorts

    d. Average time is quadratic.

24. Use invariants to show that the method `selectionSort` is correct.

25. Describe an iterative version of `mergesort`. Define an appropriate invariant and show the correctness of your algorithm.

26. One criterion used to evaluate sorting algorithms is stability. A sorting algorithm is **stable** if it does not exchange items that have the same sort key. Thus, items with the same sort key (possibly differing in other ways) will maintain their positions relative to one another. For example, you might want to take an array of students sorted by name and sort it by year of graduation. Using a stable sorting algorithm to sort the array by year will ensure that within each year the students will remain sorted by name. Some applications mandate a stable sorting algorithm. Others do not. Which of the sorting algorithms described in this chapter are stable?

27. When we discussed the radix sort, we sorted a hand of cards by first ordering the cards by rank and then by suit. To implement a radix sort for this example, you could use two characters to represent a card, if you used T to represent a 10. For example, S2 is the 2 of spades and HT is the 10 of hearts.

a. Show a trace of the radix sort for the following cards:

S2, HT, D6, S4, C9, CJ, DQ, ST, HQ, DK

b. Suppose that you did not use T to represent a 10—that is, suppose that H10 is the 10 of hearts—and that you padded the two-character strings on the right with a blank to form three-character strings. How would a radix sort order the entire deck of cards in this case?

Programming Problems

1. Write a Java program that reads *n* number of elements and sorts them by any of the following algorithms, depending upon the user's choice:

   a. Selection sort

   b. Bubble sort

   c. Insertion sort

   d. Merge sort

2. A program that has this selection sort static method available:

   ```
   void SELECTSORT(int[ ] data, int n);
   ```

   This program also has an integer array called A, with 10 elements.

   Write two method activations:

   a. The first call uses the `SELECTSORT` method to sort all elements of A;

   b. The second call uses the `SELECTSORT` method to sort elements from `A[4]` to `A[8]` of the array

3. a. Modify the partition algorithm for `quicksort` so that S_1 and S_2 will never be empty.

   b. Another partitioning strategy for `quicksort` is possible. Let an index `low` traverse the array segment `theArray [first..last]` from `first` to `last` and stop when it encounters the first item that is greater than the pivot item. Similarly, let a second index `high` traverse the array segment from `last` to `first` and stop when it encounters the first item that is smaller than the pivot item. Then swap these two items, increment `low`, decrement `high`, and continue until `high` and `low` meet somewhere in the middle. Implement this version of `quicksort` in Java. How can you ensure that the regions S_1 and S_2 are not empty?

   c. There are several variations of this partitioning strategy. What other strategies can you think of? How do they compare to the two that have been given?

4. Implement the radix sort of an array by using an ADT queue for each group.

5. Implement a radix sort of a linked list of integers.

6. A doubly circular linked list contains five elements. Write a program that sorts those elements in an ascending order.

7. A class *STN* contains the I.D. number, name, and scores of students at a university. Write a program that creates an array of 60 students of class *STN*. Write a method that sorts the students according to their scores (you can use any sorting algorithm).

8. Shellsort (named for its inventor, Donald Shell) is an improved insertion sort. Rather than always exchanging adjacent items—as in insertion sort—Shellsort can exchange items that are far apart in the array. Shellsort arranges the array so that every h^{th} item forms a sorted subarray. For every h in a decreasing sequence of values, Shellsort arranges the array. For example, if h is 5, every fifth item forms a sorted subarray. Ultimately, if h is 1, the entire array will be sorted.

    One possible sequence of h's begins at $n/2$ and halves n until it becomes 1. By using this sequence, and by replacing 1 with h and 0 with $h-1$ in *insertionSort*, we get the following method for Shellsort:

```
public static <T extends Comparable<? super T>>
        void shellsort(T[] theArray, int n) {
   int loc;
   T nextItem;
   for (int h = n/2; h > 0; h = h/2) {
      for (int unsorted = h; unsorted < n; ++unsorted) {
         nextItem = theArray[unsorted];
         loc = unsorted;
         while ((loc >= h) &&
                (theArray[loc-h].compareTo(nextItem) > 0)) {
            theArray[loc] = theArray[loc-h];
            loc = loc - h;
         } // end while
         theArray[loc] = nextItem;
      } // end for unsorted
   } // end for h
} // end shellsort
```

   Add a counter to the methods *insertionSort* and *shellsort* that counts the number of comparisons that are made. Run the two methods with arrays of various sizes. On what size does the difference in the number of comparisons become significant?

CHAPTER 11

Trees

The data organizations presented in previous chapters are linear in that items are one after another. The ADTs in this chapter organize data in a nonlinear, hierarchical form, whereby an item can have more than one immediate successor. In particular, this chapter discusses the specifications, implementations, and relative efficiency of the ADT binary tree and the ADT binary search tree. These ADTs are basic to the next three chapters.

585

The previous chapters discussed ADTs whose operations fit into at least one of these general categories:

General categories of data-management operations

- Operations that insert data into a data collection
- Operations that delete data from a data collection
- Operations that ask questions about the data in a data collection

The form of operations on position-oriented ADTs

The ADTs list, stack, and queue are all **position oriented,** and their operations have the form

- Insert a data item into the ith *position* of a data collection.
- Delete a data item from the ith *position* of a data collection.
- Ask a question about the data item in the ith *position* of a data collection.

As you have seen, the ADT list places no restriction on the value of i, while the ADTs stack and queue do impose some restrictions. For example, the operations of the ADT stack are restricted to inserting into, deleting from, and asking a question about one end—the top—of the stack. Thus, although they differ with respect to the flexibility of their operations, lists, stacks, and queues manage an association between data items and *positions.*

The form of operations on value-oriented ADTs

The ADT sorted list is **value oriented.** Its operations are of the form

- Insert a data item containing the *value x.*
- Delete a data item containing the *value x.*
- Ask a question about a data item containing the *value x.*

Although these operations, like position-oriented operations, fit into the three general categories of operations listed earlier—they insert data, delete data, and ask questions about data—they are based upon *values* of data items instead of *positions.*

This chapter discusses two major ADTs: the binary tree and the binary search tree. As you will see, the binary tree is a position-oriented ADT, but it is not linear as are lists, stacks, and queues. Thus, you will not reference items in a binary tree by using a position number. Our discussion of the ADT binary tree provides an important background for the more useful binary search tree, which is a value-oriented ADT. Although a binary search tree is also not linear, it has operations similar to those of a sorted list, which is linear.

In the next chapter, you will see two more value-oriented ADTs: the ADT table and the ADT priority queue. The implementations of both of these ADTs can use the ideas presented in this chapter.

11.1 Terminology

You use **trees** to represent relationships. Previous chapters informally used tree diagrams to represent the relationships between the calls of a recursive algorithm. For example, the diagram of the *rabbit* algorithm's recursive calls in

Figure 3-11 of Chapter 3 is actually a tree. Each call to *rabbit* is represented by a box, or **node,** or **vertex,** in the tree. The lines between the nodes (boxes) are called **edges.** For this tree, the edges indicate recursive calls. For example, the edges from *rabbit*(7) to *rabbit*(6) and *rabbit*(5) indicate that subproblem *rabbit*(7) makes calls to *rabbit*(6) and *rabbit*(5).

All trees are **hierarchical** in nature. Intuitively, hierarchical means that a "parent-child" relationship exists between the nodes in the tree. If an edge is between node *n* and node *m*, and node *n* is above node *m* in the tree, then *n* is the **parent** of *m*, and *m* is a **child** of *n*. In the tree in Figure 11-1, nodes *B* and *C* are children of node *A*. Children of the same parent—for example, *B* and *C*—are called **siblings.** Each node in a tree has at most one parent, and exactly one node—called the **root** of the tree—has no parent. Node *A* is the root of the tree in Figure 11-1. A node that has no children is called a **leaf** of the tree. The leaves of the tree in Figure 11-1 are *C, D, E,* and *F.*

> Trees are hierarchical

The parent-child relationship between the nodes is generalized to the relationships **ancestor** and **descendant.** In Figure 11-1, *A* is an ancestor of *D*, and thus *D* is a descendant of *A*. Not all nodes are related by the ancestor or descendant relationship: *B* and *C*, for instance, are not so related. However, the root of any tree is an ancestor of every node in that tree. A **subtree** in a tree is any node in the tree together with all of its descendants. A **subtree of a node** *n* is a subtree rooted at a child of *n*. For example, Figure 11-2 shows a subtree of the tree in Figure 11-1. This subtree has *B* as its root and is a subtree of the node *A*.

> A subtree is any node and its descendants

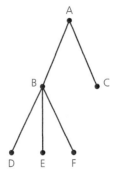

FIGURE 11-1

A general tree

FIGURE 11-2

A subtree of the tree in Figure 11-1

Because trees are hierarchical in nature, you can use them to represent information that itself is hierarchical in nature—for example, organization charts and family trees, as Figure 11-3 depicts. It may be disconcerting to discover, however, that the nodes in the family tree in Figure 11-3b that represent Caroline's parents (John and Jacqueline) are the children of the node that represents Caroline! That is, the nodes that represent Caroline's ancestors are the descendants of Caroline's node. It's no wonder that computer scientists often seem to be confused by reality.

Formally, a **general tree** T is a set of one or more nodes such that T is partitioned into disjoint subsets:

- A single node r, the root

- Sets that are general trees, called subtrees of r

Thus, the trees in Figures 11-1 and 11-3a are general trees.

The primary focus of this chapter will be on binary trees. Formally, a **binary tree** is a set T of nodes such that either

Formal definition of a binary tree

- T is empty, or

- T is partitioned into three disjoint subsets:

    - A single node r, the root

    - Two possibly empty sets that are binary trees, called **left** and **right subtrees** of r

The trees in Figures 3-11a and 11-3b are binary trees. Notice that each node in a binary tree has no more than two children. A binary tree is not a special kind of general tree, because a binary tree can be empty, whereas a general tree cannot.

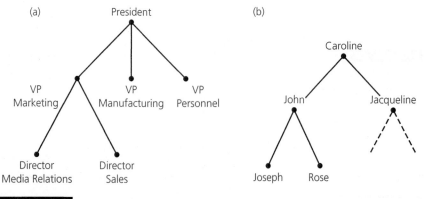

(a)

President

VP Marketing   VP Manufacturing   VP Personnel

Director Media Relations   Director Sales

(b)

Caroline

John   Jacqueline

Joseph   Rose

FIGURE 11-3

(a) An organization chart; (b) a family tree

The following intuitive restatement of the definition of a binary tree is useful:

T is a binary tree if either

- T has no nodes, or
- T is of the form

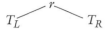

where r is a node and T_L and T_R are both binary trees

Notice that the formal definition agrees with this intuitive one: If r is the root of T, then the binary tree T_L is the left subtree of node r and T_R is the right subtree of node r. If T_L is not empty, its root is the **left child** of r, and if T_R is not empty, its root is the **right child** of r. Notice that if both subtrees of a node are empty, that node is a leaf.

As an example of how you can use a binary tree to represent data in a hierarchical form, consider Figure 11-4. The binary trees in this figure represent algebraic expressions that involve the binary operators +, −, *, and /. To represent an expression such as $a - b$, you place the operator in the root node and the operands a and b into the left and right children, respectively, of the root. (See Figure 11-4a.) Figure 11-4b represents the expression $a - b/c$; a subtree represents the subexpression b/c. A similar situation exists in Figure 11-4c, which represents $(a - b) * c$. The leaves of these trees contain the expressions' operands, while other tree nodes contain the operators. Parentheses do not appear in these trees. The binary tree provides a hierarchy for the operations—that is, the tree specifies an unambiguous order for evaluating an expression.

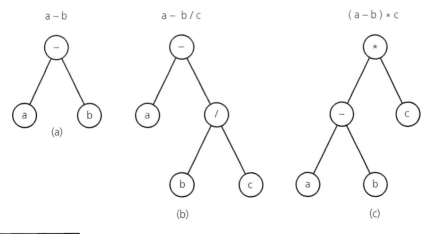

FIGURE 11-4

Binary trees that represent algebraic expressions

The nodes of a tree typically contain values. A **binary search tree** is a binary tree that is in a sense sorted according to the values in its nodes. For each node n, a binary search tree satisfies the following three properties:

Properties of a binary search tree

- n's value is greater than all values in its left subtree T_L.

- n's value is less than all values in its right subtree T_R.

- Both T_L and T_R are binary search trees.

Figure 11-5 is an example of a binary search tree. As its name suggests, a binary search tree organizes data in a way that facilitates searching it for a particular data item. Later, this chapter discusses binary search trees in detail.

The height of trees. Trees come in many shapes. For example, although the binary trees in Figure 11-6 all contain the same nodes, their structures are

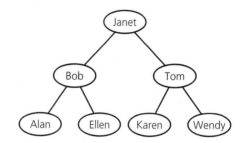

FIGURE 11-5

A binary search tree of names

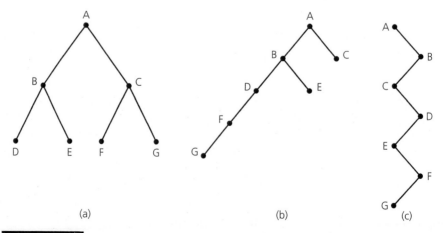

FIGURE 11-6

Binary trees with the same nodes but different heights

quite different. Although each of these trees has seven nodes, some are "taller" than others. The **height of a tree** is the number of nodes on the longest path from the root to a leaf. For example, the trees in Figure 11-6 have respective heights of 3, 5, and 7. Many people's intuitive notion of height would lead them to say that these trees have heights of 2, 4, and 6. Indeed, many authors define height to agree with this intuition. However, the definition of height used in this book leads to a cleaner statement of many algorithms and properties of trees.

There are other equivalent ways to define the height of a tree T. One way uses the following definition of the **level** of a node n:

Level of a node

- If n is the root of T, it is at level 1.

- If n is not the root of T, its level is 1 greater than the level of its parent.

For example, in Figure 11-6a, node A is at level 1, node B is at level 2, and node D is at level 3.

The **height** of a tree T in terms of the levels of its nodes is defined as follows:

Height of a tree in
terms of levels

- If T is empty, its height is 0.

- If T is not empty, its height is equal to the maximum level of its nodes.

Apply this definition to the trees in Figure 11-6 and show that their heights are, respectively, 3, 5, and 7, as was stated earlier.

For binary trees, it is often convenient to use an equivalent recursive definition of height:

Recursive definition
of height

- If T is empty, its height is 0.

- If T is a nonempty binary tree, then because T is of the form

$$T_L \overset{\displaystyle r}{\diagup \diagdown} T_R$$

the height of T is 1 greater than the height of its root's taller subtree; that is,

$$height(T) = 1 + max\{height(T_L), height(T_R)\}$$

Later, when we discuss the efficiency of searching a binary search tree, it will be necessary to determine the maximum and minimum heights of a binary tree of n nodes.

Full, complete, and balanced binary trees. In a **full binary tree** of height h, all nodes that are at a level less than h have two children each. Figure 11-7 depicts a full binary tree of height 3. Each node in a full binary tree has left and right subtrees of the same height. Among binary trees of height h, a full binary tree has as many leaves as possible, and they all are at level h. Intuitively, a full binary tree has no missing nodes.

FIGURE 11-7

A full binary tree of height 3

When proving properties about full binary trees—such as how many nodes they have—the following recursive definition of a full binary tree is convenient:

A full binary tree

- If *T* is empty, *T* is a full binary tree of height 0.

- If *T* is not empty and has height $h > 0$, *T* is a full binary tree if its root's subtrees are both full binary trees of height $h - 1$.

This definition closely reflects the recursive nature of a binary tree.

A **complete binary tree** of height h is a binary tree that is full down to level $h - 1$, with level h filled in from left to right, as Figure 11-8 illustrates. More formally, a binary tree *T* of height h is complete if

A complete binary tree

1. All nodes at level $h - 2$ and above have two children each, and

2. When a node at level $h - 1$ has children, all nodes to its left at the same level have two children each, and

3. When a node at level $h - 1$ has one child, it is a left child

Full binary trees are complete

Parts 2 and 3 of this definition formalize the requirement that level h be filled in from left to right. Note that a full binary tree is complete.

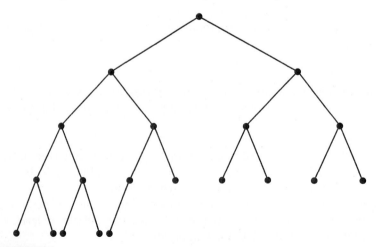

FIGURE 11-8

A complete binary tree

Finally, a binary tree is **height balanced,** or simply **balanced,** if the height of any node's right subtree differs from the height of the node's left subtree by no more than 1. The binary trees in Figures 11-8 and 11-6a are balanced, but the trees in Figures 11-6b and 11–6c are not balanced. A complete binary tree is balanced.

Complete binary trees are balanced

The following is a summary of the major tree terminology presented so far.

KEY CONCEPTS

Summary of Tree Terminology

General tree	A set of one or more nodes, partitioned into a root node and subsets that are general subtrees of the root.
Parent of node n	The node directly above node n in the tree.
Child of node n	A node directly below node n in the tree.
Root	The only node in the tree with no parent.
Leaf	A node with no children.
Siblings	Nodes with a common parent.
Ancestor of node n	A node on the path from the root to n.
Descendant of node n	A node on a path from n to a leaf.
Subtree of node n	A tree that consists of a child (if any) of n and the child's descendants.
Height	The number of nodes on the longest path from the root to a leaf.
Binary tree	A set of nodes that is either empty or partitioned into a root node and one or two subsets that are binary subtrees of the root. Each node has at most two children, the left child and the right child.
Left (right) child of node n	A node directly below and to the left (right) of node n in a binary tree.
Left (right) subtree of node n	In a binary tree, the left (right) child (if any) of node n plus its descendants.
Binary search tree	A binary tree where the value in any node n is greater than the value in every node in n's left subtree, but less than the value of every node in n's right subtree.
Empty binary tree	A binary tree with no nodes.
Full binary tree	A binary tree of height h with no missing nodes. All leaves are at level h and all other nodes each have two children. (continues)

Summary of Tree Terminology (continued)

Complete binary tree	A binary tree of height h that is full to level $h - 1$ and has level h filled in from left to right.
Balanced binary tree	A binary tree in which the left and right subtrees of any node have heights that differ by at most 1.

11.2 The ADT Binary Tree

As an abstract data type, the binary tree has operations that add and remove nodes and subtrees. By using these basic operations, you can build any binary tree. Other operations set or retrieve the data in the root of the tree and determine whether the tree is empty.

Traversal operations that *visit* every node in a binary tree are also typical. "Visiting" a node means "doing something with or to" the node. Chapter 5 introduced the concept of traversal for a linked list: Beginning with the list's first node, you visit each node sequentially until you reach the end of the linked list. Chapter 9 showed how to implement a Java iterator to facilitate traversal of the list. Traversal of a binary tree, however, visits the tree's nodes in one of several different orders. The three standard orders are called preorder, inorder, and postorder, and they are described in the next section along with an iterator for binary trees.

The operations available for a particular ADT binary tree depend on the type of binary tree being implemented. Thus, we will first develop an abstract class representing a binary tree, containing only the most basic binary tree operations. Later, we will extend this abstract class to provide additional binary tree operations.

Basic Operations of the ADT Binary Tree

The first task is to define the operations that are common to all binary tree implementations. Here is a summary:

Basic Operations of the ADT Binary Tree

1. Create an empty binary tree.
2. Create a one-node binary tree, given an item.
3. Remove all nodes from a binary tree, leaving it empty.
4. Determine whether a binary tree is empty.
5. Determine what data is the binary tree's root.
6. Set the data in the binary tree's root (may not be implemented by all binary trees).

Notice that we included in this basic set of operations an operation that changes the item in the root. For some binary trees, such an operation would not be desirable, and may not be implemented. The operation should throw an exception to indicate this.

The following pseudocode specifies these basic operations in more detail.

KEY CONCEPTS

Pseudocode for the Basic Operations of the ADT Binary Tree

```
+createBinaryTree()
// Creates an empty binary tree.

+createBinaryTree(in rootItem:TreeItemType)
// Creates a one-node binary tree whose root contains
// rootItem.

+makeEmpty()
// Removes all of the nodes from a binary tree, leaving an
// empty tree.

+isEmpty():boolean {query}
// Determines whether a binary tree is empty.

+getRootItem():TreeItemType throws TreeException {query}
// Retrieves the data item in the root of a nonempty
// binary tree. Throws TreeException if the tree is
// empty.

+setRootItem(in rootItem:TreeItemType)
           throws UnsupportedOperationException
// Sets the data item in the root of a binary tree. Throws
// UnsupportedOperationException if the method is not
// implemented.
```

As you can see, we must still specify other operations for building the tree. One possible set of operations is presented next.

General Operations of the ADT Binary Tree

As was mentioned earlier, the particular operations provided for an ADT binary tree depend on the kind of binary tree we are designing. This section specifies some general operations for a binary tree, with the assumption that we are adding these operations to the basic operations of the ADT binary tree specified before. A UML diagram for a binary tree is shown in Figure 11-9.

```
              ┌─────────────────────────────┐
              │         BinaryTree          │
              ├─────────────────────────────┤
              │ root                        │
              │ left subtree                │
              │ right subtree               │
              ├─────────────────────────────┤
              │ createBinaryTree()          │
              │ makeEmpty()                 │
              │ isEmpty()                   │
              │ getRootItem()               │
              │ setRootItem()               │
              │ attachLeft()                │
              │ attachRight()               │
              │ attachLeftSubtree()         │
              │ attachRightSubtree()        │
              │ detachLeftSubtree()         │
              │ detachRightSubtree()        │
              │ getLeftSubtree()            │
              │ getRightSubtree()           │
              └─────────────────────────────┘
```

FIGURE 11-9

UML diagram for the class *BinaryTree*

KEY CONCEPTS

Pseudocode for the General Operations of the ADT Binary Tree

```
+createBinaryTree(in rootItem:TreeItemType,
                  in leftTree:BinaryTree,
                  in rightTree:BinaryTree)
// Creates a binary tree whose root contains rootItem and
// has leftTree and rightTree, respectively, as its left
// and right subtrees.

+setRootItem(in newItem:TreeItemType)
// Replaces the data item in the root of a binary tree
// with newItem, if the tree is not empty. If the
// tree is empty, creates a root node whose data item
// is newItem and inserts the new node into the tree.
```

(continues)

KEY CONCEPTS

Pseudocode for the General Operations
of the ADT Binary Tree (continued)

```
+attachLeft(in newItem:TreeItemType) throws TreeException
// Attaches a left child containing newItem to the root of
// a binary tree. Throws TreeException if the binary
// tree is empty (no root node to attach to) or a left
// subtree already exists (should explicitly detach it
// first).

+attachRight(in newItem:TreeItemType) throws TreeException
// Attaches a right child containing newItem to the root of
// a binary tree. Throws TreeException if the binary
// tree is empty (no root node to attach to) or a left
// subtree already exists (should explicitly detach it
// first).

+attachLeftSubtree(in leftTree:BinaryTree) throws TreeException
// Attaches leftTree as the left subtree of the
// root of a binary tree and makes leftTree empty
// so that it cannot be used as a reference into this tree.
// Throws TreeException if the binary tree is empty
// (no root node to attach to) or a left subtree already
// exists (should explicitly detach it first).

+attachRightSubtree(in rightTree:BinaryTree) throws TreeException
// Attaches rightTree as the right subtree of the
// root of a binary tree and makes rightTree empty
// so that it cannot be used as a reference into this tree.
// Throws TreeException if the binary tree is empty
// (no root node to attach to) or a right subtree already
// exists (should explicitly detach it first).

+detachLeftSubtree():BinaryTree throws TreeException
// Detaches and returns the left subtree of a binary tree's
// root. Throws TreeException if the binary tree is empty
// (no root node to detach from).

+detachRightSubtree():BinaryTree throws TreeException
// Detaches and returns the right subtree of a binary tree's
// root. Throws TreeException if the binary tree is empty
// (no root node to detach from).
```

You can use these operations, for example, to build the binary tree in Figure 11-6b, in which the node labels represent character data. The following pseudocode constructs the tree from the subtree *tree1* rooted at *"F"*, the subtree *tree2* rooted at *"D"*, the subtree *tree3* rooted at *"B"*, and the subtree *tree4* rooted at *"C"*. Initially, these subtrees exist but are empty.

Using ADT binary tree operations to build a binary tree

```
tree1.setRootItem("F")
tree1.attachLeft("G")

tree2.setRootItem("D")
tree2.attachLeftSubtree(tree1)

tree3.setRootItem("B")
tree3.attachLeftSubtree(tree2)
tree3.attachRight("E")

tree4.setRootItem("C")
// tree in Fig 11-6b
binTree.createBinaryTree("A", tree3, tree4)
```

The traversal operations are considered in detail next.

Traversals of a Binary Tree

A traversal algorithm for a binary tree visits each node in the tree. While visiting a node, you do something with or to the node. For the purpose of this discussion, assume that visiting a node simply means displaying the data portion of the node.

With the recursive definition of a binary tree in mind, you can construct a recursive traversal algorithm as follows. According to the definition, the binary tree T is either empty or is of the form

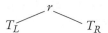

If T is empty, the traversal algorithm takes no action—an empty tree is the base case. If T is not empty, the traversal algorithm must perform three tasks: It must display the data in the root r, and it must traverse the two subtrees T_L and T_R, each of which is a binary tree smaller than T.

The general form of a recursive traversal algorithm

Thus, the general form of the recursive traversal algorithm is

```
+traverse(in binTree:BinaryTree)
// Traverses the binary tree binTree.

  if (binTree is not empty) {
    traverse(Left subtree of binTree's root)
    traverse(Right subtree of binTree's root)
  } // end if
```

This algorithm is not quite complete, however. It is missing the instruction to display the data in the root. When traversing any binary tree, the algorithm has three choices of when to visit the root r. It can visit r before it traverses both of r's subtrees, it can visit r after it has traversed r's left subtree T_L but before it traverses r's right subtree T_R, or it can visit r after it has traversed both of r's subtrees. These traversals are called **preorder, inorder,** and **postorder,** respectively. Figure 11-10 shows the results of these traversals for a given binary tree.

The preorder traversal algorithm is as follows:

Preorder traversal

```
+preorder(in binTree:BinaryTree)
// Traverses the binary tree binTree in preorder.
// Assumes that "visit a node" means to display
// the node's data item.

  if (binTree is not empty) {
     Display the data in the root of binTree
     preorder(Left subtree of binTree's root)
     preorder(Right subtree of binTree's root)
  }  // end if
```

The preorder traversal of the tree in Figure 11-10a visits the nodes in this order: 60, 20, 10, 40, 30, 50, 70. If you apply preorder traversal to a binary tree that represents an algebraic expression, such as any tree in Figure 11-4,

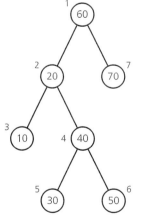 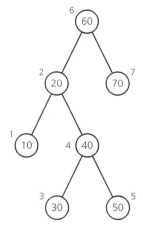 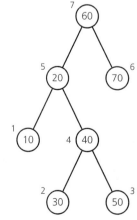

(a) Preorder: 60, 20, 10, 40, 30, 50, 70   (b) Inorder: 10, 20, 30, 40, 50, 60, 70   (c) Postorder: 10, 30, 50, 40, 20, 70, 60

(Numbers beside nodes indicate traversal order.)

FIGURE 11-10

Traversals of a binary tree: (a) preorder; (b) inorder; (c) postorder

and display the nodes as you visit them, you will obtain the prefix form of the expression.[1]

Inorder traversal

The inorder traversal algorithm is as follows:

```
+inorder(in binTree:BinaryTree)
// Traverses the binary tree binTree in inorder.
// Assumes that "visit a node" means to display
// the node's data item.

  if (binTree is not empty) {
    inorder(Left subtree of binTree's root)
    Display the data in the root of binTree
    inorder(Right subtree of binTree's root)
  }  // end if
```

The result of the inorder traversal of the tree in Figure 11-10b is 10, 20, 30, 40, 50, 60, 70. If you apply inorder traversal to a binary search tree, you will visit the nodes in order according to their data values. Such is the case for the tree in Figure 11-10b.

Postorder traversal

Finally, the postorder traversal algorithm is as follows:

```
+postorder(in binTree:BinaryTree)
// Traverses the binary tree binTree in postorder.
// Assumes that "visit a node" means to display
// the node's data item.

  if (binTree is not empty) {
    postorder(Left subtree of binTree's root)
    postorder(Right subtree of binTree's root)
    Display the data in the root of binTree
  }  // end if
```

The result of the postorder traversal of the tree in Figure 11-10c is 10, 30, 50, 40, 20, 70, 60. If you apply postorder traversal to a binary tree that represents an algebraic expression, such as any tree in Figure 11-4, and display the nodes as you visit them, you will obtain the postfix form of the expression.[2]

Each of these traversals visits every node in a binary tree exactly once. Thus, n visits occur for a tree of n nodes. Each visit performs the same operations on each node, independently of n, so it must be O(1). Thus, each tra-

Traversal is O(n)

versal is O(n).

As we discussed in Chapter 9, an iterator class can be developed in conjunction with a collection of objects. In this case, the objects are stored in the nodes of a binary tree, and the order in which this collection is iterated could

---

1. The prefix expressions are (a) $-ab$; (b) $-a/bc$; (c) $*-abc$.
2. The postfix expressions are (a) $ab-$; (b) $abc/-$; (c) $ab-c*$.

be based on preorder, inorder, or postorder traversal of the tree. This allows users of the binary tree class to visit each node of the tree and specify the action to be performed on each item in the tree. The implementation details of such an iterator will be discussed shortly.

Possible Representations of a Binary Tree

You can implement a binary tree by using the constructs of Java in one of three general ways. Two of these approaches use arrays, but the typical implementation uses references. In each case, the described data structures would be private data fields of a class of binary trees.

To illustrate the three approaches, we will implement a binary tree of names. Each node in this tree contains a name, and, because the tree is a binary tree, each node has at most two descendant nodes.

An array-based representation. If you use a Java class to define a node in the tree, you can represent the entire binary tree by using an array of tree nodes. Each tree node contains a data portion—a name in this case—and two indexes, one for each of the node's children, as the following Java statements indicate:

```java
public class TreeNode<T> {
    private T item;            // data item in the tree
    private int leftChild;     // index to left child
    private int rightChild;    // index to right child
    ...
    // constructors and methods appear here
}   // end TreeNode

public class BinaryTreeArrayBased<T> {
    protected final int MAX_NODES = 100;
    protected ArrayList<TreeNode<T>> tree;
    protected int root; // index of tree's root
    protected int free; // index of next unused array
                        // location

    ...
    // constructors and methods
}   // end BinaryTreeArrayBased
```

The constants and data fields are declared *protected* in *BinaryTreeArrayBased* so that they will be directly accessible by the subclasses.

The variable *root* is an index to the tree's root within the array *tree*. If the tree is empty, *root* is −1. Both *leftChild* and *rightChild* within a node are indexes to the children of that node. If a node has no left child, *leftChild* is −1; if a node has no right child, *rightChild* is −1.

As the tree changes due to insertions and deletions, its nodes may not be in contiguous elements of the array. Therefore, this implementation requires

A free list keeps track of available nodes

you to establish a list of available nodes, which is called a **free list.** To insert a new node into the tree, you first obtain an available node from the free list. If you delete a node from the tree, you place it into the free list so that you can reuse the node at a later time. The variable *free* is the index to the first node in the free list and, arbitrarily, the *rightChild* field of each node in the free list is the index of the next node in the free list.[3] Figure 11-11 contains a binary tree and the data fields for its array-based implementation.

An array-based representation of a complete tree. The previous implementation works for any binary tree, even though the tree in Figure 11-11 is complete. If you know that your binary tree is complete, you can use a simpler array-based implementation that saves memory. As you saw earlier in this chapter, a complete tree of height h is full to level $h - 1$ and has level h filled from left to right.

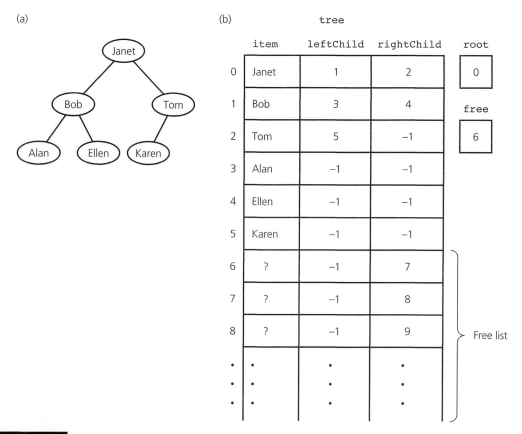

FIGURE 11-11

(a) A binary tree of names; (b) its array-based implementation

---

3. This free list is actually an array-based linked list, as Programming Problem 10 of Chapter 5 describes.

Figure 11 12 shows the complete binary tree of Figure 11-11a with its nodes numbered according to a standard level-by-level scheme. The root is numbered 0, and the children of the root (the next level of the tree) are numbered, left to right, 1 and 2. The nodes at the next level are numbered, left to right, 3, 4, and 5. You place these nodes into the array *tree* in numeric order. That is, *tree[i]* contains the node numbered *i*, as Figure 11-13 illustrates. Now, given any node *tree[i]*, you can easily locate both of its children and its parent: Its left child (if it exists) is *tree[2*i+1]*, its right child (if it exists) is *tree[2*i+2]*, and its parent (if *tree[i]* is not the root) is *tree[(i-1)/2]*.

This array-based representation requires a complete binary tree. If nodes were missing from the middle of the tree, the numbering scheme would be thrown off, and the parent-child relationship among nodes would be ambiguous. This requirement implies that any changes to the tree must maintain its completeness.

> If the binary tree is complete and remains complete, you can use a memory-efficient array-based implementation

As you will see in the next chapter, an array-based representation of a binary tree is useful in the implementation of the ADT priority queue.

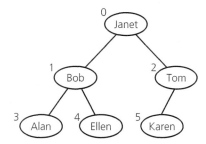

FIGURE 11-12

Level-by-level numbering of a complete binary tree

0	Janet
1	Bob
2	Tom
3	Alan
4	Ellen
5	Karen
6	
7	

FIGURE 11-13

An array-based implementation of the complete binary tree in Figure 11-12

A reference-based representation.   You can use Java references to link the nodes in the tree. Thus, you can represent a tree by using the following Java classes:

```
class TreeNode<T> {
  T item;
  TreeNode<T> leftChild;
  TreeNode<T> rightChild;
  . . .
  // constructors
}  // end TreeNode

public abstract class BinaryTreeBasis<T> {
  protected TreeNode root;
  . . .
  // constructors and methods appear here
}  // end BinaryTreeBasis
```

The class *TreeNode* is analogous to the class *Node* that we used in Chapter 5 for a linked list. The data fields of *TreeNode* are declared package access only. Within the class *BinaryTreeBasis*, the external reference *root* references the tree's root. If the tree is empty, *root* is *null*. Figure 11-14 illustrates this implementation.

The root of a nonempty binary tree has a left subtree and a right subtree, each of which is a binary tree. In a reference-based implementation, *root* references the root *r* of a binary tree, *root.leftChild* references the root of the left subtree of *r*, and *root.rightChild* references the root of the right subtree of *r*.

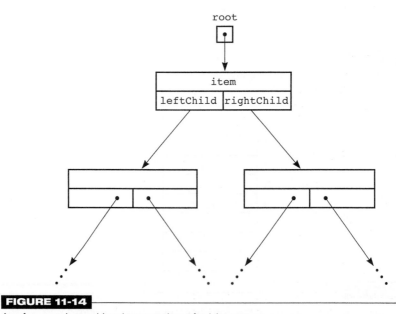

FIGURE 11-14

A reference-based implementation of a binary tree

The section that follows provides the details for a reference-based implementation of the ADT binary tree.

A Reference-Based Implementation of the ADT Binary Tree

The following classes provide a generic reference-based implementation for the ADT binary tree described earlier. A discussion of several implementation details follows these classes. The specification of pre- and postconditions is left as an exercise.

```java
class TreeNode<T> {
  T item;
  TreeNode<T> leftChild;
  TreeNode<T> rightChild;

  public TreeNode(T newItem) {
  // Initializes tree node with item and no children.
    item = newItem;
    leftChild  = null;
    rightChild = null;
  }  // end constructor

  public TreeNode(T newItem,
                  TreeNode<T> left, TreeNode<T> right) {
  // Initializes tree node with item and
  // the left and right children references.
    item = newItem;
    leftChild  = left;
    rightChild = right;
  }  // end constructor

}  // end TreeNode
```
A node in a binary tree

```java
public class TreeException extends RuntimeException {
  public TreeException(String s) {
    super(s);
  }  // end constructor
} // end TreeException
```
An exception class

```java
public abstract class BinaryTreeBasis<T> {
  protected TreeNode<T> root;

  public BinaryTreeBasis() {
    root = null;
  }  // end default constructor

  public BinaryTreeBasis(T rootItem) {
    root = new TreeNode<T>(rootItem, null, null);
  }  // end constructor
```
An abstract class of basic tree operators

```java
public boolean isEmpty() {
// Returns true if the tree is empty, else returns false.
  return root == null;
}  // end isEmpty

public void makeEmpty() {
// Removes all nodes from the tree.
  root = null;
}  // end makeEmpty

public T getRootItem() throws TreeException {
// Returns the item in the tree's root.
  if (root == null) {
    throw new TreeException("TreeException: Empty tree");
  }
  else {
    return root.item;
  }  // end if
}  // end getRootItem

public abstract void setRootItem(T newItem);
  // Throws UnsupportedOperationException if operation
  // is not supported.

}  // end BinaryTreeBasis
```

BinaryTreeBasis will be used as the base class for the implementation of particular binary trees. It is declared as an abstract class because it is used for inheritance purposes only; there can be no direct instances of this class. *BinaryTreeBasis* declares the root of the tree as a protected item so that the subclasses will have direct access to the root of the tree. It also provides methods to check for an empty tree, to make the tree empty, and to retrieve the contents of the root node. Setting the contents of the root node is left to a subclass, since different kinds of binary trees may have varying requirements regarding the value in the root node of the tree. Some implementations may not support the operation *setRootItem*, they should be implemented to throw *UnsupportedOperationException*.

The following class implements the general operations of a binary tree and is derived from *BinaryTreeBasis*.

A class that extends
**BinaryTreeBasis
<T>**

```java
public class BinaryTree<T> extends BinaryTreeBasis<T> {

public BinaryTree() {
}  // end default constructor
```

```java
public BinaryTree(T rootItem) {
  super(rootItem);
} // end constructor

public BinaryTree(T rootItem,
                  BinaryTree<T> leftTree,
                  BinaryTree<T> rightTree) {
  root = new TreeNode<T>(rootItem, null, null);
  attachLeftSubtree(leftTree);
  attachRightSubtree(rightTree);
} // end constructor

public void setRootItem(T newItem) {
  if (root != null) {
    root.item = newItem;
  }
  else {
    root = new TreeNode<T>(newItem, null, null);
  } // end if
} // end setRootItem

public void attachLeft(T newItem) {
  if (!isEmpty() && root.leftChild == null) {
    // assertion: nonempty tree; no left child
    root.leftChild = new TreeNode<T>(newItem, null, null);
  } // end if
} // end attachLeft

public void attachRight(T newItem) {
  if (!isEmpty() && root.rightChild == null) {
    // assertion: nonempty tree; no right child
    root.rightChild = new TreeNode<T>(newItem, null, null);
  } // end if
} // end attachRight

public void attachLeftSubtree(BinaryTree<T> leftTree)
                                  throws TreeException {
  if (isEmpty()) {
    throw new TreeException("TreeException:  Empty tree");
  }
  else if (root.leftChild != null) {
    // a left subtree already exists; it should have been
    // deleted first
    throw new TreeException("TreeException: " +
                      "Cannot overwrite left subtree");
  }
```

```java
    else {
      // assertion: nonempty tree; no left child
      root.leftChild = leftTree.root;
      // don't want to leave multiple entry points into
      // our tree
      leftTree.makeEmpty();
    }  // end if
  }  // end attachLeftSubtree

  public void attachRightSubtree(BinaryTree<T> rightTree)
                                 throws TreeException {
    if (isEmpty()) {
      throw new TreeException("TreeException:  Empty tree");
    }
    else if (root.rightChild != null) {
      // a right subtree already exists; it should have been
      // deleted first
      throw new TreeException("TreeException: " +
                         "Cannot overwrite right subtree");
    }
    else {
      // assertion: nonempty tree; no right child
      root.rightChild = rightTree.root;
      // don't want to leave multiple entry points into
      // our tree
      rightTree.makeEmpty();
    }  // end if
  }  // end attachRightSubtree

  protected BinaryTree(TreeNode<T> rootNode) {
    root = rootNode;
  }  // end protected constructor

  public BinaryTree<T> detachLeftSubtree()
                       throws TreeException {
    if (isEmpty()) {
      throw new TreeException("TreeException:  Empty tree");
    }
    else {
      // create a new binary tree that has root's left
      // node as its root
      BinaryTree<T> leftTree;
      leftTree = new BinaryTree<T>(root.leftChild);
      root.leftChild = null;
      return leftTree;
    }  // end if
  }  // end detachLeftSubtree
```

```
   public BinaryTree<T> detachRightSubtree()
                      throws TreeException {
     if (isEmpty()) {
       throw new TreeException("TreeException:  Empty tree");
     }
     else {
       BinaryTree <T> rightTree;
       rightTree = new BinaryTree<T>(root.rightChild);
       root.rightChild = null;
       return rightTree;
     }   // end if
   }   // end detachRightSubtree
} // end BinaryTree
```

The class *BinaryTree* has more constructors than previous classes you have seen. They allow you to define binary trees in a variety of circumstances. Two of these public constructors refer back to the abstract class *BinaryTreeBasis*, with a third public constructor implemented within *BinaryTree*. With these constructors you can construct a binary tree

- That is empty

- From data for its root, which is its only node

- From data for its root and the root's two subtrees

For example, the following statements invoke these three constructors:

Sample uses of public constructors

```
BinaryTree<Integer> tree1 = new BinaryTree<Integer>();
BinaryTree<Integer> tree2 = new BinaryTree<Integer>(root2);
BinaryTree<Integer> tree3 = new BinaryTree<Integer>(root3);
BinaryTree<Integer> tree4 = new BinaryTree<Integer>(root4,
                                        tree2, tree3);
```

In these statements, *tree1* is an empty binary tree; *tree2* and *tree3* have only root nodes, whose data is *root2* and *root3*, respectively; and *tree4* is a binary tree whose root contains *root4* and has subtrees *tree2* and *tree3*.

The class also contains a protected constructor, which creates a tree from a reference to a root node. For example,

```
leftTree = new BinaryTree<T>(root.leftChild)
```

constructs a tree *leftTree* whose root is the node that *root.leftChild* references. Although the methods *detachLeftSubtree* and *detachRightSubtree* use this constructor, it should not be available to clients of the class, because they do not have access to node references. Thus, this constructor is not public.

Some methods should not be public

Note that *attachLeftSubtree* and *attachRightSubtree* call *makeEmpty* with the subtree as an argument after the subtree has been attached to the invoking tree. This causes the root of the subtree as it existed in the client to be set to *null*. Thus, the client will not be able to access and manipulate the subtree directly, a violation of abstraction of the tree.

Tree Traversals Using an Iterator

We will use the tree traversals to determine the order in which an iterator will visit the nodes of a tree. The tree iterator will implement the Java *Iterator* interface and will provide methods to set the iterator to the type of traversal desired. Since the abstract class *BinaryTreeBasis* has sufficient information to perform a traversal, we will define the iterator using this class. This will allow the iterator class to be used by any subclass of the *BinaryTreeBasis*.

As we mentioned in Chapter 9, a class that implements the *Iterator* interface must provide three methods: *next()*, *hasNext()*, and *remove()*. We will not implement the *remove()* method in this version of the iterator for two reasons: First, the semantics of removing a node from a tree may depend on the type of tree you are working with (for example, a binary search tree). Second, the class *BinaryTree* itself does not provide a method for removing nodes from the tree.

The iterator class for the binary tree should be placed in the same package as *BinaryTreeBasis*. Doing so will give the iterator access to the root of the tree and, in turn, to all of the nodes of the tree. This access is necessary for the implementation of the iterator.

You must implement the recursive traversal operations carefully so that you do not violate the wall of the ADT. For example, the method *inorder*, whose declaration is

```
void inorder(TreeNode treeNode);
```

has as a parameter the reference *treeNode*, which eventually references every node in the tree. Because this parameter clearly depends on the tree's reference-based implementation, *inorder* is not suitable as a public method. The method *inorder*, in fact, is a private method, which the public method *setInorder* calls.

The implementation presented here for the iterator of a binary tree assumes that the iteration order will be set by calling *setPreorder*, *setInorder*, or *setPostorder*. Until one of these methods is called, the iterator will not provide any items from the tree (*hasNext* returns *false*). Recall from Chapter 9 that the behavior of an iterator is unspecified if the underlying collection is modified in any way other than by calling the method *remove()* while the iteration is in progress. Thus, if the binary tree is altered after the iteration order has been set, the changes to the tree will not be reflected in the iteration.

Implement traversals so that the action to be performed remains on the client's side of the wall

Here is the definition of the tree iterator class *TreeIterator*:

```java
import java.util.LinkedList;
public class TreeIterator<T> implements java.util.Iterator<T> {
  private BinaryTreeBasis<T> binTree;
  private TreeNode<T> currentNode;
  private LinkedList <TreeNode<T>> queue; // from JCF

  public TreeIterator(BinaryTreeBasis<T> bTree) {
    binTree = bTree;
    currentNode = null;
    // empty queue indicates no traversal type currently
    // selected or end of current traversal has been reached
    queue = new LinkedList <TreeNode<T>>();
  } // end constructor

  public boolean hasNext() {
    return !queue.isEmpty();
  } // end hasNext

  public T next()
          throws java.util.NoSuchElementException {
    currentNode = queue.remove();
    return currentNode.item;
  } // end next

  public void remove()
              throws UnsupportedOperationException {
    throw new UnsupportedOperationException();
  } // end remove

  public void setPreorder() {
    queue.clear();
    preorder(binTree.root);
  } // setPreOrder

  public void setInorder() {
    queue.clear();
    inorder(binTree.root);
  } // end setInorder

  public void setPostorder() {
    queue.clear();
    postorder(binTree.root);
  } // end setPostorder
```

```java
    private void preorder(TreeNode<T> treeNode) {
      if (treeNode != null) {
        queue.add(treeNode);
        preorder(treeNode.leftChild);
        preorder(treeNode.rightChild);
      } // end if
    }  // end preorder

    private void inorder(TreeNode<T> treeNode) {
      if (treeNode != null) {
        inorder(treeNode.leftChild);
        queue.add(treeNode);
        inorder(treeNode.rightChild);
      } // end if
    }  // end inorder

    private void postorder(TreeNode<T> treeNode) {
      if (treeNode != null) {
        postorder(treeNode.leftChild);
        postorder(treeNode.rightChild);
        queue.add(treeNode);
      } // end if
    }  // end postorder
}  // end TreeIterator
```

The class *TreeIterator* uses a queue (using the *LinkedList* class from the JCF) to maintain the current traversal of the nodes in the tree. This traversal order is placed in a queue when the client selects the desired traversal method. If a new traversal is set in the middle of an iteration, the queue is cleared first, and then the new traversal is generated.

The following statements create an iterator that will perform a preorder traversal of a tree *tree4*:

```java
TreeIterator<T> treeIterator = new TreeIterator<T>(tree4);
treeIterator.setPreorder();
```

Here is an example that uses the iterator to print out the nodes of the tree using the preorder traversal:

```java
System.out.println("Preorder traversal:");
while (treeIterator.hasNext()) {
  System.out.println(treeIterator.next());
}  // end while
```

To demonstrate how to use *BinaryTree* and *TreeIterator*, we build and then traverse the binary tree in Figure 11-10:

```
public static void main(String[] args) {                    A sample program
    BinaryTree<Integer> tree3 = new BinaryTree<Integer>(70);

    // build the tree in Figure 11-10
    BinaryTree<Integer> tree1 = new BinaryTree<Integer>();
    tree1.setRootItem(40);
    tree1.attachLeft(30);
    tree1.attachRight(50);

    BinaryTree<Integer> tree2 = new BinaryTree<Integer>();
    tree2.setRootItem(20);
    tree2.attachLeft(10);
    tree2.attachRightSubtree(tree1);

    BinaryTree<Integer> binTree =    // tree in Figure 11-10
            new BinaryTree<Integer>(60, tree2, tree3);

    TreeIterator<Integer> btIterator =
            new TreeIterator<Integer>(binTree);
    btIterator.setInorder();

    while (btIterator.hasNext()) {
        System.out.println(btIterator.next());
    }   // end while

    BinaryTree<Integer> leftTree = binTree.detachLeftSubtree();
    TreeIterator<Integer> leftIterator =
                        new TreeIterator<Integer>(leftTree);

    // iterate through the left subtree
    leftIterator.setInorder();
    while (leftIterator.hasNext()) {
        System.out.println(leftIterator.next());
    }   // end while

    // iterate through binTree minus left subtree
    btIterator.setInorder();
    while (btIterator.hasNext()) {
        System.out.println(btIterator.next());
    }   // end while
}   // end main
```

Here, *binTree* is the tree in Figure 11-10. Its inorder traversal is 10, 20, 30, 40, 50, 60, 70. The inorder traversal of the left subtree of *binTree*'s root (the subtree rooted at 20) is 10, 20, 30, 40, 50. The inorder traversal of *leftTree* produces the same result. Since *leftTree* is actually detached from *binTree*, the final traversal of *binTree* is 60, 70.

One disadvantage of this implementation of the traversal is that it performs a lot of computations that may never be used. Not only is a queue of node references created, but also the recursion stores activation records on an implicit stack. Besides the time requirement, O(n) additional space is used by the recursion for a tree with n nodes. In contrast, the space requirement for a nonrecursive traversal of the tree would be only O(*height of the tree*). Programming Problem 6 asks you to explore this issue further.

Nonrecursive traversal (*optional*).   Before leaving the topic of traversals, let's develop a nonrecursive traversal algorithm to illustrate further the relationship between stacks and recursion that was discussed in Chapter 7. In particular, we will develop a nonrecursive inorder traversal for the reference-based implementation of a binary tree.

The conceptually difficult part of a nonrecursive traversal is determining where to go next after a particular node has been visited. To gain some insight into this problem, consider how the recursive *inorder* method works:

```
+inorder(in treeNode:TreeNode)
// Recursively traverses a binary tree in inorder.
```

if (treeNode != null) {

Recursive calls from points 1 and 2

```
    inorder(treeNode.leftChild)  // point 1
    queue.enqueue(treeNode)
    inorder(treeNode.rightChild) // point 2
  } // end if
```

The method has its recursive calls marked as points 1 and 2.

During the course of the method's execution, the value of the reference *treeNode* actually marks the current position in the tree. Each time *inorder* makes a recursive call, the traversal moves to another node. In terms of the stack that is implicit to recursive methods, a call to *inorder* pushes the new value of *treeNode*—that is, a reference to the new current node—onto the stack. At any given time, the stack contains references to the nodes along the path from the tree's root to the current node n, with the reference to n at the top of the stack and the reference to the root at the bottom. Note that n is possibly "empty"—that is, it may be indicated by a *null* value for *treeNode* at the top of the stack.

Study recursive inorder's implicit stack to gain insight into a nonrecursive traversal algorithm

Figure 11-15 partially traces the execution of *inorder* and shows the contents of the implicit stack. The first four steps of the trace show the stack as *treeNode* references first 60, then 20, then 10, and then becomes *null*. The recursive calls for these four steps are from point 1 in *inorder*.

Now consider what happens when *inorder* returns from a recursive call. The traversal retraces its steps by backing up the tree from a node n to its

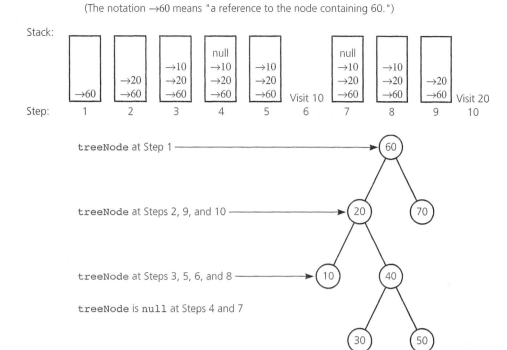

(The notation →60 means "a reference to the node containing 60.")

Stack:

Step: 1 2 3 4 5 Visit 10 6 7 8 9 Visit 20 10

treeNode at Step 1 ──────────────→ 60

treeNode at Steps 2, 9, and 10 ──────────→ 20   70

treeNode at Steps 3, 5, 6, and 8 ─────────→ 10   40

treeNode is null at Steps 4 and 7

30   50

FIGURE 11-15

Contents of the implicit stack as ***treeNode*** progresses through a given tree during a recursive inorder traversal

parent p, from which the recursive call to n was made. Thus, the reference to n is popped from the stack and the reference to p comes to the top of the stack, as occurs in Step 5 of the trace in Figure 11-15. (n happens to be empty in this case, so *null* is popped from the stack.)

What happens next depends on which subtree of p has just been traversed. If you have just finished traversing p's left subtree (that is, if n is the left child of p and thus the return is made to point 1 in *inorder*), control is returned to the statement that displays the data in node p. Such is the case for Steps 6 and 10 of the trace in Figure 11-15. Figure 11-16a illustrates Steps 9 and 10 in more detail.

After the data in p has been displayed, a recursive call is made from point 2 and the right subtree of p is traversed. However, if, as Figure 11-16b illustrates, you have just traversed p's right subtree (that is, if n is the right child of p and thus the return is made to point 2), control is returned to the end of the method. As a consequence, another return is made, the reference to p is popped off the stack, and you go back up the tree to p's parent, from which the recursive call to p was made. In this latter case, the data in p is not displayed—it was displayed before the recursive call to n was made from point 2.

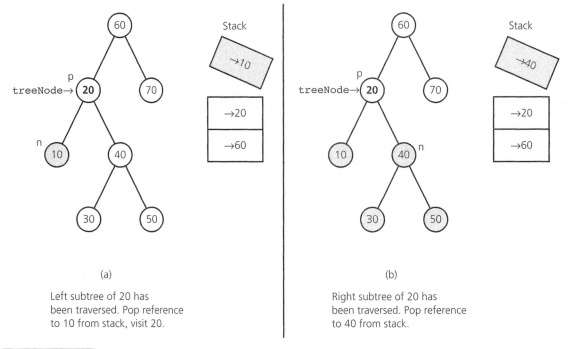

(a)

Left subtree of 20 has
been traversed. Pop reference
to 10 from stack, visit 20.

(b)

Right subtree of 20 has
been traversed. Pop reference
to 40 from stack.

FIGURE 11-16

Traversing (a) the left and (b) the right subtrees of 20

Actions at a return
from a recursive call
to *inorder*

Thus, two facts emerge from the recursive version of *inorder* when a return is made from a recursive call:

■ The implicit recursive stack of references is used to find the node *p* to which the traversal must go back.

■ Once the traversal backs up to node *p*, it either visits *p* (for example, displays its data) or backs farther up the tree. It visits *p* if *p*'s left subtree has just been traversed; it backs up if its right subtree has just been traversed. The appropriate action is taken simply as a consequence of the point—1 or 2—to which control is returned.

You could directly mimic this action by using an iterative method and an explicit stack, as long as some bookkeeping device kept track of which subtree of a node had just been traversed. However, you can use the following observation both to eliminate the need for the bookkeeping device and to speed up the traversal somewhat. Consider the tree in Figure 11-17. After you have finished traversing the subtree rooted at node *R*, there is no need to return to nodes *C* and *B*, because the right subtrees of these nodes have already been traversed. You can instead return directly to node *A*, which is the nearest ancestor of *R* whose right subtree has not yet been traversed.

This strategy of not returning to a node after its right subtree has been traversed is simple to implement: You place a reference to a node in the stack only before the node's left subtree is traversed, but not before its right subtree is

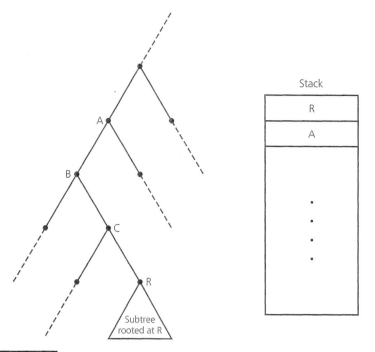

Stack

R
A
·
·
·
·

FIGURE 11-17

Avoiding returns to nodes *B* and *C*

traversed. Thus, in Figure 11-17, when you are at node *R*, the stack contains *A* and *R*, with *R* on top. Nodes *B* and *C* are not in the stack, because you have visited them already and are currently traversing their right subtrees. On the other hand, *A* is in the stack because you are currently traversing its left subtree. When you return from node *R*, nodes *B* and *C* are thus bypassed because you have finished with their right subtrees and do not need to return to these nodes. Thus, you pop *R*'s reference from the stack and go directly to node *A*, whose left subtree has just been traversed. You then visit *A*, pop its reference from the stack, and traverse *A*'s right subtree.

This nonrecursive traversal strategy is captured by then following pseudocode, assuming a reference-based implementation. Exercise 17 at the end of this chapter asks you to trace this algorithm for the tree in Figure 11-15.

Nonrecursive inorder traversal

```
+inorderTraverse(in treeNode:TreeNode)
// Nonrecursively traverses a binary tree in inorder.

   // initialize
   Create an empty stack visitStack
   curr = treeNode          // start at root treeNode
   done = false
```

```
while (!done) {
  if (curr != null) {
    // place reference to node on stack before
    // traversing node's left subtree
    visitStack.push(curr)

    // traverse the left subtree
    curr = curr.leftChild
  }

  else {// backtrack from the empty subtree and visit
        // the node at the top of the stack; however,
        // if the stack is empty, you are done
    if (!visitStack.isEmpty()) {
      curr = visitStack.pop()
      queue.enqueue(curr)

      // traverse the right subtree
      // of the node just visited
      curr = curr.rightChild
    }

    else {
      done = true
    }  // end if
  }  // end if
}  // end while
```

Eliminating recursion can be more complicated than the example given here. However, the general case is beyond the scope of this book.

11.3 The ADT Binary Search Tree

Searching for a particular item is one operation for which the ADT binary tree is ill suited. The binary search tree is a binary tree that corrects this deficiency by organizing its data by value. Recall that each node n in a binary search tree satisfies the following three properties:

- n's value is greater than all values in its left subtree T_L.

- n's value is less than all values in its right subtree T_R.

- Both T_L and T_R are binary search trees.

This organization of data enables you to search a binary search tree for a particular data item, given its value instead of its position. As you will see, certain conditions make this search efficient.

A binary search tree is often used in situations where the instances stored in the tree contain many different fields of information. For example, each item in a binary search tree might contain a person's name, ID number, address, telephone number, and so on. In general, such an item is called a **record** and will be an instance of a Java class. To determine whether a particular person is in the tree, you could provide the data for all components, or **fields,** of the record, but typically you would provide only one field—the ID number, for example. Thus, the request

Find the record for the person whose ID number is 123456789

is feasible if the ID number uniquely describes the person. By making this request, not only can you determine whether a person is in a binary search tree, but, once you find the person's record, you can also access the other data about the person.

A field such as an ID number is called a **search key,** or simply a **key,** because it identifies the record that you seek. This portion of the record may involve more than one field, and it will need to be compared to the key of other records. It is important that the value of the search key remain the same as long as the item is stored in the tree. Changing the search key of an existing element in the tree could make that element or other tree elements impossible to find. Thus, the search-key value should not be modifiable. Also, this search-key data type (or one of its superclasses) should implement the *Comparable* interface. This suggests the use of a *KeyedItem* class for items of the tree. The class *KeyedItem* will contain the search key as a data field and a method for accessing the search key. The class is declared abstract since it is only used to derive other classes and appears as follows:

> A data item in a binary search tree has a specially designated search key

```
public abstract class KeyedItem<KT extends
                             Comparable<? super KT>> {
    private KT searchKey;

    public KeyedItem(KT key) {
        searchKey = key;
    }  // end constructor

    public KT getKey() {
        return searchKey;
    } // end getKey
} // end KeyedItem
```

Classes for the items that are in a binary search tree must extend *KeyedItem.* Such classes will have only the constructor available for initializing the search key. Thus, the search-key value cannot be modified once an item is created.

As an example of a class that extends *KeyedItem,* suppose we want to create a class *Person* as just described, in which the person's ID number is used as the search key.

```
public class Person extends KeyedItem<String> {
  // inherits method getKey that returns the search key
  private FullName name;
  private String phoneNumber;
  private Address address;

  public Person(String id, FullName name, String phone,
                Address addr) {
    super(id);    // sets the key value to String id
    this.name = name;
    phoneNumber = phone;
    address = addr;
  }  // end constructor

  public String toString() {
    return getKey() + " # " + name;
  } // end toString

  // other methods would appear here
}  // end Person
```

Notice that the class *Person* inherits the *getKey* method to return the field that has been designated as the key. This will be the value that is used to search for a record in the tree. The *Person* class could easily be designed to use a key that involves more than one value. For example, if the key is the person's first name and last name, you can use the class *FullName* as presented on page 223–224 of Chapter 4, since it implements the *Comparable* interface. The class *Person* would then provide the person's full name as the key by replacing the generic parameter with *Fullname* to yield the following:

```
public class Person extends KeyedItem <Fullname> {
  private String idNumber;
  private String phoneNumber;
  private Address address;

  public Person(String id, Fullname name,
                String phone, Address addr) {
    super(name);
    idNumber = id;
    phoneNumber = phone;
    address = addr;
  } // end constructor
  ...
  // other methods appear here
```

The data fields of *Person* have been revised by omitting *name* and adding *idNumber*.

For simplicity, we will assume that the search key uniquely identifies the records in your binary search tree. In this case, you can restate the recursive definition of a binary search tree as follows:

For each node n, a binary search tree satisfies the following three properties:

A recursive definition of a binary search tree

□ n's search key is greater than all search keys in n's left subtree T_L.

□ n's search key is less than all search keys in n's right subtree T_R.

□ Both T_L and T_R are binary search trees.

As an ADT, the binary search tree has operations that are like the operations for the ADTs you studied in previous chapters in that they involve inserting, deleting, and retrieving data. In the implementations of the position-oriented ADTs list, stack, and queue, insertion and deletion into the ADT was independent of the value of the data. In the binary search tree, however, the insertion, deletion, and retrieval operations are by search-key value, not by position. The search key facilitates the search process, since we need to know only the key information to find a particular record or to determine the proper position for a data item in the tree. The traversal operations that you just saw for a binary tree apply to a binary search tree without change, because a binary search tree is a binary tree.

The operations that extend the basic ADT binary tree to the ADT binary search tree are as follows:

KEY CONCEPTS

Operations of the ADT Binary Search Tree

1. Insert a new item into a binary search tree.

2. Delete the item with a given search key from a binary search tree.

3. Retrieve the item with a given search key from a binary search tree.

4. Traverse the items in a binary search tree in preorder, inorder, or postorder.

The UML diagram in Figure 11-18 shows the basic tree operations in the class *BinaryTreeBasis*, which is then used to derive the classes *BinaryTree* and *BinarySearchTree*. The *TreeIterator* is based upon the class *BinaryTreeBasis*, and can be used by instances of both *BinaryTree* and *BinarySearchTree*.

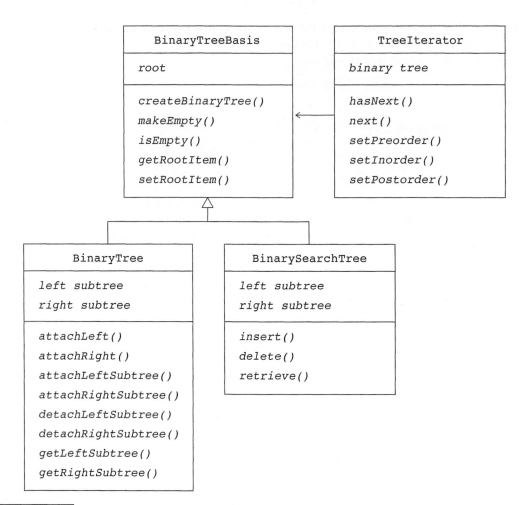

FIGURE 11-18
UML diagram for the binary tree implementations

The following pseudocode specifies the first three operations in more detail. As you soon will see, you can use the class *TreeIterator* developed earlier to perform traversals of a binary search tree.

KEY CONCEPTS

Pseudocode for the Operations of the ADT Binary Search Tree

```
+insert(in newItem:TreeItemType)
// Inserts newItem into a binary search tree whose items
// have distinct search keys that differ from newItem's
// search key.

+delete(in searchKey:KeyType) throws TreeException
// Deletes from a binary search tree the item whose search
// key equals searchKey. If no such item exists, the
// operation fails and throws TreeException.

+retrieve(in searchKey:KeyType):TreeItemType
// Returns the item in a binary search
// tree whose search key equals searchKey. Returns
// null if no such item exists.
```

Figure 11-19 is a binary search tree *nameTree* of names. Each node in the tree is actually a record that represents the named person. That is, if the search key for each record is the person's name, you see only the search keys in the picture of the tree.

For example,

```
firstRecord = nameTree.retrieve("Karen")
```

retrieves Karen's record into *firstRecord*. If you insert a record *secondRecord* into *nameTree* that describes Sarah by invoking

```
nameTree.insert(secondRecord)
```

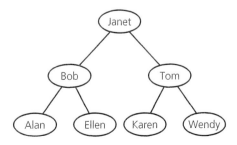

FIGURE 11-19

A binary search tree

you will be able to retrieve that record later and still be able to retrieve Karen's record. If you delete Janet's record by using

```
nameTree.delete("Janet")
```

you will still be able to retrieve the records for Karen and Sarah. Finally, if an iterator *nameIterator* is declared for *nameTree*, you display the name records as follows:

```
TreeIterator<Person> nameIterator =
                        new TreeIterator<Person>(nameTree);
nameIterator.setInorder();
System.out.println("Inorder traversal:");
while (nameIterator.hasNext()) {
  System.out.println(nameIterator.next());
}  // end while
```

This will display in alphabetical order the names of the people that *nameTree* represents.

Algorithms for the Operations of the ADT Binary Search Tree

Consider again the binary search tree in Figure 11-19. Each node in the tree contains data for a particular person. The person's first name is the search key, and that is the only data item you see in the figure.

Because a binary search tree is recursive by nature, it is natural to formulate recursive algorithms for operations on the tree. Suppose that you want to locate Ellen's record in the binary search tree of Figure 11-19. Janet is in the root node of the tree, so if Ellen's record is present in the tree it must be in Janet's left subtree, because the search key Ellen is before the search key Janet alphabetically. From the recursive definition, you know that Janet's left subtree is also a binary search tree, so you use exactly the same strategy to search this subtree for Ellen. Bob is in the root of this binary search tree, and, because the search key Ellen is greater than the search key Bob, Ellen's record must be in Bob's right subtree. Bob's right subtree is also a binary search tree, and it happens that Ellen is in the root node of this tree. Thus, the search has located Ellen's record.

A search algorithm for a binary search tree

The following pseudocode summarizes this search strategy:

```
+search(in bst:BinarySearchTree, in searchKey:KeyType)
// Searches the binary search tree bst for the item
// whose search key is searchKey.

  if (bst is empty) {
    The desired record is not found
  }
```

```
else if (searchKey == search key of root's item) {
    The desired record is found
}
else if (searchKey < search key of root's item) {
    search(Left subtree of bst, searchKey)
}
else {
    search(Right subtree of bst, searchKey)
}  // end if
```

As you will see, this *search* algorithm is the basis of the insertion, deletion, and retrieval operations on a binary search tree.

Many different binary search trees can contain the names Alan, Bob, Ellen, Janet, Karen, Tom, and Wendy. For example, in addition to the tree in Figure 11-19, each tree in Figure 11-20 is a valid binary search tree for these names. Although

Several different binary search trees are possible for the same data

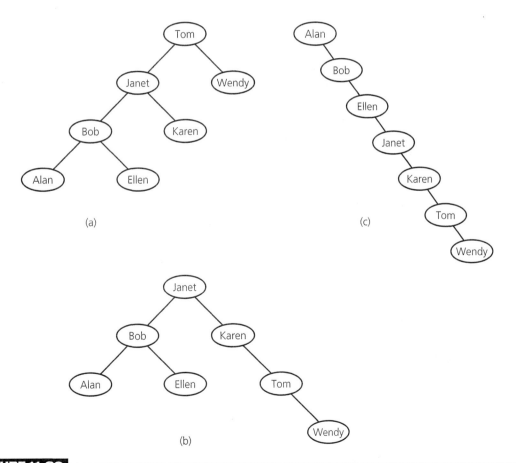

Binary search trees with the same data as in Figure 11-19

these trees have different shapes, the shape of the tree in no way affects the validity of the `search` algorithm. The algorithm requires only that a tree be a binary search tree.

The method `search` works more efficiently on some trees than on others, however. For example, with the tree in Figure 11-20c, the `search` algorithm inspects every node before locating Wendy. In fact, this binary tree really has the same structure as a sorted linear linked list and offers no advantage in efficiency. In contrast, with the full tree in Figure 11-19, the `search` algorithm inspects only the nodes that contain the names Janet, Tom, and Wendy. These names are exactly the names that a binary search of the sorted array in Figure 11-21 would inspect. Later in this chapter, you will learn more about how the shape of a binary search tree affects `search`'s efficiency and how the insertion and deletion operations affect this shape.

The algorithms that follow for insertion, deletion, retrieval, and traversal assume the reference-based implementation of a binary tree that was discussed earlier in this chapter. With minor changes, the basic algorithms also apply to other implementations of the binary tree. Also keep in mind the assumption that the items in the tree have unique search keys.

Insertion.   Suppose that you want to insert a record for Frank into the binary search tree of Figure 11-19. As a first step, imagine that you instead want to *search* for the item with a search key of Frank. The `search` algorithm first searches the tree rooted at Janet, then the tree rooted at Bob, and then the tree rooted at Ellen. It then searches the tree rooted at the right child of Ellen. Because this tree is empty, as Figure 11-22 illustrates, the `search` algorithm has reached a base case and will terminate with the report that Frank is not present. What does it mean that `search` looked for Frank in the right subtree of Ellen? For one thing, it means that if Frank were the right child of Ellen, `search` would have found Frank there.

This observation indicates that a good place to insert Frank is as the right child of Ellen. Because Ellen has no right child, the insertion is simple, requiring only that Ellen's `rightChild` field reference a node containing Frank. More important, Frank belongs in this location—`search` will look for Frank here. Specifically, inserting Frank as the right child of Ellen will preserve the tree's binary search tree property. Because `search`, when searching for Frank, would follow a path that leads to the right child of Ellen, you are assured that Frank is in the proper relation to the names above it in the tree.

Use **search** to determine the insertion point

Using `search` to determine where in the tree to insert a new name always leads to an easy insertion. No matter what new item you insert into the tree, `search` will always terminate at an empty subtree. Thus, `search` always tells

Alan	Bob	Ellen	Janet	Karen	Tom	Wendy
0	1	2	3	4	5	6

FIGURE 11-21

An array of names in sorted order

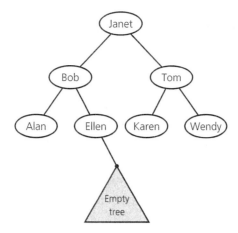

FIGURE 11-22

Empty subtree where **search** terminates

you to insert the item as a new leaf. Because adding a leaf requires only a change of the appropriate reference in the parent, the work required for an insertion is virtually the same as that for the corresponding search.

The following high-level pseudocode describes this insertion process:

First draft of the insertion algorithm

```
insertItem(in treeNode:TreeNode, in newItem:TreeItemType)
// Inserts newItem into the binary search tree of
// which treeNode is the root.
  Let parentNode be the parent of the empty subtree
      at which search terminates when it seeks
      newItem's search key

  if (Search terminated at parentNode's left subtree) {
    Set leftChild of parentNode to reference newItem
  }
  else {
    Set rightChild of parentNode to reference newItem
  }  // end if
```

The appropriate reference—*leftChild* or *rightChild*—of node *parentNode* must be set to reference the new node. The recursive nature of the *search* algorithm provides an elegant means of setting the reference, provided that you return *treeNode* as the result of the method, as you will see. Thus, *insertItem* is refined as follows:

Refinement of the insertion algorithm

```
+insertItem(in treeNode:TreeNode, in newItem:TreeItemType)
// Inserts newItem into the binary search tree of
// which treeNode is the root.
```

```
if (treeNode is null) {
    Create a new node and let treeNode reference it
    Create a new node with newItem as the data portion
    Set the references in the new node to null
}

else if (newItem.getKey() < treeNode.item.getKey()) {
    treeNode.leftChild = insertItem(treeNode.leftChild, newItem)
}
else {
    treeNode.rightChild = insertItem(treeNode.rightChild, newItem)
}  // end if

return treeNode
```

How does this recursive algorithm set *leftChild* and *rightChild* to reference the new node? The situation is quite similar to the recursive insertion method for the sorted linked list that you saw in Chapter 5. If the tree was empty before the insertion, the external reference to the root of the tree would be *null* and the method would not make a recursive call. When this situation occurs, a new tree node must be created and initialized. The method then returns the reference to this node, which should be made the new root of the tree. Figure 11-23a illustrates insertion into an empty tree.

The general case of *insertItem* is similar to the special case for an empty tree. When the formal parameter *treeNode* becomes *null*, the corresponding actual argument is the *leftChild* or *rightChild* reference in the parent of the empty subtree; that is, this reference has the value *null*. This reference was passed to the *insertItem* method by one of the recursive calls

```
insertItem(treeNode.leftChild, newItem)
```

or

```
insertItem(treeNode.rightChild, newItem)
```

As in the case of the empty tree, the method will return the reference to a new node, which then must be set as either the parent's left child or the parent's right child. Thus, you complete the insertion by using either *leftChild* to make the node the new left child of the parent, or *rightChild* to make the node the new right child of the parent. Parts *b* and *c* of Figure 11-23 illustrate the general case of insertion.

You can use *insertItem* to create a binary search tree. For example, beginning with an empty tree, if you insert the names Janet, Bob, Alan, Ellen, Tom, Karen, and Wendy in order, you will get the binary search tree in Figure 11-19. It is interesting to note that the names Janet, Bob, Alan, Ellen, Tom, Karen, and Wendy constitute the preorder traversal of the tree in Figure 11-19.

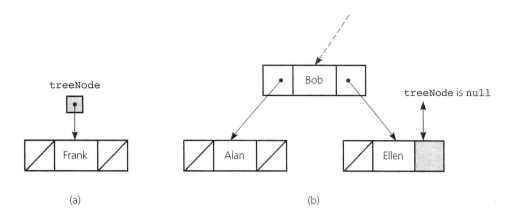

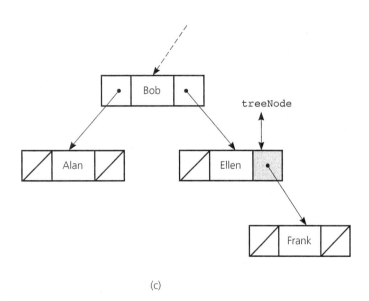

FIGURE 11-23

(a) Insertion into an empty tree; (b) search terminates at a leaf; (c) insertion at a leaf

Thus, if you take the output of a preorder traversal of a binary search tree and use it with *insertItem* to create a binary search tree, you will obtain a duplicate tree.

To copy a tree, traverse it in preorder and insert each item visited into a new tree

By inserting the previous names in a different order, you will get a different binary search tree. For example, by inserting the previous names in alphabetic order, you will get the binary search tree in Figure 11-20c.

Deletion. The deletion operation is a bit more involved than insertion. First, you use the *search* algorithm to locate the item with the specified search key

First draft of the deletion algorithm

and then, if it is found, you must remove the item from the tree. A first draft of the algorithm follows:

```
+deleteItem(in rootNode:TreeNode, in searchKey:KeyType)
// Deletes from the binary search tree (with root
// rootNode) the item whose search key equals
// searchKey. If no such item exists, the operation
// fails and throws TreeException.
   Locate (by using the search algorithm) the item i
       whose search key equals searchKey

  if (item i is found) {
    Remove item i from the tree
  }
  else {
    throw a tree exception
  }  // end if
```

The essential task here is

```
Remove item i from the tree
```

Three cases for the node N containing the item to be deleted

Assuming that deleteItem locates item i in a particular node N, there are three cases to consider:

1. N is a leaf.

2. N has only one child.

3. N has two children.

Case 1: Set the reference in a leaf's parent to **null**

The first case is the easiest. To remove the leaf containing item i, you need only set the reference in its parent to null. The second case is a bit more difficult. If N has only one child, you have two possibilities:

Case 2: Two possibilities for a node with one child

■ N has only a left child.

■ N has only a right child.

The two possibilities are symmetrical, so it is sufficient to illustrate the solution for a left child. In Figure 11-24a, L is the left child of N, and P is the parent of N. N can be either the left child or the right child of P. If you deleted N from the tree, L would be without a parent, and P would be without one of its children. Suppose you let L take the place of N as one of P's children, as in Figure 11-24b. Does this adoption preserve the binary search tree property?

Let N's parent adopt N's child

If N is the left child of P, for example, all of the search keys in the subtree rooted at N are less than the search key in P. Thus, all of the search keys in the subtree rooted at L are less than the search key in P. Therefore, after N is removed and L is adopted by P, all of the search keys in P's left subtree are still less than the search key in P. This deletion strategy thus preserves the binary

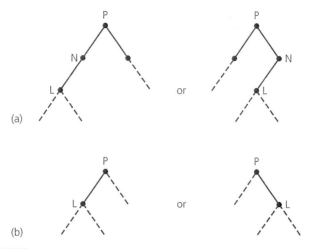

FIGURE 11-24

(a) *N* with only a left child—*N* can be either the left or right child of *P*; (b) after deleting node *N*

search tree property. A parallel argument holds if *N* is a right child of *P*, and therefore the binary search tree property is preserved in either case.

The most difficult of the three cases occurs when the item to be deleted is in a node *N* that has two children, as in Figure 11-25. As you just saw, when *N* has only one child, the child replaces *N*. However, when *N* has two children, these children cannot both replace *N*: *N*'s parent has room for only one of *N*'s children as a replacement for *N*. A different strategy is necessary.

> Case 3: *N* has two children

In fact, you will not delete *N* at all. You can find another node that is easier to delete and delete it instead of *N*. This strategy may sound like cheating. After all, the programmer who requests

```
nameTree.delete(searchKey)
```

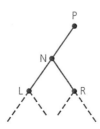

FIGURE 11-25

N with two children

expects that the item whose search key equals `searchKey` will be deleted from the ADT binary search tree. However, the programmer expects only that the *item* will be deleted and has no right, because of the wall between the program and the ADT implementation, to expect a particular *node* in the tree to be deleted.

Deleting an item
whose node has two
children

Consider, then, an alternate strategy. To delete from a binary search tree an item that resides in a node N that has two children, take the following steps:

1. Locate another node M that is easier to remove from the tree than the node N.

2. Copy the item that is in M to N, thus effectively deleting from the tree the item originally in N.

3. Remove the node M from the tree.

What kind of node M is easier to remove than the node N? Because you know how to delete a node that has no children or one child, M could be such a node. You have to be careful, though. Can you choose any node and copy its data into N? No, because you must preserve the tree's status as a binary search tree. For example, if in the tree of Figure 11-26, you copied the data from M to N, the result would no longer be a binary search tree.

What data item, when copied into the node N, will preserve the tree's status as a binary search tree? All of the search keys in the left subtree of N are less than the search key in N, and all of the search keys in the right subtree of N are greater than the search key in N. You must retain this property when you replace the search key x in node N with the search key y. There are two suitable possibilities for the value y: It can come immediately after or immediately before x in the sorted order of search keys. If y comes immediately after x, then clearly all search keys in the left subtree of N are smaller than y, because they are all smaller than x, as Figure 11-27 illustrates. Further, all search keys

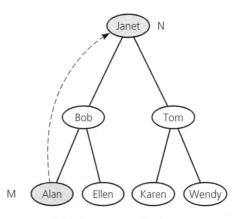

FIGURE 11-26

Not any node will do

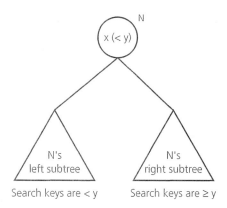

Search keys are < y   Search keys are ≥ y

FIGURE 11-27

Search key *x* can be replaced by *y*

in the right subtree of N are greater than or equal to y, because they are greater than x and, by assumption, there are no search keys in the tree between x and y. A similar argument illustrates that if y comes immediately before x in the sorted order, it is greater than or equal to all search keys in the left subtree of N and smaller than all search keys in the right subtree of N.

You can thus copy into N either the item whose search key is immediately after N's search key[4] or the item whose search key is immediately before it. Suppose that, arbitrarily, you decide to use the node whose search key y comes immediately after N's search key x. This search key is called x's **inorder successor.**[5] How can you locate this node? Because N has two children, the inorder successor of its search key is in the leftmost node of N's right subtree. That is, to find the node that contains y, you follow N's `rightChild` reference to its right child R, which must be present because N has two children. You then descend the tree rooted at R by taking left branches at each node until you encounter a node M with no left child. You copy the item in this node M into node N and then, because M has no left child, you can remove M from the tree as one of the two easy cases. (See Figure 11-28.)

> The inorder successor of N's search key is in the leftmost node in N's right subtree

A more detailed high-level description of the deletion algorithm follows:

> Second draft of the deletion algorithm

```
+deleteItem(in rootNode:TreeNode, in searchKey:KeyType)
// Deletes from the binary search tree (with root rootNode)
// the item whose search key equals searchKey. If no such
// item exists, the operation fails and throws TreeException.

   Locate (by using the search algorithm) the
      item whose search key equals searchKey; it
      occurs in node i
```

---

4. N's search key is the search key of the data item in N.
5. We also will use the term N's **inorder successor** to mean the inorder successor of N's search key.

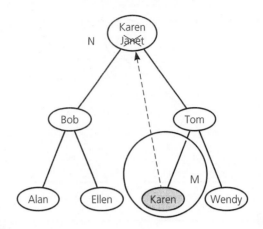

FIGURE 11-28

Copying the item whose search key is the inorder successor of *N*'s search key

```
if (item is found in node i) {
   deleteNode(i)  // defined next
}
else {
   throw a tree exception
}  // end if


+deleteNode(in treeNode:TreeNode):TreeNode
// Deletes the item in treeNode. Returns
// the root node of the resulting tree.

if (treeNode is a leaf) {
   Remove treeNode from the tree
}
else if (treeNode has only one child c) {
   if (c was a left child of its parent p){
      Make c the left child of p
   }
   else {
      Make c the right child of p
   }  // end if
}
else { // treeNode has two children
   Find the item contained in treeNode's
       inorder successor
   Copy the item into treeNode
   Remove treeNode's inorder successor by using the
       previous technique for a leaf or a node
       with one child
}  // end if
return reference to root node of resulting tree
```

In the following refinement, *search*'s algorithm is adapted and inserted directly into *deleteItem*. Also, the method *deleteNode* uses the method *findLeftmost* to find the item in the node *M*, that is, the inorder successor of node *N*. The item in *M* is saved for later replacement of the item in node *N*. Next, *deleteLeftmost* deletes *M* from the tree. The saved item then replaces the item in node *N*, thus deleting it from the binary search tree.

Final draft of the deletion algorithm

```
+deleteItem(in rootNode:TreeNode, in searchKey:KeyType):TreeNode
// Deletes from the binary search tree (with root
// rootNode) the item whose search key equals searchKey.
// Returns the root node of the resulting tree.
// If no such item exists, the operation
// fails and throws TreeException.

  if (rootNode is null) {
    throw TreeException // item not found
  }
  else if (searchKey equals the key in rootNode item) {
   // delete the rootNode; a new root of the tree is
   // returned
    newRoot = deleteNode(rootNode, searchKey)
    return newRoot
  }
  else if (searchKey is less than the key in rootNode item) {
    newLeft = deleteItem(rootNode.leftChild, searchKey)
    rootNode.leftChild = newLeft
    return rootNode // returns rootNode with new left
                    // subtree
  }
  else { // search the right subtree
    newRight = deleteItem(rootNode.rightChild, searchKey)
    rootNode.rightChild = newRight
    return rootNode // returns rootNode with new right
                    // subtree
} // end if

+deleteNode(in treeNode:TreeNode):TreeNode
// Deletes the item in the node referenced by treeNode.
// Returns the root node of the resulting tree.

  if (treeNode is a leaf) {
    // remove leaf from the tree
   return null
  }
```

```
  else if (treeNode has only one child c) {
    // c replaces treeNode as the child of
    // treeNode's parent
    if (c is the left child of treeNode) {
      return treeNode.leftChild
    }
    else {
      return treeNode.rightChild
    }  // end if
  }
  else { // treeNode has two children
    // find the inorder successor of the search key in
    // treeNode: it is in the leftmost node of the
    // subtree rooted at treeNode's right child
    replacementItem = findLeftMost(treeNode.rightChild)
    replacementRChild = deleteLeftmost(treeNode.rightChild)
    Set treeNode's item to replacementItem
    Set treeNode's right child to replacementRChild
    return treeNode
  }  // end if


+findLeftmost(in treeNode:TreeNode):TreeNode
// Returns the item that is the leftmost
// descendant of the tree rooted at treeNode.
  if (treeNode.leftChild == null) {
    // this is the node you want, so return its item
    return treeNode.item
  }
  else {
    return findLeftmost(treeNode.leftChild)
  }  // end if


+deleteLeftmost(in treeNode:TreeNode):TreeNode
// Deletes the node that is the leftmost
// descendant of the tree rooted at treeNode.
// Returns subtree of deleted node.

  if (treeNode.leftChild == null) {
    // this is the node you want; it has no left
    // child, but it might have a right subtree

    // the return value of this method is a
    // child reference of treeNode's parent; thus, the
    // following "moves up" treeNode's right subtree
    return treeNode.rightChild
  }
```

```
else {
   replacementLChild = deleteLeftmost(treeNode.leftChild)
   treeNode.leftChild = replacementLChild
   return treeNode
}  // end if
```

Observe that, as in the case of the *insertItem* method, the actual argument that corresponds to *rootNode* either is one of the references of the parent of *N*, as Figure 11-29 depicts, or is the external reference to the root, in the case where *N* is the root of the original tree. In either case *rootNode* references *N*. Thus, any change you make to *rootNode* by calling the method *deleteNode* with actual argument *rootNode* changes the reference in the parent of *N*. The recursive method *deleteLeftmost*, which is called by *deleteNode* if *N* has two children, also uses this strategy to remove the inorder successor of the node containing the item to be deleted.

Exercise 30 at the end of this chapter describes an easier deletion algorithm. However, that algorithm tends to increase the height of the tree, and, as you will see later, an increase in height can decrease the efficiency of searching the tree.

Retrieval.   By refining the *search* algorithm, you can implement the retrieval operation. Recall that the *search* algorithm is

```
+search(in bst:BinarySearchTree, in searchKey:KeyType)
// Searches the binary search tree bst for the item
// whose search key is searchKey.

  if (bst is empty) {
     The desired record is not found
  }
```

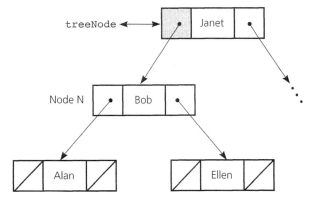

Any change to treeNode while deleting node N (Bob) changes leftChild of Janet

FIGURE 11-29

Recursive deletion of node *N*

```
else if (searchKey == search key of bst's root item) {
  The desired record is found
}
else if (searchKey < search key of bst's root item) {
  search(Left subtree of bst, searchKey)
}
else {
  search(Right subtree of bst, searchKey)
}  // end if
```

retrieveItem is a refinement of **search**

The retrieval operation must return the item with the desired search key if it exists; otherwise it must return a *null* reference. The retrieval algorithm, therefore, appears as follows:

```
+retrieveItem(in treeNode:TreeNode,
              in searchKey:KeyType):TreeItemType
// Returns the item (treeItem) whose search
// key equals searchKey from the binary search tree
// that has treeNode as its root. The operation
// returns a null reference if no such item
// exists.

  if (treeNode == null) {
    treeItem = null  // tree is empty
  }
  else if (searchKey == treeNode.item.getKey()) {
    // item is in the root of some subtree
    treeItem = treeNode.item
  }
  else if (searchKey < treeNode.item.getKey()) {
    // search the left subtree
    treeItem =
    retrieveItem(treeNode.leftChild, searchKey)
  }
  else { // search the right subtree
    treeItem =
    retrieveItem(treeNode.rightChild, searchKey)
  }  // end if

  return treeItem
```

Traversal.   The traversals for a binary search tree are the same as the traversals for a binary tree. You should be aware, however, that an inorder traversal of a binary search tree will visit the tree's nodes in sorted search-key order. Before seeing the proof of this statement, recall the inorder traversal algorithm:

```
+inorder(in bst:BinarySearchTree)
// Traverses the binary tree bst in inorder.

  if (bst is not empty) {
    inorder(Left subtree of bst's root)
    Process the root of bst
    inorder(Right subtree of bst's root)
  } // end if
```

THEOREM 11-1.   The inorder traversal of a binary search tree T will visit its nodes in sorted search-key order.

PROOF.   The proof is by induction on h, the height of T.

Basis: $h = 0$. When T is empty, the algorithm does not visit any nodes. This is the proper sorted order for the zero names that are in the tree!

Inductive hypothesis: Assume that the theorem is true for all k, $0 < k < h$. That is, assume for all k $(0 < k < h)$ that the inorder traversal visits the nodes in sorted search-key order.

Inductive conclusion: You must show that the theorem is true for $k = h > 0$. T has the form

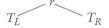

Because T is a binary search tree, all the search keys in the left subtree T_L are less than the search key in the root r, and all the search keys in the right subtree T_R are greater than the search key in r. The `inorder` algorithm will visit all the nodes in T_L, then visit r, and then visit all the nodes in T_R. Thus, the only concern is that `inorder` visit the nodes within each of the subtrees T_L and T_R in the correct sorted order. But because T is a binary search tree of height h, each subtree is a binary search tree of height less than h. Therefore, by the inductive hypothesis, `inorder` visits the nodes in each subtree T_L and T_R in the correct sorted search-key order. (**End of proof.**)

It follows from this theorem that `inorder` visits a node's inorder successor immediately after it visits the node.

> Use inorder traversal to visit nodes of a binary search tree in search-key order

A Reference-Based Implementation of the ADT Binary Search Tree

A Java reference-based implementation of the ADT binary search tree follows. Notice the protected methods that implement the recursive algorithms. These methods are not public, because clients do not have access to node references.

The methods could be private, but making them protected enables a derived class to use them directly.

```java
import SearchKeys.KeyedItem;

// ADT binary search tree.
//  Assumption: A tree contains at most one item with a
//              given search key at any time.

public class BinarySearchTree<T extends KeyedItem<KT>,
                              KT extends Comparable<? super KT>>
     extends BinaryTreeBasis<T> {
// inherits isEmpty(), makeEmpty(), getRootItem(), and
// the use of the constructors from BinaryTreeBasis

  public BinarySearchTree() {
  }  // end default constructor

  public BinarySearchTree(T rootItem) {
    super(rootItem);
  }  // end constructor

  public void setRootItem(T newItem)
            throws UnsupportedOperationException {
    throw new UnsupportedOperationException();
  }  // end setRootItem

  public void insert(T newItem) {
    root = insertItem(root, newItem);
  }  // end insert

  public T retrieve(KT searchKey) {
    return retrieveItem(root, searchKey);
  }  // end retrieve

  public void delete(KT searchKey) throws TreeException {
    root = deleteItem(root, searchKey);
  }  // end delete

  public void delete(T item) throws TreeException {
    root = deleteItem(root, item.getKey());
  }  // end delete

  protected TreeNode<T> insertItem(TreeNode<T> tNode,
                                   T newItem) {
    TreeNode<T> newSubtree;
    if (tNode == null) {
```

```java
      // position of insertion found; insert after leaf
      // create a new node
      tNode = new TreeNode<T>(newItem, null, null);
      return tNode;
    } // end if
    T nodeItem = tNode.item;

    // search for the insertion position

    if (newItem.getKey().compareTo(nodeItem.getKey()) < 0) {
      // search the left subtree
      newSubtree = insertItem(tNode.leftChild, newItem);
      tNode.leftChild = newSubtree;
      return tNode;
    }
    else { // search the right subtree
      newSubtree = insertItem(tNode.rightChild, newItem);
      tNode.rightChild = newSubtree;
      return tNode;
    } // end if
  } // end insertItem

  protected T retrieveItem(TreeNode<T> tNode,
                           KT searchKey) {
    T treeItem;
    if (tNode == null) {
      treeItem = null;
    }
    else {
      T nodeItem = tNode.item;
      if (searchKey.compareTo(nodeItem.getKey()) == 0) {
        // item is in the root of some subtree
        treeItem = tNode.item;
      }
      else if (searchKey.compareTo(nodeItem.getKey()) < 0) {
        // search the left subtree
        treeItem = retrieveItem(tNode.leftChild, searchKey);
      }
      else { // search the right subtree
        treeItem = retrieveItem(tNode.rightChild, searchKey);
      } // end if
    } // end if
    return treeItem;
  } // end retrieveItem

  protected TreeNode<T> deleteItem(TreeNode<T> tNode,
                                   KT searchKey) {
    // Calls: deleteNode.
```

```
                    TreeNode<T> newSubtree;
                    if (tNode == null) {
                       throw new TreeException("TreeException: Item not found");
                    }
                    else {
                       T nodeItem = tNode.item;
                       if (searchKey.compareTo(nodeItem.getKey()) == 0) {
                          // item is in the root of some subtree
                          tNode = deleteNode(tNode);  // delete the item
                       }
                       // else search for the item
                       else if (searchKey.compareTo(nodeItem.getKey()) < 0) {
                          // search the left subtree
                          newSubtree = deleteItem(tNode.leftChild, searchKey);
                          tNode.leftChild = newSubtree;
                       }
                       else { // search the right subtree
                          newSubtree = deleteItem(tNode.rightChild, searchKey);
                          tNode.rightChild = newSubtree;
                       }  // end if
                    }  // end if
                    return tNode;
                 }  // end deleteItem

                 protected TreeNode<T> deleteNode(TreeNode<T> tNode) {
                    // Algorithm note: There are four cases to consider:
                    //    1. The tNode is a leaf.
                    //    2. The tNode has no left child.
                    //    3. The tNode has no right child.
                    //    4. The tNode has two children.
                    // Calls: findLeftmost and deleteLeftmost
                    T replacementItem;

                    // test for a leaf
                    if ( (tNode.leftChild == null) &&
                         (tNode.rightChild == null) ) {
                       return null;
                    }  // end if leaf

                    // test for no left child
                    else if (tNode.leftChild == null) {
                       return tNode.rightChild;
                    }  // end if no left child

                    // test for no right child
                    else if (tNode.rightChild == null) {
```

```
      return tNode.leftChild;
   }  // end if no right child

   // there are two children:
   // retrieve and delete the inorder successor
   else {
      replacementItem = findLeftmost(tNode.rightChild);
      tNode.item = replacementItem;
      tNode.rightChild = deleteLeftmost(tNode.rightChild);
      return tNode;
   }  // end if
}  // end deleteNode

protected T findLeftmost(TreeNode<T> tNode)  {
   if (tNode.leftChild == null) {
      return tNode.item;
   }
   else {
      return findLeftmost(tNode.leftChild);
   }  // end if
}  // end findLeftmost

protected TreeNode<T> deleteLeftmost(TreeNode<T> tNode) {
   if (tNode.leftChild == null) {
      return tNode.rightChild;
   }
   else {
      tNode.leftChild = deleteLeftmost(tNode.leftChild);
      return tNode;
   }  // end if
}  // end deleteLeftmost

}  // end BinarySearchTree
```

The class *TreeIterator* developed earlier in the chapter can be used with *BinarySearchTree*. It would also make sense to implement the *remove* method, since *BinarySearchTree* provides a method for deleting a node from the tree. Exercise 32 at the end of this chapter asks you to explore this possibility.

The Efficiency of Binary Search Tree Operations

You have seen binary search trees in many shapes. For example, even though the binary search trees in Figures 11-19 and 11-20c have seven nodes each, they have radically different shapes and heights. You saw that to locate Wendy in Figure 11-20c, you would have to inspect all seven nodes, but you can locate Wendy in Figure 11-19 by inspecting only three nodes (Janet, Tom, and Wendy). Consider now the relationship between the height of a binary search tree and the efficiency of the retrieval, insertion, and deletion operations.

Each of these operations compares the specified value `searchKey` to the search keys in the nodes along a **path** through the tree. This path always starts at the root of the tree and, at each node *N*, follows the left or right branch, depending on the comparison of `searchKey` to the search key in *N*. The path terminates at the node that contains `searchKey` or, if `searchKey` is not present, at an empty subtree. Thus, each retrieval, insertion, or deletion operation requires a number of comparisons equal to the number of nodes along this path. This means that the maximum number of comparisons that each operation can require is the number of nodes on the longest path through the tree. In other words, the *maximum number of comparisons that these operations can require is equal to the height of the binary search tree*. What, then, are the maximum and minimum heights of a binary search tree of *n* nodes?

> The maximum number of comparisons for a retrieval, insertion, or deletion is the height of the tree

> *n* is the maximum height of a binary tree with *n* nodes

The maximum and minimum heights of a binary search tree. You can maximize the height of a binary tree with *n* nodes simply by giving each internal node (nonleaf) exactly one child, as shown in Figure 11-30. This process will result in a tree of height *n*. An *n*-node tree with height *n* strikingly resembles a linear linked list.

A minimum-height binary tree with *n* nodes is a bit more difficult to obtain. As a first step, consider the number of nodes that a binary tree with a given height *h* can have. For example, if *h* = 3, the possible binary trees include those in Figure 11-31. Thus, binary trees of height 3 can have between 3 and 7 nodes. In addition, Figure 11-31 shows that 3 is the minimum height for a binary tree with 4, 5, 6, or 7 nodes. Similarly, binary trees with more than 7 nodes require a height greater than 3.

> Except for the last level, each level of a minimum-height binary tree must contain as many nodes as possible

Intuitively, to minimize the height of a binary tree given *n* nodes, you must fill each level of the tree as completely as possible. A complete tree meets this requirement (although it does not matter whether the nodes on the last level are filled left

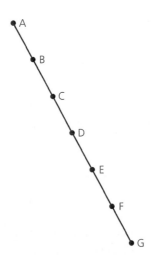

FIGURE 11-30

A maximum-height binary tree with seven nodes

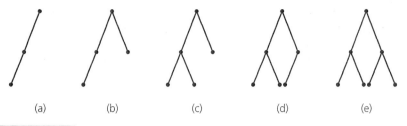

(a)   (b)   (c)   (d)   (e)

FIGURE 11-31

Binary trees of height 3

to right). In fact, trees *b*, *c*, *d*, and *e* of Figure 11-31 are complete trees. If a complete binary tree of a given height *h* is to have the maximum possible number of nodes, it should be full (as in Figure 11-31e). Figure 11-32 counts these nodes by level and shows the following:

THEOREM 11-2. A full binary tree of height $h \geq 0$ has $2^h - 1$ nodes.

A formal proof by induction of this theorem is left as an exercise.

It follows then that

THEOREM 11-3. The maximum number of nodes that a binary tree of height *h* can have is $2^h - 1$.

You cannot add nodes to a full binary tree of height *h* without increasing its height. The formal proof of this theorem, which closely parallels that of Theorem 11-2, is left as an exercise.

	Level	Number of nodes at this level	Number of nodes at this and previous levels
	1	$1 = 2^0$	$1 = 2^1 - 1$
	2	$2 = 2^1$	$3 = 2^2 - 1$
	3	$4 = 2^2$	$7 = 2^3 - 1$
	4	$8 = 2^3$	$15 = 2^4 - 1$
	.	.	.
	.	.	.
	.	.	.
	h	2^{h-1}	$2^h - 1$

FIGURE 11-32

Counting the nodes in a full binary tree of height *h*

The following theorem uses Theorems 11-2 and 11-3 to determine the minimum height of a binary tree that contains some given number of nodes.

THEOREM 11-4. The minimum height of a binary tree with n nodes is $\lceil \log_2(n + 1) \rceil$.[6]

PROOF. Let h be the smallest integer such that $n \le 2^h - 1$. To find the minimum height of a binary tree with n nodes, first establish the following facts:

1. *A binary tree whose height is $\le h - 1$ has $< n$ nodes.*

   By Theorem 11-3, a binary tree of height $h - 1$ has at most $2^{h-1} - 1$ nodes. If it is possible that $n \le 2^{h-1} - 1 < 2^h - 1$, then h is not the smallest integer such that $n \le 2^h - 1$. Therefore, n must be greater than $2^{h-1} - 1$ or, equivalently, $2^{h-1} - 1 < n$. Because a binary tree of height $h - 1$ has at most $2^{h-1} - 1$ nodes, it must have fewer than n nodes.

2. *There exists a complete binary tree of height h that has exactly n nodes.*

   Consider the full binary tree of height $h - 1$. By Theorem 11-2, it has $2^{h-1} - 1$ nodes. As you just saw, $n > 2^{h-1} - 1$ because h was selected so that $n \le 2^h - 1$. You can thus add nodes to the full tree from left to right until you have n nodes, as Figure 11-33 illustrates. Because $n \le 2^h - 1$ and a binary tree of height h cannot have more than $2^h - 1$ nodes, you will reach n nodes by the time level h is filled up.

3. *The minimum height of a binary tree with n nodes is the smallest integer h such that $n \le 2^h - 1$.*

   If h is the smallest integer such that $n \le 2^h - 1$, and if a binary tree has height $\le h - 1$, then by fact 1, it has fewer than n nodes. Because by fact 2 there is a binary tree of height h that has exactly n nodes, h must be as small as possible.

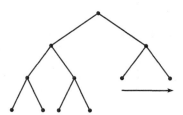

FIGURE 11-33

Filling in the last level of a tree

---

6. The **ceiling of X**, which $\lceil X \rceil$ denotes, is X rounded up. For example, $\lceil 6 \rceil = 6$, $\lceil 6.1 \rceil = 7$, and $\lceil 6.8 \rceil = 7$.

The previous discussion implies that

$$2^{h-1} - 1 < n \leq 2^h - 1$$
$$2^{h-1} < n + 1 \leq 2^h$$
$$h - 1 < \log_2(n + 1) \leq h$$

If $\log_2(n + 1) = h$, the theorem is proven. Otherwise, $h - 1 < \log_2(n + 1) < h$ implies that $\log_2(n + 1)$ cannot be an integer. Therefore, round $\log_2(n + 1)$ up to get h.

Thus, $h = \lceil \log_2(n + 1) \rceil$ is the minimum height of a binary tree with n nodes. **(End of proof.)**

Complete trees and full trees with n nodes thus have heights of $\lceil \log_2(n + 1) \rceil$, which, as you just saw, is the theoretical minimum. This minimum height is the same as the maximum number of comparisons a binary search must make to search an array with n elements. Thus, if a binary search tree is complete and therefore balanced, the time it takes to search it for a value is about the same as that required for a binary search of an array. On the other hand, as you go from balanced trees toward trees with a linear structure, the height approaches the number of nodes n. This number is the same as the maximum number of comparisons that you must make when searching a linked list of n nodes.

Complete trees and full trees have minimum height

The height of an n-node binary search tree ranges from $\lceil \log_2(n + 1) \rceil$ to n

However, the outstanding efficiency of the operations on a binary search tree hinges on the assumption that the height of the binary search tree is $\lceil \log_2(n + 1) \rceil$. What will the height of a binary search tree actually be? The factor that determines the height of a binary search tree is the order in which you perform the insertion and deletion operations on the tree. Recall that, starting with an empty tree, if you insert names in the order Alan, Bob, Ellen, Janet, Karen, Tom, Wendy, you would obtain a binary search tree of maximum height, as shown in Figure 11-20c. On the other hand, if you insert names in the order Janet, Bob, Tom, Alan, Ellen, Karen, Wendy, you would obtain a binary search tree of minimum height, as shown in Figure 11-19.

Insertion in search-key order produces a maximum-height binary search tree

Which of these situations should you expect to encounter in the course of a real application? It can be proven mathematically that if the insertion and deletion operations occur in a random order, the height of the binary search tree will be quite close to $\log_2 n$. Thus, in this sense, the previous analysis is not unduly optimistic. However, in a real-world application, is it realistic to expect the insertion and deletion operations to occur in random order? In many applications, the answer is yes. There are, however, applications in which this assumption would be dubious. For example, the person preparing the previous sequence of names for the insertion operations might well decide to "help you out" by arranging the names to be inserted into sorted order. This arrangement, as has been mentioned, would lead to a tree of maximum height. Thus, while in many applications you can expect the behavior of a binary search tree to be excellent, you should be wary of the possibility of poor performance due to some characteristic of a given application.

Insertion in random order produces a near-minimum-height binary search tree

Is there anything you can do if you suspect that the operations might not occur in a random order? Similarly, is there anything you can do if you have an enormous number of items and need to ensure that the height of the tree is close to $\log_2 n$? Chapter 13 presents variations of the basic binary search tree that are guaranteed always to remain balanced.

Figure 11-34 summarizes the order of the retrieval, insertion, deletion, and traversal operations for the ADT binary search tree.

Treesort

You can use the ADT binary search tree to sort an array of records efficiently into search-key order. To simplify the discussion, however, we will sort an array of integers into ascending order, as we did with the sorting algorithms in Chapter 10.

The basic idea of the algorithm is simple:

Treesort uses a binary search tree

```
+treesort(inout anArray:ArrayType, in n:integer)
// Sorts the n integers in array anArray into
// ascending order.

    Insert anArray's elements into a binary search tree
        bTree

    Traverse bTree inorder. As you visit bTree's nodes, copy
        their data items into successive locations of anArray
```

An inorder traversal of the binary search tree *bTree* visits the integers in *bTree*'s nodes in ascending order.

A treesort can be quite efficient. As Figure 11-34 indicates, each insertion into a binary search tree requires $O(\log n)$ operations in the average case and $O(n)$ operations in the worst case. Thus, *treesort*'s *n* insertions require $O(n * \log n)$ operations in the average case and $O(n^2)$ operations in the worst case. The traversal of the tree involves one copy operation for each of the *n* elements and so is $O(n)$. Since $O(n)$ is less than $O(n * \log n)$ and $O(n^2)$, treesort is $O(n * \log n)$ in the average case and $O(n^2)$ in the worst case.

Treesort. Average case: $O(n * \log n)$; worst case: $O(n^2)$

Operation	Average case	Worst case
Retrieval	O(log n)	O(n)
Insertion	O(log n)	O(n)
Deletion	O(log n)	O(n)
Traversal	O(n)	O(n)

FIGURE 11-34

The order of the retrieval, insertion, deletion, and traversal operations for the reference-based implementation of the ADT binary search tree

Saving a Binary Search Tree in a File

Imagine a program that maintains the names, addresses, and telephone numbers of your friends and relatives. While the program is running, you can enter a name and get the person's address and phone number. If you terminate program execution, the program must save its database of people in a form that it can recover at a later time.

If the program uses a binary search tree to represent the database, it must save the tree's data in a file so that it can later restore the tree. You could save the tree by simply adding the `java.io.Serializable` interface to the various classes in the implementation of the binary search tree. Exercise 36 at the end of this chapter asks you to decide which classes would need to have this interface specified. Suppose, however, that you want to define the interface `java.io.Serializable` only on the items you are storing in the tree. We will consider two different algorithms for saving and restoring a binary search tree. The first algorithm restores a binary search tree to its original shape. The second restores a binary search tree to a shape that is balanced.

Saving a binary search tree and then restoring it to its original shape.
The first algorithm restores a binary search tree to exactly the same shape it had before it was saved. For example, consider the tree in Figure 11-35a. If you save the tree in preorder, you get the sequence 60, 20, 10, 40, 30, 50, 70. If you then use the binary search tree *insert* to insert these values into a tree that is initially empty, you will get the original tree. Figure 11-35b shows this sequence of insertion operations in pseudocode.

*Use a preorder traversal and **insert** to save and then restore a binary search tree in its original shape*

Saving a binary search tree and then restoring it to a balanced shape.
Can you do better than the previous algorithm? That is, do you necessarily want the restored tree to have its original shape? Recall that you can organize a given set of data items into binary search trees with many different shapes. Although the shape of a binary search tree has no effect whatsoever on the correctness of the ADT operations, it will affect the efficiency of those operations. Efficient operations are assured if the binary search tree is balanced.

A balanced binary search tree increases the efficiency of the ADT operations

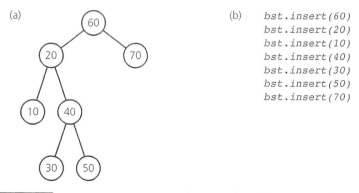

(a)

(b)
```
bst.insert(60)
bst.insert(20)
bst.insert(10)
bst.insert(40)
bst.insert(30)
bst.insert(50)
bst.insert(70)
```

FIGURE 11-35

(a) A binary search tree **bst**; (b) the sequence of insertions that result in this tree

The algorithm that restores a binary search tree to a balanced shape is surprisingly simple. In fact, you can even guarantee a restored tree of minimum height—a condition stronger than balanced. To gain some insight into the solution, consider a full tree, because it is balanced. If you save a full tree in a file by using an inorder traversal, the file will be in sorted order, as Figure 11-36 illustrates. A full tree with exactly $n = 2^h - 1$ nodes for some height h has the exact middle of the data items in its root. The left and right subtrees of the root are full trees of $2^{h-1} - 1$ nodes each (that is, half of $n - 1$, since n is odd or, equivalently, $n/2$). Thus, you can use the following recursive algorithm to create a full binary search tree with n nodes, provided you either know or can determine n beforehand.

Building a full binary search tree

```
+readFull(in inputFile:FileType, in n:integer):TreeNode
// Builds a full binary search tree from n sorted values
// in a file and returns the tree's root.

   if (n > 0) {
      treeNode = a new node with null child references
      // construct the left subtree
      Set treeNode's left child to readFull(inputFile, n/2)

      // get the root
      Read item from file into treeNode's item

      // construct the right subtree
      Set treeNode's right child to readFull(inputFile, n/2)
   }  // end if

   return treeNode
```

Surprisingly, you can construct the tree directly by reading the sorted data sequentially from the file.

This algorithm for building a full binary search tree is simple, but what can you do if the tree to be restored is not full (that is, if it does not have $n = 2^h - 1$ nodes for some h)? The first thing that comes to mind is that the restored

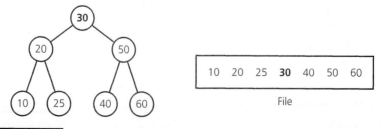

FIGURE 11-36

A full tree saved in a file by using inorder traversal

tree should be complete—full up to the last level, with the last level filled in from left to right. Actually, because you care only about minimizing the height of the restored tree, it does not matter where the nodes on the last level go, as Figure 11-37 shows.

The *readFull* algorithm is essentially correct even if the tree is not full. However, you do have to be a bit careful when computing the sizes of the left and right subtrees of the tree's root. If *n* is odd, both subtrees are of size *n*/2, as before. (The root is automatically accounted for.) If *n* is even, however, you have to account for the root and the fact that one of the root's subtrees will have one more node than the other. In this case, you can arbitrarily choose to put the extra node in the left subtree. The following algorithm makes these compensations:

```
+readTree(in inputFile:FileType, in n:integer):TreeNode
// Builds a minimum-height binary search tree from n sorted
// values in a file. Will return the tree's root.

  if (n > 0) {
     treeNode = reference to new node with null
                child references
     // construct the left subtree
     Set treeNode's left child to readTree(inputFile, n/2)

     // get the root
     Read item from file into treeNode's item

     // construct the right subtree
     Set treeNode's right child to
         readTree(inputFile, (n-1)/2)
  } // end if

  return treeNode
```

Building a minimum-height binary search tree

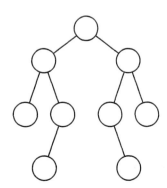

A tree of minimum height that is not complete

You should trace this algorithm and convince yourself that it is correct for both even and odd values of *n*.

To summarize, you can easily restore a tree as a balanced binary search tree if the data is sorted—that is, if it has been produced from the inorder traversal—and you know the number *n* of nodes in the tree. You need *n* so that you can determine the middle item and, in turn, the number of nodes in the left and right subtrees of the tree's root. Knowing these numbers is a simple matter of counting nodes as you traverse the tree and then saving the number in a file that the restore operation can read.

Note that *readTree* would be an appropriate protected method of *BinarySearchTree*, if you also had a public method to call it.

The JCF Binary Search Algorithm

The Java Collections Framework provides two binary search methods to find a specified element in a sorted *java.util.List*. The first is based upon the natural ordering of the elements:

```
static <T> int
    binarySearch(List<? extends Comparable<? super T>> list, T key)
```

The second is based upon a specified *Comparator*:

```
static <T> int
    binarySearch(List<? extends T> list, T key,
                 Comparator<? super T> c)
```

The JCF *sort* methods shown in Chapter 10 can be used to sort the list before calling *binarySearch*. Both methods assume the list is in ascending order and if the element is found, its index in the list is returned (a value >= 0). If the element is not found, a negative value is returned. This value, *-(insertIndex)-1* can be used to determine the insertion point for the element in the sorted list, even if the element should be inserted at the end of the list. For example, if the *binarySearch* method returns –2, *insertIndex* would be 1.

The *binarySearch* methods run in logarithmic time if the elements in the *List* can be access directly in constant time (also known as random access). If the *List* does not implement the *RandomAccess* interface and is large, the *binarySearch* algorithm will do an iterator-based binary search that runs in linear time.

The following program demonstrates the use of the *binarySearch* algorithm on a sorted list:

```
import java.util.List;
import java.util.LinkedList;
import java.util.Collections;
import java.util.Arrays;

public class JCFSearchEx {
    public static void main(String args[]) {
```

```
String[] names = {"Janet", "Michael", "Pat", "Craig",
                  "Andrew", "Sarah", "Evan", "Anita"};

LinkedList<String> namelist = new LinkedList<String>();
namelist.addAll(Arrays.asList(names));
Collections.sort(namelist);
String name = "Maite";

int loc = Collections.binarySearch(namelist, name);
if (loc < 0) {
  System.out.println(name + " should be inserted to position "
                     + (-(loc+1)) + "\n");
  namelist.add(-(loc+1), name);
  System.out.println(namelist);
} else {
  System.out.println(name + " was found in location "
                     + loc + "\n");
}   // end if
}   // end main
}   // end JCFSearchEx
```

11.4 General Trees

This chapter ends with a brief discussion of general trees and their relationship to binary trees. Consider the general tree in Figure 11-38. The three children *B*, *C*, and *D* of node *A*, for example, are siblings. The leftmost child *B* is called the **oldest child,** or **first child,** of *A*. One way to implement this tree uses the same node structure that we used for a reference-based binary tree. That is, each node has two references: The left one references the node's oldest child and the right one references the node's next sibling. Thus, you can use the data structure in Figure 11-39 to implement the tree in Figure 11-38. Notice that the structure in Figure 11-39 also represents the binary trees:general trees;general treestree pictured in Figure 11-40.

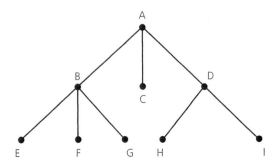

FIGURE 11-38

A general tree

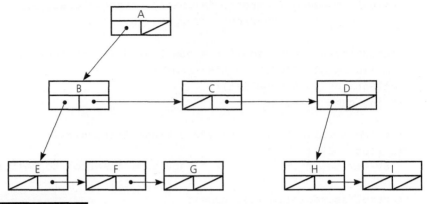

A reference-based implementation of the general tree in Figure 11-38

An *n*-ary tree is a generalization of a binary tree whose nodes each can have no more than *n* children. The tree in Figure 11-38 is an *n*-ary tree with *n* = 3. You can, of course, use the implementation just described for an *n*-ary tree. However, because you know the maximum number of children for each node, you can let each node reference its children directly. Figure 11-41 illustrates such a representation for the tree in Figure 11-38. This tree is shorter than the tree in Figure 11-40.

Exercise 35 at the end of this chapter discusses general trees further.

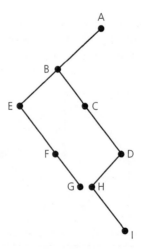

The binary tree that Figure 11-39 represents

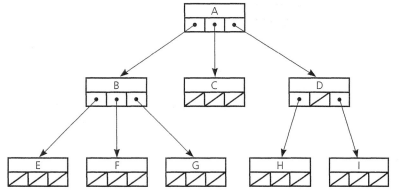

FIGURE 11-41

An implementation of the *n*-ary tree in Figure 11-38

Summary

1. Binary trees provide a hierarchical organization of data, which is important in many applications.

2. The implementation of a binary tree is usually reference based. If the binary tree is complete, an efficient array-based implementation is possible.

3. Traversing a tree is a useful operation. Intuitively, traversing a tree means to visit every node in the tree. Because the meaning of "visit" is application dependent, the traversal operations are implemented using an iterator.

4. The binary search tree allows you to use a binary search–like algorithm to search for an item with a specified value.

5. Binary search trees come in many shapes. The height of a binary search tree with n nodes can range from a minimum of $\lceil \log_2(n + 1) \rceil$ to a maximum of n. The shape of a binary search tree determines the efficiency of its operations. The closer a binary search tree is to a balanced tree (and the farther it is from a linear structure), the closer the behavior of the `search` algorithm will be to a binary search (and the farther it will be from the behavior of a linear search).

6. An inorder traversal of a binary search tree visits the tree's nodes in sorted search-key order.

7. The treesort algorithm efficiently sorts an array by using the binary search tree's insertion and traversal operations.

8. If you save a binary search tree's data in a file while performing an inorder traversal of its nodes, you can restore the tree as a binary search tree of minimum height. If you save a binary search tree's data in a file while performing a preorder traversal of its nodes, you can restore the tree to its original form.

Cautions

1. If you use an array-based implementation of a complete binary tree, you must be sure that the tree remains complete as a result of insertions or deletions.

2. Operations on a binary search tree can be quite efficient. In the worst case, however—when the tree approaches a linear shape—the performance of its operations degrades and is comparable to that of a linear linked list. If you must avoid such a situation for a given application, you should use the balancing methods presented in Chapter 13.

Self-Test Exercises

1. Consider the tree in Figure 11-42. What node or nodes are

   a. The tree's root

   b. Parents

   c. Children of the parents in Part *b*

   d. Siblings

   e. Ancestors of 60

   f. Descendants of 70

   g. Leaves

2. What are the levels of all nodes in the tree in

   a. Figure 11-6b

   b. Figure 11-6c

3. What is the height of the tree in Figure 11-42?

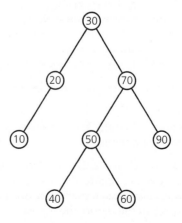

FIGURE 11-42

A tree for Self-Test Exercises 1, 3, 7, and 11 and for Exercises 7 and 14

4. Consider the binary trees in Figure 11-31. Which are complete? Which are full? Which are balanced?

5. What are the preorder, inorder, and postorder traversals of the binary tree in Figure 11-6a?

6. Beginning with an empty binary search tree, what binary search tree is formed when you insert the following values in the order given: J, N, B, A, W, E, T?

7. Starting with an empty binary search tree, in what order should you insert items to get the binary search tree in Figure 11-42?

8. Represent the full binary tree in Figure 11-36 with an array.

9. What complete binary tree does the array in Figure 11-43 represent?

10. Is the tree in Figure 11-44 a binary search tree?

11. Using the tree in Figure 11-42, trace the algorithm that searches a binary search tree, given a search key of

   a. 50

   b. 80

   In each case, list the nodes in the order in which the search visits them.

5	1	2	8	6	10	3	9	4	7
0	1	2	3	4	5	6	7	8	9

FIGURE 11-43

An array for Self-Test Exercise 9

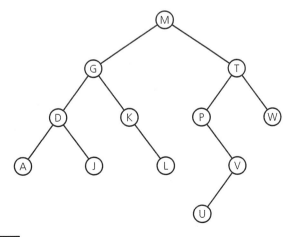

FIGURE 11-44

A tree for Self-Test Exercise 10 and for Exercise 2a

12. Trace the treesort algorithm as it sorts the following array into ascending order: 20 80 40 25 60 30.

13. a. What binary search tree results when you execute `readTree` with a file of the six integers 2, 4, 6, 8, 10, 12?

   b. Is the resulting tree's height a minimum? Is the tree complete? Is it full?

Exercises

1. Write a Java program that can find the total number of nodes in a binary search tree.

2. What are the preorder, inorder, and postorder traversals of the binary trees in

   a. Figure 11-44   b. Figure 11-6b   c. Figure 11-6c

3. Consider the binary search tree in Figure 11-45. The numbers simply label the nodes so that you can reference them; they do not indicate the contents of the nodes.

   a. Which node must contain the inorder successor of the value in the root? Explain.

   b. In what order will an inorder traversal visit the nodes of this tree? Indicate this order by listing the labels of the nodes in the order that they are visited.

4. Beginning with an empty binary search tree, what binary search tree is formed when you insert the following values in the order given?

   a. T, N, W, J, E, A, B

   b. J, A, N, E, T, B, W

   c. J, T, E, N, B, A, W

5. Draw the complete binary tree that is formed when the following values are inserted in the order given: 3, 12, 5, 16, 6, 9.

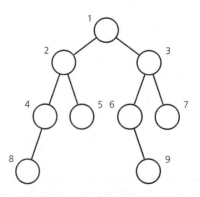

FIGURE 11-45

A binary search tree for Exercise 3

6. Write a Java program which can find the smallest element in a binary search tree in a non-recursive way.

7. Consider the binary search tree in Figure 11-42.

   a. What tree results after you insert the nodes 80, 65, 75, 45, 35, and 25, in that order?

   b. After inserting the nodes mentioned in Part *a*, what tree results when you delete the nodes 50 and 20?

8. a. What is the maximum number of nodes in a binary tree with 8 levels?

   b. What is the maximum and minimum number of levels of a tree with 2,011 nodes?

   c. What is the maximum and minimum number of leaves in a tree with 10 levels?

9. Given the following data: 10, 15, 5, 18, 14, 6, 20, 9

   a. What binary search tree is created by inserting the data in the order given?

   b. Given a search key of 12, trace the algorithm that searches the binary search tree that you created in Part *a*. List the nodes in the order in which the search visits them.

10. The *NULL* reference is used to indicate the absence of child in a tree node. Write a JAVA program which will determine the number of *NULL* references in a binary tree.

11. Given the ADT binary tree operations as defined in this chapter, what tree or trees does the following sequence of statements produce?

```java
public void Ex11() {
    BinaryTree<Integer> t1 = new BinaryTree<Integer>(2);
    t1.attachLeft(5);

    BinaryTree<Integer> t2 = new BinaryTree<Integer>(8);
    t2.attachLeft(6);
    t2.attachRight(7);

    t1.attachRightSubtree(t2);

    BinaryTree<Integer> t3 = new BinaryTree<Integer>(7);
    t2.attachLeft(3);
    t2.attachRight(1);

    BinaryTree<Integer> t4 = new BinaryTree<Integer>(1, t1, t3);
} // end Ex11
```

12. Consider a method *isLeaf()* that returns *true* if an instance of *BinaryTree* is a one-node tree—that is, if it consists of only a leaf—and returns *false* otherwise.

   a. Add the method of *isLeaf* to *BinaryTree* so that the method is available to clients of the class.

   b. If *isLeaf* were not a member of *BinaryTree*, would a client of the class be able to implement *isLeaf*? Explain.

13. The operation

    ```
    replace(in replacementItem:TreeItemType):boolean
    ```

    locates, if possible, the item in a binary search tree with the same search key as `replacementItem`. If the tree contains such an item, `replace` replaces it with `replacementItem`. Thus, the fields of the original item are updated.

    a. Add the operation `replace` to the reference-based implementation of the ADT binary search tree given in this chapter. The operation should replace an item without altering the tree structure.

    b. Instead of adding `replace` as an operation of the ADT binary search tree, implement it as a client of `BinarySearchTree`. Will the shape of the binary tree remain the same?

14. Suppose that you traverse the binary search tree in Figure 11-42 and write the data item in each node visited to a file. You plan to read this file later and create a new binary search tree by using the ADT binary search tree operation `insert`. In creating the file, in what order should you traverse the tree so that the new tree will have exactly the same shape and nodes as the original tree? What does the file look like after the original tree is traversed?

15. Consider an array-based implementation of a binary search tree `bst`. Figure 11-11 presents such a representation for a particular binary search tree.

    a. Depict the array in an array-based implementation for the binary search tree in Figure 11-20a.

    b. Show the effect of each of the following sequential operations on the array in Part *a* of this exercise. For simplicity, assume that tree items are names.

    ```
    bst.insert(new Name("Doug"));
    bst.delete(new Name("Karen"));
    bst.delete(new Name("Andrew"));
    bst.insert(new Name("Sarah"));
    ```

    c. Repeat Parts *a* and *b* of this exercise for the tree in Figure 11-21b.

    d. Write an inorder traversal algorithm for this array-based implementation.

16. Duplicates in an ADT could mean either identical items or, more subtly, items that have identical search keys but with differences in other fields. If duplicates are allowed in a binary search tree, it is important to have a convention that determines the relationship between the duplicates. Items that duplicate the root of a tree should either all be in the left subtree or all be in the right subtree, and, of course, this property must hold for every subtree.

    a. Why is this convention critical to the effective use of the binary search tree?

    b. This chapter stated that you can delete an item from a binary search tree by replacing it with the item whose search key either immediately follows or immediately precedes the search key of the item to be deleted. If duplicates are allowed, however, the choice between inorder successor and inorder predecessor is no longer arbitrary. How does the convention of putting duplicates in either the left or right subtree affect this choice?

17. Complete the trace of the nonrecursive inorder traversal algorithm that Figure 11-15 began. Show the contents of the implicit stack as the traversal progresses.

18. Write a program which will convert a given binary search tree into a linked list data structure. All the data in the linked list should be in sorted order.

19. Given the recursive nature of a binary tree, a good strategy for writing a Java method that operates on a binary tree is often first to write a recursive definition of the task. Given such a recursive definition, a Java implementation is often straight-forward.

    Write recursive definitions that perform the following tasks on arbitrary binary trees. Implement the definitions in Java. Must your methods be members of `Binary Tree`? For simplicity, assume that each data item in the tree is an *integer* object and that there are no duplicates.

    a. Count the number of nodes in the tree. (*Hint:* If the tree is empty, the count is 0. If the tree is not empty, the count is 1 plus the number of nodes in the root's left subtree plus the number of nodes in the root's right subtree.)

    b. Compute the height of a tree.

    c. Find the maximum element.

    d. Find the sum of the elements.

    e. Find the average of the elements.

    f. Find a specific item.

    g. Determine whether one item is an ancestor of another (that is, whether one item is in the subtree rooted at the other item).

    h. Determine the highest level that is full or, equivalently, has the maximum number of nodes for that level. (See Exercise 25.)

20. Consider a nonempty binary tree with two types of nodes: **min** nodes and **max** nodes. Each node has an integer value initially associated with it. You can define the **value** of such a **minimax** tree as follows:

    ■ If the root is a min node, the value of the tree is equal to the *minimum* of

        □ The integer stored in the root

        □ The value of the left subtree, but only if it is nonempty

        □ The value of the right subtree, but only if it is nonempty

    ■ If the root is a max node, the value of the tree is equal to the *maximum* of the above three values.

    Figure 11-46a shows a completed minimax tree.

    a. Compute the value of the minimax tree in Figure 11-46. Each node is labeled with its initial value.

    b. Write a general solution in Java for representing and evaluating these trees.

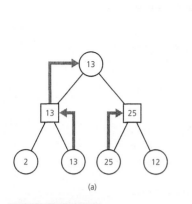
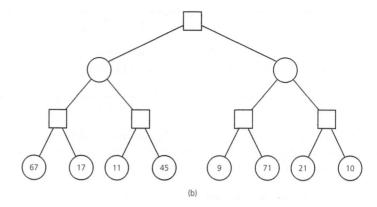

(a)   (b)

FIGURE 11-46

A minimax tree for Exercise 20

* 21. A binary search tree with a given set of data items can have several different struc-
      tures that conform to the definition of a binary search tree. If you are given a list of
      data items, does at least one binary search tree whose preorder traversal matches
      the order of the items on your list always exist? Is there ever more than one binary
      search tree that has the given preorder traversal?

  22. Determine the height of a binary search tree (BST) in the worst case condition, if
      the number of keys is 1000.

  23. Write pseudocode for a method that performs a range query for a binary search
      tree. That is, the method should visit all items that have a search key in a given
      range of values (such as all values between 100 and 1,000).

  24. Write a JAVA program which will traverse a given binary search tree in non-
      recursive order.

  25. What is the maximum number of nodes that a binary tree can have at level n?
      Prove your answer by using induction. Use this fact to do the following:

      a. Rewrite the formal definition of a complete tree of height h.

      b. Derive a closed form for the formula

      $$\sum_{i=1}^{h} 2^{i-1}$$

      What is the significance of this sum?

  26. Write a program to find the largest path from the root node to the leaf node of a
      given binary search tree.

  27. A binary tree is **strictly binary** if every nonleaf node has exactly two children.
      Prove by induction on the number of leaves that a strictly binary tree with n leaves
      has exactly $2n - 1$ nodes.

28. Consider two algorithms for traversing a binary tree. Both are nonrecursive algorithms that use an extra ADT for bookkeeping. Both algorithms have the following basic form:

```
Put the root of the tree in the ADT
while (the ADT is not empty) {
  Remove a node from the ADT and call it n
  Visit n
  if (n has a left child) {
    Put the child in the ADT
  } // end if
  if (n has a right child) {
     Put the child in the ADT
  } // end if
} // end while
```

The difference between the two algorithms is the method for choosing a node *n* to remove from the ADT.

Algorithm 1: Remove the newest (most recently added) node from the ADT.

Algorithm 2: Remove the oldest (earliest added) node from the ADT.

   a. In what order would each algorithm visit the nodes of the tree in Figure 11-19?

   b. For each algorithm, describe an appropriate ADT for doing the bookkeeping. What should the ADT data be? Do not use extra memory unnecessarily for the bookkeeping ADT. Also, note that the traversal of a tree should not alter the tree in any way.

29. Describe how to save a binary tree in a file so that you can later restore the tree to its original shape. Compare the efficiencies of saving and restoring a binary tree and a binary search tree.

30. Design another algorithm to delete nodes from a binary search tree. This algorithm differs from the one described in this chapter when the node *N* has two children. First let *N*'s right child take the place of the deleted node *N* in the same manner in which you delete a node with one child. Next reconnect *N*'s left child (along with its subtree, if any) to the left side of the node containing the inorder successor of the search key in *N*.

31. Write iterative methods to perform insertion and deletion operations on a binary search tree.

32. Use inheritance to derive the class `BSTTreeIterator` from the class `TreeIterator` and implement the method `remove`. Is the traversal affected when a node of the tree is removed? Does this depend on the implementation of the iterator?

33. If you know in advance that you often access a given item in a binary search tree several times in a row before accessing a different item, you will search for the same item repeatedly. One way to address this problem is to add an extra bookkeeping component to your implementation. That is, you can maintain a last-accessed reference that will always reference the last item that any binary search tree operation accessed. Whenever you perform such an operation, you can check the search key of the item most recently accessed before performing the operation.

    Revise the implementation of the ADT binary search tree to add this new feature by adding the data field `lastAccessed` to the class.

664 Chapter 11 Trees

34. The motivation for using a doubly linked list is the need to locate and delete a node in a list without traversing the list. The analogy for a binary search tree is to maintain parent references. That is, every node except the root will have a reference to its parent in the tree. Write insertion and deletion operations for this tree.

35. A node in a general tree, such as the one in Figure 11-38, can have an arbitrary number of children.

    a. Describe a Java implementation of a general tree in which every node contains an array of child references. Write a recursive preorder traversal method for this implementation. What are the advantages and disadvantages of this implementation?

    b. Consider the implementation of a general tree that this chapter described. Each node has two references: The left one references the node's oldest child and the right one references the node's next sibling. Write a recursive preorder traversal method for this implementation.

    c. Every node in a binary tree *T* has at most two children. Compare the oldest-child/next-sibling representation of *T* described in Part *b* to the left-child/right-child representation of a binary tree described in this chapter. Does one representation simplify the implementation of the ADT operations? Are the two representations ever the same?

36. The section "Saving a Binary Search Tree in a File" mentions that you can save a binary search tree in a file by adding the interface *java.io.Serializable* to the various classes involved in the implementation of the tree. Name all of these classes when the binary search tree contains instances of the class *Person* presented in this chapter.

Programming Problems

1. Write an array-based implementation of the ADT binary search tree that uses dynamic memory allocation. Use a data structure like the one in Figure 11-11.

2. Repeat Programming Problem 1 for complete binary trees.

3. Write a Java program that learns about a universe of your choice by asking the user yes/no questions. For example, your program might learn about animals by having the following dialogue with its user. (User responses are in uppercase.)

```
Think of an animal and I will guess it.
Does it have legs? YES
Is it a cat? YES
I win! Continue? YES

Think of an animal and I will guess it.
Does it have legs? NO
Is it a snake? YES
I win! Continue? YES

Think of an animal and I will guess it.
Does it have legs? NO
Is it a snake? NO
I give up. What is it? EARTHWORM
```

```
Please type a question whose answer is yes for an
earthworm and no for a snake:
DOES IT LIVE UNDERGROUND?
Continue? YES

Think of an animal and I will guess it.
Does it have legs? NO
Does it live underground? NO
Is it a snake? NO
I give up. What is it? FISH
Please type a question whose answer is yes for a
fish and no for a snake:
DOES IT LIVE IN WATER?
Continue? NO

Good-bye.
```

The program begins with minimal knowledge about animals: It knows that cats have legs and snakes do not. When the program incorrectly guesses "snake" the next time, it asks for the answer and also asks for a way to distinguish between snakes and earthworms.

The program builds a binary tree of questions and animals. A YES response to a question is stored in the question's left child; a NO response is stored in the question's right child.

4. Write a program that maintains the names, addresses, and telephone numbers of your friends and relatives and thus serves as an address book. You should be able to enter, delete, modify, or search this data. The person's name should be the search key, and initially you can assume that the names are unique. The program should be able to save the address book in a file for use later.

   Design a class to represent the people in the address book and another class to represent the address book itself. This class should contain a binary search tree of people as a data field.

   You can enhance this problem by adding birth dates to the database and by adding an operation that lists everyone who satisfies a given criterion. For example, it might list people born in a given month or people who live in a given state. You should also be able to list everyone in the database.

5. Write a program that provides a way for you to store and retrieve telephone numbers. Design a user interface that provides the following operations:

   Add: Adds a person's name and phone number to the phone book.

   Delete: Deletes a given person's name and phone number from the phone book, given only the name.

   Find: Locates a person's phone number, given only the person's name.

   Change: Changes a person's phone number, given the person's name and new phone number.

   Quit: Quits the application, after first saving the phone book in a text file.

   You can proceed as follows:

   ■ Design and implement the class *Person*, which represents the name and phone number of a person. You will store instances of this class in the phone book.

- Design and implement the class *PhoneBook*, which represents the phone book. The class should contain a binary search tree as a data field. This tree contains the people in the book.

- Add methods that use a text file to save and restore the tree.

- Design and implement the class *Menu*, which provides the program's user interface.

The program should read data from a text file when it begins and save data into a text file when the user quits the program.

6. In this chapter, a single iterator class was created to perform any one of the three binary tree traversals. The user could specify which of the traversals to use by calling *setPreorder*, *setInorder*, or *setPostorder*. An alternative implementation is based on creating a separate iterator class for each of the traversals. Also, as was mentioned in this chapter, the space and time requirements of the traversal can be minimized if the traversals are based on nonrecursive algorithms.

For example, the following pseudocode demonstrates how the method *inorderTraverse* presented in this chapter can be modified slightly and called from the method *next* in the iterator. The original version of *inorderTraverse* used a queue to store the entire traversal. This version of the method will produce the next node in the traversal only as needed. It is therefore slightly different in that the statement that queued a node is replaced with a return of the node.

```
+inorderTraverse(in treeNode:TreeNode):TreeItemType
// Nonrecursively traverses a binary tree
// inorder.
  curr = treeNode     // start at treeNode
  done = false
  while (!done) {
    if (curr != null) {
      visitStack.push(curr)
      // traverse the left subtree
      curr = curr.leftChild
    }
    else {
      if (!visitStack.isEmpty()) {
        curr = visitStack.pop()
        return curr.item
      }
      else {
        done = true
      }  // end if
    }  // end if
  }  // end while
```

Implement an iterator class for each of the three traversals using nonrecursive methods such that the storage requirements are never greater than O(*height of the tree*).

CHAPTER 12

Tables and Priority Queues

This chapter considers the ADT table, which is appropriate for problems that must manage data by value. Several table implementations—which use arrays, linked lists, and binary search trees—will be presented, along with their advantages and disadvantages.

To make an intelligent choice among the various possible table implementations, you must analyze the efficiency with which each of the implementations supports the table operations. For example, this chapter analyzes the efficiency of array-based and reference-based table implementations and concludes that, in many applications, the implementations do not support the table operations as efficiently as possible. This conclusion motivates the use of a more sophisticated table implementation based on binary search tree.

This chapter also introduces an important variation of the table, the ADT priority queue. This ADT provides operations for easily retrieving and deleting the item with the largest value. Although you can implement a priority queue by using a binary search tree, a simpler tree structure, known as a heap, is often more appropriate for this purpose.

12.1 The ADT Table

The previous chapter introduced value-oriented ADTs whose operations are of the form

- Insert a data item containing the value *x*.

- Delete a data item containing the value *x*.

- Ask a question about a data item containing the value *x*.

Applications that require such value-oriented operations are extremely prevalent, as you might imagine. For example, the tasks

- *Find the phone number of John Smith*

- *Delete all the information about the employee with ID number 12908*

involve values instead of positions. This section presents another example of a value-oriented ADT.

The name of an ADT often suggests images of familiar objects that possess properties resembling those of the ADT. For example, the name "stack" might remind you of a stack of dishes. What does the name "table" bring to mind? If you had heard the question before you began reading this book, you might have answered, "My favorite mahogany coffee table." However, your answer now should be something more like, "A table of the major cities of the world," such as the one in Figure 12-1.

This table of cities contains several pieces of information about each city. Its design allows you to look up this information. For example, if you wanted to know the population of London, you could scan the column of city names, starting at the top, until you came to London. Because the cities are listed in alphabetical order, you could also mimic a binary search. You could begin the search near

City	Country	Population
Athens	Greece	2,500,000
Barcelona	Spain	1,800,000
Cairo	Egypt	9,500,000
London	England	9,400,000
New York	U.S.A.	7,300,000
Paris	France	2,200,000
Rome	Italy	2,800,000
Toronto	Canada	3,200,000
Venice	Italy	300,000

FIGURE 12-1

An ordinary table of cities

the middle of the table, determine in which half London lies, and recursively apply the binary search to the appropriate half. As you know, a binary search is far more efficient than scanning the entire table from the beginning.

If, however, you wanted to find which of the major cities are in Italy, you would have no choice but to scan the entire table. The alphabetical order of the city names does not help you for this problem at all. The table's arrangement facilitates the search for a given city, but other types of questions require a complete scan of the table.

The ADT **table,** or **dictionary,** also allows you to look up information easily and has a special operation for this purpose. Typically, the items in the ADT table are records that contain several pieces of data. You can facilitate the retrieval of an item by basing the search on a specified search key. In the table of cities, for example, you could designate `city` as the search key if you often needed to retrieve the information about a city. You can devise implementations of a table that allow the rapid retrieval of the item(s) whose search key matches some specified value. However, if you need to retrieve item(s) based on a value of a non-search-key portion of each record, you will have to inspect the entire table. Therefore, the choice of a search key sends the ADT implementer the following message:

The ADT table uses a search key to identify its items

> *Arrange the data to facilitate the search for an item, given the value of its search key.*

The basic operations that define the ADT table are as follows:

KEY CONCEPTS

Operations of the ADT Table
1. Create an empty table.
2. Determine whether a table is empty.
3. Determine the number of items in a table.
4. Insert a new item into a table.
5. Delete the item with a given search key from a table.
6. Retrieve the item with a given search key from a table.
7. Traverse the items in a table in sorted search-key order.

For simplicity, we will assume that all items in the table have distinct search keys. Under this assumption, the insertion operation must reject an attempt to insert an item whose search key is the same as an item already in the table. The following pseudocode specifies in more detail the operations for an ADT table of items with distinct search keys. Figure 12-2 shows a UML diagram for the class Table.

KEY CONCEPTS

Pseudocode for the Operations of the ADT Table

```
// TableItem type is the type of the items stored in the
// table, KeyType is the type of the search-key value.

+createTable()
// Creates an empty table.

+tableIsEmpty():boolean {query}
// Determines whether a table is empty.

+tableLength():integer {query}
// Determines the number of items in a table.

+tableInsert(in newItem:TableItemType) throws
                                        TableException
// Inserts newItem into a table whose items have distinct
// search keys that differ from newItem's search key.
// Throws TableException if the insertion is not
// successful.

+tableDelete(in searchKey:KeyType)
// Deletes from a table the item whose search key equals
// searchKey. Returns false if no such item exists.
// Returns true if the deletion was successful.

+tableRetrieve(in searchKey:KeyType):TableItemType
// Returns the item in a table whose search
// key equals searchKey. Returns null
// if no such item exists.

+tableTraverse():TableItemType
// Traverses a table in sorted search-key order.
```

Various sets of
table operations
are possible

Our table assumes
distinct search keys

Other tables could
allow duplicate
search keys

You should realize that these operations are only one possible set of table operations. The client may require either a subset of these operations or other operations not listed here to fit the application at hand. It may also be convenient to modify the definitions of some of the operations. For example, these operations assume that no two table items have the same values in their search keys. However, in many applications it is quite reasonable to expect duplicate search-key values. If this is the case, you must redefine several of the operations to eliminate the ambiguity that would arise from duplicate search-key values. For example, which item should *tableRetrieve* return if several items have

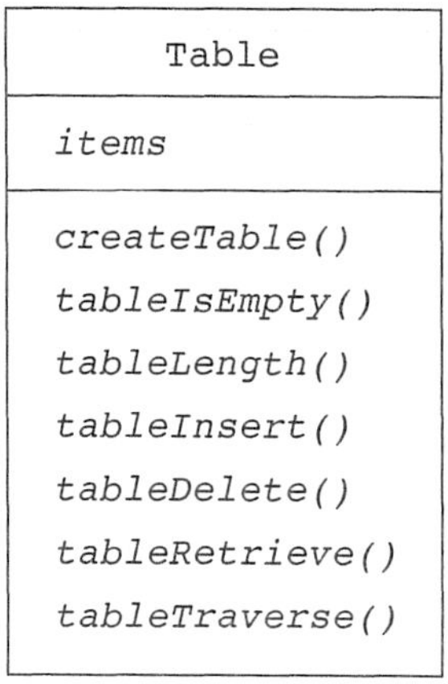

```
        ┌─────────────────────────┐
        │          Table          │
        ├─────────────────────────┤
        │ items                   │
        ├─────────────────────────┤
        │ createTable()           │
        │ tableIsEmpty()          │
        │ tableLength()           │
        │ tableInsert()           │
        │ tableDelete()           │
        │ tableRetrieve()         │
        │ tableTraverse()         │
        └─────────────────────────┘
```

FIGURE 12-2

UML diagram for the class `Table`

the specified value in their search keys? You should tailor your definition of the ADT table to the problem at hand.

Although the operations `tableInsert`, `tableDelete`, and `tableRetrieve` in the previous set of operations are sufficient for some applications, you cannot do several significant things without additional operations. For instance, you cannot perform an important task such as

Display all the table items

because you cannot retrieve a data item unless you know the value of its search key. Thus, you cannot display the entire table unless you can traverse the table.

In defining the traversal operation, you must specify the order in which `tableTraverse` should visit the items. One common specification is to visit the items sorted by the search key, but perhaps you do not care in what order the traversal visits the items. As you will see, the way you define `tableTraverse`—if you define it at all—may affect the way that you implement the table.

The concept of a search key for the table items is essential to the implementation of the table. It is important that the value of the search key remain the same as long as the item is stored in the table. Changing the search key of an existing element in the table could make that element or other table elements impossible to find. Thus, the search-key value should not be modifiable. This suggests the use of a class for items of the table; the class will contain the search key and a method for accessing the search-key data field. This is the same class that appeared in Chapter 11:

```java
package SearchKeys;

public abstract class KeyedItem<KT extends
                        Comparable <? super KT>> {
   private KT searchKey;
```

```
    public KeyedItem(KT key) {
      searchKey = key;
    }   // end constructor

    public KT getKey() {
      return searchKey;
    }   // end getKey
}   // end KeyedItem
```

Recall that classes that extend *KeyedItem* will have only the constructor available for initializing the search key. Thus, the search-key value cannot be modified once an item is created, which meets our requirement.

Suppose that the items in the table are instances of the following class:

```
import SearchKeys.KeyedItem;

public class City extends KeyedItem<String> {
  private String city;      // city's name
  private String country;   // city's country
  private int     pop;      // city's population
  . . .
  // implementation of methods for accessing private
  // data fields
}   // end City
```

and you want to perform tasks on this table such as

Tasks that use *city* as the search key

- *Display, in alphabetical order, the name of each city and its population*

- *Increase the population of each city by 10 percent*

- *Delete all cities with a population of less than 1,000,000*

Each task suggests that you designate *city* as the search key. The class *City* contains all the information for a city, including the city name (returned by the inherited method *getKey*), country, and population. Here is a Java definition of *City*:

```
import SearchKeys.KeyedItem;

public class City extends KeyedItem<String> {
  // city's name will be designated as search key
  private String country;   // city's country
  private int     pop;      // city's population

  public City(String theCity, String theCountry,
              int newPop) {
```

```
  super(theCity); // makes city name the search key
  country = theCountry;
  pop = newPop;
} // end constructor

public String toString() {
  return getKey() + ", " + country + "   " + pop;
} // end toString

// The methods getCountry, setCountry, getPopulation,
// and setPopulation appear here.

...

} // end City
```

The first task requires you to write the city names in alphabetical order. Thus, *tableTraverse* must visit items alphabetically by search key. One way to implement *tableTraverse* is to define an iterator for the ADT table. You can use an instance of this iterator class to access each table item and then pass it to a method such as *displayItem*, which appears in pseudocode as follows:

+displayItem(in anItem:TableItemType)   First task

```
  Display anItem.getCity()
  Display anItem.getPopulation()
```

The iterator's visitation order is immaterial for the other two tasks. To perform the second task, you pass each item that the iterator visits to a method *updatePopulation*:

+updatePopulation(in anItem:TableItemType)   Second task

```
  anItem.setPopulation(1.1 * anItem.getPopulation())
```

To perform the third task, you pass each item that the iterator visits to a method *deleteSmall*:

+deleteSmall(inout table:Table, in anItem:TableItemType)   Third task

```
  if (anItem.getPopulation() < 1,000,000)
    table.tableDelete(anItem)
```

However, this task is not as simple as it may seem. By deleting an item, you alter the table during the traversal with the iterator. Which item will the iterator visit next? Clearly, it should visit the one after the deleted item, but will it do so, or will it skip that item? Usually, you use the iterator's *remove* method to perform a deletion when an iterator is in use. Doing so clarifies the semantics of the deletion with respect to the iterator. The definition of the iterators for the two table implementations presented later in this chapter, and in particular the *remove* operation, are left as programming problems.

The following interface *TableInterface* summarizes the table operations. Note that the first data-type parameter reflects the type of item in the table, the second is the data type for the search key.

```
package Tables;
import SearchKeys.KeyedItem;


public interface
        TableInterface<T extends KeyedItem<KT>,
                        KT extends Comparable <? super KT>> {


// Table operations:
// Precondition for all operations:
// No two items of the table have the same search key.
// The table's items are sorted by search key.

  public boolean tableIsEmpty();
  // Determines whether a table is empty.
  // Postcondition: Returns true if the table is
  // empty; otherwise returns false.

  public int tableLength();
  // Determines the length of a table.
  // Postcondition: Returns the number of items in the
  // table.

  public void tableInsert(T newItem) throws TableException;
  // Inserts an item into a table in its proper sorted
  // order according to the item's search key.
  // Precondition: The item to be inserted into the
  // table is newItem, whose search key differs from
  // all search keys presently in the table.
  // Postcondition: If the insertion was successful,
  // newItem is in its proper order in the table.
  // Otherwise, the table is unchanged, and
  // TableException is thrown.

  public boolean tableDelete(KT searchKey);
  // Deletes an item with a given search key from a
  // table.
  // Precondition: searchKey is the search key of the
  // item to be deleted.
```

```
// Postcondition: If the item whose search key equals
// searchKey existed in the table, the item was
// deleted and method returns true. Otherwise, the
// table is unchanged and the method returns false.

public T tableRetrieve(KT searchKey);
// Retrieves an item with a given search key from a
// table.
// Precondition: searchKey is the search key of the
// item to be retrieved.
// Postcondition: If the retrieval was successful,
// the table item with the matching search key is
// returned. If no such item exists, the method
// returns a null reference.

}   // end TableInterface
```

Selecting an Implementation

In the previous chapters, ADT implementations were either array based or reference based. That is, you used either an array or a linked list to store the ADT's items. Such implementations are called **linear** because they represent items one after another in a data structure and thus mirror the flat, listlike appearance of the table of cities in Figure 12-1.

Linear implementations of a table are certainly possible and fall into four categories:

Four categories of linear implementations

- Unsorted, array based

- Unsorted, reference based

- Sorted (by search key), array based

- Sorted (by search key), reference based

The unsorted implementations store the items in no particular order; they can insert a new item into any convenient location. The sorted implementations, however, must insert a new item into its proper position as determined by the value of its search key. Whether sorted or unsorted, the array-based and reference-based linear implementations have the basic structures shown in Figure 12-3. Both implementations maintain a count of the current number of items in the table. As you will see, the unsorted and sorted implementations have their relative advantages and disadvantages.

At this point in your study of ADTs, you have other choices for a table implementation. For instance, you can implement the ADT table by using an ADT list, sorted list, or binary search tree. The binary search tree implementation, as illustrated in Figure 12-4, is an example of a **nonlinear implementation** and offers several advantages over linear implementations. Among these advantages is the opportunity to reuse the implementation of the ADT binary search

A binary search tree implementation is nonlinear

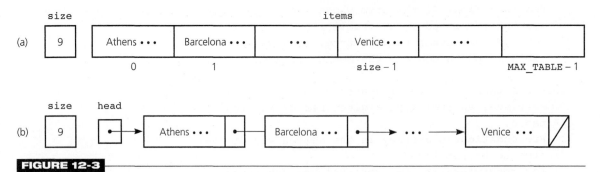

FIGURE 12-3

The data fields for two sorted linear implementations of the ADT table for the data in Figure 12-1: (a) array-based; (b) reference-based

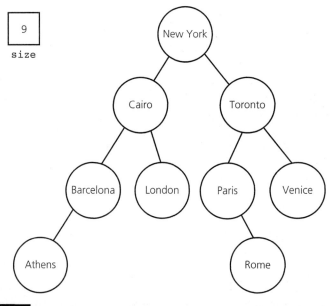

FIGURE 12-4

The data fields for a binary search tree implementation of the ADT table for the data in Figure 12-1

tree given in Chapter 11. Implementations based on the ADTs list and sorted list also share this advantage, and they are left for you to consider as programming problems.

A major goal of this chapter is to indicate how the requirements of a particular application influence the selection of an implementation. The discussion here elaborates on the comments made in Chapter 10 in the section

"Keeping Your Perspective." Some applications require all of the operations of the ADT table given earlier; others require either a subset of them or additional operations. Before choosing an implementation of the ADT table, you as problem solver should carefully analyze which operations you really need for the application at hand. It is tempting to want all possible operations, but this strategy is a poor one, because often one implementation supports some of the operations more efficiently than another implementation does. Therefore, if you include an operation that you never use, you might end up with an implementation of the ADT that does not best suit your purpose.

What operations are needed?

In addition to knowing what operations are needed for a given application, the ADT implementer should know approximately how often the application will perform each operation. Although some applications may require many occurrences of every operation, other applications may not. For example, if you maintained a table of major cities such as the one in Figure 12-1, you would expect to perform many more retrieval operations than insertions or deletions. Thus, if you seldom insert items, you can tolerate a table implementation that results in an inefficient insertion operation, as long as frequently used operations are efficient. Of course, as Chapter 10 mentioned, if an ADT operation is to be used in a life-or-death situation, that operation must be efficient, even if you rarely need it. The necessary operations, their expected frequency of occurrence, and their required response times are therefore some factors that influence which implementation of an ADT you should select for a particular application. You should, however, remain conscious of factors other than efficiency, as discussed in Chapter 10.

How often is each operation required?

Consider now several different application scenarios, each of which requires a particular mix of the table operations. The analysis of various implementations of the ADT table will illustrate some of the basic concerns of the analysis of algorithms. You will see, given an application, how to select an implementation that supports in a reasonably efficient manner the required mix of table operations.

Scenario A: Insertion and traversal in no particular order. Mary's sorority plans to raise money for a local charity. Tired of previous fund-raisers, Mary suggests a brainstorming session to discover a new money-making strategy. As sorority members voice their ideas, Mary records them by inserting each new thought into a table. Later, she will print a report of all the ideas currently in the table. Assume that the organization of the report is irrelevant—the items can be sorted or unsorted. Also assume that operations such as retrieval, deletion, or traversal in sorted order either do not occur or occur so infrequently that they do not influence your choice of an implementation.

For this application, maintaining the items in a sorted order has no advantage. In fact, by not maintaining a sorted order, the *tableInsert* operation can be quite efficient. For either unsorted linear implementation, you can insert a new item into any convenient location. For an unsorted array-based implementation, you can easily insert a new item after the last item in the array—that is, at location *items[size]*. Figure 12-5a shows the result of this

An unsorted order is efficient

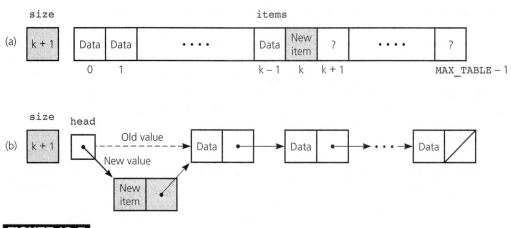

FIGURE 12-5

Insertion for unsorted linear implementations: (a) array-based; (b) reference-based

insertion after `size` has been updated. For a reference-based implementation, you can simply insert a new item at the beginning of the linked list. As Figure 12-5b illustrates, `head` references the new item, and the new item references the item previously first on the list. Thus, not only can you insert a new item quickly into either unsorted implementation of a table, but also the `tableIn-sert` operation is O(1): It requires a constant time for either implementation regardless of the table size.

Array based versus reference based

Should you choose the array-based or the reference-based implementation? As you have seen with other ADTs, an implementation that uses dynamically allocated memory is appropriate if you do not have a good estimate of the maximum possible size of the table. Mary's brainstorming session likely falls into this category. On the other hand, if you know that the table's maximum size is not drastically larger than its expected size,[1] the choice is mostly a matter of style.

Should you consider a binary search tree implementation for this application? Because such an implementation orders the table items, it does more work than the application requires. In fact, as you saw in Chapter 11, insertion into a binary search tree is O(log n) in the average case.

Scenario B: Retrieval. When you use a word processor's thesaurus to look up synonyms for a word, you use a retrieval operation. If an ADT table represents the thesaurus, each table item is a record that contains both the word—which is the search key—and the word's synonyms. Frequent retrieval operations require a table implementation that allows you to search efficiently for an

---

1. Chapter 5, in the section "Comparing Array-Based and Reference-Based Implementations," discussed how the expected and maximum number of items in an ADT affect an array-based implementation.

item, given its search-key value. Typically, you cannot alter the thesaurus, so no insertion or deletion operations are necessary.

For an array-based implementation, you can use a binary search to retrieve a particular word's record, if the array is sorted. On the other hand, for a reference-based implementation, you must traverse the linked list from its beginning until you encounter the word in the list. The binary search performs this retrieval in significantly less time than is required to traverse a linked list. Two questions come to mind at this point:

A sorted array-based implementation can use a binary search

Questions

1. Is a binary search of a linked list possible?

2. How much more efficient is a binary search of an array than a sequential search of a linked list?

Can you perform a binary search under a reference-based implementation? Yes, but too inefficiently to be practical. Consider the very first step of the binary search algorithm:

A binary search is impractical with a reference-based implementation

```
Look at the "middle" item in the table
```

If n items are in a linked list, how can you possibly get to the middle item of the list? You can traverse the list from the beginning until you have visited $n/2$ items. But, as you will see in the answer to the second question, just this first step will often take longer than the entire binary search of an array. Further, you would have the same problem of finding the "middle" element at each recursive step. It is thus not practical to perform a binary search for the linear reference-based implementation. This observation is extremely significant.

On the other hand, if n items are in an array `items`, the middle item is at location $n/2$ and can be accessed directly. Thus, a binary search of an array requires considerably less time than an algorithm that must inspect every item in the table. What does "considerably less time" mean? As you know, without the ability to perform a binary search, you may have to inspect every item in the table, either to locate an item with a particular value in its search key or to determine that such an item is not present. In other words, if a table has size n, you will have to inspect as many as n items; thus, such a search is $O(n)$. How much better can you do with a binary search? Recall from Chapter 10 that a binary search is $O(\log_2 n)$ in its worst case and that an $O(\log_2 n)$ algorithm is substantially more efficient than an $O(n)$ algorithm. For example, $\log_2 1024 = 10$ and $\log_2 1,048,576 = 20$. For a large table, the binary search has an enormous advantage.

If you know the table's maximum size, a sorted array-based implementation is appropriate for frequent retrievals

Since a thesaurus is probably large, you must choose an implementation for which a binary search is practical. As you have just seen, this observation eliminates the linear reference-based implementations. The sorted array-based implementation is fine here, since you know the size of the thesaurus.

The binary search tree implementation is also a good choice for retrieval-dominated applications. As you saw in Chapter 11, searching a binary search tree is $O(\log n)$ if the tree is balanced. Since the thesaurus does not change, you can create a balanced tree that remains balanced and be assured of an efficient search.

If you do not know the table's maximum size, use a binary search tree implementation

Scenario C: Insertion, deletion, retrieval, and traversal in sorted order.
If your local library has computerized its catalog of books, you perform a retrieval operation when you access this catalog. The library staff uses insertion and deletion operations to update the catalog and a traversal to save the entire catalog in a file. Presumably, retrieval is the most frequent operation, but the other operations are not infrequent enough to ignore. (Otherwise, this scenario would be the same as Scenario B!)

To insert into a table an item that has the value X in its search key, you must first determine where the item belongs in the table's sorted order. Similarly, to delete from the table an item that has the value X in its search key, you must first locate the item. Thus, both the `tableInsert` and `tableDelete` operations perform the following steps:

Both insertion and deletion perform these two steps

1. Find the appropriate position in the table.

2. Insert into (or delete from) this position.

Use an array-based implementation for Step 1

Step 1 is far more efficient if the table implementation is array based instead of reference based. For an array-based implementation, you can use a binary search to determine—in the case of insertion—where the new item X belongs and—in the case of deletion—where the item is located. On the other hand, for a reference-based implementation, you know from the discussion in Scenario B that a binary search is impractical, and so you must traverse the list from its beginning until you encounter the appropriate location in the list. You also saw in Scenario B that it takes significantly less time to perform a binary search of an array than it does to traverse a linked list.

Thus, because it facilitates a binary search, the array-based implementation is superior with respect to Step 1 of `tableInsert` and `tableDelete`. However, as you may have guessed, the reference-based implementation is better for Step 2, the actual insertion or deletion of the item. Under the array-based implementation, `tableInsert` must shift array items to make room for the new item (see Figure 12-6a), while `tableDelete` must shift array items to fill in the gap created when the item is removed. The worst case would require that every array item be shifted. On the other hand, under the reference-based implementation, you can accomplish this second step simply by changing at most two references, as Figure 12-6b illustrates.

Use a reference-based implementation for Step 2

A sorted array-based implementation shifts data during insertions and deletions

When you take Steps 1 and 2 together, you will find that the sorted array-based and sorted reference-based implementations of `tableInsert` or `tableDelete` both require roughly the same amount of time—they are both O(n). Neither implementation supports these operations particularly well. The binary search tree implementation, however, combines the best features of the two linear implementations. Because it is reference based, you avoid shifting data, and the table can grow dynamically as needed. You can also retrieve items from a binary search tree efficiently.

The sorted linear implementations are comparable here, but none are suitable

Summary. An unsorted array-based implementation of the ADT table can efficiently insert an item at the end of an array. A deletion, however, will

items

(a)

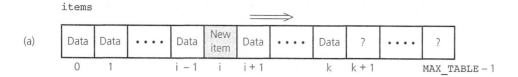

Data	Data	• • • •	Data	New item	Data	• • • •	Data	?	• • • •	?

0   1   i − 1   i   i + 1   k   k + 1   MAX_TABLE − 1

head

(b)

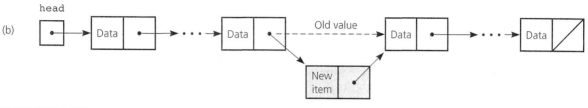

Insertion for sorted linear implementations: (a) array-based; (b) reference-based

usually require shifting data so that no hole remains in the array. Because the items are unsorted, retrieval will require a sequential search.

A sorted array-based implementation usually requires shifting data during both insertions and deletions. Retrieval, however, can use an efficient binary search because the items are sorted.

An unsorted reference-based implementation can efficiently insert an item at the beginning of a linked list. A deletion will require a sequential search but no data shifts. Retrieval will also require a sequential search.

A sorted reference-based implementation requires a sequential search but no data shifts during both insertions and deletions. Retrieval will also require a sequential search.

Although these linear implementations are less sophisticated and generally require more time than the binary search tree implementation, they are nevertheless useful for many applications. Because linear implementations are easy to understand conceptually, they are appropriate for tables that will contain only a small number of items. In such cases, efficiency is not as great a concern as simplicity and clarity. Even when a table is large, a linear implementation may still be appropriate for applications that can use an unsorted table and have few deletions.

Despite certain difficulties, linear implementations of a table can be appropriate

The nonlinear, binary search tree implementation of the ADT table can be a better choice, in general, than the linear implementations. If an n-node binary search tree has minimum height—that is, has height $\lceil \log_2(n + 1) \rceil$—the binary search tree implementation of the ADT table certainly succeeds where the linear implementations failed: You can, with efficiency comparable to that of a binary search, locate an item in both the retrieval operation and the first steps of the insertion and deletion operations. In addition, the reference-based implementation of the binary search tree permits dynamic allocation of its nodes, and so it can handle a table whose maximum size is unknown. This implementation also efficiently performs the second step of

A binary search tree implementation is a better choice, in general

the insertion and deletion operations: The actual insertion and removal of a node requires only a few reference changes (plus a short traversal to the inorder successor if the node to be removed has two children) rather than the possible shifting of all the table items, as the array-based implementations require. The binary search tree implementation therefore combines the best aspects of the two linear implementations, yet avoids their disadvantages.

As the previous chapter showed, however, the height of a binary search tree depends on the order in which you perform the insertion and deletion operations on the tree and can be as large as *n*. If the insertion and deletion operations occur in a random order, the height of the binary search tree will be quite close to its minimum value. You do need to watch for a possible increase in the tree's height, however, and the resulting decrease in performance. If instead you use a variation of the binary search tree that remains balanced—as Chapter 13 describes—you can keep the height of the tree near $\log_2 n$.

> A balanced binary search tree increases the efficiency of the ADT table operations

Figure 12-7 summarizes the order of the insertion, deletion, retrieval, and traversal operations for the table implementations discussed in this chapter.

A Sorted Array-Based Implementation of the ADT Table

If the binary search tree implementation of the ADT table is so good, you might wonder why you needed to study the linear implementations at all. There are three reasons. The first and foremost of these is perspective. Chapter 9 spoke of the dangers of overanalyzing a problem. If the size of the problem is small, the difference in efficiency among the possible solutions is likely insignificant. In particular, if the size of the table is small, a linear implementation is adequate and simple to understand.

> Perspective, efficiency, and motivation are reasons for studying the linear implementations

The second reason is efficiency: A linear implementation can be quite efficient for certain situations. For example, a linear implementation was best for Scenario A, where the predominant operations are insertion and traversal in no particular order. For Scenario B, where the predominant operation is retrieval, the sorted array-based implementation is adequate, if the maximum number of items is known. For these situations, a concern for simplicity suggests that you use a linear implementation and not a binary search tree, even for large tables.

	Insertion	Deletion	Retrieval	Traversal
Unsorted array-based	O(1)	O(n)	O(n)	O(n)
Unsorted pointer-based	O(1)	O(n)	O(n)	O(n)
Sorted array-based	O(n)	O(n)	O(log n)	O(n)
Sorted pointer-based	O(n)	O(n)	O(n)	O(n)
Binary search tree	O(log n)	O(log n)	O(log n)	O(n)

FIGURE 12-7

The average-case order of the operations of the ADT table for various implementations

The third reason is motivation. By seeing scenarios for which the linear implementations are not adequate, you are forced to look beyond arrays and consider other implementations, such as the binary search tree. Actually looking at both a linear implementation and a binary search tree implementation allows you to see these inadequacies more clearly.

The following sorted array-based implementation assumes unique search keys. Exercise 7 at the end of this chapter asks you to remove this assumption. The pre- and postconditions are omitted to save space, but they are the same as those given earlier in this chapter in *TableInterface*.

```java
package Tables;
import SearchKeys.KeyedItem;
import java.util.ArrayList;


// ********************************************************
// ADT table.
// Sorted array-based implementation.
// Assumption: A table contains at most one item with a
//             given search key at any time.
// ********************************************************

public class
      TableArrayBased<T extends KeyedItem<KT>,
                    KT extends Comparable<? super KT>>
      implements TableInterface<T, KT> {
  final int MAX_TABLE = 100;      // maximum size of table
  protected ArrayList<T> items;    // table items

  public TableArrayBased() {
    items = new ArrayList<T>(MAX_TABLE);
  }  // default constructor

  public boolean tableIsEmpty() {
    return tableLength()==0;
  } // end tableIsEmpty

  public int tableLength() {
    return items.size();
  }  // end tableLength

  public void tableInsert(T newItem) throws TableException {
  // Calls: position.
    if (tableLength() < MAX_TABLE) {
      // there is room to insert;
      // locate the position where newItem belongs
      int spot = position(newItem.getKey());
```

```
         if ((spot < tableLength()) &&
             (items.get(spot).getKey()).compareTo(
                                         newItem.getKey())==0) {
       // we have found a duplicate key
       throw new TableException("Table Exception: " +
                    "Insertion failed, duplicate key item");
       }
       else {
         // ArrayList automatically shifts items to make room
         // for the new item
         items.add(spot, newItem);
       }   // end if
     }
     else {
       throw new TableException("TableException: Table full");
     } // end if
   }   // end tableInsert

   public boolean tableDelete(KT searchKey) {
   // Calls: position.
     // locate the position where searchKey exists/belongs
     int spot = position(searchKey);
     // is searchKey present in the table?
     boolean success = (spot <= tableLength()) &&
             (items.get(spot).getKey().compareTo(searchKey)==0);
     if (success) {
       // searchKey in table
       // ArrayList automatically shifts items
       items.remove(spot);
     }   // end if

     return success;
   }   // end tableDelete

   public T tableRetrieve(KT searchKey) {
   // Calls: position.

     // locate the position where searchKey exists/belongs
     int spot = position(searchKey);
     // is searchKey present in table?
     boolean success = (spot < tableLength()) &&
             (items.get(spot).getKey().compareTo(searchKey)==0);
     if (success) {
       return items.get(spot);  // item present; retrieve it
     }
     else {
       return null;
```

```
   }  // end if
}  // end tableRetrieve

protected int position(KT searchKey) {
// Finds the position of a table item or its insertion
// point.
// Precondition: searchKey is the value of the search key
// sought in the table.
// Postcondition: Returns the index (between 0 and size - 1)
// of the item in the table whose search key equals
// searchKey. If no such item exists, returns the position
// (between 0 and size) that the item would occupy if
// inserted into the table. The table is unchanged.
   int pos = 0;
   while ((pos < tableLength()) &&
        (searchKey.compareTo(items.get(pos).getKey()) > 0)) {
     pos++;
   }  // end while
   return pos;
}  // end position

}  // end TableArrayBased
```

A Binary Search Tree Implementation of the ADT Table

Although linear implementations are suited to specific applications, they are not good as general-purpose implementations of the ADT table.

The following nonlinear reference-based implementation uses a binary search tree to represent the items in the ADT table. That is, class *TableBSTBased* has a binary search tree as one of its data fields. In this way, *TableBSTBased* reuses the class *BinarySearchTree* from the previous chapter. The pre- and postconditions are omitted to save space, but they are the same as those given earlier in this chapter.

```
package Tables;
import BinaryTrees.BinarySearchTree;
import BinaryTrees.TreeException;
import SearchKeys.KeyedItem;

// Assumes that the binary search tree created in Chapter 11
// is contained in a package called BinaryTrees.

// ***********************************************************
// Implementation of a table using a binary search tree.
// Assumption: A table contains at most one item with a
//             given search key at any time.
// ***********************************************************
```

```java
public class
      TableBSTBased<T extends KeyedItem<KT>,
                    KT extends Comparable<? super KT>>
      implements TableInterface<T, KT> {
// binary search tree that contains the table's items
  protected BinarySearchTree<T,KT> bst;
  protected int size;        // number of items in the table

  public TableBSTBased() {
    bst = new BinarySearchTree<T,KT>();
    size = 0;
  }  // end default constructor

// table operations:
  public boolean tableIsEmpty() {
    return size == 0;
  }  // end tableIsEmpty

  public int tableLength() {
    return size;
  }  // end tableLength

  public void tableInsert(T newItem) throws TableException {
    if (bst.retrieve(newItem.getKey()) == null) {
      bst.insert(newItem);
      ++size;
    }
    else {
      throw new TableException("Table Exception: Insertion"
                             + " failed, duplicate key item");
    } // end if
  }  // end tableInsert

  public T tableRetrieve(KT searchKey) {
    return bst.retrieve(searchKey);
  }  // end tableRetrieve

  public boolean tableDelete(KT searchKey) {
    try {
      bst.delete(searchKey);
    }  // end try
    catch (TreeException e) {
      return false;
    }  //end catch
    --size;
    return true;
  }  // end tableDelete
```

```
  protected void setSize(int newSize) {
    size = newSize;
  }  // end setSize

}  // end TableBSTBased
```

The following statements demonstrate how to use this class in a program that requires the ADT table:

```
import Tables.*;
```
A sample program

```
class TestTable {
  public static void displayCity(City c) {
    System.out.println(c.getCity());
  }  // end displayCity

  // Main entry point
  public static void main(String[] args) {
    TableInterface<City, String> chart =
                    new TableBSTBased<City, String>();
    City c;

    c = new City("Narragansett, RI", "USA", 16361);
    chart.tableInsert(c);
    c = new City("Ocracoke, NC", "USA", 769);
    chart.tableInsert(c);

    System.out.println(chart.tableRetrieve("Narragansett, RI"));
    System.out.println(chart.tableLength());

    // If a table iterator class called TableIteratorBST
    // is available for the class TableBSTBased (as created
    // in Programming Problem 2, you can also do the
    // following:
    TreeIteratorBST<City> iter = new TableIteratorBST<City>(chart);
    while (iter.hasNext()) {
      displayCity(iter.next());
    } // end while

  } // end main
} // end TestTable
```

12.2 The ADT Priority Queue: A Variation of the ADT Table

The ADT table organizes its data by search key, facilitating the retrieval of a particular item, given its search key. Thus, the ADT table is appropriate when you have a database to maintain and search by value, such as the table of cities described earlier in this chapter. Consider now applications for which another ADT, related to the ADT table, would be more appropriate.

Imagine a person who visits a hospital's emergency room (ER). When any patient enters the hospital, a staff member enters a record about that person into a database for later retrieval by nurses, doctors, and the billing department. In addition, the staff must keep track of the emergency room patients and decide when each person will receive care.

The ADT table would be an appropriate choice for the hospital's general database. What ADT should the ER staff use for their patients? The ADT table would facilitate the treatment of ER patients in alphabetic order by name or in numeric order by ID number. A queue would enable the treatment of patients in the order of arrival. In either case, Ms. Zither, who was just rushed to the ER with acute appendicitis, would have to wait for Mr. Able to have a splinter removed. Clearly, the ER staff should assign some measure of urgency, or **priority,** to the patients waiting for treatment. The next available doctor should treat the patient with the highest priority. The ADT that the ER staff needs should produce this patient upon request.

Another example of the use of priorities is your list of daily or weekly tasks. Suppose that your "to do" list for this week contains the following items:

Send a birthday card to Aunt Mabel.

Start the research paper for world history.

Finish reading Chapter 12 of *Walls and Mirrors.*

Make plans for Saturday night.

When you consult your list, you most likely will attend to the task that, for you, has the highest priority.

A **priority value** indicates, for example, a patient's priority for treatment or a task's priority for completion. What quantity should you use for this priority value? Many reasonable possibilities exist, including a simple ranking from 1 to 10. Let's arbitrarily decide that the largest priority value indicates the highest priority. The priority value becomes a part of the record that represents an item. You insert each item into an ADT and then ask the ADT for the item that has the highest priority.

Such an ADT is known as a **priority queue.** More formally, a priority queue is an ADT that provides the following operations:

You can organize data by priorities

You usually prioritize your list of tasks

A priority queue orders by priority values

KEY CONCEPTS

Operations of the ADT Priority Queue
1. Create an empty priority queue.
2. Determine whether a priority queue is empty.
3. Insert a new item into a priority queue.
4. Retrieve and then delete the item in a priority queue with the highest priority value.

Figure 12-8 shows a UML diagram for a class of priority queues.

The following pseudocode specifies in more detail the operations for an ADT priority queue:

KEY CONCEPTS

Pseudocode for the Operations of the ADT Priority Queue

```
// PQItemType is the type of the items
// stored in the priority queue.

+createPQueue()
// Creates an empty priority queue.

+pqIsEmpty():boolean {query}
// Determines whether a priority queue is empty.

+pqInsert(in newItem:PQItemType) throws PQueueException
// Inserts newItem into a priority queue. Throws
// PQueueException if priority queue is full.

+pqDelete():PQItemType
// Retrieves and then deletes the item in a priority queue
// with the highest priority value.
```

These operations resemble a subset of the operations of the ADT table. The significant difference is the *pqDelete* operation. Whereas the sequence of table operations *tableRetrieve–tableDelete* allows you to retrieve and delete an item that has a specified value in its search key, *pqDelete* allows you to retrieve and delete the item with the highest priority value. Notice that

Priority queue ***pqDelete*** *is the difference between a priority queue and a table*

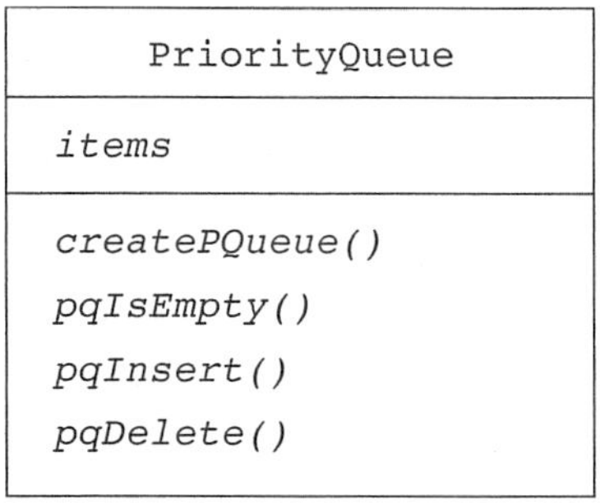

PriorityQueue
items
createPQueue() pqIsEmpty() pqInsert() pqDelete()

FIGURE 12-8

UML diagram for a class of priority queues

pqDelete, unlike *tableRetrieve* and *tableDelete*, is not told the value in question. Because in general you will not know what the highest priority value is, *tableRetrieve* and *tableDelete* could not easily perform this task. On the other hand, you could not use *pqDelete* to retrieve and delete an item with some specified value.

The ADT priority queue and the ADT table are thus both similar and dissimilar, a fact that their implementations reflect. To begin, consider some of the table

Possible implementations

implementations as implementations for a priority queue. The sorted linear implementations are appropriate if the number of items in the priority queue is small. The array-based implementation maintains the items sorted in ascending order of priority value, so that the item with the highest priority value is at the end of the array, as Figure 12-9a illustrates. Thus, *pqDelete* simply returns the item in *items[size-1]* and decrements *size*. However, the *pqInsert* operation, after

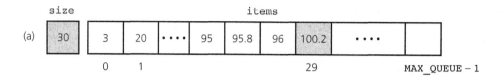

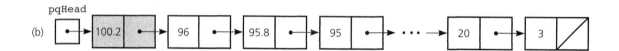

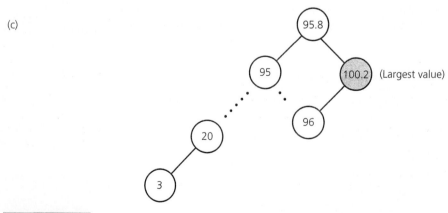

FIGURE 12-9

Some implementations of the ADT priority queue: (a) array based; (b) reference based; (c) binary search tree

using a binary search to find the correct position for the insertion, must shift the array elements to make room for the new item.

The linear reference-based implementation, shown in Figure 12-9b, maintains the items sorted in descending order of priority value, so that the item with the highest priority value is at the beginning of the linked list. Thus, *pqDelete* simply returns the item that *pqHead* references and then changes *pqHead* to reference the next item. The *pqInsert* operation, however, must traverse the list to find the correct position for the insertion. Thus, the linear implementations of priority queues suffer from the same trade-offs as the linear implementations of tables.

Instead, consider a binary search tree as an implementation of a priority queue, as Figure 12-9c illustrates. Although the *pqInsert* operation is the same as *tableInsert*, the *pqDelete* operation has no direct analogue among the table operations. It must locate the item with the highest priority value, without knowing what that value is. The task is not difficult, however, because this item is always in the rightmost node of the tree. (Why?) You thus need only follow *rightChild* references until you encounter a node with a *null rightChild* reference. (Methods analogous to the binary search tree's *findLeftmost* and *deleteLeftmost* can accomplish this task.) Removing this node from the tree is particularly easy because it has at most one child.

A binary search tree implementation is thus good for both a table and a priority queue. Tables and priority queues have different uses, however. Some table applications primarily involve retrieval and traversal operations and thus do not affect the balance of the binary search tree. Priority queues, on the other hand, do not have retrieval and traversal operations, so all their applications involve insertions and deletions, which can affect the shape of the binary search tree. You could use a balanced variation of the binary search tree from Chapter 13; however, if you know the maximum size of the priority queue, a better choice might be an array-based implementation of a heap, which is described next. The heap implementation is often the most appropriate one for a priority queue, but it is not at all appropriate as an implementation of a table.

Heaps

A **heap** is an ADT that is similar to a binary search tree, although it differs from a binary search tree in two significant ways. First, while you can view a binary search tree as sorted, a heap is ordered in a much weaker sense. This order, however, is sufficient for the efficient performance of the priority-queue operations. Second, while binary search trees come in many different shapes, heaps are always complete binary trees.

A heap differs from a binary search tree in two ways

A heap is a complete binary tree

A heap is a special complete binary tree

1. That is empty

or

2. Whose root contains a search key greater than or equal to the search key in each of its children, and

3. Whose root has heaps as its subtrees

In our definition of a heap, the root contains the item with the largest search key. Such a heap is also known as a **maxheap.** A **minheap,** on the other hand, places the item with the smallest search key in its root. Exercise 16 considers the minheap further.

Figure 12-10 contains a UML diagram for the class Heap. The pseudocode for the heap follows.

KEY CONCEPTS

Pseudocode for the Operations of the ADT Heap

```
// HeapItemType is the type of the items stored
// in the heap

+createHeap()
// Creates an empty heap.

+heapIsEmpty():boolean {query}
// Determines whether a heap is empty.

+heapInsert(in newItem:HeapItemType) throws HeapException
// Inserts newItem into a heap. Throws HeapException
// if heap is full.

+heapDelete():HeapItemType
// Retrieves and then deletes a heap's root item.
// This item has the largest search key.
```

Because a heap is a complete binary tree, you can use an array-based implementation of a binary tree, as you saw in Chapter 11, if you know the maximum size of the heap. For example, Figure 12-11 shows a heap along with its array representation. The search key in a heap node is greater than or

Heap
items
createHeap() heapIsEmpty() heapInsert() heapDelete()

FIGURE 12-10

UML diagram for the class Heap

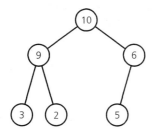

0	10
1	9
2	6
3	3
4	2
5	5

FIGURE 12-11

A heap with its array representation

equal to the search keys in each of the node's children. Further, in a heap, the search keys of the children have no relationship; that is, you do not know which child contains the larger search key.

An array-based implementation of a heap.   Let the following data fields represent the heap:

- *items:* an array of heap items

- *size:* an integer equal to the number of items in the heap

> An array and an integer counter are the data fields for an array-based implementation of a heap

The array *items* corresponds to the array-based representation of a tree. (To simplify the following discussion, assume that the heap items are integers.)

heapDelete.   First consider the *heapDelete* operation. Where is the largest search key in the heap? Because the search key in every node is greater than or equal to the search key in either of its children, the largest search key must be in the root of the tree. Thus, the first step of the *heapDelete* operation is

> *heapDelete*'s first step

```
// return the item in the root
rootItem = items[0]
```

That was easy, but you must also remove the root. When you do so, you are left with two disjoint heaps, as Figure 12-12a indicates. Therefore, you need to transform the remaining nodes back into a heap. To begin this transformation, you take the item in the last node of the tree and place it in the root, as follows:

> *heapDelete*'s second step produces a semiheap

```
// copy the item from the last node into the root
items[0] = items[size-1]

// remove the last node
--size
```

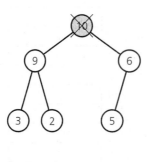
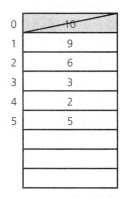

(a)

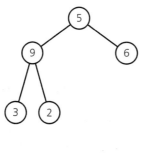

(b)

FIGURE 12-12

(a) Disjoint heaps; (b) a semiheap

As Figure 12-12b suggests, the result of this step is *not* necessarily a heap. It is, however, a complete binary tree whose left and right subtrees are both heaps. The only problem is that the item in the root may be (and usually is) out of place. Such a structure is called a **semiheap.** You thus need a way to transform a semiheap into a heap. One strategy allows the item in the root to *trickle down* the tree until it reaches a node in which it will not be out of place; that is, the item will come to rest in the first node where its search key would be greater than (or equal to) the search key of each of its children. To accomplish this, you first compare the search key in the root of the semiheap to the search keys in its children. If the root has a smaller search key than the larger of the search keys in its children, you swap the item in the root with that of the larger child. (The larger child is the child whose search key is greater than the search key of the other child.)

Figure 12-13 illustrates the `heapDelete` operation. Although the value 5 trickles down to its correct position after only one swap, in general more swaps may be necessary. In fact, once the items in the root and the larger child *C* have been swapped, *C* becomes the root of a semiheap. (Notice that node *C*

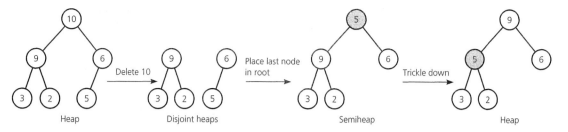

Delete 10   Place last node in root   Trickle down

Heap   Disjoint heaps   Semiheap   Heap

FIGURE 12-13

Deletion from a heap

does not move; only its value changes.) This strategy suggests the following recursive algorithm:

heapDelete's final step transforms the semiheap into a heap

```
+heapRebuild(inout items:ArrayType, in root:integer,
            in size:integer)
// Converts a semiheap rooted at index root into a heap.

  // Recursively trickle the item at index root down to
  // its proper position by swapping it with its larger
  // child, if the child is larger than the item.
  // If the item is at a leaf, nothing needs to be done.

  if (the root is not a leaf) {
    // root must have a left child
    child = 2 * root + 1                // left child index

    if (the root has a right child) {
      rightChild = child + 1            // right child index
      if (items[rightChild].getKey() > items[child].getKey()) {
        child = rightChild             // larger child index
      }  // end if
    }  // end if

    // if the item in the root has a smaller search key
    // than the search key of the item in the larger
    // child, swap items
    if (items[root].getKey() < items[child].getKey()) {
      Swap items[root] and items[child]

      // transform semiheap rooted at child into a heap
      heapRebuild(items, child, size)
    }  // end if
  }  // end if

  // else root is a leaf, so you are done
```

Figure 12-14 illustrates *heapRebuild*'s recursive calls.
Now the *heapDelete* operation uses *heapRebuild* as follows:

```
// return the item in the root
rootItem = items[0]

// copy the item from the last node into the root
items[0] = items[size-1]

// remove the last node
--size

// transform the semiheap back into a heap
heapRebuild(items, 0, size)
return rootItem
```

***heapDelete*'s**
efficiency

Consider briefly the efficiency of *heapDelete*. Because the tree is stored in an array, the removal of a node requires you to swap array elements. These swaps may concern you, but they do not necessarily indicate that the algorithm is inefficient. Since array contents are references, swapping will be very fast. The data in the objects need not be copied. At most, how many array elements will you have to swap? After *heapDelete* copies the item in the last node of the tree into the root, *heapRebuild* trickles this item down the tree until its appropriate place is found. This item travels down a single path from the root to, at worst, a leaf. Therefore, the number of array items that *heapRebuild* must swap is no greater than the height of the tree. The height of a complete binary tree with n nodes is always $\lceil \log_2(n + 1) \rceil$, as you know from Chapter 11.

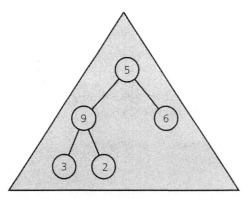
First semiheap passed to heapRebuild

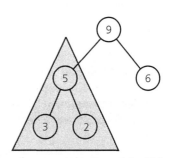
Second semiheap passed to heapRebuild

FIGURE 12-14

Recursive calls to ***heapRebuild***

Each swap requires three reference changes, so *heapDelete* requires

$$3 * \lceil \log_2(n + 1) \rceil + 1$$

reference changes. Thus, *heapDelete* is O(log *n*), which is, in fact, quite efficient.   **heapDelete** is O(log *n*)

heapInsert.   The strategy for the *heapInsert* algorithm is the opposite of that for *heapDelete*. A new item is inserted at the bottom of the tree, and it trickles up to its proper place, as Figure 12-15 illustrates. It is easy to trickle up a node, because the parent of the node in *items[i]*—other than a root—is always stored in *items[(i-1)/2]*. The pseudocode for *heapInsert* is   Insertion strategy

```
// insert newItem into the bottom of the tree
items[size] = newItem

// trickle new item up to appropriate spot in the tree
place = size
parent = (place-1)/2
while ( (parent >= 0) and
        (items[place] > items[parent]) ) {
  Swap items[place] and items[parent]
  place = parent
  parent = (place-1)/2
}  // end while

Increment size
```

The efficiency of *heapInsert* is like that of *heapDelete*. That is, *heapInsert*, at worst, has to swap array elements on a path from a leaf to the root. The number of swaps, therefore, cannot exceed the height of the tree. Because the height of the tree, which is complete, is always $\lceil \log_2(n + 1) \rceil$, *heapInsert* is also O(log *n*).   **heapInsert** is O(log *n*)

Given that the *Heap* implementation does not require a method to search elements in the *Heap* by search-key, the generic implementation of *Heap* uses

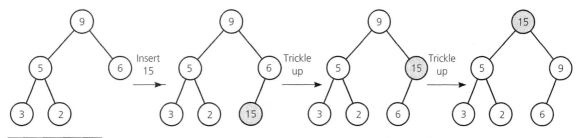

FIGURE 12-15

Insertion into a heap

only one formal data-type parameter. To arrange the elements properly though, some method of comparing the objects must be provided. This implementation uses a technique similar to that found in many of the implementations in the Java Collections Framework by allowing either a natural ordering of the elements through the *Comparable* interface, or by providing a *Comparator* object to the constructor. The assumption is that if a *Comparator* object is not provided, the element type used as the actual data-type parameter implements the *Comparable* interface. Note that the formal data-type parameter does not extend the *Comparable* interface, if it did so, you would be needlessly requiring the element to implement the *Comparable* interface when a *Comparator* object is provided.

```java
package Heaps;
import java.util.ArrayList;
import java.util.Comparator;

public class Heap<T> {
  private ArrayList<T> items;    // array of heap items
  private Comparator<? super T> comparator;

  public Heap() {
    items = new ArrayList<T>();
  }  // end default constructor

  public Heap(Comparator<? super T> comparator) {
    items = new ArrayList<T>();
    this.comparator = comparator;
  }  // end default constructor

// heap operations:
  public boolean heapIsEmpty() {
  // Determines whether a heap is empty.
  // Precondition: None.
  // Postcondition: Returns true if the heap is empty;
  // otherwise returns false.
    return items.size()==0;
  } // end heapIsEmpty

  public void heapInsert(T newItem)
        throws HeapException, ClassCastException {
  // Inserts an item into a heap.
  // Precondition: newItem is the item to be inserted.
  // Postcondition: If the heap was not full, newItem is
  // in its proper position; otherwise HeapException is
  // thrown.
    if (!items.add(newItem)) {
      // problem adding element to ArrayList item for heap
```

```
        throw new HeapException("HeapException: heapInsert failed");
    } else {
        // trickle new item up to its proper position
        int place = items.size()-1;
        int parent = (place - 1)/2;
        while ((parent >= 0) &&
                (compareItems(items.get(place), items.get(parent))) < 0) {
            // swap items[place] and items[parent]
            T temp = items.get(parent);
            items.set(parent, items.get(place));
            items.set(place, temp);

            place = parent;
            parent = (place - 1)/2;
        }   // end while
    } // end else
} // end heapInsert

public T heapDelete() {
// Retrieves and deletes the item in the root of a heap.
// This item has the largest search key in the heap.
// Precondition: None.
// Postcondition: If the heap is not empty, returns the
// item in the root of the heap and then deletes it. However,
// if the heap is empty, removal is impossible and the
// method returns null.
    T rootItem = null;
    int loc;
    if (!heapIsEmpty()) {
        rootItem = items.get(0);
        loc = items.size()-1;
        // if we remove the item first, it may make the ArrayList items
        // empty, then set() won't work
        items.set(0, items.get(loc));
        items.remove(loc);
        heapRebuild(0);
    }   // end if
    return rootItem;
} // end heapDelete

protected void heapRebuild(int root) {
// if the root is not a leaf and the root's search key
// is less than the larger of the search keys in the
// root's children
    int child = 2 * root + 1;  // index of root's left
                               // child, if any
    if ( child < items.size() ) {
```

```
                    // root is not a leaf, so it has a left child at child
                    int rightChild = child + 1;   // index of right child,
                                                  // if any

                    // if root has a right child, find larger child
                    if ((rightChild < items.size()) &&
                        (compareItems(items.get(rightChild),items.get(child)))
                                                                   < 0) {
                      child = rightChild;     // index of larger child
                    } // end if

                    // if the root's value is smaller than the
                    // value in the larger child, swap values
                    if (compareItems(items.get(root), items.get(child)) > 0) {
                      T temp = items.get(root);
                      items.set(root, items.get(child));
                      items.set(child, temp);
                      // transform the new subtree into a heap
                      heapRebuild(child);
                    }   // end if
                  }   // end if
                  // if root is a leaf, do nothing
                } // end heapRebuild

              private int compareItems(T item1, T item2) {
                if (comparator == null) {
                return ((Comparable <T>)item1).compareTo(item2);
                } else {
                  return comparator.compare(item1, item2);
                } // end if
              } // end compare
            } // end Heap
```

A Heap Implementation of the ADT Priority Queue

Priority-queue operations and heap operations are analogous

Once you have implemented the ADT heap, the implementation of the ADT priority queue is straightforward, because priority-queue operations are exactly analogous to heap operations. The priority value in a priority-queue item corresponds to a heap item's search key. Thus, the implementation of the priority queue can reuse the class *Heap*. That is, the class *PriorityQueue* has an instance of *Heap* as its data field:

```
package PriorityQueues;
import Heaps.Heap;
import Heaps.HeapException;
import java.util.Comparator;
```

```java
// *************************************************************
// Assumes that Heap implementation is in package Heaps.
// PriorityQueue class implementation.
// *************************************************************

public class PriorityQueue<T>{
  private Heap<T> h;

  public PriorityQueue() {
    h = new Heap<T>();
  }  // end default constructor

  public PriorityQueue(Comparator<? super T> comparator) {
    h = new Heap<T>(comparator);
  }  // end default constructor

  // priority-queue operations:
  public boolean pqIsEmpty() {
    return h.heapIsEmpty();
  }  // end pqIsEmpty

  public void pqInsert(T newItem) throws PriorityQueueException {
    try {
      h.heapInsert(newItem);
    }  // end try
    catch (HeapException e) {
      throw new PriorityQueueException(
            "PQueueException: Problem inserting to Priority Queue");
    }  // end catch
  }  // end pqInsert

  public T pqDelete() {
    return h.heapDelete();
  }  // end pqDelete

}  // end PriorityQueue
```

How does a heap compare to a binary search tree as an implementation of a priority queue? If you know the maximum number of items in the priority queue, the heap is the better implementation.

Because a heap is complete, it is always balanced, which is its major advantage. If the binary search tree is balanced, both implementations will have the same average performance for n items: They both will be O(log n). The height of a binary search tree, however, can increase during insertions and deletions, greatly exceeding $\log_2 n$ and degrading the implementation's efficiency to O(n) in the worst case. The heap implementation avoids this decrease in performance.

The heap implementation requires knowledge of the priority queue's maximum size

A heap is always balanced

In the next chapter, you will see how to keep a binary search tree balanced, but the operations that do this are far more complex than the heap operations. Do not think, however, that a heap can replace a binary search tree as a table implementation; as was stated earlier, a heap is not appropriate in this role. If this fact is not apparent to you, try to perform the table operation `tableRetrieve` on a heap, or try to traverse a heap in search-key order.

Finite, distinct priority values.   If you have a finite number of distinct priority values, such as the integers 1 through 20, many items will likely have the same priority value. You could place items whose priority values are the same in the order in which you encounter them.

A heap of queues accommodates this situation, with one queue for each distinct priority value. To insert an item into the priority queue, you add a queue for the item's priority value to the heap, if it is not already there. Then you insert the item into the corresponding queue. To delete an item from a priority queue, you delete the item at the front of the queue that corresponds to the highest priority value in the heap. If this deletion leaves the queue empty, you remove it from the heap.

Programming Problem 7 at the end of this chapter treats distinct priority values further.

A heap of queues (margin note)

Heapsort

As its name implies, the heapsort algorithm uses a heap to sort an array *anArray* of items that are in no particular order. The first step of the algorithm transforms the array into a heap. One way to accomplish this transformation is to use the *heapInsert* method to insert the items into the heap one by one.

A more efficient method of building a heap out of the items of *anArray* is possible, however. For example, assume that the initial contents of *anArray* are as shown in Figure 12-16a. First you imagine the array as a binary tree by assigning the items of *anArray* to the tree's nodes, beginning with the root and proceeding left to right down the tree. Figure 12-16b shows the resulting tree. Next, you transform this tree into a heap by calling *heapRebuild* repeatedly. *heapRebuild* transforms a semiheap—a tree whose subtrees are both heaps but whose root may be out of place—into a heap. But are there any semiheaps in the

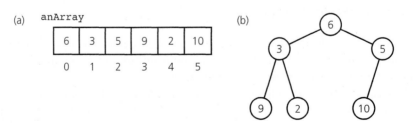

FIGURE 12-16

(a) The initial contents of *anArray*; (b) *anArray*'s corresponding binary tree

tree for *heapRebuild* to work on? Although the tree in Figure 12-16b is not a semiheap, if you look at its leaves you will find semiheaps—that is, each leaf is a semiheap. (In fact, each leaf is a heap, but for the sake of simplicity, ignore this fact.) You first call *heapRebuild* on the leaves from right to left. You then move up the tree, knowing that by the time you reach a node *s*, its subtrees are heaps, and thus *heapRebuild* will transform the semiheap rooted at *s* into a heap.

The following algorithm transforms the array *anArray* of *n* items into a heap and is the first step of the heapsort algorithm:

Building a heap from
an array of items

```
for (index = n - 1 down to 0)
    // Assertion: the tree rooted at index is a semiheap
    heapRebuild(anArray, index, n)
    // Assertion: the tree rooted at index is a heap
```

Actually, you can replace *n - 1* with *n/2* in the previous *for* statement. Exercise 21 at the end of this chapter asks you to explain why this improvement is possible. Figure 12-17 traces this algorithm for the array in Figure 12-16a.

After transforming the array into a heap, heapsort partitions the array into two regions—the Heap region and the Sorted region—as Figure 12-18 illustrates. The Heap region is in *anArray[0..last]*, and the Sorted region is in *anArray[last+1..n-1]*. Initially, the Heap region is all of *anArray* and the Sorted region is empty—that is, *last* is equal to *n - 1*.

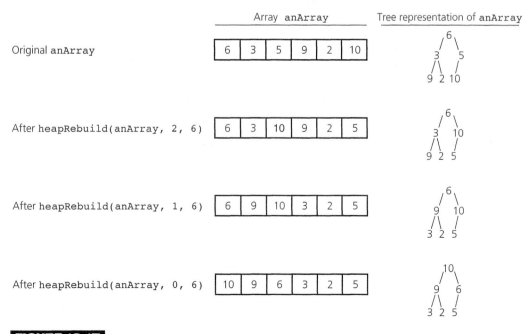

FIGURE 12-17

Transforming an array *anArray* into a heap

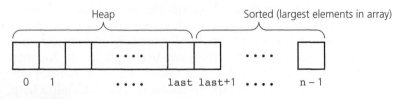

FIGURE 12-18

Heapsort partitions an array into two regions

Each step of the algorithm moves an item *I* from the Heap region to the Sorted region. The invariant of the heapsort algorithm is

- After Step *k*, the Sorted region contains the *k* largest values in `anArray`, and they are in sorted order—that is, `anArray[n-1]` is the largest, `anArray[n-2]` is the second largest, and so on.

- The items in the Heap region form a heap.

So that the invariant holds, *I* must be the item that has the largest value in the Heap region, and therefore *I* must be in the root of the heap. To accomplish the move, you exchange the item in the root of the heap with the last item in the heap—that is, you exchange `anArray[0]` with `anArray[last]`—and then decrement the value of `last`. As a result, the item just swapped from the root into `anArray[last]` becomes the smallest item in the Sorted region (and is in the first position of the Sorted region). After the move, you must transform the Heap region back into a heap because the new root may be out of place. You can accomplish this transformation by using `heapRebuild` to trickle down the item now in the root so that the Heap region is once again a heap.

The following algorithm summarizes the steps:

```
+heapSort(in anArray:ArrayType, in n:integer)
// Sorts anArray[0..n-1].

  // build initial heap
  for (index = n - 1 down to 0) {
    // Invariant: the tree rooted at index is a semiheap
    heapRebuild(anArray, index, n)
    // Assertion: the tree rooted at index is a heap
  }  // end for
  // Assertion: anArray[0] is the largest item in heap
  // anArray[0..n-1]

  // initialize the regions
  last = n - 1

  // Invariant: anArray[0..last] is a heap,
  // anArray[last+1..n-1] is
  // sorted and contains the largest items of A
```

```
for (step = 1 through n) {
  // move the largest item in the heap region -- that
  // is, the root anArray[0] -- to the beginning of the
  // Sorted region by swapping items
  Swap anArray[0] and anArray[last]

  // expand the Sorted region, shrink the Heap region
  Decrement last

  // make the Heap region a heap again
  heapRebuild(anArray, 0, last)
}  // end for
```

Figure 12-19 completes the trace of the pseudocode heapsort that Figure 12-17 began. The Java implementation of heapsort is left as an exercise.

The analysis of the efficiency of heapsort is similar to that of mergesort, as given in Chapter 10. Both algorithms are $O(n * \log n)$ in both the worst and average cases. Heapsort has an advantage over mergesort in that it does not require a second array. Quicksort is also $O(n * \log n)$ in the average case but is $O(n^2)$ in the worst case. Even though quicksort has poor worst-case efficiency, it is generally the preferred sorting method.

Heapsort is $O(n * \log n)$

12.3 Tables and Priority Queues in the JCF

The Java Collections Framework provides collections that act as tables. These classes are called **maps** because their elements consist of (*key, value*) pairs, where a *key* is used to retrieve a corresponding *value*, in other words, a *key* maps to a *value*. The JCF distinguishes maps from collections. Collections are used to hold single values, such as `List` and `Queue`. Within the JCF, single value collections are contained in one hierarchy with three branches, one for sets, a second for lists, and a third for queues. Maps are used to hold two values, a key that maps to a particular value. The JCF places maps in a second hierarchy that includes `HashMap` and `TreeMap`.

Also note that these (*key, value*) pairs differ slightly from the search-key implementation presented in this chapter and the last. Our search-key value was embedded within the element. With (*key, value*) pairs, the search-key is a separate, standalone component.

The JCF does include a class for priority queues call `PriorityQueue`, but has no direct support for heaps or heap algorithms. The `PriorityQueue` class will be discussed at the end of this section.

The JCF *Map* Interface

The JCF provides an interface `Map` that is the root in the hierarchy of the map components. This `Map` interface provides the basis for numerous other interfaces, abstract classes, and implementations of different kinds of maps in the JCF.

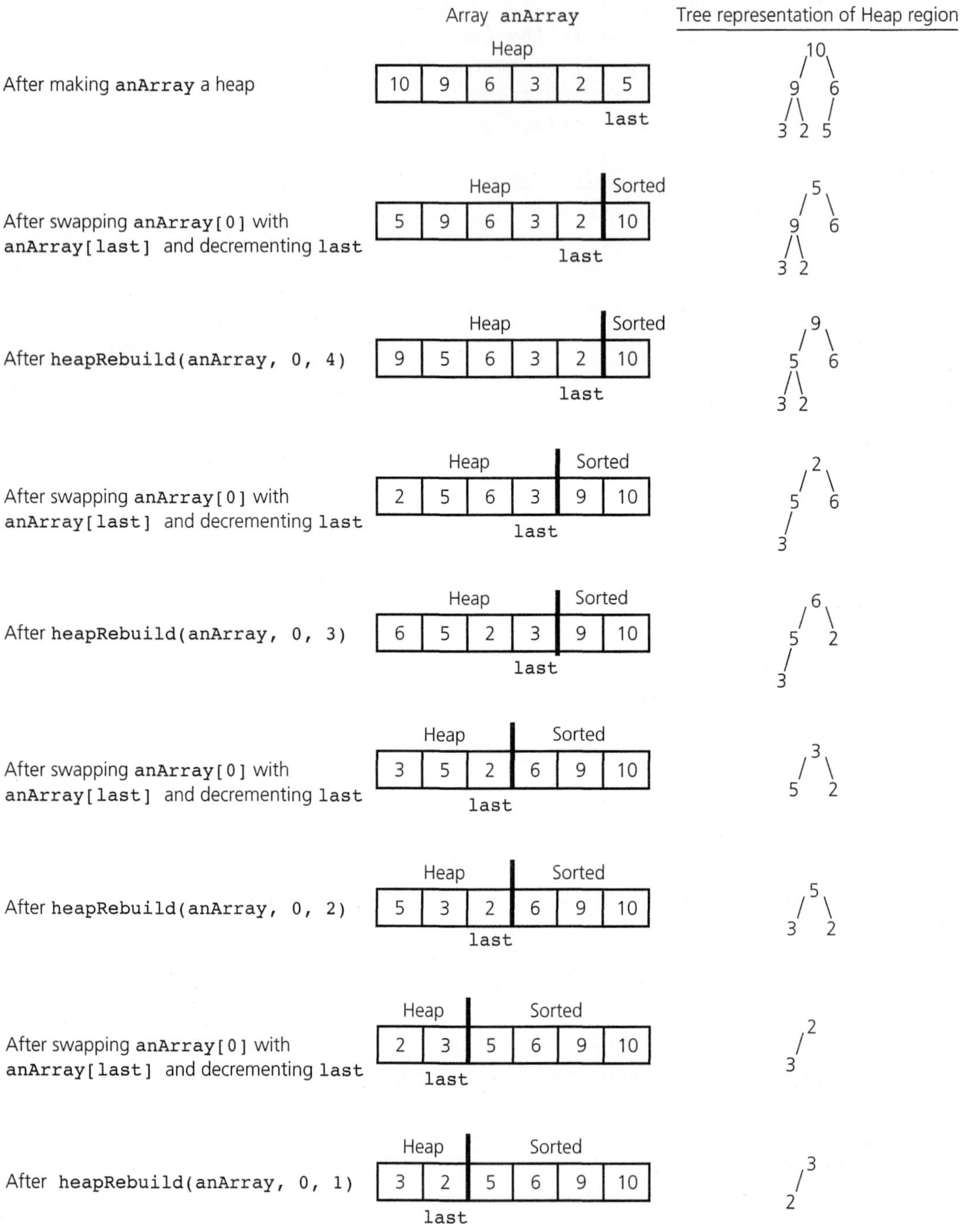

FIGURE 12-19

A trace of the pseudocode heapsort, beginning with the heap in Figure 12-17

continues

	Heap		Sorted			
	2	3	5	6	9	10

After swapping `anArray[0]` with
`anArray[last]` and decrementing `last`   last

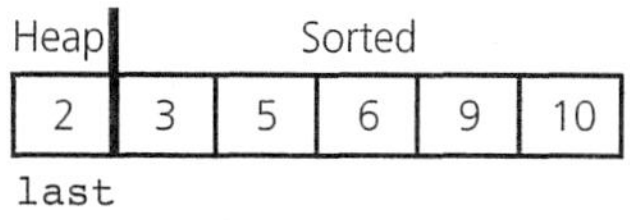

Array is sorted

FIGURE 12-19

The `Map` interface provides the framework necessary for creating classes for objects that map keys to values. It is assumed that these key-values are unique, and that each key can map to only one value. Here is a partial listing of the `Map` interface:

```
public interface Map<K,V> {
  void clear();
    // Removes all mappings from this map (optional operation).

  boolean containsKey(Object key);
    // Returns true if this map contains a mapping for the specified
    // key.

  boolean containsValue(Object value);
    // Returns true if this map maps one or more keys to the
    // specified value.

  Set<Map.Entry<K,V>> entrySet();
    // Returns a set view of the mappings contained in this map.

  V get(Object key);
    // Returns the value to which this map maps the specified key.

  boolean isEmpty();
    // Returns true if this map contains no key-value mappings.

  Set<K> keySet();
    // Returns a set view of the keys contained in this map.

  V put(K key, V value);
    // Associates the specified value with the specified key in this
    // map (optional operation).

  V remove(Object key);
    // Removes the mapping for this key from this map if it is
    // present (optional operation).
```

```
    int size();
      // Returns the number of key-value mappings in this map.

    Collection<V> values();
      // Returns a collection view of the values contained in this
      // map.
}  // end Map
```

Note that the `Map` interface provides a method *put* for adding (*key*, *value*) pairs, and the methods *get* and *remove* to respectively retrieve and remove values by their key. The interface also provides the method *keySet* for retrieving all of the map keys as a set, the method *values* for retrieving all of the values as a collection, and the method *entrySet* to retrieve all of the map entries as a set. The results of these methods are often referred to as *collection views* of the map, since they are returning collections from the map. Note that the methods *keySet* and *entrySet* return a `Set`, a subinterface of `Collection`. The `Set` interface is discussed in the next section.

If you want the collection views to be returned in ascending order by key value, then you would use the map interface `SortedMap`. It is expected that any implementation of `SortedMap` allows for the natural ordering of the keys, or provides for a `Comparator` object to be provided upon construction of a sorted map instance.

The *entrySet* method returns the map entries as a set of `Map.Entry<K,V>`, shown below.

```
public static interface Map.Entry<K,V> {

    boolean equals(Object o);
      // Compares the specified object with this entry for equality.

    K getKey();
      // Returns the key corresponding to this entry.

    V getValue();
      // Returns the value corresponding to this entry.

    int hashCode();
      // Returns the hash code value for this map entry.

    V setValue(V value);
      // Replaces the value corresponding to this entry with the
      // specified value (optional operation).
}  // end Map.Entry
```

The method *entrySet* is the only method that returns the map entries using this data type, so if you wish to work with the entries in the `Map` in this fashion, you must retrieve this set, and use a set iterator to traverse the result.

It is assumed that once you create an entry in a map, that the key-value should not be modified, it should be implemented as a nonmutable object. If this value is allowed to change, the behavior of the map is not specified. If an entry is added for a key that is already in the *Map*, the original mapping is removed, and the new entry is inserted into the map, maintaining unique key-values in the map.

Two popular JCF map implementations are *HashMap* and *TreeMap*. The class *HashMap* provides a hash table implementation of the *Map* interface. Hash tables are discussed in the next chapter. The class *TreeMap* provides a red-black tree implementation of the *SortedMap* interface. Red-black trees are also discussed in the next chapter. An example using the class *HashMap* is shown at the end of the next section.

The JCF *Set* Interface

The *Set* interface, like *Map*, is an ordered collection, but it only stores single value entries. The difference between a *Set* and a *Collection* is that a *Set* does not allow for duplicate elements as determined by the result of applying the *equals* method. Here is a partial listing of the *Set* interface:

```
interface Set<T> extends Collection<T> {

  boolean add(T o);
    // Adds the specified element to this set if it is not already
    // present (optional operation).

  boolean addAll(Collection<? extends T> c);
    // Adds all of the elements in the specified collection to this set
    // if they're not already present (optional operation).

  void clear();
    // Removes all of the elements from this set (optional operation).

  boolean contains(Object o);
    // Returns true if this set contains the specified element.

  boolean isEmpty();
    // Returns true if this set contains no elements.

  Iterator<T> iterator();
    // Returns an iterator over the elements in this set.

  boolean remove(Object o);
    // Removes the specified element from this set if it is
    // present (optional operation).

  boolean removeAll(Collection<?> c);
```

```
// Removes from this set all of its elements that are contained
// in the specified collection (optional operation).

boolean retainAll(Collection<?> c);
// Retains only the elements in this set that are contained in the
// specified collection (optional operation).

int size();
// Returns the number of elements in this set (its cardinality).

} // end Set
```

As with the keys in the *Map* interface, it is recommended that the elements of the set be nonmutable; the behavior of the set is not guaranteed if the value of an object is modified after it is inserted into the set. In particular, the implementation may not be able to determine if the value is changed to an equal value already in the set. If you want the set elements to be available in sorted order, there is a subinterface called *SortedSet*.

Two popular JCF set implementations are *HashSet* and *TreeSet*. The class *HashSet* provides a hash table implementation of the *Set* interface using *HashMap*. The class *TreeSet* uses a *TreeMap* implementation of the *SortedSet* interface.

You will notice that the mathematical operations of set union, difference, and intersection appear to be absent. But note that these operations can be achieved through the use of the methods *addAll*, *retainAll*, and *removeAll* as follows:

```
HashSet<Integer> setA = new HashSet<Integer>();

setA.add(2);
setA.add(3);
setA.add(5);
setA.add(8);
System.out.println("setA => " + setA);

HashSet<Integer> setB = new HashSet<Integer>();

setB.add(1);
setB.add(3);
setB.add(7);
setB.add(9);
System.out.println("setB => " + setB);

// Set union
HashSet<Integer> unionSet = new HashSet<Integer>(setA);
unionSet.addAll(setB);
System.out.println("setA union setB => " + unionSet);
```

```
// Set intersection
HashSet<Integer> intSet = new HashSet<Integer>(setA);
intSet.retainAll(setB);
System.out.println("setA intersect setB => " + intSet);

// Set difference (setA - setB)
HashSet<Integer> diffSet = new HashSet<Integer>(setA);
diffSet.removeAll(setB);
System.out.println("setA - setB => " + diffSet);
```

The output of this code is as follows:

```
setA => [2, 8, 3, 5]
setB => [9, 1, 3, 7]
setA union setB => [2, 9, 8, 1, 3, 7, 5]
setA intersect setB => [3]
setA - setB => [2, 8, 5]
```

The following program creates two versions of a telephone book, one unsorted (using *HashMap*), and the other sorted (using *SortedMap*). You will also see the use of *HashSet* and *Set* in processing of the telephone book.

```
import java.util.*;

public class MapSetExample {

  static public void main(String[] args) {
    // create some data for the keys, use names
    String[] name = {"Smith, Jackson",
                     "Prichard, Marlene",
                     "Hayden, Sarah",
                     "Records, Hal",
                     "Prichard, Marlene"};

    // create corresponding values for the keys
    String[] phone = {"212-555-4444",
                      "806-555-6565",
                      "401-555-5220",
                      "445-555-3241",
                      "715-555-9087"};

    // Declare a map to contain the names and phone numbers
    HashMap<String, String> phoneBook = new HashMap<String, String>();

    // Insert the names and phone number pairs into the map.
    // When the duplicate key "Prichard, Marlene" is inserted, should
    // replace original entry.
```

```java
    for (int i=0; i<name.length; i++) {
      phoneBook.put(name[i], phone[i]);
    } // end phone

    // print the contents of the map
    Set<Map.Entry<String,String>> resultSet = phoneBook.entrySet();
    Iterator<Map.Entry<String,String>> iter = resultSet.iterator();
    Map.Entry<String, String> entry;

    System.out.println("Contents of phone book, using HashMap");
    while (iter.hasNext()) {
      entry = iter.next();
      System.out.println(entry.getKey() + "\t\t" + entry.getValue());
    } // end while
    System.out.println("\n");

    // Retrieve a map value
    System.out.println("Search for " + name[2]);
    System.out.println("  - phone number is " +
                       phoneBook.get(name[2]));

    // Declare a sorted map to contain the names and phone numbers
    TreeMap<String, String> phoneBookSorted =
        new TreeMap<String, String>();

    // insert the names and phone number pairs into the map
    // when the duplicate key "Prichard, Marlene" is inserted, should
    // replace original entry
    for (int i=0; i<name.length; i++) {
      phoneBookSorted.put(name[i], phone[i]);
    } // end phone
    System.out.println("\n");

    // print the contents of the map
    Set<Map.Entry<String,String>> sortedSet =
        phoneBookSorted.entrySet();
    iter = sortedSet.iterator();
    System.out.println("Contents of sorted phone book, using TreeMap");
    while (iter.hasNext()) {
      entry = iter.next();
      System.out.println(entry.getKey() + "\t\t" + entry.getValue());
    } // end while
  } // end main
} // // end MapSetExample
```

This program produces the following output:

```
Contents of phone book, using HashMap
Records, Hal          445-555-3241
Smith, Jackson        212-555-4444
Hayden, Sarah         401-555-5220
Prichard, Marlene     715-555-9087

Search for Hayden, Sarah
  - phone number is 401-555-5220

Contents of sorted phone book, using TreeMap
Hayden, Sarah         401-555-5220
Prichard, Marlene     715-555-9087
Records, Hal          445-555-3241
Smith, Jackson        212-555-4444
```

The JCF *PriorityQueue* Class

The *PriorityQueue* class is an implementation of the abstract class *AbstractQueue*. The *PriorityQueue* class has a single data-type parameter with ordered elements. As we have seen with *SortedMap* and *SortedTree*, *PriorityQueue* relies on the natural ordering of the elements as provided by the *Comparable* interface or through the use of a *Comparator* object supplied when the priority queue is created. The elements in the queue are ordered in ascending order.

The priority queue processes the least element (the *head* of the queue) when any of the retrieval or removal operations are used. Additions to the queue are inserted so that the ascending order of the elements in the priority queue is maintained.

Here is a partial listing of the *PriorityQueue* class:

```
public class PriorityQueue<T> extends AbstractQueue<T>
                              implements Serializable

  PriorityQueue(int initialCapacity)
    // Creates a PriorityQueue with the specified initial
    // capacity that orders its elements according to their
    // natural ordering (using Comparable).

  PriorityQueue(int initialCapacity, Comparator<? super T> comparator)
    // Creates a PriorityQueue with the specified initial capacity that
    // orders its elements according to the specified comparator.

  // Other constructors available...

  boolean add(T o)
    // Adds the specified element to this queue.
```

```
void clear()
   // Removes all elements from the priority queue.

boolean contains(Object o)
   // Returns true if this priority queue contains the specified
   // element.

Comparator<? super T> comparator()
   // Returns the comparator used to order this collection, or null
   // if this collection is sorted according to its elements natural
   // ordering (using Comparable).

T element()
   // Retrieves, but does not remove, the head of this priority queue.

Iterator<T> iterator()
   // Returns an iterator over the elements in this queue.

boolean offer(T o)
   // Inserts the specified element into this priority queue.

T peek()
   // Retrieves, but does not remove, the head of this queue,
   // returning null if this queue is empty.

T poll()
   // Retrieves and removes the head of this queue, or null if this
   // queue is empty.

boolean remove(Object o)
   // Removes a single instance of the specified element from this
   // queue, if it is present.

int size()
   // Returns the number of elements in this collection.
} // end PriorityQueue
```

A priority queue can be provided with an initial capacity that will grow as needed. The implementation provides $O(\log(n))$ time for the methods that modify the priority queue contents (*offer*, *poll*, *remove*, and *add*). The methods *remove* and *contains* provide $O(n)$ time, and the retrieval methods (*peek*, *element*, and *size*) are of $O(1)$ time.

Like we have seen with other classes in the JCF, two different methods are offered for insertion, retrieval, and removal. Be sure to check the specifications carefully in determining which version will be best for your application. For example, *peek* and *element* are both methods for retrieving but not removing an element from the priority queue. They differ in that *peek* will return *null* if the priority queue is empty, and *element* will throw *NoSuchElementException* if this queue is empty.

The following program demonstrates the use of a priority queue of integer values:

```
static public void main(String[] args) {

   PriorityQueue<Integer> pq = new PriorityQueue<Integer>(10);
   pq.offer(87);
   pq.offer(2);
   pq.offer(10);
   pq.offer(5);

   System.out.println("The elements will be processed in this order:");
   System.out.print(pq.remove());
   while (!pq.isEmpty()) {
     System.out.print(", " + pq.remove());
   }
   System.out.println();
} // end main
```

Here is the output of the program:

```
The elements will be processed in this order:

   2, 5, 10, 87
```

Summary

1. The ADT table supports value-oriented operations, such as

   Retrieve all the information about John Smith

2. The linear implementations (array based and reference based) of a table are adequate only in limited situations, such as when the table is small, or for certain operations. In those situations, the simplicity of a linear implementation may be an advantage. A linear implementation of a table, however, is not suitable as a general-purpose, reusable class.

3. A nonlinear reference-based (binary search tree) implementation of the ADT table provides the best aspects of the two linear implementations. The reference-based implementation allows the table to grow dynamically and allows insertions and deletions of data to occur through just a few reference changes. In addition, the binary search tree allows you to use a binary search-like algorithm when searching for an item with a specified value. These characteristics make a nonlinear table implementation far superior to the linear implementations in many applications.

4. A priority queue is a variation of the ADT table. Its operations allow you to retrieve and remove the item with the highest priority value.

5. A heap that uses an array-based representation of a complete binary tree is a good implementation of a priority queue when you know the maximum number of items that will be stored at any one time.

6. Heapsort, like mergesort, has good worst-case and average-case behaviors, but neither algorithm is as good in the average case as quicksort. Heapsort has an advantage over mergesort in that it does not require a second array.

Cautions

1. When defining an ADT to solve a particular problem, do not request unnecessary operations. The proper choice of an implementation depends on the mix of requested operations, and if you request an operation that you do not need, you might get an implementation that does not best support what you are really doing.

2. A linear array-based implementation of the ADT table must shift the references to the data during a deletion and during an insertion in sorted order. These shifts can be time consuming, particularly for large tables.

3. Although a linear reference-based implementation of the ADT table eliminates the need to shift the references to the data, it does not support the insertion and deletion operations any more efficiently than does an array-based implementation, because you cannot perform a binary search in a reasonable fashion.

4. Usually a binary search tree can support the operations of the ADT table quite efficiently. However, in the worst case, when the tree approaches a linear shape, the performance of the table operations is comparable to that of a linear reference-based implementation. If a given application cannot tolerate poor performance, you should use the table implementations presented in Chapter 13.

5. Although a heap is a good implementation of a priority queue, it is not appropriate for a table. Specifically, a heap does not support the sorted *tableRetrieve* and traversal operations efficiently.

Self-Test Exercises

1. Using the operations of the ADT table, write pseudocode for a *tableReplace* operation that replaces the table item whose search key is x with another item whose search key is also x.

2. Does the array in Figure 12-20 represent a heap?

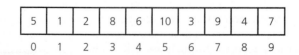

5	1	2	8	6	10	3	9	4	7
0	1	2	3	4	5	6	7	8	9

FIGURE 12-20

Array for Self-Test Exercises 2 and 7 and Exercise 22

3. Is the full binary tree in Figure 11-36 a semiheap? Is it a heap?

4. Consider the heap in Figure 12-11. Draw the heap after you insert 12 and then remove 12.

5. What does the initially empty heap *h* contain after the following sequence of pseudocode operations?

```
h.heapInsert(2)
h.heapInsert(3)
h.heapInsert(4)
h.heapInsert(1)
h.heapInsert(9)
item = h.heapDelete()
h.heapInsert(7)
h.heapInsert(6)
item = h.heapDelete()
h.heapInsert(5)
```

6. What does the heap that represents the initially empty priority queue *pq* contain after the following sequence of pseudocode operations?

```
pq.pqInsert(5)
pq.pqInsert(9)
pq.pqInsert(6)
pq.pqInsert(7)
pq.pqInsert(3)
pq.pqInsert(4)
item = pq.pqDelete()
pq.pqInsert(9)
pq.pqInsert(2)
item = pq.pqDelete()
```

7. Execute the pseudocode statements

```
for (index = n - 1 down to 0)
   heapRebuild(anArray, index, n)
```

on the array in Figure 12-20.

Exercises

1. Complete the sorted array-based implementation of the ADT table.

2. The operation `tableReplace(replacementItem)` locates, if possible, the item in a table with the same search key as `replacementItem`. If the table contains such an item, `tableReplace` replaces it with `replacementItem`. Thus, the fields of the original item are updated.

   a. Write implementations of `tableReplace` for the five implementations (four linear ones and the binary search tree) of the ADT table described in this chapter.

   b. For the binary search tree implementation of the ADT table, under what circumstances can `tableReplace` replace an item without altering the structure of the binary search tree? (See Exercise 13 in Chapter 11.)

3. Let us assume that the following elements are in a heap.

90	60	16	30	15	8	7

What is the root element of the heap after 3 consecutive deletions?

4. When you use a word processor's spell checker, it compares the words in your document with words in a dictionary. You can add new words to the dictionary as necessary. Thus, this dictionary needs frequent retrievals and occasional insertions. Which implementation of the ADT table would be most efficient as a spellchecker's dictionary?

5. A Java compiler uses a **symbol table** to keep track of the identifiers that a program uses. When the compiler encounters an identifier, it searches the symbol table to see whether that identifier has already been encountered. If the identifier is new, it is inserted into the table. Thus, the symbol table needs only insertion and retrieval operations. Which implementation of the ADT table would be most efficient as a symbol table?

6. Write a Java program that makes a heap out of the following data that are read from command line arguments.

82	64	3	27	5	16	97	87	20

7. The implementations of the ADT table given in this chapter make the following assumption: At any time, a table contains at most one item with a given search key. Although the definition of an ADT required for a specific application may not allow duplicates, it is probably wise to test for them rather than simply to assume that they will not occur. Why?

    Modify the table implementations so that they test for—and disallow—any duplicates. What table operations are affected? What are the implications for the unsorted linear implementations?

8. Although disallowing duplicates in the ADT table (see Exercise 7) is reasonable for some applications, it is just as reasonable to have an application that will allow duplicates.

    a. What are the implications of inserting duplicate items that are identical? What are the implications of duplicate items for the deletion and retrieval operations?

    b. What are the implications of inserting items that are not identical but have the same search key? Specifically, what would the implementations of `tableInsert`, `tableDelete`, and `tableRetrieve` do?

9. Write a program for a priority queue where the data is stored in a circular queue in a sorted order depending upon the priority value of each element. At the time of deletion the values are always deleted from the front.

10. Write a Java program which reads ten elements from the user and then sorts them using a HEAP SORT algorithm.

11. Given the following minheap h in Figure 12-21, show what the heap h would look like after each of the following pseudocode operations:

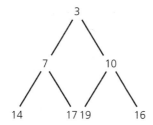

FIGURE 12-21

Minheap for Exercise 11

    a. *h.heapInsert(9)*

    b. *h.heapInsert(6)*

    c. *h.heapDelete()*

12. Given the following maxheap *h* in Figure 12-22, show what the heap *h* would look like after each of the following pseudocode operations:

    a. *h.heapInsert(19)*

    b. *h.heapInsert(16)*

    c. *h.heapDelete()*

13. Draw the maxheap that is created by using the array: 12, 17, 3, 9, 2, 13, 7, 19.

14. Prove that the root of a heap contains the largest search key in the tree.

15. Write a Java program that deletes the elements from a heap. After the deletion, it should repair the heap.

16. Revise the implementation of *heapInsert* and *heapRebuild* so that the actual swaps of items are unnecessary.

17. Suppose that you have two items with the same priority value. How does the order in which you insert these items into a priority queue affect the order in which they will be deleted? What can you do if you need elements with equal priority value to be served on a first-come, first-served basis?

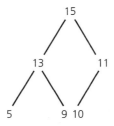

FIGURE 12-22

Minheap for Exercise 12

18. Create a priority queue using the following data:

    3:26, 7:36, 18:6, 90:26, 99:1, 22:13

    The first number represents the data and the second number represents its priority. Assume that the queue gives higher priority to a higher value.

19. Suppose that you wanted to maintain the index of the item with the smallest priority value in a maxheap. That is, in addition to a *removeMax* operation, you might want to support a *retrieveMin* operation. How difficult would it be to maintain this index within the *pqInsert* and *removeMax* operations?

20. Suppose that after you have placed several items into a priority queue, you need to adjust one of their priority values. For example, a particular task in a priority queue of tasks could become either more or less urgent. How can you adjust a heap if a single priority value changes?

21. Show that within the pseudocode for the method *heapsort* you can replace the statement

    ```
    for (index = n-1 down to 0)
    ```

    with

    ```
    for (index = n/2 down to 0)
    ```

22. Trace the action of *heapSort* on the array in Figure 12-20.

23. Implement the priority queue in question no. 5 using the heap tree algorithm.

24. Revise *heapSort* so that it sorts an array into descending order.

Programming Problems

1. Write the sorted reference-based, unsorted array-based, and unsorted reference-based implementations of the ADT table described in this chapter.

2. Write iterator classes for the two table classes presented in this chapter, *TableArrayBased* and *TableBSTBased*. Be sure to include an implementation of the *remove* operation.

3. Write unsorted and sorted implementations of the ADT table that use, respectively, the ADTs list and sorted list, which Chapter 4 described.

4. Repeat Programming Problem 4 of Chapter 11, using the ADT table as the address book.

5. Implement the symbol table described in Exercise 5 by reusing the class *TableArrayBased*.

6. As Figure 12-9 illustrates, you can use data structures other than a heap to implement the ADT priority queue.

    a. Write the Java class for the reference-based implementation that Figure 12-9b represents.

b. Write the Java class for the binary search tree implementation that Figure 12-9c represents.

c. Implement the classes that you wrote in Parts *a* and *b*.

7. Suppose that you wanted to implement a priority queue whose priority values are the integers 1 through 20.

a. Implement the priority queue as a heap of queues, as described in this chapter.

b. Another solution uses an array of 20 queues, one for each priority value. Use this approach to implement the priority queue.

8. Write an interactive program that will monitor the flow of patients in a large hospital. The program should account for patients checking in and out of the hospital and should allow access to information about a given patient. In addition, the program should manage the scheduling of three operating rooms. Doctors make a request that includes a patient's name and a priority value between 1 and 10 that reflects the urgency of the operation. Patients are chosen for the operating room by priority value, and patients with the same priority are served on a first-come, first-served basis.

The user should use either one-letter or one-word commands to control the program. As you design your solution, try to identify the essential operations (excuse the pun) that you must perform on the data, and only then choose an appropriate data structure for implementation. This approach will allow you to maintain the wall between the main part of the program and the implementations. An interesting exercise would be to recast this problem as an event-driven simulation.

CHAPTER 13

Advanced Implementations of Tables

Although Chapter 12 described the advantages of using the binary search tree to implement the ADT table, the efficiency of this implementation suffers when the tree loses its balance. This chapter introduces several advanced implementations of the table. First examined are various other search trees, which remain balanced in all situations and thus enable table operations whose efficiency is comparable to a binary search.

This chapter then considers a completely different implementation of the ADT table that, for many applications, is even more efficient than a search-tree implementation. In principle the algorithm, which is called hashing, locates a data item by performing a calculation on its search-key value, rather than by searching for it.

Finally, the chapter considers data organizations that support diverse kinds of operations simultaneously. For example, you might want to organize data in first-in, first-out order, but you also might require the data to be in sorted order. The challenge is to design cooperative data structures to manage the data.

13.1 Balanced Search Trees

As you saw in the previous chapter, the efficiency of the binary search tree implementation of the ADT table is related to the tree's height. The operations *tableRetrieve*, *tableInsert*, and *tableDelete* follow a path from the root of the tree to the node that contains the desired item (or, in the case of the insertion operation, to the node that is to become the parent of the new item). At each node along the path, you compare a given value to the search key in the node and determine which subtree to search next. Because the maximum number of nodes on such a path is equal to the height of the tree, the maximum number of comparisons that the table operations can require is also equal to this height.

As you know, the height of a binary search tree of n items ranges from a maximum of n to a minimum of $\lceil \log_2(n + 1) \rceil$. As a consequence, locating a particular item in a binary search tree requires between n and $\lceil \log_2(n + 1) \rceil$ comparisons. Thus, a search of a binary search tree can be as inefficient as a sequential search of a linked list or as efficient as a binary search of an array. Efficiency was the primary reason for developing the binary search tree implementation of the table: We wanted to perform a search of a linked structure as efficiently as we could perform a binary search of an array. Thus, we certainly want the most optimistic behavior of the binary search tree.

The height of a binary search tree is sensitive to the order of insertions and deletions

What affects the height of a binary search tree? As you learned in Chapter 11, the height of the tree is quite sensitive to the order in which you insert or delete items. For example, consider a binary search tree that contains the items[1] 10, 20, 30, 40, 50, 60, and 70. If you inserted the items into the tree in ascending order, you would obtain a binary search tree of maximum height, as shown in Figure 13-1a. If, on the other hand, you inserted the items in the order 40, 20, 60, 10, 30, 50, 70, you would obtain a balanced binary search tree of minimum height, as shown in Figure 13-1b.

Various search trees can retain their balance despite insertions and deletions

As you can see, if you use the algorithms in Chapter 11 to maintain a binary search tree, insertions and deletions can cause the tree to lose its balance and approach a linear shape. Such a tree is no better than a linked list. For this reason, it is desirable in many applications to use one of several variations of the binary search tree. Such trees can absorb insertions and deletions without a deterioration of their balance and are easier to maintain than a minimum-height binary search tree. In addition, you can search these trees almost as efficiently as you can search a minimum-height binary search tree. This chapter discusses the better-known search trees to give you a sense of the possibilities. We continue to assume that the search keys in a tree are unique, that is, that there are no duplicates.

---

1. As in Chapter 11, tree items are records that each contain a search key. The tree diagrams in this chapter will show only these search keys, and the discussions will often treat an item as if it consisted solely of its search key.

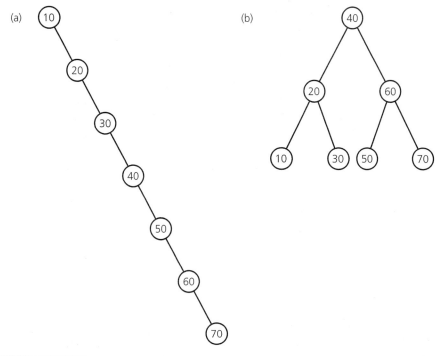

FIGURE 13-1

A binary search tree of (a) maximum height; (b) minimum height

2-3 Trees

A **2-3 tree** is a tree in which each internal node (nonleaf) has either two or three children, and all leaves are at the same level. For example, Figure 13-2 shows a 2-3 tree of height 3. A node with two children is called a **2-node**—the nodes in a binary tree are all 2-nodes—and a node with three children is called a **3-node**.

A 2-3 tree is not a binary tree, because a node can have three children; nevertheless, a 2-3 tree does resemble a full binary tree. If a particular 2-3 tree

A 2-3 tree is not binary

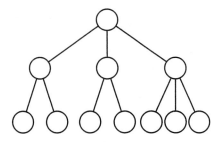

FIGURE 13-2

A 2-3 tree of height 3

does not contain 3-nodes—a possibility, according to the definition—it is like a full binary tree, because all of its internal nodes have two children and all of its leaves are at the same level. If, on the other hand, some of the internal nodes of a 2-3 tree do have three children, the tree will contain more nodes than a full binary tree of the same height. Therefore, a 2-3 tree of height h always has at least as many nodes as a full binary tree of height h; that is, it always has at least $2^h - 1$ nodes. To put this another way, a 2-3 tree with n nodes never has height greater than $\lceil \log_2(n + 1) \rceil$, the minimum height of a binary tree with n nodes.

A 2-3 tree is never taller than a minimum-height binary tree

Given these observations, a 2-3 tree might be useful as an implementation of the ADT table. Indeed, this is the case if the 2-3 tree orders its nodes to make it useful as a search tree. The following recursive definition[2] of a 2-3 tree specifies this order:

A 2-3 tree

T is a 2-3 tree of height h if

1. T is empty (a 2-3 tree of height 0).

or

2. T is of the form

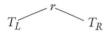

where r is a node that contains one data item and T_L and T_R are both 2-3 trees, each of height $h - 1$. In this case, the search key in r must be greater than each search key in the left subtree T_L and smaller than each search key in the right subtree T_R.

or

3. T is of the form

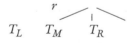

where r is a node that contains two data items and T_L, T_M, and T_R are 2-3 trees, each of height $h - 1$. In this case, the smaller search key in r must be greater than each search key in the left subtree T_L and smaller than each search key in the **middle subtree** T_M. The larger search key in r must be greater than each search key in the middle subtree T_M and smaller than each search key in the right subtree T_R.

This definition implies the following rules for how you may place data items in the nodes of a 2-3 tree.

---

2. Just as we distinguish between a binary tree and a binary search tree, we could distinguish between a 2-3 tree and a "2-3 search tree." The previous description would define a 2-3 tree, and the definition given here would define a 2-3 search tree. Most people, however, do not make such a distinction and use the term "2-3 tree" to mean "2-3 search tree"; we will also.

KEY CONCEPTS

Rules for Placing Data Items in the Nodes of a 2-3 Tree

1. A 2-node, which has two children, must contain a single data item whose search key is greater than the left child's search key(s) and less than the right child's search key(s), as Figure 13-3a illustrates.

2. A 3-node, which has three children, must contain two data items whose search keys S and L satisfy the following relationships, as Figure 13-3b illustrates: S is greater than the left child's search key(s) and less than the middle child's search key(s); L is greater than the middle child's search key(s) and less than the right child's search key(s).

3. A leaf may contain either one or two data items.

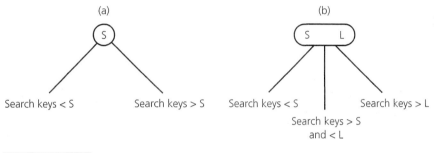

FIGURE 13-3

Nodes in a 2-3 tree: (a) a 2-node; (b) a 3-node

Thus, the items in a 2-3 tree are ordered by their search keys. For example, the tree in Figure 13-4 is a 2-3 tree.

Items in a 2-3 tree are ordered

You can represent any node in a 2-3 tree with the following class:

A node in a 2-3 tree

```
import SearchKeys.KeyedItem;

class TreeNode<T> {
    T smallItem;
    T largeItem;
    TreeNode<T> leftChild;
    TreeNode<T> midChild;
    TreeNode<T> rightChild;

// constructors appear here
    . . .
}  // end TreeNode
```

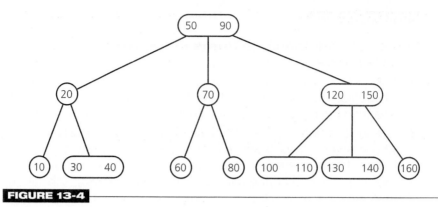

FIGURE 13-4

A 2-3 tree

When a node contains only one data item, you can place it in *smallItem* and use *leftChild* and *midChild* to reference the node's children. To be safe, you can place *null* in *rightChild*.

    Now consider the traversal, retrieval, insertion, and deletion operations for a 2-3 tree. The algorithms for these operations are recursive. You can avoid distracting implementation details by defining the base case for these recursive algorithms to be a leaf rather than an empty subtree. As a result, the algorithms must assume that they are not passed an empty tree as an argument.

Traversing a 2-3 tree.   You can traverse a 2-3 tree in sorted search-key order by performing the analogue of an inorder traversal:

Traversal in sorted order

```
+inorder(in ttTree:TwoThreeTree)
// Traverses the nonempty 2-3 tree, ttTree, in sorted
// search-key order.

  if (ttTree's root node r is a leaf) {
    Visit the data item(s)
  }
  else if (r has two data items) {
    inorder(left subtree of ttTree's root)
    Visit the first data item
    inorder(middle subtree of ttTree's root)
    Visit the second data item
    inorder(right subtree of ttTree's root)
  }
  else  { // r has one data item
    inorder(left subtree of ttTree's root)
    Visit the data item
    inorder(right subtree of ttTree's root)
  }  // end if
```

Searching a 2-3 tree. The ordering of items in a 2-3 tree is analogous to the ordering for a binary search tree and allows you to search a 2-3 tree efficiently for a particular item. In fact, the retrieval operation for a 2-3 tree is quite similar to the retrieval operation for a binary search tree, as you can see from the following pseudocode:

Searching a 2-3 tree is efficient

```
+retrieveItem(in ttTree:TwoThreeTree,
              in searchKey:KeyType):TreeItemType
// Returns from the nonempty 2-3 tree ttTree the
// item whose search key equals searchKey. The operation
// fails and returns null if no such item exists,

  if (searchKey is in ttTree's root node r) {
    // the item has been found
    treeItem = the data portion of r
  }
  else if (r is a leaf) {
    treeItem = null  // failure
  }

  // else search the appropriate subtree
  else if (r has two data items) {
    if (searchKey < smaller search key of r) {
      treeItem = retrieveItem(r's left subtree, searchKey)
    }
    else if (searchKey < larger search key of r) {
      treeItem = retrieveItem(r's middle subtree, searchKey)
    }
    else {
      treeItem = retrieveItem(r's right subtree, searchKey)
    }  // end if
  }

  else { // r has one data item
    if (searchKey < r's search key) {
      treeItem = retrieveItem(r's left subtree, searchKey)
    }
    else {
      treeItem = retrieveItem(r's right subtree, searchKey)
    }  // end if
  }  // end if
```

Have you gained anything by using a 2-3 tree rather than a binary search tree to implement the ADT table? You can search the 2-3 tree and the shortest binary search tree with about the same efficiency, because

- A binary search tree with n nodes cannot be shorter than $\lceil \log_2(n + 1) \rceil$
- A 2-3 tree with n nodes cannot be taller than $\lfloor \log_2(n + 1) \rfloor$

■ A node in a 2-3 tree has at most two items

Searching a 2-3 tree is not *more* efficient than searching a binary search tree, however. This observation may surprise you because, after all, the nodes of a 2-3 tree can have three children, and hence a 2-3 tree might indeed be shorter than the shortest possible binary search tree. Although true, this advantage in height is offset by the extra time required to compare a given value with two search-key values instead of only one. In other words, although you might visit fewer nodes when searching a 2-3 tree, you might have to make more comparisons at each node. As a consequence, the number of comparisons required to search a 2-3 tree for a given item is *approximately equal* to the number of comparisons required to search a binary search tree that is *as balanced as possible*. This number is approximately $\log_2 n$.

If you can search a 2-3 tree and a balanced binary search tree with approximately the same efficiency, why then should you use a 2-3 tree? Although maintaining the balance of a binary search tree is difficult in the face of insertion and deletion operations, maintaining the shape of a 2-3 tree is relatively simple. For example, consider the two trees in Figure 13-5. The first tree is a binary search tree and the second is a 2-3 tree. Both trees contain the same data items. The binary search tree is as balanced as possible, and thus you can search both it and the 2-3 tree for an item with approximately the same efficiency. If, however, you perform a sequence of insertions on the binary search tree—by using the insertion algorithm of Chapter 11—the tree can quickly lose its balance, as Figure 13-6a indicates. As you soon will see, you can perform the same sequence of insertions on the 2-3 tree without a degradation in the tree's shape—it will retain its structure, as Figure 13-6b shows.

The new values (32 through 39) that were inserted into the binary search tree of Figure 13-5a appear along a single path in Figure 13-6a. The insertions increased the height of the binary search tree from 4 to 12—an increase of 8. On the other hand, the new values have been spread throughout the 2-3 tree in Figure 13-6b. As a consequence, the height of the resulting tree is only 1 greater than the height of the original 2-3 tree in Figure 13-5b. We demonstrate these insertions into the original 2-3 tree next.

Searching a 2-3 tree is $O(\log_2 n)$

Maintaining the shape of a 2-3 tree is relatively easy

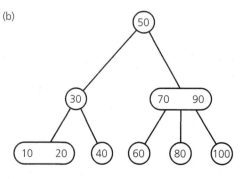

(a) A balanced binary search tree; (b) a 2-3 tree with the same elements

FIGURE 13-5

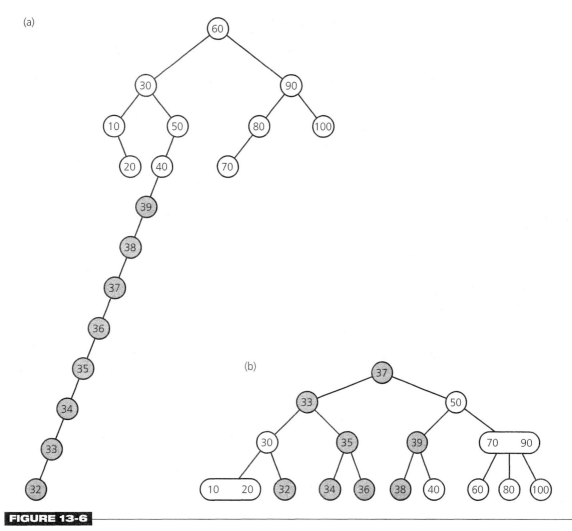

FIGURE 13-6

(a) The binary search tree of Figure 13-5a after a sequence of insertions; (b) the 2-3 tree of Figure 13-5b after the same insertions

Inserting into a 2-3 tree. Because the nodes of a 2-3 tree can have either two or three children and can contain one or two values, you can insert items into the tree while maintaining its shape. The following paragraphs informally describe the sequence of insertions that produced the 2-3 tree shown in Figure 13-6b. Figure 13-5b shows the original tree.

Insert 39. As is true with a binary search tree, the first step in inserting a node into a 2-3 tree is to locate the node at which the search for 39 would terminate. To do this, you can use the search strategy of the `retrieveItem` algorithm given previously; an unsuccessful search will always terminate at a leaf.

Insertion into a 2-node leaf is simple

With the tree in Figure 13-5b, the search for 39 terminates at the leaf <40>.[3] Since this node contains only one item, you can simply insert the new item into this node. The result is the 2-3 tree in Figure 13-7.

Insert 38.   In a similar manner, you would search the tree in Figure 13-7 for 38 and find that the search terminates at the node <39 40>. As a conceptual first step, you should place 38 in this node, as Figure 13-8a illustrates.

Insertion into a 3-node causes it to divide

This placement is problematic because a node cannot contain three values. You divide these three values, however, into the smallest (38), middle (39), and largest (40) values. You can move the middle value (39) up to the node's parent p and separate the remaining values, 38 and 40, into two nodes that you attach to p as children, as Figure 13-8b indicates. Since you chose to move up the middle value of <38 39 40>, the parent correctly separates the values of its children; that is, 38 is less than 39, which is less than 40. The result of the insertion is the 2-3 tree in Figure 13-8c.

Insert 37.   The insertion of 37 into the tree in Figure 13-8c is easy because 37 belongs in a leaf that currently contains only one value, 38. The result of this insertion is the 2-3 tree in Figure 13-9.

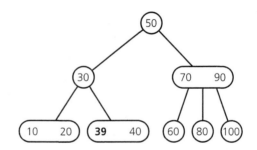

FIGURE 13-7

After inserting 39

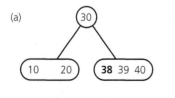   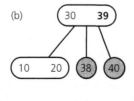   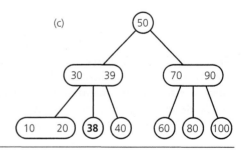

FIGURE 13-8

(a), (b) The steps for inserting 38; (c) the resulting tree

---

3. Here, the angle brackets denote a node and its contents.

Insert 36. The search strategy determines that 36 belongs in the node <37 38> of the tree in Figure 13-9. Again, as a conceptual first step, place it there, as Figure 13-10a indicates.

Because the node <36 37 38> now contains three values, you divide it—as you did previously—into the smallest (36), middle (37), and largest (38) values. You then move the middle value (37) up to the node's parent p, and attach to p—as children—nodes that contain the smallest (36) and largest (38) values, as Figure 13-10b illustrates.

This time, however, you are not finished: You have a node <30 37 39> that contains three values and has four children. This situation is familiar, with the slight difference that the overcrowded node is not a leaf but rather has four

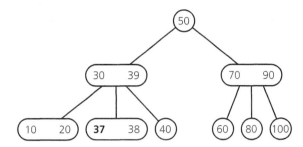

FIGURE 13-9

After inserting 37

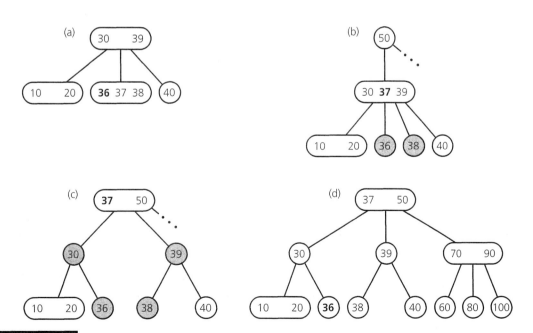

FIGURE 13-10

(a), (b), (c) The steps for inserting 36; (d) the resulting tree children. As you did before, you divide the node into the smallest (30), middle (37), and largest (39) values and then move the middle value up to the node's parent. Because you are splitting an internal node, you now must account for its four children; that is, what happens to nodes <10 20>, <36>, <38>, and <40>, which were the children of node <30 37 39>? The solution is to attach the left pair of children (nodes <10 20> and <36>) to the smallest value (30) and attach the right pair of children (nodes <38> and <40>) to the largest value (39), as shown in Figure 13-10c. The final result of this insertion is the 2-3 tree in Figure 13-10d.

Insert 35, 34, and 33. Each of these insertions is similar to the previous ones. Figure 13-11 shows the tree after the three insertions.

Before performing the final insertion of the value 32, consider the 2-3 tree's insertion strategy.

The insertion algorithm. To insert an item I into a 2-3 tree, you first locate the leaf at which the search for I would terminate. You insert the new item I into the leaf, and if the leaf now contains only two items, you are done. However, if the leaf contains three items, you must **split** it into two nodes, n_1 and n_2. As Figure 13-12 illustrates, you place the smallest[4] item S into n_1, place the largest item L into n_2, and move the middle item M up to the original leaf's parent. Nodes n_1 and n_2 then become children of the parent. If the parent now has only three children (and contains two items)—as is true here— you are finished. On the other hand, if the parent now has four children (and contains three items), you must split it, as follows.

You split an internal node n that contains three items by using the process just described for a leaf, except that you must also take care of n's four children. As Figure 13-13 illustrates, you split n into n_1 and n_2, place n's smallest item S into n_1, attach n's two leftmost children to n_1, place n's largest item L

> When a leaf contains three items, split it into two nodes

> When an internal node contains three items, split it into two nodes and accommodate its children

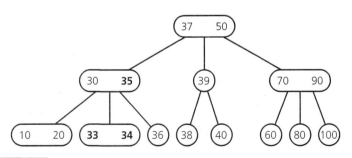

The tree after the insertion of 35, 34, and 33

---

4. "Smallest item" means the item with the smallest search key. Analogously, the terms "middle item" and "largest item" will also be used.

into n_2, attach n's two rightmost children to n_2, and move n's middle item M up to n's parent.

After this, the process of splitting a node and moving an item up to the parent continues recursively until a node is reached that had only one item before the insertion and thus has only two items after it takes on a new item. Notice in the previous sequence of insertions that the tree's height never increased from its original value of 3. In general, *an insertion will not increase the height of the tree* as long as there is at least one node containing only one item on the path from the root to the leaf into which the new item is inserted. The insertion strategy of a 2-3 tree has thus postponed the growth of the

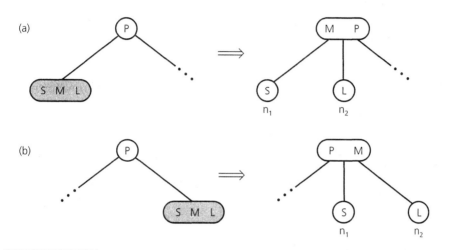

FIGURE 13-12

Splitting a leaf in a 2-3 tree

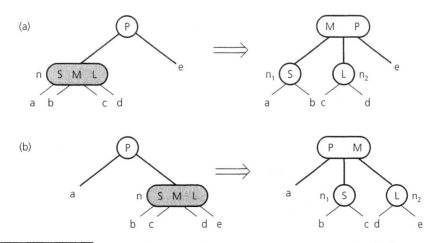

FIGURE 13-13

Splitting an internal node in a 2-3 tree

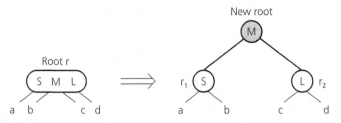

FIGURE 13-14

Splitting the root of a 2-3 tree

tree's height much more effectively than the strategy of a basic binary search tree did.

When the height of a 2-3 tree does grow, it does so from the top. An increase in the height of a 2-3 tree will occur if every node on the path from the root of the tree to the leaf into which the new item is inserted contains two items. In this case, the recursive process of splitting a node and moving an item up to the node's parent will eventually reach the root r. When this occurs you must split r into r_1 and r_2 exactly as you would any other internal node. However, you must create a new node that contains the middle item of r and becomes the parent of r_1 and r_2. Thus, the new node is the new root of the tree, as Figure 13-14 illustrates.

The following algorithm summarizes the entire insertion strategy:

When the root contains three items, split it into two nodes and create a new root node

2-3 tree insertion algorithm

```
+insertItem(in ttTree:TwoThreeTree, in newItem:TreeItemType)
// Inserts newItem into a 2-3 tree ttTree whose items have
// distinct search keys that differ from newItem's search
// key.

  Let sKey be the search key of newItem
  Locate the leaf leafNode in which sKey belongs
  Add newItem to leafNode

  if (leafNode now has three items) {
     split(leafNode)
  }  // end if


split(inout n:TreeNode)
// Splits node n, which contains 3 items. Note: if n is
// not a leaf, it has 4 children.

  if (n is the root) {
     Create a new node p
  }
  else {
     Let p be the parent of n
  }  // end if
```

```
Replace node n with two nodes, n1 and n2, so that p is
    their parent

Give n₁ the item in n with the smallest search-key value
Give n₂ the item in n with the largest search-key value

if (n is not a leaf) {
  n₁ becomes the parent of n's two leftmost children
  n₂ becomes the parent of n's two rightmost children
}  // end if

Move the item in n that has the middle
    search-key value up to p

if (p now has three items) {
  split(p)
}  // end if
```

Insert 32.   To be sure that you fully understand the insertion algorithm, go through the steps of inserting 32 into the 2-3 tree in Figure 13-11. The result should be the tree shown in Figure 13-6b.

Once again, compare this tree with the binary search tree in Figure 13-6a and notice the dramatic advantage of the 2-3 tree's insertion strategy.

Deleting from a 2-3 tree.   The deletion strategy for a 2-3 tree is the inverse of its insertion strategy. Just as a 2-3 tree spreads insertions throughout the tree by splitting nodes when they become too full, it spreads deletions throughout the tree by merging nodes when they become empty. As an illustration of the 2-3 tree's deletion strategy, consider the deletion of 70, 100, and 80 from the tree in Figure 13-5b.

Delete 70.   By searching the tree, you will discover that 70 is in the node <70 90>. Because you always want to begin the deletion process at a leaf, the first step is to swap 70 with its inorder successor—the value that follows it in the sorted order. Because 70 is the smaller of the two values in the node, its inorder successor (80) is the smallest value in the node's middle subtree. (The inorder successor of an item in an internal node will always be in a leaf.) After the swap, the tree appears as shown in Figure 13-15a. The value 80 is in a legal position of the search tree because it is larger than all the values in its node's left subtree and smaller than all the values in its node's right subtree. The value 70 is not in a legal position, but this is of no concern, because the next step is to delete this value from the leaf.

Swap the value to be deleted with its inorder successor

In general, after you delete a value from a leaf, another value may remain in the leaf (because the leaf contained two values before the deletion). If this is the case, you are done, because a leaf of a 2-3 tree can contain a single value. In this example, however, once you delete 70 from the leaf, the node is left without a value, as Figure 13-15b indicates.

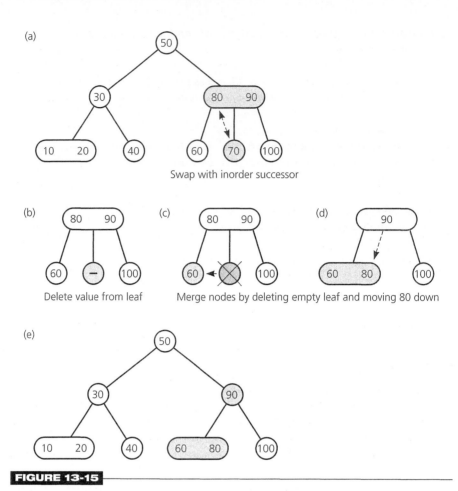

FIGURE 13-15

(a), (b), (c), (d) The steps for deleting 70; (e) the resulting tree

You then delete the node, as Figure 13-15c illustrates. At this point you see that the parent of the deleted node contains two values (80 and 90) but has two children (60 and 100). This situation is not allowed in a 2-3 tree. (See Rule 1.) You can remedy the problem by moving the smaller value (80) down from the parent into the left child, as Figure 13-15d illustrates. Deleting the leaf node and moving a value down to a sibling of the leaf is called **merging** the leaf with its sibling.

Merge nodes

The 2-3 tree that results from this deletion is shown in Figure 13-15e.

Delete 100. The search strategy discovers that 100 is in the leaf <100> of the tree in Figure 13-15e. When you delete the value from this leaf, the node becomes empty, as Figure 13-16a indicates. In this case, however, no merging of nodes is required, because the sibling <60 80> can spare a value. That is, the sibling has two values, whereas a 2-3 tree requires only that it have at least one

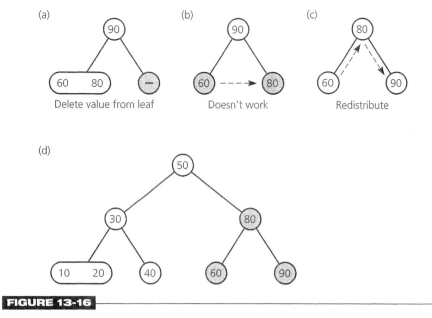

FIGURE 13-16

(a), (b), (c) The steps for deleting 100; (d) the resulting tree

value. If you simply move the value 80 into the empty node—as Figure 13-16b illustrates—you find that the search-tree order is destroyed: The value in 90's right child is 80, whereas it should be greater than 90. The solution to this problem is to redistribute the values among the empty node, its sibling, and its parent. Here you can move the larger value (80) from the sibling into the parent and move the value 90 down from the parent into the node that had been empty, as Figure 13-16c shows. This distribution preserves the search-tree order, and you have thus completed the deletion. The resulting 2-3 tree is shown in Figure 13-16d.

Redistribute values

Delete 80.   The search strategy finds that 80 is in an internal node of the tree in Figure 13-16d. You thus must swap 80 with its inorder successor, 90, as Figure 13-17a illustrates. When you delete 80 from the leaf, the node becomes empty. (See Figure 13-17b.) Because the sibling of the empty node has only one value, you cannot redistribute as you did in the deletion of 100. Instead you must merge the nodes, bringing the value 90 down from the parent and removing the empty leaf, as Figure 13-17c indicates.

You are not yet finished, however, because the parent now contains no values and has only one child. You must recursively apply the deletion strategy to this internal node without a value. First, you should check to see if the node's sibling can spare a value. Because the sibling <30> contains only the single value 30, you cannot redistribute—you must merge the nodes. The merging of two internal nodes is identical to the merging of leaves, except that the child <60 90> of the empty node must be adopted. Because the sibling of the empty node contains only

(a)

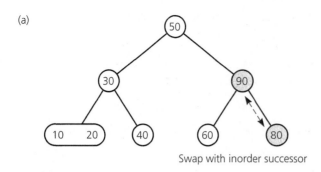

Swap with inorder successor

(b)

(c)

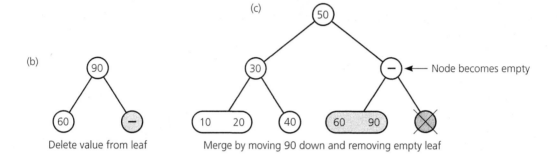

Delete value from leaf

Node becomes empty

Merge by moving 90 down and removing empty leaf

(d)

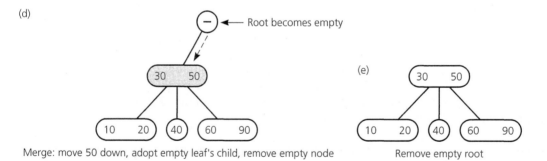

Root becomes empty

(e)

Merge: move 50 down, adopt empty leaf's child, remove empty node

Remove empty root

FIGURE 13-17

The steps for deleting 80

one value (and hence can have only two children, as stated in Rule 1), it can become the parent of <60 90> only if you bring the value 50 down from the sibling's parent. The tree now appears as shown in Figure 13-17d. Note that this operation preserves the search property of the tree.

Now the parent of the merged nodes is left with no values and only a single child. Usually, you would apply the recursive deletion strategy to this node, but this case is special because the node is the root. Because the root is empty and has only one child, you can simply remove it, allowing <30 50> to become the root of the tree, as Figure 13-17e illustrates. This deletion has thus caused the height of the tree to shrink by 1.

To summarize, we have deleted 70, 100, and 80 from the 2-3 tree in Figure 13-5b and obtained the 2-3 tree in Figure 13-18b. In contrast, after deleting 70, 100, and 80 from the balanced binary search tree in Figure 13-5a, you are left with the tree in Figure 13-18a. Notice that the deletions affected only one part of the binary search tree, causing it to lose its balance. The left subtree has not been affected at all, and thus the overall height of the tree has not been diminished.

The deletion algorithm. In summary, to delete an item I from a 2-3 tree, you first locate the node n that contains it. If n is not a leaf, you find I's inorder successor and swap it with I. As a result of the swap, the deletion always begins at a leaf. If the leaf contains an item in addition to I, you simply delete I and you are done. On the other hand, if the leaf contains only I, deleting I would leave the leaf without a data item. In this case you must perform some additional work to complete the deletion.

You first check the siblings of the now-empty leaf. If a sibling has two items, you redistribute the items among the sibling, the empty leaf, and the leaf's parent, as Figure 13-19a illustrates. If no sibling of the leaf has two items, you merge the leaf with an adjacent sibling by moving an item down from the leaf's parent into the sibling—it had only one item before, so it has room for another—and removing the empty leaf. This case is shown in Figure 13-19b.

Redistribute values

By moving an item down from a node n, as just described, you might cause n to be left without a data item and with only one child. If so, you recursively apply the deletion algorithm to n. Thus, if n has a sibling with two items (and three children), you redistribute the items among n, the sibling, and n's parent. You also give n one of its sibling's children, as Figure 13-19c indicates.

If n has no sibling with two items, you merge n with a sibling, as Figure 13-19d illustrates. That is, you move an item down from the parent and let the

Merge nodes

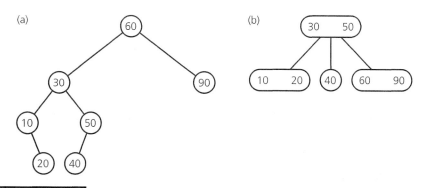

FIGURE 13-18

Results of deleting 70, 100, and 80 from (a) the binary search tree of Figure 13-5a and (b) the 2-3 tree of Figure 13-5b

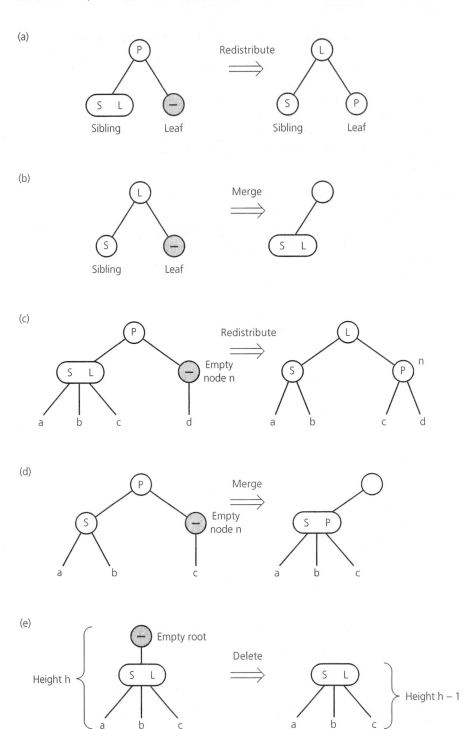

FIGURE 13-19

(a) Redistributing values; (b) merging a leaf; (c) redistributing values and children;
(d) merging internal nodes; (e) deleting the root

sibling adopt *n*'s one child. (At this point you know that the sibling previously had only one item and two children.) You then remove the empty leaf. If the merge causes *n*'s parent to be without an item, you recursively apply the deletion process to it.

If the merging continues so that the root of the tree is without an item (and has only one child), you simply remove the root. When this step occurs, the height of the tree is reduced by 1, as Figure 13-19e illustrates.

A high-level statement of the algorithm for deleting from a 2-3 tree is shown below:

2-3 tree deletion algorithm

```
+deleteItem(in ttTree:TwoThreeTree, in searchKey:KeyType)
// Deletes from the 2-3 tree the item whose
// search key equals searchKey. If the deletion is
// successful, the method returns true.
// If no such item exists, the operation fails and
// returns false.

   Attempt to locate item theItem whose search key
       equals searchKey

  if (theItem is present) {
    if (theItem is not in a leaf) {
      Swap item theItem with its inorder successor, which
          will be in a leaf theLeaf
    }  // end if

    // the deletion always begins at a leaf
    Delete item theItem from leaf theLeaf

    if (theLeaf now has no items) {
      fix(theLeaf)
    }  // end if
    return true
  }

  else {
    return false
  }  // end if

+fix(in n:TreeNode)
// Completes the deletion when node n is empty by either
// removing the root, redistributing values, or merging
// nodes. Note: if n is internal, it has one child.

  if (n is the root) {
    Remove the root
  }
```

```
else {
  Let p be the parent of n

  if (some sibling of n has two items) {
    Distribute items appropriately among n, the
        sibling, and p
    if (n is internal) {
      Move the appropriate child from sibling to n
    }  // end if
  }

  else   { // merge the node
    Choose an adjacent sibling s of n
    Bring the appropriate item down from p into s

    if (n is internal) {
      Move n's child to s
    }  // end if

    Remove node n

    if (p is now empty) {
      fix(p)
    }  // end if
  }    // end if

}  // end if
```

The details of the Java implementation of the preceding insertion and deletion algorithms for 2-3 trees are rather involved. The implementation is left as a challenging exercise (Programming Problem 2).

You might be concerned about the overhead that the insertion and deletion algorithms incur in the course of maintaining the 2-3 structure of the tree. That is, after the search strategy locates either the item or the position for the new item, the insertion and deletion algorithms sometimes have to perform extra work, such as splitting and merging nodes. However, this extra work is not a real concern. A rigorous mathematical analysis would show that the extra work required to maintain the structure of a 2-3 tree after an insertion or a deletion is not significant. In other words, when analyzing the efficiency of the *insertItem* and *deleteItem* algorithms, it is sufficient to consider only the time required to locate the item (or the position for the insertion). Given that a 2-3 tree is always balanced, you can search a 2-3 tree in all situations with the logarithmic efficiency of a binary search. Thus, the 2-3 tree implementation of the ADT table is guaranteed to provide efficient table operations. Although a binary search tree that is as balanced as possible minimizes the amount of work required to implement the operations of the ADT table, its balance is difficult to maintain. A 2-3 tree is a compromise—although

A 2-3 tree is always balanced

A 2-3 implementation of a table is $O(\log_2 n)$ for all table operations searching it may not be quite as efficient as searching a binary search tree of minimum height, it is relatively simple to maintain.

2-3-4 Trees

If a 2-3 tree is so good, are trees whose nodes can have more than three children even better? To an extent, the answer is yes. A **2-3-4 tree** is like a 2-3 tree, but it also allows **4-nodes,** which are nodes that have four children and three data items. For example, Figure 13-20 shows a 2-3-4 tree of height 3 that has the same items as the 2-3 tree in Figure 13-6b. As you will see, you can perform insertions and deletions on a 2-3-4 tree with fewer steps than a 2-3 tree requires.

T is a 2-3-4 tree of height h if

1. T is empty (a 2-3-4 tree of height 0). A 2-3-4 tree

or

2. T is of the form

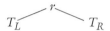

where r is a node that contains one data item and T_L and T_R are both 2-3-4 trees, each of height $h - 1$. In this case, the search key in r must be greater than each search key in the left subtree T_L and smaller than each search key in the right subtree T_R.

or

3. T is of the form

where r is a node that contains two data items and T_L, T_M, and T_R are 2-3-4 trees, each of height $h - 1$. In this case, the smaller search key in r must be greater than each search key in the left subtree T_L and smaller than each search key in the middle subtree T_M. The larger search key in r

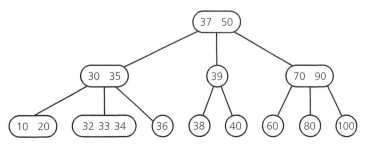

FIGURE 13-20

A 2-3-4 tree with the same items as the 2-3 tree in Figure 13-6b

must be greater than each search key in T_M and smaller than each search key in the right subtree T_R.

or

4. T is of the form

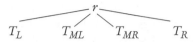

where r is a node that contains three data items and T_L, T_{ML}, T_{MR}, and T_R are 2-3-4 trees, each of height $h - 1$. In this case, the smallest search key in r must be greater than each search key in the left subtree T_L and smaller than each search key in the **middle-left subtree** T_{ML}. The middle search key in r must be greater than each search key in T_{ML} and smaller than each search key in the **middle-right subtree** T_{MR}. The largest search key in r must be greater than each search key in T_{MR} and smaller than each search key in the right subtree T_R.

This definition implies the following rules for how you may place data items in the nodes of a 2-3-4 tree:

KEY CONCEPTS

Rules for Placing Data Items in the Nodes of a 2-3-4 Tree

1. A 2-node, which has two children, must contain a single data item whose search keys satisfy the relationships pictured earlier in Figure 13-3a.

2. A 3-node, which has three children, must contain two data items whose search keys satisfy the relationships pictured earlier in Figure 13-3b.

3. A 4-node, which has four children, must contain three data items whose search keys S, M, and L satisfy the following relationships, as Figure 13-21 illustrates: S is greater than the left child's search key(s) and less than the middle-left child's search key(s); M is greater than the middle-left child's search key(s) and less than the middle-right child's search key(s); L is greater than the middle-right child's search key(s) and less than the right child's search key(s).

4. A leaf may contain either one, two, or three data items.

Although a 2-3-4 tree has more efficient insertion and deletion operations than a 2-3 tree, it also has greater storage requirements due to the additional data fields in its 4-nodes, as the following Java class indicates:

A 2-3-4 tree requires more storage than a 2-3 tree

A node in a 2-3-4 tree

```
class TreeNode<T> {
    T smallItem;
    T middleItem;
```

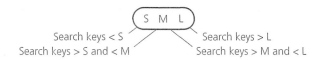

Search keys < S
Search keys > S and < M
Search keys > L
Search keys > M and < L

A 4-node in a 2-3-4 tree

```
   T largeItem;
   TreeNode<T> leftChild;
   TreeNode<T> lMidChild;
   TreeNode<T> rMidChild;
   TreeNode<T> rightChild;

// constructors appear here
     .   .   .
}  // end TreeNode
```

As you will see later, however, you can transform a 2-3-4 tree into a special binary tree that reduces the storage requirements.

Searching and traversing a 2-3-4 tree. The search algorithm and the traversal algorithm for a 2-3-4 tree are simple extensions of the corresponding algorithms for a 2-3 tree. For example, to search the tree in Figure 13-20 given the search key 31, you would search the left subtree of the root, because 31 is less than 37; search the middle subtree of the node <30 35>, because 31 is between 30 and 35; and terminate the search at the left child reference of <32 33 34>, because 31 is less than 32, deducing that no item in the tree has a search key of 31. Exercise 8 at the end of the chapter asks you to complete the details of searching and traversing a 2-3-4 tree.

Inserting into a 2-3-4 tree. The insertion algorithm for a 2-3-4 tree, like the insertion algorithm for a 2-3 tree, splits a node by moving one of its items up to its parent node. For a 2-3 tree, the search algorithm traces a path from the root to a leaf and then backs up from the leaf as it splits nodes. To avoid this return path after reaching a leaf, the insertion algorithm for a 2-3-4 tree splits 4-nodes as soon as it encounters them on the way down the tree from the root to a leaf. As a result, when a 4-node is split and an item is moved up to the node's parent, the parent cannot possibly be a 4-node and so can accommodate another item.

Split 4-nodes as they are encountered

As an example of the algorithm, consider the tree in Figure 13-22a. This one-node tree is the result of inserting 60, 30, and 10 into an initially empty 2-3-4 tree.

Insert 20. While determining the insertion point, you begin at the root and encounter the 4-node <10 30 60>, which you split by moving the middle value 30 up. Since the node is the root, you create a new root, move 30 into it, and attach two children, as Figure 13-22b illustrates. You continue the search for 20 by examining the left subtree of the root, since 20 is less than 30. The insertion results in the tree in Figure 13-22c.

Insert 50 and 40. The insertions of 50 and 40 do not require split nodes and result in the tree in Figure 13-23.

Insert 70. As you search Figure 13-23 for 70's insertion point, you encounter the 4-node <40 50 60>, since 70 is greater than 30. You split this 4-node by moving 50 up to the node's parent <30>, to get the tree in Figure 13-24a. You then insert 70 into the leaf <60>, as Figure 13-24b illustrates.

Insert 80 and 15. These insertions do not require split nodes and result in the tree in Figure 13-25.

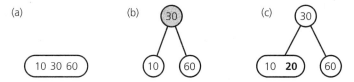

FIGURE 13-22

Inserting 20 into a one-node 2-3-4 tree

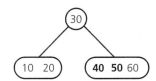

FIGURE 13-23

After inserting 50 and 40

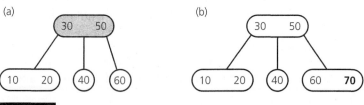

FIGURE 13-24

The steps for inserting 70

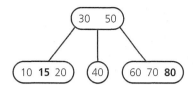

FIGURE 13-25

After inserting 80 and 15

Insert 90. As you search Figure 13-25 for 90's insertion point, you traverse the root's right subtree, since 90 is greater than 50, and encounter the 4-node <60 70 80>. You split this 4-node into two nodes and move 70 up to the root, as Figure 13-26a indicates. Finally, since 90 is greater than 70, you insert 90 into the leaf <80> to get the tree in Figure 13-26b.

Insert 100. As you begin to search Figure 13-26b, you immediately encounter a 4-node at the tree's root. You split this node into two nodes and move 50 up to a new root, as Figure 13-27a indicates. After continuing the search, you insert 100 into <80 90> to get the tree in Figure 13-27b.

Splitting 4-nodes during insertion. As you have just seen, you split each 4-node as soon as you encounter it during your search from the root to a leaf that will accommodate the new item to be inserted. The 4-node will either

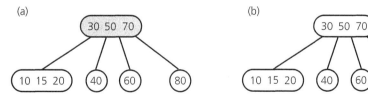

FIGURE 13-26

The steps for inserting 90

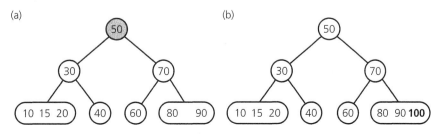

FIGURE 13-27

The steps for inserting 100

- Be the root, or

- have a 2-node parent, or

- have a 3-node parent.

Figure 13-28 illustrates how to split a 4-node that is the tree's root. You have seen two previous examples of this: We split <10 30 60> in Figure 13-22a, resulting in the tree in Figure 13-22b. We also split <30 50 70> during the insertion of 100 into the tree in Figure 13-26b, giving us the tree in Figure 13-27a.

Figure 13-29 illustrates the two possible situations that you can encounter when you split a 4-node whose parent is a 2-node. For example, when you split <40 50 60> during the insertion of 70 into the tree in Figure 13-23, you get the tree in Figure 13-24a.

Figure 13-30 illustrates the three possible situations that you can encounter when you split a 4-node whose parent is a 3-node. For example, when you

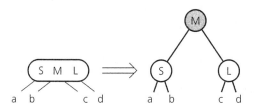

FIGURE 13-28

Splitting a 4-node root during insertion

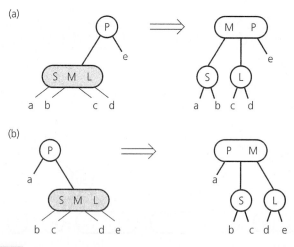

FIGURE 13-29

Splitting a 4-node whose parent is a 2-node during insertion

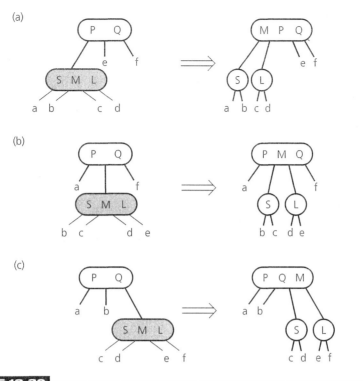

Splitting a 4-node whose parent is a 3-node during insertion

split <60 70 80> during the insertion of 90 into the tree in Figure 13-25, you get the tree in Figure 13-26a.

Deleting from a 2-3-4 tree.   The deletion algorithm for a 2-3-4 tree has the same beginning as the deletion algorithm for a 2-3 tree. You first locate the node *n* that contains the item *theItem* that you want to delete. You then find *theItem*'s inorder successor and swap it with *theItem* so that the deletion will always be at a leaf. If that leaf is either a 3-node or a 4-node, you simply remove *theItem*. If you can ensure that *theItem* does not occur in a 2-node, you can perform the deletion in one pass through the tree from root to leaf, unlike deletion from a 2-3 tree. That is, you will not have to back away from the leaf and restructure the tree.

   To accomplish this goal, you transform each 2-node that you encounter during the search for *theItem* into either a 3-node or a 4-node. Several cases are possible, depending on the configuration of the 2-node's parent and nearest sibling. (Arbitrarily, a node's nearest sibling is its left sibling, unless the node is a left child, in which case its nearest sibling is to its right.) That is, either the parent or the sibling could be a 2-node, a 3-node, or a 4-node. For example, if the next node that you will encounter is a 2-node and both its parent and nearest sibling

Transform each 2-node into a 3-node or a 4-node

are 2-nodes, apply the transformation that Figure 13-28 illustrates, but in reverse; if the parent is a 3-node, apply the transformation that Figure 13-29 illustrates, but in reverse; and if the parent is a 4-node, apply the transformation that Figure 13-30 illustrates, but in reverse.

The details of deletion are left to you as a challenging exercise (Exercise 8).

2-3 and 2-3-4 trees are attractive because their balance is easy to maintain

Concluding remarks. The advantage of both 2-3 and 2-3-4 trees is their easy-to-maintain balance, not their shorter height. Even if a 2-3 tree is shorter than a balanced binary search tree, the reduction in height is offset by the increased number of comparisons that the search algorithm may require at each node. The situation is similar for a 2-3-4 tree, but its insertion and deletion algorithms require only one pass through the tree and so are simpler than those for a 2-3 tree. This decrease in effort makes the 2-3-4 tree more attractive than the 2-3 tree.

Insertion and deletion algorithms for a 2-3-4 tree require fewer steps than those for a 2-3 tree

Allowing nodes with more than four children is counterproductive

Should we consider trees whose nodes have even more than four children? Although a tree whose nodes can each have 100 children would be shorter than a 2-3-4 tree, its search algorithm would require more comparisons at each node to determine which subtree to search. Thus, allowing the nodes of a tree to have many children is counterproductive. Such a search tree is appropriate, however, when it is implemented in external storage, because moving from node to node is far more expensive than comparing the data values in a node. In such cases, a search tree with the minimum possible height is desirable, even at the expense of additional comparisons at each node. Chapter 15 will discuss external search trees further.

Red-Black Trees

A 2-3-4 tree requires more storage than a binary search tree

A 2-3-4 tree is attractive because it is balanced and its insertion and deletion operations use only one pass from root to leaf. On the other hand, a 2-3-4 tree requires more storage than a binary search tree that contains the same data because a 2-3-4 tree has nodes that must accommodate up to three data items. A typical binary search tree is inappropriate, however, because it might not be balanced.

A red-black tree has the advantages of a 2-3-4 tree but requires less storage

You can use a special binary search tree—**a red-black tree**—to represent a 2-3-4 tree and retain the advantages of a 2-3-4 tree without the storage overhead. The idea is to represent each 3-node and 4-node in a 2-3-4 tree as an equivalent binary tree. To distinguish between 2-nodes that appeared in the original 2-3-4 tree and 2-nodes that were generated from 3-nodes and 4-nodes, you use red and black child references. Let all the child references in the original 2-3-4 tree be black; use red child references to link the 2-nodes that result when you split 3-nodes and 4-nodes.

Figures 13-31 and 13-32 indicate how to represent, respectively, a 4-node and a 3-node as binary trees. Because there are two possible ways to represent a 3-node as a binary tree, a red-black representation of a 2-3-4 tree is not unique. Figure 13-33 gives a red-black representation for the 2-3-4 tree in Figure 13-20. In all of these figures, a dashed line represents a red reference and a solid line represents a black reference.

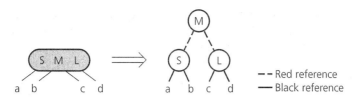

FIGURE 13-31

Red-black representation of a 4-node

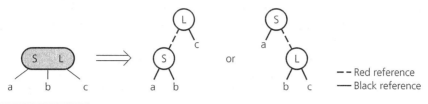

FIGURE 13-32

Red-black representation of a 3-node

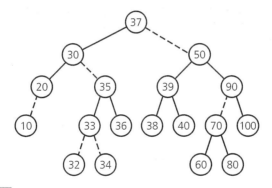

FIGURE 13-33

A red-black tree that represents the 2-3-4 tree in Figure 13-20

A node in a red-black tree is similar to a node in a binary search tree, but it must also store the reference colors, as the following Java class indicates:

```
public enum Color {RED, BLACK}

class TreeNode<T> {
    T item;
    TreeNode<T> leftChild;
    TreeNode<T> rightChild;
    Color leftColor;
```

A node in a red-black tree

```
        Color rightColor;

// constructors appear here
        .   .   .
}   // end TreeNode
```

Even with the reference colors, a node in a red-black tree requires less storage than a node in a 2-3-4 tree. (Why? See Self-Test Exercise 6.) Keep in mind that the transformations in Figures 13-31 and 13-32 imply a change in node structure.

Searching and traversing a red-black tree.   Since a red-black tree is a binary search tree, you can search and traverse it by using the algorithms for a binary search tree. You simply ignore the color of the references.

Inserting into and deleting from a red-black tree.   Because a red-black tree actually represents a 2-3-4 tree, you simply need to adjust the 2-3-4 insertion algorithms to accommodate the red-black representation. Recall that while searching a 2-3-4 tree, you split each 4-node that you encounter, so it is sufficient to reformulate that process in terms of the red-black representation. For example, Figure 13-31 shows the red-black representation of a 4-node. Thus, to identify a 4-node in its red-black form, you look for a node that has two red references.

Suppose that the 4-node is the root of the 2-3-4 tree. Figure 13-28 shows how to split the root into 2-nodes. By comparing this figure with

Splitting the equivalent of a 4-node requires only simple color changes

Figure 13-31, you see that to perform an equivalent operation on a red-black tree, you simply change the color of its root's references to black, as Figure 13-34 illustrates.

Figure 13-29 shows how to split a 4-node whose parent is a 2-node. If you reformulate this figure by using the red-black notation given in Figures 13-31 and 13-32, you get Figure 13-35. Notice that this case also requires only color changes within the red-black tree.

Finally, Figure 13-30 shows how to split a 4-node whose parent is a 3-node. Note that each configuration before a split in Figure 13-30 has two red-black representations, as Figure 13-36 illustrates. (Apply the transformations that Figures 13-31 and 13-32 describe to Figure 13-30.) As you can see

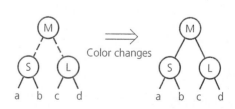

FIGURE 13-34

Splitting a red-black representation of a 4-node that is the root

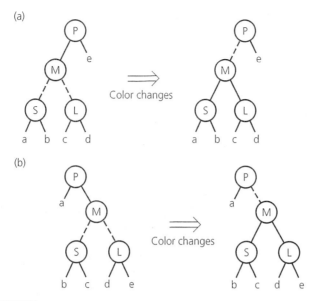

FIGURE 13-35

Splitting a red-black representation of a 4-node whose parent is a 2-node

from Figure 13-36, each pair of representations transforms into the same red-black configuration. Of the six possibilities given in Figure 13-36, only two require simple color changes. The others also require changes to the references themselves. These reference changes, which are called **rotations,** result in a shorter tree.

Reference changes called rotations result in a shorter tree

The deletion algorithm follows in an analogous fashion from the 2-3-4 deletion algorithm. Since insertion and deletion operations on a red-black tree frequently require only color changes, they are more efficient than the corresponding operations on a 2-3-4 tree.

Exercise 11 asks you to complete the details of the insertion and deletion algorithms.

AVL Trees

An **AVL tree**—named for its inventors, Adel'son-Vel'skii and Landis—is a balanced binary search tree. Since the heights of the left and right subtrees of any node in a balanced binary tree differ by no more than 1, you can search an AVL tree almost as efficiently as a minimum-height binary search tree. This section will simply introduce you to the notion of an AVL tree—the oldest form of balanced binary tree—and leave the details for another course.

An AVL tree is a balanced binary search tree

It is, in fact, possible to rearrange any binary search tree of n nodes to obtain a binary search tree with the minimum possible height $\lceil \log_2(n + 1) \rceil$. Recall, for example, the algorithms developed in Chapter 11 that use a file to save and restore a binary search tree. You can start with an arbitrary binary search tree, save its values in a file, and then construct from these same values a

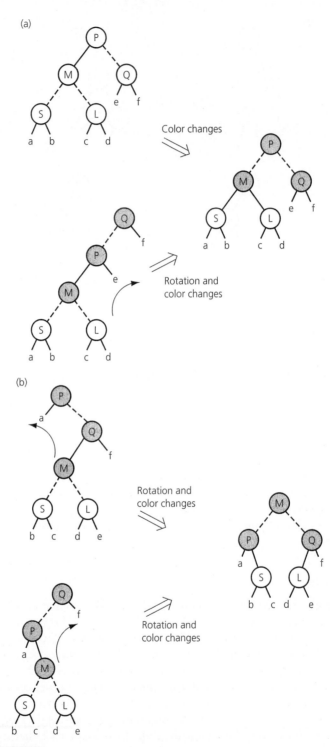

FIGURE 13-36

Splitting a red-black representation of a 4-node whose parent is a 3-node

(continues)

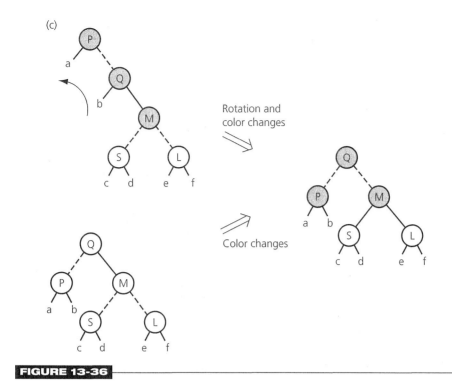

(c)

Rotation and color changes

Color changes

FIGURE 13-36

new binary search tree of minimum height. Although this approach may be appropriate in the context of a table that occasionally is saved and restored, it requires too much work to be performed every time an insertion or deletion leaves the tree unbalanced. The cost of repeatedly rebuilding the tree could very well outweigh the benefit of searching a tree of minimum height.

The AVL method is a compromise. It maintains a binary search tree with a height close to the minimum, but it is able to do so with far less work than would be necessary to keep the height of the tree exactly equal to the minimum. The basic strategy of the AVL method is to monitor the shape of the binary search tree. You insert or delete nodes just as you would for any binary search tree, but after each insertion or deletion, you check that the tree is still an AVL tree. That is, you determine whether any node in the tree has left and right subtrees whose heights differ by more than 1. For example, suppose that the binary search tree in Figure 13-37a is the result of a sequence of insertions and deletions. The heights of the left and right subtrees of the root 30 differ by 2. You can restore this tree's AVL property—that is, its balance—by rearranging its nodes. For instance, you can **rotate** the tree so that the node 20 becomes the root, with left child 10 and right child 30, as in Figure 13-37b. Notice that you cannot arbitrarily rearrange the tree's nodes, because you must take care not to destroy the search tree's ordering property in the course of the rebalancing.

An AVL tree maintains a height close to the minimum

Rotations restore the balance

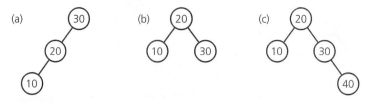

FIGURE 13-37

(a) An unbalanced binary search tree; (b) a balanced tree after rotation; (c) a balanced tree after insertion

Rotations are not necessary after every insertion or deletion. For example, you can insert 40 into the AVL tree in Figure 13-37b and still have an AVL tree. (See Figure 13-37c.) However, when a rotation is necessary to restore a tree's AVL property, the rotation will be one of two possible types. Let's look at an example of each type.

Suppose that you have the tree in Figure 13-38a after the insertion or deletion of a node. (Perhaps you obtained this tree by inserting 60 into an AVL tree.) An imbalance occurs at the node 20; that is, 20's left and right sub-trees differ in height by more than 1. A **single rotation** to the left is necessary to obtain the balanced tree in Figure 13-38b: 40 becomes the parent of 20, which adopts 30 as its right child. Figure 13-39 shows this rotation in a more general form. It shows, for example, that before the rotation, the left and right subtrees of the node 40 have heights h and $h + 1$, respectively. After the rotation, the tree is balanced and, in this particular case, has decreased in height from $h + 3$ to $h + 2$. Figures 13-40 and 13-41 show examples of a single left rotation that restores a tree's balance but does not affect its height. An analogous single right rotation would produce a mirror image of these examples.

A more complex rotation may be necessary. For example, consider the tree in Figure 13-42a, which is the result of nodes being added to or deleted from an AVL tree. The left and right subtrees of 20 differ in height by more than 1. A **double rotation** is necessary to restore this tree's balance. Figure 13-42b shows the result of a left rotation about 20, and Figure 13-42c shows the

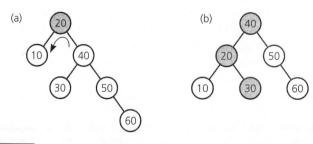

FIGURE 13-38

(a) An unbalanced binary search tree; (b) a balanced tree after a single left rotation

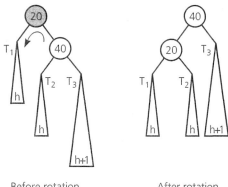

Before rotation   After rotation

FIGURE 13-39

Before and after a single left rotation that decreases the tree's height

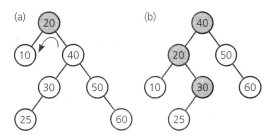

FIGURE 13-40

(a) An unbalanced binary search tree; (b) a balanced tree after a single left rotation

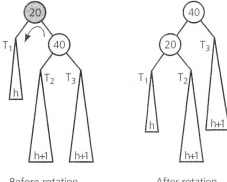

Before rotation   After rotation

FIGURE 13-41

Before and after a single left rotation that does not affect the tree's height

result of a right rotation about 40. Figure 13-43 illustrates this double rotation in a more general form. Mirror images of these figures provide examples of other possible double rotations.

It can be proven that the height of an AVL tree with n nodes will always be very close to the theoretical minimum of $\lceil \log_2(n + 1) \rceil$. The AVL tree implementation of a table is, therefore, one implementation that guarantees a binary searchlike efficiency. Usually, however, implementations that use either a 2-3-4 tree or a red-black tree will be simpler.

An AVL tree implementation of a table is more difficult than other implementations

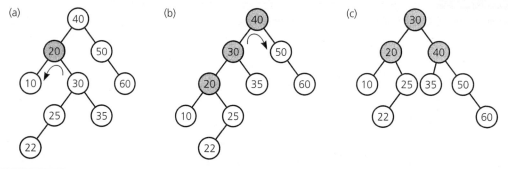

FIGURE 13-42

(a) Before; (b) during; and (c) after a double rotation

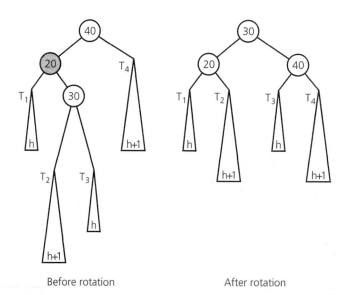

Before rotation   After rotation

FIGURE 13-43

Before and after a double rotation that decreases the tree's height

13.2 Hashing

The binary search tree and its balanced variants, such as 2-3, 2-3-4, red-black, and AVL trees, provide excellent implementations of the ADT table. They allow you to perform all of the table operations quite efficiently. If, for example, a table contains 10,000 items, the operations *tableRetrieve*, *tableInsert*, and *tableDelete* each require approximately $\log_2 10{,}000 = 13$ steps. As impressive as this efficiency may be, situations do occur for which the search-tree implementations are not adequate.

As you know, time can be vital. For example, when a person calls the 911 emergency system, the system detects the caller's telephone number and searches a database for the caller's address. Similarly, an air traffic control system searches a database of flight information, given a flight number. Clearly these searches must be rapid.

A radically different strategy is necessary to locate (and insert or delete) an item virtually instantaneously. Imagine an array *table* of n items—with each array slot capable of holding a single table item—and a seemingly magical box called an "address calculator." Whenever you have a new item that you want to insert into the table, the address calculator will tell you where you should place it in the array. Figure 13-44 illustrates this scenario.

Table operations without searches

You can thus easily perform an insertion into the table as follows:

```
+tableInsert (in newItem:TableItemType)

   i = the array index that the address calculator
          gives you for newItem's search key
   table[i] = newItem
```

An insertion is O(1); that is, it requires constant time.

You also use the address calculator for the *tableRetrieve* and *tableDelete* operations. If you want to retrieve an item that has a particular search key, you

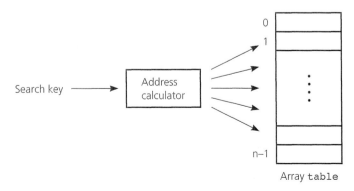

FIGURE 13-44

Address calculator

simply ask the address calculator to tell you where it would insert such an item. Because you would have inserted the item earlier by using the `tableInsert` algorithm just given, if the desired item is present in the table, it will be in the array location that the address calculator specifies.

Thus, the retrieval operation appears in pseudocode as follows:

```
+tableRetrieve(in searchKey:KeyType):TableItemType
// Returns table item that has a matching searchKey.
// If not found, returns null.

  i = the array index that the address calculator
        gives you for an item whose search key
        equals searchKey

  if (table[i].getKey() equals searchKey) {
    return table[i]
  }
  else {
    return null
  }  // end if
```

Similarly, the pseudocode for the deletion operation is

```
+tableDelete(in searchKey:KeyType)
// Deletes item that has a matching searchKey. If
// successful, returns true; otherwise, returns false.
  i = the array index that the address calculator
        gives you for an item whose search key
        equals searchKey

  success = (table[i].getKey() equals searchKey)
  if (success) {
    Delete the item from table[i]
  }  // end if
  return success
```

It thus appears that you can perform the operations `tableRetrieve`, `tableInsert`, and `tableDelete` virtually instantaneously. You never have to search for an item; instead, you simply let the address calculator determine where the item should be. The amount of time required to carry out the operations is $O(1)$ and depends only on how quickly the address calculator can perform this computation.

If you are to implement such a scheme, you must, of course, be able to construct an address calculator that can, with very little work, tell you where a given item should be. Address calculators are actually not as mysterious as they seem; in fact, many exist that can approximate the idealized behavior just described. Such an address calculator is usually referred to as a **hash function.** The scheme just described is an idealized description of a method known as **hashing,** and the array `table` is called the **hash table.**

A hash function tells you where to place an item in an array called a hash table

To understand how a hash function works, consider the 911 emergency system mentioned earlier. If, for each person, the system had a record whose search key was the person's telephone number, it could store these records in a search tree. Although searching a tree would be fast, faster access to a particular record would be possible by storing the records in an array `table`, as follows. You store the record for a person whose telephone number is *num* into `table[num]`. Retrieval of the record, then, is almost instantaneous given its search key *num*. For example, you can store the record for the telephone number 123-4567 in `table[1234567]`. If you can spare ten million memory locations for `table`, this approach is fine. You need not use memory so extravagantly, however, since 911 systems are regional. If you consider only one telephone exchange, for example, you can store the record for the number 123-4567 in `table[4567]` and get by with an array `table` of 10,000 locations.

The transformation of 1234567 into an array index 4567 is a simple example of a hash function. A hash function *h* must take an arbitrary integer *x* and map it into an integer that you can use as an array index. In our example, such indexes would be in the range 0 through 9999. That is, *h* is a function such that for any integer *x*,

A hash function maps an integer into an array index

$h(x) = i$, where *i* is an integer in the range 0 through 9999

Since the database contains records for every telephone number in a particular exchange, the array `table` is completely full. In this sense, our example is not typical of hashing applications and serves only to illustrate the idea of a hash function. What if many fewer records were in the array? Consider, for example, an air traffic control system that stores a record for each current flight according to its four-digit flight number. You could store a record for Flight 4567 in `table[4567]`, but you still would need an array of 10,000 locations, even if only 50 flights were current.

A different hash function would save memory. If you allow space for a maximum of 101 flights, for example, so that the array `table` has indexes 0 through 100, the necessary hash function *h* should map any four-digit flight number into an integer in the range 0 through 100.

If you have such a hash function *h*—and you will see several suggestions for hash functions later—the table operations are easy to write. For example, in the `tableRetrieve` algorithm, the step

```
i = the array index that the address calculator
        gives you for an item whose search key
        equals searchKey
```

is implemented simply as

```
i = h(searchKey)
```

In the previous example, `searchKey` would be the flight number.

The table operations appear to be virtually instantaneous. But is hashing really as good as it sounds? If it really were this good, there would have been little reason for developing all those other table implementations. Hashing would beat them hands down!

Why is hashing not quite as simple as it seems? You might first notice that since the hashing scheme stores the items in an array, it would appear to suffer from the familiar problems associated with a fixed-size implementation. Obviously, the hash table must be large enough to contain all of the items that you want to store. This requirement is not the crux of the implementation's difficulty, however, for—as you will see later—there are ways to allow the hash table to grow dynamically. The implementation has a major pitfall, even given the assumption that the number of items to be stored will never exceed the size of the hash table.

Ideally, you want the hash function to map each x into a unique integer i. The hash function in the ideal situation is called a **perfect hash function.** In fact, it is possible to construct perfect hash functions if you know all of the possible search keys that *actually* occur in the table. You have this knowledge for the 911 example, since everyone is in the database, but not for the air traffic control example. Usually, you will not know the values of the search keys in advance.

In practice, a hash function can map two or more search keys x and y into the *same* integer. That is, the hash function tells you to store two or more items in the same array location `table[i]`. This occurrence is called a **collision.** Thus, even if fewer than 101 items were present in the hash table `table[0..100]`, h could very well tell you to place more than one item into the same array location. For example, if two items have search keys 4567 and 7597, and if

$$h(4567) = h(7597) = 22$$

h will tell you to place the two items into the same array location, `table[22]`. That is, the search keys 4567 and 7597 have collided.

Even if the number of items that can be in the array at any one time is small, the only way to avoid collisions completely is for the hash table to be large enough that each possible search-key value can have its own location. If, for example, social security numbers were the search keys, you would need an array location for each integer in the range 000000000 through 999999999. This situation would certainly require a good deal of storage! Because reserving vast amounts of storage is usually not practical, **collision-resolution schemes** are necessary to make hashing feasible. Such resolution schemes usually require that the hash function place items evenly throughout the hash table.

To summarize, a typical hash function must

- Be easy and fast to compute

- Place items evenly throughout the hash table

A perfect hash function maps each search key into a unique location of the hash table

A perfect hash function is possible if you know all the search keys

Collisions occur when the hash function maps more than one item into the same array location

Requirements for a hash function

Note that the size of the hash table affects the ability of the hash function to distribute the items evenly throughout the table. The requirements of a hash function will be discussed in more detail later in this chapter.

Consider now several hash functions and collision-resolution schemes.

Hash Functions

It is sufficient to consider hash functions that have an arbitrary integer as an argument. Why? If a search key is not an integer, you can simply map the search key into an integer, which you then hash. At the end of this section, you will see one way to convert a string into an integer.

It is sufficient for hash functions to operate on integers

There are many ways to convert an arbitrary integer into an integer within a certain range, such as 0 through 100. Thus, there are many ways to construct a hash function. Many of these functions, however, will not be suitable. Here are several simple hash functions that operate on positive integers.

Selecting digits.   If your search key is the nine-digit employee ID number 001364825, you could select the fourth digit and the last digit, to obtain 35 as the index to the hash table. That is,

$h(001364825) = 35$ (*select the fourth and last digits*)

Therefore, you would store the item whose search key is 001364825 in `table[35]`.

You do need to be careful about which digits you choose in a particular situation. For example, the first three digits of a Social Security number are based on the geographic region in which the number was assigned. If you select only these digits, you will map all people from the same state into the same location of the hash table.

Digit-selection hash functions are simple and fast, but generally they do not evenly distribute the items in the hash table. A hash function really should utilize the entire search key.

Digit selection does not distribute items evenly in the hash table

Folding.   One way to improve upon the previous method of selecting digits is to add the digits. For example, you can add all of the digits in 001364825 to obtain

$0 + 0 + 1 + 3 + 6 + 4 + 8 + 2 + 5 = 29$ (*add the digits*)

Therefore, you would store the item whose search key is 001364825 in `table[29]`. Notice that if you add all of the digits from a nine-digit search key,

$0 \leq h(\text{search key}) \leq 81$

That is, you would use only `table[0]` through `table[81]` of the hash table. To change this situation or to increase the size of the hash table, you can group the digits in the search key and add the groups. For example, you could form three groups of three digits from the search key 001364825 and add them as follows:

$$001 + 364 + 825 = 1{,}190$$

For this hash function,

$$0 \leq h(\text{search key}) \leq 3 * 999 = 2{,}997$$

You can apply more than one hash function to a single search key

Clearly, if 2,997 is larger than the size of the hash table that you want, you can alter the groups that you choose. Perhaps not as obvious is that you can apply more than one hash function to a search key. For example, you could select some of the digits from the search key before adding them, or you could either select digits from the previous result 2,997 or apply folding to it once again by adding 29 and 97.

Modulo arithmetic. Modulo arithmetic provides a simple and effective hash function that we will use in the rest of this chapter. For example, consider the function[5]

$$h(x) = x \bmod \textit{tableSize}$$

where the hash table `table` has *tableSize* elements. In particular, if *tableSize* is 101, $h(x) = x \bmod 101$ maps any integer x into the range 0 through 100. For example, h maps 001364825 into 12.

For $h(x) = x \bmod \textit{tableSize}$, many x's map into `table[0]`, many x's map into `table[1]`, and so on. That is, collisions occur. However, you can distribute the table items evenly over all of `table`—thus reducing collisions—by choosing a prime number as *tableSize*. The reasoning behind choosing a prime number is discussed later in this chapter in the section "What Constitutes a Good Hash Function?" For instance, 101 in the previous example is prime. The choice of table size will also be discussed in more detail later in this chapter. For now, realize that 101 is used here as a simple example of a prime table size. For the typical table, 101 is much too small.

The table size should be prime

Converting a character string to an integer. If your search key is a character string—such as a name—you could convert it into an integer before applying the hash function $h(x)$. To do so, you could first assign each character in the string an integer value. For example, for the word "NOTE" you could assign the ASCII values 78, 79, 84, and 69, to the letters N, O, T, and E, respectively. Or, if you assign the values 1 through 26 to the letters A through Z, you could assign 14 to N, 15 to O, 20 to T, and 5 to E.

If you now simply add these numbers, you will get an integer, but it will not be unique to the character string. For example, the string "TONE" will give you the same result. Instead, write the numeric value for each character in

---

5. Remember that this book uses "mod" as an abbreviation for the mathematical operation modulo. In Java, the modulo operator is %.

binary and concatenate the results. If you assign the values 1 through 26 to the letters A through Z, you obtain the following for the string "NOTE":

N is 14, or 01110 in binary

O is 15, or 01111 in binary

T is 20, or 10100 in binary

E is 5, or 00101 in binary

Concatenating the binary values gives you the binary integer

01110011111010000101

which is 474,757 in decimal. You can apply the hash function x mod *tableSize* for $x = 474{,}757$.

Now consider a more efficient way to compute 474,757. Rather than converting the previous binary number to decimal, you can evaluate the expression

$$14 * 32^3 + 15 * 32^2 + 20 * 32^1 + 5 * 32^0$$

This computation is possible because we have represented each character as a 5-bit binary number, and 2^5 is 32.

By factoring this expression, you can minimize the number of arithmetic operations. This technique is called **Horner's rule** and results in

$$((14 * 32 + 15) * 32 + 20) * 32 + 5$$

Horner's rule minimizes the number of computations

Although both of these expressions have the same value, the result in either case could very well be larger than a typical computer can represent; that is, an overflow can occur.

Since we plan to use the hash function

$h(x) = x$ mod *tableSize*

you can prevent an overflow by applying the modulo operator after computing each parenthesized expression in Horner's rule. The implementation of this algorithm is left as an exercise.

Resolving Collisions

Consider the problems caused by a collision. Suppose that you want to insert an item whose search key is 4567 into the hash table `table`, as was described previously. The hash function $h(x) = x$ mod 101 tells you to place the new item in `table[22]`, because 4567 mod 101 is 22. Suppose, however, that `table[22]` already contains an item, as Figure 13-45 illustrates. If earlier you had placed 7597 into `table[22]` because 7597 mod 101 equals 22, where do you place the new item? You certainly do not want to disallow the insertion on the grounds that the table is full: You could have a collision even when inserting into a table that contains only one item!

Two general approaches to collision resolution are common. One approach allocates another location *within* the hash table to the new item. A

Two approaches to collision resolution

second approach changes the structure of the hash table so that each location `table[i]` can accommodate more than one item. The collision-resolution schemes described next exemplify these two approaches.

Approach 1: Open addressing. During an attempt to insert a new item into a table, if the hash function indicates a location in the hash table that is already occupied, you **probe** for some other empty, or open, location in which to place the item. The sequence of locations that you examine is called the **probe sequence.**

Such schemes are said to use **open addressing.** The concern, of course, is that you must be able to find a table item efficiently after you have inserted it. That is, the `tableDelete` and `tableRetrieve` operations must be able to reproduce the probe sequence that `tableInsert` used and must do so efficiently.

The difference among the various open-addressing schemes is the method used to probe for an empty location. We briefly describe three such methods.

Linear probing. In this simple scheme to resolve a collision, you search the hash table sequentially, starting from the original hash location. More specifically, if `table[h(searchKey)]` is occupied, you check `table [h(searchKey)+1]`, `table[h(searchKey)+2]`, and so on until you find an available location. Figure 13-46 illustrates the placement of four items that all hash into the same location `table[22]` of the hash table, assuming a hash function $h(x) = x \bmod 101$. Typically, you *wrap around* from the last table location to the first table location if necessary.

Begin at the hash location and search the table sequentially

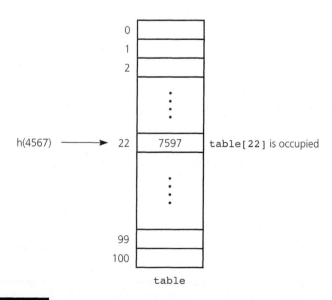

FIGURE 13-45

A collision

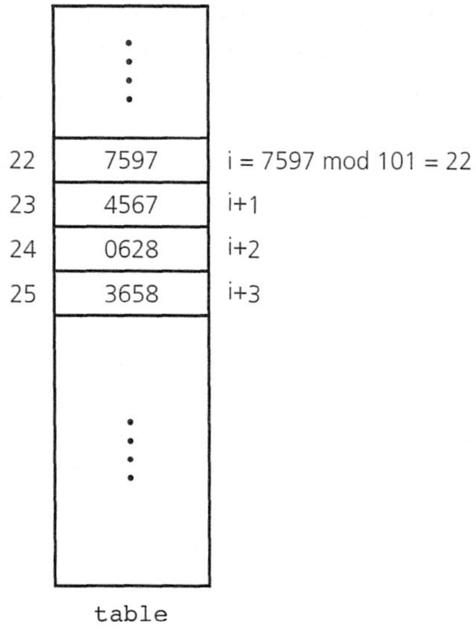

22	7597	i = 7597 mod 101 = 22
23	4567	i+1
24	0628	i+2
25	3658	i+3

table

FIGURE 13-46

Linear probing with $h(x) = x \bmod 101$

In the absence of deletions, the implementation of *tableRetrieve* under this scheme is straightforward. You need only follow the same probe sequence that *tableInsert* used until you either find the item you are searching for, reach an empty location, which indicates that the item is not present, or visit every table location.

Deletions, however, add a slight complication. The *tableDelete* operation itself is no problem. You merely find the desired item, as in *tableRetrieve*, and delete it, making the location empty. But what happens to *tableRetrieve* after deletions? The new empty locations that *tableDelete* created along a probe sequence could cause *tableRetrieve* to stop prematurely, incorrectly indicating a failure. You can resolve this problem by allowing a table location to be in one of three states: occupied (currently in use), empty (has not been used), or deleted (was once occupied but is now available). You then modify the *tableRetrieve* operation to continue probing when it encounters a location in the deleted state. Similarly, you modify *tableInsert* to insert into either empty or deleted locations.

Three states: occupied, empty, deleted

One of the problems with the linear-probing scheme is that table items tend to **cluster** together in the hash table. That is, the table contains groups of consecutively occupied locations. This phenomenon is called **primary clustering.** Clusters can get close to one another and, in fact, merge into a larger cluster. Large clusters tend to get even larger. ("The rich get richer.") Thus, one part of the table might be quite dense, even though another part has relatively few items. Primary clustering causes long probe searches and therefore decreases the overall efficiency of hashing.

Clustering can be a problem

Quadratic probing. You can virtually eliminate primary clusters simply by adjusting the linear probing scheme just described. Instead of probing consecutive locations from the original hash location $table[h(searchKey)]$, you check locations $table[h(searchKey)+1^2]$, $table[h(searchKey)+2^2]$, $table[h(searchKey)+3^2]$, and so on until you find an available location. Figure 13-47 illustrates this open-addressing scheme—which is called **quadratic probing**—for the same items that appear in Figure 13-46.

Unfortunately, when two items hash into the same location, quadratic probing uses the same probe sequence for each item. This phenomenon—called **secondary clustering**—delays the resolution of the collision. Although the analysis of quadratic probing remains incomplete, it appears that secondary clustering is not a problem.

Double hashing. Double hashing, which is yet another open-addressing scheme, drastically reduces clustering. The probe sequences that both linear probing and quadratic probing use are *key independent*. For example, linear probing inspects the table locations sequentially no matter what the hash key is. In contrast, double hashing defines *key-dependent* probe sequences. In this scheme, the probe sequence still searches the table in a linear order, starting at the location $h_1(key)$, but a second hash function h_2 determines the size of the steps taken.

Although you choose h_1 as usual, you must follow these guidelines for h_2:

$$h_2(key) \neq 0$$
$$h_2 \neq h_1$$

A hash address and a step size determine the probe sequence

Guidelines for the step-size function h_2

	⋮	
22	7597	i = 7597 mod 101 = 22
23	4567	i+1²
24		
25		
26	0628	i+2²
	⋮	
31	3658	i+3²
	⋮	

table

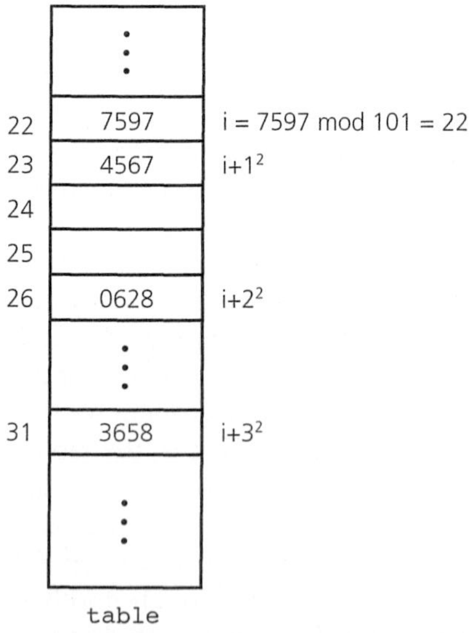

FIGURE 13-47

Quadratic probing with $h(x) = x \bmod 101$

Clearly, you need a nonzero step size $h_2(key)$ to define the probe sequence. In addition, h_2 must differ from h_1 to avoid clustering.

For example, let h_1 and h_2 be the primary and secondary hash functions defined as

$h_1(key) = key \bmod 11$

$h_2(key) = 7 - (key \bmod 7)$

Primary and secondary hash functions

where a hash table of only 11 items is assumed, so that you can readily see the effect of these functions on the hash table. If $key = 58$, h_1 hashes key to table location 3 (58 mod 11), and h_2 indicates that the probe sequence should take steps of size 5 (7 – 58 mod 7). In other words, the probe sequence will be 3, 8, 2 (wraps around), 7, 1 (wraps around), 6, 0, 5, 10, 4, 9. On the other hand, if $key = 14$, h_1 hashes key to table location 3 (14 mod 11), and h_2 indicates that the probe sequence should take steps of size 7 (7 – 14 mod 7), and so the probe sequence would be 3, 10, 6, 2, 9, 5, 1, 8, 4, 0.

Each of these probe sequences visits *all* the table locations. This phenomenon always occurs if the size of the table and the size of the probe step are relatively prime, that is, if their greatest common divisor is 1. Because the size of a hash table is commonly a prime number, it will be relatively prime to all step sizes.

Figure 13-48 illustrates the insertion of 58, 14, and 91 into an initially empty hash table. Since $h_1(58)$ is 3, you place 58 into `table[3]`. You then find that $h_1(14)$ is also 3, so to avoid a collision, you step by $h_2(14) = 7$ and place 14 into `table[3 + 7]`, or `table[10]`. Finally, $h_1(91)$ is 3 and $h_2(91)$

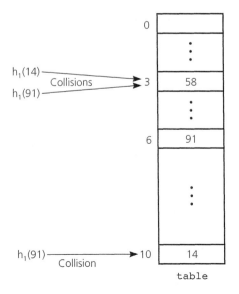

FIGURE 13-48

Double hashing during the insertion of 58, 14, and 91

is 7. Since `table[3]` is occupied, you probe `table[10]` and find that it, too, is occupied. You finally store 91 in `table[(10 + 7) % 11]`, or `table[6]`.

Using more than one hash function is called **rehashing.** While more than two hash functions can be desirable, such schemes are difficult to implement.

Increasing the size of the hash table.   With any of the open-addressing schemes, as the hash table fills, the probability of a collision increases. At some point, a larger hash table becomes desirable. If you use a resizeable array for the hash table, you can increase its size whenever the table becomes too full.

You cannot simply double the size of the array, as we did in earlier chapters, because the size of the hash table must remain prime. In addition, you do not copy the items from the original hash table to the new hash table. If your hash function is *x* mod *tableSize*, it changes as *tableSize* changes. Thus, you need to apply your new hash function to every item in the old hash table before placing it into the new hash table.

Approach 2: Restructuring the hash table.   Another way to resolve collisions is to change the structure of the array `table`—the hash table—so that it can accommodate more than one item in the same location. We describe two such ways to alter the hash table.

Each hash-table location can accommodate more than one item

Buckets.   If you define the hash table `table` so that each location `table[i]` is itself an array called a **bucket,** you then can store the items that hash into `table[i]` in this array. The problem with this approach, of course, is choosing the size *B* of each bucket. If *B* is too small, you will only have postponed the problem of collisions until *B* + 1 items map into some array location. If you attempt to make *B* large enough so that each array location can accommodate the largest number of items that might map into it, you are likely to waste a good deal of storage.

A bucket is an element of a hash table that is itself an array

Separate chaining.   A better approach is to design the hash table as an array of linked lists. In this collision-resolution method, known as **separate chaining,** each entry `table[i]` is a reference to a linked list—the **chain**—of items that the hash function has mapped into location *i*, as Figure 13-49 illustrates. The following classes for the ADT table assume an implementation that uses a hash table and separate chaining:

Each hash-table location is a linked list

```
class ChainNode<K, V> {
  private K key;
  private V value;
  ChainNode<K, V> next;

  public ChainNode(K newKey, V newValue,
                   ChainNode<K, V> nextNode) {
    key = newKey;
    value = newValue;
    next = nextNode;
```

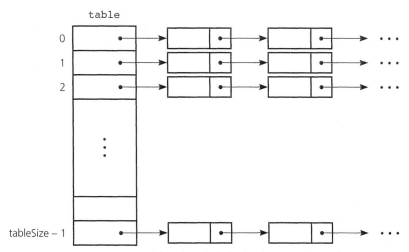

Each location of the hash table contains a reference to a linked list

FIGURE 13-49

Separate chaining

```
  }  // end constructor

  public V getValue() {
    return value;
  }  // end getValue

  public K getKey() {
    return key;
  }  // end getKey

} // end ChainNode

// ***********************************************************
// Hash table implementation.
// Assumption: A table contains at most one item with a
//             given search key at any time.
// Note: This code will compile with a warning about the use
// of unchecked or unsafe operations. This is due to the
// cast in method tableRetrieve.  Exercise X asks you to
// rewrite this implementation using ArrayList to avoid this
// warning.
// ***********************************************************

public class HashTable<K, V> {
  public final int HASH_TABLE_SIZE = 101;
  private ChainNode[] table;      // hash table
  private int size = 0;           // size of ADT table
```

```
public HashTable() {
   table = new ChainNode[HASH_TABLE_SIZE];
}  // end default constructor

// table operations
public boolean tableIsEmpty() {
   return size==0;
}  // end tableIsEmpty

public int tableLength() {
   return size;
}  // end tableLength

// Programming Problem 4 asks you to implement the following
// methods.

public void tableInsert(K key, V value)
                              throws HashException {
   // ...
}  // end tableInsert

public boolean tableDelete(K searchKey) {

   // ...
   return true;   // added for compilation
}  // end tableDelete

public V tableRetrieve(K searchKey) {
   // ...
   return null;   // added for compilation
} // end tableRetrieve

public int hashIndex(K key) {
   // ...
}  // end hashIndex

}  // end HashTable
```

Items are stored in the table using *ChainNode*, which expects *<key, value>* pairs as first presented in Chapter 12. This node class is similar to the one that we used with linked lists in Chapter 5, except that it is generic and holds two data values, one for the key, the other for the corresponding value. The *ChainNode* class provides the method *getKey* to retrieve the key, and the method *getValue* to retrieve the value.

In the *HashTable* class, the *hashIndex* method needs to generate a hash index value. Since the *hashIndex* method does not usually have access to the internal structure of the search key, it must rely on methods available in the class `Object` and the interface `Comparable`. The `Object` class has two methods that are likely to be used in the implementation of `hashIndex`: `toString` and `hashCode`. The `hashIndex` method could use `toString` with the techniques involving strings discussed earlier in the chapter. The `hashIndex` method could also simply call `hashCode`, a method that returns a unique value for each unique object. The `hashIndex` method of the class `HashTable` should take care of ensuring that the value generated is in an appropriate range and should resolve collisions if needed.

When you insert a new item into the table, you simply place it at the beginning of the linked list that the hash function indicates. The following pseudocode describes the insertion algorithm:

```
+tableInsert(in searchKey:KeyType, in value:ValueType)

  if (table not full) {
    searchKey = the search key of newItem
    i = hashIndex(searchKey)
    node = reference to a new node containing searchKey and value
    node.next = table[i]
    table[i] = node
  }
  else { // table full
    throw new HashException()
  }  // end if
```

When you want to retrieve an item, you search the linked list that the hash function indicates. The following pseudocode describes the retrieval algorithm:

```
+tableRetrieve(in searchKey:KeyType):ValueType

  i = hashIndex(searchKey)
  node = table[i]

  while ((node ≠ null) && (node.getKey() ≠ searchKey)){
    node = node.next
  }  // end while

  if (node != null) {
    return node.getValue()
  }

  else {
    return null
  }  // end if
```

The deletion algorithm is very similar to the retrieval algorithm and is left as an exercise. (See Exercise 14.)

Separate chaining successfully resolves collisions

Separate chaining is thus a successful method of resolving collisions. With separate chaining, the size of the ADT table is dynamic and can exceed the size of the hash table, since each linked list can be as long as necessary. As you will see in the next section, the length of these linked lists affects the efficiency of retrievals and deletions.

The Efficiency of Hashing

The load factor measures how full a hash table is

An analysis of the average-case efficiency of hashing involves the **load factor** α, which is the ratio of the current number of items in the table to the maximum size of the array `table`. That is,

$$\alpha = \frac{\textit{Current number of table items}}{\textit{tableSize}}$$

α is a measure of how full the hash table `table` is. As `table` fills, α increases and the chance of collision increases, so search times increase. Thus, hashing efficiency decreases as α increases.

Unlike the efficiency of earlier table implementations, the efficiency of hashing does not depend solely on the number n of items in the table. While it is true that for a fixed *tableSize*, efficiency decreases as n increases, for a given n you can choose *tableSize* to increase efficiency. Thus, when determining *tableSize*, you should estimate the largest possible n and select *tableSize* so that α is small. As you will see shortly, α should not exceed 2/3.

Unsuccessful searches generally require more time than successful searches

Hashing efficiency for a particular search also depends on whether the search is successful. An unsuccessful search requires more time in general than a successful search. The following analyses[6] enable a comparison of collision-resolution techniques.

Linear probing.   For linear probing, the approximate average number of comparisons that a search requires is

$$\frac{1}{2}\left[1 + \frac{1}{1-\alpha}\right]$$ for a successful search, and

$$\frac{1}{2}\left[1 + \frac{1}{(1-\alpha)^2}\right]$$ for an unsuccessful search

As collisions increase, the probe sequences increase in length, causing increased search times. For example, for a table that is two-thirds full ($\alpha = 2/3$), an average unsuccessful search might require at most five comparisons, or probes, while an average successful search might require at most two

---

6. D. E. Knuth, *Searching and Sorting*, vol. 3 of *The Art of Computer Programming* (Menlo Park, CA: Addison-Wesley, 1973).

comparisons. To maintain efficiency, it is important to prevent the hash table from filling up.

Do not let the hash table get too full

Quadratic probing and double hashing. The efficiency of both quadratic probing and double hashing is given by

$$\frac{-\log_e(1 - \alpha)}{\alpha} \quad \text{for a successful search, and}$$

$$\frac{1}{1 - \alpha} \quad \text{for an unsuccessful search}$$

On average, both methods require fewer comparisons than linear probing. For example, for a table that is two-thirds full, an average unsuccessful search might require at most three comparisons, or probes, while an average successful search might require at most two comparisons. As a result, you can use a smaller hash table for both quadratic probing and double hashing than you can for linear probing. However, because they are open-addressing schemes, all three methods suffer when you are unable to predict the number of insertions and deletions that will occur. If your hash table is too small, it will fill up, and search efficiency will decrease.

Open-addressing schemes require a good estimate of the number of insertions and deletions
Insertion is instantaneous

Separate chaining. Since the `tableInsert` operation places the new item at the beginning of a linked list within the hash table, it is O(1). The `tableRetrieve` and `tableDelete` operations, however, are not as fast. They each require a search of the linked list of items, so ideally you would like for these linked lists to be short.

For separate chaining, *tableSize* is the number of linked lists, not the maximum number of table items. Thus, it is entirely possible, and even likely, that the current number of table items *n* exceeds *tableSize*. That is, the load factor α, or *n/tableSize*, can exceed 1. Since *tableSize* is the number of linked lists, *n/tableSize*—that is, α—is the average length of each linked list.

Some searches of the hash table are unsuccessful because the relevant linked list is empty. Such searches are virtually instantaneous. For an unsuccessful search of a nonempty linked list, however, `tableRetrieve` and `tableDelete` must examine the entire list, that is, α items in the average case. On the other hand, a successful search must examine a nonempty linked list. In the average case, the search will locate the item in the middle of the list. That is, after determining that the linked list is not empty, the search will examine $\alpha/2$ items.

Thus, the efficiency of the retrieval and deletion operations under the separate-chaining approach is

$$1 + \frac{\alpha}{2} \quad \text{for a successful search, and}$$

$$\alpha \quad \text{for an unsuccessful search}$$

Average-case efficiency of retrievals and deletions

Even if the linked lists typically are short, you should still estimate the worst case. If you seriously underestimate *tableSize* or if most of the table items happen to hash into the same location, the number of items in a linked list could be quite large. In fact, in the worst case, all *n* items in the table could be in the same linked list!

As you can see, the time that a retrieval or deletion operation requires can range from almost nothing—if the linked list to be searched either is empty or has only a couple of items in it—to the time required to search a linked list that contains all the items in the table, if all the items hashed into the same location.

Comparing methods. Figure 13-50 plots the relative efficiency of the collision-resolution schemes just discussed. When the hash table *table* is about half full—that is, when α is 0.5—the methods are nearly equal in efficiency. As the table fills and α approaches 1, separate chaining is the most efficient. Does this mean that we should discard all other search methods in favor of hashing with separate chaining?

No. The analyses here are average-case analyses. Although an implementation of the ADT table that uses hashing might often be faster than one that uses a search tree, in the worst case it can be much slower. If you can afford

In the worst case, a hashing implementation of a table can be much slower than other implementations

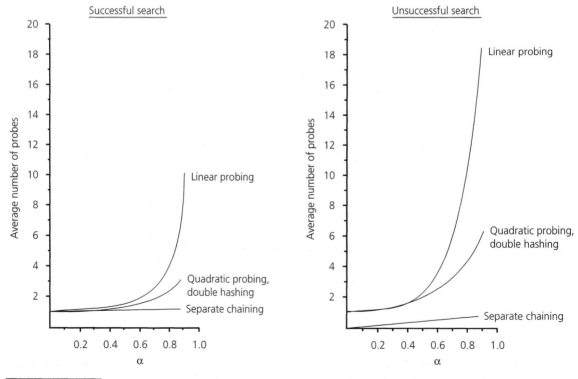

FIGURE 13-50

The relative efficiency of four collision-resolution methods

both an occasional slow search and a large *tableSize*—that is, a small α—then hashing can be an attractive table implementation. However, if you are performing a life-and-death search for your city's poison control center, a search-tree implementation would at least provide you with a guaranteed bound on its worst-case behavior.

What Constitutes a Good Hash Function?

Before concluding this introduction to hashing, consider in more detail the issue of choosing a hash function to perform the address calculations for a given application. A great deal has been written on this subject, most of which is beyond the mathematical level of this book. However, this section will present a brief summary of the major concerns.

■ **A hash function should be easy and fast to compute.** If a hashing scheme is to perform table operations almost instantaneously and in constant time, you certainly must be able to calculate the hash function rapidly. Most of the common hash functions require only a single division (like the modulo function), a single multiplication, or some kind of "bit-level" operation on the internal representation of the search key. In all these cases, the requirement that the hash function be easy and fast to compute is satisfied.

■ **A hash function should scatter the data evenly throughout the hash table.** Unless you use a perfect hash function—which is usually impractical to construct—you typically cannot avoid collisions entirely. For example, to achieve the best performance from a separate-chaining scheme, each entry *table[i]* should contain approximately the same number of items in its chain; that is, each chain should contain approximately *n/tableSize* items (and thus no chain should contain significantly more than *n/tableSize* items). To accomplish this goal, your hash function should scatter the search keys evenly throughout the hash table.

> You cannot avoid collisions entirely

There are two issues to consider with regard to how evenly a hash function scatters the search keys.

■ **How well does the hash function scatter random data?** If every search-key value is equally likely, will the hash function scatter the search keys evenly? For example, consider the following scheme for hashing nine-digit ID numbers:

table[0..39] is the hash table, and
the hash function is $h(x)$ = (first two digits of *x*) mod 40

The question is, given the assumption that all employee ID numbers are equally likely, does a given ID number *x* have equal probability of hashing into any one of the 40 array locations? For this hash function, the answer is no. Only ID numbers that start with 19, 59, and 99 map into *table[19]*, while only ID numbers that start with 20 and 60 map into *table[20]*. In general, three different ID *prefixes*—that is, the first two digits of an ID number—map into each array location 0 through 19, while only two different prefixes map into each array location 20 through 39. Since all ID numbers are equally likely—and thus all prefixes 00 through 99 are equally likely—a given ID number is 50 percent more likely to hash into one of the locations 0 through 19 than it is to hash into one of the locations 20 through 39. As a result, each array location 0 through 19 would contain, on average, 50 percent more items than each location 20 through 39.

Thus, the hash function

A function that does not scatter random data evenly

$$h(x) = (\text{first two digits of } x) \bmod 40$$

does not scatter random data evenly throughout the array `table[0..39]`. On the other hand, it can be shown that the hash function

A function that does scatter random data evenly

$$h(x) = x \bmod 101$$

does, in fact, scatter random data evenly throughout the array `table[0..100]`.

■ **How well does the hash function scatter nonrandom data?** Even if a hash function scatters random data evenly, it may have trouble with nonrandom data. In general, no matter what hash function you select, it is always possible that the data will have some unlucky pattern that will result in uneven scattering. Although there is no way to guarantee that a hash function will scatter all data evenly, you can greatly increase the likelihood of this behavior.

As an example, consider the following scheme:

`table[0..99]` is the hash table, and
the hash function is $h(x) = $ first two digits of x

If every ID number is equally likely, h will scatter the search keys evenly throughout the array. But what if every ID number is not equally likely? For instance, a company might assign employee IDs according to department, as follows:

10xxxxx	Sales
20xxxxx	Customer Relations
. . .	
90xxxxx	Data Processing

Under this assignment, only 9 out of the 100 array locations would contain any items at all. Further, those locations corresponding to the largest departments (Sales, for example, which corresponds to `table[10]`) would contain more items than those locations corresponding to the smallest departments. This scheme certainly does not scatter the data evenly.

Much research has been done into the types of hash functions that you should use to guard against various types of patterns in the data. The results of this research are really in the province of more advanced courses, but two general principles can be noted here:

1. The calculation of the hash function should *involve the entire search key*. Thus, for example, computing a modulo of the entire ID number is much safer than using only its first two digits.

General require-
ments of a hash
function

2. If a hash function uses modulo arithmetic, *the base should be prime;* that is, if h is of the form

$$h(x) = x \bmod tableSize$$

then *tableSize* should be a prime number. This selection of *tableSize* is a safeguard against many subtle kinds of patterns in the data (for example, search keys whose digits are likely to be multiples of one another). Although each application can have its own particular kind of patterns and thus should be analyzed on an individual basis, choosing *tableSize* to be prime is an easy way to safeguard against some common types of patterns in the data.

Table Traversal: An Inefficient Operation under Hashing

For many applications, hashing provides the most efficient implementation of the ADT table. One important table operation—traversal in sorted order—performs poorly when hashing implements the table. As mentioned earlier, a good hash function scatters items as randomly as possible throughout the array, so that no ordering relationship exists between the search keys that hash into `table[i]` and those that hash into `table[i + 1]`. As a consequence, if you must traverse the table in sorted order, you first would have to sort the items. If sorting were required frequently, hashing would be a far less attractive implementation than a search tree.

Items hashed into
`table[i]` and
`table[i+1]`
have no ordering
relationship

Traversing a table in sorted order is really just one example of a whole class of operations that hashing does not support well. Many similar operations that you often wish to perform on a table require that the items be ordered. For example, consider an operation that must find the table item with the smallest or largest value in its search key. If you use a search-tree implementation, these items are in the leftmost and rightmost nodes of the tree, respectively. If you use a hashing implementation, however, you do not know where these items are—you would have to search the entire table. A similar type of operation is a **range query,** which requires that you retrieve all items whose search keys fall into a given range of values. For example, you might want to retrieve all items whose search keys are in the range 129 to 755. This task is relatively easy to perform by using a search tree (see Exercise 3), but if you use hashing, there is no efficient way to answer the range query.

Hashing versus bal-
anced search trees

In general, if an application requires any of these ordered operations, you should probably use a search tree. Although the *tableRetrieve*, *tableInsert*, and *tableDelete* operations are somewhat more efficient when you use hashing to implement the table instead of a balanced search tree, the balanced search tree supports these operations so efficiently itself that, in most contexts, the difference in speed for these operations is negligible (whereas the advantage of the search tree over hashing for the ordered operations is significant).

In the context of external storage, however, the story is different. For data that is stored externally, the difference in speed between hashing's implementation of *tableRetrieve* and a search tree's implementation may well be significant. In an external setting, it is not uncommon to see a hashing implementation of the *tableRetrieve* operation and a search-tree implementation of the ordered operations used simultaneously.

The JCF *Hashtable* and *TreeMap* Classes

Two of the ADTs discussed in this chapter have a direct implementation in the JCF. The first, *Hashtable*, is a hash table implementation, and the second, *TreeMap*, is a red-black tree implementation. Both of these implementations are contained in the *Map* hierarchy portion of the JCF as discussed in the last chapter.

The *Hashtable* Class

As discussed in the hash table section earlier in this chapter, the JCF *Hashtable* class maps keys to values. The objects used as keys and values must be not be *null*. As suggested in the implementation of the hash table presented in this chapter, the method *hashCode*, as inherited from the class object is used to generate a hash index. If you wish to use a different hashing algorithm, you must override the *hashCode* method in the class used for the keys. The *equals* method for the keys should also be redefined accordingly.

Here is a partial listing of the *Hashtable* class:

```
public class Hashtable<K,V>
  extends Dictionary<K,V>
  implements Map<K,V>, Cloneable, Serializable {

  Hashtable()
    // Constructs a new, empty hashtable with a default
    // capacity (11) and load factor, which is 0.75.

  Hashtable(int initialCapacity)
    // Constructs a new, empty hashtable with the specified
    // capacity and load factor, which is 0.75.

  Hashtable(int initialCapacity, float loadFactor)
    // Constructs a new, empty hashtable with the specified
    // initial capacity and the specified load factor.
```

```
void clear()
   // Clears this hashtable so that it contains no keys.

boolean contains(Object value)
   // Tests if some key maps into the specified value in this
   // hashtable.

boolean containsKey(Object key)
   // Tests if the specified object is a key in this
   //  hashtable.

boolean containsValue(Object value)
   // Returns true if this Hashtable maps one or more keys to
   // this value.

Set<Map.Entry<K,V>> entrySet()
   // Returns a Set view of the entries contained in this
   // Hashtable.

V get(Object key)
   // Returns the value to which the specified key is mapped
   // in this Hashtable.

boolean isEmpty()
   // Tests if this hashtable maps no keys to values.

Set<K> keySet()
   // Returns a Set view of the keys contained in this
   // Hashtable.

V put(K key, V value)
   // Maps the specified key to the specified value in this
   // Hashtable.

void putAll(Map<? extends K,? extends V> t)
   // Copies all of the mappings from the specified Map to
   // this Hashtable. These mappings will replace any
   // mappings that this Hashtable had for any of the keys
   // currently in the specified Map.

protected void rehash()
   // Increases the capacity of and internally reorganizes
   // this Hashtable, in order to accommodate and access its
   // entries more efficiently.
```

```
V remove(Object key)
  // Removes the key (and its corresponding value) from this
  // Hashtable.

int size()
  // Returns the number of keys in this Hashtable.

String toString()
  // Returns a string representation of this Hashtable
  // object in the form of a set of entries, enclosed in
  // braces and separated by the ASCII characters ", "
  // (comma and space).

Collection<V> values()
  // Returns a collection view of the values contained in
  // this map.

} // end HashTable
```

Note that the constructors for the *HashTable* can be used to specify an *initial capacity* and a *load factor*. The *initial capacity* is the number of buckets in the hash table when it is first created, with the default value of 11. Like the implementation shown in this chapter for a hash table, the collision-resolution method used is separate chaining, leading to a sequential search within each bucket when a collision occurs. The *load factor* is a measure used to indicate how full the table is allowed to get before the capacity is increased automatically (which is implementation dependent). The default load factor is 0.75, which is considered to be a value that offers a good tradeoff between time and space costs. The implementation guarantees no automatic rehashing of the table will occur as long as the capacity exceeds the number of entries divided by the load factor.

A rehashing of the table can also be done by calling the rehash method. But understand that rehashing the table is considered to be an expensive operation—done automatically or by request. Hence, it is important to choose an initial capacity that is realistic with respect to the number of entries expected in the hash table.

Here is a simple example that creates a hash table that maps names to ages. It uses the names as the keys, and the ages as the values:

```
Hashtable<String, Integer> ht = new Hashtable<String, Integer>();

// Placing items into the hash table
ht.put("Sarah", 17);
ht.put("Mike", 57);
ht.put("Janet", 51);
ht.put("Andrew", 20);
```

```
// Retrieving items from the hash table
System.out.println("Janet  => " + ht.get("Janet"));
System.out.println("Mike   => " + ht.get("Mike"));
System.out.println("Nobody => " + ht.get("Nobody"));
```

The output of the above code is as follows:

```
Janet  => 51
Mike   => 57
Nobody => null
```

The `TreeMap` Class

The JCF *TreeMap* class is a red-black tree implementation of the *SortedMap* interface. The *SortedMap* interface specifies that when *sets* of keys, <key, value> pairs, or values are returned (using the methods *keySet*, *entrySet*, and *values* respectively), an iteration over the returned set will be based upon an ascending order of the key values. As we have seen in previous JCF classes, the ordering of the keys will be based upon either a natural ordering using the *Comparable* interface, or a user supplied *Comparator* object. It is important that, whether the *Comparable* interface or a *Comparator* object is used, their implementations must be consistent with the equals method.

The *TreeMap* implementation guarantees O(log *n*) time cost for methods used to insert, retrieve, and remove values in the tree map. It also guarantees O(log *n*) time cost for searching the map for a key.

Here is a partial listing of the *TreeMap* class:

```
public class TreeMap<K,V>
  extends AbstractMap<K,V>
  implements SortedMap<K,V>, Cloneable, Serializable {

  TreeMap()
    // Constructs a new, empty map, sorted according to the
    // keys' natural order.

  TreeMap(Comparator<? super K> c)
    // Constructs a new, empty map, sorted according to the
    // given comparator.

  void clear()
    // Removes all mappings from this TreeMap.

  Comparator<? super K> comparator()
    // Returns the comparator used to order this map, or null
    // if this map uses its keys' natural order.
```

```
boolean containsKey(Object key)
   // Returns true if this map contains a mapping for the
   // specified key.

boolean containsValue(Object value)
   // Returns true if this map maps one or more keys to the
   // specified value.

Set<Map.Entry<K,V>> entrySet()
   // Returns a set view of the mappings contained in this
   // map.

K firstKey()
   // Returns the first (lowest) key currently in this sorted
   // map.

V get(Object key)
   // Returns the value to which this map maps the specified
   // key.

SortedMap<K,V> headMap(K toKey)
   // Returns a view of the portion of this map whose keys
   // are strictly less than toKey.

K lastKey()
   // Returns the last (highest) key currently in this sorted
   // map.

V put(K key, V value)
   // Associates the specified value with the specified key
   // in this map.

void putAll(Map<? extends K,? extends V> map)
   // Copies all of the mappings from the specified map to
   // this map.

V remove(Object key)
   // Removes the mapping for this key from this TreeMap if
   // present.

int size()
   // Returns the number of key-value mappings in this
   // map.

SortedMap<K,V> subMap(K fromKey, K toKey)
   // Returns a view of the portion of this map whose
   // keys range from fromKey, inclusive, to toKey,
   // exclusive.
```

```
SortedMap<K,V> tailMap(K fromKey)
  // Returns a view of the portion of this map whose keys
  // are greater than or equal to fromKey.

Collection<V> values()
  // Returns a collection view of the values contained in
  // this map.
}  // end TreeMap
```

The *TreeMap* class provides methods to create submaps of a *TreeMap*. A submap is like a subset; it is a map that contains a subset of the <key, value> pairs from the original map. There are three different methods that return submaps, each with a return type of *SortedMap*. The first, called *headMap*, returns a submap whose keys are strictly less than the *toKey* parameter. The second, called *subMap*, creates a submap that contains a range of map elements that are greater than or equal to the key *fromKey*, but less than the value *toKey*. Lastly, the method *tailMap* creates a submap whose keys are greater than or equal to the parameter *fromKey*.

   Below is a simple example that uses a *TreeMap* to store phone book entries and print all of the entries that begin with the letter "H."

```
TreeMap<String, String> phoneBook =
                             new TreeMap<String, String>();
phoneBook.put("Smith, Jackson", "212-555-4444");
phoneBook.put("Prichard, Marlene F.", "806-555-6565");
phoneBook.put("Hayden, Sarah", "401-555-5220");
phoneBook.put("Records, H.", "445-555-3241");
phoneBook.put("Harrington, J. R.", "617-555-1962");
phoneBook.put("Sousa, Keith", "252-555-0607");

// Return all of the entries such that "H" <= key value <
// "I", in other words, all of the names that start with H
SortedMap results = phoneBook.subMap("H","I");

if (results.isEmpty()) {
   System.out.println("Sorry, no names beginning with H found.");
} else {
   // Set up an iterator so we can print the entries in
   // result
   Iterator<Map.Entry<String, String>> iter =
                             results.entrySet().iterator();
   Map.Entry<String, String> entry;
   while (iter.hasNext()) {
     entry = iter.next();
     System.out.println(entry.getKey() + "\t: " + entry.getValue());
   }  // end while
}  // end if
```

The output of the above program is:

```
Harrington, J. R.  : 617-555-1962
Hayden, Sarah      : 401-555-5220
```

13.3 Data with Multiple Organizations

Many applications require a data organization that simultaneously supports several different data-management tasks. One simple example involves a waiting list of customers, that is, a queue of customer records. In addition to requiring the standard queue operations *isEmpty, enqueue, dequeue,* and *peek,* suppose that the application frequently requires a listing of the customer records in the queue. This listing is more useful if the records appear sorted by customer name. You thus need a traversal operation that visits the customer records in sorted order.

This scenario presents an interesting problem. If you simply store the customer records in a queue, they will not, in general, be sorted by name. If, on the other hand, you just store the records in sorted order, you will be unable to process the customers on a first-come, first-served basis. Apparently, this problem requires you to organize the data in two different ways.

One solution is to maintain two independent data structures, one organized to support the sorted traversal and the other organized to support the queue operations. Figure 13-51 depicts reference-based implementations of a sorted linked list of customer records and a queue of the same records. The reference-based data structures are a good choice because they do not require an estimate of the maximum number of customer records that must be stored. Note that although figures throughout the text have shown the data within the nodes of the data structure, in reality it is the references to the objects that are actually stored in the data structure. As Figure 13-51 shows, the two data structures share one set of data items.

How well does this scheme support the required operations? The operations that only *retrieve* data are easy to perform and require no coordination between the two data structures. You can obtain a sorted list of customer records by traversing the sorted linked list, and you can perform the queue *peek* operation by inspecting the record at the front of the queue.

The insertion and deletion operations are, however, more difficult to perform because they must *modify* both data structures. That is, the insertion and deletion operations are done separately on the two data structures.

The insertion operation has two steps:

1. Insert the new customer record at the back of the queue. This step requires only a few reference changes.

2. Insert the new customer record into its proper position in the sorted linked list. This step requires a traversal of the sorted linked list.

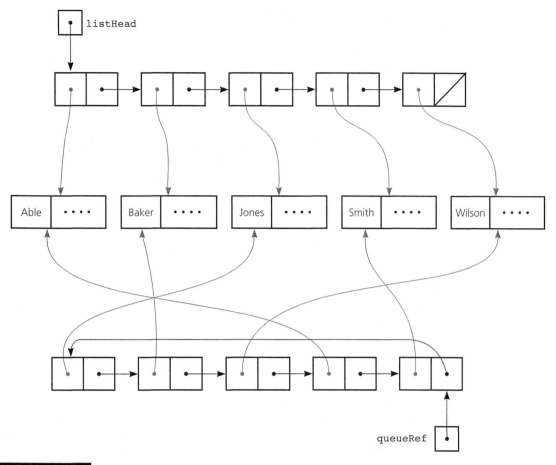

FIGURE 13-51

Two data structures that share the same data: (a) a sorted linked list; (b) a reference-based queue

Similarly, the deletion operation has two steps:

1. Delete the customer at the front of the queue, but retain a copy of the name for the next step. This step requires only a few reference changes. Note that this deletion removes a node from the queue but does not deallocate the customer records as it is still referenced by the sorted list.

2. Search the sorted linked list for the name just removed from the queue, and delete from the list the customer record containing this name. This step requires a traversal of the sorted linked list.

Thus, although the scheme efficiently supports a traversal of the sorted list and the queue *peek* operation, insertion and deletion require a search of the sorted linked list (whereas in a queue alone *enqueue* and *dequeue* require only a small, constant number of steps). Can you improve on this scheme? One possibility is to store the customer records in a binary search tree rather than a

Several independent data structures do not support all operations efficiently

sorted linked list. This approach would allow you to perform the second steps of the insertion and deletion operations much more efficiently. While the binary search tree strategy is certainly an improvement over the original scheme, the insertion and deletion operations would still require significantly more work than they would for a normal queue.

A different kind of scheme, one that supports the deletion operation almost as efficiently as if you were maintaining only a queue, is possible by allowing the data structures to communicate with each other. This concept is demonstrated here first with a sorted linked list and a queue, and then with more-complex structures, such as a binary search tree.

Interdependent data structures provide a better way to support a multiple organization of data

In the data structure shown in Figure 13-52, the sorted linked list contains references to customer records, and the queue contains references to the nodes containing the customer records. That is, each entry of the queue references the node in the sorted linked list for the customer at the given queue position. As you will soon see, this scheme significantly improves the efficiency of the *dequeue* operation.

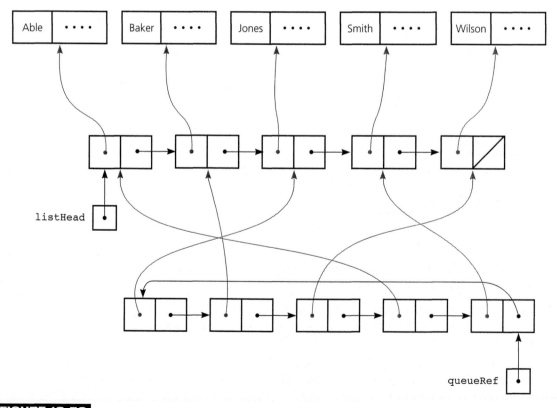

FIGURE 13-52

A queue referencing a sorted linked list

The efficiency of a traversal of the sorted list and the queue's *peek* and *enqueue* operations does not differ significantly from that of the original scheme that Figure 13-51 depicts. You still traverse the sorted linked list as before. However, you perform *peek* and *enqueue* as follows:

```
+peek():ItemType
```

```
Let nodeRef be the reference stored at the front of
    the queue (nodeRef references the node, which is
    in the sorted linked list, that contains the
    record for the customer at the front of the
    queue)

return item in the node that nodeRef references
```

```
+enqueue(in newItem:ItemType)
```

```
Find the proper position for newItem in the sorted
    linked list
Insert a node that contains newItem into this
    position
Insert a reference to the new node at the back of
    the queue
```

The real benefit of the new scheme is in the implementation of the *dequeue* operation:

```
+dequeue()
```

```
Delete the item at the front of the queue and
    retain its reference nodeRef (nodeRef
    references the node that contains the customer
    record to be deleted)

Delete from the sorted linked list the node
    that nodeRef references
```

Because the front of the queue contains a reference to the node *N* that you want to delete from the sorted linked list, there is no need to search the linked list. You have a reference to the appropriate node, and all you need to do is delete it.

There is one big problem, however. Because you are able to go directly to node *N* without traversing the linked list from its beginning, you have no trailing reference to the node that precedes *N* on the list! Recall that you must have a trailing reference to delete *N*. As the scheme now stands, the only way to obtain the trailing reference is to traverse the linked list from its beginning, but this requirement negates the advantage gained by having the queue reference the linked list. However, as you saw in Chapter 5, you can solve this problem by replacing the singly linked list in Figure 13-52 with a doubly linked list, as shown in Figure 13-53. (See Programming Problem 8.)

A doubly linked list is required

To summarize, you have seen a fairly good scheme for implementing the queue operations plus a sorted traversal. The only operation whose efficiency you might improve significantly is *enqueue*, since you still must traverse the linked list to find the proper place to insert a new customer record.

The choice to store the customer records in a linear linked list was made to simplify the discussion. A more efficient scheme has the queue reference a binary search tree rather than a linked list. This data structure allows you to perform the *enqueue* operation in logarithmic time, assuming that the tree remains balanced. To support the *dequeue* operation efficiently, however, you need a doubly linked tree. That is, each node in the tree must reference its parent so that you can easily delete the node that the front of the queue references. Figure 13-54 illustrates this data structure; its implementation, which is somewhat difficult, is the subject of Programming Problem 9.

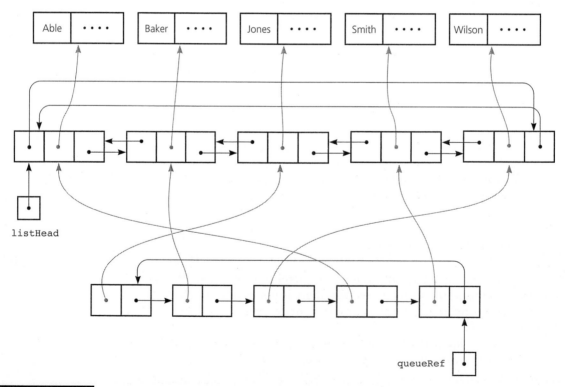

FIGURE 13-53

A queue referencing into a doubly linked list

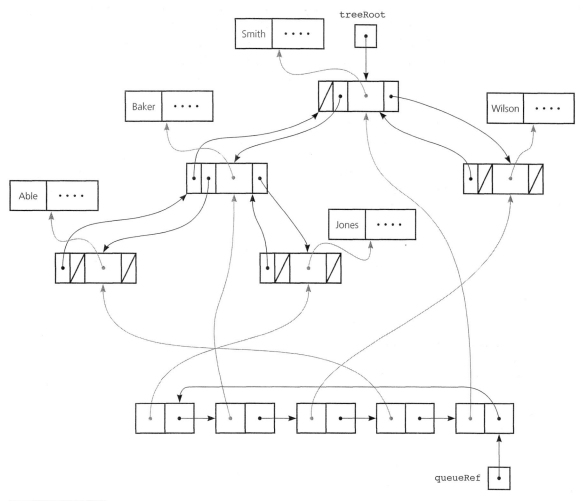

FIGURE 13-54

A queue referencing a doubly linked binary search tree

Summary

1. A 2-3 tree and a 2-3-4 tree are variants of a binary search tree. The internal nodes of a 2-3 tree can have either two or three children. The internal nodes of a 2-3-4 tree can have either two, three, or four children. Allowing the number of children to vary permits the insertion and deletion algorithms to maintain easily the balance of the tree.

2. The insertion and deletion algorithms for a 2-3-4 tree require only a single pass from root to leaf and, therefore, are more efficient than the corresponding algorithms for a 2-3 tree.

3. A red-black tree is a binary tree representation of a 2-3-4 tree that requires less storage than a 2-3-4 tree. Insertions and deletions for a red-black tree are more efficient than the corresponding operations on a 2-3-4 tree.

4. An AVL tree is a binary search tree that is guaranteed to remain balanced. The insertion and deletion algorithms perform rotations in the event that the tree starts to stray from a balanced shape.

5. Hashing as a table implementation calculates where the data item should be rather than searching for it. Hashing allows for very efficient retrievals, insertions, and deletions.

6. The hash function should be extremely easy to compute—it should require only a few operations—and it should scatter the search keys evenly throughout the hash table.

7. A collision occurs when two different search keys hash into the same array location. Two ways to resolve collisions are through probing and chaining.

8. Hashing does not efficiently support operations that require the table items to be ordered—for example, traversing the table in sorted order.

9. When table operations such as traversal are not important to a particular application, if you know the maximum number of table items and if you have ample storage, hashing is a table implementation that is simpler and faster than balanced search tree implementations. Tree implementations, however, are dynamic and do not require you to estimate the maximum number of table items.

10. You can impose several independent organizations on a given set of data. For example, you can store records in a sorted doubly linked list and impose a FIFO order by using a queue of references to the list.

Cautions

1. Even though search trees that allow their nodes to have more than two children are shorter than binary search trees, they are not necessarily easier to search: More comparisons are necessary at each node to determine which subtree should be searched next.

2. A hashing scheme, in general, must provide a means of resolving collisions. Choose a hash function that keeps the number of collisions to a minimum. You should be careful to avoid a hash function that will map more items into one part of the hash table than into another.

3. To improve the performance of hashing, either change the hash function or increase the size of the hash table. Do not use complex collision-resolution schemes.

4. Hashing is not a good table implementation if you frequently require operations that depend on some order of the table's items. For example, if you frequently need to either traverse the table in sorted order or find the item with the largest search-key value, you probably should not use hashing.

Self-Test Exercises

1. What is the result of inserting 5, 40, 10, 20, 15, and 30—in the order given—into an initially empty 2-3 tree? Note that insertion of one item into an empty 2-3 tree will create a single node that contains the inserted item.

2. a. What is the result of deleting the 10 from the 2-3 tree that you created in Self-Test Exercise 1?

   b. What is the result of inserting 3 and 4 into the 2-3 tree that you created in Self-Test Exercise 1?

3. a. Repeat Self-Test Exercise 1 for a 2-3-4 tree.

   b. Insert 3 and 4 into the tree that you created in Part *a*.

4. What red-black tree represents the 2-3-4 tree in Figure 13-27a?

5. If your application of the ADT table involves only retrieval—such as the application in Scenario B of Chapter 12 that searched a thesaurus—what tree would provide for the most efficient table implementation: a balanced binary search tree, a 2-3 tree, a 2-3-4 tree, or a red-black tree?

6. Why does a node in a red-black tree require less memory than a node in a 2-3-4 tree?

7. Write the pseudocode for the `tableDelete` operation when linear probing is used to implement the hash table.

8. What is the probe sequence that double hashing uses when

   $h_1(key) = key \bmod 11$, $h_2(key) = 7 - (key \bmod 7)$, and $key = 19$

9. If $h(x) = x \bmod 7$ and separate chaining resolves collisions, what does the hash table look like after the following insertions occur: 8, 10, 24, 15, 32, 17? Assume that each table item contains only a search key.

Exercises

1. Execute the following sequence of operations on an initially empty ADT table *t* that is implemented as

   a. A binary search tree

   b. A 2-3 tree

   c. A 2-3-4 tree

   d. A red-black tree

   e. An AVL tree

   and show the underlying tree after each operation:

   ```
   t.tableInsert(17)
   t.tableInsert(78)
   t.tableInsert(20)
   t.tableInsert(57)
   t.tableInsert(51)
   ```

```
t.tableDelete(17)
t.tableInsert(60)
t.tableInsert(70)
t.tableInsert(40)
t.tableDelete(57)
t.tableInsert(90)
t.tableInsert(19)
t.tableDelete(20)
t.tableDelete(70)
```

2. What are the advantages of implementing the ADT table with a 2-3 tree instead of a binary search tree? Why do you not, in general, maintain a completely balanced binary search tree?

3. Write a pseudocode method that performs a range query for a 2-3 tree. That is, the method should visit all items that have a search key in a given range of values (such as all values between 100 and 1,000).

4. Given the following 2-3 tree in Figure 13-55, draw the tree that results after inserting m, a, d, x, and z into the tree.

5. Given the following 2-3 tree in Figure 13-56 draw the tree that results after removing r, e, h, and b from the tree.

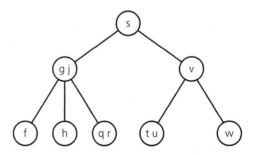

FIGURE 13-55

A 2-3 Tree for Exercise 4

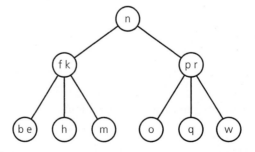

FIGURE 13-56

A 2-3 Tree for Exercise 5

6. Construct an red and black tree with following elements:
   13, 8, 7, 11, 6, 17, 15, 25, 22, 27.

7. Assume that the tree in Figure 13-5b is a 2-3-4 tree, and insert 39, 38, 37, 36, 35, 34, 33, and 32 into it. What 2-3-4 tree results?

8. Write pseudocode for the insertion, deletion, retrieval, and traversal operations for a 2-3-4 tree.

9. Write a program which stores the elements in a hashed list, after reading them from a user. If any collision occurs, it resolves it by quadratic probing.

10. What 2-3-4 tree does the red-black tree in Figure 13-57 represent?

11. Write pseudocode for the insertion, deletion, retrieval, and traversal operations for a red-black tree.

12. Construct an AVL tree with the following elements: 9, 20, 10, 40, 36, 47, 16, and 12.

13. Write pseudocode for the table operations `tableInsert`, `tableDelete`, and `tableRetrieve` when the implementation uses hashing and linear probing to resolve collisions.

14. Write pseudocode for the `tableDelete` operation when the implementation uses hashing and separate chaining to resolve collisions.

15. The success of a hash-table implementation of the ADT table is related to the choice of a good hash function. A good hash function is one that is easy to compute and that will evenly distribute the possible data. Comment on the appropriateness of the following hash functions. What patterns would hash to the same location?

   a. The hash table has size 2,048. The search keys are English words. The hash function is

   $h(key)$ = (sum of positions in alphabet of key's letters) mod 2048

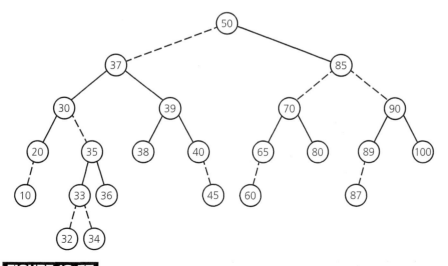

FIGURE 13-57

A red-black tree for Exercise 10

b. The hash table has size 2,048. The keys are strings that begin with a letter. The hash function is

$h(key)$ = (position in alphabet of first letter of key) mod 2048

Thus, "BUT" maps to 2. How appropriate is this hash function if the strings are random? What if the strings are English words?

c. The hash table is 10,000 entries long. The search keys are integers in the range 0 through 9999. The hash function is

$h(key) = (key * random)$ truncated to an integer

where $random$ represents a sophisticated random-number generator that returns a real value between 0 and 1.

d. The hash table is 10,000 entries long ($HASH\_TABLE\_SIZE$ is 10000). The search keys are integers in the range 0 through 9999. The hash function is given by the following Java method:

```java
public int hashIndex(int x) {
  for (int i = 1; i <= 1000000; ++i) {
    x = (x * x) % HASH_TABLE_SIZE;
  }  // end for
  return x;
}  // end hashIndex
```

Programming Problems

1. Implement the ADT table by using a 2-3-4 tree.

2. Implement the ADT table by using a 2-3 tree. (This implementation is more diffi-cult than the 2-3-4 implementation.)

3. Implement the ADT table by using a red-black tree.

4. Exercise 5 in Chapter 12 describes a compiler's symbol table, which keeps track of the program's identifiers. Write an implementation of a symbol table that uses hashing. Use the hash function $h(x)$ = x mod $tableSize$ and the algorithm that involves Horner's rule, as described in the section "Hash Functions," to convert a variable into an integer x. Resolve collisions by using separate chaining. (See the code given on pages 772 to 774 of this chapter.)

   Since you add an item to the table only if it is not already present, does the time required for an insertion increase?

5. Write a program that uses a hashing algorithm to create an inventory. After creating the hashed inventory list, write a driven code that allows the user to:

a. Search for any element in the list

b. Insert a new element into the list (with a collision resolving mechanism)

c. Display the contents of the inventory

6. Repeat Programming Problem 4, but allocate the hash table dynamically. If the hash table becomes more than half full, increase its size to the first prime number greater than 2 * *tableSize*.

7. Repeat Programming Problem 4, but experiment with variations of chaining. For example, you could use a binary search tree or a 2-3-4 tree instead of a linked list.

8. Implement the operations of the ADT queue as well as a sorted traversal operation for a queue that references a doubly linked list, as shown in Figure 13-53.

9. Implement the operations of the ADT queue as well as a sorted traversal operation for a queue that references a doubly linked binary search tree, as shown in Figure 13-54. You will need the insertion and deletion operations for a binary search tree that contains parent references, as discussed in Exercise 34 of Chapter 11.

10. Repeat Programming Problem 4 of Chapter 11, using the ADT table as the address book. Use a balanced search tree to implement the table.

11. Implement the symbol table described in Exercise 5 of Chapter 12 using hashing.

12. Modify the `HashMap` implementation found in this chapter so that the user can specify a load factor and a capacity as seen in the JCF `Hashtable` class. Be sure to include a rehash method as described in the `Hashtable` documentation.

CHAPTER 14

Graphs

Graphs are an important mathematical concept that have significant applications not only in computer science, but also in many other fields. You can view a graph as a mathematical construct, a data structure, or an abstract data type. This chapter provides an introduction to graphs that allows you to view a graph in any of these three ways. It also presents the major operations and applications of graphs that are relevant to the computer scientist.

14.1 Terminology

You are undoubtedly familiar with graphs: Line graphs, bar graphs, and pie charts are in common use. The simple line graph in Figure 14-1 is an example of the type of graph that this chapter considers: a set of points that are joined by lines. Clearly, graphs provide a way to illustrate data. However, graphs also represent the relationships among data items, and it is this feature of graphs that is important here.

$G = \{V, E\}$; that is, a graph is a set of vertices and edges

A **graph** G consists of two sets: a set V of **vertices**, or **nodes**, and a set E of **edges** that connect the vertices. For example, the campus map in Figure 14-2a is a graph whose vertices represent buildings and whose edges represent the sidewalks between the buildings. This definition of a graph is more general than the definition of a line graph. In fact, a line graph, with its points and lines, is a special case of the general definition of a graph.

Adjacent vertices are joined by an edge

A path between two vertices is a sequence of edges

A simple path passes through a vertex only once

A cycle is a path that begins and ends at the same vertex

A connected graph has a path between each pair of distinct vertices

A **subgraph** consists of a subset of a graph's vertices and a subset of its edges. Figure 14-2b shows a subgraph of the graph in Figure 14-2a. Two vertices of a graph are **adjacent** if they are joined by an edge. In Figure 14-2b, the Library and the Student Union are adjacent. A **path** between two vertices is a sequence of edges that begins at one vertex and ends at another vertex. For example, there is a path in Figure 14-2a that begins at the Dormitory, leads first to the Library, then to the Student Union, and finally back to the Library. Although a path may pass through the same vertex more than once, as the path just described does, a **simple path** may not. The path Dormitory–Library–Student Union is a simple path. A **cycle** is a path that begins and ends at the same vertex; a **simple cycle** is a cycle that does not pass through other vertices more than once. The path Library–Student Union–Gymnasium–Dormitory–Library is a simple cycle in the graph in Figure 14-2a. A graph is **connected** if each pair of distinct vertices has a path between them. That is, in a connected graph you can get from any vertex to any other vertex by following a path. Figure 14-3a shows a connected graph. Notice that a connected graph does not necessarily have an edge between every pair of vertices. Figure 14-3b shows a **disconnected** graph.

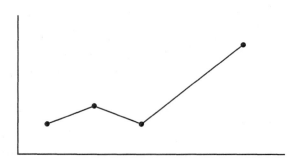

FIGURE 14-1

An ordinary line graph

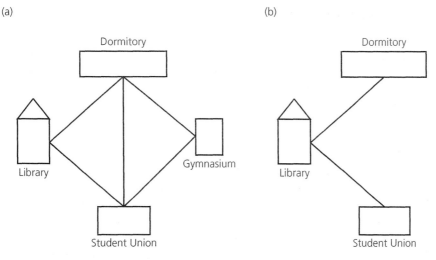

FIGURE 14-2

(a) A campus map as a graph; (b) a subgraph

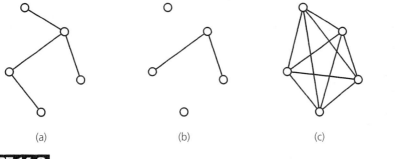

FIGURE 14-3

Graphs that are (a) connected; (b) disconnected; and (c) complete

In a **complete graph,** each pair of distinct vertices has an edge between them. The graph in Figure 14-3c is complete. Clearly, a complete graph is also connected, but the converse is not true; notice that the graph in Figure 14-3a is connected but is not complete.

Since a graph has a *set* of edges, a graph cannot have duplicate edges between vertices. However, a **multigraph,** as illustrated in Figure 14-4a, does allow multiple edges. A graph's edges cannot begin and end at the same vertex. Figure 14-4b shows such an edge, which is called a **self edge,** or **loop.**

You can label the edges of a graph. When these labels represent numeric values, the graph is called a **weighted graph.** The graph in Figure 14-5a is a weighted graph whose edges are labeled with the distances between cities.

All of the previous graphs are examples of **undirected** graphs because the edges do not indicate a direction. That is, you can travel in either direction along the edges between the vertices of an undirected graph. In contrast, each

A complete graph has an edge between each pair of distinct vertices

A complete graph is connected

A multigraph has multiple edges and so is not a graph

The edges of a weighted graph have numeric labels

Each edge in a directed graph has a direction

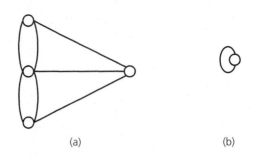

FIGURE 14-4

(a) A multigraph is not a graph; (b) a self edge is not allowed in a graph

edge in a **directed graph,** or **digraph,** has a direction and is called a **directed edge.** Although each distinct pair of vertices in an undirected graph has only one edge between them, a directed graph can have two edges between a pair of vertices, one in each direction. For example, the airline flight map in Figure 14-5b is a directed graph. There are flights in both directions between Providence and New York, but, although there is a flight from San Francisco to Albuquerque, there is no flight from Albuquerque to San Francisco. You can convert an undirected graph to a directed graph by replacing each edge with two edges that point in opposite directions.

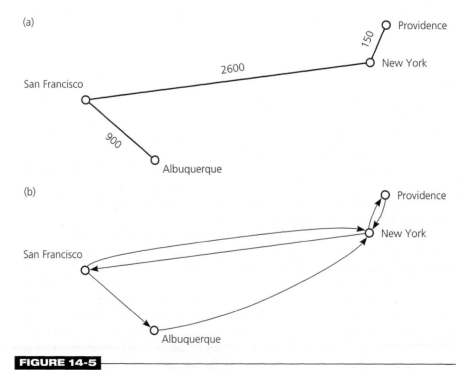

FIGURE 14-5

(a) A weighted graph; (b) a directed graph

The definitions just given for undirected graphs apply also to directed graphs, with changes that account for direction. For example, a **directed path** is a sequence of directed edges between two vertices, such as the directed path in Figure 14-5b that begins in Providence, goes to New York, and ends in San Francisco. However, the definition of adjacent vertices is not quite as obvious for a digraph. If there is a directed edge from vertex x to vertex y, then y is **adjacent** to x. (Alternatively, y is a **successor** of x, and x is a **predecessor** of y.) It does not necessarily follow, however, that x is adjacent to y. Thus, in Figure 14-5b, Albuquerque is adjacent to San Francisco, but San Francisco is not adjacent to Albuquerque.

> In a directed graph, vertex y is adjacent to vertex x if there is a directed edge from x to y

14.2 Graphs as ADTs

You can treat graphs as abstract data types. Insertion and deletion operations are somewhat different for graphs than for other ADTs that you have studied in that they apply to either vertices or edges. You can define the ADT graph so that its vertices either do or do not contain values. A graph whose vertices do not contain values represents only the relationships among vertices. Such graphs are not unusual, because many problems have no need for vertex values. However, the following operations of the ADT graph do assume that the graph's vertices contain values.

KEY CONCEPTS

Operations of the ADT Graph

1. Create an empty graph.

2. Determine whether a graph is empty.

3. Determine the number of vertices in a graph.

4. Determine the number of edges in a graph.

5. Determine whether an edge exists between two given vertices. For weighted graphs, return weight value.

6. Insert a vertex in a graph whose vertices have distinct search keys that differ from the new vertex's search key.

7. Insert an edge between two given vertices in a graph.

8. Delete a particular vertex from a graph and any edges between the vertex and other vertices.

9. Delete the edge between two given vertices in a graph.

10. Retrieve from a graph the vertex that contains a given search key.

Several variations of this ADT are possible. For example, if the graph is directed, you can replace occurrences of "edges" in the previous operations with "directed edges." You can also add traversal operations to the ADT. Graph-traversal algorithms are discussed in the section "Graph Traversals."

Implementing Graphs

Adjacency matrix

The two most common implementations of a graph are the adjacency matrix and the adjacency list. An **adjacency matrix** for a graph with n vertices numbered $0, 1, \ldots, n-1$ is an n by n array $matrix$ such that $matrix[i][j]$ is 1 (or $true$) if there is an edge from vertex i to vertex j, and 0 (or $false$) otherwise. Figure 14-6 shows a directed graph and its adjacency matrix. Notice that the diagonal entries $matrix[i][i]$ are 0, although sometimes it can be useful to set these entries to 1. You should choose the value that is most convenient for your application.

When the graph is weighted, you can let $matrix[i][j]$ be the weight that labels the edge from vertex i to vertex j, instead of simply 1, and let $matrix[i][j]$ equal ∞ instead of 0 when there is no edge from vertex i to vertex j. For example, Figure 14-7 shows a weighted undirected graph and its adjacency matrix. Notice that the adjacency matrix for an undirected graph is symmetrical; that is, $matrix[i][j]$ equals $matrix[j][i]$.

Vertices can have values

Our definition of an adjacency matrix does not mention the value, if any, in a vertex. If you need to associate values with vertices, you can use a second array, $values$, to represent the n vertex values. The $values$ array is one-dimensional, and $values[i]$ is the value in vertex i.

(a)

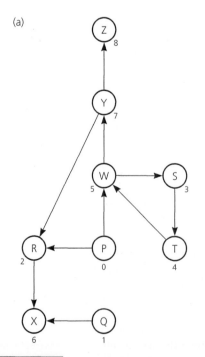

(b)

		0	1	2	3	4	5	6	7	8
		P	Q	R	S	T	W	X	Y	Z
0	P	0	0	1	0	0	1	0	0	0
1	Q	0	0	0	0	0	0	1	0	0
2	R	0	0	0	0	0	0	1	0	0
3	S	0	0	0	0	1	0	0	0	0
4	T	0	0	0	0	0	1	0	0	0
5	W	0	0	0	1	0	0	0	1	0
6	X	0	0	0	0	0	0	0	0	0
7	Y	0	0	1	0	0	0	0	0	1
8	Z	0	0	0	0	0	0	0	0	0

FIGURE 14-6

(a) A directed graph and (b) its adjacency matrix

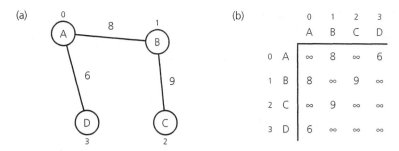

FIGURE 14-7

(a) A weighted undirected graph and (b) its adjacency matrix

An **adjacency list** for a graph with n vertices numbered $0, 1, \ldots, n-1$ Adjacency list
consists of n linked lists. The ith linked list has a node for vertex j if and only if
the graph contains an edge from vertex i to vertex j. This node can contain the
vertex j's value, if any. If the vertex has no value, the node needs to contain
some indication of the vertex's identity. Figure 14-8 shows a directed graph
and its adjacency list. You can see, for example, that vertex 0 (P) has edges to
vertex 2 (R) and vertex 5 (W). Thus, the first linked list in the adjacency list
contains nodes for R and W.

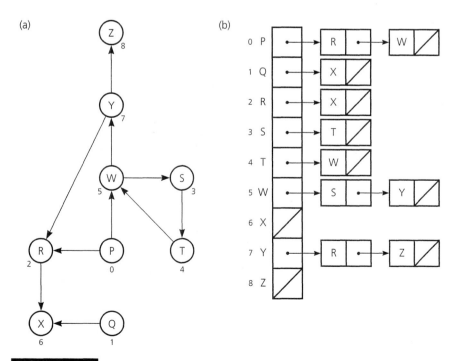

FIGURE 14-8

(a) A directed graph and (b) its adjacency list

Figure 14-9 shows an undirected graph and its adjacency list. The adjacency list for an undirected graph treats each edge as if it were two directed edges in opposite directions. Thus, the edge between *A* and *B* in Figure 14-9a appears as edges from *A* to *B* and from *B* to *A* in Figure 14-9b. The graph in part *a* happens to be weighted; you can include the edge weights in the nodes of the adjacency list, given in part *b*.

Which of these two implementations of a graph—the adjacency matrix or the adjacency list—is better? The answer depends on how your particular application uses the graph. For example, the two most commonly performed graph operations are

> Two common operations on graphs

1. Determine whether there is an edge from vertex *i* to vertex *j*

2. Find all vertices adjacent to a given vertex *i*

> An adjacency matrix supports operation 1 more efficiently

The adjacency matrix supports the first operation somewhat more efficiently than does the adjacency list. To determine whether there is an edge from *i* to *j* by using an adjacency matrix, you need only examine the value of `matrix[i][j]`. If you use an adjacency list, however, you must traverse the ith linked list to determine whether a vertex corresponding to vertex *j* is present.

> An adjacency list supports operation 2 more efficiently

The second operation, on the other hand, is supported more efficiently by the adjacency list. To determine all vertices adjacent to a given vertex *i*, given the adjacency matrix, you must traverse the ith row of the array; however, given the adjacency list, you need only traverse the ith linked list. For a graph with *n* vertices, the ith row of the adjacency matrix always has *n* entries, whereas the ith linked list has only as many nodes as there are vertices adjacent to vertex *i*, a number typically far less than *n*.

Consider now the space requirements of the two implementations. On the surface it might appear that the matrix implementation requires less memory than the linked list implementation, because each entry in the matrix is simply an integer, whereas each linked list node contains both a value to identify the

(a)   (b)

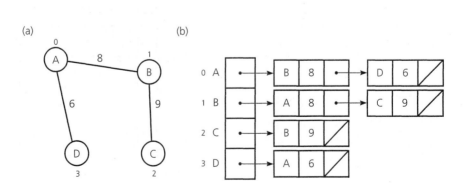

FIGURE 14-9

(a) A weighted undirected graph and (b) its adjacency list

vertex and a reference to the next node. The adjacency matrix, however, always has n^2 entries, whereas the number of nodes in an adjacency list equals the number of edges in a directed graph or twice that number for an undirected graph. Even though the adjacency list also has n head references, it often requires less storage than an adjacency matrix.

An adjacency list often requires less space than an adjacency matrix

Thus, when choosing a graph implementation for a particular application, you must consider such factors as what operations you will perform most frequently on the graph and the number of edges that the graph is likely to contain. For example, Chapter 7 presented the HPAir problem, which was to determine whether an airline provided a sequence of flights from an origin city to a destination city. The flight map for that problem, is in fact, a directed graph and appeared earlier in this chapter in Figure 14-8a. Figures 14-6b and 14-8b show, respectively, the adjacency matrix and adjacency list for this graph. Because the most frequent operation was to find all cities (vertices) adjacent to a given city (vertex), the adjacency list would be the more efficient implementation of the flight map. The adjacency list also requires less storage than the adjacency matrix, which you can demonstrate as an exercise.

Implementing a Graph Class Using the JCF

The ADT graph is not included as part of the Java Collections Framework. In this section, a `Graph` class will be implemented using classes from the JCF. Graph classes and their accompanying algorithms can be implemented in many different ways. The `Graph` class in this section is an undirected, weighted graph. It is implemented with an adjacency list, which consists of a vector of maps. The vector elements represent the vertices of the graph. The map for each vertex contains element pairs, which consist of an adjacent vertex and an edge weight. There are numerous choices within the JCF for the actual adjacency list. This implementation uses the `TreeSet` class, an implementation of `SortedMap`. This allows the list of adjacent vertices (the keys) to be stored in sorted order.

The number of vertices in the graph is determined by an integer argument passed to the `Graph` constructor. An `Edge` class hold the two vertices of an edge and the edge weight. Many of the methods in the `Graph` class utilize the `Edge` class. For example, the client application can add an edge to the graph by passing an `Edge` object to the `addEdge` method. Here is the code for the `Edge` class and the `Graph` class:

```
class Edge {

    private Integer v, w;    // The vertices of the edge.
    private int weight;      // The weight of the edge.

    public Edge(Integer first, Integer second, int edgeWeight) {
        // Constructor. Creates an edge from v to w with weight
        // edgeWeight.
        // Precondition: None.
        // Postcondition: The edge is created.
```

```
      v = first;
      w = second;
      weight = edgeWeight;
    } // end constructor

    public int getWeight() {
      // Returns the edge weight
      return weight;
    } // end getWeight

    public Integer getV() {
      // Returns the first vertex of the edge
      return v;
    } // end getV

    public Integer getW() {
      // Returns the second vertex of the edge
      return w;
    } // end getW
  } // end Edge


  class Graph {
    private int numVertices; // number of vertices in the graph
    private int numEdges;    // number of edges in the graph

    // For each vertex, we need to keep track of the edges,
    // so for each edge, we need to store the second vertex and
    // the edge weight. This can be done as a <key, value> pair,
    // with the second vertex as the key, and the weight as the
    // value. The TreeMap data structure is used to store a list
    // these (key, value) pairs for each vertex, accessible as
    // adjList.get(v).
    private Vector<TreeMap<Integer, Integer>> adjList;

    public Graph(int n) {
      // Constructor for weighted graph.
      // Precondition: The number of vertices n should be
      // greater than zero.
      // Postcondition: Initializes the graph with n vertices.
      numVertices = n;
      numEdges = 0;
      adjList = new Vector<TreeMap<Integer, Integer>>();
      for (int i=0; i<numVertices; i++) {
        adjList.add(new TreeMap<Integer, Integer>());
      } // end for
    } // end constructor
```

```java
public int getNumVertices() {
   // Determines the number of vertices in the graph.
   // Precondition: None.
   // Postcondition: Returns the number of vertices in
   // the graph.
   return numVertices;
} // end getNumVertices

public int getNumEdges() {
   // Determines the number of edges in the graph.
   // Precondition: None.
   // Postcondition: Returns the number of edges in
   // the graph.
   return numEdges;
} // end getNumEdges

public int getEdgeWeight(Integer v, Integer w) {
   // Determines the weight of the edge between vertices
   // v and w.
   // Precondition: The edge must exist in the graph.
   // Postcondition: Returns the weight of the edge.
   return adjList.get(v).get(w);
} // end getWeight

public void addEdge(Integer v, Integer w, int wgt) {
   // Adds an edge from v to w with weight wgt to the graph.
   // Precondition: The vertices contained within
   // edge e exist in the graph.
   // Postcondition: An edge from v to w is part of the
   // graph.

   // Add the edge to both v's and w's adjacency list
   adjList.get(v).put(w, wgt);
   adjList.get(w).put(v, wgt);
   numEdges++;
} // end addEdge

public void addEdge(Edge e) {
   // Adds an edge to the graph.
   // Precondition: The vertices contained within
   // edge e exist in the graph.
   // Postcondition: Edge e is part of the graph.

   // Extract the vertices and weight from the edge e
   Integer v = e.getV();
   Integer w = e.getW();
   int weight = e.getWeight();
```

```
        addEdge(v, w, weight);
    } // end addEdge

    public void removeEdge(Edge e) {
        // Removes an edge from the graph.
        // Precondition: The vertices contained in the edge e
        // exist in the graph.
        // Postcondition: Edge e is no longer part of the graph.

        // Extract the vertices from the edge e
        Integer v = e.getV();
        Integer w = e.getW();

        // Remove the edge from v's and w's adjacency list
        adjList.get(v).remove(w);
        adjList.get(w).remove(v);
        numEdges--;
    } // end remove

    public Edge findEdge(Integer v, Integer w) {
        // Finds the edge connecting v and w.
        // Precondition: The edge exists.
        // Postcondition: Returns the edge with the weight.
        int wgt = adjList.get(v).get(w);
        return new Edge(v, w, wgt);
    } // end findEdge

    // package access
    TreeMap<Integer,Integer> getAdjList(Integer v) {
        // Returns the adjacency list for given vertex
        // Precondition: The vertex exists in the graph
        // Postcondition: Returns the associated adjacency
        // list.
        return adjList.get(v);
    } // end getAdjList

} // end Graph
```

The programming problems at the end of the chapter ask you to add other methods and exception handling to the *Graph* class, modify the class to represent a directed graph, and to rewrite the *Graph* class as a template.

14.3 Graph Traversals

The solution to the HPAir problem in Chapter 7 involved an exhaustive search of the graph in Figure 14-8a to determine a directed path from the origin vertex (city) to the destination vertex (city). The algorithm *searchS* started at a given vertex and traversed edges to other vertices until it either found the desired vertex or determined that no (directed) path existed between the two vertices.

What distinguishes *searchS* from a standard graph traversal is that *searchS* stops when it first encounters the designated destination vertex. A **graph-traversal algorithm,** on the other hand, will not stop until it has visited *all of the vertices that it can reach*. That is, a graph traversal that starts at vertex *v* will visit all vertices *w* for which there is a path between *v* and *w*. Unlike a tree traversal, which always visits *all* of the nodes in a tree, a graph traversal does not necessarily visit all of the vertices in the graph unless the graph is connected. In fact, a graph traversal visits every vertex in the graph if and only if the graph is connected, regardless of where the traversal starts. (See Exercise 18.) Thus, you can use a graph traversal to determine whether a graph is connected.

A graph traversal visits all of the vertices that it can reach

A graph traversal visits all vertices only if the graph is connected

If a graph is not connected, a graph traversal that begins at vertex *v* will visit only a subset of the graph's vertices. This subset is called the **connected component** containing *v*. You can determine all of the connected components of a graph by repeatedly starting a traversal at an unvisited vertex.

A connected component is the subset of vertices visited during a traversal that begins at a given vertex

If a graph contains a cycle, a graph-traversal algorithm can loop indefinitely. To prevent such a misfortune, the algorithm must mark each vertex during a visit and must never visit a vertex more than once.

Two basic graph-traversal algorithms, which apply to either directed or undirected graphs, are presented next. These algorithms visit the vertices in different orders, but if they both start at the same vertex, they will visit the same set of vertices. Figure 14-10 shows the traversal order for the two algorithms when they begin at vertex *v*.

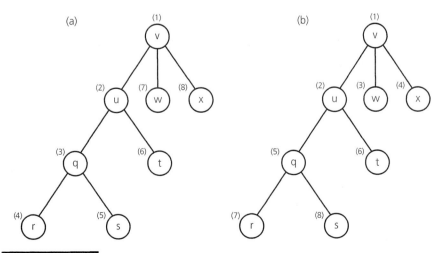

FIGURE 14-10

Visitation order for (a) a depth-first search; (b) a breadth-first search

Depth-First Search

DFS traversal goes
as far as possible
from a vertex before
backing up

From a given vertex v, the **depth-first search (DFS)** strategy of graph traversal proceeds along a path from v as deeply into the graph as possible before backing up. That is, after visiting a vertex, a DFS visits, if possible, an unvisited adjacent vertex.

The DFS strategy has a simple recursive form:

Recursive DFS tra-
versal algorithm

```
+dfs(in v:Vertex)
// Traverses a graph beginning at vertex v by using a
// depth-first search: Recursive version.

   Mark v as visited
   for (each unvisited vertex u adjacent to v)
      dfs(u)
```

Choose an order in
which to visit adja-
cent vertices

The depth-first search algorithm does not completely specify the order in which it should visit the vertices adjacent to v. One possibility is to visit the vertices adjacent to v in sorted (that is, alphabetic or numerically increasing) order. This possibility is natural either when an adjacency matrix represents the graph or when the nodes in each linked list of an adjacency list are linked in sorted order.

As Figure 14-10a illustrates, the DFS traversal algorithm marks and then visits each of the vertices v, u, q, and r. When the traversal reaches a vertex—such as r—that has no unvisited adjacent vertices, it backs up and visits, if possible, an unvisited adjacent vertex. Thus, the traversal backs up to q and then visits s. Continuing in this manner, the traversal visits vertices in the order given in the figure.

An iterative version of the DFS algorithm is also possible by using a stack:

An iterative DFS tra-
versal algorithm
uses a stack

```
+dfs(in v:Vertex)
// Traverses a graph beginning at vertex v by using a
// depth-first search: Iterative version.

  s.createStack()

  // push v onto the stack and mark it
  s.push(v)
  Mark v as visited

  // loop invariant: there is a path from vertex v at the
  // bottom of the stack s to the vertex at the top of s
  while (!s.isEmpty()) {
    if (no unvisited vertices are adjacent to
        the vertex on the top of the stack)
      s.pop()  // backtrack
    }
```

```
else {
    Select an unvisited vertex u adjacent to
        the vertex on the top of the stack
    s.push(u)
    Mark u as visited
    }   // end if
}   // end while
```

The *dfs* algorithm is similar to the *searchS* algorithm of Chapter 7, but the while statement in *searchS* terminates when the top of the stack is *destination*.

For another example of a DFS traversal, consider the graph in Figure 14-11. Figure 14-12 shows the contents of the stack as the previous method *dfs* visits vertices in this graph, beginning at vertex *a*. Because the graph is connected, a DFS traversal will visit every vertex. In fact, the traversal visits the vertices in this order: *a, b, c, d, g, e, f, h, i*.

The vertex from which a depth-first traversal embarks is the vertex that it visited most recently. This *last visited, first explored* strategy is reflected both in the explicit stack of vertices that the iterative *dfs* uses and in the implicit stack of vertices that the recursive *dfs* generates with its recursive calls.

Breadth-First Search

After visiting a given vertex *v*, the **breadth-first search (BFS)** strategy of graph traversal visits every vertex adjacent to *v* that it can before visiting any other vertex. As Figure 14-10b illustrates, after marking and visiting *v*, the BFS traversal algorithm marks and then visits each of the vertices *u*, *w*, and *x*. Since no other vertices are adjacent to *v*, the BFS algorithm visits, if possible, all unvisited vertices adjacent to *u*. Thus, the traversal visits *q* and *t*. Continuing in this manner, the traversal visits vertices in the order given in the figure.

A BFS traversal will not embark from any of the vertices adjacent to *v* until it has visited all possible vertices adjacent to *v*. Whereas a DFS is a *last visited,*

> BFS traversal visits all vertices adjacent to a vertex before going forward

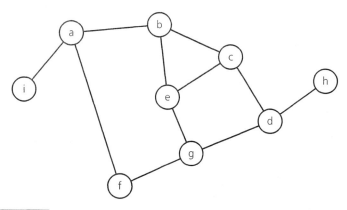

FIGURE 14-11

A connected graph with cycles

Node visited	Stack (bottom to top)
a	a
b	a b
c	a b c
d	a b c d
g	a b c d g
e	a b c d g e
(backtrack)	a b c d g
f	a b c d g f
(backtrack)	a b c d g
(backtrack)	a b c d
h	a b c d h
(backtrack)	a b c d
(backtrack)	a b c
(backtrack)	a b
(backtrack)	a
i	a i
(backtrack)	a
(backtrack)	(empty)

FIGURE 14-12

The results of a depth-first traversal, beginning at vertex *a*, of the graph in Figure 14-11

An iterative BFS traversal algorithm uses a queue

first explored strategy, a BFS is a *first visited, first explored* strategy. It is not surprising, then, that a breadth-first search uses a queue. An iterative version of this algorithm follows.

```
+bfs(in v:Vertex)
// Traverses a graph beginning at vertex v by using a
// breadth-first search: Iterative version.

  q.createQueue()

  // add v to queue and mark it
  q.enqueue(v)
  Mark v as visited

  while (!q.isEmpty()) {
      w = q.dequeue()

      // loop invariant: there is a path from vertex w to
      // every vertex in the queue q
```

```
    for (each unvisited vertex u adjacent to w) {
        Mark u as visited
        q.enqueue(u)
    }  // end for
}  // end while
```

Figure 14-13 shows the contents of the queue as *bfs* visits vertices in the graph in Figure 14-11, beginning at vertex *a*. In general, a breadth-first search will visit the same vertices as a depth-first search, but in a different order. In this example, the BFS traversal visits all of the vertices in this order: *a, b, f, i, c, e, g, d, h.*

A recursive version of BFS traversal is not as simple as the recursive version of DFS traversal. Exercise 19 at the end of this chapter asks you to think about why this is so.

A recursive BFS traversal algorithm is possible, but not simple

Implementing a BFS Iterator Class Using the JCF

A breadth-first search iterator for the *LinkedList* class in the previous section can be implemented using the JCF *LinkedList* collection. The *BFSIterator*

Node visited	Queue (front to back)
a	a
	(empty)
b	b
f	b f
i	b f i
	f i
c	f i c
e	f i c e
	i c e
g	i c e g
	c e g
	e g
d	e g d
	g d
	d
	(empty)
h	h
	(empty)

FIGURE 14-13

The results of a breadth-first traversal, beginning at vertex *a*, of the graph in Figure 14-11

class uses the *LinkedList* class as a queue to keep track of the order the vertices should be processed to create a breadth-first iteration of the graph. The *BFSIterator* has a constructor that given a graph, initiates the methods used to determine the BFS order of the vertices for the graph. The graph is searched by processing the vertices from each vertex's adjacency list in the order that they were pushed onto the queue. The code for the *BFSIterator* class follows.

```
class BFSIterator implements Iterator<Integer> {

  private Graph g;          // The graph to be iterated.
  private int numVertices;  // The number of vertices in the graph.
  private int count;        // Used to mark the order the
                            // vertices are visited.
  private int[] mark;       // Keeps track of the order that
                            // the vertices are visited.
  private int iter;         // Used for the iteration.

  public BFSIterator(Graph g) {
    // Creates an iterator for the graph g.
    // Precondition: The graph g is a non-empty graph.
    // Postcondition: Completes the Breadth-first search
    // of graph g, ready for iteration.
    this.g = g;
    numVertices = g.getNumVertices();
    mark = new int[numVertices];
    Arrays.fill(mark,0,numVertices,-1);

    count = 0;
    iter = -1;
    startSearch();
  } // end constructor

  public boolean hasNext() {
    // Determines if there is another vertex in the BFS
    // iteration of the graph.
    // Precondition: None.
    // Postcondition: Returns true if there are more vertices
    // in the BFS iteration, otherwise returns false.
    return (iter >=0) && (iter < numVertices);
  } // end hasNext

  public Integer next() throws NoSuchElementException {
    // Returns the next vertex in the BFS iteration
    // of the graph.
    // Precondition: The BFS iteration has more vertices.
    // Postcondition: Returns next element in the BFS
    // iteration, if none exists, throws an exception.
```

```java
    if (hasNext()) {
      return mark[iter++];
    } else {
      throw new NoSuchElementException();
    }   // end if
} // end next

public void remove() {
  // Not implemented, vertices cannot be removed
  // from the graph using the iterator.
  throw new UnsupportedOperationException();
} // end remove

protected void startSearch() {
  // Searches each unvisited vertex.
  // Precondition: The vertex exists in the graph.
  // Postcondition: Completes a breadth-first search
  // with each unvisited vertex.

  for (int v=0; v < numVertices; v++) {
    if (mark[v] == -1) {
      search(v);
    } // end if
  } // end for

  // Breadth-first search completed, initialize
  // iterator.
  iter = 0;
} // end startSearch

protected void search(Integer vertex) {
  // Traverse the graph beginning at vertex v by using
  // a breadth-first search.
  // Precondition: The vertex v is in the graph.
  // Postcondition: Completes a breadth-first search
  // starting from vertex.

  LinkedList<Integer> q = new LinkedList<Integer>();
  TreeMap<Integer, Integer> m;
  Set<Integer> connectedVertices;
  Integer v;

  // This gets it started at vertex v
  q.add(vertex);

  while (!q.isEmpty()) {
    v = q.remove();
```

```
        if (mark[v] == -1) {
          mark[v] = count++;

          m = g.getAdjList(v);
          connectedVertices = m.keySet();
          for (Integer w : connectedVertices) {
            if (mark[w] == -1) {
              q.add(w);
            } // end if
          } // end for
        } // end if

      } // end while
    } // end search

  } // end BFS
```

14.4 Applications of Graphs

There are many useful applications of graphs. This section surveys some of these common applications.

Topological Sorting

A directed graph without cycles, such as the one in Figure 14-14, has a natural order. For example, vertex *a* precedes *b*, which precedes *c*. Such a graph has significance in ordinary life. If the vertices represent academic courses, the graph represents the prerequisite structure for the courses. For example, course *a* is a prerequisite to course *b*, which is a prerequisite to both courses *c* and *e*. In what order should you take all seven courses so that

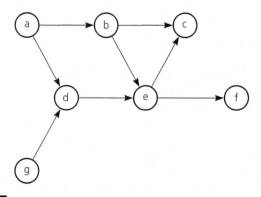

FIGURE 14-14

A directed graph without cycles

you will satisfy all prerequisites? There is a linear order, called a **topological order,** of the vertices in a directed graph without cycles that answers this question. In a list of vertices in topological order, vertex x precedes vertex y if there is a directed edge from x to y in the graph.

The vertices in a given graph may have several topological orders. For example, two topological orders for the vertices in Figure 14-14 are

a, g, d, b, e, c, f

and

a, b, g, d, e, f, c

If you arrange the vertices of a directed graph linearly and in a topological order, the edges will all point in one direction. Figure 14-15 shows two versions of the graph in Figure 14-14 that correspond to the two topological orders just given.

Arranging the vertices into a topological order is called **topological sorting.** There are several simple algorithms for finding a topological order. First, you could find a vertex that has no successor. You remove from the graph the vertex and all edges that lead to it, and add it to the beginning of a list of vertices. You add each subsequent vertex that has no successor to the beginning of the list. When the graph is empty, the list of vertices will be in topological order. The following pseudocode describes this algorithm:

```
+topSort1(in theGraph:Graph)
// Arranges the vertices in graph theGraph into a
// topological order and places them in list aList
// Returns aList.

    n = number of vertices in theGraph
    for (step = 1 through n) {
        Select a vertex v that has no successors
        aList.add(1, v)
```

A simple topological sorting algorithm

(a)

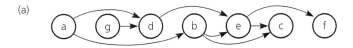

(b)

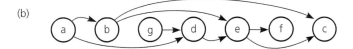

FIGURE 14-15

The graph in Figure 14-14 arranged according to the topological orders (a) *a, g, d, b, e, c, f* and (b) *a, b, g, d, e, f, c*

```
        Delete from theGraph vertex v and its edges
    } // end for
    return aList
```

When the traversal ends, the list *aList* of vertices will be in topological order. Figure 14-16 traces this algorithm for the graph in Figure 14-14. The resulting topological order is the one that Figure 14-15a represents.

Another algorithm is a simple modification of the iterative depth-first search algorithm. First you push all vertices that have no predecessor onto a

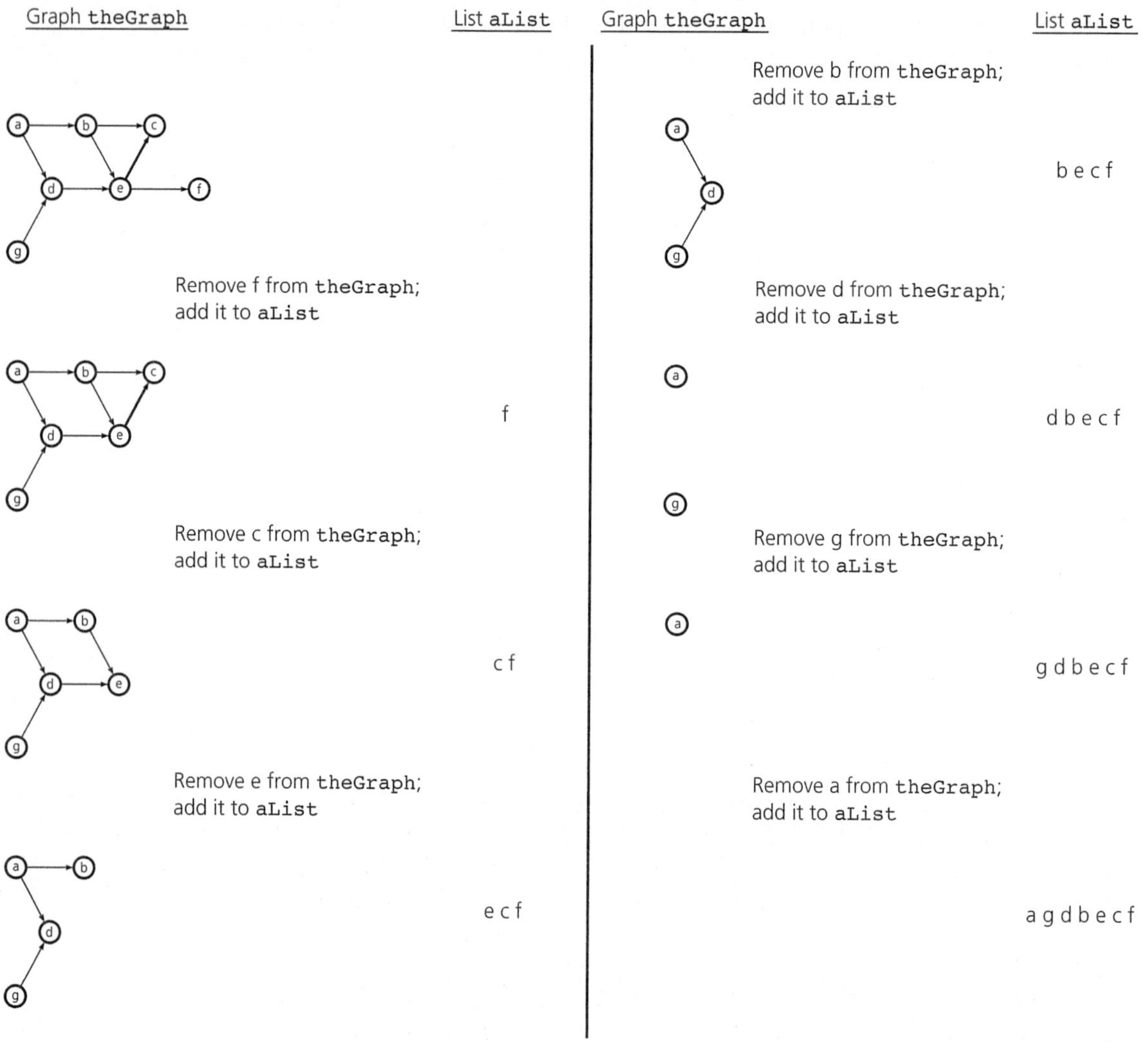

Remove f from theGraph; add it to aList

Remove c from theGraph; add it to aList

Remove e from theGraph; add it to aList

Remove b from theGraph; add it to aList

Remove d from theGraph; add it to aList

Remove g from theGraph; add it to aList

Remove a from theGraph; add it to aList

FIGURE 14-16

A trace of **topSort1** for the graph in Figure 14-14

stack. Each time you pop a vertex from the stack, you add it to the beginning of a list of vertices. The pseudocode for this algorithm is

```
+topSort2(in theGraph:Graph):List
// Arranges the vertices in graph theGraph into a
// topological order and places them in list aList.
// Returns aList.

    s.createStack()
    for (all vertices v in the graph theGraph) {
        if (v has no predecessors) {
            s.push(v)
            Mark v as visited
        }  // end if
    }  // end for

while (!s.isEmpty()) {
    if (all vertices adjacent to the vertex on
            the top of the stack have been visited) {
        v = s.pop()
        aList.add(1, v)
    }
    else {
        Select an unvisited vertex u adjacent to
          the vertex on the top of the stack
        s.push(u)
        Mark u as visited
    }  // end if
}  // end while
return aList
```

The DFS topological sorting algorithm

When the traversal ends, the list `aList` of vertices will be in topological order. Figure 14-17 traces this algorithm for the graph in Figure 14-14. The resulting topological order is the one that Figure 14-15b represents.

Spanning Trees

A tree is a special kind of undirected graph, one that is connected but has no cycles. Each vertex in the graph in Figure 14-3a could be the root of a different tree. Although all trees are graphs, not all graphs are trees. The nodes (vertices) of a tree have a hierarchical arrangement that is not required of all graphs.

A **spanning tree** of a connected undirected graph *G* is a subgraph of *G* that contains all of *G*'s vertices and enough of its edges to form a tree. For example, Figure 14-18 shows a spanning tree for the graph in Figure 14-11. The dashed lines in Figure 14-18 indicate edges that were omitted from the graph to form the tree. There may be several spanning trees for a given graph.

A tree is an undirected connected graph without cycles

Action	Stack s (bottom to top)	List aList (beginning to end)
Push a	a	
Push g	a g	
Push d	a g d	
Push e	a g d e	
Push c	a g d e c	
Pop c, add c to aList	a g d e	c
Push f	a g d e f	c
Pop f, add f to aList	a g d e	f c
Pop e, add e to aList	a g d	e f c
Pop d, add d to aList	a g	d e f c
Pop g, add g to aList	a	g d e f c
Push b	a b	g d e f c
Pop b, add b to aList	a	b g d e f c
Pop a, add a to aList	(empty)	a b g d e f c

FIGURE 14-17

A trace of *topSort2* for the graph in Figure 14-14

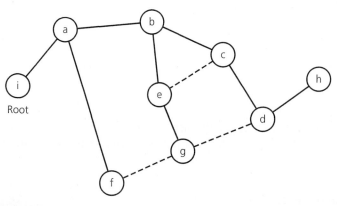

FIGURE 14-18

A spanning tree for the graph in Figure 14-11

If you have a connected undirected graph with cycles and you remove edges until there are no cycles, you will obtain a spanning tree for the graph. It is relatively simple to determine whether a graph contains a cycle. One way to make this determination is based on the following observations about undirected graphs:

1. **A connected undirected graph that has *n* vertices must have at least *n* − 1 edges.** To establish this fact, recall that a connected graph has a path between every pair of vertices. Suppose that, beginning with *n* vertices, you choose one vertex and draw an edge between it and any other vertex. Next, draw an edge between this second vertex and any other unattached vertex. If you continue this process until you run out of unattached vertices, you will get a connected graph like the ones in Figure 14-19. If the graph has *n* vertices, it has *n* − 1 edges. In addition, if you remove an edge, the graph will not be connected.

2. **A connected undirected graph that has *n* vertices and exactly *n* − 1 edges cannot contain a cycle.** To see this, begin with the previous observation: To be connected, a graph with *n* vertices must have at least *n* − 1 edges. If a connected graph did have a cycle, you could remove any edge along that cycle and still have a connected graph. Thus, if a connected graph with *n* vertices and *n* − 1 edges did contain a cycle, removing an edge along the cycle would leave you with a connected graph with only *n* − 2 edges, which is impossible according to observation 1.

3. **A connected undirected graph that has *n* vertices and more than *n* − 1 edges must contain at least one cycle.** For example, if you add an edge to any of the graphs in Figure 14-19, you will create a cycle within the graph. This fact is harder to establish and is left as an exercise. (See Exercise 17 at the end of this chapter.)

Observations about undirected graphs that enable you to detect a cycle

Thus, you can determine whether a connected graph contains a cycle simply by counting its vertices and edges.

It follows, then, that a tree, which is a connected undirected graph without cycles, must connect its *n* nodes with *n* − 1 edges. Thus, to obtain the spanning tree of a connected graph of *n* vertices, you must remove edges along cycles until *n* − 1 edges are left.

Simply count a graph's vertices and edges to determine whether it contains a cycle

Two algorithms for determining a spanning tree of a graph are based on the previous traversal algorithms and are presented next. In general, these algorithms will produce different spanning trees for any particular graph.

The DFS spanning tree.   One way to determine a spanning tree for a connected undirected graph is to traverse the graph's vertices by using a depth-first search. As you traverse the graph, mark the edges that you follow. After the traversal

FIGURE 14-19

Connected graphs that each have four vertices and three edges is complete, the graph's vertices and marked edges form a spanning tree, which is called the **depth-first search (DFS) spanning tree.** (Alternatively, you can remove the unmarked edges from the graph to form the spanning tree.) Simple modifications to the previous iterative and recursive versions of *dfs* result in algorithms to create a DFS spanning tree. For example, the recursive algorithm follows:

DFS spanning tree algorithm

```
+dfsTree(in v:Vertex)
// Forms a spanning tree for a connected undirected graph
// beginning at vertex v by using depth-first search:
// Recursive version.

    Mark v as visited

    for (each unvisited vertex u adjacent to v) {
        Mark the edge from u to v
        dfsTree(u)
    }  // end for
```

When you apply this algorithm to the graph in Figure 14-11, you get the DFS spanning tree rooted at vertex *a* shown in Figure 14-20. The figure indicates the order in which the algorithm visits vertices and marks edges. You should reproduce these results by tracing the algorithm.

The BFS spanning tree. Another way to determine a spanning tree for a connected undirected graph is to traverse the graph's vertices by using a breadth-first search. As you traverse the graph, mark the edges that you follow. After the traversal is complete, the graph's vertices and marked edges form a spanning tree, which is called the **breadth-first search (BFS) spanning tree.** (Alternatively, you can remove the unmarked edges from the graph to form the spanning tree.) You can modify the previous iterative version of *bfs* by

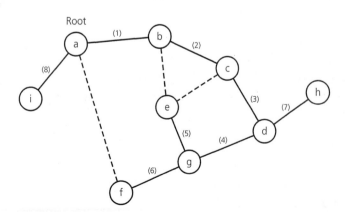

The DFS spanning tree algorithm visits vertices in this order: a, b, c, d, g, e, f, h, i. Numbers indicate the order in which the algorithm marks edges.

FIGURE 14-20

The DFS spanning tree rooted at vertex *a* for the graph in Figure 14-11 marking the edge between *w* and *u* before you add *u* to the queue. The result is the following iterative algorithm to create a BFS spanning tree.

```
+bfsTree(in v:Vertex)
// Forms a spanning tree for a connected undirected graph
// beginning at vertex v by using breadth-first search:
// Iterative version.

   q.createQueue()

   // add v to queue and mark it
   q.enqueue(v)
   Mark v as visited

   while (!q.isEmpty() {
      w = q.dequeue()

      // loop invariant: there is a path from vertex w to
      // every vertex in the queue q
      for (each unvisited vertex u adjacent to w) {
         Mark u as visited
         Mark edge between w and u
         q.enqueue(u)
      }  // end for
   }  // end while
```

When you apply this algorithm to the graph in Figure 14-11, you get the BFS spanning tree rooted at vertex *a* shown in Figure 14-21. The figure indicates the order in which the algorithm visits vertices and marks edges. You should reproduce these results by tracing the algorithm.

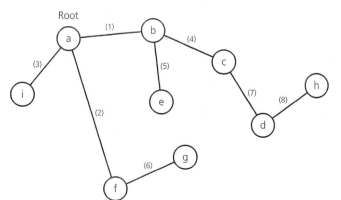

The BFS spanning tree algorithm visits vertices in this order: a, b, f, i, c, e, g, d, h. Numbers indicate the order in which the algorithm marks edges.

FIGURE 14-21

The BFS spanning tree rooted at vertex *a* for the graph in Figure 14-11

Minimum Spanning Trees

Imagine that a developing country hires you to design its telephone system so that all the cities in the country can call one another. Obviously, one solution is to place telephone lines between every pair of cities. However, your engineering team has determined that due to the country's mountainous terrain, it is impossible to put lines between certain pairs of cities. The team's report contains the weighted undirected graph in Figure 14-22. The vertices in the graph represent n cities. An edge between two vertices indicates that it is feasible to place a telephone line between the cities that the vertices represent, and each edge's weight represents the installation cost of the telephone line. Note that if this graph is not connected, you will be unable to link all of the cities with a network of telephone lines. The graph in Figure 14-22 is connected, however, making the problem feasible.

If you install a telephone line between each pair of cities that is connected by an edge in the graph, you will certainly solve the problem. However, this solution may be too costly. From observation 1 in the previous section, you know that $n - 1$ is the minimum number of edges necessary for a graph of n vertices to be connected. Thus, $n - 1$ is the minimum number of lines that can connect n cities.

If the cost of installing each line is the same, the problem is reduced to one of finding any spanning tree of the graph. The total installation cost—that is, the **cost of the spanning tree**—is the sum of the costs of the edges in the spanning tree. However, as the graph in Figure 14-22 shows, the cost of installing each line varies. Because there may be more than one spanning tree, and because the cost of different trees may vary, you need to solve the problem by selecting a spanning tree with the least cost; that is, you must select a spanning tree for which the sum of the edge weights (costs) is minimal. Such a tree is called the **minimum spanning tree,** and it need not be unique. Although there may be several minimum spanning trees for a particular graph, their costs are equal.

A minimum spanning tree of a connected undirected graph has a minimal edge-weight sum

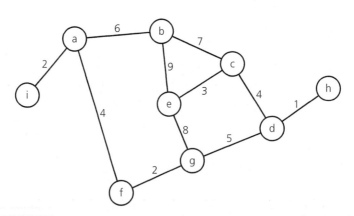

FIGURE 14-22

A weighted, connected, undirected graph

One simple algorithm, called Prim's algorithm, finds a minimum spanning tree that begins at any vertex. Initially, the tree contains only the starting vertex. At each stage, the algorithm selects a least-cost edge from among those that begin with a vertex in the tree and end with a vertex not in the tree. The latter vertex and least-cost edge are then added to the tree. The following pseudocode describes this algorithm:

Minimum spanning
tree algorithm

```
+PrimsAlgorithm(in v:Vertex)
// Determines a minimum spanning tree for a weighted,
// connected, undirected graph whose weights are
// nonnegative, beginning with any vertex v.
    Mark vertex v as visited and include it in the minimum
        spanning tree

    while (there are unvisited vertices) {
        Find the least-cost edge (v, u) from a visited
            vertex v to some unvisited vertex u
        Mark u as visited
        Add the vertex u and the edge (v, u) to the minimum
            spanning tree
    }  // end while
```

Figure 14-23 traces `PrimsAlgorithm` for the graph in Figure 14-22, beginning at vertex *a*. Edges added to the tree appear as solid lines, while edges under consideration appear as dashed lines.

It is not obvious that the spanning tree that `PrimsAlgorithm` determines will be minimal. However, the proof that `PrimsAlgorithm` is correct is beyond the scope of this book.

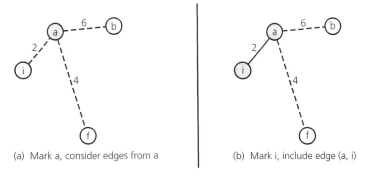

(a) Mark a, consider edges from a   (b) Mark i, include edge (a, i)

FIGURE 14-23

A trace of **PrimsAlgorithm** for the graph in Figure 14-22, beginning at vertex *a*

(continues)

FIGURE 14-23

(continued)

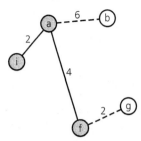

(c) Mark f, include edge (a, f)

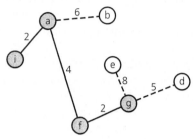

(d) Mark g, include edge (f, g)

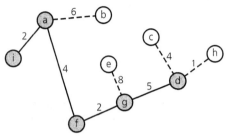

(e) Mark d, include edge (g, d)

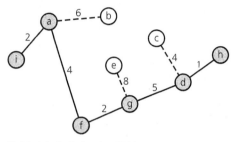

(f) Mark h, include edge (d, h)

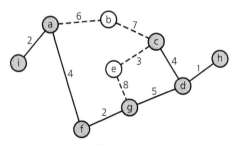

(g) Mark c, include edge (d, c)

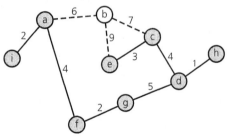

(h) Mark e, include edge (c, e)

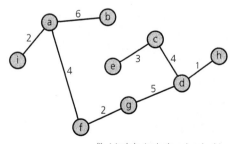

(i) Mark b, include edge (a, b)

Shortest Paths

Consider once again a map of airline routes. A weighted directed graph can represent this map: The vertices are cities, and the edges indicate existing flights between cities. The edge weights represent the mileage between cities (vertices); as such, the weights are not negative. For example, you could combine the two graphs in Figure 14-5 to get such a weighted directed graph.

Often for weighted directed graphs you need to know the shortest path between two particular vertices. The **shortest path** between two given vertices in a weighted graph is the path that has the smallest sum of its edge weights. Although we use the term "shortest," realize that the weights could be a measure other than distance, such as the cost of each flight in dollars or the duration of each flight in hours. The sum of the weights of the edges of a path is called the path's **length**, **weight**, or **cost**.

The shortest path between two vertices in a weighted graph has the smallest edge-weight sum

For example, the shortest path from vertex 0 to vertex 1 in the graph in Figure 14-24a is not the edge between 0 and 1—its cost is 8—but rather the path from 0 to 4 to 2 to 1, with a cost of 7. For convenience, the starting vertex, or origin, is numbered 0 and the other vertices are numbered from 1 to $n - 1$. Notice the graph's adjacency matrix in Figure 14-24b.

The following algorithm, which is attributed to E. Dijkstra, actually determines the shortest paths between a given origin and *all* other vertices. The algorithm uses a set *vertexSet* of selected vertices and an array *weight*, where *weight*[v] is the weight of the shortest (cheapest) path from vertex 0 to vertex v that passes through vertices in *vertexSet*.

Finding the shortest paths between vertex 0 and all other vertices

If v is in *vertexSet*, the shortest path involves only vertices in *vertexSet*. However, if v is not in *vertexSet*, then v is the only vertex along the path that is not in *vertexSet*. That is, the path ends with an edge from a vertex in *vertexSet* to v.

Initially, *vertexSet* contains only vertex 0, and *weight* contains the weights of the single-edge paths from vertex 0 to all other vertices. That is, *weight*[v] equals *matrix*[0][v] for all v, where *matrix* is the adjacency matrix. Thus, initially *weight* is the first row of *matrix*.

After this initialization step, you find a vertex v that is not in *vertexSet* and that minimizes *weight*[v]. You add v to *vertexSet*. For all (unselected) vertices u not in *vertexSet*, you check the values *weight*[u] to ensure that they are indeed

(a) Origin

(b)

	0	1	2	3	4
0	∞	8	∞	9	4
1	∞	∞	1	∞	∞
2	∞	2	∞	3	∞
3	∞	∞	2	∞	7
4	∞	∞	1	∞	∞

FIGURE 14-24

(a) A weighted directed graph and (b) its adjacency matrix

minimums. That is, can you reduce *weight*[*u*]—the weight of a path from vertex 0 to vertex *u*—by passing through the newly selected vertex *v*?

To make this determination, break the path from 0 to *u* into two pieces and find their weights as follows:

$$weight[v] = \text{weight of the shortest path from 0 to } v$$
$$matrix[v][u] = \text{weight of the edge from } v \text{ to } u$$

Then compare *weight*[*u*] with *weight*[*v*] + *matrix*[*v*][*u*] and let

$$weight[u] = \text{the smaller of the values } weight[u] \text{ and}$$
$$weight[v] + matrix[v][u]$$

The pseudocode for **Dijkstra's shortest-path algorithm** is as follows:

The shortest-path algorithm

```
+shortestPath(in theGraph:Graph, in weight:WeightArray)
// Finds the minimum-cost paths between an origin vertex
// (vertex 0) and all other vertices in a weighted directed
// graph theGraph. The array weight contains theGraph's
// weights which are nonnegative.

    // Step 1: initialization
    Create a set vertexSet that contains only vertex 0
    n = number of vertices in theGraph
    for (v = 0 through n - 1) {
      weight[v] = matrix[0][v]
    }  // end for
    // Steps 2 through n
```

Loop invariant

```
    // Invariant: For v not in vertexSet, weight[v] is the
    // smallest weight of all paths from 0 to v that pass
    // through only vertices in vertexSet before reaching v.
    // For v in vertexSet, weight[v] is the smallest weight
    // of all paths from 0 to v (including paths outside
    // vertexSet), and the shortest path from 0 to v lies
    // entirely in vertexSet.
    for (step = 2 through n) {
      Find the smallest weight[v] such that v is not in
          vertexSet
      Add v to vertexSet

      // Check weight[u] for all u not in vertexSet
      for (all vertices u not in vertexSet) {
        if (weight[u] > weight[v] + matrix[v][u]) {
          weight[u] = weight[v] + matrix[v][u]
        }  // end if
      }  // end for
    }  // end for
```

The loop invariant states that once a vertex v is placed in *vertexSet, weight[v]* is the weight of the absolutely shortest path from 0 to v and will not change.

Figure 14-25 traces the algorithm for the graph in Figure 14-24a. The algorithm takes the following steps:

Step 1.   *vertexSet* initially contains vertex 0, and *weight* is initially the first row of the graph's adjacency matrix, shown in Figure 14-24b.

A trace of the shortest-path algorithm

Step 2.   *weight[4]* = 4 is the smallest value in *weight*, ignoring *weight[0]* because 0 is in *vertexSet*. Thus, v = 4, so add 4 to *vertexSet*. For vertices not in *vertexSet*—that is, for u = 1, 2, and 3—check whether it is shorter to go from 0 to 4 and then along an edge to u instead of directly from 0 to u along an edge. For vertices 1 and 3, it is not shorter to include vertex 4 in the path. However, for vertex 2 notice that *weight[2]* = ∞ > *weight[4]* + *matrix[4][2]* = 4 + 1 = 5. Therefore, replace *weight[2]* with 5. You can also verify this conclusion by examining the graph directly, as Figure 14-26a shows.

Step 3.   *weight[2]* = 5 is the smallest value in *weight*, ignoring *weight[0]* and *weight[4]* because 0 and 4 are in *vertexSet*. Thus, v = 2, so add 2 to *vertexSet*. For vertices not in *vertexSet*—that is, for u = 1 and 3— check whether it is shorter to go from 0 to 2 and then along an edge to u instead of directly from 0 to u along an edge. (See parts b and c of Figure 14-26.)

Notice that

weight[1] = 8 > *weight[2]* + *matrix[2][1]* = 5 + 2 = 7. Therefore, replace *weight[1]* with 7.

weight[3] = 9 > *weight[2]* + *matrix[2][3]* = 5 + 3 = 8. Therefore, replace *weight[3]* with 8.

Step 4.   *weight[1]* = 7 is the smallest value in *weight*, ignoring *weight[0]*, *weight[2]*, and *weight[4]* because 0, 2, and 4 are in *vertexSet*. Thus, v = 1, so add 1 to *vertexSet*. For vertex 3, which is the only vertex not in *vertexSet*, notice that *weight[3]* = 8 < *weight[1]* + *matrix[1][3]* = 7 + ∞, as Figure 14-26d shows. Therefore, leave *weight[3]* as it is.

Step 5.   The only remaining vertex not in *vertexSet* is 3, so add it to *vertexSet* and stop.

Step	v	vertexSet	weight[0]	weight[1]	weight[2]	weight[3]	weight[4]
1	–	0	0	8	∞	9	4
2	4	0, 4	0	8	5	9	4
3	2	0, 4, 2	0	7	5	8	4
4	1	0, 4, 2, 1	0	7	5	8	4
5	3	0, 4, 2, 1, 3	0	7	5	8	4

FIGURE 14-25

A trace of the shortest-path algorithm applied to the graph in Figure 14-24a

(a)
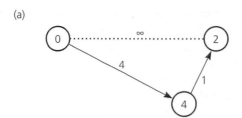

Step 2. The path 0–4–2 is
shorter than 0–2

(b)
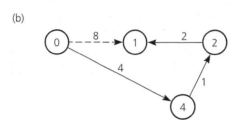

Step 3. The path 0–4–2–1 is
shorter than 0–1

(c)
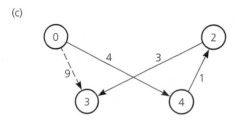

Step 3 continued. The path 0–4–2–3 is
shorter than 0–3

(d)
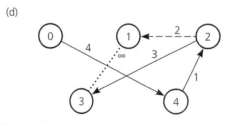

Step 4. The path 0–4–2–3 is
shorter than
0–4–2–1–3

FIGURE 14-26

Checking *weight*[*u*] by examining the graph: (a) *weight*[2] in Step 2; (b) *weight*[1] in Step 3; (c) *weight*[3] in Step 3; (d) *weight*[3] in Step 4

The final values in *weight* are the weights of the shortest paths. These values appear in the last line of Figure 14-25. For example, the shortest path from vertex 0 to vertex 1 has a cost of *weight*[1], which is 7. This result agrees with our earlier observation about Figure 14-24. We saw then that the shortest path is from 0 to 4 to 2 to 1. Also, the shortest path from vertex 0 to vertex 2 has a cost of *weight*[2], which is 5. This path is from 0 to 4 to 2.

The weights in *weight* are the smallest possible, as long as the algorithm's loop invariant is true. The proof that the loop invariant is true is by induction on *step*, and is left as a difficult exercise. (See Exercise 20.)

Circuits

A **circuit** is simply another name for a type of cycle that is common in the statement of certain problems. Recall that a cycle in a graph is a path that begins and ends at the same vertex. Typical circuits either visit every vertex once or visit every edge once.

Probably the first application of graphs occurred in the early 1700s when Euler (pronounced "oiler") proposed a bridge problem. Two islands in a river are joined to each other and to the river banks by several bridges, as Figure 14-27a illustrates. The bridges correspond to the edges in the multigraph in Figure 14-27b, and the land masses correspond to the vertices. The problem asked whether you can begin at a vertex v, pass through every edge exactly once, and terminate at v. Euler demonstrated that no solution exists for this particular configuration of edges and vertices.

For simplicity, we will consider an undirected graph rather than a multigraph. A path in an undirected graph that begins at a vertex *v*, passes through every edge in the graph exactly once, and terminates at *v* is called a **Euler circuit.** Euler showed that a Euler circuit exists if and only if each vertex touches an even number of edges. Intuitively, if you arrive at a vertex along one edge, you must be able to leave the vertex along another edge. If you cannot, you will not be able to reach all of the vertices.

> A Euler circuit begins at a vertex *v*, passes through every edge exactly once, and terminates at *v*

Finding a Euler circuit is like drawing each of the diagrams in Figure 14-28 without lifting your pencil or redrawing a line, but ending at your starting point. No solution is possible for Figure 14-28a, but you should be able to find one easily for Figure 14-28b. Figure 14-29 contains undirected graphs based on Figure 14-28. In Figure 14-29a, vertices *h* and *i* each touch an odd

(a)   (b)

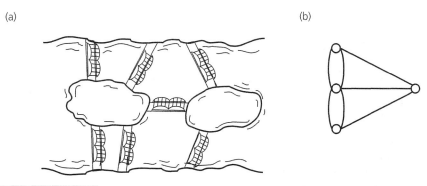

FIGURE 14-27

(a) Euler's bridge problem and (b) its multigraph representation

number of edges (three), so no Euler circuit is possible. On the other hand, each vertex in Figure 14-29b touches an even number of edges, making a Euler circuit feasible. Notice also that the graphs are connected. If a graph is not connected, a path through *all* of the vertices would not be possible.

Let's find a Euler circuit for the graph in Figure 14-29b, starting arbitrarily at vertex *a*. The strategy uses a depth-first search that marks edges instead of vertices as they are traversed. Recall that a depth-first search traverses a path from *a* as deeply into the graph as possible. By marking edges instead of vertices, you will return to the starting vertex; that is, you will find a cycle. In this example, the cycle is *a*, *b*, *e*, *d*, *a*, if we visit the vertices in alphabetical order, as Figure 14-30a shows. Clearly this is not the desired circuit, because we have not visited every edge. We are not finished, however.

To continue, find the first vertex along the cycle *a*, *b*, *e*, *d*, *a* that touches an unvisited edge. In our example, the desired vertex is *e*. Apply our modified depth-first search, beginning with this vertex. The resulting cycle is *e*, *f*, *j*, *i*, *e*. Next you join this cycle with the one you found previously. That is, when you reach *e* in the first cycle, you travel along the second cycle before

(a)   (b)

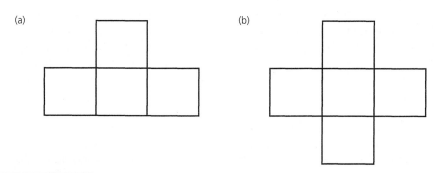

FIGURE 14-28

Pencil and paper drawings

(a)   (b)

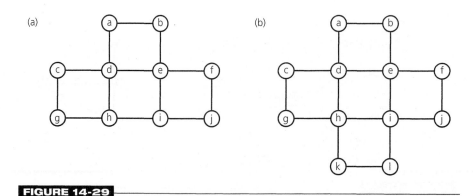

FIGURE 14-29

Connected undirected graphs based on the drawings in Figure 14-28

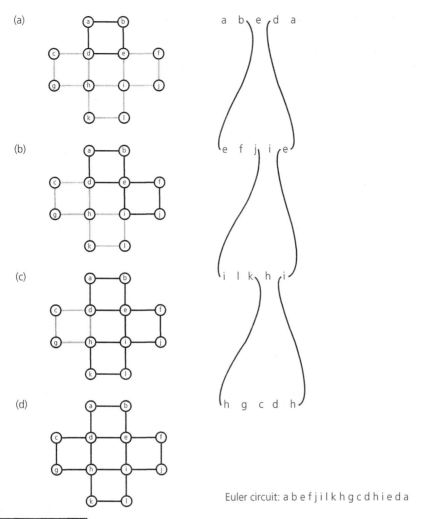

Euler circuit: a b e f j i l k h g c d h i e d a

FIGURE 14-30

The steps to determine a Euler circuit for the graph in Figure 14-29b

continuing in the first cycle. The resulting path is *a, b, e, f, j, i, e, d, a,* as Figure 14-30b shows.

The first vertex along our combined cycle that touches an unvisited edge is *i*. Beginning at *i*, our algorithm determines the cycle *i, l, k, h, i*. Joining this to our combined cycle results in the path *a, b, e, f, j, i, l, k, h, i, e, d, a.* (See Figure 14-30c.) The first vertex along this combined cycle that touches an unvisited edge is *h*. From *h*, we find the cycle *h, g, c, d, h*. Joining this to our combined cycle results in the Euler circuit *a, b, e, f, j, i, l, k, h, g, c, d, h, i, e, d, a.* (See Figure 14-30d.)

Some Difficult Problems

The next three applications of graphs have solutions that are beyond the scope of this book.

A Hamilton circuit begins at a vertex *v*, passes through every vertex exactly once, and terminates at *v*

The traveling salesperson problem.   A **Hamilton circuit** is a path that begins at a vertex *v*, passes through every vertex in the graph exactly once, and terminates at *v*. Determining whether or not an arbitrary graph contains a Hamilton circuit can be difficult. A well-known variation of this problem—the traveling salesperson problem—involves a weighted graph that represents a road map. Each edge has an associated cost, such as the mileage between cities or the time required to drive from one city to the next. The salesperson must begin at an origin city, visit every other city exactly once, and return to the origin city. However, the circuit traveled must be the least expensive.

Unfortunately for this traveler, solving the problem is no easy task. Although a solution does exist, it is quite slow, and no better solution is known.

The three utilities problem.   Imagine three houses *A*, *B*, and *C* and three utilities *X*, *Y*, and *Z* (such as telephone, water, and electricity), as Figure 14-31 illustrates. If the houses and the utilities are vertices in a graph, is it possible to connect each house to each utility with edges that do not cross one another? The answer to this question is no.

A planar graph can be drawn so that no two edges cross

A graph is **planar** if you can draw it in a plane in at least one way so that no two edges cross. The generalization of the three utilities problem determines whether a given graph is planar. Making this determination has many important applications. For example, a graph can represent an electronic circuit where the vertices represent components and the edges represent the connections between

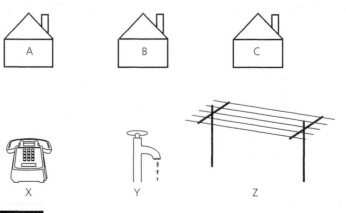

FIGURE 14-31

The three utilities problem

components. Is it possible to design the circuit so that the connections do not cross? The solutions to these problems are also beyond the scope of this book.

The four-color problem.   Given a planar graph, can you color the vertices so that no adjacent vertices have the same color, if you use at most four colors? For example, the graph in Figure 14-11 is planar because none of its edges cross. You can solve the coloring problem for this graph by using only three colors. Color vertices *a, c, g,* and *h* red; color vertices *b, d, f,* and *i* blue; and color vertex *e* green.

The answer to our question is yes, but it is difficult to prove. In fact, this problem was posed more than a century before it was solved in the 1970s with the use of a computer.

Summary

1. The two most common implementations of a graph are the adjacency matrix and the adjacency list. Each has its relative advantages and disadvantages. The choice should depend on the needs of the given application.

2. Graph searching is an important application of stacks and queues. Depth-first search is a graph-traversal algorithm that uses a stack to keep track of the sequence of visited vertices. It goes as deep into the graph as it can before backtracking. Breadth-first search uses a queue to keep track of the sequence of visited vertices. It visits all possible adjacent vertices before traversing further into the graph.

3. Topological sorting produces a linear order of the vertices in a directed graph without cycles. Vertex *x* precedes vertex *y* if there is a directed edge from *x* to *y* in the graph.

4. Trees are connected undirected graphs without cycles. A spanning tree of a connected undirected graph is a subgraph that contains all of the graph's vertices and enough of its edges to form a tree. DFS and BFS traversals produce DFS and BFS spanning trees.

5. A minimum spanning tree for a weighted undirected graph is a spanning tree whose edge-weight sum is minimal. Although a particular graph can have several minimum spanning trees, their edge-weight sums will be the same.

6. The shortest path between two vertices in a weighted directed graph is the path that has the smallest sum of its edge weights.

7. A Euler circuit in an undirected graph is a cycle that begins at vertex *v*, passes through every edge in the graph exactly once, and terminates at *v*.

8. A Hamilton circuit in an undirected graph is a cycle that begins at vertex *v*, passes through every vertex in the graph exactly once, and terminates at *v*.

Cautions

1. When searching a graph, realize that the algorithm might take wrong turns. For example, you must eliminate the possibility of cycling within the algorithm; the algorithm must be able to backtrack when it hits a dead end.

Self-Test Exercises

1. Describe the graphs in Figure 14-32. For example, are they directed? Connected? Complete? Weighted?

2. Use the depth-first strategy and the breadth-first strategy to traverse the graph in Figure 14-32a, beginning with vertex 0. List the vertices in the order in which each traversal visits them.

3. Write the adjacency matrix for the graph in Figure 14-32a.

4. Add an edge to the directed graph in Figure 14-14 that runs from vertex d to vertex b. Write all possible topological orders for the vertices in this new graph.

5. Is it possible for a connected undirected graph with 5 vertices and 4 edges to contain a simple cycle? Explain.

6. Draw the DFS spanning tree whose root is vertex 0 for the graph in Figure 14-33.

7. Draw the minimum spanning tree whose root is vertex 0 for the graph in Figure 14-33.

8. What are the shortest paths from vertex 0 to each vertex of the graph in Figure 14-24a? (Note the weights of these paths in Figure 14-25.)

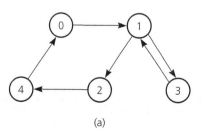

(a)

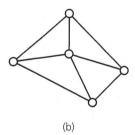

(b)

FIGURE 14-32

Graphs for Self-Test Exercises 1, 2, and 3

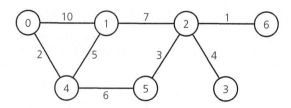

FIGURE 14-33

A graph for Self-Test Exercises 6 and 7 and Exercises 1 and 4

Exercises

When given a choice of vertices to visit, the traversals in the following exercises should visit vertices in sorted order.

1. Give the adjacency matrix and adjacency list for

   a. The weighted graph in Figure 14-33

   b. The directed graph in Figure 14-34

2. Show that the adjacency list in Figure 14-8b requires less memory than the adjacency matrix in Figure 14-6b.

3. Consider Figure 14-35 and answer the following:

   a. Will the adjacency matrix be symmetrical?

   b. Provide the adjacency matrix.

   c. What does the sum of each row of the adjacency matrix represent?

   d. Provide the adjacency list.

4. Describe an adjacency matrix for a complete graph.

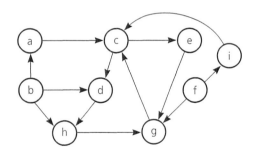

FIGURE 14-34

A graph for Exercise 1

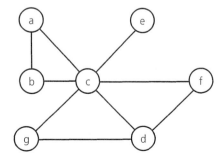

FIGURE 14-35

A graph for Exercises 3 and 12

5. a Do any complete graphs have Euler circuits? If so, describe the characteristics of such graphs.

b. Do any complete graphs have Hamiltonian circuits? If so, describe the charac-teristics of such graphs.

6. Use both the depth-first strategy and the breadth-first strategy to traverse the graph in Figure 14-33, beginning with vertex 0, and the graph in Figure 14-36, beginning with vertex *b*. List the vertices in the order in which each traversal visits them.

7. By modifying the DFS traversal algorithm, write pseudocode for an algorithm that determines whether a graph contains a cycle.

8. Using the topological sorting algorithm *topSort1*, write the topological order of the vertices for each graph in Figure 14-37.

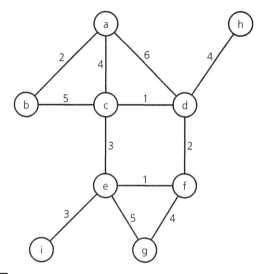

FIGURE 14-36

A graph for Exercises 6 and 12

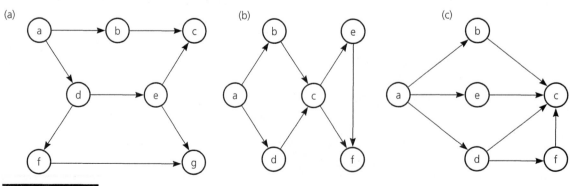

FIGURE 14-37

Graphs for Exercises 6, 8, 9, and 10

9. Trace the DFS topological sorting algorithm *topSort2*, and indicate the resulting topological order of the vertices for each graph in Figure 14-37.

10. Revise the topological sorting algorithm *topSort1* by removing predecessors instead of successors. Trace the new algorithm for each graph in Figure 14-37.

11. Trace the DFS and BFS spanning tree algorithms, beginning with vertex *a* of the graph in Figure 14-11, and show that the spanning trees are the trees in Figures 14-20 and 14-21, respectively.

12. Draw the DFS and BFS spanning trees rooted at *a* for the graph in Figure 14-35. Then draw the minimum spanning tree rooted at *a* for this graph.

13. For the graph in Figure 14-38:

    a. Draw all the possible spanning trees.

    b. Draw the minimum spanning tree.

14. Write pseudocode for an iterative algorithm that determines a DFS spanning tree for an undirected graph. Base your algorithm on the traversal algorithm *dfs*.

15. Draw the minimum spanning tree for the graph in Figure 14-22 when you start with

    a. Vertex *e*

    b. Vertex *d*

* 16. Trace the shortest-path algorithm for the graph in Figure 14-39, letting vertex 0 be the origin.

* 17. Implement the shortest-path algorithm in Java. How can you modify this algorithm so that any vertex can be the origin?

* 18. Determine a Euler circuit for the graph in Figure 14-40. Why is one possible?

* 19. Prove that a connected undirected graph with *n* vertices and more than $n - 1$ edges must contain at least one simple cycle. (See observation 3 in the section "Spanning Trees.")

* 20. Prove that a graph-traversal algorithm visits every vertex in the graph if and only if the graph is connected, regardless of where the traversal starts.

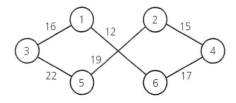

FIGURE 14-38

A graph for Exercise 13

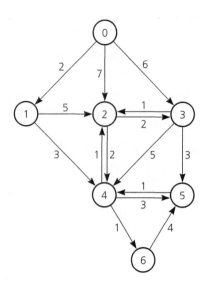

FIGURE 14-39

A graph for Exercise 16

* 21. Although the DFS traversal algorithm has a simple recursive form, a recursive BFS traversal algorithm is not straightforward.

    a. Explain why this fact is true.

    b. Write the pseudocode for a recursive version of the BFS traversal algorithm.

* 22. Prove that the loop invariant of Dijkstra's shortest-path algorithm is true by using a proof by induction on *step*.

Programming Problems

1. Modify the *Graph* class presented in the section "Graphs as ADTs" to include the following methods:

```
public Graph()
    // default constructor, creates an empty graph

public Integer addVertex()
```

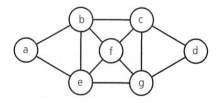

FIGURE 14-40

A graph for Exercise 18

```
   // Adds a vertex to the graph, returns the Vertex index

   public boolean isEdge(Integer v, Integer w) {
      // Determines if an edge exists between vertices v and w
```

Add exception handling to the class as well.

2. Modify the *Graph* class presented in the section "Graphs as ADTs" to represent a directed or undirected graph. Once the graph has been created as a directed or undirected graph, that aspect of the graph cannot be changed. Add exception handling to the class as well.

3. Implement a template version of the *Graph* class presented in the section "Graphs as ADTs." The template parameter will represent the value associated with each vertex. An additional vector of vertices will hold the data, and additional methods should be provided to allow the client application to add or remove vertex information.

4. Implement the ADT graph as a Java class, using an adjacency matrix to represent the graph. Allow the graph to be either weighted or unweighted and either directed or undirected. Include DFS and BFS traversals.

5. Extend Programming Problem 4 by adding ADT operations such as *isConnected* and *hasCycle*. Also, include operations that perform a topological sort for a directed graph without cycles, determine the DFS and BFS spanning trees for a connected graph, and determine a minimum spanning tree for a connected undirected graph.

6. The HPAir problem was the subject of Programming Problems 11, 12, and 13 of Chapter 7. Revise these problems by implementing the ADT flight map as a derived class of the graph class that you wrote for Programming Problem 4.

CHAPTER 15

External Methods

All of the previous table implementations assume that the data items reside in the computer's internal memory. Many real-world applications, however, require a table so large that it greatly exceeds the amount of available internal memory. In such situations, you must store the table on an external storage device such as a disk and perform table operations there.

This chapter considers the problem of data management in an external environment by using a random access file as a model of external storage. In particular, this chapter discusses how to sort the data in an external file by modifying the mergesort algorithm and how to search an external file by using generalizations of the hashing and search-tree schemes developed previously.

15.1 A Look at External Storage

You use external storage when your program reads data from and writes data to a file. Also, when you use a word processing program, for example, and choose Save, the program saves your current document in a file. This action enables you to exit the program and then use it later to retrieve your document for revision. This is one of the advantages of external storage: It exists beyond the execution period of a program. In this sense, it is "permanent" instead of volatile like internal memory.

External storage exists after program execution

Another advantage of external storage is that, in general, there is far more of it than internal memory. If you have a table of one million data items, each of which is a record of moderate size, you will probably not be able to store the entire table in internal memory at one time. On the other hand, this much data can easily reside on an external disk. As a consequence, when dealing with tables of this magnitude, you cannot simply read the entire table into memory when you want to operate on it and then write it back onto the disk when you are finished. Instead, you must devise ways to operate on data—for example, sort it and search it—while it resides externally.

Generally, there is more external storage than internal memory

In general, you can create files for either sequential access or random access. To access the data stored at a given position in a **sequential access file,** you must advance the file window beyond all the intervening data. In this sense, a sequential access file resembles a linked list. To access a particular node in the list, you must traverse the list from its beginning until you reach the desired node. In contrast, a **random access file** allows you to access the data at a given position directly. A random access file resembles an array in that you can access the element at *data[i]* without first accessing the elements before *data[i]*.

Random access files are essential for external tables

Without random access files, it would be impossible to support the table operations efficiently in an external environment. Many programming languages, including Java, support both sequential access and random access of files. However, to permit a language-independent discussion, we will construct a model of random access files that illustrates how a programming language that does not support such files might implement them. This model will be a simplification of reality but will include the features necessary for this discussion.

Imagine that a computer's memory is divided into two parts: internal memory and external memory, as Figure 15-1 illustrates. Assume that an executing program, along with its nonfile data, resides in the computer's internal

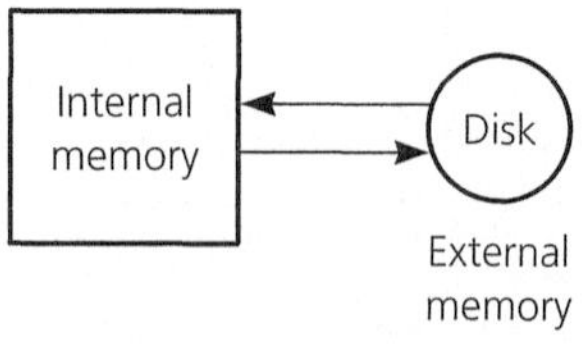

Internal memory

Disk

External memory

FIGURE 15-1

Internal and external memory

memory; the permanent files of a computer system reside in the external memory. Further assume that the external storage devices have the characteristics of a disk (although some systems use other devices).

A file consists of **data records.** A data record can be anything from a simple value, such as an integer, to an aggregate structure, such as an employee record. For simplicity, assume that the data records in any one file are all of the same type.

The records of a file are organized into one or more **blocks,** as Figure 15-2 shows. The size of a block—that is, the number of bits of data it can contain—is determined by both the hardware configuration and the system software of the computer. In general, an individual program has no control over this size. Therefore, the number of records in a block is a function of the size of the records in the file. For example, a file of integer records will have more records per block than a file of employee records.

A file contains records that are organized into blocks

Much as you number the elements of an array, you can number the blocks of a file in a linear sequence. With a random access file, a program can read a given block from the file by specifying its block number, and similarly, it can write data out to a particular block. In this regard a random access file resembles an array of arrays, with each block of the file analogous to a single array entry, which is itself an array that contains several records.

In this random access model, *all input and output is at the block level rather than at the record level.* That is, you can read and write a block of records, but you cannot read or write an individual record. Reading or writing a block is called a **block access.**

Random access input and output involves blocks instead of records

The algorithms in this chapter assume commands for reading and writing blocks. The statement

```
buf.readBlock(dataFile, i)
```

will read the ith block of the file `dataFile` and place it in an object `buf`. This object must accommodate the many records that each block of the file `dataFile` contains. For example, if each block contains 100 employee records, `buf` must

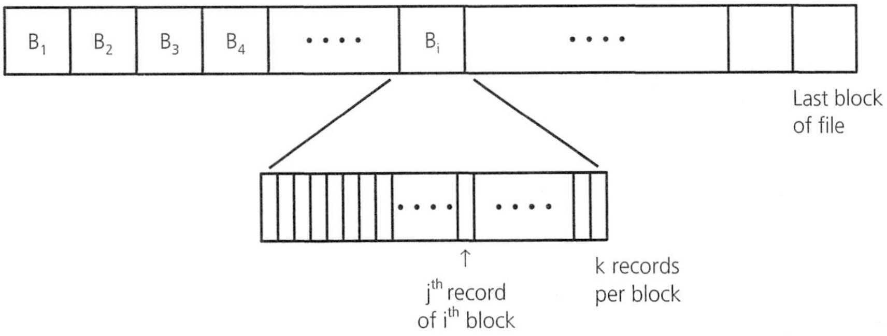

FIGURE 15-2

A file partitioned into blocks of records

A buffer stores data temporarily
store at least 100 employee records. The object *buf* is called a **buffer,** which is a location that temporarily stores data as it makes its way from one process or location to another.

Once the system has read a block into *buf*, the program can process—for example, inspect or modify—the records in the block. Also, because the records in the object *buf* are only copies of the records in the file *dataFile*, if a program does modify the records in *buf*, it must write *buf* back out to *dataFile*, so that the file also reflects the modifications. We assume that the statement

```
buf.writeBlock(dataFile, i)
```

will write the contents of *buf* to the ith block of the file *dataFile*. If *dataFile* contains *n* blocks, the statement

```
buf.writeBlock(dataFile, n + 1)
```

will append a new block to *dataFile*, and thus the file can grow dynamically, just as a Java file can.

Again, realize that these input and output commands allow you to read and write only entire blocks. As a consequence, even if you need to operate on only a single record of the file, you must access an entire block. For example, suppose that you want to give employee Smith a $1,000 raise. If Smith's record is in block *i* (how to determine the correct block is discussed later in the chapter), you would perform the following steps:

Updating a portion of a record within a block

```
// read block i from file dataFile into buffer buf
buf.readBlock(dataFile, i)

Find the entry buf.getRecord(j) that contains the
    record whose search key is "Smith"

// increase the salary portion of Smith's record
((buf.getRecord(j)).setSalary((buf.getRecord(j)).salary()
                + 1000)

// write changed block back to file dataFile
buf.writeBlock(dataFile, i)
```

The time required to read or write a block of data is typically much longer than the time required to operate on the block's data once it is in the computer's internal memory.[1] For example, you typically can inspect every record

---

1. Data enters or leaves a buffer at a rate that differs from the record-processing rate. (Hence, a buffer between two processes compensates for the difference in the rates at which they operate on data.)

in the buffer *buf* in less time than that required to read a block into the buffer. As a consequence, you should reduce the number of required block accesses. In the previous pseudocode, for instance, you should process as many records in *buf* as possible before writing it to the file. You should pay little attention to the time required to operate on a block of data once it has been read into internal memory.

Reduce the number of block accesses

Interestingly, several programming languages, including Java, have commands to make it *appear* that you can access records one at a time. In general, however, the system actually performs input and output at the block level and perhaps hides this fact from the program. For example, if a programming language includes the statement

```
rec.readRecord(dataFile, i)
// Reads the ith record of file dataFile into rec.
```

the system probably accesses the entire block that contains the ith record. Our model of input and output therefore approximates reality reasonably well.

In most external data-management applications, the time required for block accesses typically dominates all other factors. The rest of the chapter discusses how to sort and search externally stored data. The goal will be to reduce the number of required block accesses.

Block access time is the dominant factor when considering an algorithm's efficiency

15.2 Sorting Data in an External File

This section considers the following problem of sorting data that resides in an external file:

> An external file contains 1,600 employee records. You want to sort these records by Social Security number. Each block contains 100 records, and thus the file contains 16 blocks B_1, B_2, and so on to B_{16}. Assume that the program can access only enough internal memory to manipulate about 300 records (three blocks' worth) at one time.

A sorting problem

Sorting the file might not sound like a difficult task, because you have already seen several sorting algorithms earlier in this book. There is, however, a fundamental difference here in that the file is far too large to fit into internal memory all at once. This restriction presents something of a problem because the sorting algorithms presented earlier assume that all the data to be sorted is available at one time in internal memory (for example, that it is all in an array). Fortunately, however, we can remove this assumption for a modified version of mergesort.

The basis of the mergesort algorithm is that you can easily merge two sorted segments—such as arrays—of data records into a third sorted segment that is the combination of the two. For example, if S_1 and S_2 are sorted segments of records, the first step of the merge is to compare the first record of each segment and select the record with the smaller search key. If the record from S_1 is selected, the next step is to compare the second record of S_1 to the first record of S_2. This process is continued until all of the records have been considered. The key observation is that at any step, the merge never needs to look beyond the *leading edge* of either segment.

This observation makes a mergesort appropriate for the problem of sorting external files, if you modify the algorithm appropriately. Suppose that the 1,600 records to be sorted are in the file F and that you are not permitted to alter this file. You have two work files, F_1 and F_2. One of the work files will contain the sorted records when the algorithm terminates. The algorithm has two phases: Phase 1 sorts each block of records, and Phase 2 performs a series of merges.

External mergesort

Phase 1. Read a block from F into internal memory, sort its records by using an internal sort, and write the sorted block out to F_1 before you read the next block from F. After you process all 16 blocks of F, F_1 contains 16 **sorted runs** R_1, R_2, and so on to R_{16}; that is, F_1 contains 16 blocks of records, with the records within each block sorted among themselves, as Figure 15-3a illustrates.

Phase 2. Phase 2 is a sequence of merge steps. Each merge step merges pairs of sorted runs to form larger sorted runs. Each merge step doubles the number of blocks in each sorted run and thus halves the total number of sorted runs. For example, as Figure 15-3b shows, the first merge step merges eight pairs of sorted runs from F_1 (R_1 with R_2, R_3 with R_4, . . . , R_{15} with R_{16}) to form eight sorted runs, each two blocks long, which are written to F_2. The next merge step merges four pairs of sorted runs from F_2 (R_1 with R_2, R_3 with R_4, . . . , R_7 with R_8) to form four sorted runs, each four blocks long, which are written back to F_1, as Figure 15-3c illustrates. The next step merges the two pairs of sorted runs from F_1 to form two sorted runs, which are written to F_2. (See Figure 15-3d.) The final step merges the two sorted runs into one, which is written to F_1. At this point, F_1 will contain all of the records of the original file in sorted order.

Merging sorted runs in Phase 2

Given this overall strategy, how can you merge the sorted runs at each step of Phase 2? The statement of the problem provides only sufficient internal memory to manipulate at most 300 records at once. However, in the later steps of Phase 2, runs contain more than 300 records each, so you must merge the runs a piece at a time. To accomplish this merge, you must divide the program's internal memory into three buffers, *in1*, *in2*, and *out*, each capable of holding 100 records (the block size). You read block-sized pieces of the runs into the two *in* buffers and merge them into the *out* buffer. Whenever an *in* buffer is exhausted—that is, when all of its elements have been copied to *out*—you read the next piece of the run into the *in* buffer; whenever the *out* buffer becomes full, you write this completed piece of the new sorted run to one of the files.

Consider how you can perform the first merge step. You start this step with the pair of runs R_1 and R_2, which are in the first and second blocks, respectively, of the file F_1. (See Figure 15-3a.) Because at this first merge step each run contains only one block, an entire run can fit into one of the *in*

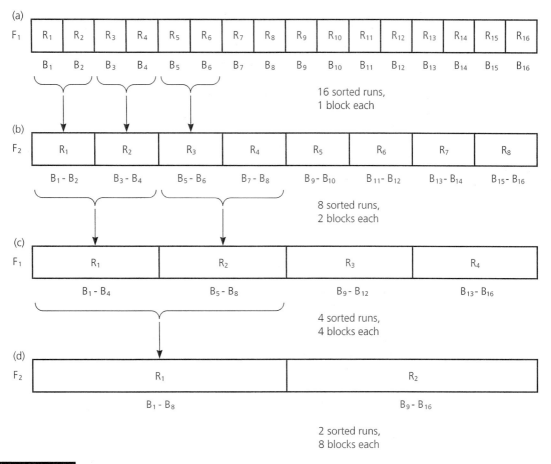

FIGURE 15-3

(a) 16 sorted runs, 1 block each, in file F_1; (b) 8 sorted runs, 2 blocks each, in file F_2; (c) 4 sorted runs, 4 blocks each, in file F_1; (d) 2 sorted runs, 8 blocks each, in file F_2

buffers. You can thus read R_1 and R_2 into the buffers *in1* and *in2*, and then merge *in1* and *in2* into *out*. However, although the result of merging *in1* and *in2* is a sorted run two blocks long (200 records), *out* can hold only one block (100 records). Thus, when *out* becomes full in the course of the merge, you write its contents to the first block of F_2, as Figure 15-4a illustrates. The merging of *in1* and *in2* into *out* then resumes. The buffer *out* will become full for a second time only after all of the records in *in1* and *in2* are exhausted. At that time, write the contents of *out* to the second block of F_2. You merge the remaining seven pairs from F in the same manner and append the resulting runs to F_2.

This first merge step is conceptually a bit easier than the others because the initial runs are only one block in size, and thus each can fit entirely into one of the *in* buffers. What do you do in the later steps when the runs to be merged

(a)

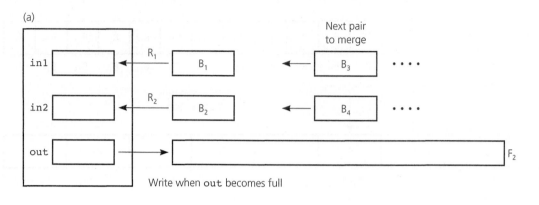

(b)

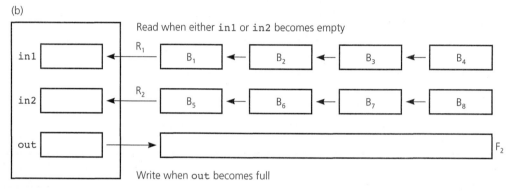

FIGURE 15-4

(a) Merging single blocks; (b) merging long runs

are larger than a single block? Consider, for example, the merge step in which you must merge runs of four blocks each to form runs of eight blocks each. (See Figure 15-3c.) The first pair of these runs to be merged is in blocks 1 through 4 and 5 through 8 of F_1.

The algorithm will read the first block of R_1—which is the first block B_1 of the file—into *in1*, and it will read the first block of R_2—which is B_5—into *in2*, as Figure 15-4b illustrates. Then, as it did earlier, the algorithm merges *in1* and *in2* into *out*. The complication here is that as soon as you finish moving all of the records from either *in1* or *in2*, you must read the next block from the corresponding run. For example, if you finish *in2* first, you must read the next block of R_2—which is B_6—into *in2* before the merge can continue. The algorithm thus must detect when the *in* buffers become exhausted as well as when the *out* buffer becomes full.

A high-level description of the algorithm for merging arbitrary-sized sorted runs R_i and R_j from F_1 into F_2 is as follows:

Pseudocode to merge sorted runs

Read the first block of R_i into in1
Read the first block of R_j into in2

```
while (either in1 or in2 is not exhausted) {
  Select the smaller "leading" record of in1 and in2
      and place it into the next position of out (if
      one of the buffers is exhausted, select the
      leading record from the other)

  if (out is full) {
    Write its contents to the next block of F₂
  }  // end if
  if (in1 is exhausted and blocks remain in Rᵢ) {
    Read the next block into in1
  }  // end if
  if (in2 is exhausted and blocks remain in Rⱼ) {
    Read the next block into in2
  }  // end if
}  // end while
```

A pseudocode version of the external sorting algorithm follows. Notice that it uses *readBlock* and *writeBlock*, as introduced in the previous section, and assumes a method *copyFile* that copies a file. To avoid further complications, the solution assumes that the number of blocks in the file is a power of 2. This assumption allows the algorithm always to pair off the sorted runs at each step of the merge phase, avoiding special end-of-file testing that would obscure the algorithm. Also note that the algorithm uses two temporary files and copies the final sorted temporary file to the designated output.

```
+externalMergesort(in unsortedFileName:String,
                   in sortedFileName:String)
// Sorts a file by using an external mergesort.
// Precondition: unsortedFileName is the name of an external
// file to be sorted. sortedFileName is the name that the
// method will give to the resulting sorted file.
// Postcondition: The new file named sortedFileName is sorted.
// The original file is unchanged. Both files are closed.
// Calls: blockSort, mergeFile, and copyFile.
// Simplifying assumption: The number of blocks in the
// unsorted file is an exact power of 2.

  Associate unsortedFileName with the file variable inFile
      and sortedFileName with the file variable outFile

  // Phase 1: sort file block by block and count the blocks
  blockSort(inFile, tempFile1, numberOfBlocks)

  // Phase 2: merge runs of size 1, 2, 4, 8,...,
  // numberOfBlocks/2 (uses two temporary files and a toggle
  // that keeps track of the files for each merge step)
```

A pseudocode mergesort method

```
      toggle = 1

      for (size = 1 through numberOfBlocks/2 with
                                        increments of size) {
        if (toggle == 1) {
          mergeFile(tempFile1, tempFile2, size, numberOfBlocks)
        }
        else {
          mergeFile(tempFile2, tempFile1, size, numberOfBlocks)
        }  // end if
        toggle = -toggle
      }  // end for

      // copy the current temporary file to outFile
      if (toggle == 1) {
        copyFile(tempFile1, outFile)
      }
      else {
        copyFile(tempFile2, outFile)
      }  // end if
```

The method *externalMergesort* calls *blockSort* and *mergeFile*, which calls *mergeRuns*. The pseudocode for these methods follows.

```
blockSort(in inFile:File, in outFile:File,
          in numberOfBlocks:integer)
// Sorts each block of records in a file.
// Precondition: The file variable inFile is associated
// with the file to be sorted.
// Postcondition: The file associated with the file variable
// outFile contains the blocks of inFile. Each block is
// sorted; numberOfBlocks is the number of blocks processed.
// Both files are closed.
// Calls: readBlock and writeBlock to perform random access
// input and output, and sortBuffer to sort a buffer.

  Prepare inFile for input
  Prepare outFile for output

  numberOfBlocks = 0
  while (more blocks in inFile remain to be read) {
    ++numberOfBlocks
    buffer.readBlock(inFile, numberOfBlocks)
    sortBuffer(buffer)  // sort with some internal sort
    buffer.writeBlock(outFile, numberOfBlocks)
  }  // end while

  Close inFile and outFile
```

```
// end blockSort


+mergeFile(in inFile:File, in outFile:File,
          in runSize:integer,
          in numberOfBlocks:integer)
// Merges blocks from one file to another.
// Precondition: inFile is an external file that contains
// numberOfBlocks sorted blocks organized into runs of
// runSize blocks each.
// Postcondition: outFile contains the merged runs of
// inFile. Both files are closed.
// Calls: mergeRuns.

  Prepare inFile for input
  Prepare outFile for output

  for (next = 1 through numberOfBlocks with increments
                                        of 2 * runSize) {
    // Invariant: runs in outFile are ordered
    mergeRuns(inFile, outFile, next, runSize)
  }  // end for
  Close inFile and outFile
// end mergeFile


+mergeRuns(in fromFile:File, in toFile:File,
          in start:integer, in size:integer)
// Merges two consecutive sorted runs in a file.
// Precondition: fromFile is an external file of sorted runs
// open for input. toFile is an external file of sorted runs
// open for output. start is the block number of the first
// run on fromFile to be merged; this run contains size
// blocks.
//    Run 1: block start to block start + size - 1
//    Run 2: block start + size to start + (2 * size) - 1
// Postcondition: The merged runs from fromFile are appended
// to toFile. The files remain open.

  // initialize the input buffers for runs 1 and 2
  in1.readBlock(fromFile, first block of Run 1)
  in2.readBlock(fromFile, first block of Run 2)

  // Merge until one of the runs is finished. Whenever an
  // input buffer is exhausted, the next block is read.
  // Whenever the output buffer is full, it is written.
  while (neither run is finished) {
```

```
       // Invariant: out and each block in toFile are ordered
       Select the smaller "leading edge" of in1 and in2, and
           place it in the next position of out

     if (out is full) {
       out.writeBlock(toFile, next block of toFile)
     }  // end if

     if (in1 is exhausted and blocks remain in Run 1) {
       in1.readBlock(fromFile, next block of Run 1)
     }  // end if

     if (in2 is exhausted and blocks remain in Run 2) {
       in2.readBlock(fromFile, next block of Run 2)
     }  // end if
   }  // end while

   // Assertion: exactly one of the runs is complete

   // append the remainder of the unfinished input
   // buffer to the output buffer and write it

   while (in1 is not exhausted) {
     // Invariant: out is ordered
     Place next item of in1 into the next position of out
   }  // end while

   while (in2 is not exhausted) {
     // Invariant: out is ordered
     Place next item of in2 into the next position of out
   }  // end while

   out.writeBlock(toFile, next block of toFile)

   // finish off the remaining complete blocks

   while (blocks remain in Run 1) {
     // Invariant: each block in toFile is ordered
     in1.readBlock(fromFile, next block of Run 1)
     in1.writeBlock(toFile, next block of toFile)
   }  // end while

   while (blocks remain in Run 2) {
     // Invariant: Each block in toFile is ordered
     in2.readBlock(fromFile, next block of Run 2)
     in2.writeBlock(toFile, next block of toFile)
   }  // end while
// end mergeRuns
```

15.3 External Tables

This section discusses techniques for organizing records in external storage so that you can efficiently perform ADT table operations such as retrieval, insertion, deletion, and traversal. Although this discussion will only scratch the surface of this topic, you do have a head start: Two of the most important external table implementations are variations of the 2-3 tree and hashing, which you studied in Chapter 13.

    Suppose you have a random access file of records that are to be table items. The file is partitioned into blocks, as described earlier in this chapter. One of the simplest table implementations stores the records in order by their search key, perhaps sorting the file by using the external mergesort algorithm developed in the previous section. Once it is sorted, you can easily traverse the file in sorted order by using the following algorithm:

A simple external table implementation: records stored in search-key order

```
+traverseTable(in dataFile:File, in numberOfBlocks:integer,
              in recordsPerBlock:integer)
// Traverses the sorted file dataFile in sorted order,
// visiting each node.

  // read each block of file dataFile into an
  // internal buffer buf
  for (blockNumber = 1 through numberOfBlocks) {
    buf.readBlock(dataFile, blockNumber)
    // visit each record in the block
    for (recordNumber = 1 through recordsPerBlock) {
      Visit record buf.getRecord(recordNumber-1)
    }  // end for
  }  // end for
```

Sorted-order traversal

To perform the *tableRetrieve* operation on the sorted file, you can use a binary search algorithm as follows:

Retrieval by using a binary search

```
+tableRetrieve(in dataFile:File, in recordsPerBlock:integer,
              in first:integer, in last:integer,
              in searchKey:KeyType):TableItemType
// Searches blocks first through last of file dataFile and
// returns the record whose search key equals
// searchKey. The operation fails and returns null
// if no such item exists.

  if (first > last or nothing is left to read from dataFile) {
    return null
  }
  else {
    // read the middle block of file dataFile into buffer buf
    mid = (first + last)/2
    buf.readBlock(dataFile, mid)
```

```
if ( (searchKey >= (buf.getRecord(0)).getKey()) &&
     (searchKey <= (buf.getRecord(recordsPerBlock-1)).getKey()) ) {
   // desired block is found
   Search buffer buf for record buf.getRecord(j)
       whose search key equals searchKey
   if (record is found) {
     tableItem = buf.getRecord(j)
     return tableItem
   }
    else {
      return null
   }  // end if
}
// else search appropriate half of the file
else if (searchKey < (buf.getRecord(0)).getKey()) {
   return tableRetrieve(dataFile, recordsPerBlock,
                         first, mid-1, searchKey)
}
else {
   return tableRetrieve(dataFile, recordsPerBlock,
                         mid+1, last, searchKey)
}  // end if
}  // end if
```

The `tableRetrieve` algorithm recursively splits the file in half and reads the middle block into the object *buf*. Splitting a file segment requires that you know the numbers of the first and last blocks of the segment. You would pass these values as arguments, along with the file variable, to `tableRetrieve`.

Once you have read the middle block of the file segment into *buf*, you determine whether a record whose search key equals *searchKey* could be in this block. You can make this determination by comparing *searchKey* to the smallest search key in *buf*—which is in *buf.getRecord(0)*—and to the largest search key in *buf*, which is in *buf.getRecord(recordsPerBlock-1)*. If *searchKey* does not lie between the values of the smallest and largest search keys in *buf*, you must recursively search one of the halves of the file (which half to search depends on whether *searchKey* is less than or greater than the search keys in the block you just examined). If, on the other hand, *searchKey* does lie between the values of the smallest and largest search keys of the block in *buf*, you must search *buf* for the record. Because the records within the block *buf* are sorted, you could use a binary search on the records within this block. However, the number of records in the block *buf* is typically small, and thus the time required to scan the block sequentially is insignificant compared to the time required to read the block from the file. It is therefore common simply to scan the block sequentially.

This external implementation of the ADT table is not very different from the internal sorted array-based implementation. As such, it has many of the same advantages and disadvantages. Its main advantage is that because the records are sorted sequentially, you can use a binary search to locate the block that contains a given search key. The main disadvantage of the implementation is that, as is the case with an array-based implementation, the `tableInsert` and `tableDelete` operations must shift table items. Shifting records in an external file is, in general, far more costly than shifting array items. A file may contain an enormous number of large records, which are organized as several thousand blocks. As a consequence, the shifting could require a prohibitively large number of block accesses.

`tableInsert` and `tableDelete` for an external implementation of the ADT table can require many costly block accesses due to shifting records

Consider, for example, Figure 15-5. If you insert a new record into block *k*, you must shift the records not only in block *k*, but also in every block after it. As a result, you must shift some records across block boundaries. Thus, for each of these blocks, you must read the block into internal memory, shift its records by using an assignment such as

`buf.setRecord(i+1, buf.getRecord(i))`

and write the block to the file so that the file reflects the change. This large number of block accesses makes the external sorted buffer-based implementation practical only for tables in which insertions and deletions are rare. (See Exercise 1 at the end of this chapter.)

Indexing an External File

Two of the best external table implementations are variations of the internal hashing and search-tree schemes. The biggest difference between the internal and external versions of these implementations is that in the external versions, it is often advantageous to organize an **index** to the data file rather than to organize the data file itself. An index to a data file is conceptually similar to other indexes with which you are familiar. For example, consider a library catalog. Rather than looking all over the library for a particular title, you can simply search the catalog. The catalog is typically organized alphabetically by title (or by author), so it is a simple matter to locate the appropriate entry. The entry for each book contains an indication (for example, a Library of Congress number) of where on the shelves you can find the book.

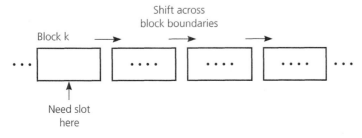

FIGURE 15-5

Shifting across block boundaries

Using a catalog to index the books in a library has at least three benefits:

Advantages of a
library catalog

- Because each catalog entry is much smaller than the book it represents, the entire catalog for a large library can fit into a small space. A patron can thus locate a particular book quickly.

- The library can organize the books on the shelves in any way, without regard to how easy it will be for a patron to scan the shelves for a particular book. To locate a particular book, the patron searches the catalog for the appropriate entry.

- The library can have different types of catalogs to facilitate different types of searches. For example, it can have one catalog organized by title and another organized by author.

Now consider how you can use an index to a data file to much the same advantage as the library catalog. As Figure 15-6 illustrates, you can leave the data file in a disorganized state and maintain an organized index to it. When you need to locate a particular record in the data file, you search the index for the corresponding entry, which will tell you where to find the desired record in the data file.

An index to a data
file

An index to the data file is simply a file, called the **index file,** that contains an **index record** for each record in the data file, just as a library catalog contains an entry for each book in the library. An index record has two parts: a **key,** which contains the same value as the search key of its corresponding record in the data file, and a **pointer,** which shows the number of the block in the data file that contains this data record. You thus can determine which block of the data file contains the record whose search key equals $searchKey$ by searching the index file for the index record whose key equals $searchKey$.

Maintaining an index to a data file has benefits analogous to those provided by the library's catalog:

Advantages of an
index file

- In general, an index record will be much smaller than a data record. While the data record may contain many components, an index record contains

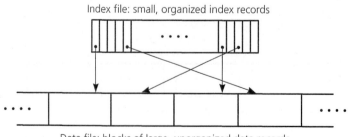

Index file: small, organized index records

Data file: blocks of large, unorganized data records

FIGURE 15-6

A data file with an index

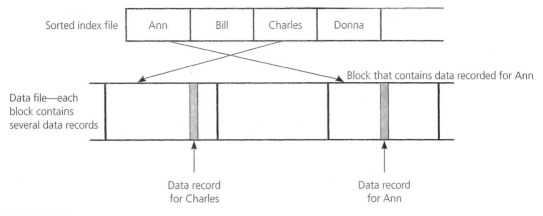

FIGURE 15-7

A data file with a sorted index file

only two: a key, which is also part of the data record, and a single integer pointer, which is the block number. Thus, just as a library catalog occupies only a small fraction of the space occupied by the books it indexes, an index file is only a fraction of the size of the data file. As you will see, the small size of the index file often allows you to manipulate it with fewer block accesses than you would need to manipulate the data file.

■ Because you do not need to maintain the data file in any particular order, you can insert new records in any convenient location, such as at the end of the file. As you will see, this flexibility eliminates the need to shift the data records during insertions and deletions.

■ You can maintain several indexes simultaneously. Just as a library can have one catalog organized by title and another organized by author, you can have one index file that indexes the data file by one search key (for example, an index file that consists of <name, pointer> records), and a second index file that indexes the data file by another search key (for example, an index file that consists of <socSec, pointer> records). Such **multiple indexing** is discussed briefly at the end of this chapter.

Although you do not organize the data file, you must organize the index file so that you can search and update it rapidly. Before considering how to organize an index file by using either hashing or search-tree schemes, first consider a less complex organization that illustrates the concepts of indexing. In particular, let the index file simply store the index records sequentially, sorted by their keys, as shown in Figure 15-7.

Organize the index file but not the data file

To perform the *tableRetrieve* operation, for example, you can use a binary search on the index file as follows:

```
tableRetrieve(in tIndex:File, in tData:File,
              in searchKey:KeyType):TableItemType
// Returns the record whose search key
```

Retrieval by search-
ing an index file

```
// equals searchKey, where tIndex is the index file and
// tData is the data file. The operation fails and returns
// null if no such record exists.

if (no blocks are left in tIndex to read) {
  return null
}
else {
  // read the middle block of index file into buf
  mid = number of middle block of index file tIndex
  buf.readBlock(tIndex, mid)
  num = indexRecordsPerBlock
  if ((searchKey >= (buf.getRecord(0)).getKey()) &&
      (searchKey <= buf.getRecord(indexRecPerBlock-1).getKey())) {

    // desired block of index file found
    Search buf for index file record buf.getRecord(j)
       whose key value equals searchKey

    if (index record buf.getRecord(j) is found) {
      blockNum = number of the data-file block to
                 which buf.getRecord(j) points
      data.readBlock(tData, blockNum)
      Find data record data.getRecord(k) whose search
         key equals searchKey
      tableItem = data.getRecord(k)
      return tableItem
    }
    else {
      return null
    }  // end if
  }

  else if (tIndex is one block in size) {
    return null  // no more blocks in file
  }

  // else search appropriate half of index file
  else if (searchKey < (buf.getRecord(0)).getKey()) {
    return tableRetrieve(first half of tIndex, tData,
                         searchKey)
  }
  else {
    return tableRetrieve(second half of tIndex, tData,
                         searchKey)
  }  // end if
}  // end if
```

Because the index records are far smaller than the data records, the index file contains far fewer blocks than the data file. For example, if the index records are one-tenth the size of the data records and the data file contains 1,000 blocks, the index file will require only about 100 blocks. As a result, the use of an index cuts the number of block accesses in `tableRetrieve` down from about $\log_2 1000 \approx 10$ to about $1 + \log_2 100 \approx 8$. (The one additional block access is into the data file once you have located the appropriate index record.)

An index file reduces the number of required block accesses for table operations

The reduction in block accesses is far more dramatic for the `tableInsert` and `tableDelete` operations. In the implementation of an external table discussed earlier in this section, if you insert a record into or delete a record from the first block of data, for example, you have to shift records in every block, requiring that you access all 1,000 blocks of the data file. (See Figure 15-5.)

However, when you perform an insertion or a deletion by using the index scheme, you have to shift only index records. When you use an index file, you do not keep the data file in any particular order, so you can insert a new data record into any convenient location in the data file. This flexibility means that you can simply insert a new data record at the end of the file or at a position left vacant by a previous deletion (as you will see). As a result, you never need to shift records in the data file. However, you do need to shift records in the index file to create an opening for a corresponding index entry in its proper sorted position. Because the index file contains many fewer blocks than the data file (100 versus 1,000 in the previous example), the maximum number of block accesses required is greatly reduced. A secondary benefit of shifting index records rather than data records is a reduction in the time requirement for a single shift. Because the index records themselves are smaller, the time required for the statement `buf.setRecord(i+1, buf.getRecord(i))` is decreased.

Shift index records instead of data records

Deletions under the index scheme reap similar benefits. Once you have searched the index file and located the data record to be deleted, you can simply leave its location vacant in the data file, and thus you need not shift any data records. You can keep track of the vacant locations in the data file (see Exercise 2), so that you can insert new data records into the vacancies, as was mentioned earlier. The only shifting required is in the index file to fill the gap created when you remove the index record that corresponds to the deleted data record.

Even though this scheme is an improvement over maintaining a sorted data file, in many applications it is far from satisfactory. The 100 block accesses that could be required to insert or delete an index record often would be prohibitive. Far better implementations are possible when you use either hashing or search trees to organize the index file.

An unsorted data file with a sorted index is more efficient than a sorted data file, but other schemes are even better

External Hashing

The external hashing scheme is quite similar to the internal scheme described in Chapter 13. In the internal hashing scheme, each entry of the array `table` contains a reference to the beginning of the list of items that hash into that location. In the external hashing scheme, each entry of *table* contains a block pointer to the beginning of a list, but here each list consists of *blocks of index records*. In other words, you hash an index file rather than the data file, as Figure 15-8 illustrates. (In many applications the array *table* is itself so large that you must keep it in external storage—for example, in the first K blocks of the index file. To avoid this extra detail, you can assume here that the array *table* is an internal array.)

You hash the index file instead of the data file

Associated with each entry *table[i]* is a linked list of blocks of the index file, as you can see in Figure 15-8. Each block of *table[i]*'s linked list contains index records whose keys (and thus whose corresponding data records' search keys) hash into location *i*. To form the linked lists, you must reserve space in each block for a block pointer—the integer block number of the next block in the chain—as Figure 15-9 illustrates. That is, in this linked list, the

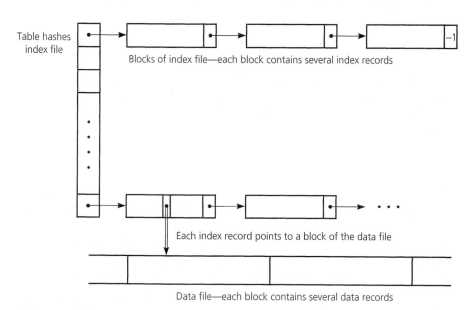

Table hashes index file

Blocks of index file—each block contains several index records

Each index record points to a block of the data file

Data file—each block contains several data records

FIGURE 15-8

A hashed index file

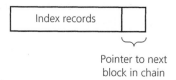

Index records

Pointer to next block in chain

FIGURE 15-9

A single block with a pointer

block pointers are integers, not Java references. A pointer value of −1 is used as a *null* pointer.

Retrieval under external hashing of an index file. The `tableRetrieve` operation appears in pseudocode as follows:

```
+tableRetrieve(in tIndex:File, in tData:File,
               in searchKey:KeyType):TableItemType
// Returns the item whose search key equals searchKey,
// where tIndex is the index file, which is hashed, and
// tData is the data file. The operation fails and returns
// null if no such record exists.

  // apply the hash function to the search key
  i = h(searchKey)

  // find the first block in the chain of index blocks —
  // these blocks contain index records that hash into
  // location i
  p = table[i]

  // if p == -1, no values have hashed into location i
  if (p != -1) {
    buf.readBlock(tIndex, p)
  }  // end if



  // search for the block with the desired index record
  while (p != -1 and buf does not contain an index record
                        whose key value equals searchKey) {
    p = number of next block in chain
    // if p == -1, you are at the last block in the chain
    if (p != -1) {
      buf.readBlock(tIndex, p)
    }  // end if
  }  // end while

  // retrieve the data item if present
  if (p != -1) {
    // buf.getRecord(j) is the index record whose
    // key value equals searchKey
    blockNum = number of the data-file block to
               which buf.getRecord(j) points
    data.readBlock(tData, blockNum)
    Find data record data.getRecord(k) whose search key
        equals searchKey
    tableItem = data.getRecord(k)
```

```
    return tableItem
  }
  else {
    return null
  }  // end if
```

Insertion under external hashing of an index file.   The external hashing versions of `tableInsert` and `tableDelete` are also similar to the internal hashing versions. The major difference is that, in the external environment, you must insert or delete both a data record and the corresponding index record.

To insert a new data record whose search key is `searchKey`, you take the following steps:

1. **Insert the data record into the data file.** Because the data file is not ordered, the new record can go anywhere you want. If a previous deletion has left a free slot in the middle of the data file, you can insert it there. (See Exercise 2.)

   If no slots are free, you insert the new data record at the end of the last block, or, if necessary, you append a new block to the end of the data file and store the record there. In either case, let p denote the number of the block that contains this new data record.

2. **Insert a corresponding index record into the index file.** You need to insert into the index file an index record that has key value `searchKey` and reference value p. (Recall that p is the number of the block in the data file into which you inserted the new data record.) Because the index file is hashed, you first apply the hash function to `searchKey`, letting

   `i = h(searchKey)`

   You then insert the index record `<searchKey, p>` into the chain of blocks that the entry `table[i]` points to. You can insert this record into any block in the chain that contains a free slot, or, if necessary, you can allocate a new block and link it to the beginning of the chain.

Deletion under external hashing of an index file.   To delete the data record whose search key is `searchKey`, you take the following steps:

1. **Search the index file for the corresponding index record.** You apply the hash function to `searchKey`, letting

   `i = h(searchKey)`

   You then search the chain of index blocks pointed to by the entry `table[i]` for an index record whose key value equals `searchKey`. If you do not find such a record, you can conclude that the data file does not contain a record whose search key equals `searchKey`. However, if you find an index record <searchKey, p>, you delete it from the index file after noting the block number p, which indicates where in the data file you can find the data record to be deleted.

2. **Delete the data record from the data file.** You know that the data record is in block p of the data file. You simply access this block, search the block for the record, delete the record, and write the block back to the file.

Observe that for each of the operations tableRetrieve, tableInsert, and tableDelete, the number of block accesses is very low. You never have to access more than one block of the data file, and at worst you have to access all of the blocks along a single hash chain of the index file. You can take measures to keep the length of each of the chains quite short (for example, one or two blocks long), just as you can with internal hashing. You should make the size of the array table large enough so that the average length of a chain is near one block, and the hash function should scatter the keys evenly. If necessary, you can even structure each chain as an external search tree—a **B-tree**—by using the techniques described in the next section.

The hashing implementation is the one to choose when you need to perform the operations tableRetrieve, tableInsert, and tableDelete on a large external table. As is the case with internal hashing, however, this implementation is not practical for certain other operations, such as sorted traversal, retrieval of the smallest or largest item, and range queries that require ordered data. When these types of operations are added to the basic table operations tableRetrieve, tableInsert, and tableDelete, you should use a search-tree implementation instead of hashing.

Choose external hashing for **tableRetrieve**, **tableInsert**, and **tableDelete** operations

B-Trees

Another way to search an external table is to organize it as a balanced search tree. Just as you can apply external hashing to the index file, you can organize the index file, not the data file, as an external search tree. The implementation developed here is a generalization of the 2-3 tree of Chapter 13.

You can organize the blocks of an external file into a tree structure by using block numbers for child pointers. In Figure 15-10a, for example, the blocks are organized into a 2-3 tree. Each block of the file is a node in the tree and contains three child pointers, each of which is the integer block number of the child. A child pointer value of −1 plays the role of a null pointer, and thus, for example, a leaf will contain three child pointers with the value −1.

If you organized the index file into a 2-3 tree, each node (block of the index file) would contain either one or two index records, each of the form <key, pointer>, and three child pointers. The pointer portion of an index record has nothing to do with the tree structure of the index file; pointer indicates the block (in the data file) that contains the data record whose search key equals key. (See Figure 15-10b.) To help avoid confusion, the pointers in the tree structure of the index file will be referred to as **child pointers.**

Organize the index file as an external 2-3 tree

You must organize the index records in the tree so that their keys obey the same search-tree ordering property as an internal 2-3 tree. This organization

(a)

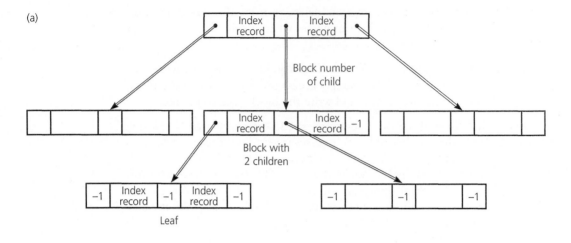

(b)

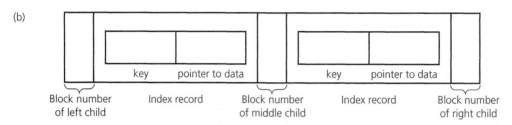

FIGURE 15-10

(a) Blocks organized into a 2-3 tree; (b) a single node of the 2-3 tree

allows you to retrieve the data record with a given value in its search key as
follows:

Retrieval when the
index file is a 2-3
tree

```
+tableRetrieve(in tIndex:File, in tData:File, in rootNum:integer,
              in searchKey:KeyType):TableItemType
// Returns the record whose search key equals searchKey. tIndex
// is the index file, which is organized as a 2-3 tree. rootNum
// is the block number (of the index file) that contains the
// root of the tree. tData is the data file. The operation
// fails and returns a null reference if no such record exists.
    if (no blocks are left in tIndex to read) {
       return null
    }
    else {
       // read from index file into buf the
       // block that contains the root of the 2-3 tree
       buf.readBlock(tIndex, rootNum)

       // search for the index record whose key value
       // equals searchKey
```

```
if (searchKey is in the root) {
  blockNum = number of the data-file block that
            index record specifies
  data.readBlock(tData, blockNum)
  Find data record data.getRecord(k) whose search key
      equals searchKey
  tableItem = data.getRecord(k)
  return tableItem
}
// else search the appropriate subtree
else if (the root is a leaf) {
  return null
} // end else if
else {
  child = block number of root of
          appropriate subtree
  return tableRetrieve(tIndex, tData, child,
                       searchKey)
}  // end if
}  // end if
```

You also can perform insertions and deletions in a manner similar to the internal version, with the addition that you must insert records into and delete records from both the index file and the data file (as was the case in the external hashing scheme described earlier). In the course of insertions into and deletions from the index file, you must split and merge nodes of the tree just as you do for the internal version. You perform insertions into and deletions from the data file—which, recall, is not ordered in any way—exactly as described for the external hashing implementation. You thus can support the table operations fairly well by using an external version of the 2-3 tree.

However, you can generalize the 2-3 tree to a structure that is even more suitable for an external environment. Recall the discussion in Chapter 13 about search trees whose nodes can have many children. Adding more children per node reduces the height of the search tree but increases the number of comparisons at each node during the search for a value.

An external 2-3 tree is adequate, but an improvement is possible

In an external environment, however, the advantage of keeping a search tree short far outweighs the disadvantage of performing extra work at each node. As you traverse the search tree in an external environment, you must perform a block access for each node visited. Because the time required to access a block of an external file is, in general, far greater than the time required to process the data in that block once it has been read in, the overriding concern is to reduce the number of block accesses required. This fact implies that you should attempt to reduce the height of the tree, even at the expense of requiring more comparisons at each node. In an external search tree, you should thus allow each node to have as many children as possible, with only the block size as a limiting factor.

Keep an external search tree short

How many children can a block of some fixed size accommodate? If a node is to have m children, clearly you must be able to fit m child pointers in the node. In addition to child pointers, however, the node must also contain index records.

Before you can answer the question of how many children a block can accommodate, you must first consider this related question: If a node N in a search tree has m children, how many key values—and thus how many index records—must it contain?

Binary search tree: the number of records and children per node

In a binary search tree, if the node N has two children, it must contain one key value, as Figure 15-11a indicates. You can think of the key value in node N as separating the key values in N's two subtrees—all of the key values in N's left subtree are less than N's key value, and all of the key values in N's right subtree are greater than N's key value. When you are searching the tree for a given key value, the key value in N tells you which branch to take.

2-3 tree: the number of records and children per node

Similarly, if a node N in a 2-3 tree has three children, it must contain two key values. (See Figure 15-11b.) These two values separate the key values in N's three subtrees—all of the key values in the left subtree are less than N's smaller key value, all of the key values in N's middle subtree lie between N's two key values, and all of the key values in N's right subtree are greater than N's larger key value. As is the case with a binary search tree, this requirement allows a search algorithm to know which branch to take at any given node.

General search tree: the number of records and children per node

In general, if a node N in a search tree is to have m children, it must contain $m - 1$ key values to separate the values in its subtrees correctly. (See Figure 15-11c.) Suppose that you denote the subtrees of N as S_0, S_1, and so on to S_{m-1} and denote the key values in N as K_1, K_2, and so on to K_{m-1} (with

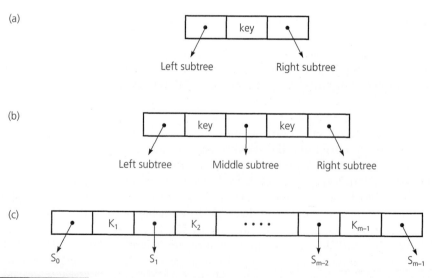

(a)

Left subtree   Right subtree

(b)

Left subtree   Middle subtree   Right subtree

(c)

S_0 S_1 S_{m-2} S_{m-1}

FIGURE 15-11

(a) A node with two children; (b) a node with three children; (c) a node with m children

$K_1 < K_2 < \cdots < K_{m-1}$). The key values in N must separate the values in its subtrees as follows:

- All the values in subtree S_0 must be less than the key value K_1.

- For all i, $1 \leq i \leq m - 2$, all the values in subtree S_i must lie between the key values K_i and K_{i+1}.

- All the values in subtree S_{m-1} must be greater than the key value K_{m-1}.

If every node in the tree obeys this property, you can search the tree by using a generalized version of a search tree's retrieval algorithm. Thus, you can perform the `tableRetrieve` operation as follows:

```
+tableRetrieve(in tIndex:File, in tData:File, in rootNum:integer,
               in searchKey:KeyType):TableItemType
// Returns the record whose search key
// equals searchKey. tIndex is the index file, which is
// organized as a search tree. rootNum is the block number
// (of the index file) that contains the root of the tree.
// tData is the data file. The operation fails and returns
// null if no such record exists.

  if (no blocks are left in tIndex to read) {
    return null
  }
  else {
    // read from index file into internal buffer buf the
    // block that contains the root of the tree
    buf.readBlock(tIndex, rootNum)

    // search for the index record whose key value
    // equals searchKey
    if (searchKey is one of the K_i in the root) {
      blockNum = number of the data-file block that
                 index record specifies
      data.readBlock(tData, blockNum)
      Find data record data.getRecord(k) whose search key
          equals searchKey
      tableItem = data.getRecord(k)
      return tableItem
    }
    // else search the appropriate subtree
    else if (the root is a leaf) {
      return null
    }
    else {
      Determine which subtree S_i to search
      child = block number of the root of S_i
```

Retrieval with a general external search tree

```
        return tableRetrieve(tIndex, tData, child, searchKey)
    }  // end if
}  // end if
```

Now return to the question of how many children the nodes of the search tree can have—that is, how big can m be? If you wish to organize the index file into a search tree, the items that you store in each node will be records of the form <key, pointer>. Thus, if each node in the tree (which, recall, is a block of the index file) is to have m children, it must be large enough to accommodate m child **pointers** and $m - 1$ records of the form <key, pointer>. You should choose m to be the largest integer such that m child **pointers** (which, recall, are integers) and $m - 1$ <key, pointer> records can fit into a single block of the file. Actually, the algorithms are somewhat simplified if you always choose an odd number for m. That is, you should choose m to be the largest odd integer such that m child pointers and $m - 1$ index records can fit into a single block.

Number of children per node

Ideally, then, you should structure the external search tree so that every internal node has m children, where m is chosen as just described, and all leaves are at the same level, as is the case with full trees and 2-3 trees. For example, Figure 15-12 shows a full tree whose internal nodes each have five children. Although this search tree has the minimum possible height, its balance is too difficult to maintain in the face of insertions and deletions. As a consequence, you must make a compromise. You can still insist that all the

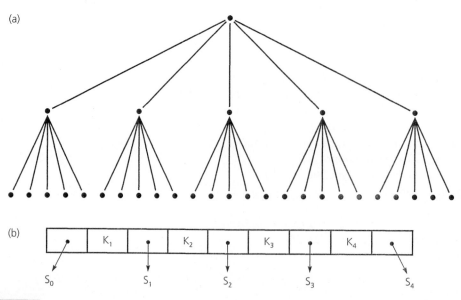

FIGURE 15-12

(a) A full tree whose internal nodes have five children; (b) the format of a single node leaves of the search tree be at the same level—that is, that the tree be balanced—but you must allow each internal node to have between *m* and [*m*/2] + 1 children. (The [ ] notation means *greatest integer in*. Thus, [5/2] is 2, for example.)

This type of search tree is known as a **B-tree of degree** *m* and has the following characteristics:

- All leaves are at the same level.   B-tree of degree m

- Each node contains between *m* – 1 and [*m*/2] records, and each internal node has one more child than it has records. An exception to this rule is that the root of the tree can contain as few as one record and can have as few as two children. This exception is necessitated by the insertion and deletion algorithms described next.

A 2-3 tree is a B-tree of degree 3. Furthermore, the manner in which the B-tree insertion and deletion algorithms maintain the structure of the tree is a direct generalization of the 2-3 tree's strategy of splitting and merging nodes.   A 2-3 tree is a B-tree of degree 3

The B-tree insertion and deletion algorithms are illustrated next by means of an example. Assume that the index file is organized into a B-tree of degree 5—that is, 5 is the maximum and 3 is the minimum number of children that an internal node (other than the root) in the tree can have. (Typically, a B-tree will be of a higher degree, but the diagrams would get out of hand!)

Insertion into a B-tree. To insert a data record with search key 55 into the tree shown in Figure 15-13, you take the following steps:

1. **Insert the data record into the data file.** First you find block *p* in the data file into which you can insert the new record. As was true with the external hashing implementation, block *p* is either any block with a vacant slot or a new block.

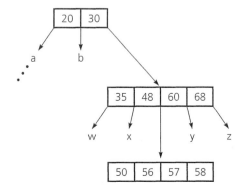

FIGURE 15-13

A B-tree of degree 5

2. **Insert a corresponding index record into the index file.** You now must insert the index record <55, *p*> into the index file, which is a B-tree of degree 5. The first step is to locate the leaf of the tree in which this index record belongs by determining where the search for 55 would terminate.

Suppose that this is the leaf *L* shown in Figure 15-14a. Conceptually, you insert the new index record into *L*, causing it to contain five records (Figure 15-14b). Since a node can contain only four records, you must split *L* into L_1 and L_2. With an action analogous to the splitting of a node in a 2-3 tree, L_1 gets the two records with the smallest key values, L_2 gets

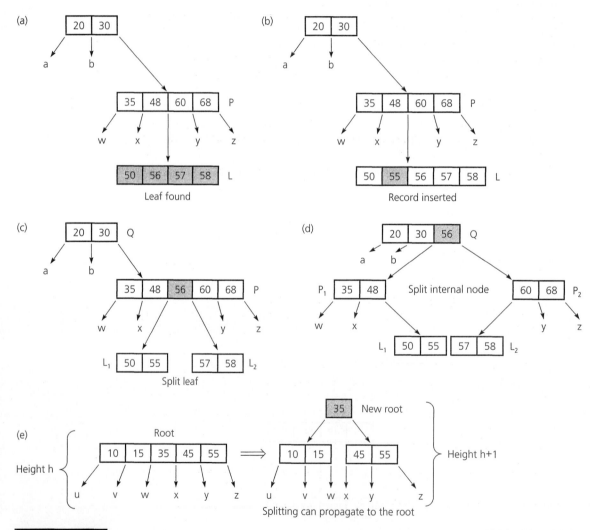

FIGURE 15-14

The steps for inserting 55

the two records with the largest key values, and the record with the middle key value (56) is moved up to the parent P. (See Figure 15-14c.)

In this example, P now has six children and five records, so it must be split into P_1 and P_2. The record with the middle key value (56) is moved up to P's parent, Q. Then P's children must be distributed appropriately, as happens with a 2-3 tree when an internal node is split. (See Figure 15-14d.)

At this point the insertion is complete, since P's parent Q now contains only three records and has only four children. In general, though, an insertion might cause splitting to propagate all the way up to the root (Figure 15-14e). If the root must be split, the new root will contain only one record and have only two children—the definition of a B-tree allows for this eventuality.

Deletion from a B-tree.   To delete a data record with a given search key from a B-tree, you take the following steps:

1. **Locate the index record in the index file.** You use the search algorithm to locate the index record with the desired key value. If this record is not already in a leaf, you swap it with its inorder successor. (See Exercise 8.) Suppose that the leaf L shown in Figure 15-15a contains the index record with the desired key value, 73. After noting the value p of the pointer in this index record (you will need p in Step 2 to delete the data record), you remove the index record from L (Figure 15-15b). Because L now contains only one value (recall that a node must contain at least two values) and since L's siblings cannot spare a value, you merge L with one of the siblings and bring down a record from the parent P (Figure 15-15c). Notice that this step is analogous to the merge step for a 2-3 tree. However, P now has only one value and two children, and since its siblings cannot spare a record and child, you must merge P with its sibling P_1 and bring a record down from P's parent, Q. Since P is an internal node, its children must be adopted by P_1. (See Figure 15-15d.)

   After this merge, P's parent Q is left with only two children and one record. In this case, however, Q's sibling Q_1 can spare a record and a child, so you redistribute children and records among Q_1, Q, and the parent S to complete the deletion. (See Figure 15-15e.) If a deletion ever propagates all the way up to the root, leaving it with only one record and only two children, you are finished because the definition of a B-tree allows this situation. If a future deletion causes the root to have a single child and no records, you remove the root so that the tree's height decreases by 1, as Figure 15-15f illustrates. The deletion of the index record is complete, and you now must delete the data record.

2. **Delete the data record from the data file.** Prior to deleting the index record, you noted the value p of its pointer. Block p of the data file contains the data record to be deleted. Thus, you simply access block p, delete the data record, and write the block back to the file. The high-level pseudocode for the insertion and deletion algorithms parallels that of the 2-3 tree and is left as an exercise.

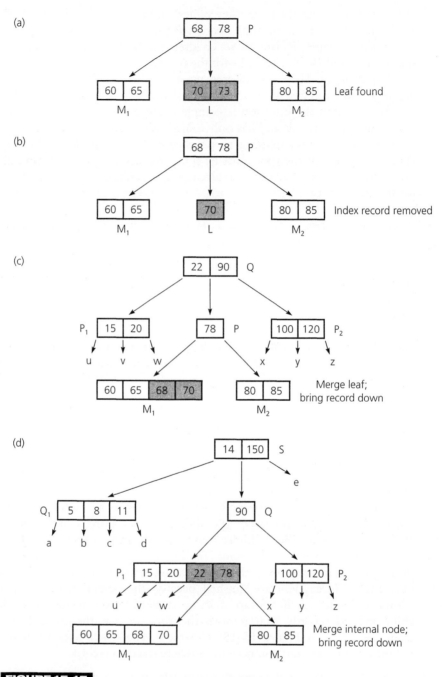

FIGURE 15-15

The steps for deleting 73

(continues)

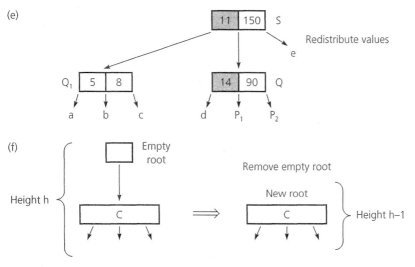

FIGURE 15-15

(continued)

Traversals

Now consider the operation *traverseTable* in sorted order, which is one of the operations that hashing does not support at all efficiently. Often an application requires only that the traversal display the search keys of the records. If such is the case, the B-tree implementation can efficiently support the operation, because you do not have to access the data file. You can visit the search keys in sorted order by using an inorder traversal of the B-tree, as follows:

Accessing only the search key of each record, but not the data file

```
+traverseTable(in blockNum:integer, in m:integer)
// Traverses in sorted order an index file that is organized
// as a B-tree of degree m. blockNum is the block number of
// the root of the B-tree in the index file.

   if (blockNum != -1) {
      // read the root into internal buffer buf
      buf.readBlock(indexFile, blockNum)

      // traverse the children

      // traverse S0
      Let p be the block number of the 0th child of buf
      traverseTable(p, m)

      for (i = 1 through m - 1) {
         Display key Ki of buf
```

Inorder traversal of a B-tree index file

```
                    // traverse S_i
                    Let p be the block number of the i^th child of buf
                    traverseTable(p, m)
             }   // end for
      }   // end if
```

This traversal accomplishes the task with the minimum possible number of block accesses because each block of the index file is read only once. This algorithm, however, assumes that enough internal memory is available for a recursive stack of h blocks, where h is the height of the tree. In many situations this assumption is reasonable—for example, a 255-degree B-tree that indexes a file of 16 million data records has a height of no more than 3. When internal memory cannot accommodate h blocks, you must use a different algorithm. (See Exercise 12.)

Accessing the entire data record

If the traversal must display the entire data record (and not just the search key), the B-tree implementation is less attractive. In this case, as you traverse the B-tree, you must access the appropriate block of the data file. The traversal becomes

Sorted-order traversal of a data file indexed with a B-tree

```
+traverseTable(in blockNum:integer, in m:integer)
// Traverses in sorted order a data file that is indexed
// with a B-tree of degree m. blockNum is the block number
// of the root of the B-tree.

  if (blockNum != -1) {
    // read the root into internal buffer buf
    buf.readBlock(indexFile, blockNum)

    // traverse S_0
    Let p be the block number of the 0^th child of buf
    traverseTable(p, m)
    for (i = 1 through m - 1) {
      Let p_i be the pointer in the i^th index record of buf
      data.readBlock(dataFile, p_i)
      Extract from data the record whose search key equals K_i
      Display the data record

      // traverse S_i
      Let p be the block number of the i^th child of buf
      traverseTable(p, m)
    }   // end for
  }   // end if
```

Generally, the previous traversal is unacceptable

This traversal requires you to read a block of the data file before you display each data record; that is, the number of data-file block accesses is equal to the number of data records. In general, such a large number of block accesses would not be acceptable. If you must perform this type of traversal frequently, you probably would modify the B-tree scheme so that the data file itself was kept nearly sorted.

Multiple Indexing

Before concluding the discussion of external implementations, let's consider the multiple indexing of a data file. Chapter 13 presented a problem in which you had to support multiple organizations for data stored in internal memory. Such a problem is also common for data stored externally. For example, suppose that a data file contains a collection of employee records on which you need to perform two types of retrievals:

```
retrieveN(in aName:NameType):ItemType
// Retrieves the item whose search key contains the
// name aName.

retrieveS(in ssn:SSNType):ItemType
// Retrieves the item whose search key contains the
// Social Security number ssn.
```

One solution to this problem is to maintain two independent index files to the data file. For example, you could have one index file that contains index records of the form `<name, pointer>` and a second index file that contains index records of the form `<socSec, pointer>`. These index files could both be hashed, could both be B-trees, or could be one of each, as Figure 15-16 indicates. The

Multiple index files allow multiple data organizations

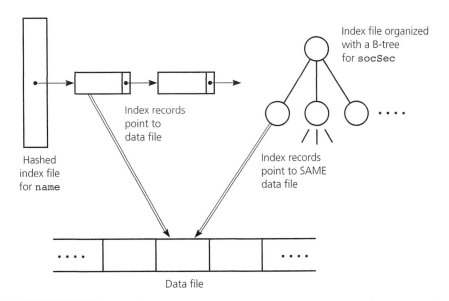

FIGURE 15-16
Multiple index files

choice would depend on the operations you wanted to perform with each search key. (Similarly, if an application required extremely fast retrievals on *socSec* and also required operations such as traverse in sorted *socSec* order and range queries on *socSec*, it might be reasonable to have two *socSec* index files—one hashed, the other a B-tree.)

While you can perform each retrieval operation by using only one of the indexes (that is, use the *name* index for *retrieveN* and the *socSec* index for *retrieveS*), insertion and deletion operations must update both indexes. For example, the delete-by-name operation *deleteN(Jones)* requires the following steps:

A deletion by name must update both indexes

1. Search the *name* index file for Jones and delete the index record.

2. Delete the appropriate data record from the data file, noting the *socSec* value *ssn* of this record.

3. Search the *socSec* index file for *ssn* and delete this index record.

In general, the price paid for multiple indexing is more storage space and an additional overhead for updating each index whenever you modify the data file.

This chapter has presented, at a very high level, the basic principles of managing data in external storage. The details of implementing the algorithms depend heavily on your specific computing system. Particular situations often mandate either variations of the methods described here or completely different approaches. In future courses and work experience, you will undoubtedly learn much more about these techniques.

Summary

1. An external file is partitioned into blocks. Each block typically contains many data records, and a block is generally the smallest unit of transfer between internal and external memory. That is, to access a record, you must access the block that contains it.

2. You can access the ith block of a random access file without accessing the blocks that precede it. In this sense, random access files resemble arrays.

3. You can modify the mergesort algorithm, presented in Chapter 10, so that it can sort an external file of records without requiring all of the records to be in internal memory at one time.

4. An index to a data file is a file that contains an index record for each record in the data file. An index record contains both the search key of the corresponding data record and the number of the block in the data file that contains the data record.

5. You can organize the index file by using either hashing or a B-tree. These schemes allow you to perform the basic table operations by using only a few block accesses.

6. You can have several index files for the same data file. Such multiple indexing allows you to perform different types of operations efficiently, such as retrieve by name and retrieve by Social Security number.

Cautions

1. Before you can process (for example, inspect or update) a record, you must read it from an external file into internal memory. Once you modify a record, you must write it back to the file.

2. Block accesses are typically quite slow when compared to other computer operations. Therefore, you must carefully organize a file so that you can perform tasks by using only a few block accesses. Otherwise, response time can be very poor.

3. If a record is inserted into or deleted from a data file, you must make the corresponding change to the index file. If a data file has more than one index file, you must update each index file. Thus, multiple indexing has an overhead.

4. Although external hashing generally permits retrievals, insertions, and deletions to be performed more quickly than does a B-tree, it does not support such operations as sorted traversals or range queries. This deficiency is one motivation for multiple indexing.

Self-Test Exercises

1. Consider two files of 1,600 employee records each. The records in each file are organized into sixteen 100-record blocks. One file is sequential access and the other is random access. Describe how you would append one record to the end of each file.

2. Trace `externalMergesort` with an external file of 16 blocks. Assume that the buffers `in1`, `in2`, and `out` are each one block long. List the calls to the various methods in the order in which they occur.

3. Trace the retrieval algorithm for an indexed external file when the search key is less than all keys in the index. Assume that the index file stores the index records sequentially, sorted by their search keys, and contains 20 blocks of 50 records each. Also, assume that the data file contains 100 blocks, and each block contains 10 employee records. List the calls to the various methods in the order in which they occur.

4. Repeat Self-Test Exercise 3, but this time assume that the search key equals the key in record 26 of block 12 of the index. Also assume that record 26 of the index points to block 98 of the data file.

Exercises

1. Assuming the existence of `readBlock` and `writeBlock` methods, write a pseudocode program for shifting data to make a gap at some specified location of a sorted file. Pay particular attention to the details of shifting the last item out of one block and into the first position of the next block. You can assume that the last record of the file is in record `lastRec` of block `lastBlock` and that `lastBlock` is not full. (Note that this assumption permits shifting without allocating a new block to the file.)

2. The problem of managing the blocks of an external data file indexed by either a B-tree or an external hashing scheme is similar to that of managing memory for internal structures. When an external structure such as a data file needs more memory (for

example, to insert a new record), it gets a new block from a **free list** that the system manages. That is, if the file contains N blocks, the system can allocate to it an $(N + 1)^{\text{th}}$ block. When the file no longer needs a block, you can deallocate it and return it to the system.

The complication in the management of external storage is that a block allocated to a file may have available space interspersed with data. For example, after you have deleted a record from the middle of a data file, the block that contained that record will have space available for at least one record. Therefore, you must be able to keep track of blocks that have space available for one or more records as well as recognize when blocks are completely empty (so that you can return them to the system).

Assuming the existence of `allocateBlock` and `returnBlock` methods that get empty blocks from and return empty blocks to the system, write pseudocode implementations of the following external memory-management methods:

```
getSlot(in dataFile:File):BlockInfoType
// Determines the block number (blockNum) and record
// number (recNum) of an available slot in file
// dataFile. Places this info in a BlockInfoType object
// for return. A new block is allocated to the file from
// the system if necessary.

freeSlot(in dataFile:File, in blockInfo:BlockInfoType)
// Gets recNum and blockNum from blockInfo.
// Makes record recNum in block blockNum of file
// dataFile available. The block is returned to the
// system if it becomes empty.
```

What data structure is appropriate to support these operations? You may assume that you can distinguish slots of a block that do not contain a record from those that do. You can make this distinction either by having a convention for *null* values within a record or by adding an empty/full flag.

3. Describe pseudocode algorithms for insertion into and deletion from a table implemented externally with a hashed index file.

4. Execute the following sequence of operations on an initially empty ADT table *t* that is implemented as a B-tree of degree 5. Note that insertion into an empty B-tree will create a single node that contains the inserted item.

```
t.tableInsert(10)
t.tableInsert(100)
t.tableInsert(30)
t.tableInsert(80)
t.tableInsert(50)
t.tableDelete(10)
t.tableInsert(60)
t.tableInsert(70)
t.tableInsert(40)
t.tableDelete(80)
t.tableInsert(90)
t.tableInsert(20)
t.tableDelete(30)
t.tableDelete(70)
```

5. Given a B-tree of degree 5 and a height of 3:

    a. What is the maximum number of nodes (including the root)?

    b. What is the maximum number of records that can be stored?

6. Given the following B-tree of degree 7 in Figure 15-17, draw the B-tree that results after the insertion of m, o, y, r, c, i, k, w, and h.

7. Given the following B-tree of degree 7 in Figure 15-18, draw the B-tree that results after the removal of s, t, p, m, k, and e.

8. Describe a pseudocode algorithm for finding an item's inorder successor in an external B-tree.

9. Describe pseudocode algorithms for insertion into and deletion from an ADT table implemented with an index file organized as a B-tree.

10. Write a *rangeQuery* method for a B-tree in pseudocode. (See Exercise 3 of Chapter 13.) Assume that only the key values are needed (as opposed to the entire data record).

11. Implement the hashing scheme for a given set of keys using the chaining method. Maintain the chains in the descending order of the keys.
    Write a menu driven code to implement insert, delete and search functions for this hashing scheme.

12. The B-tree traversal algorithm presented in this chapter assumes that internal memory is large enough to accommodate the recursive stack that contains up to h blocks, where h is the height of the B-tree. If you are in an environment where this assumption is not true, modify the traversal algorithm so that the recursive stack contains block numbers rather than the actual blocks. How many block accesses does your algorithm have to perform?

13. a. Write pseudocode B-tree implementations of traversals and range queries that need to access entire data records, not simply the search keys. How many block accesses do your methods require?

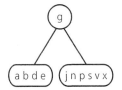

FIGURE 15-17

A B-tree for Exercise 6

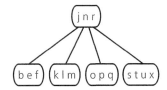

FIGURE 15-18

A B-tree for Exercise 7

b. To reduce the number of block accesses required by these operations, various modifications of the basic B-tree structure are frequently used. The central idea behind such structures is to keep the data file itself sorted. First, assume that you can keep the data file in sequential sorted order—that is, the records are sorted within each block and the records in B_{i-1} are less than the records in B_i for $i = 2, 3$, and so on to the number of blocks in the file. Rewrite your implementations of the traversal and range-query operations to take advantage of this fact. How many block accesses do these operations now require?

c. Because it is too inefficient to maintain a sequentially sorted data file in the face of frequent insertions and deletions, a compromise scheme is often employed. One such possible compromise is as follows. If a data record belongs in block B and B is full, a new block is allocated and linked to B, allowing the new record to be inserted into its proper sorted location. The difficulty is that you must now view each index record in the B-tree as indicating the first of possibly several blocks in a chain of blocks that might contain the corresponding data record. Rewrite the `table-Insert`, `tableDelete`, `tableRetrieve`, `traverseTable`, and `rangeQuery` operations in terms of this implementation. What is the effect on their efficiency?

14. Write an iterative (nonrecursive) version of internal `mergesort`, as given in Chapter 10, that is based on the external version that this chapter describes. That is, merge sorted runs that double in size at each pass of the array.

Programming Problems

1. a. Implement the `externalMergesort` algorithm in Java by using the class `RandomAccessFile`. Assume that the file to be sorted is a file of type `int` and that each block contains one integer. Further assume that the file contains 2^n integers for some integer n.

b. Now assume that each block contains many integers. Write Java methods that simulate `readBlock` and `writeBlock`. Implement `externalMergesort` by using these methods.

c. Extend your implementation of `externalMergesort` by removing the restriction that the file contains 2^n blocks.

2. Implement the ADT table by using a sorted index file, as described in the section "Indexing an External File."

3. Implement an ADT table that uses a sorted index file using the JCF Map interface.

4. Implement a simple dictionary application, such as the one described in Exercise 4 of Chapter 12, using the external table of Programming Problem 3.

5. Implement the ADT table by using a hashed index file, as described in the section "External Hashing."

6. Implement the ADT table by using a B-tree, as described in the section "B-Trees."

7. Repeat Programming Problem 5 of Chapter 11, using an external table to implement `PhoneBook`.

APPENDIX A

A Comparison of Java to C++

The following examples will help you compare a construct in C++ with the equivalent construct in Java.

``// Java comment on a single line
/* Java comment
that crosses multiple lines */
/** Javadoc-style comments */```	```// C++ comment on a single line
/* C++ comment
that crosses multiple lines */```
``// Java uses packages to group
// related classes together```	```// C++ uses libraries to group
// related functions and classes
// together```
``// Java class
// Each member has an access
// modifier (public, private,
// protected, or none for
// package access)
class Person {
  private String name;
  protected int age;
  double gpa;
  public Person() {
  } // end default constructor
  ...
} // end Person``` | ```// C++ class - by default, all
// members are private unless
// labeled otherwise, no package access

class Person {
  string name;
protected:
  int age;
  double gpa;
public:
  Person();
}; // end Person``` |
| ```// No equivalent in Java, a class
// containing only public data
// could be used``` | ```// C++ structure - by default, all
// members are public unless
// labeled otherwise
struct person {
  string name;
  int   age;
  double gpa;
}; // end person``` |
| ```// Java supports single inheritance
// of classes. Interfaces can be
// used to specify additional
// behavior``` | ```// C++ supports multiple
// inheritance``` |

```// Java provides generics to handle` `// parameterized types` `public class Stack <T> {` ` private T temp;` ` ` ` public void push(T newItem) {` ` ...` ` } // end push` `} // end Stack` ```	```// C++ provides generics to handle` `// parameterized types` `template <class T>` `class Stack {` ` private:` ` T temp;` ` ` ` public:` ` void push(const T&);` ` ` ` ...` `} // end Stack` ` ` `template <class T>` `void Stack<T>::push(const T& newItem) {` ` ...` `}` ```
```// Java does not rely on a` `// preprocessor;` `// functionality is provided by the` `// Java language itself` ```	```// C++ uses a preprocessor for` `// compiler directives such as file` `// inclusion` ```
```// Java methods must appear as part` `// of a class` ```	```// C++ can have stand-alone functions` ```
```// Java constant` `// Must be declared within a class` `// or a method` `final int SIZE = 50;` ```	```// C++ constant` `// Can be declared globally or` `// within a class or a function` `const int SIZE = 50;` ```
```// Java valued method` `public boolean isLeapYear(int year) {` `// Returns true if year is a leap` `// year; otherwise returns false.` ` boolean leap = false;` ` boolean yearEndsIn00 = (year % 100 == 0);` ` if (yearEndsIn00 && (year % 400 == 0))` ` leap = true;` ` else if (!yearEndsIn00 && (year % 4 == 0))` ` leap = true;` ` return leap;` `} // end isLeapYear` ```	```// C++ valued function` `bool isLeapYear(int year) {` `// Returns true if year is a leap` `// year; otherwise returns false.` ` bool leap = false;` ` bool yearEndsIn00 = (year % 100 == 0);` ` if (yearEndsIn00 && (year % 400 == 0))` ` Leap = true;` ` else if (!yearEndsIn00 &&` ` (year % 4 == 0))` ` leap = true;` ` return leap;` `} // end isLeapYear` ```

```
// Java variable declarations          // C++ variable declarations
// Variables must be declared          // Variables can be declared
// within a class or a method          // globally as well as within
int        day, month, year;           // classes and methods
double     power, x;                   int     day, month, year;
char       response;                   double  power, x;
boolean    done;                       char    response;
// Simple reference declaration; no    bool    done;
// object is instantiated until the    // Objects can be declared
// new operator is used. Java          // statically using the default
// supports only dynamic allocation    // constructor
// of objects                          Sphere ball;
Sphere ball;                           // Also by using a constructor with
// Creating an object using a          // parameters
// default constructor                 Sphere ball(1.0);
Sphere ball = new Sphere();            // Dynamic allocation is supported
// Using constructor with              // using pointers and the new
// parameters                          // operator
Sphere ball = new Sphere(1.0);         Sphere *ball = new Sphere();
```

```
// Equality in Java                    // Equality in C++
// == and != check for shallow         // == and != check for shallow
// equality                            // equality
// For object equality, must           // For object equality, must
// override the equals method from     // provide the functions operator
// class Object                        // == and operator !=, for example
```

```
// Java array, primitive types         // C++ array
double[] r = new double[SIZE];         typedef double arrayType[SIZE];
double[] s = new double[SIZE];         arrayType r;
                                       double    s[SIZE];
for (int i = 0; i < SIZE; i++) {
  r[i] = 0.0;                          for (int i = 0; i < SIZE; ++i) {
} // end for                             r[i] = 0.0;
                                       } // end for
// Java array using objects and references
Sphere[] marbles = new Sphere[SIZE];
for (int i=0; i < SIZE; i++) {
  marbles[i] = new Sphere(0.3);
} // end for
```

```
// Java Standard Output                // C++ Standard Output
System.out.println("Enter month and " + cout << "Enter month and day "
     "day for year " + year +               << "for year" << year
     "as integers: ");                      << " as integers: ";
```

```
// Java Scanner class can be used      // C++ Standard input
// with standard input                 cin >> x >> y;
import java.util.Scanner;
Scanner kbInput = new Scanner(System.in);
x = kbInput.nextInt();
y = kbInput.nextDouble();
```

Unicode Character Codes (ASCII Subset)

Dec	Char	Dec	Char	Dec	Char	Dec	Char
0	NUL	32	(blank)	64	@	96	` (reverse quote)
1	STX	33	!	65	A	97	a
2	SOT	34	"	66	B	98	b
3	ETX	35	#	67	C	99	c
4	EOT	36	$	68	D	100	d
5	ENQ	37	%	69	E	101	e
6	ACK	38	&	70	F	102	f
7	BEL	39	' (apostrophe)	71	G	103	g
8	BS	40	(	72	H	104	h
9	HT	41	)	73	I	105	i
10	LF	42	*	74	J	106	j
11	VT	43	+	75	K	107	k
12	FF	44	, (comma)	76	L	108	l
13	CR	45	–	77	M	109	m
14	SO	46	.	78	N	110	n
15	SI	47	/	79	O	111	o
16	DLE	48	0	80	P	112	p
17	DC1	49	1	81	Q	113	q
18	DC2	50	2	82	R	114	r
19	DC3	51	3	83	S	115	s
20	DC4	52	4	84	T	116	t
21	NAK	53	5	85	U	117	u
22	SYN	54	6	86	V	118	v
23	ETB	55	7	87	W	119	w
24	CAN	56	8	88	X	120	x
25	EM	57	9	89	Y	121	y
26	SUB	58	:	90	Z	122	z
27	ESC	59	;	91	[	123	{
28	FS	60	<	92	\	124		
29	GS	61	=	93	]	125	}
30	RS	62	>	94	^	126	~
31	US	63	?	95	_ (underscore)	127	DEL

Note: The codes 0 through 31 and 127 are for control characters that do not print.

APPENDIX C

Java Resources

Java Web Sites

Sun Microsystems, a subsidiary of Oracle Corporation, released the Java platform in 1995. Oracle now maintains some of the best Web sites of information on Java at

`http://java.com` and `http://www.oracle.com/technetwork/java/index.html`

Of particular interest is the Java Standard Edition version 6 (also know as version 1.6). This is the version of the Java Development Kit (JDK) used to compile all of the code contained in this text. You can download it in english from the following page:

`http://www.java.com/en/download/`

The last section of this appendix lists some of the more popular Integrated Development Environments (IDEs) that are available for free and work in conjunction with Java SE 6.

You can also browse the Java SE 6 API documentation and find other useful resources on Java including tutorials on the following Web page:

`http://download.oracle.com/javase/`

Using Java SE 6

This section summarizes the commands used to compile and execute Java applications within an MS-DOS window on a PC running Windows. These commands also work in a command window of most Unix machines.

Follow the instructions specified on the download page *http://www.java.com/en/download/* to unpack and install Java SE 6 on your system. After you install Java from this Web site, it will ask to close your browser, and when it re-opens, you can verify that the installation was successful.

The following discussion assumes that you have created a simple Java program in the file Hello.java as follows:

```java
public class Hello {
  public static void main(String[] args) {
    System.out.println("Hello World");
  } // end main
} // end Hello
```

Compiling a Java program. To compile the Java program `Hello.java`, use the command `javac` followed by the name of the Java program as follows:

```
javac Hello.java
```

Java expects that your file name will be consistent with the name of the class it contains, and that it will end with `.java`.

If your program contains errors, they will be listed on the screen. If the program compiles successfully, you will see no messages, and a new file called `Hello.class` will appear in your folder or directory. This file contains the bytecode for your program.

Running a Java program. Java programs are executed using the Java Virtual Machine (JVM). To run your program using the JVM, use the command `java` followed by the name of the *.class* file created by the Java compiler:

```
java Hello
```

Note that you should not include the `.class` extension. At this point, the program is executed and produces the following output:

```
Hello World
```

The Web site for this textbook contains all of the code contained in this text, plus further instructions for compiling and using the code.

Integrated Development Environments (IDEs)

An IDE is a set of tools that make it easier to develop code. They provide a window-based environment for writing and editing source code, and typically provide highlighting of keywords. They often are bundled with debugging tools, a viewer for browsing class structures, and in some cases, drag-and-drop utilities for building graphical user interfaces.

There are many free IDEs available that work with Java SE 6. Unfortunately, it is beyond the scope of this appendix to demonstrate these IDEs. Here is a list of just a few more popular ones:

Eclipse	http://www.eclipse.org
Netbeans	http://www.netbeans.org
BlueJ	http://www.bluej.org
JGrasp	http://www.jgrasp.org

APPENDIX D

Mathematical Induction

Many proofs of theorems or invariants in computer science use a technique called **mathematical induction,** or simply **induction.** Induction is a principle of mathematics that is like a row of dominoes standing on end. If you push the first domino, all the dominoes will fall one after another. What is it about the dominoes that allows us to draw this conclusion? If you know that when one domino falls the next domino will fall, then pushing the first domino will cause them all to fall in succession. More formally, you can show that all the dominoes will fall if you can show that the following two facts are true:

- The first domino falls.

- For any $k \geq 1$, if the kth domino falls, the $(k + 1)^{\text{th}}$ domino will fall.

The principle of mathematical induction is an axiom that is stated as follows:

AXIOM D-1.   The principle of mathematical induction. A property $P(n)$ that involves an integer n is true for all $n \geq 0$ if the following are true:

1. P(0) is true.
2. If P(k) is true for any k $\geq$ 0, then P(k + 1) is true.

A **proof by induction on** n is one that uses the principle of mathematical induction. Such a proof consists of the two steps given in Axiom D-1. The first step is called the **basis,** or **base case.** The second step is the **inductive step.** We usually break the inductive step into two parts: the **inductive hypothesis** ("if $P(k)$ is true for any $k \geq 0$") and the **inductive conclusion** ("then $P(k + 1)$ is true").

Example 1

The following recursive method, which is given here in pseudocode, computes x^n:

```
power2(x, n)

    if (n == 0)
        return 1
    else
        return  x * power2(x, n-1)
```

You can prove that *power2* returns x^n for all $n \geq 0$ by using the following proof by induction on *n*:

Basis.   **Show that the property is true when n = 0.** That is, you must show that *power2(x, 0)* returns x^0, which is 1. However, as you can see from the definition of *power2*, *power2(x, 0)* is 1.

Now you must establish the inductive step. By assuming that the property is true when $n = k$ (the inductive hypothesis), you must show that the property is true when $n = k + 1$ (the inductive conclusion).

Inductive hypothesis.   **Assume that the property is true when n = k.** That is, assume that

power2(x, k) $= x^k$

Inductive conclusion.   **Show that the property is true when n = k + 1.** That is, you must show that *power2(x, k + 1)* returns the value x^{k+1}. By definition of the method *power2*,

power2(x, k + 1) $=$ x * power2(x, k)

By the inductive hypothesis, *power2(x, k)* returns the value x^k, so

power2(x, k + 1) $=$ x * x^k
$\qquad\qquad\qquad\quad = x^{k+1}$

which is what you needed to show to establish the inductive step.

The inductive proof is thus complete. We demonstrated that the two steps in Axiom D-1 are true, so the principle of mathematical induction guarantees that *power2* returns x^n for all $n \geq 0$. (**End of proof.**)

Example 2

Prove that

$$1 + 2 + \cdots + n = \frac{n(n+1)}{2} \quad \text{when } n \geq 1$$

It will be helpful to let S_n represent the sum $1 + 2 + \cdots + n$.

Basis.   Sometimes the property to be proven is trivial when $n = 0$, as is the case here. You can use $n = 1$ as the basis instead. (Actually, you can use any value of $n \geq 0$ as the basis, but a value of 0 or 1 is typical.)

You need to show that the sum S_1, which is simply 1, is equal to $1(1 + 1)/2$. This fact is obvious.

Inductive hypothesis. Assume that the formula is true when $n = k$; that is, assume that $S_k = k(k + 1)/2$.

Inductive conclusion. Show that the formula is true when $n = k + 1$. To do so, you can proceed as follows:

$$
\begin{aligned}
S_{k+1} &= (1 + 2 + \cdots + k) + (k + 1) && \text{(definition of } S_{k+1}) \\
&= S_k + (k + 1) && \text{(definition of } S_k) \\
&= k(k + 1)/2 + (k + 1) && \text{(inductive hypothesis)} \\
&= (k(k + 1) + 2(k + 1))/2 && \text{(common denominator)} \\
&= (k + 1)(k + 2)/2 && \text{(factorization)}
\end{aligned}
$$

The last expression is $n(n + 1)/2$ when n is $k + 1$. Thus, if the formula for S_k is true, the formula for S_{k+1} is true. Therefore, by the principle of mathematical induction, the formula is true when $n \geq 1$. (**End of proof.**)

Example 3

Prove that $2^n > n^2$ when $n \geq 5$.

Basis. Here is an example where the base case is not $n = 0$ or 1, but instead is $n = 5$. It is obvious that the relationship is true when $n = 5$ because

$$2^5 = 32 > 5^2 = 25$$

Inductive hypothesis. Assume that the relationship is true when $n = k \geq 5$; that is, assume that $2^k > k^2$ when $k \geq 5$.

Inductive conclusion. Show that the relationship is true when $n = k + 1$; that is, show that $2^{k+1} > (k + 1)^2$ when $k \geq 5$. To do so, you can proceed as follows:

$$
\begin{aligned}
(k + 1)^2 &= k^2 + (2k + 1) && \text{(square } k + 1) \\
&< k^2 + k^2 \text{ when } k \geq 5 && (2k + 1 < k^2; \text{ see Exercise 3)} \\
&< 2^k + 2^k \text{ when } k \geq 5 && \text{(inductive hypothesis)} \\
&= 2^{k+1}
\end{aligned}
$$

Therefore, by the principle of mathematical induction, $2^n > n^2$ when $n \geq 5$. (**End of proof.**)

Sometimes, the inductive hypothesis in Axiom D-1 is not sufficient. That is, you may need to assume more than $P(k)$. The following axiom is a stronger form of the principle of mathematical induction:

AXIOM D-2. The principle of mathematical induction (strong form). A property $P(n)$ that involves an integer n is true for all $n \geq 0$ if the following are true:

1. $P(0)$ is true.

2. If $P(0)$, $P(1)$, . . . , $P(k)$ are true for any $k \geq 0$, then $P(k + 1)$ is true.

Notice that the inductive hypothesis of Axiom D-2 ("If $P(0)$, $P(1)$, . . . , $P(k)$ are true for any $k \geq 0$") includes the inductive hypothesis of Axiom D-1 ("If $P(k)$ is true for any $k \geq 0$").

Example 4

Prove that every integer greater than 1 can be written as a product of prime integers.

Recall that a prime number is one that is divisible only by 1 and itself. The inductive proof is as follows:

Basis.   The statement that you must prove involves integers greater than 1. Thus, the base case is $n = 2$. However, 2 is a prime number and, therefore, it trivially is a product of prime numbers.

Inductive hypothesis.   Assume that the property is true for each of the integers 2, 3, . . . , k, where $k \geq 2$.

Inductive conclusion.   Show that the property is true when $n = k + 1$; that is, show that $k + 1$ can be written as a product of prime numbers.

If $k + 1$ is a prime number, there is nothing more to show. However, if $k + 1$ is not a prime number, it must be divisible by an integer x such that $1 < x < k + 1$. Thus,

$$k + 1 = x * y$$

where $1 < y < k + 1$. Notice that x and y are each less than or equal to k, so the inductive hypothesis applies. That is, x and y can each be written as a product of prime numbers. Clearly $x * y$, which is equal to $k + 1$, must be a product of prime numbers. Because the formula holds for $n = k + 1$, it holds for all $n \geq 2$ by the principle of mathematical induction. (**End of proof.**)

Example 5

Chapter 3 discusses the following recursive definition:

$$rabbit(1) = 1$$

$$rabbit(2) = 1$$

$$rabbit(n) = rabbit(n - 1) + rabbit(n - 2) \text{ when } n > 2$$

Prove that

$$rabbit(n) - (a^n - b^n)/\sqrt{5}$$

where $a = (1 + \sqrt{5})/2$ and $b = (1 - \sqrt{5})/2 = 1 - a$.

Basis. Because *rabbit*(0) is undefined, begin at $n = 1$. Some algebra shows that $rabbit(1) = (a^1 - b^1)/\sqrt{5} = 1$. However, notice that *rabbit*(2) is also a special case. That is, you cannot compute *rabbit*(2) from *rabbit*(1) by using the recurrence relationship given here. Therefore, the basis in this inductive proof must include $n = 2$.

When $n = 2$, some more algebra will show that $rabbit(2) = (a^2 - b^2)/\sqrt{5} = 1$. Thus, the formula is true when n is either 1 or 2.

Inductive hypothesis. Assume that the formula is true for all n such that $1 \leq n \leq k$, where k is at least 2.

Inductive conclusion. Show that the formula is true for $n = k + 1$. To do so, you can proceed as follows:

$$rabbit(k + 1) = rabbit(k) + rabbit(k - 1) \qquad \text{(recurrence relation)}$$
$$= [(a^k - b^k) + (a^{k-1} - b^{k-1})]/\sqrt{5} \quad \text{(inductive hypothesis)}$$
$$= [a^{k-1}(a + 1) - b^{k-1}(b + 1)]/\sqrt{5} \text{ (factorization)}$$
$$= [a^{k-1}(a^2) - b^{k-1}(b^2)]/\sqrt{5} \qquad (a + 1 = a^2; b + 1 = b^2)$$
$$= (a^{k+1} - b^{k+1})/\sqrt{5}$$

Because the formula holds for $n = k + 1$, it holds for all $n > 2$ by the principle of mathematical induction. (**End of proof.**)

Note that the previous proof requires that you show that $a + 1 = a^2$ and $b + 1 = b^2$. Although simple algebra will demonstrate the validity of these equalities, exactly how did we discover them after the factorization step? Some experience with inductive proofs will give you the confidence to determine and verify the auxiliary relationships—such as $a + 1 = a^2$—that are necessary in a proof. Here, after we introduced the factors $(a + 1)$ and $(b + 1)$, we observed that if these factors were equal to a^2 and b^2, respectively, we could finish the proof. Thus, we tried to show that $a + 1 = a^2$ and $b + 1 = b^2$; indeed, we were successful. Inductive proofs often require adventurous algebraic manipulations!

Self-Test Exercises

The answers to all Self-Test Exercises are at the back of this book.

1. Prove that $1 + 2^1 + 2^2 + \cdots + 2^m = 2^{m+1} - 1$ for all $m \geq 0$.
2. Prove that the sum of the first n odd positive integers is n^2.
3. Prove that $rabbit(n) \geq a^{n-2}$ when $n \geq 2$ and $a = (1 + \sqrt{5})/2$.

Exercises

1. Prove that the sum of the first n even positive integers is $n(n + 1)$.

2. Prove that $1^2 + 2^2 + \cdots + n^2 = n(n + 1)(2n + 1)/6$ for all $n \geq 1$.

3. Prove that $2n + 1 < n^2$ for all $n \geq 3$.

4. Prove that $n^3 - n$ is divisible by 6 for all $n \geq 0$.

5. Prove that $2^n > n^3$ when $n \geq 10$.

6. Prove that $n! > n^3$ when n is large enough.

7. Recall the following recursive definition from Chapter 2:

$c(n, 0) = 1$
$c(n, n) = 1$
$c(n, k) = c(n - 1, k - 1) + c(n - 1, k)$ when $0 < k < n$
$c(n, k) = 0$ when $k > n$

   a. Prove that $c(n, 0) + c(n, 1) + \cdots + c(n, n) = 2^n$.
      Hint: Use $c(n + 1, 0) = c(n, 0)$ and $c(n + 1, n) = c(n, n)$.

   b. Prove that $(x + y)^n = \displaystyle\sum_{k=0}^{n} c(n, k)\, x^k y^{n-k}$

8. Prove that $rabbit(n) \leq a^{n-1}$ when $n \geq 1$ and $a = (1 + \sqrt{5})/2$.

9. Suppose that the rabbit population doubles every year. If you start with two rabbits, find and prove a formula that predicts the rabbit population after n years.

Glossary

abstract base class   A class without instances that forms the basis of other classes that descend from it. An abstract base class contains zero or more abstract methods.

abstract method   A method that must be overridden in the derived class. If the derived class does not override the abstract method from the abstract base class, the derived class must also be declared abstract.

abstract data type (ADT)   A collection of data values together with a set of well-specified operations on that data.

abstraction   See *data abstraction* and *procedural abstraction*.

access time   The time required to access a particular item in a data structure such as an array, a linked list, or a file.

activation record   A record that contains a method's local environment at the time of and as a result of the call to the method.

address   A number that labels a location in a computer's memory.

adjacency list   The *n* linked lists that implement a graph of *n* vertices numbered 0, 1, . . . , $n - 1$ such that there is a node in the ith linked list for vertex *j* if and only if there is an edge from vertex *i* to vertex *j*.

adjacency matrix   An *n*-by-*n* array $graph$ that implements a graph of *n* vertices numbered 0, 1, . . . , $n - 1$ such that $graph[i][j]$ is 1 if there is an edge from vertex *i* to vertex *j*, and 0 otherwise.

adjacent vertices   Two vertices of a graph that are joined by an edge. In a directed graph, vertex *y* is adjacent to vertex *x* if there is a directed edge from vertex *x* to vertex *y*.

ADT   See *abstract data type*.

aggregate data type   A data type composed of multiple elements. Some examples of aggregate data types are arrays and files.

algorithm   A step-by-step specification of a method to solve a problem within a finite amount of time.

allocation   See *dynamic allocation* and *static allocation*.

analysis of algorithms   A branch of computer science that measures the efficiency of algorithms.

annotation   In Java, annotations are a form of metadata that can be added to a program. Uses include providing additional information to the compiler to detect errors, informing the compiler to suppress warnings, and warning of the use of deprecated elements.

ancestor class   See *superclass*.

ancestor of a node N   A node on the path from the root of a tree to N.

argument   A variable or expression that is passed to a method. An actual argument appears in a call to a method and corresponds to a formal parameter in the method's declaration. See also *parameter*.

array   A data structure that contains a fixed maximum number of elements of the same data type that are referenced directly by means of an index or subscript.

array-based implementation   An implementation of an ADT that uses an array to store the data values.

assertion   A statement that describes the state of an algorithm or program at a certain point in its execution. Java supports an assertion statement that allows you to test a condition at a certain point in a program.

autoboxing   The automatic process of converting a primitive type value to its equivalent wrapper class counterpart so that it can be used as an object. For example, the conversion of the value 5 to an *Integer* object containing 5.

average-case analysis   A determination of the average amount of time that a given algorithm requires to solve problems of size n. See also *best-case analysis* and *worst-case analysis*.

AVL tree   A balanced binary search tree in which rotations restore the tree's balance after each insertion or deletion of a node. (The AVL tree is named for its inventors Adel'son-Vel'skii and Landis.)

axiom   A mathematical rule or relationship. Axioms can be used to specify the behavior of an ADT operation.

back of a queue   The end of a queue at which items are inserted.

backtracking   A problem-solving strategy that, when it reaches an impasse, retraces its steps in reverse order before trying a new sequence of steps.

balanced binary tree   A binary tree in which the left and right subtrees of any node have heights that differ by at most 1. Also called a height-balanced tree.

base case   The known case in either a recursive definition or an inductive proof. Also called the basis or degenerate case.

base class   See *superclass*.

basis   See *base case*.

best-case analysis   A determination of the minimum amount of time that a given algorithm requires to solve problems of size n. See also *average-case analysis* and *worst-case analysis*.

BFS   See *breadth-first search*.

BFS spanning tree   A spanning tree formed by using a breadth-first search to traverse a graph's vertices.

Big O notation   A notation that uses the capital letter O to specify an algorithm's order. For example, "O($f(n)$)" means "order $f(n)$." See also *order of an algorithm*.

binary file   A file whose elements are in the computer's internal representation. A binary file is not organized into lines. Also called a general file or nontext file.

binary operator   An operator that requires two operands, for example, the + in 2 + 3. See also *unary operator*.

binary search   An algorithm that searches a sorted collection for a particular item by repeatedly halving the collection and determining which half could contain the item.

binary search tree   A binary tree in which the search key in any node N is greater than the search key in any node in N's left subtree, but less than the search key in any node in N's right subtree.

binary tree   A set of zero or more nodes, partitioned into a root node and two possibly empty sets that are binary trees. Thus, each node in a binary tree has at most two children, the left child and the right child.

binding   The association of a variable with both a memory address and the type of data the variable holds. See also *dynamic binding* and *static binding*.

block   A group of data records in a file.

block access time   The time required to read or write a block of data associated with a file.

box trace   A systematic way to trace the actions of a recursive method.

breadth-first search (BFS)   A graph-traversal strategy that visits every vertex adjacent to a vertex v that it can before it visits any other vertex. Thus, the traversal will not embark from any of the vertices adjacent to v until it has visited all possible vertices adjacent to v. See also *depth-first search*.

B-tree of degree m   A balanced search tree whose leaves are at the same level and whose nodes each contain between $m - 1$ and $[m/2]$ records. Each nonleaf has one more child than it has records. The root of the tree can contain as few as one record and can have as few as two children. Typically, a B-tree is stored in an external file.

bubble sort   A sorting algorithm that compares adjacent elements and exchanges them if they are out of order. Comparing the first two elements, the second and third elements, and so on, will move the largest (or smallest) element to the end of the array. Repeating this process will eventually sort the array into ascending (or descending) order.

bucket   A structure associated with a hash address that can accommodate more than one item. An array of buckets can be used as a hash table to resolve collisions.

buffer   A location that temporarily stores data as it makes its way from one process or location to another. A buffer enables data to leave one process or location at a different rate than the rate at which it enters another process or location, thus compensating for the difference in these rates.

bytecode   The result from a Java compiler when it translates a Java program. Bytecode must then be executed by a Java Virtual Machine. See also *compiler* and *Java Virtual Machine.*

ceiling of x   Denoted by $\lceil x \rceil$, the value of x rounded up. For example, $\lceil 6.1 \rceil = 7$.

chain   A linked list used within separate chaining, which is a collision-resolution scheme associated with hashing.

chaining   See *separate chaining.*

child of a node N   A node directly below node N in a tree.

circuit   A special cycle that passes through every vertex (or edge) in a graph exactly once.

circular doubly linked list   A doubly linked list whose first node references the list's last node and whose last node references the list's first node.

circular linked list   A linked list whose last node references the first node in the list.

class   A Java construct that enables you to define a new data type.

client   The program, module, or ADT that uses a class.

closed-form formula   A nonrecursive algebraic expression.

clustering   The tendency of items to map into groups of locations in a hash table, rather than randomly scattered locations. This difficulty, typical of the linear-probing, collision-resolution scheme in hashing, can cause lengthy search times.

code   Statements in a programming language.

coding   Implementing an algorithm in a programming language.

cohesion   The degree to which the portions of a module are related. See also *highly cohesive module.*

collision   A condition that occurs when a hash function maps two or more distinct search keys into the same location.

collision-resolution scheme   The part of hashing that assigns locations in the hash table to items with different search keys when the items are involved in a collision. See also *bucket, chain, clustering, double hashing, folding, linear probing, open addressing, probe sequence, quadratic probing,* and *separate chaining.*

compiler   A program that translates a program written in a high-level language, such as Java, into a language that a computer can execute. To achieve platform independence, a Java compiler produces bytecode, which must be executed by a Java Virtual Machine on a given computer. See also *bytecode* and *Java Virtual Machine.*

compile time   The time during which a compiler translates a program from source form into a form that can be executed. See also *run time.*

complete binary tree   A binary tree of height h that is full to level $h - 1$ and has level h filled from left to right.

complete graph   A graph that has an edge between every pair of distinct vertices.

completely balanced binary tree   A binary tree in which the left and right subtrees of any node have the same height.

connected component   For a graph that is not connected, a subset of the graph's vertices that a traversal visits beginning at a given vertex.

connected graph   A graph that has a path between every pair of distinct vertices.

constructor   A method that initializes new instances of a class. See also *default constructor*.

containment   See *has-a*.

cost of a path   The sum of the weights of the edges of a path in a weighted graph. Also called the weight or length of a path.

cost of a program   Factors such as the computer resources (computing time and memory) that a program consumes, the difficulties encountered by those who use the program, and the consequences of a program that does not behave correctly.

cost of a spanning tree   The sum of the weights of the edges in a weighted graph's spanning tree.

coupling   The degree to which the methods in a program are interdependent. See also *loosely coupled modules*.

cycle   A path in a graph that begins and ends at the same vertex. See also *circuit* and *simple cycle*.

data abstraction   A design principle that separates the operations that can be performed on a collection of data from the implementation of the operations. See also *procedural abstraction*.

data field   A component of a Java class that stores data of a particular type. See also *member* and *method*.

data flow   The flow of data between modules.

data record   An element in a file. A data record can be anything from a simple value, such as an integer, to an object, such as an employee record. See also *block* and *record*.

data structure   A construct that is defined within a programming language to store a collection of data.

deep copy of an object   A copy that includes the data structures that the object's data field(s) reference. See also *shallow copy of an object*.

default constructor   A constructor that has no parameters.

degenerate case   See *base case*.

depth-first search (DFS)   A graph-traversal strategy that proceeds along a path from a given vertex as deeply into the graph as possible before backtracking. That is, after visiting a vertex, a DFS visits, if possible, an unvisited adjacent vertex. If the traversal reaches a vertex that has no unvisited adjacent vertices, it backs up and then visits, if possible, an unvisited adjacent vertex. See also *breadth-first search*.

derived class   See *subclass.*

descendant class   See *subclass.*

descendant of a node N   A node on a path from N to a leaf of a tree.

DFS   See *depth-first search.*

DFS spanning tree   A spanning tree formed by using a depth-first search to traverse a graph's vertices.

dictionary   See *table.*

digraph   See *directed graph.*

direct access   A process that provides access to any element in a data structure by position, without the need to first access other elements in the structure. Also called random access. See also *sequential access.*

directed edge   An edge in a directed graph; that is, an edge that has a direction.

directed graph   A graph whose edges indicate a direction. Also called a digraph. See also *undirected graph.*

directed path   A sequence of directed edges that begins at one vertex and ends at another vertex in a directed graph. See also *simple path.*

disconnected graph   A graph that is not connected; that is, a graph that has at least one pair of vertices without a path between them.

divide and conquer   A problem-solving strategy that divides a problem into smaller problems, each of which is solved separately.

double hashing   A collision-resolution scheme that uses two hash functions. The hash table is searched for an unoccupied location, starting from the location that one hash function determines and considering every n^{th} location, where n is determined from a second hash function.

doubly linked list   A linked list whose nodes each contain two references, one to the next node and one to the previous node.

dummy head node   In a linked list, a first node that is not used for data but is always present. The item at the first position of the list is thus actually in the second node. See also *head record.*

dynamic allocation   The assignment of memory to a variable during program execution, as opposed to during compilation. In Java, all objects are created using dynamic allocation. See also *static allocation.*

dynamic binding   Binding that occurs during program execution. Also called late binding. See also *static binding* and *static member.*

dynamic object   A dynamically allocated object. An object whose memory is allocated at execution time and remains allocated only as long as you want.

early binding   See *static binding.*

edge   The connection between two nodes of a graph.

empty string   A string of length zero.

empty tree   A tree with no nodes.

encapsulation An information-hiding technique that combines data and operations to form an object.

event An occurrence, such as an arrival or a departure, in an event-driven simulation. See also *external event* and *internal event*.

event-driven simulation A simulation that uses events generated by a mathematical model that is based on statistics and probability. The times of events are either read as input or computed from other event times. Because only those times at which the events occur are of interest and because no action is required at times between events, the simulation can advance from the time of one event directly to the time of the next. See also *time-driven simulation*.

event list An ADT within an event-driven simulation that keeps track of arrival and departure events that will occur but have not occurred yet.

exhaustive search A search strategy that must examine every item in a collection of items before it can determine that the item sought does not exist.

exception An unusual or exceptional event that occurs during execution of a program.

exception handler Java code whose execution deals with an exception when one occurs.

extensible class A class that enables you to add capabilities to its derived classes without having access to the base class's implementation. Extensible classes can be declared abstract.

external event An event that is determined from the input data to an event-driven simulation. See also *internal event*.

external methods Algorithms that require external files because the data will not fit entirely into the computer's main memory.

external sort A sorting algorithm that is used when the collection of data will not fit in the computer's main memory all at once but must reside on secondary storage such as a disk. See also *internal sort*.

fail-safe programming A technique whereby a programmer includes checks within a program for anticipated errors.

Fibonacci sequence The sequence of integers 1, 1, 2, 3, 5, . . . defined by the recurrence relationship

$$a_1 = 1, \ a_2 = 1, \ a_n = a_{n-1} + a_{n-2} \text{ for } n > 2$$

field A data element within a record.

FIFO See *first in, first out*.

file A data structure that contains a sequence of components of the same data type. See also *binary file*, *index file*, and *text file*.

file component An indivisible piece of data in a file.

file pointer An indicator, such as an integer, that points to an element within a file. For example, an index record, which points to a data record in an external data file, contains such an indicator, namely, the number of the block that contains the data record.

file window   A marker of the current position in the file.

final class   A class that cannot be a superclass. That is, you cannot derive another class from a final class.

final data field   A data field whose value cannot change during program execution.

final method   A method that cannot be overridden by another class.

first in, first out (FIFO)   A property of a queue whereby the removal and retrieval operations access the item that was inserted first (earliest). See also *last in, first out.*

folding   A hashing technique that breaks a search key into parts and combines some or all of those parts, by using an operation such as addition, to form a hash address.

4-node   A tree node that contains three data items and has four children. See also *3-node* and *2-node.*

free list   A list of available nodes used in an array-based implementation of an ADT.

front of a queue   The end of a queue at which items are removed and retrieved.

full binary tree   A binary tree of height h with no missing nodes. All leaves are at level h, and all other nodes each have two children.

garbage collection   The return to the operating system of memory that was allocated to a program but is no longer being used.

general file   See *binary file.*

general tree   A set of one or more nodes, partitioned into a root node and subsets that are general subtrees of the root.

generic class   A specification of a class in terms of a data type parameter.

grammar   The rules that define a language.

graph   A set V of vertices, or nodes, and a set E of edges that connect the vertices.

graph traversal   A process that starts at vertex v and visits all vertices w for which there is a path between v and w. A graph traversal visits every vertex in a graph if and only if the graph is connected, regardless of where the traversal starts.

growth-rate function   A mathematical function used to specify an algorithm's order in terms of the size of the problem.

has-a   A relationship between classes whereby one class contains an instance of another class. Also called containment. See also *is-a.*

hash function   A mathematical function that maps the search key of a table item into a location that will contain the item.

hashing   A method that enables access to table items in time that is relatively constant and independent of the items by using a hash function and a scheme for resolving collisions.

hash table   An array that contains the table items, as assigned by a hash function.

head   See *head reference*.

header   See *head record*.

head reference   A reference to the first node in a linked list. Also called a head.

head record   A record that contains the external reference to the first node in a linked list, along with global information about the list, such as its length. Also called a header. See also *dummy head node*.

heap   A complete binary tree whose nodes each contain a priority value that is greater than or equal to the priority values in the node's children. Also called a maxheap. See also *minheap*.

heapsort   A sorting algorithm that first transforms an array into a heap, then removes the heap's root (the largest element) by exchanging it with the heap's last element, and finally transforms the resulting semiheap back into a heap.

height-balanced tree   See *balanced binary tree*.

height of a tree   The number of nodes on the longest path from the root of the tree to a leaf.

hierarchical relationship   The "parent-child" relationship between the nodes in a tree.

highly cohesive module   A module that performs one well-defined task. See also *cohesion*.

implement   (1) To create a program for an algorithm. (2) To use a data structure to realize an ADT.

import   To locate a program module in a library and include it in the current program.

index   (1) An integral value that references an element in an array. Also called a subscript. (2) Another name for an index file.

index file   A data structure whose entries—called index records—are used to locate items in an external file. Also called the index.

index record   An entry in an index file that points to a record in the corresponding external data file. This entry contains a search key and a file pointer.

induction   See *mathematical induction*.

inductive conclusion   See *inductive step*.

inductive hypothesis   See *inductive step*.

inductive proof   A proof that uses the principle of mathematical induction.

inductive step   The step in an inductive proof that begins with an inductive hypothesis ("if $P(k)$ is true for any $k \geq 0$") and demonstrates the inductive conclusion ("then $P(k + 1)$ is true").

infix expression   An algebraic expression in which every binary operator appears between its two operands. See also *postfix expression* and *prefix expression*.

information hiding   A process that hides certain implementation details within a module and makes them inaccessible from outside the module.

inheritance   A relationship among classes whereby a class derives properties from a previously defined class. See also *superclass* and *subclass*.

inorder successor of a node N   The inorder successor of N's search key. The inorder successor is in the leftmost node of N's right subtree.

inorder successor of x   The search key in a search tree that an inorder traversal visits immediately after x.

inorder traversal   A traversal of a binary tree that processes (visits) a node after it traverses the node's left subtree, but before it traverses the node's right subtree. See also *postorder traversal* and *preorder traversal*.

insertion sort   A sorting algorithm that considers items one at a time and inserts each item into its proper sorted position.

instance   An object that is the result of calling *new*. The operator *new* returns a reference to the instance.

interface   (1) In Java, a program component that declares methods required of a class. (2) The communication mechanisms between modules or systems.

internal event   An event that is determined by a computation within an event-driven simulation. See also *external event*.

internal node of a tree   A node that is not a leaf.

internal sort   A sorting algorithm that requires the collection of data to fit entirely in the computer's main memory. See also *external sort*.

invariant   An assertion that is always true at a particular point in an algorithm or program.

is-a   A relationship between classes whereby one class is a special case of another class. You implement an *is-a* relationship by using inheritance. See also *has-a*.

iteration   (1) A process that is repetitive. (2) A single pass through a loop.

iterative solution   A solution that involves loops.

iterator   A class that interacts with another class representing a collection of objects to provide access to either the next or previous item within the collection. An iterator provides a way to cycle through the objects in the collection.

Java Collections Framework (JCF)   A unified architecture for representing and manipulating collections in Java. It contains many commonly used collection ADTs including lists, stacks, and queues as generic classes. It also contains algorithms for common tasks such as sorting and searching.

Java Virtual Machine A program written for a particular computer that executes bytecode, which is the result of compiling a Java program. See also *bytecode* and *compiler*.

key (1) The portion of an index record that corresponds to the search key in a record in an external data file. (2) Another name for search key.

language A set of strings of symbols that adhere to the rules of a grammar.

last in, first out (LIFO) A property of a stack whereby the deletion and retrieval operations access the most recently inserted item. See also *first in, first out*.

late binding See *dynamic binding*.

leaf A tree node with no children.

left child of a node *N* A node directly below and to the left of node *N* in a tree.

left subtree of a node *N* The left child of node *N* plus its descendants in a tree.

length of a path See *cost of a path*.

level of a node The root of a tree is at level 1. If a node is not the root, its level is 1 greater than the level of its parent.

life cycle of software The phases of software development: specification, design, risk analysis, verification, coding, testing, refining, production, and maintenance.

LIFO See *last in, first out*.

linear implementation An implementation that uses either an array or a reference-based linked list.

linear linked list A linked list that is not circular.

linear probing A collision-resolution scheme that searches the hash table sequentially, starting from the original location specified by the hash function, for an unoccupied location.

linked list A list of elements, or nodes, that are linked to one another such that each element references the next element.

list An ADT whose elements are referenced by their position. See also *sorted list*.

load factor A measure of the relative fullness of a hash table, defined as the ratio of a table's current number of items to its maximum size.

local environment of a method A method's local variables, a copy of the actual value arguments, a return address in the calling routine, and the value of the method itself.

local identifier An identifier whose scope is the block that contains its declaration.

local variable A variable declared within a method and available only within that method.

loop invariant   An assertion that is true before and after each execution of a loop within an algorithm or program.

loosely coupled modules   Two or more modules that are not dependent on one another. See also *coupling*.

machine language   A language composed of the fundamental instructions that a computer can execute directly.

mathematical induction   A method for proving properties that involve nonnegative integers. Starting from a base case, you show that if a property is true for an arbitrary nonnegative integer k, then the property is true for the integer $k + 1$.

maxheap   Another name for a heap. See also *minheap*.

member   A component of a class that is either data or a method. See also *data field* and *method*.

mergesort   A sorting algorithm that divides an array into halves, sorts each half, and then merges the sorted halves into one sorted array. Mergesort can also be adapted for sorting an external file.

message   A request, in the form of a method call, that an object perform an operation.

method   A component of a class that implements a behavior of the class. See also *data field* and *member*.

minheap   A complete binary tree whose nodes each contain a priority value that is less than or equal to the priority values in the node's children. See also *maxheap*.

minimum spanning tree   A graph's spanning tree for which the sum of its edge weights is minimal among all spanning trees for the graph.

modular program   A program that is divided into isolated components, or modules, that have clearly defined purposes and interactions.

module   An individual component of a program, such as a method, a group of methods, or other block of code.

multigraph   A graphlike structure that allows duplicate edges between its vertices.

multiple indexing   A process that uses more than one index file to an external data file.

node   An element in a linked list, graph, or tree that usually contains both data and a reference to the next element in the data structure.

nontext file   See *binary file*.

object   An instance of a class.

object-oriented programming (OOP)   A software engineering technique that views a program as a collection of components called objects that interact. OOP embodies three fundamental principles: encapsulation, inheritance, and polymorphism.

object serialization   The process of transforming an object into a sequence of bytes that represent the object.

object type compatible   A characteristic of objects that enables you to use an instance of a subclass where an instance of the superclass is expected, but not the converse. The object type of an argument in a call to a method can be an instance of the subclass of the corresponding parameter's object type.

O($f(n)$)   Order $f(n)$. See *Big O notation* and *order of an algorithm*.

OOP   See *object-oriented programming*.

open   A process that prepares a stream to a file for either input or output. A state of readiness for I/O.

open addressing   A category of collision-resolution schemes in hashing that probe for an empty, or open, location in the hash table in which to place the item. See also *double hashing*, *linear probing*, and *quadratic probing*.

order of an algorithm   An algorithm's time requirement as a function of the problem size. An algorithm A is order $f(n)$ if constants k and n_0 exist such that A requires no more than $k * f(n)$ time units to solve a problem of size $n \geq n_0$. See also *Big O notation*.

order-of-magnitude analysis   An analysis of an algorithm's time requirement as a function of the problem size. See also *order of an algorithm*.

override   To redefine a method of a class within a subclass.

package   A collection of related classes.

package access member   A member of a class that is accessible only by the methods of the class and by other classes in the same package.

parameter   An identifier that appears in the declaration of a method and represents the value that the calling program will pass to the method. See also *argument*.

palindrome   A character string that reads the same from left to right as it does from right to left, for example, "deed."

parent of a node N   The node directly above node N in a tree.

partition   To divide a data structure such as an array into segments.

path   A sequence of edges in a graph that begins at one vertex and ends at another vertex. Because a tree is a special graph, you can have a path through a tree. See also *directed path* and *simple path*.

perfect hash function   An ideal hash function that maps each search key into a unique location in the hash table. Perfect hash functions exist when all possible search keys are known.

pivot element   An element that an algorithm uses to organize data by value. For example, the quicksort algorithm partitions an array about a particular element called the pivot.

planar graph   A graph that can be drawn in a plane in at least one way so that no two edges cross.

polymorphism   The ability of a variable name to represent, during program execution, instances of different but related classes that descend from a common superclass.

pop   To remove an item from a stack.

position-oriented ADT   An ADT whose operations involve the positions of its items. See also *value-oriented ADT.*

postcondition   A statement of the conditions that exist at the end of a module.

postfix expression   An algebraic expression in which every binary operator follows its two operands. See also *infix expression* and *prefix expression.*

postorder traversal   A traversal of a binary tree that processes (visits) a node after it traverses both of the node's subtrees. See also *inorder traversal* and *preorder traversal.*

precondition   A statement of the conditions that must exist at the beginning of a module in order for the module to work correctly.

predecessor   (1) In a linked list, the predecessor of node N is the node that references N. (2) In a directed graph, vertex x is a predecessor of vertex y if there is a directed edge from x to y, that is, if y is adjacent to x. See also *successor.*

prefix expression   An algebraic expression in which every binary operator precedes its two operands. See also *infix expression* and *postfix expression.*

preorder traversal   A traversal of a binary tree that processes (visits) a node before it traverses both of the node's subtrees. See also *inorder traversal* and *postorder traversal.*

primitive data type   One of the Java data types `boolean, byte, char, double, float, int, long,` or `short`.

priority queue   An ADT that orders its items by a priority value. The first item removed is the one having the highest priority value.

priority value   A value assigned to the items in a priority queue to indicate the item's priority.

private member   A member of a class that is accessible only by methods of the class.

probe sequence   The sequence of locations in the hash table that a collision-resolution scheme examines.

problem solving   The entire process of taking the statement of a problem and developing a computer program that solves that problem.

procedural abstraction   A design principle that separates the purpose and use of a module from its implementation. See also *data abstraction.*

protected member   A member of a class that is accessible by methods of the class, by derived classes, and by other classes in the same package.

public class   A class that is accessible by any other class.

public member   A member of a class that is accessible by any client of the class.

push   To add an item to a stack.

quadratic probing   A collision-resolution scheme that searches the hash table for an occupied location beginning with the original location that the hash function specifies and continuing at increments of $1^2, 2^2, 3^2$, and so on.

queue   An ADT whose first (earliest) inserted item is the first item removed or retrieved. This property is called first in, first out, or simply FIFO. Items enter a queue at its back and leave at its front.

quicksort   A sorting algorithm that partitions an array's elements around a pivot p to generate two smaller sorting problems: Sort the array's left section, whose elements are less than p, and sort the array's right section, whose elements are greater than or equal to p.

radix sort   A sorting algorithm that treats each data element as a character string and repeatedly organizes the data into groups according to the ith character in each element.

random access   See *direct access.*

random access file   A file whose elements are accessible by position without first accessing preceding elements within the file.

range query   An operation that retrieves all table items whose search keys fall into a given range of values.

rear of a queue   Another term for the back of a queue.

recognition algorithm   An algorithm, based on a language's grammar, that determines whether a given string is in the language.

record   A group of related items, called fields, that are not necessarily of the same data type. See also *data record.*

recurrence relation   A mathematical formula that generates the terms in a sequence from previous terms.

recursion   A process that solves a problem by solving smaller problems of exactly the same type as the original problem.

recursive call   A call within a method to the method itself.

red-black tree   A representation of a 2-3-4 tree as a binary tree whose nodes have red and black child references.

reference   (1) A reference variable in Java. (2) Generically, an element that references an object.

reference-based implementation   An implementation of an ADT or a data structure that uses references to organize its elements.

reference variable   A Java variable that references an object.

right child of a node *N*   A node directly below and to the right of node *N* in a tree.

right subtree of a node *N*   The right child of node *N* plus its descendants in a tree.

rightward drift   (1) In an array-based implementation of a queue, the problem of the front of the queue moving toward the end of the array.   (2) In a Java program, the problem of nested blocks bumping against the right-hand margin of the page.

root   The only node in a tree with no parent.

rotation   An operation used to maintain the balance of a red-black or AVL tree.

run time   The execution phase of a program. The time during which a program's instructions execute. See also *compile time*.

scope of an identifier   The part of a program in which an identifier has meaning.

search   A process that locates a certain item in a collection of items.

search key   The part of a record that identifies it within a collection of records. A search algorithm uses a search key to locate a record within a collection of records. Also called a key.

search tree   A tree whose organization facilitates the retrieval of its items. See also *AVL tree*, *binary search tree*, *B-tree of degree m*, *red-black tree*, *2-3 tree*, and *2-3-4 tree*.

selection sort   A sorting algorithm that selects the largest item and puts it in its correct place, then selects the next largest item and puts it in its correct place, and so on.

semiheap   A complete binary tree in which the root's left and right subtrees are both heaps.

separate chaining   A collision-resolution scheme that uses an array of linked lists as a hash table. The ith linked list, or chain, contains all items that map into location i.

sequential access   A process that stores or retrieves elements in a data structure one after another, starting at the beginning. See also *direct access*.

sequential access file   A file whose elements must be processed sequentially. That is, to process the data stored at a given position, you must advance the file window beyond all the data that precedes it.

sequential search   An algorithm that locates an item in a collection by examining items in order, one at a time, beginning with the first item.

shallow copy of an object   A copy that does not include any data structures that the object's data fields might reference. See also *deep copy of an object*.

shortest path   Between two given vertices in a weighted graph, the path that has the smallest sum of its edge weights.

siblings   Tree nodes that have a common parent.

simple cycle   A cycle in a graph that does not pass through a vertex more than once.

simple path   A path in a graph that does not pass through a vertex more than once. See also *directed path*.

simulation   A technique for modeling the behavior of both natural and artificial systems. Generally, its goal is to generate statistics that summarize the performance of an existing system or to predict the performance of a proposed system. A simulation reflects long-term average behavior of a system rather than predicting occurrences of specific events.

software engineering A branch of computer science that provides techniques to facilitate the development of computer programs.

solution Algorithms and ways to store data that solve a problem.

sorted list An ADT that maintains its elements in sorted order and retrieves them by their position number within the list. See also *list*.

sorted order The order of a collection of data that is in either ascending or descending order.

sorted run Sorted data that is part of an external sort.

sorting A process that organizes a collection of data into either ascending or descending order. See also *external sort* and *internal sort*.

sort key The part of a record that determines the sorted order of the entire record within a collection of records. A sorting algorithm uses a sort key to order records within a collection of records.

source program A program written in a programming language that needs to be compiled. For example, a Java program. Also called source code.

spanning tree A subgraph of a connected, undirected graph G that contains all of G's vertices and enough of its edges to form a tree. See also *BFS spanning tree* and *DFS spanning tree*.

stack An ADT whose most recently inserted item is the first item removed or retrieved. This property is called last in, first out, or simply LIFO. Items enter and leave a stack at its top.

static allocation The assignment of memory to a variable during compilation, as opposed to during program execution. In Java, only primitive types and references use static allocation. See also *dynamic allocation*.

static binding Binding that occurs at compilation time. Also called early binding. See also *dynamic binding* and *static member*.

static member A class member in which there is only one copy available for all instances of the class. Static members can be bound at compilation time. See also *static binding*.

stream An object that moves data into a program (an input stream) or out of a program (an output stream).

string A sequence of characters. A Java string is an object of type `String`.

structure chart An illustration of the hierarchy of modules that solve a problem.

stub A partially completed method that you use during the development and testing of other modules of a program.

subclass A class that inherits the members of another class called the superclass. Also called derived class. See also *inheritance*.

subgraph A subset of a graph's vertices and edges.

subscript See *index*.

subtree Any node in a tree, together with all of the node's descendants.

subtree of a node N A tree that consists of a child of N and the child's descendants.

successor   (1) In a linked list, the successor of node N is the node that N references. (2) In a directed graph, vertex y is a successor of vertex x if there is a directed edge from x to y, that is, if y is adjacent to x. See also *predecessor.*

superclass   A class from which another class—called a subclass—is derived. A subclass inherits ther superclass's members. Also called a base class. See also *inheritance* and *subclass.*

symmetric matrix   An n-by-n matrix A whose elements satisfy the relationship $A_{ij} = A_{ji}$.

table   An ADT whose data items are stored and retrieved according to their search-key values. Also called a dictionary.

tail reference   A reference to the last node in a linked list. Also called a tail.

tail recursion   A type of recursion in which the recursive call is the last action taken.

text file   A file of characters that are organized into lines.

3-node   A tree node that contains two data items and has three children. See also *4-node* and *2-node.*

time-driven simulation   A simulation in which the time of an event, such as an arrival or departure, is determined randomly and compared with a simulated clock. See also *event-driven simulation.*

top-down design   A process that addresses a task at successively lower levels of detail, producing independent modules.

top-down implementation   An implementation method in which you implement and test a module before implementing its submodules.

top of a stack   The end of a stack at which items are inserted, retrieved, and deleted.

topological order   A list of vertices in a directed graph without cycles such that vertex x precedes vertex y if there is a directed edge from x to y in the graph. A topological order is not unique, in general.

topological sorting   In a directed graph without cycles, the process of arranging the vertices into a topological order.

traversal   An operation that processes (visits) each element in an ADT or data structure. See also *inorder traversal, postorder traversal,* and *preorder traversal.*

tree   A connected, undirected graph without cycles. See also *binary tree* and *general tree.*

2-node   A tree node that contains one data item and has two children. See also *4-node* and *3-node.*

2-3 tree   A tree such that each internal node (nonleaf) has either two or three children, and all leaves are at the same level. A node can have a left subtree, a middle subtree, and a right subtree.

If a node has two children and contains one data item, the value of the search key in the node must be greater than the value of the search key in the left child and smaller than the value of the search key in the right child. If a node has three children and contains two data items, the value of the smaller search key in the node must be greater than the value of the search key in the left child and smaller than the value of the search key in the middle child; the value of the larger search key in the node must be greater than the value of the search key in the middle child and smaller than the value of the search key in the right child.

2-3-4 tree A tree such that each internal node (nonleaf) has either two, three, or four children, and all leaves are at the same level. A node can have a left subtree, a middle-left subtree, a middle-right subtree, and a right subtree.

If a node has two or three children, it adheres to the specifications of a 2-3 tree. If a node has four children and three data items, the value of the smaller search key in the node must be greater than the value of the search key in the left child and smaller than the value of the search key in the middle-left child; the value of the middle search key in the node must be greater than the value of the search key in the middle-left child and smaller than the value of the search key in the middle-right child; the value of the larger search key in the node must be greater than the value of the search key in the middle-right child and smaller than the value of the search key in the right child.

type compatible See *object type compatible*.

unary operator An operator that requires only one operand, for example, the – in –5. See also *binary operator*.

undirected graph A graph that has at most one edge between any two vertices and whose edges do not indicate a direction. See also *directed graph*.

user The person who uses a program.

user interface The portion of a program that provides for user input or control.

valued method A method that returns a value. See also `void` *method*.

value-oriented ADT An ADT whose operations involve the values of its data items. See also *position-oriented ADT*.

vertex A node in a graph.

visit The act of processing an item during a traversal of an ADT or a data structure.

`void` method A method that does not return a value. See also *valued method*.

weighted graph A graph whose edges are labeled with numeric values.

weight of an edge The numeric label on an edge in a weighted graph.

weight of a path See *cost of a path*.

worst-case analysis A determination of the maximum amount of time that a given algorithm requires to solve problems of size n. See also *average-case analysis* and *best-case analysis*.

Answers to Self-Test Exercises

Chapter 1

1. a. No import statement is needed, Math is contained in *java.lang*
   b. *import java.io.PrintWriter;*
   c. *import java.util.Vector;*
   d. *import java.sql.SQLException;*

2. The // comment is for a single line. The /* … */ comment is for multiple lines. The /** … */ is for Javadoc-style comments.

3. Possible *access-modifier* values are public, protected, private, or there is no modifier, which indicates package access. Possible use-modifier values are static, final, abstract, native, and synchronized.

4. a. Compiler error: The field *SimpleSphere.radius* is not visible.
   b. Compiler error: Type mismatch, cannot convert from *double* to *int*
   c. Compiler error: The method *getDiameter* is undefined for the class *SimpleSphere*.
   d. Compiler error: The *static* field *SimpleSphere.DEFAULT_RADIUS* should be accessed in a static way.

5. A "short circuit operator" in a boolean expression allows for the second argument in the expression to only be executed or evaluated if the first argument does not suffice to determine the value of the expression.

   examples: **true** || x < 5
   false&& x < 5

6. Checked exceptions must be handled locally or explicitly thrown from the method where they might occur. Unchecked exceptions occur when the error is not considered as serious and can often be prevented by fail-safe programming. Unchecked exceptions are instances of classes that are sub-classes of java.lang.RuntimeException, which relaxes the requirement, forcing the exception to be either handled locally or explicitly thrown by the method.

Chapter 2

1. There are many correct ways to specify the answer to this question, the following is one example.

   a. Specification for cell phone contact list:

       □ A contact in the contact list consists of a name, a home phone number, a work phone number, a cell phone number, and an email address.

       □ Users should be able to look up contact information by name or phone number.

       □ Users should be able to add a contact.

       □ Users should be able to delete a contact.

       □ Users should be able to modify information of a contact.

   b. Each entry in the contact list (*contactEntry*) should have the following data fields, all of type *String*:

```
ContactEntry
 -name
 -homePhone
 -workPhone
 -cellPhone
 -emailAddress
```

Each of these data fields should have methods that allow the data field to be read (*getFieldname*) or written (*setFieldname*). Preconditions for these methods may require properly formatted data, for example name in the form of *Lastname*, *Firstname*, and the telephone numbers requiring an area code. No postconditions are needed.

The contact list will be a list of contact entries (perhaps stored as an array).

```
ContactList
    -contacts - an array of contactEntry objects
```

with the following methods:

```
+createContactList()
// Create a new contact list

+add(newContact:ContactEntry):boolean
// AddnewContact to the contact list.
// Precondition: None
// Postcondition: Returns true if contact successfully
// added
```

```
+lookupByName(name:String):ContactEntry
// Searches for contact with given name
// Precondition: None
// Postcondition: Returns the contact entry corresponding
// to name. If the contact name is not in the list,
// returns null. If there are multiple contacts with the
// same name, returns the first one found.

+lookupByNumber(phoneNumber:String):ContactEntry
// Searches for contact that has phone for homePhone,
// workPhone, or cellPhone.
// Precondition: None
// Postcondition: Returns the contact entry corresponding
// to phoneNumber. If the phoneNumber is not in any of the
// contacts on the the list, returns null. If there are
// multiple contacts with the same phoneNumber, returns the
// first one found.

+delete(delContact:ContactEntry):boolean
// Deletes the contact delContact from the list
// Precondition: Contact to be deleted was previously found
// using lookupByName or lookupByNumber
// Postcondition: Returns true if contact successfully
// deleted, false otherwise

+modify(modContact:ContactEntry,
newContactInfo:ContactEntry):boolean
// Modifies the contact modContact with the information
// contained in newContactInfo
// Precondition: Contact to be modified was previously
// found using lookupByName or lookupByNumber
// Postcondition: Returns true if contact successfully
// modified, false otherwise
```

c.   UML diagram

```
┌─────────────────────────────────────────────────────────┐
│ ContactList                                              │
├─────────────────────────────────────────────────────────┤
│ -contacts:ContactEntry[*]                                │
├─────────────────────────────────────────────────────────┤
│ +createContactList()                                     │
│ +add(newContact:ContactEntry):boolean                    │
│ +lookupByName(name:String):ContactEntry                  │
│ +lookupByNumber(phoneNumber:String):ContactEntry         │
│ +delete(delContact:ContactEntry):boolean                 │
│ +modify(modContact:ContactEntry,                         │
│ newContactInfo:ContactEntry):boolean                     │
└─────────────────────────────────────────────────────────┘
                            ◇ 1
                            │
                            │ *
          ┌─────────────────────────────────────────┐
          │ ContactEntry                            │
          ├─────────────────────────────────────────┤
          │ -name:string                            │
          │ -homePhone:string                       │
          │ -workPhone:string                       │
          │ -cellPhone:string                       │
          │ -emailAddress:string                    │
          ├─────────────────────────────────────────┤
          │ +createContact(name:string)             │
          │ +getName():string                       │
          │ +setName(newName:string)                │
          │ +getHomePhone():string                  │
          │ +setHomePhone(newNum:string)            │
          │ +getWorkPhone():string                  │
          │ +setWorkPhone(newNum:string)            │
          │ +getCellPhone():string                  │
          │ +setCellPhone(newNum:string)            │
          │ +getEmail():string                      │
          │ +setEmail(newEmail:string)              │
          └─────────────────────────────────────────┘
```

2. $0 \leq \textit{index} \leq n$ and $\textit{sum} = \textit{item[0]} + \ldots + \textit{item[index]}$.

3. The equivalent $\textit{while}$ loop is as follows:

```
int index = 0;
while (index < n) {
  sum += item[index];
  index++;
} // end while
```

$0 <= \textit{index} <= n$ and $\textit{sum} = \textit{item[0]} + \ldots + \textit{item[index-1]}$

4. We can make several improvements to user interaction and programming style:

- [] Prompt the user for the input and indicate the expected form of the input. The user should also be given an option to exit the program.

- [] Give more descriptive output.

- [] Check input for obvious errors; e.g., a four-digit age entry is surely a typo and the user should be allowed to correct the error.

- [] Document the program.

- [] Use more descriptive variable names.

5.
```java
final int DZERO = 0;
final int AOTRG = 1;

void severeErrorMessage(int error) {
// ----------------------------------------------------
// Displays an error code and terminates program execution.
// Preconditions: none.
// Postconditions: An error message corresponding to the
// input errorCode is output to the standard error stream
// and the program is terminated.
// ----------------------------------------------------
   switch(error) {
     case DZERO: System.out.println("Divide by zero error.");
               break;
     case AORTG: System.out.println(
                           "Array index out of range.");
               break;
     default:    System.out.println("Unknown fatal error.");
   } // end switch

   System.exit(0); // terminate execution immediately
} // end severeErrorMessage
```

Chapter 3

1. The sum of n numbers is defined in terms of the sum of $n - 1$ numbers, which is a smaller problem of the same type. When n is 1, the sum is *anArray[0]*; this occurrence is the base case. Because $n \geq 1$ initially and n decreases by 1 at each recursive call, the base case will be reached.

2. ```java
public static void count(int n, int start) {
   // Precondition: start <= n.
   // Postcondition: Writes start, start +1, ..., n.
      if (start <= n) {
         System.out.println(start);
         count(n, start + 1);
      } // end if
   }   // end count
```

To output *1, 2, 3, ..., n* call the method as *count(n, 1)*.

3. ```java
public static double product(double anArray[], int first, int last)
   // Precondition: anArray[first..last] is an array of real numbers,
   // where first <= last.
   // Postcondition: Returns the product of the numbers in
   // anArray[first..last].
      double result;
      if (first == last) {
         result = anArray[first];
      }
      else {
         result = anArray[last] * product(anArray, first, last-1);
      }
      return result;
   }   // end product
```

4. *writeBackward*, *binarySearch*, *kSmall*, and the method *count* in Self-Test Exercise 2.

5. *c(5, 1) = 5*

6. The order of recursive calls that results from *solveTowers(3, C, A, B)* follows:

Chapter 4

1. A wall is a visualization of abstraction and modularity. Modules should be as independent as possible: Walls prevent other parts of the program from seeing the details of modules. A contract is a specification of what the module, which is behind the wall, is to do. The contract governs the slit in the wall; it specifies what is to be passed to the module and what will be passed out. The contract does not specify how to implement the module.

   These concepts help during the problem-solving process by encouraging you to divide the problem into small parts and to focus first on what you want done rather than on how to do it.

2. By assuming that the list has items at positions *i* and *j*, we know that the list operations *get* and *remove* will be successful.

```
+swap(inout aList:List, in i:integer, in j:integer)
// Swaps the ith and jth items in the list aList.

    // copy ith and jth items
    ithItem = aList.get(i)
    jthItem = aList.get(j)

    // replace ith item with jth
    aList.remove(i)
    aList.add(i, jthItem)

    // replace jth item with ith
    aList.remove(j)
    aList.add(j, ithItem)
```

   Notice that the order of operations is important because when you delete an item, *remove* renumbers the remaining items.

3. coffee, bread, cereal, milk, butter, eggs

4. Specify `createList`, `isEmpty`, `size`, and `removeAll` as you would for the ADT list.

```
+add(in item:ListItemType)
// Adds item to the beginning of the list.

+remove()
// Removes the item at the beginning of a list.

+get():ListItemType
// Returns the item at the beginning of a list.
// The list is left unchanged by this operation.
```

5.

Set
-items:itemtype array
+union(s:Set) +intersection(s:Set) +isSubset(s:Set):boolean +addElement(e:ItemType) +containsElement(e:itemType):boolean +isEmpty():boolean +size():integer

6. +*convertToSortedList(in aList:List):sortedList*
   // Creates a sorted list from the items in the list
   // aList.

   ```
   sortedList.createSortedList()
   for (index = 1 to aList.size()) {
       item = aList.get(index)
       sortedList.sortedAdd(item)
   } // end for
   return sortedList
   ```

7. Duplicate values in an ADT list are permissible and do not affect its specifications, because its operations are by position. For a sorted list, however, you need to revise the specifications to accommodate duplicates. You could either prevent the insertion of duplicate items or allow duplicates. If you do allow the insertion of duplicates, you need to decide where to insert them, whether to delete all occurrences of an item or only the first instance, and which of several duplicate items to retrieve.

8.

String
-str:char array

+charAt(i:int):char
+concat(s:String):String
+indexOf(c:char):integer
+substring(start:integer, end:integer):String
// plus many other methods as found in the
// Java String class

Chapter 5

1. a. Missing parameter for constructor, must at least supply an integer

    b.

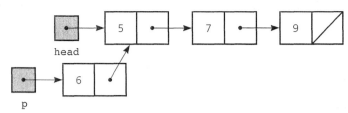

    c.

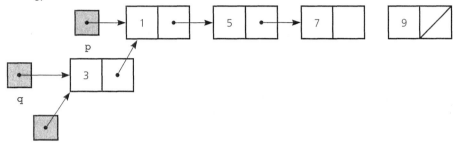

    d. The assignment q = new IntegerNode(p) must have an *int* parameter as well as a *Node*.

    e.

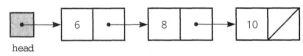

    f.

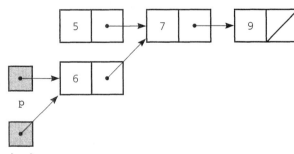

2. a. Yes, deletion of the first node in a linked list is a special case since the *head* reference must be changed to the second node in the list.

    b. No, deletion of the last node in the linked list is not a special case, the next to the last node takes the value of the *next* field in the last node, which is null.

    c. Yes, the deletion of the only node of a one-node linked list is a special case since the *head* reference must be changed to null.

    d. No, deleting the first node takes less effort than deleting the last node. Deleting the last node required traversing the list, deletion of the first node does not.

3. Assume a class *CharNode* that is analogous to *IntegerNode* (see pages 273 and 274).

   a.
```
head = new CharNode('M', null);
CharNode newNode = new CharNode('S', head);
head = newNode;
newNode = new CharNode('K', head);
head = newNode;
```

   b.
```
head = new CharNode('B');
CharNode secondNode = new CharNode('E');
head.next = secondNode;
CharNode thirdNode = new CharNode('J', null);
secondNode.next = thirdNode;
```

4. a.
```
prev.next = curr.next;
curr.next = null;
prev = null;
curr = null;
```

   b.
```
head = curr.next;
curr.next = null;
curr = null;
```

   c.
```
CharNode newNode= new CharNode('A');
newNode.next = head;
head = newNode;
```

   d. The variable *head* references a node that contains '*A*'; this node refer-ences a node that contains '*J*'. The *next* portion of the last node is *null*.

5. a. Common features of all of the nodes used in this chapter are a field to store the data, and at least one link to another node.

6. *i*, ignoring the assignments to *count* in the *for* statement.

7.
```
writeListBackward2 (reference to 'K')   // original call
  writeListBackward2 (reference to 'S')
    writeListBackward2 (reference to 'M')
      writeListBackward2 (null)
      write M
    write S
  write K
```

Chapter 6

1. The positions of the queens are given as *(row, column)* pairs.

       Solution 1: (2, 1), (4, 2), (1, 3), (3, 4)

       Solution 2: (3, 1), (1, 2), (4, 3), (2, 4)

2. *<octalNum>* = 0*<num>*

   <num> = *<digit>* | *<num><digit>*

   <digit> = 0 | 1 | 2 | 3 | 4 | 5 | 6 | 7

3. *<number>* = *<coef>* E*<sign><num>*

   <coef> = *<num>*.*<num>*

   <num> = *<digit>* | *<num><digit>*

   <digit> = 0 | 1 | 2 | 3 | 4 | 5 | 6 | 7 | 8 | 9

4. *<T>* = $ | cc*<T>*d

5. Prefix expression: - * / - * a b c d e -fg

   Postfix expression: a b * c - d / e * f g - -

6. Infix: $(a - b / (c + d * e)) - f$; postfix: $a\ b\ c\ d\ e * + / - f -$

7. No.

8. The proof that $f(n) = 2n + f(n - 1)$ has the closed-form solution $f(n) = n(n + 1)$ where $f(0) = 0$, is by induction on n.

   Basis. *Show that the property is true for n = 1.* Here, $1(1 + 1) = 2$, which is consistent with the recurrence relation's specification that $f(1) = 2(1) + 0$.
     You now must establish that

       property is true for an arbitrary k ⇒ *property is true for k + 1*

   Inductive hypothesis. *Assume that the property is true for n = k.* That is, assume that

     f(k) = k(k + 1)

   Inductive conclusion. *Show that the property is true for n = k + 1.* That is, you must show that $f(k + 1) = (k+1)(k+ 2)$. Now

$$f(k + 1) = 2(k + 1) + f(k) \qquad \text{from the recurrence relation}$$

$$= 2k + 2 + k(k + 1) \qquad \text{by the inductive hypothesis}$$

$$= k^2 + 3k + 2$$

$$= (k+1)(k+ 2)$$

   which is what you needed to show to establish that

       property is true for an arbitrary k ⇒ *property is true for k + 1*

   The inductive proof is thus complete.

Chapter 7

1. V, Z, X, Y, W.

2. *stack1*: 23 17 42 13; *stack2*: 42 49 (elements listed bottom to top).

3. Use an array-based implementation if you know the maximum string length in advance and you know that the average string length is not much shorter than the maximum length. Clearly, you would use a reference-based implementation if you could not predict the maximum string length. In addition, if the maximum string length is 300, for example, but the average string length is 30, a reference-based implementation would use less storage on average than an array-based implementation.

4. A peek operation simply returns the item from the top of the stack, leaving it on top of the stack. The pop operation removes and returns the item from the top of the stack.

5. a. When the loop ends, the stack contains one open brace and *balancedSoFar* is *true*.
   b. When the loop ends, the stack is empty and *balancedSoFar* is *true*.
   c. The stack is empty when the last close brace is encountered. When the loop ends, *balanced-SoFar* is *false*.

6. 2

7. *a b / c ∗*

8. The precedence tests control association. The ≥ test enables left-to-right association when operators have the same precedence.

9. a. Stack contains F, then F I.
   b. Stack contains F, then F G, then F G C.
   c. Stack contains H, then H G, then H G C, then H G C B, then H G C B D, then H G C B D F.

Chapter 8

1. W, Y, X, Z, V.

2. *queue1*: 23 42 13; *queue2*: 50 42 49 (elements listed front to back).

3. a.   When the *for* loop ends, the stack and queue are as follows:

Stack: a b r a c a d a b r a ← top

Queue: a b r c a d a b r a ← back

The *a* at the top of the stack matches the *a* at the front of the queue. After deleting the *a* from both ADTs, the *r* at the top of the stack does not match the *b* at the front of the queue, so the string is not a palindrome.

b.   The letters that you delete from the stack and the queue are the same, so the string is a palindrome.

c.   The letters that you delete from the stack and the queue are the same, so the string is a palindrome.

d.   When the for loop ends, the stack and queue are as follows:

Stack: x y z z y ← top

Queue: x y z z y ← back

The *y* at the top of the stack does not match the *x* at the front of the queue, so the string is not a palindrome.

4. a. 1;   b. 3;   c. 3;   d. 2;   e. 3;   f. 1;
   g. 2;   h. 2;   i. 1;   j. 1;   k. 1;   l. 2   m. 1

5. You cannot generate a departure event for a given arrival event independently of other events. So to read the file of arrival events and generate departure events, you would need to perform the same computations that the simulation performs.

6.

Time	Action	*bankQueue* (front to rear)		*eventList* (front to rear)	
29	Update *eventList* and *bankQueue*: Customer 2 enters bank	23 2		A 30 3	
	Customer 3 begins transaction, create departure event	23 2		A 30 3	D 31
30	Update *eventList* and *bankQueue*: Customer 4 enters bank	23 2	30 3	D 31	
31	Update *eventList* and *bankQueue*: Customer 3 departs	30 3		*empty*	
	Customer 4 begins transaction, create departure event	30 3		D 34	
34	Update *eventList* and *bankQueue*: Customer 4 departs	*empty*		*empty*	

Chapter 9

1. a.   `Sphere mySphere = new Sphere(2.0);`
   b.   `Ball myBall = new Ball(6.0, "Beach ball");`
   c.   `System.out.println(mySphere.diameter() + " " +`
        `myBall.diameter());`

2.
```
class Planet extends Ball {
    private double minDistance;
    private double maxDistance;

    public double minDistanceFromSun() {
        return minDistance;
    } // end minDistanceFromSun

    public double maxDistanceFromSun() {
        return maxDistance;
    } // end maxDistanceFromSun

    public void setMinDistanceFromSun(double newDistance)
        minDistance = newDistance;
    } // end setMinDistanceFromSun

    public void setMaxDistanceFromSun(double newDistance)
        maxDistance = newDistance;
    } // end setMaxDistanceFromSun
} // end Planet
```

3. a.   The method *resetBall* cannot access *radius* directly. The data field *radius* is private within the *Sphere* class, so a derived class cannot access it.

   b.   The method *resetBall* can access *radius* directly. Instead of writing *setRadius(r)* in the implementation of *resetBall*, you can write *radius = r*. This change is unnecessary, however.

4. a.   A reference can be declared as type *SortedListInterface* anywhere that a reference variable can be declared. Thus, it can be used in declaring a data field for a class, as a method parameter, or as a local variable to a method.

   b.   A class that implements *SortedListInterface* must be used when an actual instance of a sorted list needs to be created.

   c.   `SortedListInterface studentList = new`
        `SortedListReferenceBased();`

5. a.   Abstract classes and interfaces are similar in that neither can have objects directly instantiated from them.

   b.   They differ in that abstract classes can contain data fields and methods with implementations, but interfaces can contain only constants and method specifications.

6. A derived class cannot access and therefore cannot override a private method in its base class.

7. `Student s1 = new Student("Sarah", 4.0);`
   `NewClass<Student> myClass = new NewClass<Student>(s1);`
   `System.out.println("Contents of myClass => " + myClass);`

   Output:

   `Contents of myClass => Student@1f6a7b9, 1970`

   Note that the output displays *myClass* using the default *toString* method inherited from class *Object*. If the class Student provides a *toString* method, that would be used instead.

Chapter 10

1. $(n-1) + (n-2) + \cdots + 1 = n * (n-1)/2$

2. $n + (n-1) + \cdots + 2 = n * (n+1)/2 - 1$

3. a. $O(n^3)$;   b. $O(\log n)$;   c. $O(n \log n)$

4. a.   You can stop searching as soon as *searchValue* is greater than a data item, because you will have passed the point where *searchValue* would have occurred if it was in the data collection.

   b.   Sorted data, using the scheme just described in the answer to Part *a*: best case: $O(1)$; average case: $O(n)$; worst case: $O(n)$.
   Unsorted data: $O(n)$ in all cases.

   c.   Regardless of whether the data is sorted, the best case is $O(1)$ (you find the item after one comparison) and both the average and worst cases are $O(n)$ (you find the item after $n/2$ or n comparisons, respectively).

5. At each pass, the selected element is underlined.

<u>80</u>	40	25	20	30	60
<u>60</u>	40	25	20	30	80
30	<u>40</u>	25	20	60	80
<u>30</u>	20	25	40	60	80
<u>25</u>	20	30	40	60	80
20	25	30	40	60	80

6. Find the smallest instead of the largest element at each pass.

80	40	25	<u>20</u>	30	60
80	40	<u>25</u>	60	30	20
80	40	<u>30</u>	60	25	20
80	<u>40</u>	60	30	25	20
80	<u>60</u>	40	30	25	20
80	60	40	30	25	20

7.

Pass 1

80	40	25	20	30	60
25	80	25	20	30	60
25	20	80	20	30	60
25	20	30	80	30	60
25	20	30	40	80	60
25	20	30	40	60	80

Pass 2

40	25	20	30	60	80
20	40	20	30	60	80
20	25	40	30	60	80
20	25	30	40	60	80
20	25	30	40	60	80

Pass 3

25	20	30	40	60	80
20	25	30	40	60	80
20	25	30	40	60	80
20	25	30	40	60	80

There are no exchanges during Pass 4, so the algorithm will terminate.

8.
25	30	20	80	40	60
25	30	20	80	40	60
20	25	30	80	40	60
20	25	30	80	40	60
20	25	30	40	80	60
20	25	30	40	60	80

9. ■ `mergesort` sorts an array by using a mergesort to sort each half of the array.

   ■ Sorting half of an array is a smaller problem than sorting the entire array.

   ■ An array of one element is the base case.

   ■ By halving an array and repeatedly halving the halves, you must reach array segments of one element each—that is, the base case.

10. Vertical bars separate the array into regions as the partition develops. The pivot is 38.

39	12	16	38	40	27	pivot | unknown	Swap 12 with itself to move it to S_1.
39 | 12 | 16	38	40	27		pivot | S_1 | unknown	Swap 16 with itself to move it to S_1.
39 | 12 | 16 | 38	40	27		pivot | S_1 | unknown	Swap 38 with itself to move it to S_1.
39 | 12 | 16	38 | 40	27		pivot | S_1 | unknown	
39 | 12	16 | 38	40 | 27		pivot | S_1 | S_2 | unknown	Swap 27 and 40.
39	12	16 | 38 | 27	40		S_1 | pivot | S_2	

11. a. A binary search is $O(\log_2 n)$, and so is faster than a mergesort, which is $O(n \log_2 n)$.

   b. A binary search is $O(\log_2 n)$, and so is faster than displaying the array, which is $O(n)$.

Chapter 11

1. a. 30; b. 30, 20, 70, 50 c. 20, 70; 10; 50, 90; 40, 60;
   d. 20 and 70, 50 and 90, 40 and 60;
   e. 50, 70, 30; f. 50, 40, 60, 90; g. 10, 40, 60, 90;

2. a. 1: A; 2: B, C; 3: D, E; 4: F; 5: G
   b. 1: A; 2: B; 3: C; 4: D; 5: E; 6: F; 7: G

3. 4

4. Complete: b, c, d, e; Full: e; Balanced: b, c, d, e.

5. Preorder: A, B, D, E, C, F, G; Inorder: D, B, E, A, F, C, G;
   Postorder: D, E, B, F, G, C, A.

6.

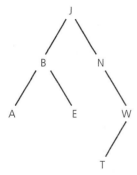

7. 30, 20, 10, 70, 50, 40, 60, 90 is one of several possible orders. (This order results from a preorder traversal of the tree.)

8. The array is 30 20 50 10 25 40 60.

9.

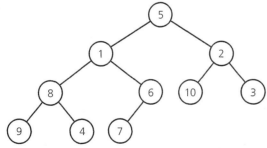

10. No. J should be in G's right subtree. U and V should be in T's right subtree.

11. The algorithm compares each given search key with the keys in the following nodes:
    a. 30, 70, 50; b. 30, 70, 90

12. Inserting the array elements into a binary search tree produces

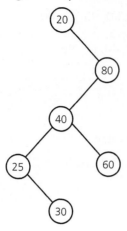

An inorder traversal of this tree results in the sorted array.

13. a.

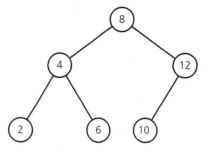

    b.   The tree has minimum height and is complete but not full.

Chapter 12

1. `tableReplace(x, replacementItem)`
   `// Precondition: replacementItem's search key is x.`
   `if (tableDelete(x))`
   `   tableInsert(replacementItem)`

2. No.

3. It is neither a semiheap nor a heap.

4. After inserting 12:   After removing 12:

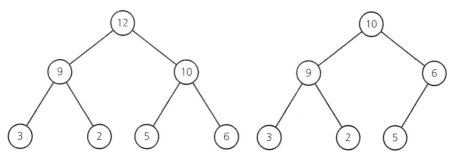

5. The array that represents the heap is 6 4 5 1 2 3.

6. The array that represents the heap is 7 5 6 4 3 2.

7. The array is 10 9 5 8 7 2 3 1 4 6.

Chapter 13

1.

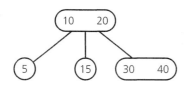

2. a.

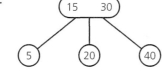

b.

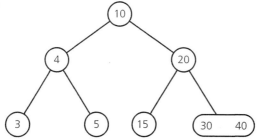

3. a.   See the answer to Self-Test Exercise 1.

b.

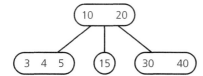

4.

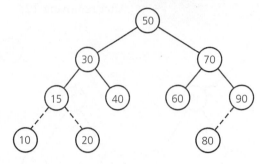

5. A balanced binary search tree.

6. Each node in a red-black tree requires memory for two references and two reference colors. These references and reference colors require no more memory than the four references in a node in a 2-3-4 tree. In addition, a node in a red-black tree requires a reference for only one data item, whereas a node in a 2-3-4 tree requires references for three data items.

7. `+tableDelete(in searchKey:KeyType) throw TableException`

```
i = h(searchKey)
while ( (table[i] is occupied and table[i].getKey() != searchKey)
        or (table[i] is deleted) ) {
    ++i
} // end if
if (table[i] is not empty) {
    // table[i].getKey() == searchKey
    Mark table[i] deleted
    return true
}
else {
    return false
} // end if
```

8. 8, 10, 1, 3, 5, 7, 9, 0, 2, 4, 6.

9. `table[1]` → 15 → 8
   `table[2]` is null
   `table[3]` → 17→ 24 → 10
   `table[4]` → 32

Chapter 14

1. a. Directed, connected;   b. Undirected, connected

2. DFS: 0, 1, 2, 4, 3; BFS: 0, 1, 2, 3, 4.

3.

	0	1	2	3	4
0	0	1	0	0	0
1	0	0	1	1	0
2	0	0	0	0	1
3	0	1	0	0	0
4	1	0	0	0	0

4. a g d b e c f

   g a d b e c f

   a g d b e f c

   g a d b e f c

5. No. See Observation 2 on page 783.

6.

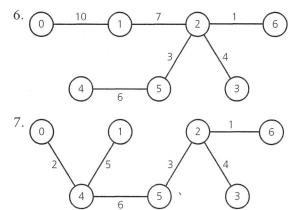

7.

8. Path 0, 4, 2, 1 has weight 7.

   Path 0, 4, 2 has weight 5.

   Path 0, 4, 2, 3 has weight 8.

   Path 0, 4 has weight 4.

Chapter 15

1. Sequential access: Copy the original file `file1` into the file `file2`. Write a new block containing the desired record and 99 blank records. Copy `file2` to the original file `file1`.

   Direct access: Create a new block containing the desired record and 99 blank records. Write the new block to the file as the 17th block.

2. `+externalMergesort(in unsortedFileName:string,`
                             `in sortedFileName:string)`

     `Associate unsortedFileName with the file variable inFile`
       `and sortedFileName with the file variable outFile`

```
blocksort(inFile, tempFile1, numBlocks)
// records in each block are now sorted; numBlocks == 16
mergeFile(tempFile1, tempFile2, 1, 16)
    mergeRuns(tempFile1, tempFile2, 1, 1)
    mergeRuns(tempFile1, tempFile2, 3, 1)
    mergeRuns(tempFile1, tempFile2, 5, 1)
    mergeRuns(tempFile1, tempFile2, 7, 1)
    mergeRuns(tempFile1, tempFile2, 9, 1)
    mergeRuns(tempFile1, tempFile2, 11, 1)
    mergeRuns(tempFile1, tempFile2, 13, 1)
    mergeRuns(tempFile1, tempFile2, 15, 1)
mergeFile(tempFile2, tempFile1, 2, 16)
    mergeRuns(tempFile2, tempFile1, 1, 2)
    mergeRuns(tempFile2, tempFile1, 5, 2)
    mergeRuns(tempFile2, tempFile1, 9, 2)
    mergeRuns(tempFile2, tempFile1, 13, 2)
mergeFile(tempFile1, tempFile2, 4, 16)
    mergeRuns(tempFile1, tempFile2, 1, 4)
    mergeRuns(tempFile1, tempFile2, 9, 4)
mergeFile(tempFile2, tempFile1, 8, 16)
    mergeRuns(tempFile2, tempFile1, 1, 8)
copyFile(tempFile1, outFile)
```

3. ```
   tableRetrieve(tIndex[1..20], tData, searchKey)
      buf.readBlock(tIndex[1..20], 10)
      tableRetrieve(tIndex[1..9], tData, searchKey)
         buf.readBlock(tIndex[1..9], 5)
         tableRetrieve(tIndex[1..4], tData, searchKey)
            buf.readBlock(tIndex[1..4], 2)
            tableRetrieve(tIndex[1..1], tData, searchKey)
               buf.readBlock(tIndex[1..1], 1)
               return null
   ```

4. ```
   tableRetrieve(tIndex[1..20], dataFile, searchKey)
      buf.readBlock(tIndex[1..20], 10)
      tableRetrieve(tIndex[11..20], dataFile, searchKey)
         buf.readBlock(tIndex[11..20], 15)
         tableRetrieve(tIndex[11..14], dataFile, searchKey)
            buf.readBlock(tIndex[11..14], 12)
            j = 26
            blockNum = 98
            dataBuf.readBlock(tData, 98)
            Find record dataBuf[k] whose search key equals searchKey
            tableItem = dataBuf[k]
            return tableItem
   ```

Appendix D

1. Proof by induction on m. When $m = 0$, $2^0 = 2^1 - 1$. Now assume that the statement is true for $m = k$; that is, assume that $1 + 2^1 + 2^2 + \cdots + 2^k = 2^{k+1} - 1$. Show that the statement is true for $m = k + 1$, as follows:

$$(1 + 2^1 + 2^2 + \cdots + 2^k) + 2^{k+1} = (2^{k+1} - 1) + 2^{k+1}$$
$$= 2^{k+2} - 1$$

2. Proof by induction on n. When $n = 1$, the first odd integer is 1 and the sum is trivially 1, which is equal to 1^2. Now assume that the statement is true for $n = k$; that is, assume that $1 + 3 + \cdots + (2k - 1) = k^2$. Show that the statement is true for $n = k + 1$, as follows:

$$[1 + 3 + \cdots + (2k - 1)] + (2k + 1) = k^2 + (2k + 1)$$
$$= (k + 1)^2$$

3. Proof by induction on n. When $n = 2$, $rabbit(2) = 1 = a^0$. Now assume that the statement is true for all $n \leq k$; that is, assume that $rabbit(n) \geq a^{n-2}$ for all $n \leq k$. Show that the statement is true for $n = k + 1$, as follows:

$$rabbit(k + 1) = rabbit(k) + rabbit(k - 1)$$
$$\geq a^{k-2} + a^{k-3}$$
$$= a^{k-3}(a + 1)$$
$$= a^{k-3}(a^2)$$
$$= a^{k-1}$$

Index

Symbols

-- operator, 34–35
% (remainder after division), 32
&& (logical and), 33
*/ (asterisk slash), 28
* (multiply), 32
/* (slash asterisk), 28
// (slash slash), 28
[ ] (bracket notation), 35
|| (logical or), 33
+ (binary add or unary plus), 32
+ operator, 61–62, 124
++ operator, 34–35
< (less than), 33
<= (less than or equal to), 33
= (assignment operator), 32
!= (not equal to) operator, 33, 270
== (equal to) operator, 33, 60, 270
> (greater than), 33
>= (greater than or equal to), 33
\ (backslash notation), 31
– (binary subtract or unary minus), 32
/ (divide), 32
( ) parentheses, 39
? wildcard, 501

Numbers

2-3 trees, 725–745, 870, 872
  B-tree of degree 27, 875
  B-trees, 869–871
  deletion algorithm, 741–744
  deletion from, 737–745
  efficiency of, 744–745

external, 869, 871
height of, 726
insertion algorithm, 734–737
insertion into, 730–737
maintaining shape of, 730
nodes in, 727–728
recursive definition, 726
rules for placing data items in nodes of, 727
searching, 729–730
traversals, 728
2-3-4 trees, 745–752
  deletion from, 751–752
  insertion into, 747–751
  middle-left subtree, 746
  middle-right subtree, 746
  rules for placing data items in nodes of, 746
  searching, 747
  splitting 4-nodes, 749–751
  traversals, 747
2-nodes, 725
3-nodes, 725–726, 753
4-nodes, 745, 749–751, 753

A

abstract classes, 493–497, 605
abstract data types (ADTs), 121–122, 222–226
  axioms for, 239–241
  binary search trees, 618–653
    algorithms for operations of, 624–639
    deletion from, 629–637
    efficiency of, 643–648

insertion into, 626–629
operations, 621–624
recursive definition, 621
reference-based implementation, 639–643
retrieval from, 637–638
saving in a file, 649–652
traversals, 638–639
treesort, 648
UML diagram, 622
binary trees, 594–608
  operations, 594–598
  reference-based implementation, 604–610
  representations of, 601–605
  traversals, 598–601
  traversals using iterator, 610–618
  UML diagram, 597
data structures and, 224–225, 242–243
defined, 224
designing, 235–239
developing, during solution design, 376–382
generic classes and, 499
graphs, 805–812
  implementing, 806–812
  implementing graph class using JCF, 809–812
  operations, 805, 808
heaps, 691–700
implementing, 242–257
Java Collections Framework (JCF) and, 314–322